THE GOSPEL ACCORDING TO

MARK

THE PREACHER'S OUTLINE & SERMON BIBLE®

THE GOSPEL ACCORDING TO

MARK

THE PREACHER'S OUTLINE & SERMON BIBLE®

NEW TESTAMENT

KING JAMES VERSION

Leadership Ministries Worldwide
Chattanooga, TN

THE PREACHER'S OUTLINE & SERMON BIBLE® - MARK
KING JAMES VERSION

Previous Editions of **The Preacher's Outline & Sermon Bible®**,
New International Version NT Copyright © 1998
King James Version NT Copyright © 1991, 1996, 2000
by Alpha-Omega Ministries, Inc.

Please address all requests for information or permission to:
Leadership Ministries Worldwide
PO Box 21310
Chattanooga, TN 37424-0310
Ph.# (423) 855-2181 FAX (423) 855-8616 E-Mail info@outlinebible.org
http://www.outlinebible.org

Library of Congress Catalog Card Number: 96-75921
ISBN Softbound Edition: 978-1-57407-003-3
ISBN Deluxe 3-Ring Edition: 978-1-57407-028-6

LEADERSHIP MINISTRIES WORLDWIDE
CHATTANOOGA, TN

Printed in the United States of America

7 8 9 10 11 16 17 18 19 20

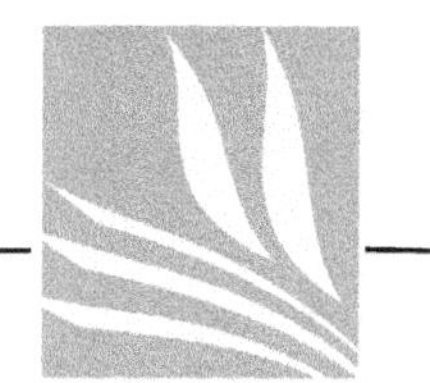

DEDICATED

To all the men and women of the world who preach and teach the Gospel of our Lord Jesus Christ and to the Mercy and Grace of God

- Demonstrated to us in Christ Jesus our Lord.

  "In whom we have redemption through His blood, the forgiveness of sins, according to the riches of His grace." (Ep.1:7)

- Out of the mercy and grace of God, His Word has flowed. Let every person know that God will have mercy upon him, forgiving and using him to fulfill His glorious plan of salvation.

  "For God so loved the world, that he gave His only begotten Son, that whosoever believeth in Him should not perish, but have everlasting life. For God sent not his son into the world to condemn the world, but that the world through him might be saved." (Jn.3:16-17)

  "For this is good and acceptable in the sight of God our Saviour; who will have all men to be saved, and to come unto the knowledge of the truth." (1 Ti.2:3-4)

6/07

The Preacher's Outline & Sermon Bible®

is written for God's servants to use in their study, teaching, and preaching of God's Holy Word...

- to share the Word of God with the world.
- to help believers, both ministers and laypersons, in their understanding, preaching, and teaching of God's Word.
- to do everything we possibly can to lead men, women, boys, and girls to give their hearts and lives to Jesus Christ and to secure the eternal life that He offers.
- to do all we can to minister to the needy of the world.
- to give Jesus Christ His proper place, the place the Word gives Him. Therefore, no work of Leadership Ministries Worldwide—no Outline Bible Resources—will ever be personalized.

ACKNOWLEDGMENTS AND BIBLIOGRAPHY

Every child of God is precious to the Lord and deeply loved. And every child as a servant of the Lord touches the lives of those who come in contact with him or his ministry. The writing ministries of the following servants have touched this work, and we are grateful that God brought their writings our way. We hereby acknowledge their ministry to us, being fully aware that there are many others down through the years whose writings have touched our lives and who deserve mention, but whose names have faded from our memory. May our wonderful Lord continue to bless the ministries of these dear servants—and the ministries of us all—as we diligently labor to reach the world for Christ and to meet the desperate needs of those who suffer so much.

THE GREEK SOURCES

Expositor's Greek Testament, Edited by W. Robertson Nicoll. Grand Rapids, MI: Eerdmans Publishing Co., 1970.

Robertson, A.T. *Word Pictures in the New Testament*. Nashville, TN: Broadman Press, 1930.

Thayer, Joseph Henry. *Greek-English Lexicon of the New Testament*. New York: American Book Co, n.d.

Vincent, Marvin R. *Word Studies in the New Testament*. Grand Rapids, MI: Eerdmans Publishing Co., 1969.

Vine, W.E. *Expository Dictionary of New Testament Words*. Old Tappan, NJ: Fleming H. Revell Co., n.d.

Wuest, Kenneth S. *Word Studies in the Greek New Testament*. Grand Rapids, MI: Eerdmans Publishing Co., 1966.

THE REFERENCE WORKS

Cruden's Complete Concordance of the Old & New Testament. Philadelphia, PA: The John C. Winston Co., 1930.

Josephus' *Complete Works*. Grand Rapids, MI: Kregel Publications, 1981.

Lockyer, Herbert. Series of books, including his books on *All the Men, Women, Miracles, and Parables of the Bible*. Grand Rapids, MI: Zondervan Publishing House, 1958–1967.

Nave's Topical Bible. Nashville, TN: The Southwestern Co., n.d.

The Amplified New Testament. (Scripture Quotations are from the Amplified New Testament, Copyright 1954, 1958, 1987 by the Lockman Foundation. Used by permission.)

The Four Translation New Testament. (Including King James, New American Standard, Williams - New Testament in the Language of the People, Beck - New Testament in the Language of Today.) Minneapolis, MN: World Wide Publications.

The New Compact Bible Dictionary, Edited by T. Alton Bryant. Grand Rapids, MI: Zondervan Publishing House, 1967.

The New Thompson Chain Reference Bible. Indianapolis, IN: B.B. Kirkbride Bible Co., 1964,

THE COMMENTARIES

Barclay, William. *Daily Study Bible Series*. Philadelphia, PA: Westminster Press, Began in 1953.

Bruce, F.F. *The Epistle to the Ephesians*. Westwood, NJ: Fleming H. Revell Co., 1968.

_____. *Epistle to the Hebrews*. Grand Rapids, MI: Eerdmans Publishing Co., 1964.

_____. *The Epistles of John*. Old Tappan, NJ: Fleming H. Revell Co., 1970.

Criswell, W.A. *Expository Sermons on Revelation*. Grand Rapids, MI: Zondervan Publishing House, 1962–66.

THE COMMENTARIES
(continued)

Greene, Oliver. *The Epistles of John*. Greenville, SC: The Gospel Hour, Inc., 1966.

_____. *The Epistles of Paul the Apostle to the Hebrews*. Greenville, SC: The Gospel Hour, Inc., 1965.

_____. *The Epistles of Paul the Apostle to Timothy & Titus*. Greenville, SC: The Gospel Hour, Inc., 1964.

_____. *The Revelation Verse by Verse Study*. Greenville, SC: The Gospel Hour, Inc., 1963.

Henry, Matthew. *Commentary on the Whole Bible*. Old Tappan, NJ: Fleming H. Revell Co.

Hodge, Charles. *Exposition on Romans & on Corinthians*. Grand Rapids, MI: Eerdmans Publishing Co., 1972–1973.

Ladd, George Eldon. *A Commentary On the Revelation of John*. Grand Rapids, MI: Eerdmans Publishing Co., 1972–1973.

Leupold, H.C. *Exposition of Daniel*. Grand Rapids, MI: Baker Book House, 1969.

Morris, Leon. *The Gospel According to John*. Grand Rapids, MI: Eerdmans Publishing Co., 1971.

Newell, William R. *Hebrews, Verse by Verse*. Chicago, IL: Moody Press, 1947.

Strauss, Lehman. *Devotional Studies in Galatians & Ephesians*. Neptune, NJ: Loizeaux Brothers, 1957.

_____. *Devotional Studies in Philippians*. Neptune, NJ: Loizeaux Brothers, 1959.

_____. *James, Your Brother*. Neptune, NJ: Loizeaux Brothers, 1956.

_____. *The Book of the Revelation*. Neptune, NJ: Loizeaux Brothers, 1964.

The New Testament & Wycliffe Bible Commentary, Edited by Charles F. Pfeiffer & Everett F. Harrison. New York: The Iverson Associates, 1971. Produced for Moody Monthly. Chicago Moody Press, 1962.

The Pulpit Commentary, Edited by H.D.M. Spence & Joseph S. Exell. Grand Rapids, MI: Eerdmans Publishing Co., 1950.

Thomas, W.H. Griffith. *Hebrews, A Devotional Commentary*. Grand Rapids, MI: Eerdmans Publishing Co., 1970.

_____. *Outline Studies in the Acts of the Apostles*. Grand Rapids, MI: Eerdmans Publishing Co., 1956.

_____. *St. Paul's Epistle to the Romans*. Grand Rapids, MI: Eerdmans Publishing Co., 1946.

_____. *Studies in Colossians & Philemon*. Grand Rapids, MI: Baker Book House, 1973.

Tyndale New Testament Commentaries. Grand Rapids, MI: Eerdmans Publishing Co., Began in 1958.

Walker, Thomas. *Acts of the Apostles*. Chicago, IL: Moody Press, 1965.

Walvoord, John. *The Thessalonian Epistles*. Grand Rapids, MI: Zondervan Publishing House, 1973.

ABBREVIATIONS

&	= and	O.T.	= Old Testament
Bc.	= because	p./pp.	= page/pages
Concl.	= conclusion	Pt.	= point
Cp.	= compare	Quest.	= question
Ct.	= contrast	Rel.	= religion
e.g.	= for example	Rgt.	= righteousness
f.	= following	Thru	= through
Illust.	= illustration	v./vv.	= verse/verses
N.T.	= New Testament	vs.	= versus

THE BOOKS OF THE OLD TESTAMENT

Book	*Abbreviation*	*Chapters*
GENESIS	Gen. or Ge.	50
Exodus	Ex.	40
Leviticus	Lev. or Le.	27
Numbers	Num. or Nu.	36
Deuteronomy	Dt. or De.	34
Joshua	Josh. or Jos.	24
Judges	Judg. or Jud.	21
Ruth	Ruth or Ru.	4
1 Samuel	1 Sam. or 1 S.	31
2 Samuel	2 Sam. or 2 S.	24
1 Kings	1 Ki. or 1 K.	22
2 Kings	2 Ki. or 2 K.	25
1 Chronicles	1 Chron. or 1 Chr.	29
2 Chronicles	2 Chron. or 2 Chr.	36
Ezra	Ezra or Ezr.	10
Nehemiah	Neh. or Ne.	13
Esther	Est.	10
Job	Job or Jb.	42
Psalms	Ps.	150
Proverbs	Pr.	31
Ecclesiastes	Eccl. or Ec.	12
The Song of Solomon	S. of Sol. or Song	8
Isaiah	Is.	66
Jeremiah	Jer. or Je.	52
Lamentations	Lam.	5
Ezekiel	Ezk. or Eze.	48
Daniel	Dan. or Da.	12
Hosea	Hos. or Ho.	14
Joel	Joel	3
Amos	Amos or Am.	9
Obadiah	Obad. or Ob.	1
Jonah	Jon. or Jona.	4
Micah	Mic. or Mi.	7
Nahum	Nah. or Na.	3
Habakkuk	Hab.	3
Zephaniah	Zeph. or Zep.	3
Haggai	Hag.	2
Zechariah	Zech. or Zec.	14
Malachi	Mal.	4

THE BOOKS OF THE NEW TESTAMENT

Book	*Abbreviation*	*Chapters*
MATTHEW	Mt.	28
Mark	Mk.	16
Luke	Lk. or Lu.	24
John	Jn.	21
The Acts	Acts or Ac.	28
Romans	Ro.	16
1 Corinthians	1 Cor. or 1 Co.	16
2 Corinthians	2 Cor. or 2 Co.	13
Galatians	Gal. or Ga.	6
Ephesians	Eph. or Ep.	6
Philippians	Ph.	4
Colossians	Col.	4
1 Thessalonians	1 Th.	5
2 Thessalonians	2 Th.	3
1 Timothy	1 Tim. or 1 Ti.	6
2 Timothy	2 Tim. or 2 Ti.	4
Titus	Tit.	3
Philemon	Phile. or Phm.	1
Hebrews	Heb. or He.	13
James	Jas. or Js.	5
1 Peter	1 Pt. or 1 Pe.	5
2 Peter	2 Pt. or 2 Pe.	3
1 John	1 Jn.	5
2 John	2 Jn.	1
3 John	3 Jn.	1
Jude	Jude	1
Revelation	Rev. or Re.	22

HOW TO USE

The Preacher's Outline & Sermon Bible®

Follow these easy steps to gain maximum benefit from The POSB.

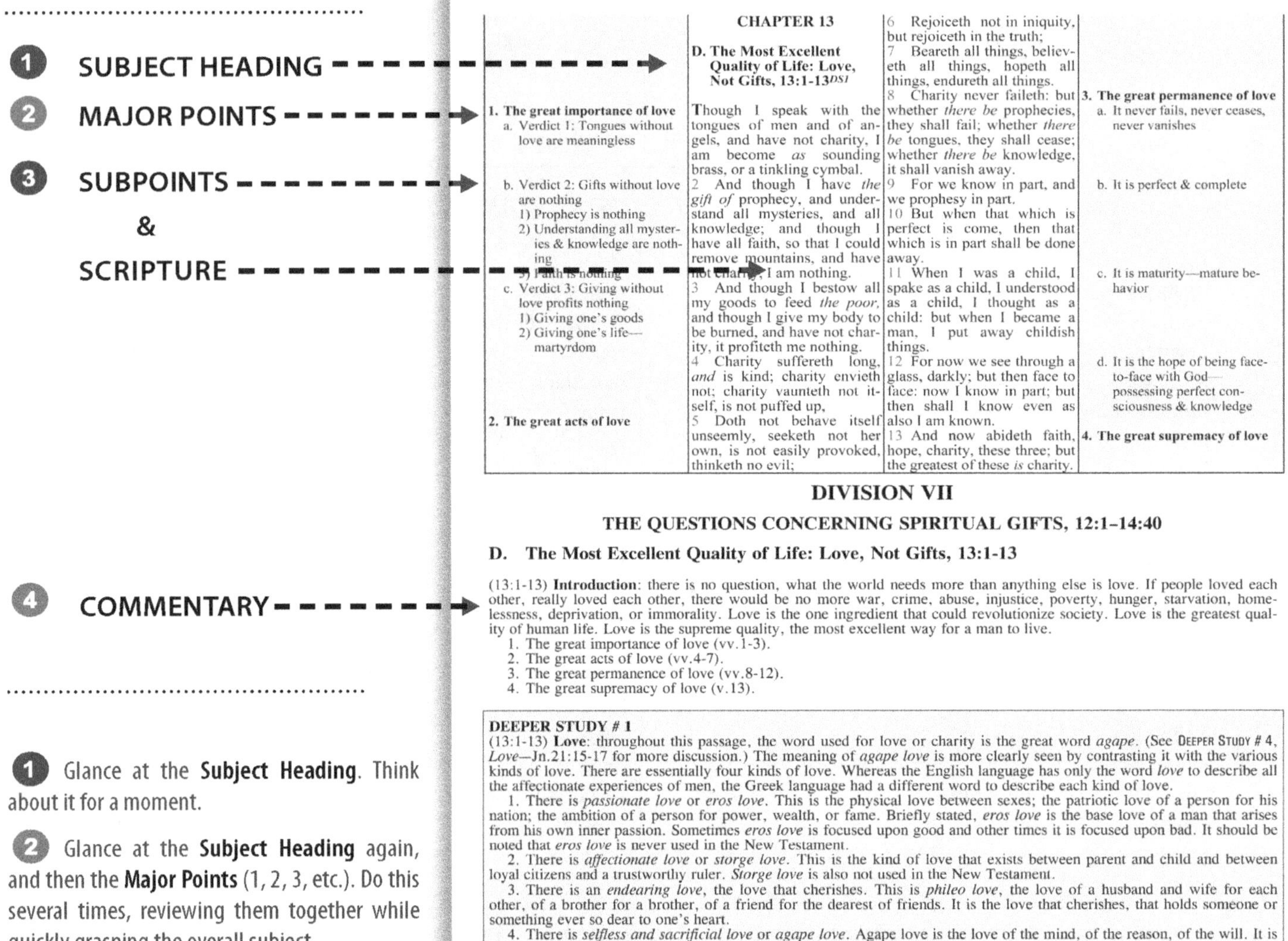

1 CORINTHIANS 13:1-13

Outline	Scripture	Scripture	Outline
	CHAPTER 13 **D. The Most Excellent Quality of Life: Love, Not Gifts, 13:1-13**[DS1]	6 Rejoiceth not in iniquity, but rejoiceth in the truth; 7 Beareth all things, believeth all things, hopeth all things, endureth all things.	
1. The great importance of love a. Verdict 1: Tongues without love are meaningless	Though I speak with the tongues of men and of angels, and have not charity, I am become *as* sounding brass, or a tinkling cymbal.	8 Charity never faileth: but whether *there be* prophecies, they shall fail; whether *there be* tongues, they shall cease; whether *there be* knowledge, it shall vanish away.	**3. The great permanence of love** a. It never fails, never ceases, never vanishes
b. Verdict 2: Gifts without love are nothing 1) Prophecy is nothing 2) Understanding all mysteries & knowledge are nothing 3) Faith is nothing	2 And though I have *the gift of* prophecy, and understand all mysteries, and all knowledge; and though I have all faith, so that I could remove mountains, and have not charity, I am nothing.	9 For we know in part, and we prophesy in part. 10 But when that which is perfect is come, then that which is in part shall be done away.	b. It is perfect & complete
c. Verdict 3: Giving without love profits nothing 1) Giving one's goods 2) Giving one's life—martyrdom	3 And though I bestow all my goods to feed *the poor,* and though I give my body to be burned, and have not charity, it profiteth me nothing.	11 When I was a child, I spake as a child, I understood as a child, I thought as a child: but when I became a man, I put away childish things.	c. It is maturity—mature behavior
	4 Charity suffereth long, *and* is kind; charity envieth not; charity vaunteth not itself, is not puffed up,	12 For now we see through a glass, darkly; but then face to face: now I know in part; but then shall I know even as also I am known.	d. It is the hope of being face-to-face with God—possessing perfect consciousness & knowledge
2. The great acts of love	5 Doth not behave itself unseemly, seeketh not her own, is not easily provoked, thinketh no evil;	13 And now abideth faith, hope, charity, these three; but the greatest of these *is* charity.	**4. The great supremacy of love**

DIVISION VII

THE QUESTIONS CONCERNING SPIRITUAL GIFTS, 12:1–14:40

D. The Most Excellent Quality of Life: Love, Not Gifts, 13:1-13

(13:1-13) **Introduction**: there is no question, what the world needs more than anything else is love. If people loved each other, really loved each other, there would be no more war, crime, abuse, injustice, poverty, hunger, starvation, homelessness, deprivation, or immorality. Love is the one ingredient that could revolutionize society. Love is the greatest quality of human life. Love is the supreme quality, the most excellent way for a man to live.

1. The great importance of love (vv.1-3).
2. The great acts of love (vv.4-7).
3. The great permanence of love (vv.8-12).
4. The great supremacy of love (v.13).

DEEPER STUDY # 1

(13:1-13) **Love**: throughout this passage, the word used for love or charity is the great word *agape*. (See DEEPER STUDY # 4, *Love*—Jn.21:15-17 for more discussion.) The meaning of *agape love* is more clearly seen by contrasting it with the various kinds of love. There are essentially four kinds of love. Whereas the English language has only the word *love* to describe all the affectionate experiences of men, the Greek language had a different word to describe each kind of love.

1. There is *passionate love* or *eros love*. This is the physical love between sexes; the patriotic love of a person for his nation; the ambition of a person for power, wealth, or fame. Briefly stated, *eros love* is the base love of a man that arises from his own inner passion. Sometimes *eros love* is focused upon good and other times it is focused upon bad. It should be noted that *eros love* is never used in the New Testament.

2. There is *affectionate love* or *storge love*. This is the kind of love that exists between parent and child and between loyal citizens and a trustworthy ruler. *Storge love* is also not used in the New Testament.

3. There is an *endearing love*, the love that cherishes. This is *phileo love*, the love of a husband and wife for each other, of a brother for a brother, of a friend for the dearest of friends. It is the love that cherishes, that holds someone or something ever so dear to one's heart.

4. There is *selfless and sacrificial love* or *agape love*. Agape love is the love of the mind, of the reason, of the will. It is the love that goes so far…

- that it loves a person even if he does not deserve to be loved
- that it actually loves the person who is utterly unworthy of being loved

1 Glance at the **Subject Heading**. Think about it for a moment.

2 Glance at the **Subject Heading** again, and then the **Major Points** (1, 2, 3, etc.). Do this several times, reviewing them together while quickly grasping the overall subject.

3 Glance at **both** the **Major Points** and **Subpoints** together while reading the **Scripture**. Do this slower than Step 2. Note how these points sit directly beside the related verse and simply restate what the Scripture is saying—in Outline form.

4 Next read the **Commentary**. Note that the *Major Point Numbers* in the Outline match those in the Commentary. A small raised number (**DS1, DS2, etc.**) at the end of a Subject Heading or Outline Point, directs you to a related **Deeper Study** in the Commentary.

Finally, read the **Thoughts** and **Support Scripture** (not shown).

As you read and re-read, pray that the Holy Spirit will bring to your attention exactly what you should preach and teach. May God bless you richly as you study and teach His Word.

The POSB contains everything you need for sermon preparation:

1. **The Subject Heading** describes the overall theme of the passage, and is located directly above the Scripture (keyed *alphabetically*).
2. **Major Points** are keyed with an outline *number* guiding you to related commentary. Note that the Commentary includes *"Thoughts"* (life application) and abundant Supporting Scriptures.
3. **Subpoints** explain and clarify the Scripture as needed.
4. **Commentary** is fully researched and developed for every point.
   - **Thoughts (in bold)** help apply the Scripture to real life.
   - **Deeper Studies** provide in-depth discussions of key words.

"Woe is unto me, if I preach not the gospel"
(1 Co.9:16)

THE GOSPEL ACCORDING TO
MARK

INTRODUCTION

AUTHOR: John Mark.

The early church fathers say that Mark was a companion of Peter. Some commentators claim that Peter furnished much of the material for the Gospel, whereas others say that Mark made notes of Peter's preaching and later used the notes to write the Gospel.

Papias says: "Mark, who was Peter's interpreter, wrote down carefully all that he remembered of what Christ had said or done, though not in order. For he had neither heard the Lord nor been His disciple; but afterwards, as I said, he had been Peter's disciple. Now Peter used to teach according to the needs, without giving an orderly summary of the Lord's sayings. So Mark was not wrong in writing down some things as he recalled them. For his one concern was this—not to omit nor to falsify anything that he had heard" (Papias, Frag.2:15. Quoted by William Barclay. *The Gospel of Mark*. "The Daily Study Bible." Philadelphia, PA: The Westminster Press, 1954, p. xvii).

Scripture gives a good deal of information about Mark (see notes—Ac.12:25; 13:13).

DATE: uncertain. Probably A.D. 67-70.

The fall of Jerusalem in A.D. 70 had not yet occurred (Mk.13). The church father, Irenaeus, says: "Matthew also issued a written Gospel among the Hebrews in their own dialect, while Peter and Paul were preaching at Rome and laying the foundations of the church. After their departure, Mark, the disciple and interpreter of Peter, did also hand down to us in writing what had been preached by Peter" (Irenaeus, *Against Heresies* III.I.1).

Note the word *departure*. It evidently means death. It is so used in referring to the Lord's death (Lu.9:31) and to Peter's impending death (2 Pe.1:15). The Anti-Marcionite Prologue says very clearly, "After the death of Peter himself, he [Mark] wrote down this same gospel...." (Quoted from *The Gospel of Mark*. Introduction. "The New Testament and Wycliffe Bible Commentary," ed. by Charles F. Pfeiffer and Everett F. Harrison. Produced for Moody Monthly by the Iversen Associates, NY, 1971, p.113.)

The deaths of Peter and Paul are thought to have occurred around A.D. 65-70. (See Introductory Notes, Author, *1 Timothy* and *2 Timothy*.) Therefore, Mark's writing would have taken place somewhere around A.D. 67-70.

TO WHOM WRITTEN: to the Roman world, the world at large, the Gentile mind.

Mark's recipients are not familiar with Jewish terms and customs, for he constantly explains them. However, they are familiar with Christian history and terms. He never explains them (for example, John the Baptist, baptism, the Holy Spirit).

PLACE WRITTEN: most likely Rome.

PURPOSE: to show that Jesus is unquestionably the Son of God.

Mark states his purpose immediately upon beginning his Gospel: "The beginning of the gospel of Jesus Christ, the Son of God" (Mk.1:1). Jesus is declared to be the Son of God at His baptism and transfiguration by the thundering voice of God, "This is my beloved Son...." (1:11; 9:7). Even demons cry out, "I know thee, who thou art, the Holy One of God" (1:24). The conclusion of the Centurion is, "Truly this was the Son of God" (15:39). Throughout His ministry Jesus Himself claims to be the Son of God time and again.

SPECIAL FEATURES:

1. *Mark* is *The Gospel of Realism*. Mark reports Jesus' life as it was with little interpretation. It is an *on-the-spot,* eyewitness account written in a straightforward manner. The account is unvarnished.
2. *Mark* is *The Gospel of Action*. The key word is *euthys* which means instantly, immediately, forthwith. It occurs well over thirty times. The Gospel paints a moving and vivid picture of the dramatic life of Christ. It rushes from event to event as if breathlessly moving toward one final ultimate climax.
3. *Mark* is *The Gospel of Humanity* or *The Gospel of Emotion*. Jesus' humanity is forcibly pictured. Jesus is the carpenter (6:3); He was moved with righteous anger (3:5; 8:33; 10:14); He became weary (4:38); He marveled at the people's unbelief (6:6); He became tired and needed rest (6:31); He was moved with compassion (6:34); He sighed (7:34; 8:12); He looked at the rich young ruler and loved him (10:21); He hungered (11:12).
4. *Mark* is *The Gospel of the Eyewitness*. Mark adds detail after detail to the events of Jesus' life, details that could come only from an eyewitness. During Jesus' temptation, He was with the wild beasts (1:13). Jesus named James and John "Boanerges" (3:17). "He was very displeased" with the disciples' rejection of little children (10:14). When Jesus foretold His death, the disciples "were amazed; and as they followed, they were afraid" (10:32). "The common people heard Him gladly" (12:37).

OUTLINE OF MARK

THE PREACHER'S OUTLINE AND SERMON BIBLE® is unique. It differs from all other Study Bibles and Sermon Resource Materials in that every Passage and Subject is outlined right beside the Scripture. When you choose any *Subject* below and turn to the reference, you have not only the Scripture but also an outline of the Scripture and Subject *already prepared for you—verse by verse.*

For a quick example, choose one of the subjects below and turn over to the Scripture; you will find this to be a marvelous help for more *organized* and *streamlined* study.

In addition, every point of the Scripture and Subject is *fully developed in a Commentary with supporting Scripture* at the end of each point. Again, this arrangement makes sermon preparation much simpler and more efficient.

Note something else: the Subjects of *Mark* have titles that are both Biblical and *practical.* The practical titles are often more appealing to people. This benefit is clearly seen for use on billboards, bulletins, church newsletters, etc.

A suggestion: for the *quickest* overview of *Mark,* first read all the Division titles (I, II, III, etc.), then come back and read the individual outline titles.

OUTLINE OF MARK

I. THE BEGINNING OF THE GOSPEL: JESUS CHRIST, THE SON OF GOD, 1:1-20

A. Jesus Christ and John the Baptist: The Good News and the Messenger of God, 1:1-8
(Matthew 3:1-12; Luke 3:1-18; John 1:19-28)
B. Jesus Christ and His Baptism: A Decision for God, 1:9-11
(Matthew 3:13-17; Luke 3:21-22; John 1:29-34)
C. Jesus Christ and His Temptation: Dealing with Temptation, 1:12-13
(Matthew 4:1-11; Luke 4:1-13)
D. Jesus Christ and His Message: The Good News of the Gospel, 1:14-15
(Matthew 4:12-17; Luke 4:14, 19-20; John 4:1-4)
E. Jesus Christ and His Disciples: The Kind of Person Called, 1:16-20
(Matthew 4:18-22; Luke 5:1-11; John 1:35-51)

II. THE SON OF GOD'S OPENING MINISTRY: JESUS' IMMEDIATE IMPACT, 1:21-3:35

A. Jesus' Teaching and Its Impact: Launching a New Ministry, 1:21-22
(Luke 4:31-32)
B. Jesus' Power Over Evil Spirits and Its Impact: Delivering the Most Enslaved, 1:23-28
(Luke 4:33-37)
C. Jesus' Power and Impact Upon Each One: Caring for the Home and the Individual, 1:29-31
(Matthew 8:14-15; Luke 4:38-39)
D. Jesus' Power and Impact Upon People in the Streets: Caring for the Whole World, 1:32-34
(Matthew 8:16-17; Luke 4:40-41)
E. Jesus' Source of Power and Its Impact: What Is the Source of Power, 1:35-39
(Luke 2:42-44)
F. Jesus' Power Over Leprosy and Its Impact: Cleansing the Most Unclean, 1:40-45
(Matthew 8:2-4; Luke 5:12-15)
G. Jesus' Power to Forgive Sin and Its Impact: Forgiveness of Sin, 2:1-12
(Matthew 9:1-8; Luke 5:17-26)
H. Jesus' Impact Upon Matthew and His Friends: Reaching the Outcast and the Sinner, 2:13-17
(Matthew 9:9-13; Luke 5:27-32)
I. Jesus' Impact Upon Young Disciples and Theologians: The Kind of Life Christ Brings, 2:18-22
(Matthew 9:14-17; Luke 5:33-39)
J. Jesus' Impact Upon Religionists: Understanding the Sabbath (Sunday), 2:23-28
(Matthew 12:1-8; Luke 6:1-5)
K. Jesus' Impact Upon Authorities and Politicians: Understanding True Religion, 3:1-6
(Matthew 12:9-14; Luke 6:6-11)
L. Jesus' Impact Upon Crowds and Evil Spirits: Seeking and Fearing Christ, 3:7-12
(Matthew 12:14-21)

M. Jesus' Impact Upon the Twelve Disciples: Calling Choice Men, 3:13-19 (Matthew 10:1-4; Luke 6:12-19; Acts 1:13-14)
N. Jesus' Impact Upon Friends: Calling Jesus Mad and Insane, 3:20-21
O. Jesus' Impact Upon Religionists: Calling Jesus Demon-Possessed, 3:22-30 (Matthew 12:22-32; Luke 11:14-20)
P. Jesus' Impact Upon His Own Family: Feeling Jesus Is an Embarrassment, 3:31-35 (Matthew 12:46-50; Luke 8:19-21)

III. THE SON OF GOD'S CONTINUING MINISTRY: JESUS' PARABLES AND HIS AUTHORITY, 4:1-6:6

A. The Parable of the Sower: How Men Receive the Word of God, 4:1-20 (Matthew 13:1-23; Luke 8:4-15)
B. The Parables Dealing with Truth: Truth and Man's Duty, 4:21-25 (Matthew 5:15-16; 10:26-27; 13:12; see Luke 8:16-18; 11:33)
C. The Parable of the Growing Seed: The Growth of Believers, 4:26-29
D. The Parable of the Mustard Seed: The Growth of God's Kingdom, 4:30-32 (Matthew 13:31-32; see Luke 13:18-19)
E. The Use of Parables by Jesus: Why Christ Used Illustrations, 4:33-34 (Matthew 13:34-35).
F. The Authority of Jesus Over Nature: Rest and Peace, 4:35-41 (Matthew 8:23-27; Luke 8:22-25)
G. The Authority of Jesus to Banish Demons: Hope for the Most Wild and Mean, 5:1-20 (Matthew 8:28-34; Luke 8:26-39)
H. The Approaches That Lay Hold of Jesus' Authority: How to Approach Jesus, 5:21-43 (Matthew 9:18-26; Luke 8:40-56)
I. The Rejection of Jesus' Authority: Why Jesus Is Rejected, 6:1-6 (Matthew 13:54-58; see Luke 4:16-30)

IV. THE SON OF GOD'S TRAINING MINISTRY: JESUS' INTENSIVE PREPARATION OF THE DISCIPLES, 6:7-8:26

A. The Sending Forth of the Disciples, 6:7-13 (Matthew 9:35-10:42; Luke 9:1-6)
B. The Death of John the Baptist: The Immoral vs. the Righteous, 6:14-29 (Matthew 14:1-14; Luke 9:7-9)
C. The Need for Rest and Its Dangers, 6:30-34 (see John 6:1-4; Luke 9:10)
D. The Attitudes Toward Human Need and Resources, 6:35-44 (Matthew 14:15-21; Luke 9:11-17; John 6:5-14)
E. Five Wise Lessons for Service, 6:45-52 (Matthew 14:22-33; John 6:16-21)
F. The Steps to Healing, 6:53-56 (Matthew 14:34-36)
G. The Emptiness of (Man-Made) Tradition, Ritual, Ceremony, Works, 7:1-13 (Matthew 15:1-9)
H. The Things That Defile, 7:14-23 (Matthew 15:10-20; see Luke 11:37-41)
I. The Steps to Caring for the Rejected, 7:24-30 (Matthew 15:21-28)
J. The Verdict Sought for One's Service: Doing All Things Well, 7:31-37 (Matthew 15:29-31)
K. The Need for Spiritual Food, Compassion, and Evangelism, 8:1-9 (Matthew 15:32-39)
L. The Fault of the Spiritually Blind, 8:10-13 (Matthew 16:1-4)
M. The Evil and Danger of Religionists and World Leaders, 8:14-21 (Matthew 16:5-12)
N. The Necessity for Caring, 8:22-26

V. THE SON OF GOD'S CLOSING MINISTRY: JESUS TEACHES THE IDEA OF GOD'S MESSIAHSHIP, NOT MAN'S MESSIAHSHIP, 8:27-9:50

A. The Great Confession of Peter: Who Jesus Is, 8:27-30 (Matthew 16:13-20; Luke 9:18-21)
B. The First Prediction of Death: God's Messiah vs. Man's Messiah, 8:31-33 (Matthew 16:21-23; Luke 9:22)

C. The Issues of God and the Issues of Men, 8:34-9:1
(Matthew 16:24-28; Luke 9:27-33)
D. The Transfiguration: A Glimpse of Heaven's Glory, 9:2-13
(Matthew 17:1-13; Luke 9:28-36)
E. The Problem of Spiritual Immaturity and Powerlessness, 9:14-29
(Matthew 17:14-21; Luke 9:37-42)
F. The Second Prediction of Death: Intensive Training in the Death of Christ, 9:30-32
(Matthew 17:22-23; Luke 9:43-45)
G. The Disciples' Terrible Ignorance of Messiahship: A Problem of Ambition, 9:33-37
(Matthew 18:1-4; Luke 9:46-48)
H. The Conditions of Tolerance, 9:38-41
(Luke 9:49-50)
I. The Terribleness of Sin, 9:42-50

VI. THE SON OF GOD'S LAST PUBLIC MINISTRY: JESUS DEALS WITH SOME SPECIAL PROBLEMS, 10:1-52

A. The Problem of Divorce, 10:1-12
(Matthew 19:1-12; see Matthew 5:31-32; Luke 16:18; 1 Cor.7:10-16)
B. The Problem of Children and the Truth About Children, 10:13-16
(Matthew 19:13-15; Luke 18:15-17)
C. The Rich Young Ruler: The Problem of Eternal Life, 10:17-22
(Matthew 19:16-22; Luke 19:18-23)
D. The Problem of Wealth and Its Dangers, 10:23-27
(Matthew 19:23-26; Luke 18:24-27).
E. The Problem of Rewards: What One Receives for Following Christ, 10:28-31
(Matthew 19:27-30; Luke 18:28-30)
F. The Third Prediction of Death: The Problem of Christ's Death, 10:32-34
(Matthew 20:17-19; Luke 18:31-34)
G. The Problem of Ambition, 10:35-45
(Matthew 20:20-28; see Luke 22:24-27)
H. The Steps for Getting Help: Blind Bartimaeus, 10:46-52
(Matthew 20:29-34; see Luke 18:35-43)

VII. THE SON OF GOD'S LAST JERUSALEM MINISTRY: JESUS' WARNING AND CONFLICT WITH RELIGIONISTS, 11:1-12:44

A. The Triumphal Entry: A Dramatic Warning, Jesus is the Messiah, 11:1-11
(Matthew 21:1-11; Luke 19:28-40; John 12:12-19)
B. The Fig Tree Cursed: A Warning Against a Fruitless Life, 11:12-14
(Matthew 21:17-20)
C. The Temple Cleansed: A Warning to Those Who Abuse God's Temple, 11:15-19
(Matthew 21:12-16; Luke 19:45-46; see John 2:13-16)
D. The Conditions of Prayer, 11:20-26
(Matthew 21:21-22)
E. The Authority of Jesus Questioned: Two Choices Concerning Jesus, 11:27-33
(Matthew 21:23-27; Luke 20:1-8)
F. The Parable of the Wicked Husbandmen: God and Israel, 12:1-12
(Matthew 21:33-46; Luke 20:9-19; see Isaiah 5:1-7).
G. The Question of Civil and Religious Power: The State or God, 12:13-17
(Matthew 22:15-22; Luke 20:20-26)
H. The Question and Proof of the Resurrection, 12:18-27
(Matthew 22:23-33; Luke 27-38)
I. The Question About the Greatest Commandment, 12:28-34
(Matthew 22:34-40; see Luke 10:25-37)
J. The Entangled Idea of the Messiah, 12:35-37
(Matthew 22:41-46; Luke 20:39-44)
K. The Warning to the Crowds and Religionists: Some Things to Guard Against, 12:38-40
(Matthew 23:5-6, 14; Luke 20:45-47)
L. The Widow's Mite: Real Giving, 12:41-44
(Luke 21:1-4)

VIII. THE SON OF GOD'S OLIVET MINISTRY: JESUS' PROPHECY OF HIS RETURN AND THE END TIME, 13:1-37

A. The Signs of the End Time, 13:1-13
(Matthew 24:1-14; Luke 21:5-19)
B. The Most Terrible Sign: The Abomination of Desolation, 13:14-23
(Matthew 24:15-28; Luke 21:20-24)
C. The Coming of the Son of Man, 13:24-27
(Matthew 24:29-31; Luke 21:25-28)
D. The End Time and Its Warning to Believers, 13:28-37
(Matthew 24:32-51; Luke 21:29-36)

IX. THE SON OF GOD'S PASSION MINISTRY: JESUS' SUPREME SACRIFICE—REJECTED AND CRUCIFIED, 14:1-15:47

A. Jesus' Death Is Plotted: A Picture of the Passover and Jesus' Death, 14:1-2
(Matthew 26:1-5; Luke 22:1-2)
B. Jesus' Anointing at Bethany: A Study of Love, 14:3-9
(Matthew 26:6-13; John 12:1-8)
C. Jesus' Betrayal: Why a Disciple Failed, 14:10-11
(Matthew 26:14-16; Luke 22:3-6)
D. Jesus' Last Chance to Judas: The Appeal to a Sinner, 14:12-21
(Matthew 26:17-25; Luke 22:21-23; John 13:21-31)
E. Jesus' Institution of the Lord's Supper, 14:22-26
(Matthew 26:26-30; Luke 22:7-20; see John 13:1-30)
F. Jesus' Prediction of Peter's Denial: How Jesus Treats Failure, 14:27-31
(Matthew 26:31-35; Luke 22:31-34; John 13:36-38)
G. Jesus in the Garden of Gethsemane: Bearing the Weight of Unspeakable Suffering, 14:32-42
(Matthew 26:36-46; Luke 22:39-46; John 18:1; see Hebrews 5:7-8; 12:3-4)
H. Jesus' Arrest: A Study of Human Character, 14:43-52
(Matthew 26:47-56; Luke 22:47-53; John 18:3-11)
I. Jesus' Trial Before the High Priest: A Look at Weak and Strong Character, 14:53-65
(Matthew 26:57-68; Luke 22:54, 63-71; see John 18:12-14, 19-24)
J. Peter's Denial: A Lesson in Failure, 14:66-72
(Matthew 26:69-72; Luke 22:54-62; John 18:15-18, 25-27)
K. Jesus' Trial Before Pilate: The Picture of a Morally Weak Man, 15:1-15
(Matthew 27:1-2; 11-25; Luke 23:1-25; John 18:28-40)
L. Jesus' Cross: An Outline of Its Mockery and Events, 15:16-41
(Matthew 27:26-56; Luke 23:26-49; John 19:16-37)
M. Jesus' Burial: A Discussion of Courage, 15:42-47
(Matthew 27:57-66; Luke 23:50-56; John 19:38-42)

X. THE SON OF GOD'S SUPREME MINISTRY: JESUS' VICTORY OVER DEATH AND HIS GREAT COMMISSION, 16:1-20

A. The Proofs of the Resurrection, 16:1-13
(Matthew 28:1-15; Luke 24:1-49; John 20:1-23)
B. The Lord's Great Commission, 16:14-20
(Matthew 28:16-20; Luke 24:46-49; John 20:21; see John 17:18; Acts 1:8)

THE GOSPEL ACCORDING TO

MARK

	CHAPTER 1	his paths straight.	
		4 John did baptize in the	b. To baptize
	I. THE BEGINNING OF THE	wilderness, and preach the	c. To preach repentance & for-
	GOSPEL: JESUS CHRIST,	baptism of repentance for the	giveness of sins
	THE SON OF GOD, 1:1-20	remission of sins.	
		5 And there went out unto	d. The impact: Many responded
	A. Jesus Christ & John the	him all the land of Judaea,	
	Baptist: The Good News	and they of Jerusalem, and	
	& The Messenger of	were all baptized of him in	
	God, 1:1-8	the river of Jordan, confess-	
	(Mt. 3:1-12; Lu. 3:1-18; Jn.	ing their sins.	
	1:19-28)	6 And John was clothed with	**4. The spirit of God's messen-**
		camel's hair, and with a gir-	**ger: Self-denial**
1. The gospel of God	The beginning of the gospel	dle of a skin about his loins;	
a. Concerns Jesus Christ,[DS1]	of Jesus Christ, the Son of	and he did eat locusts and	
the Son of God[DS2]	God;	wild honey;	
b. Began long ago: The proph-	2 As it is written in the pro-	7 And preached, saying,	**5. The message of God's mes-**
ets foretold it	phets, Behold, I send my	There cometh one mightier	**senger**
2. The promise of God to send a	messenger before thy face,	than I after me, the latchet of	a. The preeminence of Christ
messenger: To prepare for	which shall prepare thy way	whose shoes I am not worthy	b. The power of Christ
His Son	before thee.	to stoop down and unloose.	
3. The mission of God's messen-	3 The voice of one crying	8 I indeed have baptized you	
ger	in the wilderness, Prepare	with water: but he shall bap-	
a. To be a voice: "Prepare"[DS3]	ye the way of the Lord, make	tize you with the Holy Ghost.	

DIVISION I

THE BEGINNING OF THE GOSPEL: JESUS CHRIST, THE SON OF GOD, 1:1-20

A. Jesus Christ and John the Baptist: The Good News and the Messenger of God, 1:1-8

(1:1-8) **Introduction**: Mark begins his writing with the simple words "the beginning of." But the words that follow are not simple. They are profound and astounding: "the good news of Jesus Christ, the Son of God." The heart of man leaps (or should leap) with a grasping, vibrant joy: for God is, and God has sent a glorious message to mankind through One who is the Son of God.

Mark wastes no time in sharing the good news about the coming of God's Son into human history. He jumps right to the subject of God's messenger whom God sent to prepare the way for His Son.

1. The gospel of God (vv.1-2).
2. The promise of God to send a messenger: to prepare for His Son (vv.2-3).
3. The mission of God's messenger (vv.3-5).
4. The spirit of God's messenger: self-denial (v.6).
5. The message of God's messenger (vv.7-8).

1 (1:1-2) **Gospel—Jesus Christ, Deity**: Mark says two things about the beginning of the gospel or *good news* (see note, Gospel—Ro.1:1-4 for more discussion).

a. The gospel concerns "Jesus Christ, the Son of God." Note Mark's exact words: "the gospel of Jesus Christ." It is not the "gospel of Mark," but "the gospel of Jesus Christ."

1) Jesus Christ is the Subject of the gospel (see DEEPER STUDY # 1,2—Mk.1:1).
2) Jesus Christ is the Author of the gospel. By Him and through Him the gospel is created and written. He brings the *good news* of God to man. He embodies and He proclaims the *good news* about God to man (see DEEPER STUDY # 5,6—Mt.1:21; DEEPER STUDY # 3—8:20).
3) Jesus Christ is the Son of God (see notes—Jn.1:1-2; 1:34; 10:30-33; Ph.2:6; 2:7).

b. The gospel began long, long ago. Jesus Christ is the Subject and the Author of the gospel, but the gospel began long before the birth of Jesus and the ministry of John. The gospel began long ago in the *mind and plan* of God. God foretold the coming of the gospel through the prophets of old. Mark says what Paul was later to say.

> **"Having therefore obtained help of God, I continue unto this day, witnessing both to small and great, saying none other things than those which the prophets and Moses did say should come" (Ac.26:22).**

DEEPER STUDY # 1

(1:1) **Jesus** (iesous): Savior; He will save. The Hebrew form is *Joshua* (yasha), meaning Jehovah is salvation; He is the Savior (Mt.18:11; Lu.19:10; Ro.8:3; Ga.1:4; He.2:14-18; 7:25).

DEEPER STUDY # 2

(1:1) **Christ** (Christos): the words "Christ" (Christos) and "Messiah" are the same word. Messiah is the Hebrew word and Christ is the Greek word. Both words refer to the same person and mean the same thing: the *Anointed One*. The Messiah is the *Anointed One of God*. Matthew says Jesus "is called Christ" (Mt.1:16); that is, He is recognized as the *Anointed One of God*, the Messiah Himself.

In the day of Jesus Christ, people feverishly panted for the coming of the long-promised Messiah. The weight of life was harsh, hard, and impoverished. Under the Romans, the people felt that God could not wait much longer to fulfill His promise. Such longings for deliverance left the people gullible. Many arose who claimed to be the Messiah and led the trusting followers into rebellion against the Roman State. The insurrectionist Barabbas, who was set free in the place of Jesus at Jesus' trial, is an example (Mk.15:6f). (See notes—Mt.1:1; DEEPER STUDY # 3—3:11; notes—11:1-6; 11:2-3; DEEPER STUDY # 1—11:5; DEEPER STUDY # 2—11:6; note—Lu.7:21-23.)

The Messiah was thought to be several things. (See note, Davidic Prophecies—Lu.3:24-31.)

1. Nationally, He was to be the leader from David's line who would free the Jewish state as an independent nation and lead it to be the greatest nation the world had ever known.
2. Militarily, He was to be a great military leader who would lead Jewish armies victoriously over all the world.
3. Religiously, He was to be a supernatural figure straight from God who would bring righteousness over all the earth.
4. Personally, He was to be the One who would bring peace to the whole world.

Jesus Christ accepted the title of Messiah on three different occasions (Mt.16:17; Mk.14:61; Jn.4:26). The name "Jesus" shows Him to be man. The name "Christ" shows Him to be God's Anointed One, God's very own Son. *Christ* is Jesus' official title. It identifies Him officially as *Prophet* (De.18:15-19), *Priest* (Ps.110:4), and *King* (2 S.7:12-13). These three officials were always anointed with oil, a symbol of the Holy Spirit who was to perfectly anoint the Christ, the Messiah (Mt.3:16; Mk.1:10-11; Lu.3:21-22; Jn.1:32-33). (See note—Lu.3:32-38 for more discussion, verses and fulfillment.)

2 (1:2) **John the Baptist—Prophecy**: there is the promise of God to send a messenger, a forerunner to prepare the way for His Son. God promised through Malachi, the last of the Old Testament prophets:

> **"Behold, I will send my messenger, and he shall prepare the way before me" (Mal.3:1; see Mt.11:10).**

Isaiah, the most famous of the Old Testament prophets, predicted:

> **"The voice of him that crieth in the wilderness, Prepare ye the way of the Lord, make straight in the desert a highway for our God" (Is.40:3; see Mt.3:3).**

Thought 1. The Old Testament and the New Testament are one in purpose. They both point toward "the gospel" of Jesus Christ.

Thought 2. A significant fact is seen here. God knows exactly what is needed to bring the gospel to man. He knew that a forerunner was needed; therefore, He planned and promised to send a forerunner. So it is with every man. God knows what is needed to bring the gospel to all of us. However, the responsibility to respond and to obey rests with us.

> **"The kingdom of heaven is like unto a certain king, which made a marriage for his son, and sent forth his servants, saying, Tell them which are bidden, Behold, I have prepared my dinner: my oxen and my fatlings are killed, and all things are ready: come unto the marriage" (Mt.22:2-3).**
>
> **"Then said he unto him, A certain man made a great supper, and bade many: and sent his servant at supper time to say to them that were bidden, Come; for all things are now ready" (Lu.14:16-17).**
>
> **"Now then we are ambassadors for Christ, as though God did beseech you by us: we pray you in Christ's stead, be ye reconciled to God" (2 Co.5:20).**
>
> **"Behold, I stand at the door, and knock: if any man hear my voice, and open the door, I will come in to him, and will sup with him, and he with me" (Re.3:20).**
>
> **"I have sent also unto you all my servants the prophets, rising up early and sending them, saying, Return ye now every man from his evil way, and amend your doings" (Je.35:15).**

3 (1:3-5) **John the Baptist—Ministers—Baptism**: the mission of God's messenger was threefold.

a. John cried, "Prepare" (see DEEPER STUDY # 3—Mk.1:3). Note that he was crying "in the wilderness." The world is a wilderness full of dangerous, rough, uneven, thorny, and rocky roads. It is easy to get lost in the wilderness of the world, to stumble and injure oneself (see notes—Mt.18:11; DEEPER STUDY # 1—Lu.15:4). It was in the world where the messenger of God had to cry, "Prepare—prepare ye the way of the Lord."

> **"Watch ye therefore: for ye know not when the master of the house cometh, at even, or at midnight, or at the cockcrowing, or in the morning" (Mk.13:35).**

"Let your loins be girded about, and your lights burning; and ye yourselves like unto men that wait for their lord, when he will return from the wedding; that when he cometh and knocketh, they may open unto him immediately" (Lu.12:35-36).

"Wherefore come out from among them, and be ye separate, saith the Lord, and touch not the unclean thing; and I will receive you, and will be a Father unto you, and ye shall be my sons and daughters, saith the Lord Almighty" (2 Co.6:17-18).

"But in a great house there are not only vessels of gold and of silver, but also of wood and of earth; and some to honour, and some to dishonour. If a man therefore purge himself from these, he shall be a vessel unto honour, sanctified, and meet for the master's use, and prepared unto every good work" (2 Ti.2:20-21).

b. John baptized all who believed in the Messiah (see note—Mt.3:11).

c. John preached repentance and forgiveness of sins. A person was to repent, *to* turn from his sins *to* God (see DEEPER STUDY # 1, *Repentance*—Acts 17:29-30); then the person was to be baptized, "fulfilling all righteousness" (Mt.3:15). *Baptism was part of the act of repentance.* There was no true repentance without it. A man was to feel sorry for his sin, turning from his sin to God. Part of his turning to God was being baptized. John's baptism was a baptism of repentance. The person who truly repented was baptized, and his sins were forgiven (see DEEPER STUDY # 4, *Forgiveness*—Mt.26:28).

"I tell you, Nay: but, except ye repent, ye shall all likewise perish" (Lu.13:3).

"Then Peter said unto them, Repent, and be baptized every one of you in the name of Jesus Christ for the remission of sins, and ye shall receive the gift of the Holy Ghost" (Ac.2:38).

"Repent ye therefore, and be converted, that your sins may be blotted out, when the times of refreshing shall come from the presence of the Lord" (Ac.3:19).

"Repent therefore of this thy wickedness, and pray God, if perhaps the thought of thine heart may be forgiven thee" (Ac.8:22).

"If we confess our sins, he is faithful and just to forgive us our sins, and to cleanse us from all unrighteousness" (1 Jn.1:9).

"He that covereth his sins shall not prosper: but whoso confesseth and forsaketh them shall have mercy" (Pr.28:13).

"Let the wicked forsake his way, and the unrighteous man his thoughts: and let him return unto the LORD, and he will have mercy upon him; and to our God, for he will abundantly pardon" (Is.55:7).

"Only acknowledge thine iniquity, that thou hast transgressed against the LORD thy God, and hast scattered thy ways to the strangers under every green tree, and ye have not obeyed my voice, saith the LORD" (Je.3:13).

"But if the wicked will turn from all his sins that he hath committed, and keep all my statutes, and do that which is lawful and right, he shall surely live, he shall not die" (Eze.18:21).

d. John's impact was enormous. Note the word "all" (v.5). All were flocking out to him and being baptized. This was shocking, for Jews were never baptized. Baptism was only for Gentile converts to the Jewish faith (see note—Jn.1:24-26).

Thought 1. An enormous impact will be made for God if three things are true:
⇒ if the messenger is truly called of God as John was called.
⇒ if the messenger lives for God as John lived.
⇒ if the messenger witnesses and preaches for God as John witnessed and preached.

DEEPER STUDY # 3

(1:3) **Roads—Prepare**: this is a graphic scene. In ancient days, most roads were hardly more than dusty paths. When a king was about to visit a certain place, a runner would run some distance ahead of the king and shout, "Prepare! The king is coming." And the people would immediately begin to clean and level the road for the coming king. John was saying, "I am but a voice crying, 'Make ready! Prepare! The King is coming!'"

4 (1:6) **Self-Denial**: the spirit of God's messenger was self-denial.

a. His living quarters were in "the wilderness," that is, in the country. He deliberately chose to live away from the city with all its distractions and temptations. He chose to live where he could be alone with God in meditation and prayer.

b. His clothing was simple, made of camel's hide with a belt made of some other animal's skin.

c. His food was simple. It was locusts and wild honey (Le.11:22-23).

Thought 1. John knew that life was more than food and clothing and housing. He knew that he must not allow anything to distract him or the people from God...
- not living in extravagant luxury.
- not being dressed in the latest and most expensive fashion.
- not eating the most tasty dainties.

Therefore, he denied himself; he actually practiced self-denial. What a lesson for all believers, preachers, and laymen alike! (Ro.14:17).

"Then said Jesus unto his disciples, If any man will come after me, let him deny himself, and take up his cross, and follow me" (Mt.16:24).

"And whosoever doth not bear his cross, and come after me, cannot be my disciple" (Lu.14:27).

"For if ye live after the flesh, ye shall die: but if ye through the Spirit do mortify the deeds of the body, ye shall live" (Ro.8:13).

"And they that are Christ's have crucified the flesh with the affections and lusts" (Ga.5:24).

5 (1:7-8) **Preaching**: the message of God's messenger was twofold.

a. The preeminence of Christ and the *nothingness* of self. John said he himself was less than a slave. Slaves were the ones who loosed the sandals of guests and washed their feet. John said the One coming was so mighty, he was not even worthy to untie His sandals, much less wash His feet.

b. The power of Christ. John said he could minister only physical substance: water baptism, a baptism that could only point toward God. But the One coming, the Messiah, would minister spiritual reality, the baptism of the Spirit of God Himself.

Thought 1. The message of the messenger is to point to Christ and to Him alone.

Thought 2. The glorious message of the gospel is twofold.

(1) The "One mightier than I" has come, the One who rises above all men and holds the answer for all men.

"He that cometh from above is above all: he that is of the earth is earthly, and speaketh of the earth: he that cometh from heaven is above all" (Jn.3:31).

"Ye call me Master and Lord: and ye say well; for so I am" (Jn.13:13).

"Therefore let all the house of Israel know assuredly, that God hath made that same Jesus, whom ye have crucified, both Lord and Christ" (Ac.2:36).

"For to this end Christ both died, and rose, and revived, that he might be Lord both of the dead and living" (Ro.14:9).

"But to us there is but one God, the Father, of whom are all things, and we in him; and one Lord Jesus Christ, by whom are all things, and we by him" (1 Co.8:6).

"And he is the head of the body, the church: who is the beginning, the firstborn from the dead; that in all things he might have the preeminence" (Col.1:18).

(2) The One who can "baptize [immerse] us with the Holy Spirit" of God has come. The One who can fill us with "the divine nature" and save us from "the corruption that is in the world" has come (2 Pe.1:4).

"And, behold, I send the promise of my Father upon you: but tarry ye in the city of Jerusalem, until ye be endued with power from on high" (Lu.24:49).

"He that believeth on me, as the scripture hath said, out of his belly shall flow rivers of living water. (But this spake he of the Spirit, which they that believe on him should receive: for the Holy Ghost was not yet given; because that Jesus was not yet glorified" (Jn.7:38-39).

"And I will pray the Father, and he shall give you another Comforter, that he may abide with you for ever; even the Spirit of truth; whom the world cannot receive, because it seeth him not, neither knoweth him: but ye know him; for he dwelleth with you, and shall be in you. I will not leave you comfortless: I will come to you" (Jn.14:16-18).

"Nevertheless I tell you the truth; It is expedient for you that I go away: for if I go not away, the Comforter will not come unto you; but if I depart, I will send him unto you" (Jn.16:7).

"But ye shall receive power, after that the Holy Ghost is come upon you: and ye shall be witnesses unto me both in Jerusalem, and in all Judea, and in Samaria, and unto the uttermost part of the earth" (Ac.1:8).

"Then Peter said unto them, Repent, and be baptized every one of you in the name of Jesus Christ for the remission of sins, and ye shall receive the gift of the Holy Ghost" (Ac.2:38).

	B. Jesus Christ & His Baptism: A Decision for God, 1:9-11 *(Mt. 3:13-17; Lu. 3:21-22; Jn. 1:29-34)*
1. A decision & a submission made by Christ **2. A new beginning & an identification for Christ: Launched His ministry**	9 And it came to pass in those days, that Jesus came from Nazareth of Galilee, and was baptized of John in Jordan.
3. A commissioning & an empowering by the Holy Spirit	10 And straightway coming up out of the water, he saw the heavens opened, and the Spirit like a dove descending upon him:
4. An approval & an encouragement by God*DS1*	11 And there came a voice from heaven, saying, Thou art my beloved Son, in whom I am well pleased.

DIVISION I

THE BEGINNING OF THE GOSPEL: JESUS CHRIST, THE SON OF GOD, 1:1-20

B. Jesus Christ and His Baptism: A Decision for God, 1:9-11

(1:9-11) **Introduction**: Jesus' baptism pictures what happens when a person makes a decision for God.
1. A decision and a submission made by Christ (v.9).
2. A new beginning and an identification for Christ: launched His ministry (v.9).
3. A commissioning and an empowering by the Holy Spirit (v.10).
4. An approval and an encouragement by God (v.11).

1 (1:9) **Decision—Sacrifice—Surrender—Jesus Christ—Baptism**: Jesus' baptism involved a decision and a surrender, a momentous decision and a total surrender. Note the words "Jesus came from Nazareth...and was baptized in Jordan." In Nazareth, Jesus had all that most people dream about: a happy home, a close-knit family, a profitable occupation (carpenter), friends, and all the fond memories that accumulate through the years of childhood and youth. Yet, He left it all; He left Nazareth to be baptized by John in the Jordan. Why? Within Jesus' mind was the call of God to launch the mission to save the world, a mission that demanded the sacrifice of everything:

⇒ the sacrifice of all that He had in Nazareth.
⇒ the sacrifice of a long earthly life. By choosing the mission of God, He was to be killed in only thirty-six months.
⇒ the sacrifice of His Godly righteousness. He was to become the sin-bearer for the world (see note, Justification—Ro.5:1; 1 Pe.2:21-24).
⇒ the sacrifice of God's presence. In death, God was to forsake Him (see note—Mt.27:46-49).

It was a *momentous decision* for Jesus to leave Nazareth to be baptized.

⇒ By being baptized, Jesus was *surrendering totally* to God's will and mission to save the world.
⇒ By being baptized, Jesus was showing what is involved in paying the ultimate price: the price of sacrificing oneself totally for the will of God.
⇒ By being baptized, Jesus was showing the world what is involved in making a momentous decision and a total surrender to God.

Thought 1. The decision to follow Jesus is a momentous decision. It involves the total surrender of all we are and have. If we genuinely decide for Jesus, we pay the price of sacrificing self completely. However, we must remember: a decision not to follow Christ will lead to discontent and drifting, a wasted and tragic life.

"And he said to them all, If any man will come after me, let him deny himself, and take up his cross daily, and follow me" (Lu.9:23).

"So likewise, whosoever he be of you that forsaketh not all that he hath, he cannot be my disciple" (Lu.14:33).

"For if ye live after the flesh, ye shall die: but if ye through the Spirit do mortify the deeds of the body, ye shall live" (Ro.8:13).

"And they that are Christ's have crucified the flesh with the affections and lusts" (Ga.5:24).

"Yea doubtless, and I count all things but loss for the excellency of the knowledge of Christ Jesus my Lord: for whom I have suffered the loss of all things, and do count them but dung, that I may win Christ" (Ph.3:8).

2 (1:9) **Jesus Christ—Baptism**: Jesus' baptism involved a beginning and an identification. His baptism was a *beginning* in that it was the beginning of a new life, a new direction in His life. His baptism was launching the mission of God to save the world. It was an *identification* in that He was identifying with John's ministry. John was proclaiming the coming of the Messiah, the Lamb of God. Through baptism Jesus was identifying Himself as the Messiah, the Lamb of God (see notes—Mt.3:13; 3:15).

Thought 1. The decision to follow Jesus involves both baptism and the identifying of ourselves with Jesus the Messiah, the Lamb of God. If Jesus had not been baptized, He would not have identified Himself as the Messiah, nor would He have been known as the Messiah. Likewise, if we are not baptized, we do not identify ourselves with Jesus, nor are we known to be identified with Jesus.

"He that believeth and is baptized shall be saved; but he that believeth not shall be damned" (Mk.16:16).

"Repent, and be baptized every one of you in the name of Jesus Christ for the remission of sins, and ye shall receive the gift of the Holy Ghost" (Ac.2:38).

"And he commanded them to be baptized in the name of the Lord. Then prayed they him to tarry certain days" (Ac.10:48).

"And now why tarriest thou? arise, and be baptized, and wash away thy sins, calling on the name of the Lord" (Ac.22:16).

3 (1:10) **Jesus Christ—Baptism**: Jesus' baptism involved a commissioning and an empowering. This is seen in the heavens' opening and the Spirit's descending upon Him.

Jesus' commissioning was a dramatic moment. The word *opened* (schizamenous) really means rent asunder or torn apart. This could mean two things.

a. It could mean a moment like the rays of sunlight breaking through the clouds ever so brilliantly after a thunderstorm.

b. It could mean a moment when God miraculously tore apart the barrier between heaven and earth, allowing Jesus to see into the glory of heaven from where He had come.

Whatever the meaning, Jesus was being commissioned and set apart by heaven itself. God was giving His Son an experience that would make the commissioning unquestionable and unforgettable.

The empowering of Jesus was also a very dramatic moment. The Spirit of God descended upon Jesus in the form of a dove. This event was not only identifying Jesus as the Messiah, it was declaring that the Spirit of God and His power were upon Jesus. This man, Jesus of Nazareth, was being empowered by God's very own Spirit to do the work of God (see note—Jn.1:32-33).

There was also something else symbolized in the dove. The work which Jesus was to do would be the work of peace and purity (again, see note—Jn.1:32-33 for the symbolism of the dove). (Note: Luke 3:21 points out that the Spirit came to Jesus while He was praying *after having been baptized*. The Spirit's descending upon Him, not in Him, was definitely an empowering experience as well as an identifying experience.)

Thought 1. Every true believer is commissioned and empowered by God to do the work of God. Some commissioning experiences are dramatic (the heavens are torn apart); other experiences are not so dramatic (the still small voice of God's Spirit tugs at the heart with an awareness that one is called). Nevertheless, every true believer is commissioned and empowered by God's Spirit.

The *awareness* of the commission and power, however, is a different matter. Too many are not aware of God's commission and of the Spirit's presence within. What makes the difference? The first two points: one's decision and submission, one's beginning and identification. Too many of us lack a consistent commitment in both steps. As a result, we wander through life unaware of God's commission and the presence of the Spirit of God empowering us to do the task.

⇒ Too many of us do not make a decision to follow Christ totally; we do not surrender all we are and have to Christ. Therefore, we are not aware of the great call and commission of Christ.

⇒ Too many of us do not begin with Christ; we just never identify with Him. We may be baptized, but we never follow through with Christ. The world never knows that we are a follower of Christ, not a committed, genuine follower.

"Ye have not chosen me, but I have chosen you, and ordained you, that ye should go and bring forth fruit, and that your fruit should remain: that whatsoever ye shall ask of the Father in my name, he may give it you" (Jn.15:16).

"But ye shall receive power, after that the Holy Ghost is come upon you: and ye shall be witnesses unto me both in Jerusalem, and in all Judaea, and in Samaria, and unto the uttermost part of the earth" (Ac.1:8).

"But rise, and stand upon thy feet: for I have appeared unto thee for this purpose, to make thee a minister and a witness both of these things which thou hast seen, and of those things in the which I will appear unto thee" (Ac.26:16).

"Now then we are ambassadors for Christ, as though God did beseech you by us: we pray you in Christ's stead, be ye reconciled to God" (2 Co.5:20).

"Also I heard the voice of the LORD, saying, Whom shall I send, and who will go for us? Then said I, Here am I; send me" (Is.6:8).

4 (1:11) **Jesus Christ—Baptism**: Jesus' baptism involved God's approval and encouragement. As Man, Jesus Christ needed the perfect assurance of God. So much was being required of Him, and He was to pay such an enormous price to serve God (see note, Decision—Mk.1:9). He needed some clear indication, some special strength, some encouragement from God. What God did was profound: "There came a voice from heaven, saying, Thou art my beloved son, in whom I am well pleased." (See note—Mt.3:16-17.)

Thought 1. God meets the needs of His servants for assurance. He sees to it that we *know* His will and gives *assurance* that we are doing His will. He speaks to our hearts and gives signs of approval and *encouragement.*

"But of him are ye in Christ Jesus, who of God is made unto us wisdom, and righteousness, and sanctification, and redemption" (1 Co.1:30).

"Go ye therefore, and teach all nations, baptizing them in the name of the Father, and of the Son, and of the Holy Ghost: teaching them to observe all things whatsoever I have commanded you: and, lo, I am with you alway, even unto the end of the world. Amen" (Mt.28:19-20).

"The LORD is my strength and my shield; my heart trusted in him, and I am helped: therefore my heart greatly rejoiceth; and with my song will I praise him" (Ps.28:7).

"Fear thou not; For I am with thee: be not dismayed; for I am thy God: I will strengthen thee; yea, I will help thee; yea, I will uphold thee with the right hand of my righteousness" (Is.41:10).

"When thou passest through the waters, I will be with thee; and through the rivers, they shall not overflow thee: when thou walkest through the fire, thou shalt not be burned; neither shall the flame kindle upon thee" (Is.43:2).

DEEPER STUDY # 1
(1:11) **Old Testament Reference**: see Ps.2:7; Is.42:1.

	C. Jesus Christ & His Temptation: Dealing with Temptation, 1:12-13 *(Mt. 4 1-11; Lu. 4:1-13)*
1. Temptation follows decision **2. Temptation is used by the Spirit**	12 And immediately the Spirit driveth him into the wilderness.
3. Temptation is a desert or wilderness experience **4. Temptation is of Satan** **5. Temptation is met by God's help**	13 And he was there in the wilderness forty days, tempted of Satan; and was with the wild beasts; and the angels ministered unto him.

DIVISION I

THE BEGINNING OF THE GOSPEL: JESUS CHRIST, THE SON OF GOD, 1:1-20

C. Jesus Christ and His Temptation: Dealing with Temptation, 1:12-13

(1:12-13) **Introduction**: the importance of understanding temptation cannot be overstressed. The believer faces temptation every day of his life. For this reason, he needs to gain a thorough understanding of just what temptation is and how it is to be overcome. (See outlines and notes—Mt.4:1-11 for more discussion.)

1. Temptation follows decision (v.12).
2. Temptation is used by the Spirit (v.12).
3. Temptation is a desert or wilderness experience (v.13).
4. Temptation is of Satan (v.13).
5. Temptation is met by God's help (v.13).

1 (1:12) **Jesus Christ—Decision—Temptation**: Jesus was tempted right after making the decision to be baptized. His baptism was a momentous decision, for Jesus was declaring His total commitment to God and to God's mission. The decision was to lead to His death in less than thirty-six months. The point to see is that His decision was immediately attacked by Satan. Jesus was tempted immediately after His clear-cut decision to follow God and to launch God's great mission of salvation. (See DEEPER STUDY # 1,2,3—Mt.4:1-11 for more discussion.)

Thought 1. Great and wonderful things happen to a person who makes a decision for God. (See DEEPER STUDY # 1, *Salvation*—Ro.1:16 for discussion.) Satan, as the adversary of God and man, knows this; therefore, temptation always follows a decision for God. Satan always fights against a person when that person...

- is set free from selfishness and sin by God, when that person is set at liberty to live a life of love and joy and peace. (See note and DEEPER STUDY # 1—Ep.1:7.)

> **"But the fruit of the Spirit is love, joy, peace, longsuffering, gentleness, goodness, faith, meekness, temperance: against such there is no law" (Ga.5:22-23).**
>
> **"In whom we have redemption through his blood, the forgiveness of sins, according to the riches of his grace" (Ep.1:7).**

- is set free from death and the fear of death by God, when that person is set at liberty to live a life of confidence and assurance—the confidence and assurance that he has become a child of God.

> **"For ye have not received the spirit of bondage again to fear; but ye have received the Spirit of adoption, whereby we cry, Abba, Father" (Ro.8:15).**
>
> **"But when the fulness of the time was come, God sent forth his Son, made of a woman, made under the law, to redeem them that were under the law, that we might receive the adoption of sons. And because ye are sons, God hath sent forth the Spirit of his Son into your hearts, crying, Abba, Father" (Ga.4:4-6).**
>
> **"Forasmuch then as the children are partakers of flesh and blood, he also himself likewise took part of the same; that through death he might destroy him that had the power of death, that is, the devil; and deliver them who through fear of death were all their lifetime subject to bondage" (He.2:14-15).**

- is set free from condemnation and hell by God, when that person is set at liberty to live life knowing that he will never be condemned by God, that he will live forever with God, when that person knows that nothing will ever separate him from the love of Christ.

> **"Verily, verily, I say unto you, He that heareth my word, and believeth on him that sent me, hath everlasting life, and shall not come into condemnation; but is passed from death unto life" (Jn.5:24).**

"For I am persuaded, that neither death, nor life, nor angels, nor principalities, nor powers, nor things present, nor things to come, nor height, nor depth, nor any other creature, shall be able to separate us from the love of God, which is in Christ Jesus our Lord" (Ro.8:38-39).

Just imagine all that is involved in the above: the depth and the richness, the assurance and the confidence, the joy and the motivation that fills a life that receives so much. And not only does this happen to the person who truly makes a decision for God, but all this shows itself through the person's life to others. The family and friends of the new convert see the depth and richness of his changed life. The result is heartwarming: usually some of them also come to know Christ as their personal Savior.

The adversary to God and man is bound to tempt the new convert. Satan is bound to attack, attempting to overthrow the person's new decision for God. He attacks by causing the person to doubt, to question, to choose another way, to undertake another task, to seek something else. Satan knows that he cannot leave the new convert alone lest that person become strong in the Lord and in his witness for the Lord.

2 (1:12) **Jesus Christ—Temptation—Trials**: temptation is used by the Spirit. The words *driveth Him* (ekballei) mean to thrust, to cast forth, to drive forth, to force. Jesus is compelled with great force to go into the wilderness. He was driven by the Spirit to be tried. He was to be tried and tested *not to make Him fall*, but to make Him stronger and better prepared to do great things for God (see note, pt.3—Mt.4:1).

Thought 1. Trials and temptations are to be stepping stones, not stumbling stones. They are opportunities for the Spirit of God to use in making us *stronger* and *more able* to do greater things for God.

"We glory in tribulation [trials, temptations]...knowing that tribulations worketh patience; and patience, experience; and experience, hope [hope in receiving and doing things for God]" (Ro.5:3-4).

"My brethren, count it all joy when ye fall into divers temptations; knowing this, that the trying of your faith worketh patience. But let patience have her perfect work, that ye may be perfect and entire, wanting nothing. If any of you lack wisdom, let him ask of God, that giveth to all men liberally, and upbraideth not; and it shall be given him" (Js.1:2-5).

"For our light affliction, which is but for a moment, worketh for us a far more exceeding and eternal weight of glory" (2 Co.4:17).

"For this thing I besought the Lord thrice, that it might depart from me. And he said unto me, My grace is sufficient for thee: for my strength is made perfect in weakness. Most gladly therefore will I rather glory in my infirmities, that the power of Christ may rest upon me. Therefore I take pleasure in infirmities, in reproaches, in necessities, in persecutions, in distresses for Christ's sake: for when I am weak, then am I strong" (2 Co.12:8-10).

"That the trial of your faith, being much more precious than of gold that perisheth, though it be tried with fire, might be found unto praise and honour and glory at the appearing of Jesus Christ" (1 Pe.1:7).

"Beloved, think it not strange concerning the fiery trial which is to try you, as though some strange thing happened unto you: but rejoice, inasmuch as ye are partakers of Christ's sufferings; that, when his glory shall be revealed, ye may be glad also with exceeding joy" (1 Pe.4:12-13).

"And hast borne, and hast patience, and for my name's sake hast laboured, and hast not fainted" (Re.2:3).

Thought 2. After a significant decision or a mountaintop experience, it is very wise to get alone with God. One must be spiritually strengthened and prepared to follow through with the new decision.

"Let us draw near with a true heart in full assurance of faith, having our hearts sprinkled from an evil conscience, and our bodies washed with pure water" (He.10:22).

"The LORD is nigh unto them that are of a broken heart; and saveth such as be of a contrite spirit" (Ps.34:18).

"But it is good for me to draw near to God: I have put my trust in the Lord GOD, that I may declare all thy works" (Ps.73:28).

"The LORD is nigh unto all them that call upon him, to all that call upon him in truth" (Ps.145:18).

3 (1:13) **Jesus Christ—Temptation—Wilderness**: temptation is a wilderness experience. It is a discomforting, apprehensive, and threatening experience. Jesus faced all three experiences in His wilderness temptation. (See notes—Mt.4:2-4; 4:5-7; 4:8-10 for a detailed discussion of Jesus' temptation.)

⇒ He was discomforted in that His peace and security in God were disturbed. He was made immediately aware of another choice, a choice that aroused His flesh to desire the forbidden thing: bread created from rocks. (See note—Mt.4:2-4.)

⇒ He was apprehensive in that He was made immediately aware that a decision must be made, a decision that could be wrong and could result in bad consequences.

⇒ He was threatened in that if He yielded to the temptation, the consequences of sin would result and God's purpose would not be fulfilled.

Thought 1. Temptation is a wilderness experience, that is, a worldly experience. Temptation is of the wilderness and comes from the wilderness. Temptation is not civilized, comforting, peaceful, secure or safe. Note three things about the wilderness (world).

(1) The life of the wilderness...
- is covered with rocks and precipices (difficult, threatening situations) which can trip and injure.
- is often a desert (dry, empty, purposeless times) in which a person can die from thirst and hunger.
- is camouflaged with serpents (food and drink, worldly deceptions) which will strike and poison.
- is filled with ravenous beasts (both people and things, whether friend or foe) which will consume.

(2) The danger of the wilderness is that rocks, desert, serpents, or beasts will injure and consume us.
(3) The call of the wilderness is adventuresome, stimulating, challenging, and exciting. It appeals to the *nature of man.*

"For what is a man profited, if he shall gain the whole world, and lose his own soul? or what shall a man give in exchange for his soul?" (Mt.16:26).

"And be not conformed to this world: but be ye transformed by the renewing of your mind, that ye may prove what is that good, and acceptable, and perfect, will of God" (Ro.12:2).

"We all had our conversation in times past in the lusts of our flesh, fulfilling the desires of the flesh and of the mind; and were by nature the children of wrath, even as others" (Ep.2:3).

"Ye adulterers and adulteresses, know ye not that the friendship of the world is enmity with God? whosoever therefore will be a friend of the world is the enemy of God" (Js.4:4).

"Love not the world, neither the things that are in the world. If any man love the world, the love of the Father is not in him. For all that is in the world, the lust of the flesh, and the lust of the eyes, and the pride of life, is not of the Father, but is of the world" (1 Jn.2:15-16).

Thought 2. God wills us to conquer the wild, to triumph over the wilderness experience, but His presence and power are needed to conquer and triumph. Note that God sent Jesus into the wilderness only after the Spirit had come upon Him.

"There hath no temptation taken you but such as is common to man: but God is faithful, who will not suffer you to be tempted above that ye are able; but will with the temptation also make a way to escape, that ye may be able to bear it" (1 Co.10:13).

"For in that he himself hath suffered being tempted, he is able to succour them that are tempted" (He.2:18).

"The Lord knoweth how to deliver the godly out of temptations, and to reserve the unjust unto the day of judgment to be punished" (2 Pe.2:9).

4 (1:13) **Jesus Christ—Temptation**: temptation is of Satan; it is not of God (see note—Mt.4:1 for discussion. Also see DEEPER STUDY # 1—Lu.4:1-2; DEEPER STUDY # 1—Rev.12:9 for more discussion.)

Thought 1. So few people know and accept that temptation is of Satan. But the fact remains that temptation is a lie and a deception. It comes from the father of lies and deception. We must, therefore, reject temptation, for temptation kills a person eternally.

"When any one heareth the word of the kingdom, and understandeth it not, then cometh the wicked one, and catcheth away that which was sown in his heart. This is he which received seed by the way side" (Mt.13:19).

"Ye are of your father the devil, and the lusts of your father ye will do. He was a murderer from the beginning, and abode not in the truth, because there is no truth in him. When he speaketh a lie, he speaketh of his own: for he is a liar, and the father of it" (Jn.8:44).

"And supper being ended, the devil having now put into the heart of Judas Iscariot, Simon's son, to betray him" (Jn.13:2).

"Wherein in time past ye walked according to the course of this world, according to the prince of the power of the air, the spirit that now worketh in the children of disobedience" (Ep.2:2).

"Be sober, be vigilant; because your adversary the devil, as a roaring lion, walketh about, seeking whom he may devour" (1 Pe.5:8).

5 (1:13) **Jesus Christ—Temptation**: temptation is met by God's help. This is seen in three experiences of Jesus.

a. He was with the wild beasts of the wilderness, yet they did not devour Him. The beasts of the wilderness would have included the leopard, lion, bear, wild boar, jackal, scorpion, and serpent. God protected Jesus from all these for forty days.

b. He was ministered to by angels. Jesus did not have to face the temptations alone. God saw to it that He had whatever provision was necessary.

"What shall we then say to these things? If God be for us, who can be against us?" (Ro.8:31).

"For in that he himself hath suffered being tempted, he is able to succour them that are tempted" (He.2:18).

> **"My brethren, count it all joy when ye fall into divers temptations; knowing this, that the trying of your faith worketh patience. But let patience have her perfect work, that ye may be perfect and entire, wanting nothing. If any of you lack *wisdom*, let him ask of God, that giveth to all men liberally, and upbraideth not; and it shall be given him" (Js.1:2-5).**
>
> **"Submit yourselves therefore to God. Resist the devil, and he will flee from you" (Js.4:7).**
>
> **"Ye are of God, little children, and have overcome them: because greater is he that is in you, than he that is in the world" (1 Jn.4:4).**

c. He relied upon God's Word to answer the temptations (see outline and DEEPER STUDY # 1,2,3—Mt.4:1-11; Lu.4:1-13 for discussion).

Thought 1. The armor of God is the glorious provision God provides for the believer's victory over temptation (see outline and notes—Ep.6:10-20 for discussion).

	D. Jesus Christ & His Message: The Good News of God, 1:14-15 *(Mt. 4:12-17; Lu. 4:14, 19-20; Jn. 4:1-4)*
1. The good news of God was preached by Jesus[DS1] a. In Galilee b. After John was put in prison	14 Now after that John was put in prison, Jesus came into Galilee, preaching the gospel of the kingdom of God,
2. The time had come **3. The Kingdom of God was near** **4. The decision was essential: Repent & believe**[DS2]	15 And saying, The time is fulfilled, and the kingdom of God is at hand: repent ye, and believe the gospel.

DIVISION I

THE BEGINNING OF THE GOSPEL: JESUS CHRIST, THE SON OF GOD, 1:1-20

D. Jesus Christ and His Message: The Good News of the Gospel, 1:14-15

(1:14-15) **Introduction**: the *good news* of the gospel includes three emphatic points.
1. The good news of God was preached by Jesus (v.14).
2. The time had come (v.15).
3. The Kingdom of God was near (v.15).
4. The decision was essential: repent and believe (v.15).

1 (1:14) **Jesus Christ—Order of Events—Galilee**: Jesus preached the gospel. Mark says Jesus began to preach the gospel throughout Galilee when John was put in prison. This statement serves as a date to fix the approximate time that Jesus began to minister in Galilee. One year had passed between Mk.1:13 and 1:14. Mark does not cover the events that took place between the temptation of Jesus and the imprisonment of John the Baptist. They are covered by Jn.1:19-4:54. Apparently, the order of events was this:

a. Two of John's disciples, Andrew and Peter, became followers of Jesus right after Jesus' baptism (Jn.1:35-42).

b. The very next day, Jesus, accompanied by Andrew and Peter, left Judea and went into Galilee. It was there that Philip and Nathaniel became followers of Jesus (Jn.1:43-51), and that the first miracle took place at Cana (Jn.2:1-11).

c. Jesus then took His family and His followers and moved to Capernaum, which was to become His headquarters (see note—Mt.4:12-13). But He stayed there only a few days, probably just long enough to move His family's belongings.

d. The Passover was at hand, so Jesus went to Jerusalem to celebrate it (Jn.2:13). It was while there that the first cleansing of the temple and the conversation with Nicodemus about the new birth took place (Jn.2:14-3:1f).

e. Jesus then began to move about Judea and to openly preach and baptize (Jn.3:22). But His ministry posed a problem for John and aroused the opposition of the religious leaders. Consequently, He left Judea and returned to Galilee (Jn.3:23-4:3).

f. It was at this point that Mark (and also Matthew) picked up the story of Jesus' ministry. The reasons why Jesus chose Galilee to be the center for most of His ministry should be closely read (see notes—Mt.4:12; 4:12-13).

DEEPER STUDY # 1
(1:14) **Gospel**: see DEEPER STUDY # 2—1 Co.15:1-11. See Ro.1:1-4.

2 (1:15) **Fulness of Time**: first, the gospel declares that time is fulfilled. The time is fulfilled for what? For the coming of Christ, God's Messiah. It was time for the salvation of man to come upon the world scene. Two things were meant by "the time is fulfilled" or "the fulness of time" (Ga.4:4).

a. World and religious events were ready for the coming of Christ (see DEEPER STUDY # 1—Gal.4:4 for discussion).

1) The law had done its educational work. It had shown through the Jewish nation that men are terrible transgressors. Despite all of God's favor and blessings, man still failed to worship God in love. The world now had a picture of the depraved heart of man. (See Ro.3:10-18 for a clear description of man's sinfulness.)
2) The world was full of people spiritually starved. The worship of self, of pleasure, of gods, of philosophical ethics left many empty and barren. The soul was now ready to have its hunger met.
3) The world was at peace under Roman rule. The world was an open door for the spread of the gospel—without any restraint.
4) The world spoke Greek as a basic language. This made communication possible with many from all over the world.
5) The world had a system of roads for mass travel. This allowed Christian missionaries to reach the farthest parts of the earth. It also brought commercial travelers to metropolitan centers where Christian believers were concentrated.

"But when the fulness of the time was come, God sent forth his Son, made of a woman, made under the law, to redeem them that were under the law, that we might receive the adoption of sons. And because ye are sons, God hath sent forth the Spirit of his Son into your hearts, crying, Abba, Father" (Ga.4:4-6).

"For there is one God, and one mediator between God and men, the man Christ Jesus; who gave himself a ransom for all, to be testified in due time" (1 Ti.2:5-6).

"[God's elect] in hope of eternal life, which God, that cannot lie, promised before the world began" (Tit.1:2).

"Now once in the end of the world hath he appeared to put away sin by the sacrifice of himself" (He.9:26).

2. Prophetic events were ready for the coming of Christ. God had foretold that Elijah must *first* come and prepare the way (Is.40:3; Mal.3:1). Elijah came in the person of John the Baptist (Mt.11:10). But now John was passing from the scene. His ministry ob preparing the way for the Messiah was completed. It was now time for the Messiah to appear in force, proclaiming the glorious gospel of God's kingdom.

Matthew and Peter, as well as Mark, stress that "the time is fulfilled" for the Messiah to appear. The fact that the time was stressed so much points to Jesus as the true Messiah and gives additional proof to His Messiahship.

"Now when Jesus had heard that John was cast into prison, he departed into Galilee....From that time Jesus began to preach, and to say, Repent: for the kingdom of heaven is at hand" (Mt.4:12, 17).

"The word which God sent unto the children of Israel, preaching peace by Jesus Christ: (he is Lord of all:) that word, I say, ye know, which was published throughout all Judaea, and began from Galilee, after the baptism which John preached" (Ac.10:36-37).

Thought 1. Note two significant applications.

(1) God prepared the way for His Son by moving world events. He controlled history and events, and He controls all events and circumstances for the sake of His people.

"And we know that all things work together for good to them that love God, to them who are the called according to his purpose" (Ro.8:28).

(2) God fulfilled His promise to prepare the way for His Son. He will fulfill His promises to believers. He prepares the way for every genuine believer, running ahead of the believer to take care of him.

"And being fully persuaded that, what he had promised, he was able also to perform" (Ro.4:21).

"For all the promises of God in him are yea, and in him Amen, unto the glory of God by us" (2 Co.1:20).

"Yea, though I walk through the valley of the shadow of death, I will fear no evil: for thou art with me; thy rod and thy staff they comfort me" (Ps.23:4).

"When thou passest through the waters, I will be with thee; and through the rivers, they shall not overflow thee: when thou walkest through the fire, thou shalt not be burned; neither shall the flame kindle upon thee" (Is.43:2).

3 (1:15) **Kingdom of God**: second, the gospel declares that the Kingdom of God is at hand (see DEEPER STUDY # 3—Mt.19:23-24 for discussion).

"The law and the prophets were until John: since that time the kingdom of God is preached, and every man presseth into it" (Lu.16:16).

"And when he was demanded of the Pharisees, when the kingdom of God should come, he answered them and said, The kingdom of God cometh not with observation; neither shall they say, Lo here! or, lo there! for, behold, the kingdom of God is within you" (Lu.17:20-21).

"Now after that John was put in prison, Jesus came into Galilee, preaching the gospel of the kingdom of God, and saying, The time is fulfilled, and the kingdom of God is at hand: repent ye, and believe the gospel" (Mk.1:14-15).

"And he lifted up his eyes on his disciples, and said, Blessed be ye poor [in spirit]: for yours is the kingdom of God" (Lu.6:20).

"Jesus answered and said unto him, Verily, verily, I say unto thee, Except a man be born again, he cannot see the kingdom of God....Jesus answered, Verily, verily, I say unto thee, Except a man be born of water and of the Spirit, he cannot enter into the kingdom of God" (Jn.3:3, 5).

"For the kingdom of God is not meat and drink; but righteousness, and peace, and joy in the Holy Ghost" (Ro.14:17).

4 (1:15) **Repentance—Believe**: third, the gospel declares that a person must repent and believe the gospel. Both repentance and belief are essential.

a. Repentance by itself does not satisfy the law which was formerly broken. A person may repent and change from his former life, but repentance is not enough. Payment and satisfaction must be made for the laws he has already broken. This is why a person must believe in the *good news* about Jesus Christ. Jesus kept the law perfectly. He lived a sinless life

(2 Co.5:21; Heb.4:15; 7:26; 1 Pe.1:19; 2:22). He was perfectly righteous. As such, He satisfied God perfectly. He stood as the Perfect Man, the Ideal Man, the Pattern of what every man should be. And as the *Ideal Man He could stand for every man* and offer Himself to God as the *Ideal Payment*, the *Ideal Satisfaction* for all who had broken the law of God. This is the glorious gospel, the *good news* preached by Jesus Christ throughout Galilee. The person who becomes acceptable to God is the person who repents and believes in the gospel, who believes that Jesus is God's Son (Mk.1:1), that Jesus is the *Ideal Man* who has made the perfect payment, the perfect satisfaction for our sins. Jesus is the propitiation for sins (see notes—Ro.3:25; DEEPER STUDY # 1—1 Jn.2:2. Also see note, *Justification*—Ro.5:1.)

"For he hath made him to be sin for us, who knew no sin; that we might be made the righteousness of God in him" (2 Co.5:21).

"For we have not an high priest which cannot be touched with the feeling of our infirmities; but was in all points tempted like as we are, yet without sin" (He.4:15).

"Wherefore he is able also to save them to the uttermost that come unto God by him, seeing he ever liveth to make intercession for them. For such an high priest became us, who is holy, harmless, undefiled, separate from sinners, and made higher than the heavens" (He.7:25-26).

"Forasmuch as ye know that ye were not redeemed with corruptible things, as silver and gold, from your vain conversation received by tradition from your fathers; but with the precious blood of Christ, as of a lamb without blemish and without spot" (1 Pe.1:18-19).

"Who did no sin, neither was guile found in his mouth: who, when he was reviled, reviled not again; when he suffered, he threatened not; but committed himself to him that judgeth righteously: who his own self bare our sins in his own body on the tree, that we, being dead to sins, should live unto righteousness: by whose stripes ye were healed" (1 Pe.2:22-24).

b. Faith by itself does not satisfy the law. Faith without repentance, without a true change of life, is insincere. It is profession only. It presumes upon God, thinking He will excuse a self-centered life just like a grandfather who unwisely pampers and indulges a spoiled grandchild. Faith in Christ, in His satisfaction for sin, and repentance are both essential to enter the Kingdom of God. (See DEEPER STUDY # 1, *Repentance*—Acts 17:29-30 for more discussion.)

"Repent ye: for the kingdom of heaven is at hand" (Mt.3:2).

"I tell you, Nay: but, except ye repent, ye shall all likewise perish" (Lu.13:3).

"For God so loved the world, that he gave his only begotten Son, that whosoever believeth in him should not perish, but have everlasting life" (Jn.3:16).

"Then Peter said unto them, Repent, and be baptized every one of you in the name of Jesus Christ for the remission of sins, and ye shall receive the gift of the Holy Ghost" (Ac.2:38).

"Repent ye therefore, and be converted, that your sins may be blotted out, when the times of refreshing shall come from the presence of the Lord" (Ac.3:19).

"That if thou shalt confess with thy mouth the Lord Jesus, and shalt believe in thine heart that God hath raised him from the dead, thou shalt be saved. For with the heart man believeth unto righteousness; and with the mouth confession is made unto salvation" (Ro.10:9-10).

"If my people, which are called by my name, shall humble themselves, and pray, and seek my face, and turn from their wicked ways; then will I hear from heaven, and will forgive their sin, and will heal their land" (2 Chr.7:14).

"Let the wicked forsake his way, and the unrighteous man his thoughts: and let him return unto the LORD, and he will have mercy upon him; and to our God, for he will abundantly pardon" (Is.55:7).

"But if the wicked will turn from all his sins that he hath committed, and keep all my statutes, and do that which is lawful and right, he shall surely live, he shall not die" (Eze.18:21).

DEEPER STUDY # 2

(1:15) **Believe**: see DEEPER STUDY # 2—Jn.2:24; DEEPER STUDY # 3—Ac.5:32; note—Ro.10:16-17; DEEPER STUDY # 1—He.10:38 for discussion.

	E. Jesus Christ & His Disciples: The Kind of Person Called, 1:16-20 *(Mt. 4:18-22; Lu. 5:1-11; Jn. 1:35-51)*	fishers of men. 18 And straightway they forsook their nets, and followed him.	a. Their call b. Their response: Immediate & costly—gave up their business
		19 And when he had gone a little further thence, he saw	**3. They were cooperative men**
1. They were industrious, hard-working men[DS1]	16 Now as he walked by the sea of Galilee, he saw Simon and Andrew his brother casting a net into the sea: for they were fishers.	James the son of Zebedee, and John his brother, who also were in the ship mending their nets.	
		20 And straightway he called them: and they left their father Zebedee in the ship with the hired servants, and went after him.	**4. They were successful men, but also sacrificial & considerate**
2. They were visionary men: Looking for the Messiah & ready to follow Him	17 And Jesus said unto them, Come ye after me, and I will make you to become		

DIVISION I

THE BEGINNING OF THE GOSPEL: JESUS CHRIST, THE SON OF GOD, 1:1-20

E. Jesus Christ and His Disciples: The Kind of Person Called, 1:16-20

(1:16-20) **Introduction—Call**: Jesus called simple men. Note that they were *not*...
- religious leaders.
- powerful men, not the political leaders of the nation's ruling body, the Sanhedrin (see note, Sanhedrin—Mt.26:59).
- of the priestly or ministerial profession.
- students in the schools of higher learning.

Very simply, they were ordinary men, simple laymen engaged in the affairs of life just like all the laymen of their day. Having said this, however, a question needs to be asked. If these men were just ordinary people, why did Jesus call them instead of calling the more gifted? The answer lies in some very special qualities that the disciples possessed. They did have some very special qualities that made them stand out from the average layman. This passage gives a picture of these qualities, a picture of the kind of person Jesus calls. (See outline and note—Mt.4:18-22 for additional thoughts on all these points.)
1. They were industrious, hard-working men (v.16).
2. They were visionary men: looking for the Messiah and ready to follow Him (vv.17-18).
3. They were cooperative men (v.19).
4. They were successful men, but also sacrificial and considerate (v.20).

1 (1:16) **Believers—Work**: the disciples of Jesus were industrious, hard-working men. "Jesus saw Simon and Andrew casting a net into the sea." A little farther up the lake "He saw James...and John his brother...mending their nets" (v.19). Jesus has no use for the lazy, slow-moving, sloppy, nonchalant, disinterested, uncommitted workman. The person who Jesus calls is an industrious, hard-working person. A study of God's call to various persons throughout Scripture will make this fact crystal clear. For example:

⇒ Compare the call of Amos.

> **"Then answered Amos, and said to Amaziah, I was no prophet, neither was I a prophet's son; but I was a *herdman*, and a *gatherer* of sycomore fruit: and the Lord took me as I followed the flock, and the Lord said unto me, Go, prophesy unto my people Israel" (Am.7:14-15).**

⇒ Compare the call of Elisha.

> **"So he departed thence, and found Elisha the son of Shaphat, who was plowing with twelve yoke of oxen before him, and he with the twelfth: and Elijah passed by him, and cast his mantle upon him" (1 K.19:19).**

⇒ Compare the call of Saul of Tarsus, a man who was anything but lazy (Ac.9:1f).

> **"Therefore, my beloved brethren, be ye stedfast, unmoveable, always abounding in the work of the Lord, forasmuch as ye know that your labour is not in vain in the Lord" (1 Co.15:58).**

Thought 1. Note what Jesus said:

> **"For the Son of man is as a man taking a far journey, who left his house, and gave authority to his servants, and to every man his work, and commanded the porter to watch" (Mk.13:34).**
>
> **"He said therefore, A certain nobleman went into a far country to receive for himself a kingdom, and to return. And he called his ten servants, and delivered them ten pounds, and said unto them, Occupy till I come" (Lu.19:12-13).**

DEEPER STUDY # 1
(1:16) **Sea of Galilee—Lake Gennesaret—Sea of Tiberias**: a fresh water lake in northern Palestine. At its widest points, it was only about 13 miles north to south and 8 miles east to west. It would not be called a sea today because of its small size. There are several important facts to note about the Lake.

1. The Lake was known by several names: the Sea of Galilee (Mt.4:18; 15:29; Mk.1:16; 7:31); the Sea of Tiberias (Jn.6:1; 21:1); the Lake of Gennesaret (Lu.5:1); and simply the "Sea" (Jn.6:16-25) or the "Lake" (Lu.5:2; 8:22). In the Old Testament it was called the Sea of Chinnereth (meaning harp shaped, Nu.34:11; De.3:17; Jos.13:27) or Chinneroth (Jos.12:3; 1 K.15:20).
2. The Lake was surrounded by some of the richest and most heavily populated areas of Palestine. Large towns flourished along its shores, towns which play a prominent role in Scripture: Capernaum (see outline and notes—Mt.4:12-13), Bethsaida (Mk.6:45), Chorazin (Lu.10:13), Magdala (Mt.15:39), Gadara (Mk.5:1).
3. The Lake was subject to violent storms. It sat 680 feet below sea level which gave the Lake a warm climate, but it was in a pocket-like basin surrounded by steep, fast-rising hills (2000 feet high) and funnel-like mountains. The funnels or deep ravines running down through the mountains have resulted from eons of erosion. When cold-fronts move in with their fierce winds, the cold whips through the funnel-like gorges and mixes with the warm temperatures of the Lake. Unpredictable and terrifying storms result (Mt.8:23-27; Mk.4:35-41; Lu.8:22-25).

2 (1:17-18) **Call**: the disciples of Jesus were visionary men, men who were looking for the Messiah and ready to follow Him no matter the cost. This was the *quality* that distinguished the disciples from many others. Some lay persons possessed the other qualities of the disciples (as they do in every generation), but this particular quality was found in few, if in any other men. The fourth quality was a willingness to sacrifice all in order to follow Christ. Many were looking for the Messiah, but few were actually ready to follow Him. Few if any others would pay the cost of giving up their businesses and of immediately following Jesus. But these men were willing to follow Jesus, and they did follow Him.

Thought 1. Few people have a strong vision—a vision so strong that they are willing to pay any price to follow Jesus. Giving up their profession or business, home or environment, family or friends is just too costly. They lack the vision.

"He that loveth father or mother more than me is not worthy of me: and he that loveth son or daughter more than me is not worthy of me. And he that taketh not his cross, and followeth after me, is not worthy of me. He that findeth his life shall lose it: and he that loseth his life for my sake shall find it" (Mt.10:37-39).

"So likewise, whosoever he be of you that forsaketh not all that he hath, he cannot be my disciple" (Lu.14:33).

"Yea doubtless, and I count all things but loss for the excellency of the knowledge of Christ Jesus my Lord: for whom I have suffered the loss of all things, and do count them but dung, that I may win Christ" (Ph.3:8).

Thought 2. Jesus calls a person to a life of work, not to a life of ease and comfort. He calls a person to invest his life, not to waste his life.

"And he said to them all, If any man will come after me, let him deny himself, and take up his cross daily, and follow me. For whosoever will save his life shall lose it: but whosoever will lose his life for my sake, the same shall save it" (Lu.9:23-24).

"I must work the works of him that sent me, while it is day: the night cometh, when no man can work" (Jn.9:4).

"Moreover it is required in stewards, that a man be found faithful" (1 Co.4:2).

"Whatsoever thy hand findeth to do, do it with thy might; for there is no work, nor device, nor knowledge, nor wisdom, in the grave, whither thou goest" (Ec.9:10).

Thought 3. Note that the primary call is to become "fishers of men," not to become teachers, preachers, counselors, administrators, builders, fund raisers or anything else. Yet, how easily we obscure and camouflage the evangelistic ministry of the church.

"Go ye therefore, and teach all nations, baptizing them in the name of the Father, and of the Son, and of the Holy Ghost: teaching them to observe all things whatsoever I have commanded you: and, lo, I am with you alway, even unto the end of the world" (Mt.28:19-20; see Mt.20:28).

"And he said unto them, Go ye into all the world, and preach the gospel to every creature" (Mk.16:15).

"For the Son of man is come to seek and to save that which was lost" (Lu.19:10).

"Then said Jesus to them again, Peace be unto you: as my Father hath sent me, even so send I you" (Jn.20:21).

"But ye shall receive power, after the Holy Ghost is come upon you: and ye shall be witnesses unto me both in Jerusalem, and in Judaea, and in Samaria, and unto the uttermost part of the earth" (Ac.1:8).

"And the things that thou hast heard of me among many witnesses, the same commit thou to faithful men, who shall be able to teach others also. Thou therefore endure hardness, as a good soldier of Jesus Christ" (2 Ti.2:2-3).

3 (1:19) **Call**: the disciples of Jesus were cooperative men. They were brothers, and yet they were working together. The fact that they were working together says at least three things.

a. They had *good* parents who had taught them to love and care for one another.
b. They came from a closely knit family, a family that worked together.
c. They followed in the steps of their parents' teaching, maintaining a brotherly spirit throughout life.

Thought 1. The disciples' brotherly, cooperative spirit shows us three things.

(1) The need for a brotherly spirit: the kind of spirit Christ desires of His followers. The kind of kingdom Christ is building is a kingdom of followers with a brotherly spirit.

"Thou shalt love thy neighbour as thyself" (Mt.22:39).
"This is my commandment, That ye love one another, as I have loved you" (Jn.15:12; see Jn.13:35; 1 Pe.1:22).
"Be kindly affectioned one to another with brotherly love; in honour preferring one another" (Ro.12:10).

(2) The need for reaching families: brothers and sisters reaching each other.

"He first findeth his own brother Simon, and saith unto him, We have found the Messias, which is, being interpreted, the Christ. And he brought him to Jesus. And when Jesus beheld him, he said, Thou art Simon the son of Jona: thou shalt be called Cephas" (Jn.1:41-42).
"So the father knew that it was at the same hour, in the which Jesus said unto him, Thy son liveth: and himself believed, and his whole house" (Jn.4:53).
"And when she was baptized, and her household, she besought us, saying, If ye have judged me to be faithful to the Lord, come into my house, and abide there. And she constrained us" (Ac.16:15).
"And brought them out, and said, Sirs, what must I do to be saved? And they said, Believe on the Lord Jesus Christ, and thou shalt be saved, and thy house" (Ac.16:30-31).

(3) The need for parents to train up their children in the way they should go (see outline and notes—Ep.6:1-4; Col.3:20-21).

"And thou shalt teach them [God's words] diligently unto thy children, and shalt talk of them when thou sittest in thine house, and when thou walkest by the way, and when thou liest down, and when thou risest up" (De.6:7).
"Train up a child in the way he should go: and when he is old, he will not depart from it" (Pr.22:6).
"And, ye fathers, provoke not your children to wrath: but bring them up in the nurture and admonition of the Lord" (Ep.6:4).

4 (1:20) **Call**: the disciples of Jesus were successful, but sacrificial and considerate men. Zebedee and his sons, James and John, were successful businessmen. Note: the sons left their father with "hired servants." Perhaps this is the reason John was able to enter the palace of the High Priest when Jesus was being tried for treason (Jn.18:15f). He probably provided fish for the palace. (See notes—Mk.10:35-37; Jn.18:15-18.)

Note two significant facts about what is said.

a. James and John, despite their success as fellow laborers with their father, sacrificed their part of the business. They were either present owners or would be future owners by inheritance. They gave it all up to follow Jesus. This, too, was a rare quality found in few persons.

b. James and John were considerate of their father. They did not leave him alone; they would have never done that! They cared for him; they left him with "hired servants."

Thought 1. How many would sacrifice their inheritance to follow Jesus?

"One thing thou lackest: go thy way, sell whatsoever thou hast, and give to the poor, and thou shalt have treasure in heaven: and come, take up the cross, and follow me" (Mk.10:21).
"For where your treasure is, there will your heart be also" (Mt.6:21).
"And every one that hath forsaken houses, or brethren, or sisters, or father, or mother, or wife, or children, or lands, for my name's sake, shall receive an hundredfold, and shall inherit everlasting life" (Mt.19:29).

Thought 2. How many adults care enough for their parents to see to it that they have plenty of help in tending their affairs? The kind of person Jesus calls is a considerate person.

"For Moses said, Honour thy father and thy mother; and, Whoso curseth father or mother, let him die the death" (Mk.7:10).
"But if any widow have children or nephews, let them learn first to show piety at home, and to requite [repay] their parents: for that is good and acceptable before God....But if any provide not for his own, and specially for those of his own house, he hath denied the faith, and is worse than an infidel" (1 Ti.5:4, 8).
"Thou shalt rise up before the hoary [aged, elderly] head, and honor the face of the old man, and fear thy God: I am the LORD" (Le.19:32).

	II. THE SON OF GOD'S OPENING MINISTRY: JESUS' IMMEDIATE IMPACT, 1:21-3:35 **A. Jesus' Teaching & Its Impact: Launching a New Ministry, 1:21-22** *(Lu. 4:31-32)*
1. He began with worship: Immediately—in the synagogue **2. He seized the opportunity to teach**	21 And they went into Capernaum; and straightway on the sabbath day he entered into the synagogue, and taught.
3. He amazed the crowd a. His teaching, vv.14-15 b. His authority	22 And they were astonished at his doctrine: for he taught them as one that had authority, and not as the scribes.

DIVISION II

THE SON OF GOD'S OPENING MINISTRY: JESUS' IMMEDIATE IMPACT, 1:21–3:35

A. Jesus' Teaching and Its Impact: Launching a New Ministry, 1:21-22

(1:21-22) **Introduction—Jesus Christ, Ministry**: Jesus was now in the midst of launching His ministry in full force. It might be said that this was the beginning, the opening of His ministry. What Jesus did as He launched forth is important for the believer to see as he goes forth serving his Lord.

1. He began with worship: immediately—in the synagogue (v.21).
2. He seized the opportunity to teach (v.21).
3. He amazed the crowd (v.22).

1 (1:21) **Worship**: Jesus began His ministry with worship—*immediately.* Note the words "straightway [immediately] on the sabbath day He entered into the synagogue." (See DEEPER STUDY # 1,2—Mk.1:21; DEEPER STUDY # 2—Mt.4:23 for a discussion on the synagogue.)

This says several significant things.

a. Jesus launched His ministry in worship. A new ministry should always begin in worship. It should be bathed in worship.

b. Jesus was faithful to *weekly worship in the synagogue.* The synagogue, with its leaders and its worshippers, was far from perfect; yet on the Sabbath day, Jesus entered and worshipped faithfully. Such an example leaves all without excuse.

> **"And when he was departed thence, he went into their synagogue" (Mt.12:9).**
>
> **"And they went into Capernaum; and straightway on the sabbath day he entered into the synagogue, and taught" (Mk.1:21).**
>
> **"And he came to Nazareth, where he had been brought up: and, as his custom was, he went into the synagogue on the sabbath day, and stood up for to read" (Lu.4:16).**
>
> **"But when they [Paul and his companions] departed from Perga, they came to Antioch in Pisidia, and went into the synagogue on the sabbath day, and sat down" (Ac.13:14).**
>
> **"Not forsaking the assembling of ourselves together, as the manner of some is; but exhorting one another: and so much the more, as ye see the day approaching" (He.10:25).**

DEEPER STUDY # 1

(1:21) **Synagogue** (synagoge): means a gathering, a community of people. It can also mean the building in which the gathering took place. Synagogues were often held in homes. In fact, if ten Jews lived in a community, they were bound by law to conduct a synagogue meeting someplace. If there were enough Jewish citizens in a place and the local laws allowed, they constructed a synagogue building. There is no sure mention of synagogues in the Old Testament, but they are mentioned over fifty times in the New Testament.

Synagogues began to rise either during or right after the Jews returned from the Babylonian captivity. The leaders became convinced that the nation could never survive unless its people really knew and practiced the law of God. Therefore, it was established that wherever ten or more Jews lived, they were to meet together on a regular basis in a synagogue meeting. They were to study and practice the law of God. The growth of synagogues was staggering. The number can be imagined by keeping in mind how the Jews had been deported and dispersed all over the world and by remembering that wherever ten Jews lived, they were to form a synagogue meeting (see Lu.4:16f; Ac.9:2).

The head of the synagogue was the Ruler of the Synagogue. He was the administrator, handling the business affairs and overseeing the services. He arranged for speakers and readers and the men who were to pray (see Mk.5:22; Lu.13:14; Ac.18:8). There was also the chazzan or sexton or minister. He was in charge of the sacred scrolls or Scripture, the teaching of the law in actual class sessions, and the care and maintenance of the synagogue building (see Lu.4:20).

The service of the synagogue meeting was very simple. There was prayer, the reading of the Scripture (scroll), and an exposition of the Scripture. (See Lu.4:16f; Acts 13:14-52 for a picture of two services.)

As one reads the New Testament, there are two important facts to remember about the synagogue. (1) Its primary purpose was to teach the Word of God. All other functions were secondary. (2) There was no permanent preacher or teacher. It was the practice to call upon both local and visiting teachers to give an exposition of the Scripture.

These two facts explain why Jesus, and later the apostles, were able to find an open pulpit in the synagogues as they carried out their mission throughout the world (see Ac.3:1; 10:2; 13:5; 13:14-52; 18:4). (See DEEPER STUDY # 2—Mt.4:23.)

DEEPER STUDY # 2

(1:21) **Synagogue**: it is interesting to note that a Gentile centurion built this particular synagogue and gave it to the Jews as a special gift. There were both Jews and Gentile proselytes present as Jesus ministered. (See Lu.7:1-10, esp.5.)

2 (1:21) **Teaching—Time—Initiative**: Jesus seized the opportunity to teach. Note the words "straightway [immediately], He entered into the synagogue, and taught." The idea is that He excitedly entered and immediately began to teach. This was the very day He was to launch His ministry; this was the first chance He had to take the podium and teach. He immediately rushed forth, seizing the opportunity.

Thought 1. Opportunities must be seized when they present themselves. We must not let them pass. Several things can make us miss opportunities.
(1) Not looking for opportunities.
(2) Not grasping for the opportunities at the right time.
(3) Not having the initiative to grab an opportunity when it arises.
(4) Not handling the opportunity properly.

Thought 2. Jesus utilized the moment. His time was short, so He seized the opportunity to teach. Time is short. We must use every minute to the fullest, for the night is coming when no man can work. There are several mistakes made with time.
(1) We can lose time: just let it pass, never seize the opportunity.
(2) We can ignore time: pay no attention to it, give it little if any thought.
(3) We can neglect time: be unconcerned and non-caring, fail to realize its potential and exactly what could be achieved with its proper use.
(4) We can abuse time: use time to do the opposite of what we should be doing; misuse time by using it half-heartedly, sloppily, inefficiently.

"I must work the works of him that sent me, while it is day: the night cometh, when no man can work" (Jn.9:4).

"And that, knowing the time, that now it is high time to awake out of sleep: for now is our salvation nearer than when we believed. The night is far spent, the day is at hand: let us therefore cast off the works of darkness, and let us put on the armour of light" (Ro.13:11-12).

"But this I say, brethren, the time is short: it remaineth, that both they that have wives be as though they had none; and they that weep, as though they wept not; and they that rejoice, as though they rejoiced not; and they that buy, as though they possessed not; and they that use this world, as not abusing it: for the fashion of this world passeth away" (1 Co.7:29-31).

"Attend upon the Lord without distraction" (1 Co.7:35).

"See then that ye walk circumspectly, not as fools, but as wise, redeeming the time, because the days are evil" (Ep.5:15-16).

"Walk in wisdom toward them that are without, redeeming the time" (Col.4:5).

"So teach us to number our days, that we may apply our hearts unto wisdom" (Ps.90:12).

"Remember now thy Creator in the days of thy youth, while the evil days come not, nor the years draw nigh, when thou shalt say, I have no pleasure in them" (Ec.12:1).

3 (1:22) **Jesus Christ, Teaching**: Jesus astonished the crowd. The word *astonished* (ekplessonto) is a strong and expressive word. Its literal meaning is to be *struck in mind*, to *be astonished.* The people were stricken, stirred, aroused, moved by the Lord's teaching.

Jesus astonished the crowd for two reasons.

a. His message was very different (see outline and notes—Mk.1:14-15).

b. His authority was strikingly different. Note the words, "He taught them as one that had authority, and not as the scribes." Five comparisons will show this.

1) Tradition vs. authority. Other teachers relied upon esteemed men, their traditions and teachings, and quoted them as their source of authority, but not Jesus. He taught with a personal authority; He spoke independently of all others. He spoke with a certainty, a positiveness, a finality that no one else had ever done.

2) Form vs. power. Other teachers stressed ritual, ceremony, and form. Jesus stressed the need and availability of power to overcome the trials and sufferings of life.
3) Humanism (laws) vs. the spiritual (truth). Other teachers reasoned and formulated law after law, teaching that these were the way to real life. Jesus spoke about matters of the heart and life, of the soul and spirit. The answers He gave were spiritual truths, not human thought and rationalism.
4) Religion vs. life. Other teachers preached their religion; Jesus preached life—a life to be lived abundantly and eternally.
5) Profession vs. possession. Other teachers professed to follow God, but they twisted and interpreted the law of God to their own liking. What they followed was their own *man-made religion.* They were anything but followers of God. Jesus practiced and lived what He taught. His life was so different from other teachers that people sat up and took notice of what He had to say.

"Heaven and earth shall pass away: but my words shall not pass away" (Mk.13:31).

"And they were astonished at his doctrine: for his word was with power" (Lu.4:32).

"The same came to Jesus by night, and said unto him, Rabbi, we know that thou art a teacher come from God: for no man can do these miracles that thou doest, except God be with him" (Jn.3:2).

"It is the spirit that quickeneth; the flesh profiteth nothing: the words that I speak unto you, they are spirit, and they are life" (Jn.6:63).

"Jesus answered them, and said, My doctrine is not mine, but his that sent me. If any man will do his will, he shall know of the doctrine, whether it be of God, or whether I speak of myself. He that speaketh of himself seeketh his own glory: but he that seeketh his glory that sent him, the same is true, and no unrighteousness is in him" (Jn.7:16-18).

"Verily, verily, I say unto you, If a man keep my saying, he shall never see death" (Jn.8:51).

"Believest thou not that I am in the Father, and the Father in me? the words that I speak unto you I speak not of myself: but the Father that dwelleth in me, he doeth the works" (Jn.14:10).

"Whosoever transgresseth, and abideth not in the doctrine of Christ, hath not God. He that abideth in the doctrine of Christ, he hath both the Father and the Son" (2 Jn.9).

	B. Jesus' Power over Evil Spirits & Its Impact: Delivering the Most Enslaved, 1:23-28 *(Lu. 4:33-37)*	saying, Hold thy peace, and come out of him.	a. Jesus rebuked the evil spirit
		26 And when the unclean spirit had torn him, and cried with a loud voice, he came out of him.	b. The evil spirit obeyed
1. Picture 1: The need of the possessed man a. He was in the synagogue	23 And there was in their synagogue a man with an unclean spirit; and he cried out,	27 And they were all amazed, insomuch that they questioned among themselves, saying, What thing is this? what new doctrine is this? for with authority commandeth he even the unclean spirits, and they do obey him.	**3. Picture 3: The impact upon people** a. The people were amazed b. The people questioned: What power, what new revelation (teaching) is this?
b. He raged & cried out, sensed & recoiled from the purity, the holiness of Jesus c. He identified Jesus	24 Saying, Let us alone; what have we to do with thee, thou Jesus of Nazareth? art thou come to destroy us? I know thee who thou art, the Holy One of God.	28 And immediately his fame spread abroad throughout all the region round about Galilee.	c. The people spread His fame
2. Picture 2: The power of Jesus	25 And Jesus rebuked him,		

DIVISION II

THE SON OF GOD'S OPENING MINISTRY: JESUS' IMMEDIATE IMPACT, 1:21-3:35

B. Jesus' Power Over Evil Spirits and Its Impact: Delivering the Most Enslaved, 1:23-28

(1:23-28) **Introduction**: man can be delivered from all the forces of evil by the power of Jesus. He can even be delivered from unclean spirits that enslave him, no matter the grip of the enslavement. Jesus has the power to deliver man (Ro.8:31; 1 Jn.4:4). (See outline, notes and DEEPER STUDY # 1,2—Mt.8:28-34; notes—17:14-21; Lu.8:26-39.)

1. Picture 1: the need of the possessed man (vv.23-24).
2. Picture 2: the power of Jesus (vv.25-26).
3. Picture 3: the impact upon people (vv.27-28).

1 (1:23-24) **Evil Spirits**: the first picture is that of the possessed man and his need. The words *with an unclean spirit* (en pneumati akatharto) should be translated "in" (en) an unclean spirit. The man was in the grasp, in the possession of the unclean spirit. He was in the grip, captivated by the unclean spirit. He was under the spell, the will of the unclean spirit. To better understand the meaning, think of all the evil in the world, all the evil that occurs every hour and every day. Then note John's words, "The whole world lieth in the wicked [or evil] one" (en to ponero, 1 Jn.5:19). That is, the world lies under the influence, power, bondage, will, and grip of the evil one. In the very same sense, this man was possessed by an unclean spirit. (See DEEPER STUDY # 1—Mt.8:28-34 for a discussion of the Bible's teaching on evil spirits. Also see note—Lu.8:26-39.)

Note three things.

a. The possessed man, surprisingly, was in the synagogue. What was he doing there? Was he a regular attender or had he come just to hear Jesus? We are not told. But if he were a regular attender, then the synagogue was spiritually dead. How do we know this? Because the man could attend services time after time and never be helped spiritually.

> **Thought 1**. How many services are *dead*, so *lifeless* that men with evil spirits can sit in the services and never be convicted or helped spiritually?
>
> > **"Having a form of godliness, but denying the power thereof" (2 Ti.3:5).**
> >
> > **"Wherefore the Lord said, Forasmuch as this people draw near me with their mouth, and with their lips do honor me, but have removed their heart far from me, and their fear toward me is taught by the precept [tradition] of men: therefore, behold, I will proceed to do a marvelous work [work of judgment] among this people, even a marvelous work and a wonder: for the wisdom of their wise men shall perish, and the understanding of their prudent men shall be hid. Woe unto them that seek deep to hide their counsel from the LORD, and their works are in the dark, and they say, Who seeth us? and who knoweth us?" (Is.29:13-15).**
>
> **Thought 2.** How many sit in church and hear the Word of God week after week or live among believers and never make a decision to turn from their evil? They sit in service after service and brush shoulders with believers day by day, but they never decisively turn to God.
>
> > **"Ye stiffnecked and uncircumcised in heart and ears, ye do always resist the Holy Ghost: as your fathers did, so do ye" (Ac.7:51).**
> >
> > **"Hath the LORD as great delight in burnt offerings and sacrifices, as in obeying the voice of the LORD? Behold, to obey is better than sacrifice, and to hearken than the fat of rams" (1 S.15:22).**
> >
> > **"For thou desirest not sacrifice; else would I give it: thou delightest not in burnt offering" (Ps.51:16).**
> >
> > **"Keep thy foot when thou goest to the house of God, and be more ready to hear, than to give the sacrifice of fools: for they consider not that they do evil" (Ec.5:1).**

> **"And they have turned unto me the back, and not the face: though I taught them, rising up early and teaching them, yet they have not hearkened to receive instruction" (Je.32:33).**
> **"As for the word that thou hast spoken unto us in the name of the LORD, we will not hearken unto thee" (Je.44:16).**
> **"For I desired mercy, and not sacrifice; and the knowledge of God more than burnt offerings" (Ho.6:6).**
> **"But they refused to hearken, and pulled away the shoulder, and stopped their ears, that they should not hear" (Zec.7:11).**

b. The possessed man raged and cried out, sensed and recoiled from purity. The unclean spirit cried out in recognition of three things.

1) The unclean spirit cried, "What have we to do with thee, Jesus of Nazareth?" The unclean spirit was entirely different from the clean spirit of Jesus. Jesus is perfectly pure and sinless. The unclean spirit had nothing to do with the purity of Jesus. The unclean spirit was diametrically opposed to the holiness of Jesus.

Thought 1. Sin, dirt, pollution, and uncleanness do not have a part or a place with Jesus. Jesus has no uncleanness in Him whatsoever.

2) The unclean spirit recognized that Jesus had come to destroy him. Down deep within, the unclean persons know they are to judged and destroyed. They hate and despise, ignore and neglect, hide and rationalize in order to continue their unclean ways. The paradox is that they know they will be judged even while they are sinning and rebelling against God. "For this purpose the Son of God was manifested, that he might destroy the works of the devil" (1 Jn.3:8).
3) The unclean spirit identified Jesus. He said, "I know thee who thou art, the Holy One of God." He confessed Jesus. As James says, "Thou believest that there is one God; thou doest well: the devils also believe, and tremble" (Js.2:19).

Thought 1. What an indictment against so many! They deny, while devils confess.

> **"Whosoever therefore shall confess me before men, him will I confess also before my Father which is in heaven. But whosoever shall deny me before men, him will I also deny before my Father which is in heaven" (Mt.10:32-33).**
> **"Whosoever therefore shall be ashamed of me and of my words in this adulterous and sinful generation; of him also shall the Son of man be ashamed, when he cometh in the glory of his Father with the holy angels" (Mk.8:38).**
> **"Who is a liar but he that denieth that Jesus is the Christ? He is antichrist, that denieth the Father and the Son. Whosoever denieth the Son, the same hath not the Father: [but] he that acknowledgeth the Son hath the Father also" (1 Jn.2:22-23).**

Thought 2. Knowing that Jesus is the Holy One of God is not enough. A person has to believe in Christ and love Him and live a clean and pure life.

> **"Having therefore these promises, dearly beloved, let us cleanse ourselves from all filthiness of the flesh and spirit, perfecting holiness in the fear of God" (2 Co.7:1).**
> **"If a man therefore purge himself from these, he shall be a vessel unto honour, sanctified, and meet for the master's use, and prepared unto every good work" (2 Ti.2:21).**
> **"Draw nigh to God, and he will draw nigh to you. Cleanse your hands, ye sinners; and purify your hearts, ye double minded" (Js.4:8).**
> **"Come now, and let us reason together, saith the Lord: though your sins be as scarlet, they shall be as white as snow; though they be red like crimson, they shall be as wool" (Is.1:18).**
> **"Wash thine heart from wickedness, that thou mayest be saved. How long shall thy vain thoughts lodge within thee?" (Je.4:14).**

c. The possessed man identified Jesus. This point is so significant it bears repeating: "I know thee who thou art, the Holy One of God," that is, the Holy Son of God (see DEEPER STUDY # 1, Evil Spirits—Mt.8:28-34; Son of God—Jn.1:34).

Thought 1. One of the major purposes of Jesus in confronting evil spirits was to prove His Messiahship (see DEEPER STUDY # 1—Mt.8:28-34). He is the Messiah!

> **"He saith unto them, But whom say ye that I am? And Simon Peter answered and said, Thou art the Christ, the Son of the living God. And Jesus answered and said unto him, Blessed art thou, Simon Barjona: for flesh and blood hath not revealed it unto thee, but my Father which is in heaven" (Mt.16:15-17).**
> **"But Jesus held his peace. And the high priest answered and said unto him, I adjure thee by the living God, that thou tell us whether thou be the Christ, the Son of God. Jesus saith unto him, Thou hast said: nevertheless I say unto you, Hereafter shall ye see the Son of man sitting on the right hand of power, and coming in the clouds of heaven" (Mt.26:63-64).**
> **"Then he said unto them, O fools, and slow of heart to believe all that the prophets have spoken: ought not Christ to have suffered these things, and to enter into his glory?" (Lu.24:25-26).**

> **"The woman saith unto him, I know that Messias cometh, which is called Christ: when he is come, he will tell us all things. Jesus saith unto her, I that speak unto thee am he" (Jn.4:25-26).**
>
> **"Then said Jesus unto them, When ye have lifted up the Son of man, then shall ye know that I am he, and that I do nothing of myself; but as my Father hath taught me, I speak these things. And he that sent me is with me: the Father hath not left me alone; for I do always those things that please him" (Jn.8:28-29).**
>
> **"Jesus said unto her, I am the resurrection, and the life: he that believeth in me, though he were dead, yet shall he live: and whosoever liveth and believeth in me shall never die. Believest thou this? She saith unto him, Yea, Lord: I believe that thou art the Christ, the Son of God, which should come into the world" (Jn.11:25-27).**
>
> **"Even as the Son of man came not to be ministered unto, but to minister, and to give his life a ransom for many" (Mt.20:28).**
>
> **"For the Son of man is come to seek and to save that which was lost" (Lu.19:10).**
>
> **"The thief cometh not, but for to steal, and to kill, and to destroy: I am come that they might have life, and that they might have it more abundantly" (Jn.10:10).**
>
> **"This is a faithful saying, and worthy of all acceptation, that Christ Jesus came into the world to save sinners; of whom I am chief" (1 Ti.1:15).**

Thought 2. The world cries out, "What have we to do with thee, thou Jesus of Nazareth?" Why? Because He is the Son of God who demands belief and purity of life, self-denial and a life of sacrifice. "What have we to do with thee...?"

⇒ Wealth cries, "Leave us alone. Let us secure ourselves, build up, and bank more and more."
⇒ Power cries, "Leave us alone. Let us take over, exercise authority, rule and reign, dominate, maneuver and manipulate as we will."
⇒ Ego cries, "Leave us alone. Let us seek recognition, attention, esteem, honor, and praise as we wish."
⇒ Flesh cries, "Leave us alone. Let us excite, indulge, stimulate, relax, release, escape, party, revel, and carouse as we desire."

> **"And he said to them all, If any man will come after me, let him deny himself, and take up his cross daily, and follow me. For whosoever will save his life shall lose it: but whosoever will lose his life for my sake, the same shall save it" (Lu.9:23-24).**
>
> **"So likewise, whosoever he be of you that forsaketh not all that he hath, he cannot be my disciple" (Lu.14:33).**
>
> **"And take heed to yourselves, lest at any time your hearts be overcharged with surfeiting, and drunkenness, and cares of this life, and so that day come upon you unawares" (Lu.21:34).**
>
> **"For if ye live after the flesh, ye shall die: but if ye through the Spirit do mortify the deeds of the body, ye shall live" (Ro.8:13).**
>
> **"But put ye on the Lord Jesus Christ, and make not provision for the flesh, to fulfil the lusts thereof " (Ro.13:14).**
>
> **"Mortify therefore your members which are upon the earth; fornication, uncleanness, inordinate affection, evil concupiscence, and covetousness, which is idolatry" (Col.3:5).**
>
> **"Dearly beloved, I beseech you as strangers and pilgrims, abstain from fleshly lusts, which war against the soul" (1 Pe.2:11).**

2 (1:25-26) **Jesus Christ—Power—Salvation**: the second picture is that of the power of Jesus.

a. Jesus rebuked the unclean spirit. Note the words, "Hold thy peace." Jesus did not accept demonic testimony to His Messiahship. Why? Such acknowledgment was involuntary, that is, of the mind only. It was only the mental knowledge that Jesus was the Son of God. It was not of the heart nor of the will to follow Jesus. It did not come from being born again. The witness Jesus wants is the witness of a man who has made a deliberate decision to profess Him as Lord; the witness of a heart truly changed; the witness of a heart moved by the Spirit of God to confess, "Thou art the Holy One of God" (Mk.8:29; see Mk.1:34).

Note also the power of Jesus. He casts the unclean spirit out. How? By His Word, by simply saying, "Come out of him."

Thought 1. Just meditate for a moment upon the power of the Lord's Word. He simply spoke what He willed—for the unclean spirit to come out of the man—and what He willed happened. How we need to learn to depend upon His Word as we confront the unclean spirits of this world!

> **"For I am not ashamed of the gospel [the Word] of Christ: for it is the power of God unto salvation to every one that believeth; to the Jew first, and also to the Greek" (Ro.1:16).**
>
> **"For the word of God is quick, and powerful, and sharper than any twoedged sword, piercing even to the dividing asunder of soul and spirit, and of the joints and marrow, and is a discerner of the thoughts and intents of the heart" (He.4:12).**
>
> **"Is not my word like as a fire? saith the LORD; and like a hammer that breaketh the rock in pieces?" (Je.23:29).**

Thought 2. We must make the true confession of Jesus, the confession of a believing and clean heart.

> **"I beseech you therefore, brethren, by the mercies of God, that ye present your bodies a living sacrifice, holy, acceptable unto God, which is your reasonable service. And be not conformed to this world: but be ye transformed by the renewing of your mind, that ye may prove what is that good, and acceptable, and perfect, will of God" (Ro.12:1-2).**
>
> **"But he that is joined unto the Lord is one spirit. Flee fornication. Every sin that a man doeth is without the body; but he that committeth fornication sinneth against his own body" (1 Co.6:17-18).**

b. The evil spirit obeyed. Note the words *torn him* (sparasso). The words mean to be convulsed. Apparently the man had a convulsion, jerking to and fro and crying out with a loud voice.

The question is sometimes asked, Why all this? Why such a scene? Why did Jesus not calmly heal the man in a serene atmosphere? There are probably two reasons.

1) The evil and unclean spirits in the world are powerful forces, possessing enormous power to enslave and possess man. Their power could be more clearly seen in a convulsive and noisy scene. People needed to know that the evil and unclean forces of the world are the true enemies of mankind. They are the powerful forces who enslaved men with their dirty, intoxicating, and immoral habits.
2) The man was possessed by an unclean spirit. The convulsion and cry were evidence of the unclean spirit's actually being in the man.

c. The convulsion and cry demonstrated the power and Messiahship of Jesus. Jesus was actually conquering the force of evil within a man, and only God had such a power.

Thought 1. When the unclean spirit of a man is cast out, when a man really changes and is cleansed, he undergoes a convulsive experience. *Conversion* is always a convulsive experience. Change is convulsive.

> **"Repent ye therefore, and be converted, that your sins may be blotted out, when the times of refreshing shall come from the presence of the Lord" (Ac.3:19).**
>
> **"Know ye not, that to whom ye yield yourselves servants to obey, his servants ye are to whom ye obey; whether of sin unto death, or of obedience unto righteousness? But God be thanked, that ye were the servants of sin, but ye have obeyed from the heart that form of doctrine which was delivered you. Being then made free from sin, ye became the servants of righteousness" (Ro.6:16-18; see Ro.6:19-23).**
>
> **"But I see another law in my members, warring against the law of my mind, and bringing me into captivity to the law of sin which is in my members. O wretched man that I am! who shall deliver me from the body of this death? I thank God through Jesus Christ our Lord. So then with the mind I myself serve the law of God; but with the flesh the law of sin" (Ro.7:23-25).**
>
> **"Therefore if any man be in Christ, he is a new creature: old things are passed away; behold, all things are become new" (2 Co.5:17).**
>
> **"Being born again, not of corruptible seed, but of incorruptible, by the word of God, which liveth and abideth for ever" (1 Pe.1:23).**
>
> **"The law of the LORD is perfect, converting the soul: the testimony of the LORD is sure, making wise the simple" (Ps.19:7).**

3 (1:27-28) **Decision—Jesus Christ, Response to**: the third picture is that of the impact upon people. The people reacted in three ways.

a. They were amazed (ethambethesan), astonished. What the people had witnessed was unbelievable. Using no charms, no invocations, no exorcising devices, Jesus simply said, "Come out of him"; and the unclean spirit was dramatically cast out of the man. The people were shocked and stunned.

b. They questioned and buzzed among themselves, "What *thing* is this? What new power or revelation (doctrine) is this? What is God showing us? Is the revelation, the doctrine, the power from and of the Messiah? 'For with authority commandeth He even the unclean spirits, and they do obey Him.'" The people were doing just what Jesus had wanted. They were questioning if He were the Messiah.

c. They spread His fame everywhere. Imagine the conversation in the stores, businesses, homes, and streets as people travelled throughout the area and throughout the world.

Thought 1. The impact upon us should be the same. All three responses should characterize us as we witness the power of God in changing and healing lives. Yet, how *gospel-hardened* so many of us become.

> **"And the things that thou hast heard of me among many witnesses, the same commit thou to faithful men, who shall be able to teach others also" (2 Ti.2:2).**
>
> **"But sanctify the Lord God in your hearts: and be ready always to give an answer to every man that asketh you a reason of the hope that is in you with meekness and fear" (1 Pe.3:15).**
>
> **"That which we have seen and heard declare we unto you, that ye also may have fellowship with us: and truly our fellowship is with the Father, and with his Son Jesus Christ" (1 Jn.1:3).**

	C. Jesus' Power & Impact upon Each One: Caring for the Home & the Individual, 1:29-31 *(Mt. 8:14-15; Lu. 4:38-39)*
1. The worship of Jesus brought His presence into a house	29 And forthwith, when they were come out of the synagogue, they entered into the house of Simon and Andrew, with James and John.
2. The presence of Jesus brought hope to a house	30 But Simon's wife's mother lay sick of a fever, and anon they tell him of her.
3. The presence of Jesus brought healing & help to a house **4. The presence of Jesus brought devotion & service to a house**	31 And he came and took her by the hand, and lifted her up; and immediately the fever left her, and she ministered unto them.

DIVISION II

THE SON OF GOD'S OPENING MINISTRY: JESUS' IMMEDIATE IMPACT, 1:21–3:35

C. Jesus' Power and Impact Upon Each One: Caring for the Home and the Individual, 1:29-31

(1:29-31) **Introduction**: Jesus Christ cares for the individual and the home. In fact the whole thrust of His heart and purpose in coming to earth was "to seek and to save that which was lost" (Lu.19:10). His care, presence, and power are available to any individual who will invite Him into their home. This glorious truth is clearly demonstrated in this event which took place in Peter's home.

1. The worship of Jesus brought His presence into a house (v.29).
2. The presence of Jesus brought hope to a house (v.30).
3. The presence of Jesus brought healing and help to a house (v.31).
4. The presence of Jesus brought devotion and service to a house (v.31).

1 (1:29) **Worship—Devotion—Jesus Christ, Presence of**: the worship of Jesus brought His presence into a house. It was the Sabbath, and Jesus and His disciples had gone to the synagogue to worship and teach (Mk.1:21-22). The service was now over, and Jesus had apparently entered Peter's home to have lunch. Peter had probably invited Jesus to lunch. The main meal on the Sabbath came right after worship or twelve noon, which was the sixth hour (the Jewish day began at 6 a.m.).

There is a strong picture here. Worship brought Jesus into Peter's home. Peter and the other three apostles had followed Jesus to worship. Upon leaving worship, Peter invited the Lord to be a guest in his home, and Jesus accepted the invitation to fellowship with him and his family.

Thought 1. When a person truly worships the Lord and invites Him into his home, the Lord will enter and fellowship therein. He willingly becomes a guest of anyone who extends the invitation.

"Behold, I stand at the door, and knock: if any man hear my voice, and open the door, I will come in to him, and will sup with him, and he with me" (Re.3:20).

Thought 2. When a person truly worships the Lord, that person is assured of Christ's presence. Christ will live with that person no matter how humble the person's home or dwelling is. If the dwelling is nothing more than a piece of ground under the open sky, the Lord will live with that person.

"Lo, I am with you alway, even unto the end of the world. Amen" (Mt.28:20).

"Let your conversation be without covetousness; and be content with such things as ye have: for he hath said, I will never leave thee, nor forsake thee" (He.13:5).

"And it came to pass, that, while they communed together and reasoned, Jesus himself drew near, and went with them" (Lu.24:15).

Thought 3. The person or family who worships is more likely to have the presence of the Lord in their home. Worship and faithfulness to God instill a sense of God's presence in the home more than any other thing.

"For where two or three are gathered together in my name, there am I in the midst of them" (Mt.18:20).

"He that hath my commandments, and keepeth them, he it is that loveth me: and he that loveth me shall be loved of my Father, and I will love him, and will manifest myself to him" (Jn.14:21).

2 (1:30) **Hope**: the presence of Jesus brought hope to a house. Peter's mother-in-law "lay sick of a fever." It was a *great fever*, a burning fever which gripped the woman (Lu.4:38). The area was known for its swamps or marshes which were infested with disease-carrying insects. Note two things.

a. The very moment that Jesus entered the home, hope was aroused. "Immediately they told Him of her." There was a life-threatening sickness, a serious need in the home. One who had the power to help was a guest in the home. Hope was bound to be aroused.

b. The family believed that Jesus cared and could help. Note something: they had not known Jesus long. He was just beginning His ministry, yet they had already learned of His immense compassion and love, and His care and interest for people. Through this experience and many others yet to come, they were to learn to bring all their problems and sufferings to the Lord. Knowing of His care for people was bound to arouse the hope that He would help.

"Even as the Son of man came not to be ministered unto, but to minister, and to give his life a ransom for many" (Mt.20:28).

"For we have not an high priest which cannot be touched with the feeling of our infirmities; but was in all points tempted like as we are, yet without sin. Let us therefore come boldly unto the throne of grace, that we may obtain mercy, and find grace to help in time of need" (He.4:15-16).

"Casting all your care upon him; for he careth for you" (1 Pe.5:7).

"In all their affliction he was afflicted, and the angel of his presence saved them: in his love and in his pity he redeemed them; and he bare them, and carried them all the days of old" (Is.63:9).

3 (1:31) **Jesus Christ, Presence of**: the presence of Jesus brought healing and help to a house. Note several facts.

a. Jesus' response to the request was immediate. They told "Him of her [sickness]" and He immediately went to her bedside. He did not ask questions or lay down conditions. He was a guest in Peter's home, and Peter had surrendered his life to the Lord—all he was and had, including His home. Jesus loved Peter for his surrender; therefore, when Peter had a need, the Lord *immediately came* to meet that need.

b. Jesus' touch was full of compassion and authority. He loved and cared, so "He came and took her by the hand." He touched her. (Nothing can compare to a touch given from a heart of love and care. Contrast the touch of the fist, claw, and executioner.) Jesus was full of "the Godhead bodily" (Col.2:10), so He "lifted her up; and immediately the fever left her." His authority was the authority of God, and His power was the power of God.

"And Jesus came and spake unto them, saying, All power is given unto me in heaven and in earth" (Mt.28:18).

"God anointed Jesus of Nazareth with the Holy Ghost and with power: who went about doing good, and healing all that were oppressed of the devil; for God was with him" (Ac.10:38).

"Now unto him that is able to do exceeding abundantly above all that we ask or think, according to the power that worketh in us" (Ep.3:20).

Thought 1. Jesus possessed the power to meet Peter's need, that is, to heal Peter's mother-in-law. But note: He was able to help Peter because He was an invited guest in Peter's home. Think what Peter and his family would have missed if they had not invited Jesus into their home!

Thought 2. The power of Jesus' touch is enormous.

⇒ His touch has the power to cleanse from sin.

"And Jesus put forth his hand, and touched him, saying, I will; be thou clean. And immediately his leprosy was cleansed" (Mt.8:3).

⇒ His touch has the power to give sight to the blind.

"Then touched he their eyes, saying, According to your faith be it unto you. And their eyes were opened; and Jesus straitly charged them, saying, See that no man know it" (Mt.9:29-30).

⇒ His touch has the power to bless.

"And they brought young children to him, that he should touch them: and his disciples rebuked those that brought them....And he took them up in his arms, put his hands upon them, and blessed them" (Mk.10:13, 16).

⇒ His touch has the power to heal.

"And he took him aside from the multitude, and put his fingers into his ears, and he spit, and touched his tongue....And straightway his ears were opened, and the string of his tongue was loosed, and he spake plain" (Mk.7:33, 35).

4 (1:31) **Jesus Christ, Presence of—Elderly—Purpose—Ministry**: the presence of Jesus brought devotion and service to a house. Jesus healed Peter's mother-in-law so that she might serve. He did not heal her to sit and indulge her own whims and fancies and pass the time of her later years doing nothing of real value. She was elderly, the mother of Peter's wife. Jesus healed her so that she might become devoted to Him and become a servant to all. And she fulfilled her purpose: "She ministered unto them."

> **"Jesus saith unto them, My meat is to do the will of him that sent me, and to finish his work" (Jn.4:34).**
>
> **"I must work the works of him that sent me, while it is day: the night cometh, when no man can work" (Jn.9:4).**
>
> **"Wherefore I put thee in remembrance that thou stir up the gift of God, which is in thee by the putting on of my hands" (2 Ti.1:6).**
>
> **"The aged men [must] be sober, grave, temperate, sound in faith, in charity, in patience. The aged women likewise, that they be in behaviour as becometh holiness, not false accusers, not given to much wine, teachers of good things" (Tit.2:2-3).**

	D. Jesus' Power & Impact upon People in the Streets: Caring for the Whole World, 1:32-34 *(Mt. 8:16-17; Lu. 4:40-41)*
1. Jesus can be approached at all hours **2. Jesus is to be acknowledged as compassionate**	32 And at even, when the sun did set, they brought unto him all that were diseased, and them that were possessed with devils.
3. Jesus has an open door for all	33 And all the city was gathered together at the door.
4. Jesus will have compassion upon all a. He healed b. He restrained evil spirits	34 And he healed many that were sick of divers diseases, and cast out many devils; and suffered not the devils to speak, because they knew him.

DIVISION II

THE SON OF GOD'S OPENING MINISTRY: JESUS' IMMEDIATE IMPACT, 1:21-3:35

D. Jesus' Power and Impact Upon People in the Streets: Caring for the Whole World, 1:32-34

(1:32-34) **Introduction**: the world is a paradox. It is filled with both good and evil, and the good and evil are clearly seen at every hand. No matter how much men long for a perfect world, they discover that their world is desperately sick, a world...

- that is so beautiful, yet so corrupt
- that sees love, yet demonstrates hate
- that craves life, yet knows only death
- that desires more, yet deprives so many
- that has plenty, yet is starving
- that desires peace, yet is at war
- that seeks health, yet is sick

Two things are desperately needed in a sick world: (1) hearing the good news that Jesus has the power to help, and (2) coming to Jesus for help. Just imagine! The Son of God is available to help, to solve the problems of the world.

1. Jesus can be approached at all hours (v.32).
2. Jesus is to be acknowledged as compassionate (v.32).
3. Jesus has an open door for all (v.33).
4. Jesus will have compassion upon all (v.34).

1 (1:32) **Jesus Christ, Approachable**: Jesus was and can be approached at all hours. What happened is interesting. The people had heard about Jesus' teaching in the synagogue and the two miracles that had taken place. The news had spread like wildfire. It was also the Sabbath, and a Jew was not allowed to carry any kind of burden for any distance on the Sabbath. This included walking only a short distance; it even included carrying a sick person for medical help, unless it was a matter of life and death. Therefore, the people were forced by law to wait until the Sabbath was over to approach Jesus. The Jewish Sabbath began at 6 a.m. and ended at 6 p.m. Time was judged by sunrise and sundown. As soon as night came, family and friends brought their sick to Jesus, flocking to Him.

> **Thought 1.** Note when the people came to Jesus. It was not during the day, but at night. It was an inopportune time, yet they came. The hour of the day was not going to keep them away. Their sense of desperation drove them to Jesus.
>
> **Thought 2.** Jesus was tired, very fatigued. The day had been long and full of stress, yet He made Himself available, even at an odd hour. A person can approach Jesus anyplace, anytime—at any hour of the day or night.
>
> > **"Come unto me, all ye that labour and are heavy laden, and I will give your rest. Take my yoke upon you, and learn of me; for I am meek and lowly in heart: and ye shall find rest unto your souls. For my yoke is easy, and my burden is light" (Mt.11:28-30).**
> >
> > **"The Spirit of the Lord is upon me, because he hath anointed me to preach the gospel to the poor; he hath sent me to heal the brokenhearted, to preach deliverance to the captives, and recovering of sight to the blind, to set at liberty them that are bruised" (Lu.4:18).**

2 (1:32) **Jesus Christ—Compassion—Gospel**: Jesus was and is to be acknowledged as compassionate. Note the words, "When the sun did set, they brought unto Him all that were diseased." They rushed to Him to ask if He would help. They simply accepted the fact that He would help, believing and trusting in *what they had heard.*

a. They had heard that He had the power to help.

"But that ye may know that the Son of man hath power on earth to forgive sins, (then saith he to the sick of the palsy,) Arise, take up thy bed, and go unto thine house" (Mt.9:6).

"And Jesus came and spake unto them, saying, All power is given unto me in heaven and in earth" (Mt.28:18).

"How God anointed Jesus of Nazareth with the Holy Ghost and with power: who went about doing good, and healing all that were oppressed of the devil; for God was with him" (Ac.10:38).

"Now unto him that is able to do exceedingly abundantly above all that we ask or think, according to the power that worketh in us" (Ep.3:20).

b. They had heard that He was compassionate, caring, and more than willing to help.

"Casting all your care upon him; for he careth for you"(1 Pe.5:7).

"Like as a father pitieth his children, so the LORD pitieth them that fear him" (Ps.103:13).

Thought 1. What the people had heard is the crux of the gospel: Jesus has the power to help, and He cares about helping and will help. All that a person needs to do is believe the message and come to Him.

"Even as the Son of man came not to be ministered unto, but to minister, and to give his life a ransom for many" (Mt.20:28).

"Wherefore in all things it behoved him to be made like unto his brethren, that he might be a merciful and faithful high priest in things pertaining to God, to make reconciliation for the sins of the people. For in that he himself hath suffered being tempted, he is able to succour them that are tempted" (He.2:17-18).

"For we have not an high priest which cannot be touched with the feeling of our infirmities; but was in all points tempted like as we are, yet without sin. Let us therefore come boldly unto the throne of grace, that we may obtain mercy, and find grace to help in time of need" (He.4:15-16).

3 (1:33) **Access**: Jesus did have and still does have an open door for all. "All the city was gathered together at the door."

a. The news of such power and compassion could not be overlooked and ignored. It had to be searched out and sought. It would be foolish to ignore the possibility for help if help were available for the asking. Jesus was present and power was available. It was simply a matter of *gathering* at His door for help.

Thought 1. How many hear and witness the power of Jesus in the lives of family and friends, yet they ignore and overlook Him?

b. The crowd in the streets included three primary groups: the desperate who needed help, the family and friends who brought the desperate, and the observer. The observer was the curious person who had heard about Jesus and wanted to see what He was like. Note he, too, was "gathered together" with those who came to Jesus for help.

Thought 1. Our imagination makes us wonder how the observer or the curious responded to Jesus. Did they, too, begin to see needs which Jesus could meet, or did they detach themselves from the power of Him who had come with the message of God? Every church has its curiosity seekers who desperately need to see what Jesus can do for them. The great tragedy is that they are detached from Jesus. They have never experienced the power of God.

Thought 2. Note that Jesus helps the person out in the street. He does not pick and choose whom He helps; He helps all. All can claim His power if they will but come to Him.

"Come unto me, all ye that labour and are heavy laden, and I will give you rest" (Mt.11:28).

"Wherefore he is able also to save them to the uttermost that come unto God by him, seeing he ever liveth to make intercession for them" (He.7:25).

"And the Spirit and the bride say, Come. And let him that heareth say, Come. And let him that is athirst come. And whosoever will, let him take the water of life freely" (Re.22:17).

"Come now, and let us reason together, saith the LORD: though your sins be as scarlet, they shall be as white as snow; though they be red like crimson, they shall be as wool" (Is.1:18).

"Ho, every one that thirsteth, come ye to the waters, and he that hath no money; come ye, buy, and eat; yea, come, buy wine and milk without money and without price" (Is.55:1).

4 (1:34) **Jesus Christ—Power—Compassion—Salvation**: Jesus did and will have compassion. He demonstrated His Messiahship by manifesting His compassion and power over all.

a. He healed and will heal. The people were gripped with troubled minds and suffering bodies, and He healed many.

"Who his own self bare our sins in his own body on the tree, that we, being dead to sins, should live unto righteousness: by whose stripes ye were healed" (1 Pe.2:24).

"Who forgiveth all thine iniquities; who healeth all thy diseases" (Ps.103:3).

"He healeth the broken in heart, and bindeth up their wounds" (Ps.147:3).

"But he was wounded for our transgressions, he was bruised for our iniquities: the chastisement of our peace was upon him; and with his stripes we are healed" (Is.53:5).

b. He restrained and will restrain evil spirits (see outline and notes—Mk.1:25-26 for discussion).

Thought 1. The world is a diseased and suffering world brought on by a myriad of selfish sins and demon-like creatures. Is there a Savior with the power to heal and deliver, to save and set free? Yes! Jesus Christ, "the Son of Man is come to seek and to save that which was lost" (Lu.19:10).

"For God sent not his Son into the world to condemn the world; but that the world through him might be saved" (Jn.3:17).

"The thief [false teacher] cometh not, but for to steal, and to kill, and to destroy: I am come that they might have life, and that they might have it more abundantly" (Jn.10:10).

"I came not to judge the world, but to save the world" (Jn.12:47).

"This is a faithful saying, and worthy of all acceptation, that Christ Jesus came into the world to save sinners" (1 Ti.1:15).

	E. Jesus' Source of Power & Its Impact: What Is the Source of Power? 1:35-39 *(Lu. 4:42-44)*	were with him followed after him. 37 And when they had found him, they said unto him, All men seek for thee. 38 And he said unto them,	**mission**
1. Jesus' sense of prayer a. When: Morning—very early, while it was still dark b. Where: Solitary place	35 And in the morning, rising up a great while before day, he went out, and departed into a solitary place, and there prayed.	let us go into the next towns, that I may preach there also: for therefore came I forth.	
		39 And he preached in their synagogues throughout all Galilee, and cast out devils.	**3. Jesus' faithfulness** a. Preached everywhere b. Healed—cast out demons
2. Jesus' sense of a worldwide	36 And Simon and they that		

DIVISION II

THE SON OF GOD'S OPENING MINISTRY: JESUS' IMMEDIATE IMPACT, 1:21–3:35

E. Jesus' Source of Power and Its Impact: What Is the Source of Power, 1:35-39

(1:35-39) **Introduction—Power**: Where does the servant of God get power? This passage reveals in unmistakable terms the sources of Jesus' power.

1. Jesus' sense of prayer (v.35).
2. Jesus' sense of a worldwide mission (vv.36-38).
3. Jesus' faithfulness (v.39).

1 (1:35) **Prayer—Spectacular, The**: Jesus' first source of power was His *sense of prayer*. Note three facts about Jesus' prayer life in this passage.

a. When Jesus prayed. He prayed "in the morning, rising up a *great while* before day." Remember the day before had been the Sabbath, an extremely tiring day. He had taught and had expended enormous energy in teaching and ministering (Mk.5:30). He had been up late at night ministering to the whole city that had flocked to the house where He was staying (see vv.21-34). Every muscle in His body must have ached, craving rest; yet, "rising up a great while before day, He went out into a solitary place, and there prayed."

There is another critical point of instruction here as well. Early morning prayer must have been the habit of Jesus, for the fact that Jesus prayed in the early morning hours made a lasting impression upon the disciples. Remember, this is the launch of Jesus' ministry, probably the first time the disciples had an opportunity to observe Jesus' prayer life. Mark gives a detailed description, the facts of which had probably come from Peter. Mark certainly felt that the fact was important enough to emphasize, for he not only shares what Jesus' ministry was like, he also shares what Jesus' prayer life was like.

b. Where Jesus prayed. Note the words "departed into a solitary place." The solitary place is not identified. It could have been someplace out in the countryside, a quiet orchard, or an abandoned building. The fact of importance is that He had a place where He could be alone with God. He needed to be alone with God.

> **Thought 1.** If Jesus, the Son of Man, needed so much time alone with God in prayer, how much more do we? What an indictment against so many believers and their prayer life!
>
> > **"Ask, and it shall be given you; seek, and ye shall find; knock, and it shall be opened unto you" (Mt.7:7).**
> >
> > **"Hitherto have ye asked nothing in my name: ask, and ye shall receive, that your joy may be full" (Jn.16:24).**
> >
> > **"Praying always with all prayer and supplication in the Spirit, and watching thereunto with all perseverance and supplication for all saints" (Ep.6:18).**
> >
> > **"Pray without ceasing" (1 Th.5:17).**

c. Why Jesus prayed. At least three reasons are indicated in this passage.

1) Jesus was tired. The day before had drained and exhausted Him, probably to the point that every muscle in His body ached. Teaching and ministering all day sapped the strength out of His body, both mentally and emotionally. In Jesus' case it actually drained virtue out of Him (Mk.5:30). Mentally and emotionally, He was utterly exhausted. At such times the body does not want to move and the mind wanders more easily, making man more subject to temptation; therefore, prayer is desperately needed.
2) Jesus was launching His first missionary or evangelistic tour. Jesus sensed deeply that He had come forth to be an evangelist (v.38). Right before He was to launch His first tour, there was a great need to pray. The needs of people were great, and their demands would be incessant. He would be bombarded by the needs of men and by the attacks of both Satan and institutional religion. The days would be long, taxing, and exhausting. He needed the strength of God and a special anointing as He went forth launching this very special mission.
3) Jesus was confronted with the applause and praise of men. This presented the same temptation that He had faced earlier: to secure the loyalty of men by the spectacular (see note—Mt.4:5-7). Seeing the miracles, men were ready to follow Him for what they could get out of Him. Jesus needed His purpose reinforced and a special infusion of God's strength to withstand the temptation of men's applause and loyalty—applause and loyalty that arose from shallow and surface commitments.

2 (1:36-38) **Mission—Preaching**: Jesus' second source of power was His *sense of mission,* a worldwide mission. Note what happened. When Peter and the others arose from sleeping, they discovered Jesus was missing. They asked around, found out where He was, and *followed him.* The word "followed" means strongly pursued. When they found Jesus, they were emphatic, " 'All men seek for thee.' They are ready to follow you. Let's help them" (v.37).

Luke shows just how strong the urging to stay in Capernaum was by adding: "The people [themselves] sought Him, and came unto Him, and stayed Him, that He should not depart from them" (Lu.4:42). The word "stayed" is strong. It means to hold back, to hold fast. They tried their best to detain Him. They were not going to let Him leave if they could prevent Him from doing so.

The force of the urgings by the disciples and the people shows just how strongly convinced Jesus had to be of His mission. He had it made, so to speak, in Capernaum at this point in time. Note that the people were stirred and motivated to follow God, and there were tremendous needs yet to be met in the city and surrounding area. A great ministry could be performed for God right in Capernaum. There was no need to go elsewhere, not in the people's mind. Jesus' response was forceful: "Let us go into the next towns, that I may preach there also. For *therefore came I forth*" (v.38).

Jesus was thoroughly convinced: He must not be deterred nor sidetracked from His mission. Plenty of needs may still have existed, but two critical facts were being overlooked—facts which have been and are still being sadly overlooked by believers everywhere.

a. Capernaum and its people, at least many of its people, had already heard the gospel preached. If God's messenger (Jesus) had stayed in Capernaum, many throughout the world would never have heard the gospel.

b. The people in Capernaum could now share the message themselves. God's messenger (Jesus) was not really needed to continue the ministry. The people were much more likely to assume the responsibility to carry on if Jesus left. But if Jesus had stayed, the people would have left most of the responsibility up to Him. The people would not become the witnesses they should.

> **"Go ye therefore, and teach all nations, baptizing them in the name of the Father, and of the Son, and of the Holy Ghost: teaching them to observe all things whatsoever I have commanded you: and, lo, I am with you alway, even unto the end of the world. Amen" (Mt.28:19-20).**
>
> **"And he said unto them, Go ye into all the world, and preach the gospel to every creature" (Mk.16:15).**
>
> **"But ye shall receive power, after that the Holy Ghost is come upon you: and ye shall be witnesses unto me both in Jerusalem, and in all Judaea, and in Samaria, and unto the uttermost part of the earth" (Ac.1:8).**

Thought 1. The response of Jesus is a powerful lesson that is clear and striking, and hopefully convicting. So much change is needed in institutional religion if the world is truly to be reached for Jesus. Courageous voices need to be raised for believers to begin doing what Jesus did...

- ministering
- preaching (witnessing, proclaiming the gospel)
- making disciples
- moving on to other needful and unevangelized villages and towns

Thought 2. Note something of crucial importance: the exact words of Jesus. He stressed in no uncertain terms that His mission was primarily to *preach.* He set forth *the primacy of preaching* as the task of the minister. Physical needs *were* present. They still existed in Capernaum, and they existed in all the towns where He was now to go. He would meet as many of the needs as possible. But His primary task and mission was to proclaim the gospel of the Kingdom of Heaven (see DEEPER STUDY # 3—Mt.19:23-24).

> **"Then said Jesus to them again, Peace be unto you: as my Father hath sent me, even so send I you" (Jn.20:21).**

3 (1:39) **Jesus Christ—Faithfulness—Power**: Jesus' third source of power was His *faithfulness* to His mission. He preached in the synagogues throughout "all Galilee." Galilee was densely populated. There were over two hundred cities in the district (see note—Mt.4:12-13). Note two facts. (1) Jesus went everywhere preaching; He went "throughout all Galilee." He left no place untouched. Note also that He preached in the synagogues using the structure of established religion. He did this as long as He was allowed. (2) He continued to minister as well as preach. Preaching was His primary mission, but while He preached, He also ministered to the physical needs of people. People had physical, emotional, and mental needs as well as spiritual. He validated and demonstrated both His mission and deity by healing and casting out devils.

Thought 1. Faithfulness assures power. God will continue to give His power to the messenger who continues to be faithful. Likewise, He has to withdraw His power from the unfaithful messenger. He cannot give license to disobedience. A divided house cannot stand (see outline and notes—Mt.12:25-26 for more discussion).

> **"Moreover it is required in stewards, that a man be found faithful" (1 Co.4:2).**
>
> **"For we are bought with a price: therefore glorify God in your body, and in your spirit, which are God's" (1 Co.6:20).**
>
> **"As every man hath received the gift, even so minister the same one to another, as good stewards of the manifold grace of God" (1 Pe.4:10).**
>
> **"O Timothy, keep that which is committed to thy trust, avoiding profane and vain babblings, and oppositions of science falsely so called" (1 Ti.6:20).**
>
> **"That good thing which was committed unto thee keep by the Holy Ghost which dwelleth in us" (2 Ti.1:14).**

	F. Jesus' Power over Leprosy & Its Impact: Cleansing the Most Unclean, 1:40-45 *(Mt. 8:2-4; Lu. 5:12-15)*	he was cleansed.	
		43 And he straitly charged him, and forthwith sent him away;	**3. He warned the most unclean to go—sin no more**
1. He was the great hope of the most unclean[DS1]	40 And there came a leper to him, beseeching him, and kneeling down to him, and saying unto him, If thou wilt, thou canst make me clean.	44 And saith unto him, See thou say nothing to any man: but go thy way, show thyself to the priest, and offer for thy cleansing those things which Moses commanded, for a testimony unto them.	**4. He demanded that the most unclean give witness to His Messiahship**
2. He was moved with compassion for the most unclean[DS2] a. Moved to touch b. Moved to speak	41 And Jesus, moved with compassion, put forth his hand, and touched him, and saith unto him, I will; be thou clean.	45 But he went out, and began to publish it much, and to blaze abroad the matter, insomuch that Jesus could no more openly enter into the city, but was without in desert places: and they came to him from every quarter.	**5. He made a great impact** a. The news spread b. The crowds grew too large to remain in the cities: He was forced to stay out in the countryside
c. Result: It was His Word of power that cleansed & healed the most unclean	42 And as soon as he had spoken, immediately the leprosy departed from him, and		

DIVISION II

THE SON OF GOD'S OPENING MINISTRY: JESUS' IMMEDIATE IMPACT, 1:21-3:35

F. Jesus' Power Over Leprosy and Its Impact: Cleansing the Most Unclean, 1:40-45

(1:40-45) **Introduction—Leprosy**: leprosy was the most feared disease of the ancient world. The leper was considered the most unclean, revolting, and hideous person imaginable. Leprosy itself was thought to be the result of terrible sin and actually became the most dramatic type of sin in the minds of people. There was no known cure for leprosy; only God was considered powerful enough to cure the disease. Therefore, in cleansing the leper, Jesus was demonstrating His Messiahship. He was demonstrating that He had the power to cleanse the most unclean, no matter how terrible their uncleanness. (See DEEPER STUDY # 1,2,3—Mt.8:1-4 for a more detailed discussion of leprosy and for more information on this event.)

1. He was the great hope of the most unclean (v.40).
2. He was moved with compassion for the most unclean (vv.41-42).
3. He warned the most unclean to go—sin no more (v.43).
4. He demanded that the most unclean give witness to His Messiahship (v.44).
5. He made a great impact (v.45).

1 (1:40) **Jesus Christ—Seeking**: Jesus was the great hope of the most unclean. What happened was dramatic. The man was *full of leprosy* (pleres lepras) (Lu.5:12). Apparently His whole body was full of sores, perhaps some parts even eaten away by the cancerous disease. He was hopeless, for all were powerless to help him. But somewhere, somehow, he heard about Jesus and His Godly power. Hope sprung up in his heart, and he began to search for Jesus. When he found out where Jesus was, he made his way to Him. Matthew tells us that he found Jesus on the mount where Jesus was preaching the great *Sermon on the Mount* (Mt.8:1-4). He heard Jesus preach, and what Jesus said burned in his heart and turned his hope into enormous faith. As Jesus made His way down the mountain, the leper burst forth and fell at Jesus' feet. Note three things:

a. The leper (the most unclean) was so desperate and so intent on seeking Jesus' help that he forgot everything else and everyone else. He forgot all about the law's requiring him to come no closer than six feet. He forgot all about the thronging crowd that surrounded Jesus. He saw no one and thought of no one except Jesus. It was his desperate need and the enormous hope aroused in him by Jesus that drove him to race through the crowd and fall upon his face begging for help.

b. The leper worshipped Jesus. All three gospel writers throw light upon the *intensity* of the man's act.

⇒ Mark says that he knelt down (Mk.1:40).
⇒ Luke says that he fell on his face (Lu.5:12).
⇒ Matthew says that he worshipped Jesus (Mt.8:2).

c. The leper saw in Jesus the divine power of God Himself. This was evidenced by his worship of Jesus and the words spoken to Jesus. Note he did not say, "Thou canst ask of God and God will make me clean." He said, "If thou wilt, thou canst make me clean." He was saying that Jesus possessed the power of God to cleanse him.

Thought 1. The leper is a picture of the sinner. Jesus will heal any man who approaches Him as the leper did, even if he is the most unclean person on earth.

"I came not to call the righteous, but sinners to repentance" (Mk.2:17).

"And now why tarriest thou? arise, and be baptized, and wash away thy sins, calling on the name of the Lord" (Ac.22:16).

"Draw nigh to God, and he will draw nigh to you. Cleanse your hands, ye sinners; and purify your hearts, ye double minded" (Js.4:8).

DEEPER STUDY # 1
(1:40) **Leprosy**: see DEEPER STUDY # 1—Mt.8:1-4.

2 (1:41-42) **Compassion—Forgiving**: Jesus was moved with compassion for the most unclean. Looking down upon the leper, Jesus knew the man: his miserable condition, his heart, his hope, his faith. And Jesus was moved with compassion (see note and DEEPER STUDY # 2—Mt.9:36). Note what happened.

a. Jesus was moved to reach out and touch the man. He did not ignore the man. Jesus did not push the man back. He could have, for the man had no right to approach Jesus. But Jesus, knowing the man's heart, was moved with compassion; and He reached out and touched the man (the most unclean).

> **"But when he saw the multitudes, he was moved with compassion on them, because they fainted, and were scattered abroad, as sheep having no shepherd" (Mt.9:36).**
> **"And Jesus went forth, and saw a great multitude, and was moved with compassion toward them, and he healed their sick" (Mt.14:14).**
> **"Like as a father pitieth his children, so the LORD pitieth them that fear him" (Ps.103:13).**
> **"In all their affliction he was afflicted, and the angel of his presence saved them: in his love and in his pity he redeemed them; and he bare them" (Is.63:9).**

b. Jesus was moved to speak the most wonderful words known to man: "I will, be thou clean." He spoke His Word of power. Jesus wills to make every man clean. It is His will that every man be made whole. But what is so desperately needed is for every man to approach Jesus just as this poor sinful leper did.

Every man needs to approach Jesus...

- with an intense hope.
- with an intense faith.
- with an intense worship.

> **"How God anointed Jesus of Nazareth with the Holy Ghost and with power: who went about doing good, and healing all that were oppressed of the devil; for God was with him" (Ac.10:38).**
> **"Wherefore he is able also to save them to the uttermost that come unto God by him, seeing he ever liveth to make intercession for them" (He.7:25).**
> **"For all those things hath mine hand made, and all those things have been, saith the LORD: but to this man will I look, even to him that is poor and of a contrite spirit, and trembleth at my word" (Is.66:2).**

c. The result was just as Jesus willed and spoke. His Word of power cleansed and healed the man. In healing the man, Jesus demonstrated three things.

1) He cares and is moved with compassion by the plight of men, even by the most unclean.
2) He is most definitely the Son of God who possesses the very power of God to cleanse men of their sin and uncleanness. Leprosy was a type or symbol of sin, so in cleansing the man's leprosy, the man was being cleansed (healed) both physically and spiritually.
3) He is superior to the law. He reached out and touched the man—which was against the law. Lepers were by law to remain at least six feet away from others, even from family members. (See notes, *Jesus Christ, Fulfills Law*—Mt.5:17-18; DEEPER STUDY # 2—Ro.8:3 for more discussion.)

DEEPER STUDY # 2
(1:41) **Compassion**: see DEEPER STUDY # 2—Mt.9:36.

3 (1:43) **Sin, Warning Against**: Jesus charged the most unclean to go and sin no more. This point is missed with a quick, surface reading. It can be seen by noticing two facts.

a. What Jesus charged the man with (v.43) seems to be different from the directions He gives the man in verse 44. Thoughtful reading of the two verses seems to indicate this.

b. The phrase *He straitly charged him* (embrimesamenos) is a threatening phrase. It is a strong, severe warning to the man. It is the same kind of charge Jesus gave to the man who had been bedridden for thirty-eight years: "Behold, thou art made whole: sin no more, lest a worst thing come upon thee" (Jn.5:14).

Thought 1. When we are forgiven and cleansed, Christ expects us to "sin no more." We are strongly and severely warned, "lest a worst thing come upon [us]." (See outline and notes—Mt.12:43-45; Heb.2:1-4; 3:7-19; 4:1-13; 5:11-6:20; 10:26-39. See Ep.5:5-6; 2 Th.1:8; Heb.2:2-4 for more discussion.)

> **"Wash you, make you clean, put away the evil of your doings from before mine eyes; cease to do evil" (Is.1:16).**
> **"Having therefore these promises, dearly beloved, let us cleanse ourselves from all filthiness of the flesh and spirit, perfecting holiness in the fear of God" (2 Co.7:1).**
> **"If a man therefore purge himself from these, he shall be a vessel unto honour, sanctified, and meet for the master's use, and prepared unto every good work" (2 Ti.2:21).**
> **"Draw nigh to God, and he will draw nigh to you. Cleanse your hands, ye sinners; and purify your hearts, ye double minded" (Js.4:8).**

4 (1:44) **Witnessing—Pride—Church Attendance**: Jesus demanded that even the most unclean person must give witness to His Messiahship. Jesus gave the cleansed man two different charges.

a. "Say nothing to any man": "Do not boast in your cleansing. Guard against pride, against feeling that God is partial to you and that you are a favorite of God and more special than *anyone* else." Apparently there was something within this man that would tend toward pride (see note—Mt.8:4). His attention was not to be upon what had happened to him (his cleansing and healing), but upon Jesus, the compassionate and merciful One.

Thought 1. Too often we look at the sinner and say, "*But for the grace of God, there go I.*" Such is boastful and prideful. It is true that the grace of God has saved us, but God saved us not because we are favorites of His. We are not saved to compare ourselves with the sinner by going around saying (testifying) and thinking that we are above the sinner. We are saved to proclaim the grace of God to the man walking along the street. Our task is not to stand on this side of the street and testify: "But for the grace of God, there go I." Our task is to cross over the street and declare to the man: "The grace of God saves and cleanses from all sin. God has cleansed me, the sinner of sinners; His grace will cleanse you. There is cleansing and forgiveness for everyone."

b. "Go...show thyself to the priest...." Jesus demands this for three reasons.

1) The man needed to obey the law, for he was not above the law. He was to live righteously just as the law demanded. Jesus did not annul or do away with the law. He fulfilled the law; therefore, He is more than the law. The man was being taught to obey the law and more: he was being taught to obey Jesus who includes the law and more (see note—Mt.5:17-18 for discussion). His righteous act was to be his primary witness, his final act of obedience.

Thought 1. Obedience, that is, living righteously, is our primary witness for Christ. There is no real faith apart from obedience and work.

"And being made perfect, he became the author of eternal salvation unto all them that obey him" (He.5:9).

"Even so faith, if it hath not works, is dead, being alone" (Js.2:17).

2) The man must be acknowledged as *cleansed* by everyone. People would not accept him until they knew he was cleansed. The priest had to *pronounce* him clean.

Thought 1. Every cleansed person is to go to church, profess his cleansing and become a part of God's society and family of believers.

"Then they that gladly received his word were baptized: and the same day there were added unto them [the church] about three thousand souls. And they continued stedfastly in the apostles' doctrine and fellowship, and in breaking of bread, and in prayers" (Ac.2:41-42).

"Not forsaking the assembling of ourselves together, as the manner of some is; but exhorting one another: and so much the more, as ye see the day approaching" (He.10:25).

3) The priest needed to testify to the divine power of Jesus. All the people knew that only God could cure leprosy. By declaring the man cleansed, the priest would be declaring Jesus to be the Son of God, the Messiah (seeLev.14:2-20).

Thought 1. Every time a man is truly cleansed from sin, Jesus is proclaimed to be the Messiah, the Son of God. A cleansed man becomes a living testimony and witness to the power of Jesus.

"Therefore if any man be in Christ, he is a new creature: old things are passed away; behold, all things are become new. And all things are of God, who hath reconciled us to himself by Jesus Christ, and hath given to us the ministry of reconciliation; to wit, that God was in Christ, reconciling the world unto himself, not imputing their trespasses unto them; and hath committed unto us the word of reconciliation. Now then we are ambassadors for Christ, as though God did beseech you by us: we pray you in Christ's stead, be ye reconciled to God. For he hath made him to be sin for us, who knew no sin; that we might be made the righteousness of God in him" (2 Co.5:17-21).

"I write unto you, fathers, because ye have known him that is from the beginning. I write unto you, young men, because ye have overcome the wicked one. I write unto you, little children, because ye have known the Father. I have written unto you, fathers, because ye have known him that is from the beginning. I have written unto you, young men, because ye are strong, and the word of God abideth in you, and ye have overcome the wicked one. Love not the world, neither the things that are in the world. If any man love the world, the love of the Father is not in him. For all that is in the world, the lust of the flesh, and the lust of the eyes, and the pride of life, is not of the Father, but is of the world" (1 Jn.2:13-16).

5 (1:45) **Witnessing—Disobedience**: Jesus made a great impact. His fame was blazed abroad by the man. The man disobeyed Jesus (just as many of us so often do). Because of the man's disobedience, Jesus was forced to withdraw from the area. In this particular case, He had to leave because the crowds were just too large. Note: there is also a spiritual application here. When we disobey Christ, Christ is forced to withdraw. His presence is no longer sensed by us or seen by our associates. It is as though He is forced into *a desert place*. It is interesting that nothing more is said about the disobedient leper. Imagine the people who were never helped because Jesus was forced out into a desert place!

Thought 1. We may not understand the command of our Lord, but we must obey. The consequences of disobedience are too terrible, destroying lives through our lost witness.

"Awake to righteousness, and sin not; for some have not the knowledge of God: I speak this to your shame" (1 Co.15:34).

1. The setting: Jesus returned to Capernaum many months later
  a. Jesus had returned home
  b. Crowds heard & flooded the house immediately
  c. Jesus preached the Word

2. The prerequisite to being forgiven
  a. Coming to Jesus
  b. Possessing a sincere, desperate faith in Jesus' power—a faith that will not quit*DS1*

3. The reality of being forgiven
  a. Jesus saw faith
  b. Jesus forgave sins*DS2*

CHAPTER 2

G. Jesus' Power to Forgive Sin & Its Impact: Forgiveness of Sins, 2:1-12
(Mt. 9:1-8; Lu. 5:17-26)

And again he entered into
Capernaum after some days;
and it was noised that he was
in the house.
2 And straightway many
were gathered together, insomuch that there was no
room to receive them, no, not
so much as about the door:
and he preached the word unto them.
3 And they come unto him,
bringing one sick of the
palsy, which was borne of
four.
4 And when they could not
come nigh unto him for the
press, they uncovered the
roof where he was: and when
they had broken it up, they
let down the bed wherein the
sick of the palsy lay.
5 When Jesus saw their
faith, he said unto the sick of
the palsy, Son, thy sins be
forgiven thee.
6 But there were certain
of the scribes sitting there,
and reasoning in their
hearts,
7 Why doth this man thus
speak blasphemies? who can
forgive sins but God only?
8 And immediately when
Jesus perceived in his spirit
that they so reasoned within
themselves, he said unto
them, Why reason ye these
things in your hearts?
9 Whether it is easier to say
to the sick of the palsy, Thy
sins be forgiven thee; or to
say, Arise, and take up thy
bed, and walk?
10 But that ye may know
that the Son of man hath
power on earth to forgive
sins, (he saith to the sick of
the palsy,)
11 I say unto thee, Arise,
and take up thy bed, and go
thy way into thine house.
12 And immediately he
arose, took up the bed,
and went forth before
them all; insomuch that
they were all amazed, and
glorified God, saying, We
never saw it on this fashion.

4. The question aroused by being forgiven
  a. The religionists reasoned
  b. The religionists questioned: Who has the power to forgive?*DS3*

5. The source of being forgiven
  a. Jesus revealed that He knew the hearts of men
  b. Jesus revealed His God-like wisdom & fearlessness
  c. Jesus stated His purpose: To prove His Messiahship, that He is the Son of Man
  d. Jesus proved that He had the power to forgive sins

6. The impact of being forgiven
  a. The man walked before all—forgiven, healed
  b. The crowds marvelled
  c. The crowds praised God

DIVISION II

THE SON OF GOD'S OPENING MINISTRY: JESUS' IMMEDIATE IMPACT, 1:21-3:35

G. Jesus' Power to Forgive Sin and Its Impact: Forgiveness of Sin, 2:1-12

(2:1-12) **Introduction**: the man who seeks forgiveness of sins—truly seeks with a desperation that will not quit—will be forgiven. This is the great lesson learned from the man with palsy.

1. The setting: Jesus returned to Capernaum many months later (vv.1-2).
2. The prerequisite to being forgiven (vv.3-4).
3. The reality of being forgiven (v.5).
4. The question aroused by being forgiven (vv.6-7).
5. The source of being forgiven (vv.8-11).
6. The impact of being forgiven (v.12).

1 (2:1-2) **Preaching—Minister—Mission**: Jesus returned to Capernaum after many months of preaching throughout Galilee (Mk.1:39). The preaching tour had lasted about twelve months. He apparently returned to Peter's house; and as always, the news spread quickly, and the crowds began to gather and flood the house.

Note what Jesus did. He went about His *primary mission*: "He preached the Word to them." No doubt some had come for ministry, that is, to have some need met or to be healed; and some had come out of curiosity. However, note what Jesus did first of all. He did the main work of God: He proclaimed the Word of God to men who were lost eternally.

2 (2:3-4) **Forgiveness—Perseverance—Faith—Invitation**: the prerequisite to being forgiven was clearly demonstrated by what happened.

a. The man came to Jesus. Actually, this man was brought to Jesus by four other men carrying him on a cot-like pallet. Note two significant things.

1) The man was desperate for help and very hopeful, having heard about Jesus.
2) The man was counted as a very dear person by the four men. This is indicated by the extreme action they took to reach Jesus.

The point is clear: the first prerequisite to forgiveness is coming to Jesus. A person must come to Jesus for forgiveness, even if he has to be brought. Compare the invitation of God to "come":

"Come now, and let us reason together, saith the LORD: though your sins be as scarlet, they shall be as white as snow; though they be red like crimson, they shall be as wool" (Is.1:18).

"Ho, every one that thirsteth, come ye to the waters, and he that hath no money; come ye, buy, and eat; yea, come, buy wine and milk without money and without price" (Is.55:1).

"Come unto me, all ye that labour and are heavy laden, and I will give you rest" (Mt.11:28).

"And the Spirit and the bride say, Come. And let him that is athirst come. And whosoever will, let him take the water of life freely" (Re.22:17).

(See also Ge.7:1; Mt.22:4; Lu.14:17.)

b. The man and his friends possessed a sincere, desperate faith in Jesus' power—a faith that would not quit (see DEEPER STUDY # 1—Mk.2:4; notes—Mt.9:23-27; 11:22-23 for discussion. Also see Js.2:26 where faith without works [action] is said to be dead, not really existing.)

"If thou canst believe, all things are possible to him that believeth" (Mk.9:23).

DEEPER STUDY # 1

(2:4) **Houses—Persevering Faith**: many houses of Jesus' day had an outside stairway that climbed up to a second floor. The roof was easily reached from this stairway. The roof was flat and made of tile-like rocks matted together with a straw and clay-like substance. The roofs were sturdy enough for people to sit upon and carry on evening conversations and other activities (see DEEPER STUDY # 2—Mt.24:17). These men dug and scooped out an opening through the roof. They were so sure of Jesus' power to help, nothing was going to prevent them from getting to Jesus—they had an unstoppable faith.

3 (2:5) **Forgiveness**: the reality of being forgiven. Note what happened.

a. Jesus saw their faith—the faith of the man himself and the faith of the four men who brought him. The faith of the friends played a large part in the man's being healed and in his receiving forgiveness of sins. (See notes—Mt.9:2; Mk.11:23.)

"We then that are strong ought to bear the infirmities of the weak, and not to please ourselves" (Ro.15:1).

"Bear ye one another's burdens, and so fulfil the law of Christ" (Ga.6:2).

"And let us not be weary in well doing: for in due season we shall reap, if we faint not" (Ga.6:9).

"I was eyes to the blind, and feet was I to the lame. I was a father to the poor: and the cause which I knew not I search out" (Jb. 29:15-16).

"She stretcheth out her hand to the poor; yea, she reacheth forth her hands to the needy" (Pr.31:20).

"But a certain Samaritan, as he journeyed, came where he was: and when he saw him, he had compassion on him, and went to him, and bound up his wounds, pouring in oil and wine, and set him on his own beast, and brought him to an inn, and took care of him" (Lu.10:33-34).

b. Jesus proclaimed forgiveness of the man's sins. Forgiving the man's sins was far more important than healing him (Mk.2:10). A sound body assures life for only a few years at most; a sound soul assures life forever (see DEEPER STUDY # 4—Mt.26:28).

1) Jesus forgave the man's sins first. By so doing He taught that the most important thing in a man's life is for a man to seek forgiveness of sins. A man should always seek to be forgiven before anything else. Jesus wishes man to live eternally, not just for a few short years. But before he can live eternally, man must willingly come to Jesus for forgiveness of sins.
2) Jesus proclaimed forgiveness in tenderness and compassion. When a man comes to Jesus for forgiveness, Jesus does not...
    - *accuse* the man of past sins.
    - *find fault* with the man: what he has done—why he has come—from where he has come.
    - *begrudge* or *hesitate* in forgiving the man.

   When a man comes to Jesus, Jesus responds tenderly and compassionately. This is seen in the word "son." In the Greek *son* (teknon) means child. Looking upon the man lying at His feet, Jesus saw a child, and Jesus responded to the man just as any of us would respond to a child lying helpless at our feet—tenderly and compassionately.
3) Jesus proclaimed forgiveness in His own authority. It is critical to see this. He did not say, "God, forgive this man," or "God, I wish You would forgive this man." Jesus said, "Child, thy sins be forgiven thee." He forgave the sins Himself, in His own name, by His own power and authority.

The point is unmistakable. Jesus is proclaiming to be God, the very Son of God, and the people understand exactly what He is doing (vv.6-7).

Thought 1. Combine the two points: (1) Jesus proclaims forgiveness, tenderly and compassionately, and (2) He possesses the power to forgive sins because He is truly the Son of God. A man becomes a fool if he does not come to Jesus for forgiveness of sins.

"Him hath God exalted with his right hand to be a Prince and a Saviour, for to give repentance to Israel, and forgiveness of sins" (Ac.5:31).

"Be it known unto you therefore, men and brethren, that through this man is preached unto you the forgivenesss of sins" (Ac.13:38).

"In whom we have redemption through his blood, the forgiveness of sins, according to the riches of his grace" (Ep.1:7).

DEEPER STUDY # 2
(2:5) **Forgiveness**: see DEEPER STUDY # 4—Mt.26:28.

4 (2:6-7) **Blasphemy—Forgiveness**: the question aroused by being forgiven. Apparently, the ruling body in Jerusalem, the Sanhedrin, had heard about a prophet in Galilee who was carrying on an unusual ministry. Unbelievable miracles were being claimed. The prophet, who called Himself Jesus of Nazareth, needed to be checked out to make sure He was not teaching error and misleading the people; not threatening insurrection against the Jewish religion and nation which was under Roman domination. (See note—Mt.12:1-8; note and DEEPER STUDY # 1—12:10; note—15:1-20; DEEPER STUDY # 2—15:6-9.)

The Sanhedrin sent a delegation to Capernaum to investigate Jesus. The Scribes mentioned in these verses are that delegation. When the Scribes heard Jesus forgive the man's sins, they immediately saw the point Jesus was making. They began to reason in their minds and hearts: "Why does this man blaspheme? Who can forgive sins but God only? Is He claiming to be God? The promised Messiah?" (See notes—Mk.3:1-2. See outline and DEEPER STUDY # 2—Mk.3:22.)

Thought 1. The question was logical and reasonable.
(1) Most people and religions in the world ask the very same question: "Who can forgive sins but God only?" They view Jesus only as a prophet or some great man. In their minds, He could never possess the right or power to forgive sins.
(2) Some in the world simply ask, "Who can forgive sins?" And they rejoice when they find out that Jesus is the Son of God and that He does forgive sins.

"For God so loved the world, that he gave his only begotten Son, that whosoever believeth in him should not perish, but have everlasting life" (Jn.3:16).

"Jesus heard that they had cast him out; and when he had found him, he said unto him, Dost thou believe on the Son of God? He answered and said, Who is he, Lord, that I might believe on him? And Jesus said unto him, Thou hast both seen him, and it is he that talketh with thee" (Jn.9:35-37).

"Jesus said unto her, I am the resurrection, and the life: he that believeth in me, though he were dead, yet shall he live: and whosoever liveth and believeth in me shall never die. Believest thou this? She saith unto him, yea, Lord: I believe that thou art the Christ, the Son of God, which should come into the world" (Jn.11:25-27).

Thought 2. Note: If Jesus were not the Son of God, then the Scribes were correct. Jesus was speaking blasphemy. However, since He is the Son of God, He truly forgave the man's sins. The conclusion is glorious: He can forgive our sins, too.

"Then Peter said unto them, Repent, and be baptized every one of you in the name of Jesus Christ for the remission of sins, and ye shall receive the gift of the Holy Ghost" (Ac.2:38).

DEEPER STUDY # 3
(2:7) **Blasphemy**: see DEEPER STUDY # 4—Mt.9:3.

5 (2:8-11) **Forgiveness**: the source of being forgiven. Jesus revealed His power to forgive sins in four strong steps.

a. Jesus revealed that He knew the human heart: exactly what man thinks, His motives and reasonings (see note, pt.1—Mt.9:4-7 for discussion).

b. Jesus revealed His God-like wisdom and fearlessness. He suggested that He be tested with the impossible (see note, pt.2—Mt.9:4-7 for discussion).

c. Jesus stated His purpose: to prove that He is the Son of Man (see note, pt.3—Mt.9:4-7; DEEPER STUDY # 3—Mt.8:20 for discussion).

d. Jesus proved His power to forgive sins. He must be able to forgive sins, for He healed the man and caused the man to arise and walk. His power is indisputable.

Note the proof of His power to forgive sins.

⇒ Jesus *willed* the man to walk. He simply *spoke the Word* "arise," and the man arose and walked. The power was in Jesus' *will and Word.* His will is His Word, and His Word is His will.

⇒ It follows, then, that if Jesus *wills* to forgive sins, all He has to do is *speak the Word*, "Thy sins are forgiven"; and the sins are forgiven. (See Ep.1:7; 1 Jn.1:9; 1 Jn.2:1-2; Acts 5:31; 13:38; Lu.24:47.)

"Who his own self bare our sins in his own body on the tree, that we, being dead to sins, should live unto righteousness: by whose stripes ye were healed" (1 Pe.2:24).

"Who forgiveth all thine iniquities; who healeth all thy diseases" (Ps.103:3).

"But he was wounded for our transgressions, he was bruised for our iniquities: the chastisement of our peace was upon him; and with his stripes we are healed" (Is.53:5).

"Let the wicked forsake his way, and the unrighteous man his thoughts: and let him return unto the Lord, and he will have mercy upon him; and to our God, for he will abundantly pardon" (Is.55:7).

6 (2:12) **Witnessing—Faithfulness**: the impact of being forgiven.

a. The man walked before all as a living testimony to the power of Jesus to forgive and heal a man's *whole being*.
b. The crowds *marvelled* and *praised* God.

Thought 1. Jesus forgives the sin of any man, no matter how terrible the sin. When a man's sins are forgiven, it should dramatically affect both him and those who know him. However, the great tragedy is that few pay attention to the claim that sins are forgiven. They ignore the fact and go on their merry way, continuing to walk in the selfishness of this world (see 1 Jn.2:15-16).

"And the things that thou hast heard of me among many witnesses, the same commit thou to faithful men, who shall be able to teach others also" (2 Ti.2:2).

"But sanctify the Lord God in your hearts: and be ready always to give an answer to every man that asketh you a reason of the hope that is in you with meekness and fear" (1 Pe.3:15).

Outline	Scripture
	H. Jesus' Impact upon Matthew & His Friends: Reaching the Outcast & Sinner, 2:13-17 *(Mt. 9:9-13; Lu. 5:27-32)*
1. Jesus went out to the lake a. The crowds gathered b. Jesus taught them	13 And he went forth again by the sea side; and all the multitude resorted unto him, and he taught them.
2. Jesus called the outcast & the sinner[DS1] a. He passed by—saw Levi b. He called Levi to abandon all c. Impact: Levi accepted the call; he left all	14 And as he passed by, he saw Levi the son of Alphaeus sitting at the receipt of custom, and said unto him, Follow me. And he arose and followed him.
3. Jesus associated with the outcast & sinner a. Levi invited his associates & friends b. Jesus associated with them c. The impact: Many followed Him	15 And it came to pass, that, as Jesus sat at meat in his house, many publicans and sinners sat also together with Jesus and his disciples: for there were many, and they followed him.
4. Jesus answered society's attitude toward the outcast & sinner a. The religionists questioned Jesus' associations	16 And when the scribes and Pharisees saw him eat with publicans and sinners, they said unto his disciples, How is it that he eateth and drinketh with publicans and sinners?
b. Jesus' reply: His very purpose was to call sinners to repentance	17 When Jesus heard it, he saith unto them, They that are whole have no need of the physician, but they that are sick: I came not to call the righteous, but sinners to repentance.

DIVISION II

THE SON OF GOD'S OPENING MINISTRY: JESUS' IMMEDIATE IMPACT, 1:21-3:35

H. Jesus' Impact Upon Matthew and His Friends: Reaching the Outcast and Sinner, 2:13-17

(2:13-17) **Introduction**: Jesus came to seek and to save the lost. No matter how lost, how outcast, or how bad a sinner a person is, Jesus came to save the person.

1. Jesus went out to the lake (v.13).
2. Jesus called the outcast and the sinner (v.14).
3. Jesus associated with the outcast and sinner (v.15).
4. Jesus answered society's attitude toward the outcast and sinner (vv.16-17)

1 (2:13) **Faithful—Opportunity**: Jesus went forth by the lake shore, that is, by the Sea of Galilee. The mass of people now flocking to Him were so many that no building or street was large enough to hold them. The leaders of the synagogues, the religionists, were also closing the door to Him (see Mk.2:6-7). However, note the faithfulness of Jesus in preaching and teaching despite the closed doors. His mission and call was to preach, so preach He must. He would not be stopped or silenced no matter what the problems were. Note two things.

a. The crowds gathered. The words "all the multitude" show that a huge crowd followed and gathered around Him at the seashore.

> **Thought 1.** People should flock to the servant of God who truly teaches the Kingdom of God. Why? There is one simple reason: since Christ, all things are now ready for the Kingdom of God.
>
> > **"And [God] sent his servant at supper time to say to them that were bidden, Come; for all things are now ready" (Lu.14:17; see outline and notes—Lu.14:18-20 for a descriptive picture of the excuses given for not coming to Christ).**

b. He taught them. When people came to hear about the Kingdom of God, He taught them. He was the faithful servant of God, the obedient servant who laid hold of every opportunity to teach (see outline and notes—Mk.1:14-15 for more discussion).

> **Thought 1.** God's servant should lay hold of every opportunity to teach and share Christ and His kingdom. Not a single opportunity should be missed. Faithfulness and obedience to one's call are the needs of the hour.
>
> > **"Therefore, my beloved brethren, be ye stedfast, unmoveable, always abounding in the work of the Lord, forasmuch as ye know that your labour is not in vain in the Lord" (1 Co.15:58).**
> >
> > **"I must work the works of him that sent me, while it is day: the night cometh, when no man can work" (Jn.9:4).**

2 (2:14) **Tax-Collector—Outcast, The—Lost, The**: Jesus called the outcast and the sinner. At some point Jesus finished His teaching to the multitude and began walking along the seashore. As He walked along, He passed by the tax booth that had been set up to collect the taxes owed by incoming ships. Three things then happened.

a. Jesus saw Levi, the tax collector in charge of the tax station or office. All tax collectors were traitors, outcasts, and sinners in the minds of Jewish society. They were bitterly hated and ostracized. They were looked upon as having sold their souls to the Roman authorities. The vast majority were thieves, cheats, and extortioners—always adding to the legal fee in order to fill their own pockets. Most tax collectors were wealthy, and the fact that Matthew had a house large enough to accommodate a large party points toward his being rich. (See note—Mt.9:9.)

b. Jesus called Levi to abandon his profession and to follow Him. The love of money and the lust for wealth and extravagance was what made most Jewish tax collectors enter the tax-collecting service of the Romans. This tells us that Matthew, as a young man, was consumed with a greed for wealth and the so called *good things* of life. He was possessed by greed, possessed enough to betray his country and people. He was so possessed by greed that he thought he would be willing to endure a lifetime of hatred by his own people.

However in this passage, something else became evident about Matthew. The price he had paid for wealth was not worth it. His heart was cut by the piercing eyes, stinging words, isolation, and bitter hatred of the people. He ached for forgiveness and reconciliation, both with God and with his people. It is this that Jesus saw. Jesus saw hurt and the ache of it, and Jesus appealed to him to abandon his sin of greed and to follow God.

Thought 1. Note how Jesus was always looking for the opportunity to reach individuals. He had just finished teaching "all the multitude," and He was probably tired. But as He was walking away from his meeting, He saw a soul's aching and needing His attention, so He stopped to witness to the man.

"Come unto me, all ye that labour and are heavy laden, and I will give you rest. Take my yoke upon you, and learn of me; for I am meek and lowly in heart: and ye shall find rest unto your souls. For my yoke is easy, and my burden is light" (Mt.11:28-30).

"Come now, and let us reason together, saith the LORD: though your sins be as scarlet, they shall be as white as snow; though they be red like crimson, they shall be as wool" (Is.1:18).

"Ho, every one that thirsteth, come ye to the waters, and he that hath no money; come ye, buy, and eat; yea, come, buy wine and milk without money and without price" (Is.55:1).

"Come, and let us return unto the LORD: for he hath torn, and he will heal us; he hath smitten, and he will bind us up" (Ho.6:1).

c. The impact upon Matthew was volcanic and eruptive. "He arose and followed [Jesus]" immediately. Note two apparent facts.

1) Matthew already knew of Jesus. Jesus had been teaching throughout all Galilee for over a year now. Like everyone else, Matthew had certainly heard of Jesus and had probably visited some of the Lord's meetings.
2) Matthew gave up everything. In fact, the two major points to see in Matthew's call are: first, Jesus called a person who was a great *outcast* and a *sinner*; and, second, Matthew gave up everything to follow Jesus. It cost Matthew everything—his job and his enormous income. Most of the other disciples could return to their professions if things did not work out. But this was not so with Matthew. When he committed his life to Jesus, he literally committed everything. The call of Jesus disrupted his whole life (see note, *Self-Denial*—Lu.9:23 for development of this application).

"For whosoever will save his life shall lose it; but whosoever shall lose his life for my sake and the gospel's, the same shall save it. For what shall it profit a man, if he shall gain the whole world, and lose his own soul?" (Mk.8:35-36).

"And he said to them all, If any man will come after me, let him deny himself, and take up his cross daily, and follow me" (Lu.9:23).

"If any man come to me, and hate not his father, and mother, and wife, and children, and brethren, and sisters, yea, and his own life also, he cannot be my disciple" (Lu.14:26).

"So likewise, whosoever he be of you that forsaketh not all that he hath, he cannot be my disciple" (Lu.14:33).

DEEPER STUDY # 1

(2:14) **Levi—Matthew**: this Levi is the same as Matthew who wrote the first Gospel of the New Testament (see note—Mt.9:9). Apparently his given name was Levi, but Jesus changed his name to Matthew. It is significant that both Mark and Luke use his name Levi (Mk.2:14; Lu.5:27), but Matthew uses the name Jesus gave him—Matthew (Mt.9:9). The name Matthew or Matthias means the *gift of Jehovah.* When referring to himself, Matthew always stressed God's great mercy upon him. He wanted people to know that it was the glorious mercy of Jesus that had saved him, the outcast and sinner.

"But God, who is rich in mercy, for his great love wherewith he loved us, even when we were dead in sins, hath quickened us together with Christ, (by grace ye are saved)" (Ep.2:4-5).

3 (2:15) **Outcast—Sinners—Witnessing—Church**: Jesus associated with the outcast and sinner. Note three things.

a. Immediately after his conversion, Matthew invited his associates and friends to a large feast (Lu.5:29). His friends were not the respectable people of society, but other tax collectors (publicans) and sinners—the outcasts and non-religious of society. His friends were those who rejected both the restraints of society and God; they were the immoral and unjust, the thieves and the foul-mouthed, the angry and the rebellious.

Matthew had discovered something wonderful: a glorious peace and joy of heart and mind. He had found it in Jesus. In fact, *in Jesus* he had found what was actually a new life, and he desperately wanted his friends to discover the same peace and joy. So he planned a feast, and he invited all his friends to meet Jesus (see note—Mt.9:10-11).

Thought 1. Matthew did not forget his sinful friends after his conversion. He wanted them to have the wonderful, life-changing experience with Jesus that he had come to know. So he witnessed by arranging an encounter with Jesus, using the best method he knew. What a lesson for us!

Thought 2. The command of Jesus is for us to go to our families and neighbors and friends first; to go to our own *Jerusalem* (Ac.1:8. See outline and DEEPER STUDY # 1—Mt.10:6; Lu.15:8-10. See De.6:6-7; 1 Pe.3:15.)

"But ye shall receive power, after that the Holy Ghost is come upon you: and ye shall be witnesses unto me both in Jerusalem, and in all Judaea, and in Samaria, and unto the uttermost part of the earth" (Ac.1:8).

"And the things that thou hast heard of me among many witnesses, the same commit thou to faithful men, who shall be able to teach others also" (2 Ti.2:2).

b. Jesus gladly accepted the opportunity to meet with these outcasts and sinners. But note two crucial points.

1) Jesus did not meet with the outcasts and sinners to condone their sin, but to turn them from their sin. They needed to experience the same change of life that Matthew had experienced.
2) The outcasts and sinners had needs, and they were willing to confess them. They were responsive to having their needs met.

⇒ The despised tax collector and harlot.

"Whether of them twain did the will of his father? They say unto him, The first. Jesus saith unto them, Verily I say unto you, That the publicans and the harlots go into the kingdom of God before you" (Mt.21:31).

⇒ The immoral person.

"Wherefore I say unto thee, Her sins, which are many, are forgiven; for she loved much: but to whom little is forgiven, the same loveth little" (Lu.7:47).

"She said, No man, Lord. And Jesus said unto her, Neither do I condemn thee: go, and sin no more" (Jn.8:11).

⇒ The sinner.

"And the Pharisees and scribes murmured, saying, This man receiveth sinners, and eateth with them" (Lu.15:2).

⇒ The thief.

"And Jesus said unto him, Verily I say unto thee, To day shalt thou be with me in paradise" (Lu.23:43).

⇒ The rejected.

"Jesus heard that they had cast him out; and when he had found him, he said unto him, Dost thou believe on the Son of God?" (Jn.9:35).

Thought 1. Christ cannot help a person who is unwilling to confess his need. The self-righteous, self-sufficient, and self-dependent feel that they do not need help. Such feelings and beliefs, of course, are of a *fool*; for disease, accident, and death confront everyone. When they do, all who refused to confess their need will stand at the threshold of eternity, facing vast darkness and eternal condemnation.

"Whosoever therefore shall confess me before men, him will I confess also before my Father which is in heaven. But whosoever shall deny me before men, him will I also deny before my Father which is in heaven" (Mt.10:32-33).

"Who is a liar but he that denieth that Jesus is the Christ? He is antichrist, that denieth the Father and the Son. Whosoever denieth the Son, the same hath not the Father: [but] he that acknowledgeth the Son hath the Father also" (1 Jn.2:22-23).

"Whosoever shall confess that Jesus is the Son of God, God dwelleth in him, and he in God" (1 Jn.4:15).

c. The impact of Jesus upon the outcast and sinner was phenomenal: "There were many, and they followed Him."

Thought 1. The outcast and sinner of Jesus' day...

- saw His interest and acceptance, His care and compassion for any and all in need.
- saw that any person with a need was not only welcomed by Jesus, but desired.

- saw that Jesus did not act above or better, aloof or separate from sinners.
- saw that, although Jesus never compromised His message of repentance, He loved and truly forgave and offered the greatest of challenges.

Thought 2. Think...
- how uncomfortable the outcast and sinner (even the poorly dressed and unclean) feel in church and among believers today.
- how uncomfortable the church feels when the outcast and sinner, the poorly dressed and unclean slip into services. Think of the enormous hesitation the poor have to overcome just to come into church! They slip in because they sense a need, yet how often they have to sit to the side by themselves.

4 (2:16-17) **Sinner—Outcast—Society—Religion—Respectability**: Jesus answered society's attitude toward the outcast and sinner. The attitude of society has too often been the same as the Scribes' and Pharisees' attitude—that of contempt and fear.

a. The religionists and respectable of society hold contempt for the sinner because he is below their standards and discipline. They feel they are above in beliefs and self-control. The sinner is thought to be either unprincipled or not disciplined enough to live by the rules.

Thought 1. Some men are more principled and more disciplined than others. They had greater opportunity and more training as children because of parents, education, genes, environment, and resources. This must always be remembered when dealing with others. So many traits and abilities, strengths and weaknesses of men differ because of heritage and childhood opportunities.

Thought 2. There is enormous hope for every man, no matter how weak, unprincipled, or undisciplined. The hope is Jesus Christ. The man can be *born again*—truly *born again.* He can be *re-created* in Christ Jesus, made into a *new man*, a *new creature*.

"Who by him do believe in God, that raised him up from the dead, and gave him glory; that your faith and hope might be in God" (1 Pe.1:21).

"Therefore if any man be in Christ, he is a new creature: old things are passed away; behold, all things are become new" (2 Co.5:17).

"And be renewed in the spirit of your mind; and...put on the new man, which after God is created in righteousness and true holiness"(Ep.4:23-24).

"Put on the new man which is renewed in knowledge after the image of him that created him" (Col.3:10).

b. The religionists and respectable of society fear the sinner for two reasons.

1) They fear being criticized and judged for associating with such low-caste. They fear friends and neighbors' withdrawing from them because they associated with the outcast of society.
2) They fear being contaminated and led astray themselves. They fear becoming dirty and smelly, dulled and weakened in their own beliefs and principles.

The religionists questioned Jesus' association with the outcasts and sinners. Jesus' reply was forceful: "I came not to call the righteous, but sinners to repentance." Jesus made two points:

a. The first point concerned the sick (sinner). The sick person is the one who needs the physician (Him, the Savior). And note: the sick knows he is sick and he asks for the physician.

b. The second point concerned Jesus Himself, His purpose as Messiah. He came "not to call the righteous, but sinners to repentance." Note three forceful points.

1) The righteous (self-righteous) do not know they need repentance.

"For they being ignorant of God's righteousness, and going about to establish their own righteousness, have not submitted themselves unto the righteousness of God" (Ro.10:3).

"For we dare not make ourselves of the number, or compare ourselves with some that commend themselves: but they measuring themselves by themselves, and comparing themselves among themselves, are not wise" (2 Co.10:12).

"Most men will proclaim every one his own goodness: but a faithful man who can find?" (Pr.20:6).

"There is a generation that curseth their father, and doth not bless their mother" (Pr.30:12).

2) The righteous (self-righteous) do not hear the call of Christ to repent. Sinners do hear the call.

"Peter opened his mouth, and said, Of a truth I perceive that God is no respecter of persons: but in every nation he that feareth him, and worketh righteousness, is accepted with him" (Ac.10:34-35).

"There is no difference between the Jew and the Greek: for the same Lord over all is rich unto all that call upon him. For whosoever shall call upon the name of the Lord shall be saved" (Ro.10:12-13).

"Is it fit to say to a king, Thou art wicked? and to princes, Ye are ungodly? How much less to him that accepteth not the persons of princes, nor regardeth the rich more than the poor? For they all are the work of his hands" (Jb. 34:18-19).

"Whosoever therefore shall be ashamed of me and of my words in this adulterous and sinful generation; of him also shall the Son of man be ashamed, when he cometh in the glory of his Father with the holy angels" (Mk.8:38).

"Behold, I stand at the door, and knock: if any man hear my voice, and open the door, I will come in to him, and will sup with him, and he with me" (Re.3:20).

3) Christ declared that He is the Great Physician. He is the One who calls men to repentance. He is the Messiah, the Son of God Himself.

"Even as the Son of man came not to be ministered unto, but to minister, and to give his life a ransom for many" (Mt.20:28).

"Then Peter said unto them, Repent, and be baptized every one of you in the name of Jesus Christ for the remission of sins, and ye shall receive the gift of the Holy Ghost" (Ac.2:38).

"Repent ye therefore, and be converted, that your sins may be blotted out, when the times of refreshing shall come from the presence of the Lord" (Ac.3:19).

"For there is no difference between the Jew and the Greek: for the same Lord over all is rich unto all that call upon him, For whosoever shall call upon the name of the Lord shall be saved" (Ro.10:12-13).

"Who will have all men to be saved, and to come unto the knowledge of the truth. For there is one God, and one mediator between God and men, the man Christ Jesus; who gave himself a ransom for all, to be testified in due time" (1 Ti.2:4-6).

I. Jesus' Impact upon Young Disciples & Theologians: The Kind of Life Christ Brings, 2:18-22

(Mt. 9:14-17; Lu. 5:33-39)

1. Christ aroused questions about fasting[DS1]
   a. An unusual alliance: John's disciples & the Pharisees
   b. A justified question

2. Christ brings a joyous life[DS2,3]
   a. He is the bridegroom who stirs joy in His followers
   b. He stirs joy, not fasting, over a sad event

18 And the disciples of John
and of the Pharisees used to
fast: and they come and say
unto him, Why do the disciples of John and of the Pharisees fast, but thy disciples
fast not?
19 And Jesus said unto
them, Can the children of
the bride-chamber fast, while
the bridegroom is with them?
as long as they have the
bride groom with them, they
cannot fast.
20 But the days will come,
when the bridegroom shall be
taken away from them, and
then shall they fast in those
days.
21 No man also seweth a
piece of new cloth on an old
garment: else the new piece
that filled it up taketh away
from the old, and the rent is
made worse.
22 And no man putteth new
wine into old bottles: else
the new wine doth burst the
bottles, and the wine is
spilled, and the bottles will
be marred: but new wine
must be put into new bot-
tles.

3. Christ brings a seeking life
   a. He will be taken away
   b. His followers will then fast

4. Christ brings a new life
   a. He is not attaching a new life to the old life of a person
   b. He is creating a totally new life, 1 Co.5:17

5. Christ brings an adventuresome life
   a. He is not filling the old life with the new
   b. He is creating a totally new life, Jn.3:3

DIVISION II

THE SON OF GOD'S OPENING MINISTRY: JESUS' IMMEDIATE IMPACT; 1:21-3:35

I. Jesus' Impact Upon Young Disciples and Theologians: The Kind of Life Christ Brings, 2:18-22

Introduction: Jesus Christ has the power to completely change life. And He knows the desperate need and cry among men for a changed life. The changed life Christ gives is fourfold.

1. Christ aroused questions about fasting (v.18).
2. Christ brings a joyous life (v.19).
3. Christ brings a seeking life (v.20).
4. Christ brings a new life (v.21).
5. Christ brings an adventuresome life (v.22).

1 (2:18) **Fasting—Messiahship—Judging** Others: Christ aroused questions about fasting. In the Greek the words *were fasting* (esan nesteuontes) are more accurately translated "*are* fasting." The disciples of John and of the Pharisees were actually fasting when they asked Jesus this question.

What happened was probably this. Religious Jews fasted twice every week—on Mondays and Thursdays (Lu.18:12). John was strict in his observance of the law, so he had taught his disciples to observe the two fasts. But now, John's disciples had a greater reason for fasting and for seeking God's presence. John, their teacher, was in prison and facing a death sentence. Therefore, they were fasting with intense fervency, seeking God to deliver their revered prophet. They were asking every true believer (Jewish believer) to join them in their intercession and fast. Thus, they could not understand Jesus' behavior. He was claiming unmistakably to be the Messiah to whom John had pointed. The one person who should be concerned over John's fate and over religious observances should be Jesus, the Messiah. Why did He not teach faithfulness to the religious ritual of fasting? And why was he not now having His followers fast and pray for John's release? They just did not understand.

⇒ How could the *true* Messiah fail to teach faithfulness to religion?
⇒ How could the *true* Messiah not fast and intercede for God's prophet, in particular when the prophet had meant so much to the Messiah's own ministry?

The question of *Jesus' Messiahship* lay at the very root of the question. John's disciples knew that the Pharisees had also been asking how Jesus could break the rituals of religion and be the true Messiah. So they approached the Pharisees about joining them in asking Jesus the question. The two groups standing together before Jesus formed an unusual alliance. Remember, John had preached against the Pharisees and their hypocrisy, dooming them to the most horrible fate if they did not repent (see Mt.3:7-10. See DEEPER STUDY # 3, *Pharisees*—Ac.23:8.)

> **Thought 1:** A believer should not judge other believers for not keeping religious rituals. Censuring and condemning others are uncalled for. Religious rituals are not the standard by which believers are to be judged. Neither are believers the judge of other believers. Christ alone is the Judge (Ro.14:4).

> **Thought 2:** Jesus does teach fasting, but there is a right and a wrong way to fast (see note—Mt.6:16-18 for more discussion).

DEEPER STUDY # 1
(2:18) **Fasting**: see note—Mt.6:16-18; Mk.2:20.

2 (2:19) **Joy—Jesus Christ, Presence of—Conversion**: the presence of Christ brings joy—a joyous life. This is the very reason Jesus did not teach His disciples to fast as a religious ritual. There is no need to fast when the presence and joy of Jesus fills a life. Jesus used a clear picture to teach what His mission was.

What Jesus was doing was like a wedding. He said, "I am launching a new marriage of people to God. I am the Bridegroom (the Son of God Himself) who is to wed people to God, and My chosen disciples are the friends of the Bridegroom. A wedding is a joyful, not a sad, occasion that requires fasting. My presence brings joy, not sadness, to those who will follow me." (See note—Mt.9:15.)

Thought 1: The discovery of Christ and the day-by-day consciousness of His presence do bring joy to life. Christ is the secret to life and the joy in life. No matter how gloomy life may be or how far gone a person may feel, Christ can change a person's life and bring joy to the heart. Christ can convert a person from gloom and emptiness to joy and fulfillment.

"I am come that they might have life, and that they might have it more abundantly" (Jn.10:10).

"These things have I spoken unto you, that my joy might remain in you, and that your joy might be full" (Jn.15:11).

"Therefore if any man be in Christ, he is a new creature: old things are passed away; behold, all things are become new" (2 Co.5:17).

"If ye know these things, happy are ye if ye do them" (Jn.13:17).

"Whom having not seen, ye love; in whom, though now ye see him not, yet believing, ye rejoice with joy unspeakable and full of glory" (1 Pe.1:8).

"Thou wilt show me the path of life: in thy presence is fulness of joy; at thy right hand there are pleasures for evermore" (Ps.16:11).

"Therefore with joy shall ye draw water out of the wells of salvation" (Is.12:3).

DEEPER STUDY # 2
(2:19) **Jesus Christ, Bridegroom**: see DEEPER STUDY # 2—Mt.25:1-13.

DEEPER STUDY # 3
(2:19) **Wedding, Jewish**: see DEEPER STUDY # 1—Mt.25:1-13.

3 (2:20) **Man—Seeking Christ—Believers—Life**: Christ brings a seeking life. Jesus was pointed and honest. Despite the joy of His presence, He was going to be taken away. The days were coming when He would be taken away from His followers. Then they would fast.

The words "taken away" refer to the cross and Jesus' death. He was saying that once He had died, the disciples would fast. They *would seek Him—seek the joy and consciousness of His presence*. This is the first time in Mark that Jesus said He was going to die a violent death.

"And said unto them, Thus it is written, and thus it behoved Christ to suffer, and to rise from the dead the third day" (Lu.24:46).

"But God commendeth his love toward us, in that, while we were yet sinners, Christ died for us" (Ro.5:8).

"Who his own self bare our sins in his own body on the tree, that we, being dead to sins, should live unto righteousness: by whose stripes ye were healed" (1 Pe.2:24).

Jesus was saying there were two times when His followers would definitely want to fast.

a. When His presence was removed. There are times when the presence of Christ is dimmed in the believer's life. Christ seems far away and absent; there is no consciousness and no awareness of His presence. The believer needs to fast and seek the Lord's presence during these times.

"Draw nigh to God, and he will draw nigh to you. Cleanse your hands, ye sinners; and purify your hearts, ye double minded" (Js.4:8).

"Let us draw near with a true heart in full assurance of faith, having our hearts sprinkled from an evil conscience, and our bodies washed with pure water" (He.10:22).

b. When His presence was especially needed. There are times when a special manifestation, a special empowering is needed. Fasting and intense prayer draw God close to the believer, to meet the believer who so greatly needs and desires help. (See outline and notes—Mt.6:16-18 for a full discussion on fasting.)

"Howbeit this kind goeth not out but by prayer and fasting" (Mt.17:21).

Thought 1: All who will live godly in Christ Jesus shall suffer in this world (2 Ti.3:12). Therefore, the godly need the very special presence of the Lord. They must fast often, ever seeking a deeper consciousness of His presence.

"And I will pray the Father, and he shall give you another Comforter, that he may abide with you for ever; even the Spirit of truth; whom the world cannot receive, because it seeth him

not, neither knoweth him: but ye know him; for he dwelleth with you, and shall be in you. I will not leave you comfortless: I will come to you" (Jn.14:16-18).

"Men ought always to pray, and not to faint" (Lu.18:1).

"Is any among you afflicted? let him pray. Is any merry? let him sing psalms" (Js.5:13).

"Seek the LORD and his strength, seek his face continually" (1 Chr.16:11).

"The LORD is nigh unto them that are of a broken heart; and saveth such as be of a contrite spirit" (Ps.34:18).

"Be merciful unto me, O God, be merciful unto me: for my soul trusteth in thee: yea, in the shadow of thy wings will I make my refuge, until these calamities be overpast" (Ps.57:1).

"Seek the LORD, and his strength: seek his face evermore" (Ps.105:4).

"The LORD is nigh unto all them that call upon him, to all that call upon him in truth" (Ps.145:18).

4 (2:21) **Reformation—Regeneration**: Christ brings a new life. Jesus is not an old patch being sown to an old garment. He is not out to reform an old religion or an old life. His life is a completely new way of life, and His day is a completely new day. It is not the day for patching up the old; it is time to create the new. His day is a day of regeneration, not of reformation. (See outline and note—Mt.12:43-45 for more discussion.)

"But as many as received him, to them gave he power to become the sons of God, even to them that believe on his name: which were born, not of blood, nor of the will of the flesh, nor of the will of man, but of God" (Jn.1:12-13).

"Jesus answered and said unto him, Verily, verily, I say unto thee, Except a man be born again, he cannot see the kingdom of God" (Jn.3:3).

"Not by works of righteousness which we have done, but according to his mercy he saved us, by the washing of regeneration, and renewing of the Holy Ghost" (Tit.3:5).

"Being born again, not of corruptible seed, but of incorruptible, by the word of God, which liveth and abideth for ever" (1 Pe.1:23).

"Whosoever believeth that Jesus is the Christ is born of God: and every one that loveth him that begat loveth him also that is begotten of him" (1 Jn.5:1).

5 (2:22) **New Creation—Believers, Life of**: Christ brings an adventuresome life. New wine skins were elastic and would expand as the gas of fermenting wine built up pressure. Old wine skins were hardened and would not expand, but rather would explode under pressure. Jesus said that He was bringing a new elasticity to life: a new expansion, a new adventure, a new excitement, a new life.

Thought 1: The time for the new always comes in both life and history. The day for patching the old will not suffice. A new beginning and a new life must be launched or else the person faces uselessness, extinction, or death.

(1) Man himself will die in the *old garment of his flesh* unless he comes to Christ for a new beginning.

"For God so loved the world, that he gave his only begotten Son, that whosoever believeth in him should not perish, but have everlasting life" (Jn.3:16).

"Verily, verily, I say unto you, He that heareth my word, and believeth on him that sent me, hath everlasting life, and shall not come into condemnation; but is passed from death unto life" (Jn.5:24).

"Therefore if any man be in Christ, he is a new creature: old things are passed away; behold, all things are become new" (2 Co.5:17).

"That ye put off concerning the former conversation the old man, which is corrupt according to the deceitful lusts; and be renewed in the spirit of your mind; and that ye put on the new man, which after God is created in righteousness and true holiness" (Ep.4:22-24).

"And have put on the new man, which is renewed in knowledge after the image of him that created him" (Col.3:10).

(2) The programs, methods, organizations, and even religions of this world will die and become ineffective unless they are based upon Christ and His new beginning. The foundation of life is Christ and the *new garment of His righteousness* (2 Co.5:21).

Thought 2: No greater adventure can be launched than the adventuresome life that Christ gives to a person. No greater mission can be undertaken than His mission.

"Even as the Son of man came not to be ministered unto, but to minister, and to give his life a ransom for many" (Mt.20:28).

"For the Son of man is come to seek and to save that which was lost" (Lu.19:10).

"I am come that they might have life, and that they might have it more abundantly" (Jn.10:10).

"Then said Jesus to them again, Peace be unto you: as my Father hath sent me, even so send I you" (Jn.20:21).

Thought 3: We are to struggle against becoming set and fixed in our *own ways*. We are to be elastic, expanding, and adventuresome in life (see He.11:1-40).

	J. Jesus' Impact upon Religionists: Understanding the Sabbath (Sunday), 2:23-28 *(Mt. 12:1-8; Lu. 6:1-5)*	have ye never read what David did, when he had need, and was an hungred, he, and they that were with him?	**help man**[DS1] a. The illustration: David & his men were hungry
		26 How he went into the house of God in the days of Abiathar the high priest, and did eat the shewbread, which is not lawful to eat but for the priests, and gave also to them which were with him?	1) He went into the house of God 2) He ate the bread meant for priests alone 3) He shared the bread with his men
1. The Sabbath is not about rules & regulations a. Jesus passed through the grain fields b. The disciples plucked & ate some grain	23 And it came to pass, that he went through the corn fields on the sabbath day; and his disciples began, as they went, to pluck the ears of corn.	27 And he said unto them, The sabbath was made for man, and not man for the sabbath:	b. The point: The Sabbath was given to serve man, not master man
c. The religionists questioned the picking of grain on the Sabbath	24 And the Pharisees said unto him, Behold, why do they on the sabbath day that which is not lawful?	28 Therefore the Son of man is Lord also of the sabbath.	**3. The Sabbath is to be governed by the Son of Man**
2. The Sabbath was given to	25 And he said unto them,		

DIVISION II

THE SON OF GOD'S OPENING MINISTRY: JESUS' IMMEDIATE IMPACT, 1:21-3:35

J. Jesus' Impact Upon Religionists: Understanding the Sabbath (Sunday), 2:23-28

(2:23-28) **Introduction**: the Sabbath or Sunday is often abused; in fact, it is more often abused than not. A person can abuse the Sabbath by being either too strict or too loose in observing the day. In the present generation, however, the problem is not in being too strict but in being too loose. Few ever give any thought to God's command to keep the Sabbath holy.

In this passage Jesus deals with the true meaning of the Sabbath or Sunday: a critical issue for every generation (see outline and note—Mt.12:1-8 for more discussion).

1. The Sabbath is not about rules and regulations (vv.23-24).
2. The Sabbath was given to help man (vv.25-27).
3. The Sabbath is to be governed by the Son of Man (v.28).

1 (2:23-24) **Sabbath—Sunday—Judging Others**: the Sabbath (or Sunday) is not about rules and regulations. Jesus and the disciples passed through a corn field on the way to worship. They had not eaten breakfast, so the disciples began to pluck a few ears of corn and eat them. The extreme religionists, the Pharisees, saw them and accused them of breaking the Sabbath law; that is, they were charged with working on the Sabbath. Note two facts:

a. The disciples had broken the ceremonial law. The ceremonial law did not allow work on the Sabbath. The religionists were right in their accusation. The disciples had worked and broken the Sabbath law in two areas. They had plucked the corn, and they had broken the kernels off; or as Luke says, "[rubbed] them in their hands" (Lu.6:1). (See notes—Mt.12:1-8; 12:1-3 for a more detailed discussion.)

b. Jesus judged the disciples' work on the Sabbath as acceptable. He knew the law prohibited work on the Sabbath, and He knew the disciples were breaking the law—actually working on the Sabbath. Yet He did not rebuke nor correct them. He allowed them to pluck and eat the ears of corn despite the law. Why? There was one primary reason.

Resting and worshipping on Sunday or the Sabbath is important and should be observed, but Sunday or Sabbath observance is not to be rules and regulations. Some things take precedence and are more needful than rules and regulations. Jesus simply knew that the disciples' need for food was greater than their need to keep a ceremonial rule. (In reality, Jesus is teaching that religion itself, in all its ritual and ceremony, is not to be rules and regulations.)

> **Thought 1.** Rules and regulations, laws and commandments are made to help man, to govern his behavior and to show him the best way to live. Therefore, rules which guide men to rest and worship on the Sabbath or Sunday are good and beneficial.
>
> (1) Man should always follow the guides and the rules that point him to observe the Sabbath. Man needs a day of rest and worship. Man needs to be physically refreshed and spiritually revived every week.
>
> (2) Sometimes a need arises that is greater than the need for rest and worship. Jesus recognized this. When a greater need arises, it should be met. But note: a temporary need does not do away with a permanent need. Man is still to observe the Sabbath or Sunday. In the event surrounding the disciples, the temporary need for food was judged by Jesus to be greater than the need for rest and worship on the Sabbath. However, it was not to become the usual practice. The Sabbath or Sunday is permanent. Man's permanent need is to worship and rest one day a week.
>
> **"Not forsaking the assembling of ourselves together, as the manner of some is; but exhorting one another: and so much the more, as ye see the day approaching" (He.10:25).**
>
> **"It is lawful to do well on the sabbath days" (Mt.12:12).**
>
> **"Remember the sabbath day, to keep it holy" (Ex.20:8).**

"And if the people of the land bring ware or any victuals on the sabbath day to sell, that we would not buy it of them on the sabbath, or on the holy day" (Ne.10:31; see Ne.13:15).

Thought 2. When a person judges and censors another person for breaking the law, he is committing a much more serious sin: the sin of forgetting mercy and forgiveness, love and ministry.

"Judge not, that ye be not judged. For with what judgment ye judge, ye shall be judged: and with what measure ye mete, it shall be measured to you again. And why beholdest thou the mote that is in thy brother's eye, but considerest not the beam that is in thine own eye? Or how wilt thou say to thy brother, Let me pull out the mote out of thine eye; and, behold, a beam is in thine own eye? Thou hypocrite, first cast out the beam out of thine own eye; and then shalt thou see clearly to cast out the mote out of thy brother's eye" (Mt.7:1-5).

"Therefore thou art inexcusable, O man, whosoever thou art that judgest: for wherein thou judgest another, thou condemnest thyself; for thou that judgest doest the same things" (Ro.2:1).

"Who art thou that judgest another man's servant? to his own master he standeth or falleth. Yea, he shall be holden up: for God is able to make him stand" (Ro.14:4).

"Let us not therefore judge one another any more: but judge this rather, that no man put a stumblingblock or an occasion to fall in his brother's way" (Ro.14:13).

"Therefore judge nothing before the time, until the Lord come, who both will bring to light the hidden things of darkness, and will make manifest the counsels of the hearts: and then shall every man have praise of God" (1 Co.4:5).

"There is one lawgiver, who is able to save and to destroy: who art thou that judgest another?" (Js.4:12).

2 (2:25-27) **Sabbath—Sunday**: the Sabbath (or Sunday) was given to help man. Jesus proved this point by doing two things.

a. He told the story of what David had done (1 S.21:1-6). David was fleeing from Saul, and he and his men were hungry, not having eaten for some time. In their flight they came upon the tabernacle in Nob. David went in and requested food from the priests, but there was no food. There was only the showbread that was forbidden to be eaten by anyone other than the priests (see DEEPER STUDY # 2—Mt.12:3-4). Despite the law, David took five loaves, and he and his men ate the forbidden or unlawful bread.

What Jesus was doing in the illustration was twofold.

1) Jesus was saying that a great man of God, a man after God's own heart, had broken the ceremonial law of God. Yet the man of God was justified because his need for bread was greater than his keeping a ceremonial law.
2) Jesus was showing that Scripture itself gives precedence for what His disciples were doing. It was the Scripture that revealed and justified David's actions.

b. Jesus stated the point that should be self-evident: the Sabbath or Sunday is to serve man, not master man. Jesus simply said, "The Sabbath was made for man, and not man for the sabbath." Man and his needs take precedence over any ceremonial law—including the ceremonial law governing the Sabbath or Sunday. Whatever serves man the most is exactly what is to be done on the holy day. The Sabbath was made for man, not man for the Sabbath.

But note a crucial fact. Two of the greatest needs of man are for rest and worship, a day for physical refreshment and spiritual renewal every week. So the need has to be a desperate one, a need unable to be fulfilled in any other way for it to take precedence over the law. This is critical to understand, for man does not have license to break the law at every whim and fancy. Breaking the law for selfish reasons—for fleshly desires and commercial pleasure—is not what Jesus is talking about. His point is that need, a true and real need, can take *temporary precedence* over the Sabbath or Sunday law.

The Sabbath or Sunday was made for man. It is to be used for his benefit, to gain rest and a revived sense of God's presence. But it is not the master of man. Man's rest and worship may need to be temporarily interrupted in order to meet a greater need, a need that has come upon him all of a sudden (see outline, notes and DEEPER STUDY # 2, *Sabbath—Sunday*—Mt.12:3-4).

Thought 1. Man is far more important than rules and regulations; far more important than ceremony, ritual, and religion. The first duty of man is to worship God and to meet the needs of his fellow man. Nothing should ever take precedence over this first duty.

"Even as the Son of man came not to be ministered unto, but to minister, and to give his life a ransom for many" (Mt.20:28).

"Then said Jesus to them again, Peace be unto you: as my Father hath sent me, even so send I you" (Jn.20:21).

"I have showed you all things, how that so labouring ye ought to support the weak, and to remember the words of the Lord Jesus, how he said, It is more blessed to give than to receive" (Ac.20:35).

"We then that are strong ought to bear the infirmities of the weak, and not to please ourselves" (Ro.15:1).

"Bear ye one another's burdens, and so fulfil the law of Christ" (Ga.6:2).

DEEPER STUDY # 1
(2:25-26) **Showbread**: see DEEPER STUDY # 2—Mt.12:3-4.

3 (2:28) **Sabbath—Sunday**: the Sabbath (or Sunday) is to be governed by the Son of Man. Jesus, the Son of Man, gave and instituted the Sabbath. Note the two claims Jesus was making.

a. He is the true Messiah, the Son of Man (see DEEPER STUDY # 3—Mt.8:20).

b. He is the One who gave the Sabbath. Therefore, He is the Lord who governs the Sabbath. Man is to do exactly what Christ says to do on the Sabbath. (See DEEPER STUDY # 1, *Sabbath*—Mt.12:1 for the Scriptural teaching on the Sabbath or Sunday.)

> **"Therefore let all the house of Israel know assuredly, that God hath made that same Jesus, whom ye have crucified, both Lord and Christ" (Ac.2:36).**
>
> **"Him hath God exalted with his right hand to be a Prince and a Saviour, for to give repentance to Israel, and forgiveness of sins" (Ac.5:31).**
>
> **"God is faithful, by whom ye were called unto the fellowship of his Son Jesus Christ our Lord" (1 Co.1:9).**
>
> **"But to us there is but one God, the Father, of whom are all things, and we in him; and one Lord Jesus Christ, by whom are all things, and we by him" (1 Co.8:6).**
>
> **"And Jesus came and spake unto them, saying, All power is given unto me in heaven and in earth" (Mt.28:18).**
>
> **"And hath put all things under his feet, and gave him to be the head over all things to the church" (Ep.1:22).**
>
> **"[Jesus Christ] who is gone into heaven, and is on the right hand of God; angels and authorities and power being made subject unto him" (1 Pe.3:22).**

CHAPTER 3

K. Jesus' Impact upon Authorities & Politicians: Understanding True Religion, 3:1-6
(Mt. 12:9-14; Lu. 6:6-11)

And he entered again into
the synagogue; and there was
a man there which had a
withered hand.
2 And they watched him,
whether he would heal him
on the sabbath day; that they
might accuse him.
3 And he saith unto the
man which had the withered
hand, Stand forth.
4 And he saith unto them, is
it lawful to do good on the
sabbath days, or to do evil?
to save life, or to kill? But
they held their peace.
5 And when he had looked
round about on them with
anger, being grieved for the
hardness of their hearts, he
saith unto the man, Stretch
forth thine hand. And he
stretched it out: and his hand
was restored whole as the
other.
6 And the Pharisees went
forth, and straightway took
counsel with the Herodians
against him, how they might
destroy him.

1. **True religion is both worshipping & seeing those in need**
   a. Jesus entered the synagogue
   b. Jesus confronted a man with a shriveled hand
   c. Jesus confronted the religionists
2. **True religion is a willingness to stand up & obey Christ**
3. **True religion is doing good & saving lives**
   a. Not obeying rules, regulations
   b. Not refusing to face the truth
4. **True religion is righteous anger against error & evil**
   a. Feeling anger due to stubbornness[DS1]
   b. Feeling grief due to hardness
5. **True religion is restoring men to completeness, wholeness**
6. **True religion is not intrigue, nor is it destructive**

DIVISION II

THE SON OF GOD'S OPENING MINISTRY: JESUS' IMMEDIATE IMPACT, 1:21-3:35

K. Jesus' Impact Upon Authorities and Politicians: Understanding True Religion, 3:1-6

(3:1-6) **Introduction**: this was a crucial event for Jesus—the climax of five conflicts with the religionists (Scribes and Pharisees). Time and again the religionists had attacked Jesus, accusing Him of teaching a false religion. In this climactic confrontation, Jesus took the man with a withered hand and demonstrated just what true religion is. The demonstration was so clear and forceful that the religionists were stunned. What is true religion? It is five things.

1. True religion is both worshipping and seeing those in need (vv.1-2).
2. True religion is a willingness to stand up and obey Christ (v.3).
3. True religion is doing good and saving lives (v.4).
4. True religion is righteous anger against error and evil (v.5).
5. True religion is restoring men to completeness, wholeness (v.5).
6. True religion is not intrigue, nor is it destructive (v.6).

1 (3:1-2) **Jesus Christ, Opposition**: Jesus again entered the synagogue. He confronted an individual in need and a group of men who opposed Him.

a. Jesus confronted a man with a withered hand. The Greek *which had a withered hand* (exerammenen echon ten cheira) means "which had his hand withered." That is, his hand had been injured or become diseased. He was not born with a withered hand. His plight, of course, was desperate; for he was unable to work for a livelihood with a withered hand. Tradition says he was a stone mason who beseeched Jesus to heal him so that he might not have to beg in shame (see note—Mt.12:9-13).

b. Jesus confronted the religionists, probably the same delegation who had been sent earlier from the Sanhedrin to investigate His teaching (see note—Mk.2:6-7). It was their duty to protect the people from false teachers and to protect the nation from insurrectionists. Note: they were not attending the synagogue to worship God but to watch for wrong in Jesus "that they might accuse Him" (v.2).

> **Thought 1.** How many sit in church, watching and picking out wrong in others so that they might accuse them and gossip about them? Church is the place for worship and ministering to all with "withered hands"—hands that are unable to work and serve God, hands that are withered because of...
> - dead spirits
> - unlearned minds
> - disturbed emotions
> - misguided lives

2 (3:3) **Religion**: true religion is a *willingness to stand forth.* The words *stand forth* (egeirai eis to meson) actually say, "Rise up, stand up in the midst." Jesus was calling for the man's will—his willingness to do exactly what the Messiah was saying. The man had to want help enough to be willing to stand before the audience and before the scornful religionists. By such a stand, he would be *confessing his faith in Jesus and in His power to save and heal.*

> **Thought 1.** Real religion is a willingness to stand forth. Christ calls every man to *rise up, stand*, repent, and confess his faith in the Lord's power to save and heal him. (See DEEPER STUDY # 1, *Repentance*—Ac.17:29-30.)
>
> **"The blind men came to him: and Jesus saith unto them, Believe ye that I am able to do this? They said unto him, Yea, Lord" (Mt.9:28).**
>
> **"Whosoever therefore shall confess me before men, him will I confess also before my Father which is in heaven. But whosoever shall deny me before men, him will I also deny before my Father which is in heaven" (Mt.10:32-33).**

"Whosoever denieth the Son, the same hath not the Father: [but] he that acknowledgeth the Son hath the Father also" (1 Jn.2:23).

"How long wilt thou sleep, O sluggard? When wilt thou arise out of thy sleep?" (Pr.6:9).

"Arise ye, and let us go up to Zion unto the Lord our God" (Je.31:6).

"Arise ye, and depart [from sin], for this is not your rest: because it is polluted, it shall destroy you, even with a sore destruction" (Mi.2:10).

3 (3:4) **Religion**: true religion is *doing good and saving lives.* The problem the religionists had with Jesus was His breaking of their ceremonial law. People by the thousands were flocking to Jesus for help, and every time He broke the law, He was teaching the people to discredit the ceremonial law. Therefore, Jesus was a serious threat to the Jewish religion and nation and to the leaders of the nation—both civil and religious (their security, position, and power). (See notes—Mt.12:1-8; note and DEEPER STUDY # 1—12:10; note—15:1-20; DEEPER STUDY # 2—15:6-9 for a detailed discussion.)

What Jesus did was teach and show that true religion is doing good and saving lives. True religion is not rules and regulations, not ceremony and ritual, no matter how good the rules and ceremony may be. If a man has a need, true religion meets that need. Jesus drove the point home by asking two questions.

First: "Is it lawful to do good on the Sabbath day, or to do evil?" Jesus had the power to do good by healing the man. Therefore, if He did not heal the man, He would be withholding good and doing evil. Yet the ceremonial law said that no work was to be done on the Sabbath.

Second: "Is it lawful to save life, or to kill?" Jesus had the power and wanted to save the man's life; the religionists had the civil authority and wanted to kill Jesus. The religionists were actually plotting His death, and He knew it. They knew what He was asking and saying. True religion does good and saves life, it does not live by rules and regulations, ceremony and rituals; nor does it seek to isolate and cut off and kill men, even if they are judged to be threats.

Note the religionists said nothing. They refused to face the truth; they closed their minds in obstinate unbelief (see DEEPER STUDY # 4—Mt.12:24; 12:31-32 for discussion). They preferred and chose a religion of ceremony and ritual to that of doing good and saving lives.

Thought 1. True religion is doing good and saving lives.

"And to love him [God] with all the heart, and with all the understanding, and with all the soul, and with all the strength, and to love his neighbour as himself, is more than all whole burnt offerings and sacrifices" (Mk.12:33).

"Love worketh no ill to his neighbour: therefore love is the fulfilling of the law" (Ro.13:10).

"Pure religion and undefiled before God and the Father is this, To visit the fatherless and widows in their affliction, and to keep himself unspotted from the world" (Js.1:27).

"Hereby perceive we the love of God, because he laid down his life for us: and we ought to lay down our lives for the brethren. But whoso hath this world's good, and seeth his brother have need, and shutteth up his bowels of compassion from him, how dwelleth the love of God in him? My little children, let us not love in word, neither in tongue; but in deed and in truth. And hereby we know that we are of the truth, and shall assure our hearts before him" (1 Jn.3:16-19).

"For I desired mercy, and not sacrifice; and the knowledge of God more than burnt offerings" (Ho.6:6).

"He hath showed thee, O man, what is good; and what doth the LORD require of thee, but to do justly, and to love mercy, and to walk humbly with thy God?" (Mi.6:8).

4 (3:5) **Religion**: true religion is *feelings against error and evil.* Note the feelings of Jesus. He was gripped by anger—an anger that involved grief. He was angered because of "the hardness of their hearts" (see DEEPER STUDY # 1, *Grieved*—Mk.3:5. Also see DEEPER STUDY # 4—Mt.12:24; note—12:31-32 for discussion.)

"Not every one that saith unto me, Lord, Lord, shall enter into the kingdom of heaven; but he that doeth the will of my Father which is in heaven" (Mt.7:21).

"He answered and said unto them, Well hath Esaias prophesied of you hypocrites, as it is written, This people honoureth me with their lips, but their heart is far from me" (Mk.7:6).

"And why call ye me, Lord, Lord, and do not the things which I say?" (Lu.6:46).

"They profess that they know God; but in works they deny him, being abominable, and disobedient, and unto every good work reprobate" (Tit.1:16).

"My little children, let us not love in word, neither in tongue; but in deed and in truth" (1 Jn.3:18).

DEEPER STUDY # 1

(3:5) **Grieved** (sullupoumenos): to sense grief, sorrow, empathy; to suffer with a person because they are injured. In this particular passage, Jesus' anger was combined with grief over people who harmed themselves. The anger of Jesus was a grieving anger over obstinate unbelief. The people who closed their minds—who just remained obstinate in unbelief despite the evidence—aroused a grieving anger within Him.

5 (3:5) **Religion**: true religion is *restoring men to wholeness*. True religion speaks and acts. Jesus spoke, "Stretch forth thy hand." The man did, and Jesus restored the man to wholeness. True religion does not hesitate to minister and restore men. True religion is love and service, not the keeping of rules and regulations, ceremony and rituals. Rules and ceremony are helpful; they are even necessary. But they are not true religion. The essence of religion is restoring men and making them whole in the name and power of Jesus.

Thought 1. See outline and notes—Ro.12:1-21. A quick glance at the whole chapter will give an excellent description of what true religion is.

"Even as the Son of man came not to be ministered unto, but to minister, and to give his life a ransom for many" (Mt.20:28).

"Then said Jesus to them again, Peace be unto you: as my father hath sent me, even so send I you" (Jn.20:21).

"I have showed you all things, how that so labouring ye ought to support the weak, and to remember the words of the Lord Jesus, how he said, It is more blessed to give than to receive" (Ac.20:35).

"We then that are strong ought to bear the infirmities of the weak, and not to please ourselves" (Ro.15:1).

"Bear ye one another's burdens, and so fulfil the law of Christ" (Ga.6:2).

6 (3:6) **Religion**: true religion is *not intrigue nor is it destructive*. Note what had happened. Jesus had confronted the religionists with the truth. They had been shown unmistakably what true religion is. They were now faced with the dilemma: they had to either accept true religion, Jesus and His teaching, or else oppose Him. They chose to oppose Him, but they needed political help, so they went out and formed an alliance with the Herodians (see DEEPER STUDY # 2—Mt.22:16). Note a significant fact: despite enormous philosophical differences, there was no difference between the religious and political leaders in behavior (the Pharisees and the Herodians). Position, power, and security had corrupted their hearts and minds. They both plotted to destroy a person (Jesus) who opposed them. (See note—Mt.12:1-8; note and DEEPER STUDY # 1—12:10 for a detailed discussion of their opposition.) True religion is not intrigue nor is it destructive.

Thought 1. Every person is confronted with true religion in Jesus Christ. Every person is faced with the dilemma of choosing to follow the true religion or opposing Christ.

"Jesus saith unto him, I am the way, the truth, and the life: no man cometh unto the Father, but by me" (Jn.14:6).

"For there is one God, and one mediator between God and men, the man Christ Jesus; who gave himself a ransom for all, to be testified in due time" (1 Ti.2:5-6).

"And this is the record, that God hath given to us eternal life, and this life is in his Son. He that hath the Son hath life; and he that hath not the Son of God hath not life" (1 Jn.5:11-12).

Thought 2. How many within *religion* oppose Christ because of their position, power, and security? How many go along with questionable teachings, ideas, movements, and the religious fad of the day—all because they fear the reaction of the world and of their worldly-minded peers?

"And this is his commandment, That we should believe on the name of his Son Jesus Christ, and love one another, as he gave us commandment" (1 Jn.3:23).

"He that saith he abideth in him ought himself also so to walk, even as he walked" (1 Jn.2:6).

"And he said to them all, If any man will come after me, let him deny himself, and take up his cross daily, and follow me" (Lu.9:23).

"For he saith, I have heard thee in a time accepted, and in the day of salvation have I succoured thee: behold, now is the accepted time; behold, now is the day of salvation." (2 Co.6:2).

"Wherefore come out from among them, and be ye separate, saith the Lord, and touch not the unclean thing; and I will receive you, and will be a Father unto you, and ye shall be my sons and daughters, saith the Lord Almighty" (2 Co.6:17-18).

Outline	Title / Scripture	Scripture (cont.)	Outline
	L. Jesus' Impact upon Crowds & Evil Spirits: Seeking & Fearing Christ, 3:7-12 *(Mt. 12:14-21)*	came unto him.	
		9 And he spake to his disciples, that a small ship should wait on him because of the multitude, lest they should throng him.	b. Crowds crushed Him 1) Endangered His life
		10 For he had healed many; insomuch that they pressed upon him for to touch him, as many as had plagues.	2) Sought to touch Him
1. Jesus' withdrawal[DS1] **2. Jesus' impact upon people: A true seeking** a. Large crowds followed Him	7 But Jesus withdrew himself with his disciples to the sea: and a great multitude from Galilee followed him, and from Judaea,	11 And unclean spirits, when they saw him, fell down before him, and cried, saying, Thou art the Son of God.	**3. Jesus' impact upon evil spirits: A terrible fear** a. They were subject to Him b. They acknowledged His Messiahship
1) They came from near & far	8 And from Jerusalem, and from Idumaea, and from beyond Jordan; and they about Tyre and Sidon, a great multitude,	12 And he straitly charged them that they should not make him known.	c. He rebuked the evil spirit's confession
2) The reason: They heard what great things He did	when they had heard what great things he did,		

DIVISION II

THE SON OF GOD'S OPENING MINISTRY: JESUS' IMMEDIATE IMPACT, 1:21-3:35

L. Jesus' Impact Upon Crowds and Evil Spirits: Seeking and Fearing Christ, 3:7-12

(3:7-12) **Introduction—Jesus Christ, Crowds Follow**: Jesus' impact upon people was unbelievable; it was incomprehensible. In just a few months, the whole nation was aroused to seek after the One called Jesus of Nazareth, the promised Messiah. A fact that is often unnoticed is the fact covered in this passage: "A great multitude...came unto Him." The multitude is called "great" twice (v.7, 8). The crowds were enormous (remember the feeding of five thousand men, not counting the women and children). The multitudes did what we so desperately need to do: they truly sought Him, even to the point of *thronging Him* (v.9) and *pressing* or *crushing in upon Him* (v.10).

Jesus' impact upon evil spirits was just as dramatic. They were stricken to bow before Him and to acknowledge His Messiahship—two acts that desperately need to be done by men.

1. Jesus' withdrawal (v.7).
2. Jesus' impact upon people: a true seeking (vv.7-10).
3. Jesus' impact upon evil spirits: a terrible fear (vv.11-12).

1 (3:7) **Jesus Christ, Response to**: Jesus was forced to withdraw to the sea of Galilee. There seemed to be two reasons for this move.

a. The leaders, both religious and political, were now plotting His death (see note—Mt.12:14-16). He still had much to teach before He could face the end. As He had said on several occasions, His hour had not yet come. He must not allow His death—not yet. Thus, He had to move out of the synagogue into the open country.

b. The crowds had become too large for the synagogues and the cities to handle. People by the multitudes were flocking to Him, even to the point of endangering His life by the crush of bodies (see vv.8-9).

DEEPER STUDY # 1
(3:7) **Jesus Withdrew**: Mark says Jesus also withdrew in Mk.6:31, 46; 7:24, 31; 10:1; 14:34-35.

2 (3:7-10) **Jesus Christ, Impact**: the impact of Jesus upon the crowds was phenomenal. This fact is often overlooked or minimized. The crowds demonstrate how eagerly men should seek after Jesus. Note two eye-opening facts.

a. Teeming multitudes flocked to Jesus and truly sought Him.
   1) They came from all over the nation, and some even came from foreign nations.
      a) Crowds came from all over Galilee. Imagine a district so heavily populated that it embraced over two hundred cities with populations of fifteen thousand or more (see note—Mt.4:12-13). Teeming multitudes streamed to Jesus from all over the district.[1]
      b) Crowds came from Judaea and Jerusalem. This was a hundred-mile journey.
      c) Crowds came from Idumaea which lay in the deep south, bordering Palestine and Arabia. Idumaea was the Greek and Roman name for Edom or the land of Esau (Ge.25:30; 36:1, 8). The significant point is that these people traveled a great distance to reach Jesus.
      d) Crowds came from beyond Jordan which refers to the populations who lived on the east side of the Jordan River.

[1] William Barclay. *The Gospel of Matthew*, Vol.1. "The Daily Study Bible." Philadelphia, PA: The Westminster Press, 1956, p.66.

e) Crowds came from the north, from the foreign land of Phoenicia and from the nation's two major cities, Tyre and Sidon.

2) The reason the crowds flocked to Jesus is given (v.8). The people heard the testimony of those who had seen and heard Jesus themselves or else had been told by others about Jesus. The testimony that the Messiah had come—the prophet who could meet the needs of mankind—spread like wild-fire. And when the people heard, many arose, packed their bags, and "came unto Him" (v.8).

Thought 1. The importance of witnessing and talking about the marvelous work of God's grace is strongly seen in Jesus' ministry. How many more would be flocking to Jesus and following Him if we were more faithful in sharing the glorious salvation in Him.

"And when he was come into the ship, he that had been possessed with the devil prayed him that he might be with him. Howbeit Jesus suffered him not, but saith unto him, Go home to thy friends, and tell them how great things the Lord hath done for thee, and hath had compassion on thee" (Mk.5:18-19).

"Go ye therefore, and teach all nations, baptizing them in the name of the Father, and of the Son, and of the Holy Ghost: teaching them to observe all things whatsoever I have commanded you: and, lo, I am with you alway, even unto the end of the world" (Mt.28:19-20).

"But ye shall receive power, after that the Holy Ghost is come upon you: and ye shall be witnesses unto me both in Jerusalem, and in all Judaea, and in Samaria, and unto the uttermost part of the earth" (Ac.1:8).

"Speaking to yourselves in psalms and hymns and spiritual songs, singing and making melody in your heart to the Lord" (Ep.5:19).

"But sanctify the Lord God in your hearts: and be ready always to give an answer to every man that asketh you a reason of the hope that is in you with meekness and fear" (1 Pe.3:15).

"That which we have seen and heard declare we unto you, that ye also may have fellowship with us: and truly our fellowship is with the Father, and with his Son Jesus Christ" (1 Jn.1:3).

b. Multitudes thronged Him, even to the point of crushing Him and threatening His life. They pressed "to touch Him," hoping that some *virtue* from Him might flow through their body and meet their need (v.10). Jesus had to order a small boat to sit just a short distance off shore to rescue Him in case the crushing crowd became too much for Him to handle.

Thought 1. How desperately men need the same kind of fervor to seek after Jesus today. Men desperately need to touch Jesus. Men need the *virtue, the saving strength, of Jesus.*

"Ask, and it shall be given you; seek, and ye shall find; knock, and it shall be opened unto you" (Mt.7:7).

"Thence [from sin] thou shalt seek the LORD thy God, thou shalt find him, if thou seek him with all thy heart and with all thy soul" (De.4:29).

"Seek the LORD, and his strength: seek his face evermore" (Ps.105:4).

"Seek ye the LORD while he may be found, call ye upon him while he is near" (Is.55:6).

"And ye shall seek me, and find me, when ye shall search for me with all your heart" (Je.29:13).

3 (3:11-12) **Jesus Christ, Impact—Evil Spirits**: the impact of Jesus upon evil spirits was dramatic. His presence struck a terrible fear within them. Yet His power over evil spirits was both comforting and assuring to the believer (see note—Lk.8:26-39).

a. The evil spirits were subject to Jesus. They "fell down before Him." They knew Him, for He had been the greater power in the spiritual world or dimension of being. They could do nothing beyond His control. "When they saw Him, [they] fell down before Him" (v.11).

b. The evil spirits acknowledged Jesus to be the Son of God (see note—Mk.1:23-24 for more discussion). They acknowledged His Messiahship. The crowd had "pressed" to touch Jesus, hoping and praying for help; but the evil spirits "fell down before Him," being stricken to acknowledge His deity. But note: they did not fall down out of devotion—not because they were seeking Him—but they fell down because they...

- acknowledged Him to be who He claimed to be.
- feared Him, lest He cast them out, sending them to their destined hell before the end time.

Thought 1. Every *evil spirit*, every evil man needs to fall down before Christ—fearing, standing in awe, and confessing lest he be destined for hell.

"Whosoever therefore shall confess me before men, him will I confess also before my Father which is in heaven. But whosoever shall deny me before men, him will I also deny before my Father which is in heaven" (Mt.10:32-33).

"Whosoever therefore shall be ashamed of me and of my words in this adulterous and sinful generation; of him also shall the Son of man be ashamed, when he cometh in the glory of his Father with the holy angels" (Mk.8:38).

"Also I say unto you, Whosoever shall confess me before men, him shall the Son of man also confess before the angels of God" (Lu.12:8).

"That if thou shalt confess with thy mouth the Lord Jesus, and shalt believe in thine heart that God hath raised him from the dead, thou shalt be saved. For with the heart man believeth unto righteousness; and with the mouth confession is made unto salvation" (Ro.10:9-10).

"Whosoever shall confess that Jesus is the Son of God, God dwelleth in him, and he in God" (1 Jn.4:15).

"He that covereth his sins shall not prosper: but whoso confesseth and forsaketh them shall have mercy" (Pr.28:13).

c. Jesus rebuked the confession of the evil spirits (see note—Mk.1:25-26).

Thought 1. The confession Christ wants is the confession of a broken and contrite heart, a changed and repentant life.

"The LORD is nigh unto them that are of a broken heart; and saveth such as be of a contrite spirit" (Ps.34:18).

"The sacrifices of God are a broken spirit: a broken and a contrite heart, O God, thou wilt not despise" (Ps.51:17).

"For thus saith the high and lofty One that inhabiteth eternity, whose name is Holy; I dwell in the high and holy place, with him also that is of a contrite and humble spirit, to revive the spirit of the humble, and to revive the heart of the contrite ones" (Is.57:15).

"For all those things hath mine hand made, and all those things have been, saith the LORD: but to this man will I look, even to him that is poor and of a contrite spirit, and trembleth at my word" (Is.66:2).

	M. Jesus' Impact upon the Twelve Disciples: Calling Choice Men, 3:13-19 *(Mt. 10:1-4; Lu. 6:12-19; Ac. 1:13-14)*	16 And Simon he surnamed Peter; 17 And James the son of Zebedee, and John the brother of James; and he surnamed them Boanerges, which is, The sons of thunder:	**3. Men changed by Jesus**[DS4-14]
1. Men called by Jesus	13 And he goeth up into a mountain, and calleth unto him whom he would: and they came unto him.	18 And Andrew, and Philip, and Bartholomew, and Matthew, and Thomas, and James the son of Alphaeus, and Thaddaeus, and Simon the Canaanite,	
2. Men appointed by Jesus a. To be with Him b. To be sent out c. To preach[DS1,2] d. To receive authority, power[DS3]	14 And he ordained twelve, that they should be with him, and that he might send them forth to preach, 15 And to have power to heal sicknesses, and to cast out devils:	19 And Judas Iscariot, which also betrayed him: and they went into an house.	

DIVISION II

THE SON OF GOD'S OPENING MINISTRY: JESUS' IMMEDIATE IMPACT, 1:21-3:35

M. Jesus' Impact Upon the Twelve Disciples: Calling Choice Men, 3:13-19

(3:13-19) **Introduction**: Jesus calls choice men—men with hearts that are ripe to be melted and molded. He calls and appoints men, and He changes them. This is what this passage is all about: Jesus' impact upon choice men.

1. Men called by Jesus (v.13).
2. Men appointed by Jesus (vv.14-15).
3. Men changed by Jesus (vv.16-19).

1 (3:13) **Ministers, Call of**: the disciples were *men called by Jesus*. Note three facts about what happened.

a. Jesus called, picked out, and chose some choice men. Many followed Him, but there were a few who showed more interest and commitment. He noticed the ones...

- who listened with more attention.
- who were more awake and alert.
- who responded with a stirred heart.
- who showed more attachment to Him after the crowds had gone.
- who wanted to serve God with meaning and purpose.

Jesus did not look at the stature and physics of the people, not at their appearance and looks, not even at their ability and education. Jesus looked at the hearts of the people. When He saw a person listening, stirred, attached, and wanting to serve, He called that person.

b. Jesus "called...whom He would." His will was *the active power*. They did not choose Him, but He chose them. He did not call those whom the world thought more fit and educated. He called those whose hearts were right and responsive. He knew the heart, and His call was based on the principle of *heart response* (see Jn.15:16).

c. The disciples "came unto Him." The Greek means "they went away unto Him." There is the idea that they left, forsook, and went away from their former work to undertake the new work assigned by Jesus.

> **"Then Peter began to say unto him, Lo, we have left all, and have followed thee" (Mk.10:28).**
>
> **"And when they had brought their ships to land, they forsook all, and followed him....And after these things he went forth, and saw a publican, named Levi, sitting at the receipt of custom: and he said unto him, Follow me. And he left all, rose up, and followed him" (Lu.5:11, 27-28).**
>
> **"And he said to them all, If any man will come after me, let him deny himself, and take up his cross daily, and follow me, For whosoever will save his life shall lose it: but whosoever will lose his life for my sake, the same shall save it" (Lu.9:23-24).**
>
> **"So likewise, whosoever he be of you that forsaketh not all that he hath, he cannot be my disciple" (Lu.14:33).**
>
> **"And he said unto them, Verily I say unto you, there is no man that hath left house, or parents, or brethren, or wife, or childrn, for the kingdom of God's sake, who shall not receive manifold more in this present time, and in the world to come life everlasting" (Lu.18:29-30).**

2 (3:14-15) **Ministers, Call of**: the disciples were men appointed by Jesus for four specific purposes (see DEEPER STUDY # 1—Mk.3:14).

a. The disciples were appointed *to be with Jesus*. This was the first lesson Jesus wanted to teach men: that God wants man's personal fellowship and devotion before all else. God willed men to "know Him, believe Him and understand Him" above all else (Is.43:10). The disciples were to live in Jesus' presence, ever learning of Him and drawing their spiritual nourishment and strength from Him.

> **"Ye are my witnesses, saith the LORD, and my servant whom I have chosen: that ye may know and believe me, and understand that I am he: before me there was no God formed, neither shall there be after me" (Is.43:10).**
>
> **"God is faithful, by whom ye were called unto the fellowship of his Son Jesus Christ our Lord" (1 Co.1:9).**
>
> **"Yea doubtless, and I count all things but loss for the excellency of the knowledge of Christ Jesus my Lord: for whom I have suffered the loss of all things, and do count them but dung, that I may win Christ....That I may know him, and the power of his resurrection, and the fellowship of his sufferings, being made conformable unto his death" (Ph.3:8, 10).**
>
> **"Behold, I stand at the door, and knock: if any man hear my voice, and open the door, I will come in to him, and will sup with him, and he with me" (Re.3:20).**

b. The disciples were appointed to be *sent forth.* They were to be His ambassadors, His representatives who moved out into the world. They were appointed for that very purpose, to represent Him among the people of the world (see DEEPER STUDY #5, *Apostle*—Mt.10:2 for discussion).

> **"Now then we are ambassadors for Christ, as though God did beseech you by us: we pray you in Christ's stead, be ye reconciled to God" (2 Co.5:20).**
>
> **"But rise, and stand upon thy feet: for I have appeared unto thee for this purpose, to make thee a minister and a witness both of these things which thou hast seen, and of those things in the which I will appear unto thee" (Ac.26:16).**

c. The disciples were appointed *to preach.* They were to be the heralds, the messengers of Jesus Christ. He had a message for the world, and they were to proclaim His message to the world (see DEEPER STUDY # 1, 2—Mk.3:14; DEEPER STUDY # 1—Ro.1:1-7 for discussion).

> **"And as ye go, preach, saying, The kingdom of heaven is at hand" (Mt.10:7).**
>
> **"What I tell you in darkness, that speak ye in light: and what ye hear in the ear, that preach ye upon the housetops" (Mt.10:27).**
>
> **"And he said unto them, Go ye into all the world, and preach the gospel to every creature" (Mk.16:15).**
>
> **"And he sent them to preach the kingdom of God, and to heal the sick" (Lu.9:2).**
>
> **"Jesus said unto him, Let the dead bury their dead: but go thou and preach the kingdom of God" (Lu.9:60).**
>
> **"For we cannot but speak the things which we have seen and heard" (Ac.4:20).**
>
> **"Go, stand and speak in the temple to the people all the words of this life" (Ac.5:20).**
>
> **"For though I preach the gospel, I have nothing to glory of: for necessity is laid upon me; yea, woe is unto me, if I preach not the gospel!" (1 Co.9:16).**
>
> **"Then I said, I will not make mention of him, nor speak any more in his name. But his word was in mine heart as a burning fire shut up in my bones, and I was weary with forbearing, and I could not stay" (Je.20:9).**
>
> **"The lion hath roared, who will not fear? the Lord GOD hath spoken, who can but prophesy?" (Am.3:8).**

d. The disciples were appointed to *receive power*—the power to minister and to heal sicknesses and to cast out devils (see DEEPER STUDY # 3—Mk.3:15; note and DEEPER STUDY # 1,2,3—Mt.10:1 for discussion).

> **"Behold, I give unto you power to tread on serpents and scorpions, and over all the power of the enemy: and nothing shall by any means hurt you. Notwithstanding in this rejoice not, that the spirits are subject unto you; but rather rejoice, because your names are written in heaven" (Lu.10:19-20).**
>
> **"But ye shall receive power, after that the Holy Ghost is come upon you: and ye shall be witnesses unto me both in Jerusalem, and in all Judaea, and in Samaria, and unto the uttermost part of the earth" (Ac.1:8).**
>
> **"And with great power gave the apostles witness of the resurrection of the Lord Jesus: and great grace was upon them all" (Ac.4:33).**
>
> **"And they were not able to resist the wisdom and the spirit by which he spake" (Ac.6:10).**
>
> **"And what is the exceeding greatness of his power to us-ward who believe, according to the working of his mighty power" (Ep.1:19).**
>
> **"Now unto him that is able to do exceeding abundantly above all that we ask or think, according to the power that worketh in us" (Ep.3:20).**
>
> **"Wherefore I put thee in remembrance that thou stir up the gift of God, which is in thee by the putting on of my hands. For God hath not given us the spirit of fear; but of power, and of love, and of a sound mind. Be not thou therefore ashamed of the testimony of our Lord, nor of me his prisoner: but be thou partaker of the afflictions of the gospel according to the power of God" (2 Ti.1:6-8).**

DEEPER STUDY # 1
(3:14) **Ordained** (epoiese): to be made or appointed. The word is taken from the Greek word *poieo* which means to do, to make, to appoint with credentials. The word is often used to refer to a person being appointed to some high position or office. The picture is that of Jesus Christ, the Son of God, the future King of the universe, taking twelve men and appointing them to be His. He appoints (ordains) them to the *office* of being His ministers and representatives on earth.

DEEPER STUDY # 2
(3:14) **Preach** (kerusso): to be a herald; to proclaim; to publish; to evangelize. The word carries with it the idea of intense feeling, gravity, and authority—so much so that it *must* be listened to and heeded. The person who preaches is the herald of Jesus Christ; that is, his message is the message of Christ, not of someone else. The herald does not share his own opinions and views; He *proclaims* the truth of Jesus Christ (see DEEPER STUDY # 5—Mt.10:2 for more discussion).

DEEPER STUDY # 3
(3:15) **Sicknesses—Demons**: note that Mark makes a distinction between sickness and demon possession. This distinction is commonly made throughout the Gospels. Note these facts.

1. The word for power is not *dunamis*, the supernatural power of God. It is *exousia*, a delegated power or authority. The servant of God is not given the power of God to use as the servant wills, but the servant is given the authority to specifically minister by healing and casting out demons. The servant prays and speaks the word, and then God does the actual healing and casting out of the demon.
2. The emphasis of this delegated authority is casting out demons. The servant of Christ is given authority to cast out the evil spirits that rule men's lives. Note that the spiritual world or dimension of being is here acknowledged.

> **"For this purpose the Son of God was manifested, that he might destroy the works of the devil" (1 Jn.3:8).**

3 (3:16-19) **Conversion—Transformation**: the disciples were *men changed by Jesus*. But it is critical to keep in mind that each man had to be *willing* to be changed. One was not willing, Judas Iscariot. Jesus called them all, but only the ones willing to be changed were changed. (See DEEPER STUDIES # 5-15—Mk.3:16; 3:17; 3:18; 3:19 for discussion.)

> **"Therefore if any man be in Christ, he is a new creature: old things are passed away; behold, all things are become new" (2 Co.5:17).**
>
> **"I beseech you therefore, brethren, by the mercies of God, that ye present your bodies a living sacrifice, holy, acceptable unto God, which is your reasonable service. And be not conformed to this world: but be ye transformed by the renewing of your mind, that ye may prove what is that good, and acceptable, and perfect, will of God" (Ro.12:1-2).**
>
> **"Ye have not chosen me, but I have chosen you, and ordained you, that ye should go and bring forth fruit, and that your fruit should remain: that whatsoever ye shall ask of the Father in my name, he may give it you" (Jn.15:16).**

DEEPER STUDY # 4
(3:16) **Simon—Peter (Greek, petros)—Cephas (Aramaic, kepha)**: Peter was a rough-hewn fisherman. He looked, acted, and spoke like any professional fisherman at the dock of a large lake or sea. Anyone who has been around a fisherman's dock or boat can picture Peter.

1. Peter had many commendable strengths.
   a. Peter was self-sacrificing, giving up all—even his home and business—to follow Jesus (see notes—Mk.1:16-18; Mt.8:14).
   b. Peter was spiritual minded. He was the first to really grasp who Jesus was (Mt.16:16-19).
   c. Peter was childlike and humble, often responding and leaping out to Jesus as a child does to his father (Mt.14:26-29; Mk.11:21; Jn.13:6-11).
   d. Peter was trusting, sometimes casting his whole being upon Jesus (Mt.14:26-29).
   e. Peter was tenderhearted and loving, caring deeply for his Lord (Mt.26:75; Jn.21:15-17).
   f. Peter was courageous, the only disciple who defended Jesus against arrest. He was also one of the two disciples who followed Jesus through His trials and crucifixion, although he followed *afar off* (Mt.26:51; 26:58).
   g. Peter would have been judged a hard-working, industrious man by any society.
2. Peter had some glaring weaknesses.
   a. Peter was prideful and presumptuous, a man who thought he knew best and who sometimes lorded it over others. He was always depending upon human wisdom and strength, the arm of the flesh.
      ⇒ Peter thought he knew what was best for Jesus, insisting that Jesus did not have to die (Mt.16:22-23).
      ⇒ Peter tried to prevent Jesus' arrest by drawing his sword and wounding one of the arresting party (Mt.26:51; Mk.14:47; Lu.22:50).
      ⇒ Peter rebuked Jesus, overstepping the limits of his rights. When the crowd thronged Jesus, Jesus simply asked who had touched Him. Peter rebuked Jesus for asking such a question when there were so many people pressing in upon them (Lu.8:45).
      ⇒ Peter, in a self-abasing pride, refused to let Jesus wash his feet (Jn.13:6-11).

b. Peter was slow to learn and to understand truth (Mt.15:15-16).
c. Peter was self-seeking (Mt.19:27).
d. Peter was disbelieving (Mt.14:30).
e. Peter was overbearing, even to the point of instructing Jesus (Mt.16:22-23).
f. Peter had a weak, cowardly trait, being the only disciple to vocally deny Jesus (Mt.26:69-74).

3. A chart showing some of the strengths and weaknesses of Peter can be pictured as follows.

⇒ Self-sacrificing (Mt.1:16-18; Mk.8:14)	⇒ yet self-seeking (Mt.19:27)
⇒ Spiritual minded (Mt.16:16-19)	⇒ yet slow to learn spiritual truth (Mt.15:15-16)
⇒ Childlike and humble (Mk.11:21; Jn.13:6-11)	⇒ yet presumptuous and prideful (Mt.16:22-23; 26:51; Lu.8:45)
⇒ Trusting (Mt.14:26-29)	⇒ yet disbelieving (Mt.14:30)
⇒ Tenderhearted and loving (Mt.26:75; Jn.21:15-17)	⇒ yet overbearing (Mt.16:22-23; 26:51)
⇒ Courageous (Mt.26:51; 26:58)	⇒ yet cowardly (Mt.26:69-74)

Peter was changed dramatically after Jesus' resurrection and after Pentecost. The presence of the living Lord in his life empowered him. Peter was able to take charge of the frightened band of disciples and lead them to fearlessly proclaim the glorious news of the risen Savior. (See note—Mt.8:14 and Master Subject Index for additional information on Peter.)

DEEPER STUDY # 5

(3:17) **James and John**: these two men were brothers. They were the sons of Zebedee, a prosperous fisherman who was a man of high social position. Apparently he was well acquainted with the High Priest and his household, probably providing fish for the palace (see DEEPER STUDY # 1—Jn.18:15-18). Their mother was Salome, who is thought by many to be the sister of Mary, the mother of Jesus. James and John were men of *stormy tempers*, so much so that Jesus called them the *sons of thunder*. Their tempers are seen when they ask Jesus to destroy a Samaritan village with fire for rejecting Him (Lu.9:54).

The two brothers were also gripped by *worldly ambition.* They wanted the highest offices in the coming kingdom of Jesus (Mt.20:20-21). However, Jesus dramatically changed the two men. Jesus changed their stormy temper into a burning zeal and ambition for God. They became two of the greatest witnesses for God ever known. James became the first of the twelve to be martyred; and John was the longest living disciple, becoming one of the greatest literary giants of all time (*The Gospel of John, The Three Epistles of John,* and *The Revelation*). (See notes—Mk.1:20; 10:35-45; DEEPER STUDY # 1—Lu.5:10. See Introduction—The Gospel of *John* and *Revelation.*)

DEEPER STUDY # 6

(3:18) **Andrew**: Andrew was apparently the first disciple of our Lord. He had been a disciple of John the Baptist, longing for the Messianic hope. However, when John pointed out that Jesus was the Messiah, Andrew requested an interview with Jesus. From that point on, he was convinced that Jesus was the true Messiah, and Jesus granted him a very special friendship (Mk.13:3; Jn.1:35-37). Jesus met his craving for the Messianic hope and enlarged his gifts of love and caring (see Jn.1:41; 6:8-9; 12:21-22). Andrew was always helping people (Jn.6:8-9; 12:21-22).

Tradition says Andrew preached in Jerusalem and was crucified for preaching against idolatry. He was hung on a cross in the shape of an X.

DEEPER STUDY # 7

(3:18) **Philip**: Philip did not seek Jesus, but Jesus sought Philip (Jn.1:43f). This indicates that Philip was slow in responding and believing, and he almost missed the opportunity to become an apostle of Jesus. In fact, being slow to respond and fearing to act seem to be the major weaknesses of Philip. He actually did miss the opportunity to demonstrate great faith when Jesus tested his faith in feeding the multitude. He was also slow in responding when some Greeks wanted to interview Jesus (Jn.12:21-22). Again, he was slow in understanding who Jesus was (Jn.14:8f). His faith and willingness to act were in constant need of being stirred and strengthened. Jesus changed him and made him a man of strong faith. This is seen in that he stood fast and fearless even in the face of martyrdom. Tradition tells us that he died as a martyr at Hierapolis.

DEEPER STUDY # 8

(3:18) **Bartholomew—Nathanael**: little is known about this disciple other than what is given by John (see outline, notes and DEEPER STUDY # 1,2—Jn.1:46-49).

DEEPER STUDY # 9

(3:18) **Matthew—Levi**: Matthew was a tax collector, an outcast of society, a traitor to the Jewish people. He felt the alienation and rejection ever so deeply. Yet Jesus took Matthew, changed His life, and met every need of his heart (see notes and DEEPER STUDY # 1—Mt.9:9-13; DEEPER STUDY # 1—Mk.2:14. See Introduction—The Gospel of Matthew.)

DEEPER STUDY # 10

(3:18) **Thomas—Didymus** (meaning the *twin*): Thomas was a man of courage and loyalty. This is seen in his suggestion that the disciples follow Jesus even if it meant death (Jn.11:8, 16). But he was also a skeptic, a pessimist, a doubter. He was slow to understand Jesus' Messiahship (Jn.14:5-6), and he rejected the testimony of others that Jesus had actually risen from the dead. (See outline and notes—Jn.20:24-29.) However, the resurrection of Jesus changed Thomas—changed him completely. He has given to the world one of the strongest testimonies possible (Jn.20:28).

Tradition says that Thomas went to Parthia (India), carrying the gospel to that great continent. He is said to have died a martyr's death.

DEEPER STUDY # 11
(3:18) **James, the son of Alphaeus**: little is known about this James.

⇒ His father was Alphaeus or Clopos (Jn.19:25).
⇒ His mother was one of the women who stood by the cross and visited the tomb of Jesus (Jn.19:25).
⇒ He had a brother, Joses, who was also a follower of Jesus (Mk.15:40; 16:1; Jn.19:25).

It is interesting to note that Matthew's father was also named Alphaeus. Thus, it is possible that James and Matthew were brothers. Tradition says that James was a tax collector just like Matthew. If true, this would give weight to their being brothers.

James was willing to be changed by Jesus, to become a true disciple of the Lord's. He did not forsake the disciples after the crucifixion but stayed right with them. Therefore, he was present when Jesus appeared to the disciples after His resurrection and began transforming the disciples into dynamic witnesses for Him.

DEEPER STUDY # 12
(3:18) **Thaddaeus—Labbeus—Judas, Son of James**: little is known about Thaddaeus. His name (Thaddaeus) means *breast* or *one that praises* or *man of heart*. The fact that Matthew and Mark call him by the name Thaddaeus, the man of heart, reveals that he was a man with a big heart, one who gave of himself to help and minister to others. The presence of the living Lord in his heart and life could only enlarge such a heart.

DEEPER STUDY # 13
(3:18) **Simon the Canaanite—Simon the Zealot**: Simon was a member of the fanatical Jewish party known as the Zealots. The party held that God alone was to be the Ruler and Lord of the Jewish nation. They hated and bitterly opposed all foreign (Roman) domination. They preached and led revolutionary uprisings against the government when they could be formed.

The power of Jesus to change a man's heart is seen in Simon the Zealot. Simon's fanatical devotion turned him into a Zealot for Jesus. Note that he never changed the description of his fanatical nature. Even after his conversion and call, he still wanted his zeal to be known. He still wanted to be known as Simon the Zealot, one who was totally devoted to Jesus Christ, the true Messiah.

DEEPER STUDY # 14
(3:19) **Judas Iscariot**: Very simply, Judas was unwilling to have his heart and life changed by Jesus (see outlines and notes—Mt.26:14-16; 26:20-25; 27:3-5; Master Subject Index for discussion.)

	N. Jesus' Impact upon Friends: Calling Jesus Mad & Insane, *DS1* **3:20-21**
1. The crowd: Was so zealous for Jesus that He was unable to eat	20 And the multitude cometh together again, so that they could not so much as eat bread.
2. The friends or family: Acted in opposition to Jesus a. Heard of His behavior b. Thought Him insane c. Sought custody	21 And when his friends heard *of it,* they went out to lay hold on him: for they said, He is beside himself.

DIVISION II

THE SON OF GOD'S OPENING MINISTRY: JESUS' IMMEDIATE IMPACT, 1:21-3:35

N. Jesus' Impact Upon Friends: Calling Jesus Mad and Insane, 3:20-21

(3:20-21) **Introduction—Jesus Christ, Accusations Against**: the Authorized Version is probably correct in using "friends" here instead of "kinsmen" or family. Jesus' impact upon His family is discussed in Mk.3:31.

1. The crowd: was so zealous for Jesus that He was unable to eat (v.20).
2. The friends or family: acted in opposition to Jesus (v.21).

DEEPER STUDY # 1

(3:20-21) **Jesus Christ, Response to**: from this point to the end of the chapter Mark shows the difference between the feelings of the crowd and the feelings of others about Jesus. In verse 20 he shows the feelings and the support of the multitude. Then he shows the enormous contrast of the feelings of three groups who should have been the very ones to support Jesus. There are the contrasted feelings...

- of His friends—who charged Him with being mad and insane (Mk.3:21).
- of the religionists—who charged Him with being demon-possessed (Mk.3:22-30).
- of His very own family—who charged Him with being an embarrassment (Mk.3:31-35).

In the present passage, the contrast between the feelings of the multitude and Jesus' friends is clearly seen. And in the contrast much is to be learned.

1 (3:20) **Jesus Christ, Response to—Zeal—Enthusiasm—Ministers, Support of**: the zeal and enthusiasm of the crowd for Christ was great, so great that He was unable to care for Himself. He could not even find time to eat. Note two points.

a. Jesus had not called for the crowd to come; they just came. They filled the house, overflowing into the street. Some had come more out of curiosity than need, but others had come to hear and learn. Still others had come to be helped and healed.

Thought 1. Zeal and enthusiasm for Christ are so desperately lacking. Men should be flocking to Him by the multitudes, but they are not. Why?

⇒ Do they love the world and the things of the world too much (1 Jn.2:15-16)?
⇒ Do they love the flesh and its feelings too much?
⇒ Do they love pride and fame and power too much?
⇒ Do they just not know? Have they not heard (Ro.10:14-15)?
⇒ Is the witness and life of believers too weak (Ep.4:17-24)?

b. The crowd was so large and pressuring. Therefore, Christ and the disciples were unable to take care of their physical needs. However, Christ did not turn the crowd away; He ministered to them.

Thought 1. Christ ministered despite enormous inconvenience and disruption. A unique opportunity presented itself and He grasped it. He denied Himself, His own need, in order to help others. What a lesson for us!

"Come unto me, all ye that labour and are heavy laden, and I will give you rest" (Mt.11:28).

"Ho, every one that thirsteth, come ye to the waters, and he that hath no money; come ye, buy, and eat; yea, come, buy wine and milk without money and without price" (Is.55:1).

"And the Spirit and the bride say, Come. And let him that heareth say, Come. And let him that is athirst come. And whosoever will, let him take the water of life freely" (Re.22:17).

2 (3:21) **Jesus Christ, Response to**: the treatment of Jesus by some friends differed enormously from the multitude. Whereas the multitude responded to Jesus, some friends heard of His behavior and concluded that He was insane, so they sought to take custody of Him. Apparently the friends were close to the family; therefore, they cared deeply for Jesus. They felt He was in danger and wanted to help the family and Him.

Note the words "when his friends heard *of it*." The words are in italics. In the King James Version when words are in italics it means they are not in the Greek. They are added by the translator as he believes the meaning should be. In the present passage, the Greek uses a participle meaning *having heard* (akou santes). The idea is that the friends heard not only about the enormous crowds, but they heard *all about Jesus*: His phenomenal miracles, claims, and teachings; the prophetic esteem which the people heaped upon Him; the opposition which was now threatening His life. All this led the friends of the family to think He was insane. At least seven things contributed to the charge of insanity.

a. Jesus was thought to be crazed because of the zeal and enthusiasm of the crowd. It was felt that the crowd's zeal had turned His head and caused Him to overly evaluate Himself. He was reveling in their attention and adulation. It was reported that He was so caught up in the multitude's enthusiasm that He was neglecting the care of His body, even to the point of not eating meals.

b. Jesus was thought to be crazed because of the response of the people and the esteem with which they held Him. It was thought that such esteem had twisted His mind, causing Him to think too highly of Himself. There were reports that He was claiming to be the Messiah and even the Son of God Himself.

c. Jesus was thought to be crazed because He was selecting a queer band of disciples: rough-hewn fishermen (Peter, James, and John); despised and hated sinners and publicans (Matthew and probably James, the son of Alphaeus); a revolutionary zealot (Simon the Zealot); a seeker who was spiritually troubled (Nathaniel). A sane man set on religious purposes would never choose such men, not if he wished to succeed in society.

d. Jesus was thought to be crazed because His life and behavior were so radically different from normal life and behavior. What He was doing and saying was diametrically opposed to the way anything had ever been done before. He differed so much from everyone else. His very life convicted any who confronted Him, and His words demanded either acceptance or rejection.

e. Jesus was thought to be crazed because the authorities were opposing and threatening to kill Him, yet He refused to back down or flee. He even refused to move elsewhere. A normal person who had a mission to accomplish would at least flee elsewhere until he had time to regroup and plan some other way to achieve his purpose.

f. Jesus was thought to be crazed because His healing ministry necessitated some explanation. There were so many healings, so many miraculous events that a person was forced to come up with some theory. Jesus was either who He claimed, the Son of God; or He was filled with a supernatural spirit other than God's, a spirit that made Him mad, the spirit of the devil. All kinds of theories were now running rampant. There were the theories that He was...

- John the Baptist raised from the dead (Mt.14:1-2).
- Elijah, Jeremiah, or some prophet sent back to life (Mt.16:14).
- Beelzebub (Mt.12:22-32; Mk.3:22-30).
- insane (Mk.3:21).

g. Jesus was thought to be crazed because His teaching and doctrine were so different from anyone else's. In fact, what He taught often differed radically from all that *had ever* been taught. As Festus said to Paul, "Much learning doth make thee mad" (Ac.26:24).

Thought 1. Is Jesus who He claimed? Think of the alternatives:
(1) He was truly the Son of God.
(2) He was devil-possessed; that is, His power came from an evil spirit.
(3) He was insane, mad, mentally deceived, and deranged.
(4) He was deliberately lying about being the Son of God, deliberately deceiving people in order to secure a following to boost His ego.

"Then they that were in the ship came and worshipped him, saying, Of a truth thou art the Son of God" (Mt.14:33).

"The beginning of the gospel of Jesus Christ, the Son of God" (Mk.1:1).

"And I [John the Baptist] saw, and bare record that this is the Son of God" (Jn.1:34).

"For God so loved the world, that he gave his only begotten Son, that whosoever believeth in him should not perish, but have everlasting life. For God sent not his Son into the world to condemn the world; but that the world through him might be saved. He that believeth on him is not condemned: but he that believeth not is condemned already, because he hath not believed in the name of the only begotten Son of God" (Jn.3:16-18).

"Jesus heard that they had cast him out; and when he had found him, he said unto him, Dost thou believe on the Son of God? He answered and said, Who is he, Lord, that I might believe on him? And Jesus said unto him, Thou hast both seen him, and it is he that talketh with thee" (Jn.9:35-37).

"Say ye of him, whom the Father hath sanctified, and sent into the world, Thou blasphemest; because I said, I am the Son of God?" (Jn.10:36).

"Jesus said unto her, I am the resurrection, and the life: he that believeth in me, though he were dead, yet shall he live: and whosoever liveth and believeth in me shall never die. Believest thou this? She saith unto him, Yea, Lord: I believe that thou art the Christ, the Son of God, which should come into the world" (Jn.11:25-27).

"And straightway he [Paul] preached Christ in the synagogues, that he is the Son of God" (Ac.9:20).

> **"Of how much sorer punishment, suppose ye, shall he be thought worthy, who hath trodden under foot the Son of God, and hath counted the blood of the covenant, wherewith he was sanctified, an unholy thing, and hath done despite unto the Spirit of grace?" (He.10:29).**
>
> **"Whosoever shall confess that Jesus is the Son of God, God dwelleth in him, and he in God" (1 Jn.4:15).**

Thought 2. The call of the hour is: "Believe Jesus. Trust Him. He was not insane. He is truly the Son of the living God."

Thought 3. Friends can be wrong, no matter how much they esteem and love us. What they think and how they treat us can often be wrong: the friends of Jesus were wrong.

Thought 4. We must go against friends sometimes; we must vigorously surrender to God and do His will regardless of what our friends may think. If God calls us to serve Him, then serve Him we must. Friends can oppose God's will. They may have good intentions, but they cannot know God's will for another person's life. God deals, calls, and works with each of us individually and personally. Being strong and standing firm in God's call and will are desperately needed—always.

> **"Ye have not chosen me, but I have chosen you, and ordained you, that ye should go and bring forth fruit, and that your fruit should remain: that whatsoever ye shall ask of the Father in my name, he may give it you" (Jn.15:16).**
>
> **"I beseech you therefore, brethren, by the mercies of God, that ye present your bodies a living sacrifice, holy, acceptable unto God, which is your reasonable service. And be not conformed to this world: but be ye transformed by the renewing of your mind, that ye may prove what is that good, and acceptable, and perfect, will of God" (Ro.12:1-2).**
>
> **"Therefore, my beloved brethren, be ye stedfast, unmoveable, always abounding in the work of the Lord, forasmuch as ye know that your labour is not in vain in the Lord" (1 Co.15:58).**
>
> **"From that time many of his disciples went back, and walked no more with him. Then said Jesus unto the twelve, Will ye also go away? Then Simon Peter answered him, Lord, to whom shall we go? thou hast the words of eternal life" (Jn.6:66-68).**
>
> **"But the Lord said unto him, Go thy way [quit arguing]: for he is a chosen vessel unto me, to bear my name before the Gentiles, and kings, and the children of Israel" (Ac.9:15).**

	O. Jesus' Impact upon Religionists: Calling Jesus Demon-Possessed, 3:22-30 *(Mt. 12:22-32; Lu. 11:14-20)*	26 And if Satan rise up against himself, and be divided, he cannot stand, but hath an end.	c. Conclusion: Satan would be destroying his own kingdom
		27 No man can enter into a strong man's house, and spoil his goods, except he will first bind the strong man; and then he will spoil his house.	**3. Jesus' 2nd rebuttal: Satan's kingdom has been breeched**
1. The setting: An investigative committee of Scribes gave their judgment about Jesus a. The terrible charge: He is demon-possessed*DS1,2* b. The rebuttal by Jesus: A logical question	22 And the scribes which came down from Jerusalem said, He hath Beelzebub, and by the prince of the devils casteth he out devils. 23 And he called them unto him, and said unto them in parables, How can Satan cast out Satan?	28 Verily I say unto you, All sins shall be forgiven unto the sons of men, and blasphemies wherewith so-ever they shall blaspheme:	**4. Jesus' 3rd rebuttal: God's love is universal**
2. Jesus' 1st rebuttal: Internal strife always divides & destroys a. Internal strife destroys a kingdom b. Internal strife destroys a house	24 And if a kingdom be divided against itself, that kingdom cannot stand. 25 And if a house be divided against itself, that house cannot stand.	29 But he that shall blaspheme against the Holy Ghost hath never forgiveness, but is in danger of eternal damnation: 30 Because they said, He hath an unclean spirit.	**5. Jesus' 4th rebuttal: There is one danger, the unpardonable sin—ascribing God's work to the devil**

DIVISION II

THE SON OF GOD'S OPENING MINISTRY: JESUS' IMMEDIATE IMPACT, 1:21-3:35

O. Jesus' Impact Upon Religionists: Calling Jesus Demon-Possessed, 3:22-30

(3:22-30) **Introduction—Jesus Christ, Response to**: Who was Jesus Christ? Was He really of God, or was He of the devil? That is, was He evil, an imposter, a deceiver who set out to mislead the world into thinking that He was the Son of God? Is belief in Him really the only way to God? Are His teachings the *only way* to live and to experience deliverance now and eternally?

The religionists of Jesus' day believed He was evil. In fact, they believed He was an embodiment of Satan himself. This passage discusses their charge and Jesus' answer. And it challenges us to accept the truth about Jesus.

1. The setting: An investigative committee of Scribes gave their judgment about Jesus (vv.22-23).
2. Jesus' 1st rebuttal: internal strife always divides and destroys (vv.24-26).
3. Jesus' 2nd rebuttal: Satan's kingdom has been breeched (v.27).
4. Jesus' 3rd rebuttal: God's love is universal (v.28).
5. Jesus' 4th rebuttal: there is one danger, the unpardonable sin—ascribing God's work to the devil (vv.29-30).

1 (3:22-23) **Religionists, Accusations**: the Scribes, the investigative commission from Jerusalem, gave their judgment about Jesus (see notes—Mk.2:6-7; 3:1-2).

a. Their charge was terrible: "He hath Beelzebub" (see DEEPER STUDY # 1,2—Mk.3:22); that is, He was *possessed, indwelt, controlled, under the supreme power* of Beelzebub, the supernatural power of evil. Note: they were not saying that Jesus was in alliance with the devil. Their charge went much farther than an alliance. They were saying that Jesus was an incarnation of evil, of the devil himself.

The religionists and people were bitter, stinging, rough, and cutting in their accusations against Jesus.

⇒ "He hath a devil, and is mad" (Jn.10:20).
⇒ "[He is] a Samaritan, and hast a devil" (Jn.8:48).
⇒ He is born out of wedlock (Jn.8:41; Mt.1:18-19).
⇒ "[He is] a gluttonous man, and a winebibber, a friend of [cohabiter with] sinners" (Lu.7:34).

Note two things.

1) The religionists could not deny the power of Jesus: lives were being dramatically and radically changed; evil spirits were being "cast out" of people. Exorcism, the casting out of evil spirits, was not a new or unusual thing to the people of Jesus' day.
   ⇒ Jesus referred to Jewish exorcists (Mt.12:27; Lu.11:19).
   ⇒ The disciples referred to a man who professed to be a follower of Jesus and who was casting out demons in Jesus' name (Mk.9:38).
   ⇒ There was a Jewish priest who had seven sons, and each of the sons claimed to be an exorcist (Ac. 19:13-16).

The religionists were without excuse. They should have understood exorcism. The presence of evil spirits and men's attempting to cast them out were common enough occurrences for them to understand (see DEEPER STUDY # 4—Mt.12:24; 12:27-28).

The point is this: exorcism was not a *new* thing, but what Jesus was doing was new. Others were not always successful in casting out evil spirits. They failed, lacked permanent and perfect power to overcome the world of evil—but not Jesus. His power was universal and perfect, always effective. By just speaking a simple word, the most powerful results imaginable happened. Evil spirits within men, spirits which corrupted men's lives, were cast out; and the men were dramatically and forcefully changed.

The religionists could not deny the fact. They had to deal with the matter of Jesus' power. Some explanation, some theory had to be given. Their conclusion was: "He hath Beelzebub...by the prince of the devils casteth he out devils."

2) The religionists were deliberately trying to disprove Jesus' claim to be the Messiah, the Son of God. If they could prove He was an imposter, a fraud, a deceiver, an evil man misleading others, a man linked to evil and to the devil, then His claims would be disproven and the people would cease to follow Him (see notes—Mt.12:1-8; 12:9-13; note and DEEPER STUDY # 1—12:10).

b. Jesus had to answer the charge. His rebuttal was a forceful argument. He asked *the logical and irrefutable* question: "How can Satan cast out Satan?" The answer was unavoidable, inevitable: Satan would never cast out evil. If he did, he would be working against himself, and that is not his purpose. He is out to build and expand evil, not to destroy it. To say otherwise is illogical; it does not make sense. Jesus used four rebuttals to prove His point (see outline and notes of this passage).

DEEPER STUDY # 1

(3:22) **Beelzebub**: an idol god of the ancient Philistines. The name means *the god of flies*. But the Jews called the idol *the god of filth* or *the god of dung* (Beelzebub). The name was eventually ascribed to Satan as the prince of unclean spirits (see DEEPER STUDY # 1—Rev.12:9).

DEEPER STUDY # 2

(3:22) **Religionists—Jesus Christ, Opposed**: the religionists were bitter, stinging, rough, and cutting in their accusations against Jesus. "He hath a devil and is mad" (Jn.10:20). He is a "Samaritan and has a devil" (Jn.8:48); He is born out of wedlock (Jn.8:41). He is "greedy, alcoholic, a friend of sinners" (Lu.7:34).

Why did the religionists (Pharisees, Sadducees, and Scribes) oppose Jesus so vehemently? There were several reasons.

1. Religion gives a sense of security. It is the opium of the people, as Karl Marx said. It makes a person secure and comfortable with himself. Therefore, a truly professional and committed religionist opposes anything that threatens the security he has found.

2. Religionists oppose change. Every true religionist believes his way is the way, the truth, and the life. There is no reason to change so long as one's needs are being met.

3. Religion can lead to position, pride, and a sense of importance. One of the most difficult things in the world is for a person to give up his position and admit he is wrong. To do so is to deny his importance. Think about it—for this is exactly what Christ demands of every man (Lu.9:23). This is the reason so many of the gifted and the powerful of the world reject Christ and become hostile to Him (see outline—1 Co.1:26-31).

2 (3:24-26) **Strife—Division—Jesus Christ, Messiah**: the first rebuttal by Jesus was that internal strife always divides and destroys. He used two illustrations to enforce His point. (See note—Mt.12:25-26 for a more detailed explanation of this point.)

a. A kingdom divided against itself cannot stand. Civil war, internal strife, and divisiveness will cause a kingdom to fall. It cannot last, not if its subjects fight among themselves.

b. A house divided against itself cannot stand. Constant bickering and arguing will cause the house to crumble. A house cannot last, not if its subjects strive, fuss, quarrel and fight all the time. The house will break up.

c. Satan cannot be rising up against himself. He would be casting out his own evil spirits and destroying his own kingdom of evil subjects. He would be breaking his rule and reign over lives.

There is no conceivable way Jesus is from anywhere other than from God. He had nothing whatsoever to do with evil or evil spirits, except to cast them out of men's lives. He had come to free men so that they might live righteously and godly in this present world. He is God's representative among men, not Satan's. He is exactly who He claims to be, the Son of God Himself. To argue any other position is illogical. (Again, see note—Mt.12:25-26 for a detailed discussion and application of this point. Also see note, Thought 1—Mk.3:21 for Jesus' claim to be the Son of God. See note—Jn.1:34 for most of the verses referring to Jesus as the Son of God.)

"He that believeth on him is not condemned: but he that believeth not is condemned already, because he hath not believed in the name of the only begotten Son of God" (Jn.3:18).

"Say ye of him, whom the Father hath sanctified, and sent into the world, Thou blasphemest; because I said, I am the Son of God? If I do not the works of my Father, believe me not. But if I do, though ye believe not me, believe the works: that ye may know, and believe, that the Father is in me, and I in him" (Jn.10:36-38).

"Of how much sorer punishment, suppose ye, shall he be thought worthy, who hath trodden under foot the Son of God, and hath counted the blood of the covenant, wherewith he was sanctified, an unholy thing, and hath done despite unto the Spirit of grace?" (He.10:29).

3 (3:27) **Jesus Christ, Work of—Satan, Defeated**: the second rebuttal by Jesus is that Satan's kingdom had been breached. God had broken into Satan's house and kingdom by using the power of Christ to free those enslaved by Satan. Just as an invader enters a strong man's house, binds him, and then spoils his goods, so Jesus has now invaded Satan's kingdom of evil. Christ is now setting men free, free from evil spirits. Satan is now being conquered. The power of Christ is now delivering men from the world and enslavement of evil. Men can now be set free from evil—even from the evil of death itself (see Heb.2:14-15; Col.2:15; 1 Co.15:20-58. See note—Mt.12:29 for a detailed discussion of this point.)

> **"Jesus answered and said, This voice came not because of me, but for your sakes. Now is the judgment of this world: now shall the prince of this world be cast out" (Jn.12:30-31).**
>
> **"But now is Christ risen from the dead, and become the firstfruits of them that slept. For since by man came death, by man came also the resurrection of the dead. For as in Adam all die, even so in Christ shall all be made alive. But every man in his own order: Christ the firstfruits; afterward they that are Christ's at his coming" (1 Co.15:20-23).**
>
> **"And having spoiled principalities and powers, he made a show of them openly, triumphing over them in it" (Col.2:15).**
>
> **"Forasmuch then as the children are partakers of flesh and blood, he also himself likewise took part of the same; that through death he might destroy him that had the power of death, that is, the devil; and deliver them who through fear of death were all their lifetime subject to bondage" (He.2:14-15).**
>
> **"He that committeth sin is of the devil; for the devil sinneth from the beginning. For this purpose the Son of God was manifested, that he might destroy the works of the devil" (1 Jn.3:8).**

4 (3:28) **God, Love of—Forgiveness—Blasphemy**: the third rebuttal by Jesus was that God's love is universal. God forgives all sin—even blasphemy—that insults, curses, and reviles God (see DEEPER STUDY # 4—Mt.9:3). Men need to know this glorious truth. There is no sin that God does not forgive. A man can be forgiven anything, no matter how terrible or vile. He can be forgiven if he will turn to Christ, confess his sin, and repent (see DEEPER STUDY # 4, *Forgiveness*—Mt.26:28 for discussion).

The behavior of Jesus upon the cross shows just how universal God's love really is. The savage treatment and the vulgar insults inflicted upon Jesus were horrible. Such treatment shows the base, sinful nature of all men; yet Jesus prayed, "Father, forgive them" (Lu.23:34).

> **Thought 1.** God's love and forgiveness are universal. God loves every man and will forgive any man no matter how much the man has sinned and blasphemed God.
>
> > **"Be it known unto you therefore, man and brethren, that through this man is preached unto you the forgiveness of sins" (Ac.13:38).**
> >
> > **"In whom we have redemption through his blood, the forgiveness of sins, according to the riches of his grace" (Ep.1:7).**
> >
> > **"For this is good and acceptable in the sight of God our Saviour; who will have all men to be saved, and to come unto the knowledge of the truth. For there is one God, and one mediator between God and men, the man Christ Jesus; who gave himself a ransom for all, to be testified in due time" (1 Ti.2:3-6).**
> >
> > **"I, even I, am he that blotteth out thy transgressions for mine own sake, and will not remember thy sins" (Is.43:25).**
> >
> > **"I have blotted out, as a thick cloud, thy transgressions, and, as a cloud, thy sins: return unto me; for I have redeemed thee" (Is.44:22).**
> >
> > **"Let the wicked forsake his way, and the unrighteous man his thoughts: and let him return unto the LORD, and he will have mercy upon him; and to our God, for he will abundantly pardon" (Is.55:7).**

5 (3:29-30) **Sin, Unforgivable**: the fourth rebuttal by Jesus was that there is one danger—the danger of committing the unforgivable sin. The unforgivable sin is ascribing God's work to the devil (see note—Mt.12:31-32 for a detailed discussion and application of the Unpardonable Sin).

The unforgivable sin is committed by the man who continues and continues...

- to reject the *promptings* of the Holy Spirit.
- to blind himself to the illumination of the Holy Spirit.
- to willfully sin despite conviction by the Holy Spirit.
- to insist on his own way.
- to oppose the work of the Holy Spirit.
- to justify himself in his sinful behavior.

> **"He that believeth on the Son hath everlasting life: and he that believeth not the Son shall not see life; but the wrath of God abideth on him" (Jn.3:36).**
>
> **"I said therefore unto you, that ye shall die in your sins: for if ye believe not that I am he, ye shall die in your sins" (Jn.8:24).**
>
> **"Take heed, brethren, lest there be in any of you an evil heart of unbelief, in departing from the living God" (He.3:12).**

	P. Jesus' Impact upon His Own Family: Feeling Jesus Is an Embarrassment, 3:31-35 *(Mt. 12:46-50; Lu. 8:19-21)*	thy brethren without seek for thee.	
		33 And he answered them, saying, Who is my mother, or my brethren?	**2. True kinship is not just blood relationship**
1. Jesus' family a. They were standing outside b. They sent for Him—to call Him	31 There came then his brethren and his mother, and, standing without, sent unto him, calling him.	34 And he looked round about on them which sat about him, and said, Behold my mother and my brethren!	**3. True kinship is a common relationship with God** a. It is being a disciple of Christ
c. He was informed of the family's presence & embarrassment	32 And the multitude sat about him, and they said unto him, Behold, thy mother and	35 For whosoever shall do the will of God, the same is my brother, and my sister, and mother.	b. It is seeking to do God's will

DIVISION II

THE SON OF GOD'S OPENING MINISTRY: JESUS' IMMEDIATE IMPACT, 1:21-3:35

P. Jesus' Impact Upon His Own Family: Feeling Jesus Is an Embarrassment, 3:31-35

(3:31-35) **Introduction—Jesus Christ, Family**: tongues were buzzing and rumors were flying about Jesus (see outline and DEEPER STUDY # 1—Mk.3:20-21; note—3:22-30). The rumors reached Mary and her other children back in Nazareth. They became extremely concerned over Jesus' welfare and were somewhat embarrassed over Jesus. So they struck out to get Him and bring Him home before something terrible happened. When they arrived and Jesus was informed of their presence, He made a shocking claim: there is a greater family existing than the human family—a family that has supremacy over blood relationships. It is the family of God, the family of all those who do the will of God. (See outline and notes—Mt.12:46-50; Lu.8:19-21 for more discussion.)

1. Jesus' family (vv.31-32).
2. True kinship is not just blood relationship (v.33).
3. True kinship is a common relationship with God (vv.34-35).

1 (3:31-32) **Jesus Christ, Family**: Jesus' family came to take Him home. His family had not been with Him at this time. They had probably been back in Nazareth. Note the facts given.

1. They were "standing without," apparently embarrassed, not wishing to approach Jesus in front of the crowd lest a scene be created.
2. They "sent [someone else] unto Him, calling Him" to take Him home.
3. The crowd informed Him of the family's presence outside, and note: they added the words "seek for thee." The crowd was apparently aware of the family's embarrassment and thoughts that He was "beside Himself" and needed to be taken home (v.21).

Something significant had happened that brought Jesus' family to get Him and take Him home. What happened that caused Mary and His brothers to come for Him? What was so serious that they would send someone else inside to get Him instead of going in themselves or at least waiting until the meeting was over? What would cause them to seek to interrupt and stop the preaching of Jesus? (See outline and notes—Mt.12:46-50.) What would cause Jesus to proclaim such shocking words at this time (vv.34-35)? There seem to be three reasons.

a. The public, even some friends of Jesus and the family, were saying, "He is beside Himself," mad, insane (Mk.3:20-21). Two things caused this charge.

1) He was working very hard, in fact so hard that He "could not so much as eat bread" (Mk.3:20). He was swamped by people to the extent that He was forced to skip meals and do without rest. His refusing to leave the frenzied atmosphere in order to eat and rest—such behavior going on day after day and month after month—led some to wonder if He were mad, abnormal in craving the attention and adulation and frenzy of the crowds.
2) He was proclaiming Himself to be the Son of God. He made many claims that were so unusual that He was thought insane (see outlines and notes—Jn.5:1-7:53. A quick glance will show just how phenomenal Jesus' claims were and why He was so opposed by many, even by His own family.)

b. The rulers, both political and religious, were increasingly opposing Jesus. The family was alarmed and feared for His life (see outline and notes—Mt.12:1-50; Mk.3:22-30).

c. The news of His *claim* to be the Son of God reached the family, and the neighbors were saying that such a claim was preposterous, utter insanity. In addition, the neighbors and friends were whispering about His insanity and about His conflict with the leaders of the nation. All this did to Mary and the family what such news would do to any family: it caused concern and stirred a mother's deep love and responsibility for her Son. She left immediately to go for Him, to bring Him home in order to save Him from harm and the family from further embarrassment (Mt.12:14; Jn.7:1f).

Thought 1. Some penetrating questions need to be asked and answered by all of us.

⇒ How many are embarrassed by Jesus?
⇒ How many are ashamed to stand up for Jesus and His claims?
⇒ How many fear what their neighbors and friends will say if they take a stand for Jesus?
⇒ How many want to take Jesus home and lock Him up in a room where His claims will not bother anyone?

At this point a legitimate question needs to be asked: How could Mary not believe Jesus' claims after her experience with God concerning the birth of Jesus? The answer is given in an honest and open-hearted study of the Scripture.

a. Mary was a wonderful woman, the woman chosen for a very special mission: to be the person through whom God would send "His only begotten Son" into the world (Jn.3:16). But it must always be remembered that Mary was *only human.* She was a very special woman, yes; nevertheless, she was still only human. Her being special was only in that she was *highly favored* by God (Lu.1:28). Her being special was not because of any virtue or merit of her own. It was because of God, because of His mercy and His grace alone.

b. Mary's deep experience with God had happened some thirty years before. Thirty or more years is a long time for human creatures to maintain the reality and meaning of a religious experience. Human emotions rise and fall almost daily.

c. As a mother, as flesh and blood, Mary had a difficult time (as anyone in her situation would) understanding the mission and Messiahship of her Son Jesus.

1) Mary had believed God's messenger (Lu.1:45), but she had not fully understood. She apparently "kept all these things [to herself—wisely, we might add], and *pondered* them in her heart" (Lu.2:19).
2) Thirteen years later Mary had difficulty understanding the mission of her twelve year-old Son when He was found in the temple after having been lost for two days. When they found Him, He was engaged in a most unusual questioning with the temple priests. Jesus asked His mother, "[Why] is it that ye sought me? [Knew] ye not that I must be about my Father's business?" (Lu.2:49).
3) Some seventeen years after the temple experience, Mary called upon her Son to help at a wedding in Cana of Galilee. Jesus saw in the request an opportunity to begin familiarizing His mother with just who He really was, the Son of God. She was slow to grasp His purpose, so He gave her a mild rebuke, "Woman, what have I to do with thee? mine hour is not yet come" (Jn.2:4. See note—Jn.2:3-5 for a more detailed explanation.)

d. Mary had known Jesus as one of her children and as a young man for some thirty years. She had known Jesus only in a day-to-day family setting, in a day-to-day routine environment. Then all of a sudden He pulled up stakes, left home, and left what was apparently a flourishing carpentry business. The events that occurred from the moment He left happened so rapidly over the next few months and were so dramatic that Mary was bound to feel bombarded and perplexed. She and all the others who were close to Jesus were having to learn that He was not just a man, but the Son of God Himself. (See outline and notes—Mk.3:21 for other unusual acts by Jesus that caused problems for the friends and the family. Mary was bound to be concerned because of what was happening and being said about her Son.)

2 (3:33) **Brotherhood—God, Family of**: true kinship is not just blood relationship. Note two facts.

a. Jesus is not downgrading the family or human ties to blood relatives (see note—Mt.12:46-47). No one was ever more devoted to the family than Jesus. This is seen in...

- His care of Mary throughout His life (see Jn.19:26-27).
- His teaching and the teaching of His disciples throughout Scripture (see Ep.5:22-6:4).
- His impact upon society's treatment of women, children, and the family (see note—Mk.10:5; see Col.3:18-21).
- His own half-brothers who eventually became disciples (see note—Mk.6:3-4).

b. Jesus is saying that human genes, family blood and traits, are not enough to create and make a genuine family. A *true family*, a *true kinship* does not exist just because some people have common blood and traits. This is clearly seen in the pages of family histories every day. Too many families are in turmoil, divided, and torn apart. Too many families are in constant conflict ranging from mild verbal assaults to murderous assaults. There is...

- parent against child
- child against parent
- husband against wife
- sister against sister
- brother against brother
- relative against relative

Now picture the scene. Jesus is standing before the crowd. He has just been told that His mother and brothers are outside "seeking" for Him. In the event He sees a unique opportunity to teach a much needed lesson. Stretching forth His arms toward the multitude, He cries out, "Who is my mother, or my brethren?" He is proclaiming that blood relationships, family genes and traits, are not enough to create true kinship. Something more is needed.

> **"Bring forth therefore fruits worthy of repentance, and begin not to say within yourselves, We have Abraham to our father: for I say unto you, That God is able of these stones to raise up children unto Abraham" (Lu.3:8).**
>
> **"But as many as received him, to them gave he power to become the sons of God, even to them that believe on his name: which were born, not of blood, nor of the will of the flesh, nor of the will of man, but of God" (Jn.1:12-13).**
>
> **"They answered him, We be Abraham's seed, and were never in bondage to any man: how sayest thou, Ye shall be made free?" (Jn.8:33).**
>
> **"They answered and said unto him, Abraham is our father. Jesus saith unto them, If ye were Abraham's children, ye would do the works of Abraham" (Jn.8:39).**
>
> **"Then they reviled him, and said, Thou art his disciple; but we are Moses' disciples" (Jn.9:28).**
>
> **"Who by him do believe in God, that raised him up from the dead, and gave him glory; that your faith and hope might be in God" (1 Pe.1:21).**

3 (3:34-35) **God, Family of—Believers**: true kinship is based on a common relationship with God. True kinship is a spiritual relationship. God is Spirit, and those who would know and follow Him must be in spiritual union with Him. True kinship is a matter of the spirit, heart, and mind (Jn.4:23-24). All who are in *spiritual union* with God become sons and daughters of God and brothers of Jesus. They comprise the true family of God (2 Co.6:17-18; Ro.8:29).

Jesus points out two facts.

a. True kinship is based upon being a true disciple, a true follower of God. Note the words, "He looked round about on them." Matthew says that the persons Jesus was looking at were His disciples (Mt.12:49). He was saying that His true family was the disciples, those who had accepted Him as Lord and Master. It was their acceptance of Him in spirit and heart that bound them together. He was saying that all who follow Him are spiritually united. They constitute a kinship that is based upon having the same Lord and Master, a true kinship that will last forever. (See DEEPER STUDY # 3, *Fellowship*—Acts 2:42. Also see notes—Ep.2:11-18; 2:19-22 for discussion.)

> **"But as many as received him, to them gave he power to become the sons of God, even to them that believe on his name" (Jn.1:12).**
>
> **"For as many as are led by the Spirit of God, they are the sons of God. For ye have not received the spirit of bondage again to fear; but ye have received the Spirit of adoption, whereby we cry, Abba, Father. The Spirit itself beareth witness with our spirit, that we are the children of God: and if children, then heirs; heirs of God, and joint-heirs with Christ; if so be that we suffer with him, that we may be also glorified together" (Ro.8:14-17).**
>
> **"Wherefore come out from among them, and be ye separate, saith the Lord, and touch not the unclean thing; and I will receive you, and will be a Father unto you, and ye shall be my sons and daughters, saith the Lord Almighty" (2 Co.6:17-18).**
>
> **"But when the fulness of the time was come, God sent forth his Son, made of a woman, made under the law, to redeem them that were under the law, that we might receive the adoption of sons. And because ye are sons, God hath sent forth the Spirit of his Son into your hearts, crying, Abba, Father" (Ga.4:4-6).**
>
> **"For through him [Christ] we both have access by one Spirit unto the Father. Now therefore ye are no more strangers and foreigners, but fellowcitizens with the saints, and of the household of God" (Ep.2:18-19).**
>
> **"For this cause I bow my knees unto the Father of our Lord Jesus Christ, of whom the whole family in heaven and earth is named" (Ep.3:14-15).**
>
> **"For both he that sanctifieth and they who are sanctified are all of one: for which cause he is not ashamed to call them brethren" (He.2:11).**

b. True kinship is based upon doing the will of God. Jesus had given Himself to do God's will. The disciples had accepted Jesus as their Lord and Master. Therefore, they were committed to do exactly what their Lord did: the will of God. The will of God became the objective and drive of their lives. All true disciples of Jesus have the same objective: to do the will of God. Therefore, it is the spiritual commitment to do the will of God that binds all believers together.

All men who focus their lives upon the will of God are bound together spiritually, bound together to do the will of God. Jesus is saying no greater kinship exists.

Thought 1. The will of God is the law of God (see the ten commandments, Ex.20:3-17).

> **"I delight to do thy will, O my God: yea, thy law is within my heart" (Ps.40:8).**
>
> **"I beseech you therefore, brethren, by the mercies of God, that ye present your bodies a living sacrifice, holy, acceptable unto God, which is your reasonable service. And be not conformed to this world: but be ye transformed by the renewing of your mind, that ye may prove what is that good, and acceptable, and perfect, will of God" (Ro.12:1-2).**
>
> **"For this is the will of God, even your sanctification, that ye should abstain from fornication" (1 Th.4:3).**
>
> **"In every thing give thanks: for this is the will of God in Christ Jesus concerning you" (1 Th.5:18).**
>
> **"[This] is the will of God, that with well doing ye may put to silence the ignorance of foolish men" (1 Pe.2:15).**
>
> **"That he no longer should live the rest of his time in the flesh to the lusts of men, but to the will of God" (1 Pe.4:2).**

1. Jesus began a new method of teaching: The parable
  a. The setting: By the lakeshore in a boat
  b. The crowd: Very large
  c. The parable[DS1]

2. The parable: A sower or farmer sows
  a. Sows seed that does not take root
    1) Some fall by the path: Devoured
    2) Some fall upon rocky places: Withers
  b. Sows seed that does take root, but does not yield fruit—falls among thorns
  c. Sows seed that does bear fruit
  d. Sows only a few seed that bear 100 percent fruit
  e. A message heard only by spiritual ears

3. The response to the parable

CHAPTER 4

III. THE SON OF GOD'S CONTINUING MINISTRY: JESUS' PARABLES & HIS AUTHORITY, 4:1-6:6

A. The Parable of the Sower or Farmer: How Men Receive the Word of God, 4:1-20

(Mt. 13:1-23; Lu. 8:4-15)

And he began again to
teach by the sea side: and
there was gathered unto him
a great multitude, so that he
entered into a ship, and sat in
the sea; and the whole multitude
was by the sea on the
land.
2 And he taught them many
things by parables, and
said unto them in his doctrine,
3 Hearken; Behold, there
went out a sower to sow:
4 And it came to pass, as he
sowed, some fell by the way
side, and the fowls of the air
came and devoured it up.
5 And some fell on stony
ground, where it had not
much earth; and immediately
it sprang up, because it
had no depth of earth:
6 But when the sun was up,
it was scorched; and because it
had no root, it withered away.
7 And some fell among
thorns, and the thorns grew
up, and choked it, and it
yielded no fruit.
8 And other fell on good
ground, and did yield fruit
that sprang up and increased;
and brought forth,
some thirty, and some sixty,
and some an hundred.
9 And he said unto them,
He that hath ears to hear, let
him hear.
10 And when he was alone,
they that were about him
with the twelve asked of him
the parable.
11 And he said unto them,
Unto you it is given to know
the mystery of the kingdom
of God: but unto them that
are without, all these things
are done in parables:
12 That seeing they may
see, and not perceive; and
hearing they may hear, and
not understand; lest at any
time they should be converted,
and their sins should be
forgiven them.
13 And he said unto them,
Know ye not this parable?
and how then will ye know
all parables?
14 The sower soweth the
word.
15 And these are they by
the way side, where the word
is sown; but when they have
heard, Satan cometh immediately,
and taketh away the
word that was sown in their
hearts.
16 And these are they likewise
which are sown on
stony ground; who, when
they have heard the word,
immediately receive it with
gladness;
17 And have no root in
themselves, and so endure
but for a time: afterward,
when affliction or persecution
ariseth for the word's
sake, immediately they are
offended.
18 And these are they
which are sown among
thorns: such as hear the word,
19 And the cares of this
world, and the deceitfulness
of riches, and the lusts of
other things entering in,
choke the word, and it becometh
unfruitful.
20 And these are they which
are sown on good ground;
such as hear the word, and
receive it, and bring forth
fruit, some thirtyfold, some
sixty, and some an hundred.

  a. The disciples accept the parable
  b. The outsiders reject the parable—deliberately
    1) Lest they hear, see, & understand
    2) Lest they be converted & forgiven

4. The meaning of the parable
  a. The farmer sows the Word of God
  b. Some hear the Word—on the hard path
    1) The Word is heard
    2) Satan comes—takes away the Word
  c. Some hear the Word—on rocky places
    1) The Word is received excitedly
    2) The Word has no root
    3) Trial & testing come
    4) They wither away
  d. Some hear the Word—among thorns
    1) The Word is only added to life
    2) The world, riches, & possessions choke the Word
  e. Some receive the Word—on good soil—& bear fruit[DS2]
  f. Some—only a few—bear 100 percent fruit

DIVISION III

THE SON OF GOD'S CONTINUING MINISTRY: JESUS' PARABLES AND HIS AUTHORITY, 4:1-6:6

A. The Parable of the Sower or Farmer: How Men Receive the Word of God, 4:1-20

(4:1-20) **Introduction—Minister—Heart—Word of God**: there are at least two great lessons in this parable.

First, there is the lesson of sowing the seed, the lesson to the messenger of God. The messenger of God or the genuine believer is to sow the seed, the Word of God, wherever he is—no matter the difficulty, the opposition, or the discouragement. When Jesus stood before people, He knew the kind of people who sat before Him. He knew...

- the hard, closed hearts of the religionists and others.
- the shallow, deceptive enthusiasm of the poor and needy and of others.
- the worldliness of the well-to-do and of others, how entangled they were in *things* and pleasure.

He knew that many would never listen, but He also knew something else: if He just kept sowing the seed, some would bear fruit. Some soil would be fertile, craving for the truth of life and eternity. Therefore, they would "hear...receive...and bring forth fruit" (v.20). This is the reason Jesus continued on. He kept sowing, never giving in to discouragement—sowing that some might be saved and bear fruit. Jesus expects His followers to do the same, to continue on no matter the discouragement or opposition. There are some soils that are fertile, plowed, and ready to receive the seed and to bear fruit.

Second, there is the great lesson on receiving the seed, the lesson to the hearers of the Word of God. The soils, that is, human hearts, vary among men. The variance ranges all the way from hard pavement-like hearts over to soft, plowed hearts. Just what kind of heart a man has depends upon how he has lived and responded and conditioned himself throughout life.

The condition of his heart determines how he will love God and his neighbor, whether he will be responsive or close-minded. The point is that God holds a man responsible for the condition of his heart and for how he responds to the gospel.

In this parable Jesus paints the picture of various soils (hearts) and how they receive the seed, the Word of God. (See notes—Mt.13:1-9; Lu.8:4-15 for more detailed discussion and application.)

1. Jesus began a new method of teaching: the parable (vv.1-2).
2. The parable: a sower or farmer sows (vv.3-9).
3. The response to the parable (vv.10-12).
4. The meaning of the parable (vv.13-20).

1 (4:1-2) **Jesus Christ, Teaching of**: Jesus began a new method of teaching. He began to teach by parables. Note the setting was "by the seashore," and the crowd was great. The word for *great* (pleistos) means *very great*. The multitude was so great that they overflowed the seashore, and they pressed in upon Jesus so much that He was forced into a boat.

The parable was a new form of teaching for Jesus (see outlines and notes—Mt.13:10-17; see DEEPER STUDY # 1—Mk.4:2 for a detailed discussion of the parable).

DEEPER STUDY # 1

(4:2) **Parable** (parabole): literally means placing a thing by the side of something else for the purpose of comparing. The word *comparison* best describes a parable.

1. A parable is a comparison: it is an earthly event pointing out a heavenly truth. It is a comparison between the earth and heaven.
2. A parable is a comparison: the earthly story has to be delved into to discover the heavenly truth. The spiritual point is found only by active thought and effort, by actively *comparing* the physical world with the spiritual world. In fact, the more a man thinks and meditates upon a parable, the more he usually sees of the truth.

Jesus is the *Master User* of the parable. No man ever used the parable so effectively. Why did He use the parable so much? (See notes—Mt.13:10-17; Lu.8:9-10 for the reasons and for more discussion.)

2 (4:3-9) **Word of God, Receiving**: the parable Jesus told was a simple story, yet its meaning was profound. It was not understood by most (see vv.10-13). It concerned an event known by practically everyone who was familiar with sowing seed. Jesus said five things in this parable.

a. The farmer sows some seed that *does not take root*. There are two kinds of soil that bear no root at all. These two soils differ from the other soils in this very fact: there is *never* any root.

1) There is the seed that falls upon the *wayside*, the unplowed, packed down areas right outside the plowed field. The wayside joins the field, may even be a part of the field; but it is in the corners, the hard to reach areas that cannot be reached with the plow.
2) There is the seed that falls upon the *stony ground*, the rock that lies right under the surface of the ground. The rock holds the water and heat longer; therefore, the seed shoots its plant up almost immediately. But there is no root to the plant; consequently, the sun scorches and kills it.

b. The farmer sows some seed that *takes root*, but it does not yield fruit. This is seed that falls among thorns. The thorny soil is part of the field. It has been plowed, but it is deceptive ground. It looks good, but lying right underneath the soil is a mass of thorn roots ready to spring up. The fact that they were not destroyed in the plowing and that they are already in the ground means that they will spring up faster and choke the seed.

c. The farmer sows seed that *bears fruit*. This is seed that falls upon good ground. Note two things about this "good ground." It yields fruit, and when fruit appears, it increases and grows. This is the significant fact to see in the good soil.

d. The farmer sows *only a few seed that bear 100 percent fruit*. All seed in the good ground bears fruit, but each plant varies in its degree of fruitfulness. This, too, is significant. Some fruitful plants bear only 30 percent. They are very weak plants, 70 percent unfruitful. Other plants bear only 60 percent. They too are weak, being 40 percent unfruitful. There are only a few plants that bear 100 percent of their potential fruit.

e. Jesus stresses the importance of the parable. The message of the parable is heard only by the spiritual: "He that hath [spiritual] ears, let him hear" (v.9). Luke tells us that *He cried* (ephonei) out, shouted the words, which stressed the importance even more. The message was so important, so critical. Jesus wanted all to hear and understand; but He knew, brokenly, that all would not hear.

3 (4:10-12) **Word of God, Receiving**: the response to the parable is twofold.

a. The disciple hears the parable. He does not just hear the words, but he hears the message, and he hears with his heart. The disciple is receptive—willing to think and to meditate and to receive the message into his life. The disciple is willing to do exactly what the parable teaches. Thus, God reveals the mysteries of the Kingdom of God to him.

b. The unbeliever hears the parable, but not with spiritual ears. He just hears the words. Note that Jesus called unbelievers "them that are without." An unbeliever is *without*, standing on the outside; he is an *outsider*.
The *outsider* does exactly what Jesus says.

> **"Seeing, they see, yet do not perceive" (v.12).**
> **"Hearing, they hear, yet do not understand" (v.12).**

Why does the *outsider* not perceive or understand? Jesus gives the reason: "lest they be converted and forgiven" (v.12).

1) They are unwilling to receive what is taught into their lives and hearts, unwilling to change their lives, unwilling to be converted. Therefore, they shut their minds, twist the truth, and rationalize their behavior. But note: God cannot give His pearls to the swine (see Mt.7:6).
2) They experience the law of conditioning. The more they harden their minds and hearts to the truth, the harder they become. They become more and more conditioned against the truth. Their openness and sensitivity to spiritual truth dwindles more and more until it is gone. The law of spiritual conditioning says that the more we receive spiritual truth, the more we increase our capacity to understand and grow in spiritual truth. But the opposite is also true. The more we reject spiritual truth, the more we decrease our sensitivity and become hardened to spiritual truth (see notes—Mt.13:10-17).

Thought 1. There are many who are *outside...*

- who are hard-hearted against spiritual things.
- whose hearts are shallow or whose minds are superficial. They are rootless, having no depth—usually in all areas of life.
- who are worldly-minded, interested in spiritual matters only as a little *extra* added to their lives.

4 (4:13-20) **Word of God, Receiving**: the meaning of the parable is given by Jesus Himself. (See outline and notes—Mt.13:1-9 for a discussion of this point.) Note several facts.

The emphasis is upon the kind of ground which receives the seed, that is, the kind of person who receives the Word of God. All four grounds (all four types of persons) heard the Word, but each received it in a different manner. How each received the Word depended upon the kind of *ground* they were. The following chart shows this.

The wayside ground...	...is an unplowed heart...	...that results in a hardened life.
The stony ground...	...is a rootless heart...	...that results in a superficial life.
The thorny ground...	...is a worldly heart...	...that results in a strangled life.
The fruitful ground...	...is an honest and good heart...	...that results in a fruitful life.

a. The seed by the wayside: the wayside ground is an unplowed heart that results in a hardened life. The person by the wayside does hear the Word of God. He is present in church; but he is off to the side, out of the way, not involved. He lets his mind wander, thinking little, and involving himself even less. He respects Christ and the preacher and would not miss a service, but he is on the outer circle, paying little attention to the warnings and promises of the Word.

Note what happens: before the person believes, the devil comes and snatches the Word away. It is taken from the person; the person never applies the Word to his life, never really lives sacrificially for Christ. (See Judas Iscariot and see Herod who enjoyed listening to John the Baptist, Mk.6:20.)

> **"For the heart of this people is waxed gross, and their ears are dull of hearing, and their eyes have they closed; lest they should see with their eyes, and hear with their ears, and understand with their ears, and understand with their heart, and should be converted, and I should heal them" (Ac.28:27).**
>
> **"Who [the hard-hearted] being past feeling have given themselves over unto lasciviousness, to work all uncleanness with greediness" (Ep.4:19).**
>
> **"But exhort one another daily, while it is called To day; lest any of you be hardened through the deceitfulness of sin" (He.3:13).**
>
> **"Happy is the man that feareth always: but he that hardeneth his heart shall fall into mischief" (Pr.28:14).**
>
> **"He, that being often reproved hardeneth his neck, shall suddenly be destroyed, and that without remedy" (Pr.29:1).**
>
> **"But after thy hardness and impenitent heart treasurest up unto thyself wrath against the day of wrath and revelation of the righteous judgment of God" (Ro.2:5).**

b. The seed on the rock: the stony ground is a rootless heart that results in a surface, superficial life. This person hears the Word and becomes excited over it. He receives the Word, professes belief in Christ, and makes a profession of faith before the world. But he fails to count the cost, to consider the commitment, the self-denial, the sacrifice, the study, the learning, the hours and effort required. He does not apply himself to *learn Christ*; therefore, he does not become rooted and grounded in the Word. He is only a surface, superficial believer.

Again, note what happens: when trials and temptations come, he falls away. His profession is scorched and consumed, burned up by the heat of the trial and temptation. (See John Mark who at first failed to endure, Ac.13:13; Demas, Phm.1:24; and the men who discovered that following Christ cost too much, Lu.9:57-62.)

> **"And because iniquity shall abound, the love of many shall wax cold" (Mt.24:12).**

> **"But he that heareth, and doeth not, is like a man that without a foundation built an house upon the earth; against which the stream did beat vehemently, and immediately it fell; and the ruin of that house was great" (Lu.6:49).**
>
> **"And Jesus said unto him, No man, having put his hand to the plough, and looking back, is fit for the kingdom of God" (Lu.9:62).**
>
> **"But now, after that ye have known God, or rather are known of God, how turn ye again to the weak and beggarly elements [the world], whereunto ye desire again to be in bondage?" (Ga.4:9).**
>
> **"Now the just shall live by faith: but if any man draw back, my soul shall have no pleasure in him" (He.10:38).**
>
> **"For if after they have escaped the pollutions of the world through the knowledge of the Lord and Saviour Jesus Christ, they are again entangled therein, and overcome, the latter end is worse with them than the beginning. For it had been better for them not to have known the way of righteousness, than, after they have known it, to turn from the holy commandment delivered unto them. But it is happened unto them according to the true proverb, The dog is turned to his own vomit again; and the sow that was washed to her wallowing in the mire" (2 Pe.2:20-22).**
>
> **"Nevertheless I have somewhat against thee, because thou hath left thy first love. Remember therefore from whence thou art fallen, and repent, and do the first works; or else I will come unto thee quickly, and will remove thy candlestick out of his place, except thou repent" (Re.2:4-5).**

c. The seed among thorns: the thorny ground is a worldly heart that results in a strangled life. This is a person who receives the Word and *honestly tries* (professes) to live for Christ. Christ and His followers and the church and its activities appeal to him. So he joins right in, even professing Christ as he walks about his daily affairs. But there is one problem: the thorns of worldliness. He is unwilling to cut completely loose from the world: "[to] come out from among them and [to] be...separate" (2 Co.6:17-18). He lives a double life, trying to live for Christ and yet still live in the worldliness of the world. He keeps right on growing in the midst of the thorns, giving his mind and attention to the *cares* and *riches* and *pleasures* of this world.

Note what happens: fruit does appear, but it never ripens. It is never able to be plucked. The thorns choke the life out of it. It never lives to be used. (See the Rich Young Ruler, Lu.18:18f; Ananias and Sapphira, Acts 5:1f.)

> **"Therefore I say unto you, Take no thought for your life, what ye shall eat, or what ye shall drink; nor yet for your body, what ye shall put on. Is not the life more than meat, and the body than raiment?" (Mt.6:25).**
>
> **"And the cares of this world, and the deceitfulness of riches, and the lusts of other things entering in, choke the word, and it becometh unfruitful" (Mk.4:19).**
>
> **"And I will say to my soul, Soul, thou hast much goods laid up for many years; take thine ease, eat, drink, and be merry" (Lu.12:19).**
>
> **"But they that will be rich fall into temptation and a snare, and into many foolish and hurtful lusts, which drown men in destruction and perdition" (1 Ti.6:9).**
>
> **"And take heed to yourselves, lest at any time your hearts be overcharged with surfeiting, and drunkenness, and cares of this life, and so that day come upon you unawares" (Lu.21:34).**

d. The seed on good ground: the fruitful ground is an honest and good heart which results in a fruitful life. These are they who have an honest and good heart; therefore, when they hear the Word, they keep it.

> **"I am the vine, ye are the branches: He that abideth in me, and I in him, the same bringeth forth much fruit: for without me ye can do nothing" (Jn.15:5).**
>
> **"For the fruit of the Spirit is in all goodness and righteousness and truth" (Ep.5:9).**
>
> **"Being filled with the fruits of righteousness, which are by Jesus Christ, unto the glory and praise of God" (Ph.1:11).**
>
> **"That ye might walk worthy of the Lord unto all pleasing, being fruitful in every good work, and increasing in the knowledge of God" (Col.1:10).**

DEEPER STUDY # 2

(4:20) **Fruit-Bearing**: note the three steps involved in bearing fruit.

1. Hearing the Word.
2. Receiving the Word.
3. Bringing forth the Word, that is, doing and living the Word.

	B. The Parables Dealing with Truth: Truth & Man's Duty, 4:21-25 *(Mt. 5:15-16; 10:26-27; 13:12; 24:29; Lu. 8:16-18; 11:33)*	kept secret, but that it should come abroad.	
		23 If any man have ears to hear, let him hear.	c. The exhortation: A person had better hear
1. Share the truth a. The fact: Lamps are to be placed on a lampstand	21 And he said unto them, Is a candle brought to be put under a bushel, or under a bed? and not to be set on a candlestick?	24 And he said unto them, Take heed what ye hear: with what measure ye mete, it shall be measured to you: and unto you that hear shall more be given.	**2. Mark the truth** a. Pay attention, make sure you hear the truth b. The reason: Determines your reward
b. The warning: All things will be revealed; nothing is hidden—except temporarily	22 For there is nothing hid, which shall not be manifested; neither was any thing	25 For he that hath, to him shall be given: and he that hath not, from him shall be taken even that which he hath.	1) The reward of more truth 2) The judgment of losing all

DIVISION III

THE SON OF GOD'S CONTINUING MINISTRY: JESUS' PARABLES AND HIS AUTHORITY, 4:1-6:6

B. The Parables Dealing with Truth: Truth and Man's Duty, 4:21-25

(4:21-25) **Introduction**: this passage is difficult to grasp. The light reader and surface thinker will not understand what Jesus is saying. This very fact is the point Jesus was making. Grasping and knowing the truth takes time and effort and energy, and man has a twofold responsibility toward the truth. (See outline and notes—Lu.8:16-18 for more discussion.)

1. Share the truth (vv.21-23).
2. Mark the truth (vv.24-25).

1 (4:21-23) **Light—Witness—Believers**: Jesus said, Share the truth. Light is to be set in the most conspicuous place, where it can best be seen.

a. Jesus shared a very simple fact. A candle is to be placed on a candlestick. The candle or lamp is a symbol, a type of the truth. It stands for the light of the truth.

Light and truth are to be the character, the very nature and behavior of the believer. The believer is to live the truth. He is to set the candle, the truth in the most conspicuous place in his life. (See outline and notes—Mt.5:15-16 for more discussion.)

Light and truth are also to be the witness of the believer. The believer is to bear verbal witness to the truth. He is to share the candle and its light with others. He is to place the truth in the most conspicuous place.

1) A candle is not placed under a bushel basket. The basket would extinguish its light and it would no longer be able to fulfill its purpose. It could not give off its light. Its flame and light would no longer exist. However, note something: the candle would still be a candle; but it would be a candle with no purpose—hidden, as it were, under a bushel basket.
2) A candle is not put under a bed. It would carelessly set the bed on fire and destroy it. The candle would be serving the wrong purpose; it would tragically be using its flame and light for the wrong reason. It would still be a candle, but it would be a candle using its flame and light in the wrong way.

Thought 1. God gives the light of the truth to believers for a specific purpose: that it might be shared. God wants others to see and know the light, the truth and purpose of life. The believer must make sure that he does not hide or misuse the light of the truth.

"Ye are the light of the world. A city that is set on an hill cannot be hid" (Mt.5:14).

"For so hath the Lord commanded us, saying, I have set thee to be a light of the Gentiles, that thou shouldest be for salvation unto the ends of the earth" (Ac.13:47).

"For ye were sometimes darkness, but now are ye light in the Lord: walk as children of light" (Ep.5:8).

"That ye may be blameless and harmless, the sons of God, without rebuke, in the midst of a crooked and perverse nation, among whom ye shine as lights in the world" (Ph.2:15).

"Ye are all the children of light, and the children of the day: we are not of the night, nor of darkness" (1 Th.5:5).

"But ye are a chosen generation, a royal priesthood, an holy nation, a peculiar people; that ye should show forth the praises of him who hath called you out of darkness into his marvellous light" (1 Pe.2:9).

b. Jesus warned: all things shall be revealed; nothing is hid—except temporarily. Even if a believer hides the candle and keeps it secret, the day is coming when it will be revealed anyway. The Greek says, "There is nothing hid [ean me], unless, except it should be made manifest, nor has a secret thing taken place, but that it should come to light." This can mean two things. (See outline and notes—Mt.10:26-27 for more discussion).

1) Light and truth cannot be hid or extinguished or used for the wrong purpose forever. Both light and truth will break forth some day. The bushel will be lifted and the bed consumed, and the light and truth will be seen and will fulfill their original purpose.

2) If a man hides or misuses the light and truth given him, then what he has done will be revealed someday. He cannot hide and misuse the light and truth forever. A day of judgment is coming.

Thought 1. Every man is given some light, some truth (see Ro.1:20-23; 1 Co.2:12; Jn.8:32; Ro.12:3-8; Ep.4:7; 1 Co.12:7f). Each man is responsible to use what light and truth he has. He is not to hide or misuse it. He is held accountable for what he has, for what God has given him (2 Co.5:10).

"Be not thou therefore ashamed of the testimony of our Lord, nor of me his prisoner: but be thou partaker of the afflictions of the gospel according to the power of God" (2 Ti.1:8).

"But sanctify the Lord God in your hearts: and be ready always to give an answer to every man that asketh you a reason of the hope that is in you with meekness and fear" (1 Pe.3:15).

"Whosoever denieth the Son, the same hath not the Father: [but] he that acknowledgeth the Son hath the Father also" (1 Jn.2:23).

"For we must all appear before the judgment seat of Christ; that every one may receive the things done in his body, according to that he hath done, whether it be good or bad" (2 Co.5:10).

"I have set watchmen upon thy walls, O Jerusalem, which shall never hold their peace day nor night: ye that make mention of the LORD, keep not silence" (Is.62:6).

"The LORD hath brought forth our righteousness: come, and let us declare in Zion the work of the LORD our God" (Je.51:10).

2 (4:24-25) **Truth**: Jesus said mark the truth. Take heed, make sure you hear the truth. Jesus is still talking about the responsibility of the hearer: the hearer is responsible for *hearing* the truth. He is also responsible for *what* he hears and how he interprets what is being said. A man is responsible for making sure that he *has* the truth, that he possesses and knows the truth. He is responsible for *what* he hears, possesses, and knows.

Thought 1. If a man is filled with *junk*, he is responsible for the *junk*. If he is filled with the knowledge of real truth, then he is also responsible for the truth. A man is accountable for what fills his heart and mind. A man is to "take heed," keep guard, watch, make sure he hears the truth.

Jesus states why a person must take heed and make sure he hears the truth. There is a principle of truth that takes effect in every person's life, and it is pointedly clear: the measure to which a person gives himself to know the truth determines his reward. The energy, effort, and degree of commitment, the time and depth of thought—all that a person gives to know the truth—determines his reward. (See outline and notes—Mt.13:12 for more discussion.)

a. The person who gives himself to know the truth shall be given *more* truth (v.24). He shall have the truth, and he shall be given more truth (v.25).

b. The person who does not give himself to know the truth shall lose all. Everything will be taken away from him (v.25).

Thought 1. The commitment, the energy, the effort, the work, the knowledge, the degree to which a man gives himself to the truth (to God)—all determine how much God is able to entrust and give to the man. Common sense tells us this.

"Ask, and it shall be given you; seek, and ye shall find; knock, and it shall be opened unto you: for every one that asketh receiveth; and he that seeketh findeth; and to him that knocketh it shall be opened" (Mt.7:7-8).

"Study to show thyself approved unto God, a workman that needeth not to be ashamed, rightly dividing the word of truth" (2 Ti.2:15).

"As newborn babes, desire the sincere milk of the word, that ye may grow thereby: if so be ye have tasted that the Lord is gracious" (1 Pe.2:2-3).

"These were more noble than those in Thessalonica, in that they received the word with all readiness of mind, and searched the scriptures daily, whether those things were so....That they should seek the Lord, if haply they might feel after him, and find him, though he be not far from every one of us" (Ac.17:11, 27).

"Buy the truth, and sell it not; also wisdom, and instruction, and understanding" (Pr.23:23).

"Sow to yourselves in righteousness, reap in mercy; break up your fallow ground: for it is time to seek the LORD, till he come and rain righteousness upon you" (Ho.10:12).

Thought 2. God expects a man to seek after the truth. He abhors laziness, selfishness, indulgence, uselessness, worldliness, and ignorance. He holds a man responsible for hearing the truth. He expects a man...

- to look around and observe and subdue the world (Ge.1:28).
- to get up and go hear a man who knows and teaches the truth (2 Ti.1:13).
- to sit down and study the truth (the Word, Jn.17:17).
- to learn and know Christ, Who is the truth (Jn.14:6; see Ep.4:20).

Thought 3. A man is to be judged for what he has heard. He is to "take heed," to govern what he hears. He is to give himself to hear the truth.

"Casting down imaginations, and every high thing that exalteth itself against the knowledge of God, and bringing into captivity every thought to the obedience of Christ" (2 Co.10:5).

"Finally, brethren, whatsoever things are true, whatsoever things are honest, whatsoever things are just, whatsoever things are pure, whatsoever things are lovely, whatsoever things are of good report; if there be any virtue, and if there be any praise, think on these things" (Ph.4:8).

	C. The Parable of the Growing Seed: The Growth of Believers, 4:26-29	seed should spring and grow up, he knoweth not how.	
		28 For the earth bringeth forth fruit of herself; first the blade, then the ear, after	**4. The growth is sure & constant, but gradual**
1. The parable: Describes the kingdom	26 And he said, So is the kingdom of God, as if a man	that the full corn in the ear.	
2. The seed is sown by a man	should cast seed into the ground;	29 But when the fruit is brought forth, immediately	**5. The growth is consummated & harvested**
3. The growth is not of man	27 And should sleep, and rise night and day, and the	he putteth in the sickle, because the harvest is come.	

DIVISION III

THE SON OF GOD'S CONTINUING MINISTRY: JESUS' PARABLES AND HIS AUTHORITY, 4:1-6:6

C. The Parable of the Growing Seed: The Growth of Believers, 4:26-29

(4:26-29) **Introduction—Believer, Growth**: this parable tells what happens to the fruitful seed in the Parable of the Sower or Soils (Mk.4:1-20). It describes how the seed goes about growing, and the process through which it passes. The seed is the gospel and the ground is the *good ground*, either the believer individually or the church collectively. There are four things said about the fruitful seed once it has taken root, but the major point is that growth is sure; it is inevitable. Once the gospel has taken root in the heart of a believer, growth will take place. The believer will grow spiritually. This is the great promise of God, the great assurance and confidence, the great hope and encouragement to every believer.

1. The parable: describes the kingdom (v.26).
2. The seed is sown by a man (v.26).
3. The growth is not of man (v.27).
4. The growth is sure and constant, but gradual (v.28).
5. The growth is consummated and harvested (v.29).

1 (4:26) **Kingdom of God**: Jesus is describing one aspect of the Kingdom of God in this parable. The kingdom (church) and its citizens will and do grow. The kingdom is looked at in its *present state* here on earth. The Kingdom of God is growing: more and more people are being reached for God, and as they are reached, they are growing just as God wills them to grow (see DEEPER STUDY # 3, *Kingdom of God*—Mt.19:23-24 for discussion).

2 (4:26) **Gospel—Seed**: the seed is sown by a man. Note several things.

a. It is man who sows the seed. The seed has to be sown by a man; there simply is no other way it can be sown. Man is the person, the being, the means, the instrument God has chosen to share the gospel with the world.

b. It is the ground, the earth, where the seed is sown. It is the earth that God wants to reach; the earth that God wants to hear His good news. God has sent His followers out into the earth to cast forth the seed of the gospel.

> **"Go ye therefore, and teach all nations, baptizing them in the name of the Father, and of the Son, and of the Holy Ghost: teaching them to observe all things whatsoever I have commanded you: and, lo, I am with you alway, even unto the end of the world. Amen" (Mt.28:19-20).**
>
> **"And as ye go, preach, saying, The kingdom of heaven is at hand....What I tell you in darkness, that speak ye in light: and what ye hear in the ear, that preach ye upon the housetops" (Mt.10:7, 27).**
>
> **"And he said unto them, Go ye into all the world, and preach the gospel to every creature" (Mk.16:15).**
>
> **"But ye shall receive power, after that the Holy Ghost is come upon you: and ye shall be witnesses unto me both in Jerusalem, and in all Judaea, and in Samaria, and unto the uttermost part of the earth" (Ac.1:8).**
>
> **"Go, stand and speak in the temple to the people all the words of this life" (Ac.5:20).**
>
> **"And the things that thou hast heard of me among many witnesses, the same commit thou to faithful men, who shall be able to teach others also" (2 Ti.2:2).**

3 (4:27) **Gospel—Spiritual Growth—Believers**: the growth is not of man. The sower or farmer plants his seed, then he goes about his regular affairs. He sleeps and rises day by day. And while he carries on the routine of his life, the seed germinates, springs up, and grows. The point is this: the seed grows by its own virtue. The seed uses the sun, water, air, and earth to grow; but the power to germinate, to break forth and grow is of the seed itself, by its own virtue. It is not man who makes the seed grow. Man does not even know how the mysterious growth takes place. The secret of life and of growth is beyond him. He discovers, he rearranges, he develops; but he does not create, not in the real sense of *creation* (ex nihilo, out of nothing).

It is the same with the Kingdom of God, with the growth of believers both individually and collectively. Growth is not of man; growth is of God. It is the Spirit of God that takes the gospel and changes a man's heart and causes him to grow. It is the Spirit of God that recreates a man spiritually, that causes a man to be *born again* and to grow in grace (see Jn.3:3-8; Ep.2:8-9).

> **"Great is the mystery of godliness: God was manifest in the flesh...preached...believed on in the world" (1 Ti.3:16).**
> **"But as many as received him, to them gave he power to become the sons of God, even to them that believe on his name: which were born, not of blood, nor of the will of the flesh, nor of the will of man, but of God" (Jn.1:12-13).**
> **"Jesus answered and said unto him, Verily, verily, I say unto thee, Except a man be born again, he cannot see the kingdom of God" (Jn.3:3).**
> **"Jesus answered, Verily, verily, I say unto thee, Except a man be born of water and of the Spirit, he cannot enter into the kingdom of God" (Jn.3:5).**
> **"For by grace are ye saved through faith; and that not of yourselves: it is the gift of God: not of works, lest any man should boast" (Ep.2:8-9).**
> **"Not by works of righteousness which we have done, but according to his mercy he saved us, by the washing of regeneration, and renewing of the Holy Ghost" (Tit.3:5).**
> **"Being born again, not of corruptible seed, but of incorruptible, by the word of God, which liveth and abideth for ever" (1 Pe.1:23).**

Thought 1. The ground or seed can hinder and slow the process of growth. Some ground or seed bears only 30 percent fruit, some only 60 percent fruit. Very few seed bear 100 percent fruit (see outlines and notes—Mt.13:8, 23; Mk.4:13-20 for discussion).

4 (4:28) **Spiritual Growth**: the growth is sure and constant, but gradual. The words about the earth's bearing fruit *of herself* (automate) mean automatically, spontaneously, of necessity, self-moving. The idea is that the earth brings forth fruit automatically, by its very nature.

Note two facts.

a. Growth is sure, inevitable. But two conditions are essential. The ground must be "good ground," (Mk.4:20) and the seed must be sown in the ground. If these two conditions exist, then growth is both *inevitable* and unstoppable. Even a small blade of grass will find a crack in the pavement. Nothing can stop the seed from growing. (See outline and notes—Ro.8:28-39 for more discussion.)

Thought 1. The genuine believer (good ground) can rest assured: he is truly God's child, and God will complete the work of grace in his life. The grace of God planted in a person's heart is unstoppable. The believer's confidence is in God, not in his own flesh and weak efforts. Therefore, there is no reason for being down and discouraged, withdrawn and depressed.

> **"Being confident of this very thing, that he which hath begun a good work in you will perform it until the day of Jesus Christ" (Ph.1:6).**
> **"For it is God which worketh in you both to will and to do of his good pleasure" (Ph.2:13).**
> **"I am the vine, ye are the branches: He that abideth in me, and I in him, the same bringeth forth much fruit: for without me ye can do nothing" (Jn.15:5).**
> **"I know whom I have believed, and am persuaded that he is able to keep that which I have committed unto him against that day" (2 Ti.1:12).**
> **"For which cause we faint not; but though our outward man perish, yet the inward man is renewed day by day" (2 Co.4:16).**
> **"And we know that all things work together for good to them that love God, to them who are the called according to his purpose" (Ro.8:28).**

b. Growth is constant, but it is gradual, ever so gradual. The seed is sown, and then day after day and night after night passes before the blade ever springs up. Then many more days and nights pass before the ear forms. It takes weeks before the full ear of corn appears. Growth does take place; it is constant—but growth is gradual. It does take time; it does not happen overnight.

Thought 1. Growth is of God, and the believer is to trust and to wait upon God for growth. But the trust and waiting are to be active—a working trust and waiting. There is no such thing as inactive faith and waiting—not to God. Faith and waiting upon God are active; they both serve and work (see Js.2:14-18).

Thought 2. There is great abuse of this glorious truth, the truth of sure growth, of being secure in God's promises. Man has used the fact...

- to say I am secure, no matter what I do, so I can go ahead and live as I wish (see Ro.6:16, 23).
- to say God assures His kingdom and its growth, so there is no need for me to sacrifice to meet the needs of the world. (See outlines and notes—Mt.19:16-22; 19:23-26; 19:27-30.)
- to say believers and the church will grow without me, therefore I do not have to go or serve, not personally.

Thought 3. Growth requires much patience and trust.

"Now he that ministereth seed to the sower both minister bread for your food, and multiply your seed sown, and increase the fruits of your righteousness" (2 Co.9:10).

"But speaking the truth in love, may grow up into him in all things, which is the head, even Christ" (Ep.4:15).

"And sent Timotheus, our brother, and minister of God, and our fellowlabourer in the gospel of Christ, to establish you, and to comfort you concerning your faith" (1 Th.3:2).

"We are bound to thank God always for you, brethren, as it is meet, because that your faith groweth exceedingly, and the charity of every one of you all toward each other aboundeth" (2 Th.1:3).

"Meditate upon these things; give thyself wholly to them; that thy profiting may appear to all" (1 Ti.4:15).

"Therefore leaving the principles of the doctrine of Christ, let us go on unto perfection; not laying again the foundation of repentance from dead works, and of faith toward God" (He.6:1).

"As newborn babes, desire the sincere milk of the word, that ye may grow thereby: if so be ye have tasted that the Lord is gracious" (1 Pe.2:2-3).

"But grow in grace, and in the knowledge of our Lord and Saviour Jesus Christ. To him be glory both now and for ever. Amen" (2 Pe.3:18).

5 (4:29) **Spiritual Growth**: the growth is consummated and harvested. The fruit does ripen; the day does come when the corn is *fully grown* and is ready to be harvested. This can mean at least two things.

a. The believer's sowing does bear fruit. Jesus does honor His Word, and it never returns to Him void. The believer can rest assured of reaping some harvest.

Thought 1. What an encouragement to believers! How we should be challenged to work and work for our Lord! We are assured of results before we ever labor. God assures that fruit will be borne.

"For he that soweth to his flesh shall of the flesh reap corruption; but he that soweth to the Spirit shall of the Spirit reap life everlasting. And let us not be weary in well doing: for in due season we shall reap, if we faint not" (Ga.6:8-9).

"Say not ye, There are yet four months, and then cometh harvest? behold, I say unto you, Lift up your eyes, and look on the fields; for they are white already to harvest. And he that reapeth receiveth wages, and gathereth fruit unto life eternal: that both he that soweth and he that reapeth may rejoice together" (Jn.4:35-36).

"So shall my word be that goeth forth out of my mouth: it shall not return unto me void, but it shall accomplish that which I please, and it shall prosper in the thing whereto I sent it" (Is.55:11).

"Sow to yourselves in righteousness, reap in mercy; break up your fallow ground: for it is time to seek the LORD, till he come and rain righteousness upon you" (Ho.10:12).

b. The believer himself is harvested, taken on to heaven when his growth is completed. When the believer has done all that God wills for him or all that he is going to do, God then escorts the believer home forever. (See DEEPER STUDY # 1—2 Co.5:10; DEEPER STUDY # 1—1 Jn.5:16.)

"And he shall set the sheep on his right hand, but the goats on the left" (Mt.25:33; see Mt.25:34; Mk.9:41).

"And I heard a voice from heaven saying unto me, Write, Blessed are the dead which die in the Lord from henceforth: yea, saith the Spirit, that they may rest from their labours; and their works do follow them" (Re.14:13).

"The wicked worketh a deceitful work: but to him that soweth righteousness shall be a sure reward" (Pr.11:18).

1. **The parable describes the kingdom** 2. **The seed is sown**DS2	**D. The Parable of the Mustard Seed: The Growth of God's Kingdom,**DS1 **4:30-32** *(Mt. 13:31-32; Lu. 13:18-19)* 30 And he said, Whereunto shall we liken the kingdom of God? or with what comparison shall we compare it? 31 It is like a grain of mus-	tard seed, which, when it is sown in the earth, is less than all the seeds that be in the earth: 32 But when it is sown, it groweth up, and becometh greater than all herbs, and shooteth out great branches; so that the fowls of the air may lodge under the shadow of it.	a. It is sown in the ground b. It is the smallest of all seeds 3. **The seed does grow** a. The reason: It is sown b. The result: It is larger than all the plants 4. **The birds do nest under its shade**

DIVISION III

THE SON OF GOD'S CONTINUING MINISTRY: JESUS' PARABLES AND HIS AUTHORITY, 4:1-6:6

D. The Parable of the Mustard Seed: The Growth of God's Kingdom, 4:30-32

(4:30-32) **Introduction—Christianity—Church**: Jesus is describing the growth and greatness of His kingdom, that is, of Christianity. He shows how Christianity begins as the smallest of seeds and grows into the greatest of movements.

The message of the parable is a powerful message to individual believers and congregations as well as to the world-wide church. The seed of faith begins ever so small, but it grows into the greatest of bushes as it nourishes itself day by day. Mature (grown, v.32) believers and congregations alike provide lodging for the people of a turbulent world.

1. The parable describes the kingdom (v.30).
2. The seed is sown (v.31).
3. The seed does grow (v.32).
4. The birds do nest under its shade (v.32).

DEEPER STUDY # 1

(4:30-32) **Christianity—Church**: there are two interpretations of this parable.

1. Some say the birds are those in the world who find their lodging in the kingdom (the church, Christianity). The kingdom had a small beginning, but it is now growing into a stately movement. Many in the world, believers and non-believers alike, have found help and safety under its branches. Laws and institutions of mercy, justice, and honor have to a large extent evolved from this magnificent movement. This interpretation relies heavily upon the picture painted by the Old Testament. A great empire is said to be like a tree, and conquered nations are said to be like birds who lodge under its shadow (Eze.17:22-24; 31:1-6; Da.4:14).
2. Others say the birds are the children of the evil one (Satan) who see the protective covering of the kingdom and seek lodging therein.

Neither interpretation need exhaust the meaning. However, two facts should be noted.

1. Jesus was speaking to the multitudes in the first four parables. His purpose was to teach what the Kingdom of Heaven is like. It is a mixture of good and evil. He had just been vindicating His Messiahship to the Pharisees, who were set upon destroying Him ((Mt.12:1-50; 12:14). It was the same day that He began to speak in parables. His purpose was to hide the mysteries from unbelievers and to protect Himself from those who would destroy Him (Mt.12:10-17). They were the evil ones who had penetrated the kingdom. However, this needed to be known only by the true disciple, not necessarily by those who were evil.
2. The birds are used to describe the evil one in the Parable of the Seed.

1 (4:30) **Kingdom of Heaven**: Jesus described the Kingdom of Heaven, that is, the kingdom's *present state* on earth. He revealed how the kingdom, Christianity, was to begin as the smallest movement and grow into the greatest movement.

2 (4:31) **Gospel—Witnessing—Evangelism—Commitment**: the seed is sown. The words "in the earth" are significant. The earth or the world is where the seed is sown. It is the earth, the world, that needs the seed, that is, the gospel of God. And God has ordained the good news of His love to be sown upon the earth. (See DEEPER STUDY # 2—1 Co.15:1-11. See Jn.3:16; 1 Jn.2:1-2.) (See note 2, *Christianity*—Mt.13:31.)

> **"For God so loved the world, that he gave his only begotten Son, that whosoever believeth in him should not perish, but have everlasting life" (Jn.3:16).**
>
> **"That which was from the beginning, which we have heard, which we have seen with our eyes, which we have looked upon, and our hands have handled, of the Word of life; (for the life was manifested, and we have seen it, and bear witness, and show unto you that eternal life which was with the father, and was manifested unto us)" (1 Jn.1:1-2).**
>
> **"For there is no difference between the Jew and the Greek: for the same Lord over all is rich unto all that call upon him" (Ro.10:12).**
>
> **"Who will have all men to be saved, and to come unto the knowledge of the truth" (1 Ti.2:4).**

Thought 1. The farmer has to have a commitment of heart, mind, and body to sow the seed. All three are essential. Without any one of the commitments, the sowing does not get done or else it is done haphazardly. He must have...

- commitment of heart for motivation.
- commitment of mind for planning.
- commitment of body for planting.

"And thou shalt love the Lord thy God with all thy heart, and with all thy soul, and with all thy mind, and with thy strength: this is the first commandment" (Mk.12:30).

"Jesus saith unto them, My meat is to do the will of him that sent me, and to finish his work. Say not ye, There are yet four months, and then cometh harvest? behold, I say unto you, Lift up your eyes, and look on the fields; for they are white already to harvest" (Jn.4:34-35).

"I must work the works of him that sent me, while it is day: the night cometh, when no man can work" (Jn.9:4).

"I beseech you therefore, brethren, by the mercies of God, that ye present your bodies a living sacrifice, holy, acceptable unto God, which is your reasonable service. And be not conformed to this world: but be ye transformed by the renewing of your mind, that ye may prove what is that good, and acceptable, and perfect, will of God" (Ro.12:1-2).

"The night is far spent, the day is at hand: let us therefore cast off the works of darkness, and let us put on the armour of light" (Ro.13:12).

"Preach the word; be instant in season, out of season; reprove, rebuke, exhort with all long-suffering and doctrine" (2 Ti.4:2).

Thought 2. The earth is fruitless, sterile, empty, barren without the mustard seed of God. The earth becomes a wasteland; it ends without the mustard seed of God.

"Who hath divided a watercourse for the overflowing of waters, or a way for the lightning of thunder; to cause it to rain on the earth, where no man is; on the wilderness, wherein there is no man; to satisfy the desolate and waste ground; and to cause the bud of the tender herb to spring forth?" (Jb.38:25-27).

"For the nation and kingdom that will not serve thee shall perish; yea, those nations shall be utterly wasted" (Is.60:12; see Joel 1:10-13).

The fact that the mustard seed is the smallest of seeds is also significant (see DEEPER STUDY # 2, *Mustard Seed*—Mk.4:31). Just because a seed is small does not discourage or keep the farmer from sowing. He knows the enormous potential of the seed for growth and fruitfulness, so he plants. Note that the power for reproduction and bearing fruit is in the seed, not in the farmer. All the farmer has to do is sow the seed. But again, someone has to sow the seed if there is to be fruit.

Thought 1. What a lesson for believers and churches! The seed of the gospel, though ever so small, is enormously powerful.

⇒ No matter how insignificant or small we may feel in reaching others, we need to sow the gospel.

⇒ No matter how insignificant or small we may feel our church witness is, we need to sow the gospel. (See note 2—Mk.4:26 for discussion and verses of application.)

"They that sow in tears shall reap in joy. He that goeth forth and weepeth, bearing precious seed, shall doubtless come again with rejoicing, bringing his sheaves with him" (Ps.126:5-6).

"Sow to yourselves in righteousness, reap in mercy; break up your fallow ground: for it is time to seek the LORD, till he come and rain righteousness upon you" (Ho.10:12).

"For he that soweth to his flesh shall of the flesh reap corruption; but he that soweth to the Spirit shall of the Spirit reap life everlasting" (Ga.6:8).

"And he said unto them, Go ye into all the world, and preach the gospel to every creature" (Mk.16:15).

"Then said Jesus to them again, Peace be unto you: as my Father hath sent me, even so send I you" (Jn.20:21).

DEEPER STUDY # 2

(4:31) **Mustard Seed**: its seed was not actually the smallest seed known in Jesus' day. But the seed was small, and the mustard bush grew as large as some trees. It has been reported that a rider on horseback could find shade under its branches. The fact that such a small seed could produce such a huge bush caused people to use the mustard seed as a proverbial saying to describe smallness.

3 (4:32) **Christianity—The Church**: the seed does grow. Note the words "when it is sown." Again, the critical point is this: the seed has to be sown. Someone has to sow the seed if the church (Christianity) is to continue to grow. *Growth follows sowing. If there is no sowing, there is no growth. This is the law of reproduction, of fruitbearing*. The seed grows "when it is sown."

The result of sowing is growth. In dealing with Christianity and the church, the result of sowing is to see the greatest of movements (see note, *Christianity*, pt.2—Mt.13:32. Also see note—Mk.4:28 for more discussion.)

Thought 1. The growth of a tree from a small seed is nothing compared to the growth of a person who truly comes to know Christ nor to the growth of a church that is truly committed to the mission of Christ (Jn.12:24).

> **"And when the Gentiles heard this, they were glad, and glorified the word of the Lord: and as many as were ordained to eternal life believed" (Ac.13:48).**
>
> **"Be it known therefore unto you, that the salvation of God is sent unto the Gentiles, and that they will hear it" (Ac.28:28).**
>
> **"And that the Gentiles might glorify God for his mercy; as it is written, For this cause I will confess to thee among the Gentiles, and sing unto thy name" (Ro.15:9).**
>
> **"That the blessing of Abraham might come on the Gentiles through Jesus Christ; that we might receive the promise of the Spirit through faith" (Ga.3:14).**
>
> **"That the Gentiles should be fellowheirs [with Jewish believers], and of the same body, and partakers of his promise in Christ by the gospel" (Ep.3:6).**
>
> **"There shall be a handful of corn in the earth upon the top of the mountains; the fruit thereof shall shake like Lebanon: and they of the city shall flourish like grass of the earth" (Ps.72:16).**
>
> **"Of the increase of his government and peace there shall be no end, upon the throne of David, and upon his kingdom, to order it, and to establish it with judgment and with justice from henceforth even for ever. The zeal of the LORD of hosts will perform this" (Is.9:7).**
>
> **"For thou shalt break forth on the right hand and on the left; and thy seed shall inherit the Gentiles, and make the desolate cities to be inhabited" (Is.54:3).**
>
> **"Behold, thou shalt call a nation that thou knowest not, and nations that knew not thee shall run unto thee because of the LORD thy God, and for the Holy One of Israel; for he hath glorified thee" (Is.55:5).**
>
> **"Then thou shalt see, and flow together, and thine heart shall fear, and be enlarged; because the abundance of the sea shall be converted unto thee, the forces of the Gentiles shall come unto thee" (Is.60:5).**
>
> **"A little one shall become a thousand, and a small one a strong nation: I the LORD will hasten it in his time" (Is.60:22).**

4 (4:32) **Christianity—Church**: the birds do nest under its shadow. Many commentators make this point: birds feast on the seeds of the mustard bush. The very fact that the bush (the church) is present with *so much good* to be feasted upon means that many will come to its shadow (see note, *Christianity*, pts.2, 3—Mt.13:32 for discussion).

	F. The Authority of Jesus over Nature: Rest & Peace, 4:35-41 *(Mt. 8:23-27; Lu. 8:22-25)*	38 And he was in the hinder part of the ship, asleep on a pillow: and they awake him, and say unto him, Master, carest thou not that we perish?	a. The boat filled with water b. The rest & peace of Jesus: He slept **3. Rest & peace are a concern to Jesus**
1. Rest & peace are sought after a tiring day a. At evening, Jesus was fatigued, tired b. He was so fatigued, He went as He was—without any preparation c. Other ships went also	35 And the same day, when the even was come, he saith unto them, Let us pass over unto the other side. 36 And when they had sent away the multitude, they took him even as he was in the ship. And there were also with him other little ships.	39 And he arose, and rebuked the wind, and said unto the sea, Peace, be still. And the wind ceased, and there was a great calm. 40 And he said unto them, Why are ye so fearful? how is it that ye have no faith?	a. The fear of the disciples, lest they drown b. The power of Jesus to control the situation **4. Rest & peace come through two sources** a. Through faith
2. Rest & peace can be experienced despite a great storm	37 And there arose a great storm of wind, and the waves beat into the ship, so that it was now full.	41 And they feared exceedingly, and said one to another, What manner of man is this, that even the wind and the sea obey him?	b. Through Jesus, His power & His Word, 39

DIVISION III

THE SON OF GOD'S CONTINUING MINISTRY: JESUS' PARABLES AND HIS AUTHORITY, 4:1-6:6

F. The Authority of Jesus Over Nature: Rest and Peace, 4:35-41

(4:35-41) **Introduction—Messiahship—Trials**: what was the purpose of this experience? Why was a storm allowed to arise on the sea with Jesus in the boat? The answer is given in v.41. And what a marvelous purpose it was: to stir His people to ask, "What manner of man is this?" Jesus proved again that He is the Messiah! Calming the storm would do three things.

1. It would demonstrate who He is: the Sovereign Lord who has all power—even power over nature.
2. It would strengthen the belief of His followers, belief in Him as the Messiah and in His personal care as their Savior.
3. It would give to all generations a picture of His care and power to deliver through all the storms of life (trials and fearful experiences).

It does not matter what the storm or trial is nor how terrifying it may be—Jesus is able to deliver and bring about the most assuring calm. Few trials could be as terrifying as being caught in a life-threatening storm at sea. In this experience, God has demonstrated His wonderful care and power to deliver the believer through all the storms of life.

1. Rest and peace are sought after a tiring day (vv.35-36).
2. Rest and peace can be experienced despite a great storm (vv.37-38).
3. Rest and peace are a concern to Jesus (vv.38-39).
4. Rest and peace come through two sources (vv.40-41).

1 (4:35-36) **Rest—Peace**: rest and peace are sought after a tiring day. Note it was evening of the same day when Jesus sought rest and peace. He had been teaching all day to a multitude of people. The crowd had been so massive and pressing that they had forced Him off the shore into a boat (see Mk.4:1). As anyone knows, just being in such a massive throng of people struggling for space is tiring. It strains and taxes the strongest nerves. Imagine the fatigue of Jesus, having been responsible for the crowd, controlling and teaching them all day long. The fatigue and exhaustion of His body were seen in the fact that He left immediately for the other shore. He made no preparations whatsoever. Note the words, "they took Him even as He was" (v.36). Provisions, a change of clothing, notifying His family that He would be gone a while—nothing mattered but rest and peace. He was so fatigued He even slept through the storm (v.38). He just had to get away.

An interesting note that is not commented on by the other gospel writers is the simple statement: "There were also with Him other little ships" (v.36). Mark mentions this to stress His deity, His being the Son of God. There would be other witnesses to His great power and control over nature.

> **Thought 1.** Jesus sets a dynamic example in laboring to the point of fatigue and exhaustion. How many of us labor to the point that we just collapse, being unable to shower or change clothes, being so tired that we even sleep through violent storms?
>
> **"Therefore, my beloved brethren, be ye stedfast, unmoveable, always abounding in the work of the Lord, forasmuch as ye know that your labour is not in vain in the Lord" (1 Co.15:58).**
>
> **"I must work the works of him that sent me, while it is day: the night cometh, when no man can work" (Jn.9:4).**
>
> **"The night is far spent, the day is at hand: let us therefore cast off the works of darkness, and let us put on the armour of light" (Ro.13:12).**
>
> **"Preach the word; be instant in season, out of season; reprove, rebuke, exhort with all longsuffering and doctrine" (2 Ti.4:2).**

Thought 2. There are times when rest and peace are desperately needed and nothing should be allowed to interfere.

Thought 3. Note those who followed in the "little ships [boats]." Others had gone away, but these wanted more of His presence and teaching. They followed Him out of town, booking passage across the lake. Just think what they would have missed if they had turned away and not followed Him. A storm, yes! But they would have also missed experiencing His salvation and power over the storm. They would also have missed the enormous opportunity for growth in learning to trust God more and more.

"Behold, now is the accepted time; behold, now is the day of salvation" (2 Co.6:2).
"For this shall every one that is godly pray unto thee in a time when thou mayest be found: surely in the floods of great waters they shall not come nigh unto him" (Ps.32:6).

2 (4:37-38) **Rest—Peace**: rest and peace can be experienced despite a great storm. Note the words "a great storm." The idea is a severe storm with...
- rolling black clouds thundering and tumbling in upon one another.
- gusts of wind slamming into everything standing in the path of the wind's force.
- heavy drops of rain falling like pellets upon the earth.

The idea in the Greek is something like the fury of a hurricane. Such violent storms were regular occurrences on the Sea of Galilee (see DEEPER STUDY # 1—Mk.1:16).

"The ship was covered with the waves" (Mt.8:24).
"They were filled with water, and were in jeopardy" (Lu.8:23).

But note something: while all the turmoil was going on, Jesus was in the back of the ship sleeping. He was, so to speak, at rest—at peace with Himself and with others and with nature itself. He was completely without guilt or shame, completely at peace with God. He rested perfectly in the care of God. Therefore He was able to rest through the storm. (See note—Mt.8:24 for more detailed discussion.)

Thought 1. The storms or trials of life often come suddenly and violently. And too often Christ seems to be far away, asleep. What we need during the storms of life are the same rest and peace, trust and confidence in God, that Jesus had.

"For whatsoever is born of God overcometh the world: and this is the victory that overcometh the world, even our faith. Who is he that overcometh the world, but he that believeth that Jesus is the Son of God?" (1 Jn.5:4-5).
"The LORD is nigh unto them that are of a broken heart; and saveth such as be of a contrite spirit" (Ps.34:18).
"The LORD is gracious, and full of compassion; slow to anger, and of great mercy" (Ps.145:8).

3 (4:38-39) **Rest—Peace**: rest and peace are a concern to Jesus. Note something: the disciples were seasoned fishermen. No doubt they had been caught in storms before, but this storm was more violent. They feared that they were perishing. They had tried to handle the situation themselves, but the situation had gotten out of hand. They had thought Jesus would awaken on His own, as any man would; but they were wrong, and they could wait no longer.

Note the exact words of the disciples: "Master, carest thou not that we perish?" (v.38). They confessed they were perishing. They were prideful men, well-built, and very capable in their profession. They had always handled every situation before; and they had started out handling this storm. But there they stood confessing their *human inability* and their *need* for His help, the help of God Himself. (See note—Mt.8:25 for detailed thoughts.)

The response of Jesus to the plea of His disciples was dramatic. Note what Jesus did and what happened:
⇒ "He arose."
⇒ "He rebuked the wind...and the wind ceased."
⇒ "He spoke to the sea...and there was a great calm."

The words *peace, be still* (siopa pephimoso) mean literally to *be muzzled.* The use of this word *muzzled* shows the fury and violence of the storm and stresses the dramatic act of Jesus.

Thought 1. The power of Jesus to control the sea and its storms, to control nature itself, demonstrates three facts (see note 6—Mt.8:26 for more detailed thoughts).
(1) Christ is the Son of God, the Sovereign Lord over all nature and life. He not only possesses the authority of God; but, as Mark sets out to prove, He is the Son of God Himself (see DEEPER STUDY # 2—Mk.1:1).
(2) Christ can calm any storm of life for us.

"And Jesus came and spake unto them, saying, All power is given unto me in heaven and in earth" (Mt.28:18).
"And declared to be the Son of God with power, according to the spirit of holiness, by the resurrection from the dead" (Ro.1:4).

(3) Christ can strengthen us to go through any trial.

"There hath no temptation [trial] taken you but such as is common to man: but God is faithful, who will not suffer you to be tempted above that ye are able; but will with the temptation also make a way to escape, that ye may be able to bear it" (1 Co.10:13).

"Blessed be God, even the Father of our Lord Jesus Christ, the Father of mercies, and the God of all comfort; who comforteth us in all our tribulation, that we may be able to comfort them which are in any trouble, by the comfort wherewith we ourselves are comforted of God" (2 Co.1:3-4).

"Now thanks be unto God, which always causeth us to triumph in Christ, and maketh manifest the savour of his knowledge by us in every place" (2 Co.2:14).

"And the Lord shall deliver me from every evil work, and will preserve me unto his heavenly kingdom: to whom be glory for ever and ever. Amen" (2 Ti.4:18).

"Surely he shall deliver thee from the snare of the fowler, and from the noisome pestilence" (Ps.91:3).

4 (4:40-41) **Rest—Peace—Faith**: rest and peace come through two sources.

a. Through faith (see notes and DEEPER STUDY # 2—Mt.8:26 for detailed discussion and thoughts. Also see notes—Mk.11:22-23; note and DEEPER STUDY # 1—Gal.2:15-16.)

"And Jesus said unto the centurion, Go thy way; and as thou hast believed, so be it done unto thee. And his servant was healed in the selfsame hour" (Mt.8:13).

"Then touched he their eyes, saying, According to your faith be it unto you. And their eyes were opened; and Jesus straitly charged them, saying, See that no man know it" (Mt.9:29-30).

"And all things, whatsoever ye shall ask in prayer, believing, ye shall receive" (Mt.21:22).

"Jesus said unto him, If thou canst believe, all things are possible to him that believeth" (Mk.9:23).

b. Through Jesus, His power and His Word (see note—Mt.8:27 for discussion).

"But that ye may know that the Son of man hath power on earth to forgive sins, (then saith he to the sick of the palsy,) Arise, take up thy bed, and go unto thine house" (Mt.9:6).

"Come unto me, all ye that labour and are heavy laden, and I will give you rest" (Mt.11:28).

"Peace I leave with you, my peace I give unto you: not as the world giveth, give I unto you. Let not your heart be troubled, neither let it be afraid" (Jn.14:27).

"These things I have spoken unto you, that in me ye might have peace. In the world ye shall have tribulation: but be of good cheer; I have overcome the world" (Jn.16:33).

"How God anointed Jesus of Nazareth with the Holy Ghost and with power: who went about doing good, and healing all that were oppressed of the devil; for God was with him" (Ac.10:38).

"And what is the exceeding greatness of his power to us-ward who believe, according to the working of his mighty power, which he wrought in Christ, when he raised him from the dead, and set him at his own right hand in the heavenly places, far above all principality, and power, and might, and dominion, and every name that is named, not only in this world, but also in that which is to come: and hath put all things under his feet, and gave him to be the head over all things to the church" (Ep.1:19-22).

"Now unto him that is able to do exceeding abundantly above all that we ask or think, according to the power that worketh in us" (Ep.3:20).

"Wherefore in all things it behoved him to be made like unto his brethren, that he might be a merciful and faithful high priest in things pertaining to God, to make reconciliation for the sins of the people. For in that he himself hath suffered being tempted, he is able to succour them that are tempted" (He.2:17-18).

"For we have not an high priest which cannot be touched with the feeling of our infirmities; but was in all points tempted like as we are, yet without sin. Let us therefore come boldly unto the throne of grace, that we may obtain mercy, and find grace to help in time of need" (He.4:15-16).

1. **An eerie event: At night, on the lakeshore—among the tombs, see 4:35, 41**
2. **Scene 1: A man hopelessly possessed—without Jesus**
   a. He had an evil spirit
   b. He lived among the tombs[DS2]
   c. He was cut off from society
   d. He was uncontrollable, unrestrained, untamed, wild, mad, violent tempered
   e. He was naked, 15
   f. He was always inflicting wounds upon himself
3. **Scene 2: A man desperately aroused by the Son of God**
   a. He worshipped Jesus, 6
   b. He acknowledged the deity of Jesus
   c. He begged not to be tortured
4. **Scene 3: A man miraculously cleansed by the authority of Jesus**
   a. Jesus spoke the word of power, 8
   b. Jesus showed the man's great need
   c. Jesus showed the nature of evil spirits
      1) Were subject to Christ
      2) Desired a body to indwell & influence
      3) Were destroyers, malicious & violent[DS3]
5. **Scene 4: A people callously rejecting Jesus—by begging Him to leave their presence**
   a. A logical reaction: Ran to tell what had happened
   b. A logical investigation: Came to Jesus
   c. A logical account: Told of the healing & also of the pigs
   d. An illogical request: Asked Jesus to leave
   e. A tragic end: He left
6. **Scene 5: A man deliberately commissioned by Jesus**
   a. He requested discipleship
   b. He was sent home to be a witness there[DS4]
   c. He was faithful
   d. He was successful

F. The Authority of Jesus over Nature: Rest & Peace,[DS1] 4:35-41
(Mt. 8:23-27; Lu. 8:22-25)

And they came over unto the other side of the sea, into the country of the Gadarenes.
2 And when he was come out of the ship, immediately there met him out of the tombs a man with an unclean spirit,
3 Who had his dwelling among the tombs; and no man could bind him, no, not with chains:
4 Because that he had been often bound with fetters and chains, and the chains had been plucked asunder by him, and the fetters broken in pieces: neither could any man tame him.
5 And always, night and day, he was in the mountains, and in the tombs, crying, and cutting himself with stones.
6 But when he saw Jesus afar off, he ran and worshipped him.
7 And cried with a loud voice, and said, What have I to do with thee, Jesus, thou Son of the most high God? I adjure thee by God, that thou torment me not.
8 For he said unto him, Come out of the man, thou unclean spirit.
9 And he asked him, What is thy name? And he answered, saying, My name is Legion: for we are many.
10 And he besought him much that he would not send them away out of the country.
11 Now there was there nigh unto the mountains a great herd of swine feeding.
12 And all the devils besought him, saying, Send us into the swine, that we may enter into them.
13 And forthwith Jesus gave them leave. And the unclean spirits went out, and entered into the swine: and the herd ran violently down a steep place into the sea, (they were about two thousand;) and were choked in the sea.
14 And they that fed the swine fled, and told it in the city, and in the country. And they went out to see what it was that was done.
15 And they come to Jesus, and see him that was possessed with the devil, and had the legion, sitting, and clothed, and in his right mind: and they were afraid.
16 And they that saw it told them how it befell to him that was possessed with the devil, and also concerning the swine.
17 And they began to pray him to depart out of their coasts.
18 And when he was come into the ship, he that had been possessed with the devil prayed him that he might be with him.
19 Howbeit Jesus suffered him not, but saith unto him, Go home to thy friends, and tell them how great things the Lord hath done for thee, and hath had compassion on thee.
20 And he departed, and began to publish in Decapolis how great things Jesus had done for him: and all men did marvel.

DIVISION III

THE SON OF GOD'S CONTINUING MINISTRY: JESUS' PARABLES AND HIS AUTHORITY, 4:1-6:6

G. The Authority of Jesus to Banish Demons: Hope for the Most Wild and Mean, 5:1-20

(5:1-20) **Introduction**: the Spirit of God controls people to varying degrees; evil also controls people to varying degrees. Some persons are extremely controlled by evil; others are just slightly controlled.

⇒ Some men are said to be controlled by *demons*.
⇒ Mary Magdalene is said to have been possessed by seven devils (Mk.16:9).
⇒ Jesus referred to one devil's being replaced by seven devils and the last state of the man being far worse (Lu.9:26).
⇒ The man in the present passage is said to have been possessed by a Legion, that is, hordes of demons.

No matter how much a man is possessed and controlled by evil, no matter how wild and mean he is, Christ can deliver him. The man can experience a *great deliverance*. There is wonderful hope for all—even for the most wild and mean. This is the message of the present passage. (Also see note—Mt.8:28-34.)

1. An eerie event: at night, on the lakeshore—among the tombs (v.1).

2. Scene 1: a man hopelessly possessed—without Jesus (vv.2-5).
3. Scene 2: a man desperately aroused by the Son of God (vv.6-7).
4. Scene 3: a man miraculously cleansed by the authority of Jesus (vv.8-13).
5. Scene 4: a people callously rejecting Jesus—by begging Him to leave their presence (vv.14-17).
6. Scene 5: a man deliberately commissioned by Jesus (vv.18-20).

DEEPER STUDY # 1
(5:1-20) **Evil Spirits**: see DEEPER STUDY # 1—Mt.8:28-34.

1 (5:1) **Evil Spirits**: this was an eerie event. Note the words "immediately there met Him out of the tombs," and imagine the scene.

It was a stormy night, pitch dark (see Mk.4:35, 37). The boats pulled up on shore right in the midst of a seashore graveyard, and immediately a wild-acting man came running out from among the tombs. The picture was definitely eerie and scary. Five scenes are painted in the event.

2 (5:2-5) **Demon Possession—Evil Spirits**: the first scene is that of a man hopelessly possessed. He was without Jesus. The wretched condition of the demon-possessed is described in detail. Mark's purpose is to show that the man was as possessed with evil as any man could be. He had reached rock bottom. But Jesus is God, and as God He cares and has the power to deliver even the most wild and mean. (See outline and notes—Mt.8:28-31; Mk.1:23.)

a. The man had an unclean or evil spirit. Some evil, spiritual power dwelt within his body; some alien, foreign, outside power possessed and controlled the man. He represents the man who is not spiritual, the man who is not possessed and controlled by God and His Spirit (Ro.8:14).

> **"Now the works of the flesh are manifest, which are these; Adultery, fornication, uncleanness, lasciviousness, idolatry, witchcraft, hatred, variance, emulations, wrath, strife, seditions, heresies, envyings, murders, drunkenness, revellings, and such like: of the which I tell you before, as I have also told you in time past, that they which do such things shall not inherit the kingdom of God" (Ga.5:19-21).**

b. The man lived among the tombs. These were lofty, vault-like tombs, hewn out of the limestone hills (see DEEPER STUDY #2—Mk.5:3). The evil spirit caused the man to dwell in the darkest, most eerie place imaginable, and living in the dark and eeriness aggravated his condition. He represents the man who loves darkness because his deeds are evil.

> **"And this is the condemnation, that light is come into the world, and men loved darkness rather than light, because their deeds were evil" (Jn.3:19).**

c. The man was cut off from society. He did not live among the living; he lived among the dead. He represents *the living dead*; that is, all men without Christ are "dead in their sins" and are cut off from the *society of God*.

> **"Wherein in time past ye walked according to the course of this world, according to the prince of the power of the air, the spirit that now worketh in the children of disobedience: among whom also we all had our conversation in times past in the lusts of our flesh, fulfilling the desires of the flesh and of the mind; and were by nature the children of wrath, even as others" (Ep.2:2-3).**

d. The man was uncontrollable, unrestrained, untamed, wild, mad, violent tempered, often possessing super-human strength. All human efforts to help him had failed. He could not be helped, nor controlled, nor tamed. He represents the uncontrollable evil or depravity of man and the helplessness of man to deliver or save himself (see Ro.1:20-32; 3:10f; Ep.2:8-9; Tit.3:3-7. See 2 Pe.2:10-12.)

> **"Being filled with all unrighteousness, fornication, wickedness, covetousness, maliciousness; full of envy, murder, debate, deceit, malignity; whisperers, backbiters, haters of God, despiteful, proud, boasters, inventors of evil things, disobedient to parents, without understanding, covenantbreakers, without natural affection, implacable, unmerciful: who knowing the judgment of God, that they which commit such things are worthy of death, not only do the same, but have pleasure in them that do them" (Ro.1:29-32).**

e. The man was naked (see v.15), stripped of all decency and all acceptable and righteous behavior. He represents the old man who stands naked before the eyes of God and who desperately needs to be clothed with the righteousness of God and with the garments of the new man (2 Co.5:1-2, 21; Ro.13:14; Ga.3:27; Ep.4:24; Col.3:10).

> **"But put ye on the Lord Jesus Christ, and make not provision for the flesh, to fulfil the lusts thereof" (Ro.13:14).**

f. The man was a threat to himself and to others, inflicting harm upon himself. He represents the man who has become dangerous, so given over to evil that he is a threat to all. He represents the man who is totally depraved, the man who is so far gone he no longer has respect for human life, even his own; the man whose "mouth is full of cursing and bitterness" and whose "feet are swift to shed blood" (Ro.3:15). He represents the man who has fallen to the depths of the pit—so deep he can fall no further. He is hopeless in an absolute sense. No one but God could ever save him. (Now note. Jesus saved him, and this is the point. By saving the man, Jesus is saying that He is God and that, as God, He is able to save the most wild and mean, even those who are totally hopeless.)

"As it is written, there is none righteous, no, not one: there is none that understandeth, there is none that seeketh after God. They are all gone out of the way, they are together become unprofitable; there is none that doeth good, no, not one. Their throat is an open sepulchre; with their tongues they have used deceit; the poison of asps is under their lips: whose mouth is full of cursing and bitterness: their feet are swift to shed blood: destruction and misery are in their ways: and the way of peace have they not known: there is no fear of God before their eyes" (Ro.3:10-18).

DEEPER STUDY # 2
(5:3) **Tombs—Graveyards**: Jewish cemeteries were always located outside the city or town. This was necessary because Jewish law said that a person became temporarily defiled if he touched a grave. Some of the cemeteries were located around limestone hills or mountainous terrain. This enabled men to find caverns or else to hew out tombs in the limestone facing. The tombs were often large enough for a man to stand in (see DEEPER STUDY # 1—Mt.27:65-66).

3 (5:6-7) **Demon Possession—Evil Spirit, Fate of**: the second scene is that of a man desperately aroused. He was fearfully aroused by the Son of God. The man saw Jesus afar off, probably while Jesus was in the boat approaching the shore. The man ran and worshipped Jesus. Note what happened: the man acknowledged Jesus to be the Son of God, and he begged Jesus not to torment him, that is, not to send him to the abyss or to hell (see Lu.8:31). These two facts show that the man was under the control of an evil spirit. The *man* had no way to know that Jesus was the Son of God, and no *man* is sent to hell by Jesus—not in this life, not while still living.

Scripture teaches four facts about the devil and his angels (messengers, demons, evil spirits) that should always be kept in mind.

1. They believe there is One God and they tremble (Js.2:19).
2. They have nothing to do with Jesus; that is, their nature is entirely different from the clean spirit of Jesus. Evil and evil spirits are diametrically opposed to the purity and holiness of Jesus.
3. The Son of God has come to destroy the works of the devil. All evil and evil spirits are to be destroyed (1 Jn.3:8; see He.2:14-15).
4. They are doomed to everlasting torment (see DEEPER STUDY # 3, *Everlasting Fire*—Mt.25:41).

All four of these facts were involved in the behavior of the demon-possessed man. The evil spirit was trembling before the Son of God. He cried out, "What have I to do with thee, Jesus, thou Son of...God?" He was stricken with the purity and the holiness of Jesus. He was forced to bow in reverence and to beg Jesus not to doom him—not yet. (See note—Mk.1:23-24 for detailed discussion and thoughts.)

Note something: the evil spirit knew that Jesus had come to destroy evil. He knew that Jesus was going to cast him out and free the man, despite the man's utter, hopeless depravity. How marvelous the love and power of Jesus, that He frees even the most defiled!

"Even as the Son of man came not to be ministered unto, but to minister, and to give his life a ransom for many" (Mt.20:28).

"They that are whole have no need of the physician, but they that are sick: I came not to call the righteous, but sinners to repentance" (Mk.2:17).

"For the Son of man is come to seek and to save that which was lost" (Lu.19:10).

4 (5:8-13) **Evil Spirits—Spiritual Cleansing**: the third scene is that of a man miraculously cleansed. He was cleansed by the authority of Jesus. Jesus did three things in this scene.

a. Jesus spoke the word of power. He commanded the evil spirit to come out of the man.

b. Jesus revealed the man's great need, how *utterly possessed* by evil he was. Jesus led the evil spirit to identify himself. His name was Legion, referring to the Roman military legion that included over six thousand men. The point is this: the man was as desperate as a man could be, but Jesus' power was more sufficient, eternally so. He is definitely the Son of God. He could cast a legion of evil spirits out of a man.

c. Jesus revealed the nature of evil spirits. He used this occasion to teach and warn men of evil spirits. There are degrees of control by Satan just as there are degrees of control by God.

1) The evil spirit was subject to Jesus. No evil can stand up to Him. The evil spirit asked to remain in his present country. Apparently the country and its life-style were more evil and more subject to evil than other countries.
2) The evil spirit desired a body to indwell and influence (see note, pt.5—Mt.8:28-31). He asked to enter the bodies of a herd of swine. Note the plural, "devils," and the fact that there were about two thousand swine. This again stresses the enormous evil within the man, his desperate, hopeless plight.
3) The evil spirit was malicious and violent; he was a destroyer. He destroyed the herd of swine (see DEEPER STUDY #2—Mt.8:32).

Thought 1. Jesus Christ has the authority to cleanse man, no matter how mean and evil.

"But Jesus beheld them, and said unto them, With men this is impossible; but with God all things are possible" (Mt.19:26; Mk.14:36; Lu.1:37).

"And Jesus came and spake unto them, saying, All power is given unto me in heaven and in earth" (Mt.28:18).

"How God anointed Jesus of Nazareth with the Holy Ghost and with power: who went about doing good, and healing all that were oppressed of the devil; for God was with him" (Ac.10:38).

"And what is the exceeding greatness of his power to us-ward who believe, according to the working of his mighty power, which he wrought in Christ, when he raised him from the dead, and

set him at his own right hand in the heavenly places, far above all principality, and power, and might, and dominion, and every name that is named, not only in this world, but also in that which is to come: and hath put all things under his feet, and gave him to be the head over all things to the church" (Ep.1:19-22).

"Now unto him that is able to do exceeding abundantly above all that we ask or think, according to the power that worketh in us" (Ep.3:20).

DEEPER STUDY # 3
(5:12-13) **Jesus Christ, Judgment**: the question as to why Jesus would allow a herd of swine to be killed is discussed in the note Mt.5:32.

5 (5:14-17) **Jesus Christ, Response**: the fourth scene is that of a people who callously rejected God by begging Jesus to leave them. Five acts are seen here (see note—Mt.8:33-34).

a. There was the logical action: the swine keepers ran into the city to the owners of the swine to relate what had happened. The whole herd had been destroyed; it was a huge and devastating loss financially. They had to make sure the fault was not laid at their feet.

b. There was the logical investigation by the owners and city folk: they came to Jesus to investigate the loss. They saw the man's sitting before Jesus—clothed and in his right mind. (Note: when Jesus cleanses a man, the man comes to his *right mind.* He is truly cured.) They were stricken with fear of Jesus' power, for they had known the man and his hopeless condition. What power this Jesus must have!

c. There was the logical account by eyewitnesses: they shared with the owners and city folk. Note: they told the good news of what had happened to the man, but they also added what had happened to the swine. They could not get over the financial loss. They thought more of the world and its money than of God's meeting people's needs.

d. There was the illogical request: they asked Jesus to leave. "They were taken with great fear" (Lu.8:37). They were gripped with fear, not a fear of reverence and humility, but a fear of dread and hatred that He had caused so much loss and that He might punish them even more.

e. There was the tragic end: Jesus left. He did exactly what the people requested Him to do.

Thought 1. Note the devils had just what they wanted. They had caused the people to reject Jesus, choosing the riches of the world rather than Him. (Contrast the spirit of Moses, He.11:25-26.)

"Love not the world, neither the things that are in the world. If any man love the world, the love of the Father is not in him. For all that is in the world, the lust of the flesh, and the lust of the eyes, and the pride of life, is not of the Father, but is of the world" (1 Jn.2:15-16).

"For what is a man profited, if he shall gain the whole world, and lose his own soul? or what shall a man give in exchange for his soul?" (Mt.16:26).

"Set your affection on things above, not on things on the earth" (Col.3:2).

"Teaching us that, denying ungodliness and worldly lusts, we should live soberly, righteously, and godly, in this present world" (Tit.2:12).

Thought 2. Jesus granted their request: He left them. Jesus will grant our request to be left alone and to go our own way, but the result will be "leanness of soul" and rejection by God (Ps.106:15).

"But whosoever shall deny me before men, him will I also deny before my Father which is in heaven" (Mt.10:33).

"Whosoever therefore shall be ashamed of me and of my words in this adulterous and sinful generation; of him also shall the Son of man be ashamed, when he cometh in the glory of his Father with the holy angels" (Mk.8:38).

"He that loveth silver shall not be satisfied with silver; nor he that loveth abundance with increase: this is also vanity" (Ec.5:10).

"Wherefore do ye spend money for that which is not bread? and your labor for that which satisfieth not? hearken diligently unto me, and eat ye that which is good, and let your soul delight itself in fatness" (Is.55:2).

6 (5:18-20) **Witnessing**: the fifth scene is that of a man deliberately commissioned by Jesus. The man was naturally thankful, very appreciative. He immediately wanted to become a follower of Jesus, but Jesus saw something unique in the man, something that would make him a dynamic evangelist among his own people. Consequently, Jesus commissioned him to be a disciple at home. Two significant things are said about his witness: he was faithful and he was successful.

A believer must be "one that ruleth well his own house, having his children in subjection with all gravity; (for if a man know not how to rule his own house, how shall he take care of the church of God?)" (1 Ti.3:4-5).

"But if any provide not for his own, and specially for those of his own house, he hath denied the faith, and is worse than an infidel" (1 Ti.5:8).

DEEPER STUDY # 4
(5:19) **Witnessing**: Why would Jesus tell this man to proclaim the *good news* when He had instructed the leper not to spread the Word (Mk.1:44)? Jesus had just been forbidden to continue His ministry among the Gadarenes. He needed someone to carry on the work, so He commissioned this new believer.

1. **Scene 1: A large crowd gathered around Jesus**
2. **Scene 2: A ruler's desperate approach**
   a. A selfless attitude
   b. A humble attitude
   c. A pleading attitude
   d. An expectant, believing attitude
   e. The result: Jesus granted the desperate request
3. **Scene 3: A woman's hopeless approach**
   a. A last-resort attitude
   b. A shy, embarrassed, unworthy attitude
   c. An expectant, believing attitude
   d. A confessing attitude
      1) The cost of service to Jesus
      2) The insensitivity of the apostles
      3) The confession of the woman
   e. The result: Jesus granted the hopeless request
4. **Scene 4: A ruler's believing approach**
   a. Not a fearful, despairing attitude
      1) Faced devastating circumstance
      2) The answer to the terrible circumstances: Jesus' challenge to believe not fear[DS2]
   b. Not a wailing, whining attitude
      1) Social customs & influences: To express hopelessness
      2) The answer: Jesus' comfort & assurance
   c. Not a sarcastic, skeptical attitude
   d. An obedient attitude: The parents followed Jesus despite the sarcasm
   e. The result: Jesus granted the believer's request
      1) The power of Jesus: Raised the girl from the dead
      2) The amazement of the family
      3) The thoughtfulness of Jesus

H. The Approaches That Lay Hold of Jesus' Authority: How to Approach Jesus,[DS1] 5:21-43
(Mt. 9:18-26; Lu. 8:40-56)

21 And when Jesus was passed over again by ship unto the other side, much people gathered unto him: and he was nigh unto the sea.

22 And, behold, there cometh one of the rulers of the synagogue, Jairus by name; and when he saw him, he fell at his feet,

23 And besought him greatly, saying, My little daughter lieth at the point of death: I pray thee, come and lay thy hands on her, that she may be healed; and she shall live.

24 And Jesus went with him; and much people followed him, and thronged him.

25 And a certain woman, which had an issue of blood twelve years,

26 And had suffered many things of many physicians, and had spent all that she had, and was nothing bettered, but rather grew worse,

27 When she had heard of Jesus, came in the press behind, and touched his garment.

28 For she said, If I may touch but his clothes, I shall be whole.

29 And straightway the fountain of her blood was dried up; and she felt in her body that she was healed of that plague.

30 And Jesus, immediately knowing in himself that virtue had gone out of him, turned him about in the press, and said, Who touched my clothes?

31 And his disciples said unto him, Thou seest the multitude thronging thee, and sayest thou, Who touched me?

32 And he looked round about to see her that had done this thing.

33 But the woman fearing and trembling, knowing what was done in her, came and fell down before him, and told him all the truth.

34 And he said unto her, Daughter, thy faith hath made thee whole; go in peace, and be whole of thy plague.

35 While he yet spake, there came from the ruler of the synagogue's house certain which said, Thy daughter is dead: why troublest thou the Master any further?

36 As soon as Jesus heard the word that was spoken, he saith unto the ruler of the synagogue, Be not afraid, only believe.

37 And he suffered no man to follow him, save Peter, and James, and John the brother of James.

38 And he cometh to the house of the ruler of the synagogue, and seeth the tumult, and them that wept and wailed greatly.

39 And when he was come in, he saith unto them, Why make ye this ado, and weep? the damsel is not dead, but sleepeth.

40 And they laughed him to scorn. But when he had put them all out, he taketh the father and the mother of the damsel, and them that were with him, and entereth in where the damsel was lying.

41 And he took the damsel by the hand, and said unto her, Talitha cumi; which is, being interpreted, Damsel, I say unto thee, arise.

42 And straightway the damsel arose, and walked; for she was of the age of twelve years. And they were astonished with a great astonishment.

43 And he charged them straitly that no man should know it; and commanded that something should be given her to eat.

DIVISION III

THE SON OF GOD'S CONTINUING MINISTRY: JESUS' PARABLES AND HIS AUTHORITY, 4:1-6:6

H. The Approaches That Lay Hold of Jesus' Authority: How to Approach Jesus, 5:21-43

(5:21-43) **Introduction**: How can a person lay hold of Jesus and His power? This passage deals specifically with the desperate and hopeless person; it shows how the desperate person can approach Jesus and secure His help in any situation.

1. Scene 1: a large crowd gathered around Jesus (v.21).
2. Scene 2: a ruler's desperate approach (vv.22-24).
3. Scene 3: a woman's hopeless approach (vv.25-34).
4. Scene 4: a ruler's believing approach (vv.35-43).

DEEPER STUDY # 1
(5:21-43) **Faith—Believe**: the one thing that lays hold of Jesus and His power is faith (see DEEPER STUDY # 1—Mt.9:18-34. Also see notes—Mk.11:22-23; DEEPER STUDY # 2—Ga.2:16; see Jn.2:24; He.10:38.)

1 (5:21) **Jesus Christ, Response to**: crowds gathered around Jesus again. He had crossed back over the Sea of Galilee, apparently near Capernaum, His headquarters. The events that follow happened near the Sea of Galilee.

2 (5:22-24) **Desperation—Attitude—Seeking Jesus**: the first scene is that of a ruler's desperate approach (see note, *Jairus*—Mt.9:18-19). A desperate approach always lays hold of Jesus. Jesus sees and answers a person who comes to Him in desperation. A desperate approach involves four attitudes.

a. There is a selfless attitude. Jairus was a ruler, one of the most important men in the community (see note—Mt.9:18-19). The rulers were now violently opposed to Jesus and were publicly expressing their opposition. By coming to Jesus, Jairus was running the risk of arousing the hostility of his peers and of being censored. He could have easily lost his position and profession.

Something else is also noticeable. Jairus himself was approaching Jesus. Why would he leave his dying daughter's side to seek Jesus' help instead of sending someone else? Could it be that even they of his own household feared approaching Jesus because of the heated opposition? Jairus would most likely not have left his daughter's side if there had been another person willing to come to Jesus.

The point is that Jairus was desperate for help. No man could help him; this much he knew. But he had heard that Jesus could help; therefore, he set aside everything—profession, friends, family—he forgot self completely; and he went to Jesus for help.

> **"For all those things hath mine hand made, and all those things have been, saith the LORD: but to this man will I look, even to him that is poor and of a contrite spirit, and trembleth at my word" (Is.66:2).**

b. There is a humble attitude. Note the words, "he fell at His feet" (v.22). Jairus pushed and shoved his way through the crowd as rapidly as he could. When he caught his first glimpse of Jesus, his pace quickened; and when he finally reached Jesus, he "fell at Jesus' feet." This is humility at its height. The ruler willingly humbled himself and willingly...

- laid aside all his pride and dignity.
- laid aside his family and friends in all their prejudice and opposition.
- laid aside his profession with all its security, fame, and authority.

> **"Whosoever therefore shall humble himself as this little child, the same is greatest in the kingdom of heaven" (Mt.18:4).**
> **"But he giveth more grace. Wherefore he saith, God resisteth the proud, but giveth grace unto the humble" (Js.4:6).**
> **"Humble yourselves in the sight of the Lord, and he shall lift you up" (Js.4:10).**

c. There is a pleading attitude. The word *besought* (parakaleo) means to call to one's side for help, to plead, to entreat, to beg. The ruler pleaded and begged Jesus to help him.

> **"He shall call upon me, and I will answer him: I will be with him in trouble; I will deliver him, and honour him" (Ps.91:15).**
> **"Then shalt thou call, and the LORD shall answer; thou shalt cry, and he shall say, Here I am. If thou take away from the midst of thee the yoke, the putting forth of the finger, and speaking vanity" (Is.58:9).**
> **"Call unto me, and I will answer thee, and show thee great and mighty things, which thou knowest not" (Je.33:3).**

d. There is an expectant, believing attitude. The man had a little daughter twelve years old, and she was dying—"at the very point of death." Note the man's great faith: if Jesus would come and lay His hands upon her, she would be healed and live.

> **"And all things, whatsoever ye shall ask in prayer, believing, ye shall receive" (Mt.21:22).**
> **"If ye shall ask any thing in my name, I will do it" (Jn.14:14).**

e. The result and the impact of these four attitudes were powerful. Jesus granted the request of the desperate approach. Desperation—a selfless, humble, pleading, believing desperation—gets help. Jesus meets the need of the desperate who come to Him with...

- a selfless attitude
- a humble attitude
- a pleading attitude
- a believing attitude

3 (5:25-34) **Hopelessness—Attitude**: the second scene is that of a woman's hopeless approach (see note—Mt.9:20-22). This approach always lays hold of Jesus. Jesus senses the touch of the hopeless and always helps the hopeless who come to Him. A hopeless approach involves four attitudes.

a. There is the last resort attitude. The woman had been hemorrhaging for twelve years; it was uncontrollable. No one could touch her nor anything she had touched. By law she was considered unclean, so unclean that she was to be divorced by her husband (Le.15:25-27). She was to be totally cut off from society and religious worship. This particular woman had tried all she knew. She had seen "many physicians" and "spent all that she had," and yet she "grew worse." There was nowhere else to turn except to Jesus. (See note—Mt.9:20-22 for more detail of her condition.)

"Come unto me, all ye that labour and are heavy laden, and I will give you rest" (Mt.11:28).

Thought 1. When all else fails, there is Jesus. However, most people try all else before Jesus. Nevertheless, He loves us and He cares for us—enormously so. We should turn to Jesus, for He is always waiting for us—waiting even if we turn to Him as a last resort.

Thought 2. A person who has been brought to the point of helplessness and hopelessness can be helped. When there is no hope anywhere else, there is hope in Christ.

Thought 3. There is no need to reach the point of hopelessness; no need to reach the *end of our ropes*; no need to become utterly depressed. Circumstances should never be allowed to destroy us, not to the point of utter hopelessness. Nevertheless, many reach that point. The one thing to remember is that Jesus does care and will never turn away from the hopeless. He opens His arms to all who come—even to the hopeless.

b. There is the shy, embarrassed, unworthy attitude. Note the woman elbowed her way through the crowd and came up behind Jesus. She wanted to touch Jesus without being seen or noticed. Why? She was embarrassed and felt unworthy. Her hemorrhaging was a personal, intimate matter for her, something she did not want to be known and discussed. She was considered unclean; therefore, she felt unworthy to approach Jesus.

Thought 1. It is the sense of unworthiness and hopelessness that touches the heart of Jesus; it is not being shy and fearing embarrassment. Being shy and fearing embarrassment are only the attitudes that create a sense of unworthiness and hopelessness. Jesus accepts any of the hopeless who truly come to Him, no matter what causes their sense of unworthiness.

Thought 2. Embarrassing matters, personal matters, secret matters—all are understood by Christ. He wishes no one to suffer ridicule or shame. He will accept the shy, quiet approach that comes to Him.

Thought 3. There are personal, embarrassing matters that we all wish to keep secret. These sometimes cause problems for us, serious problems that drive us to the point of hopelessness. Even a shy, embarrassed attitude that approaches Jesus will be acceptable. A sense of unworthiness and hopelessness touches His heart.

"The LORD is nigh unto them that are of a broken heart; and saveth such as be of a contrite spirit" (Ps.34:18).

"The sacrifices of God are a broken spirit: a broken and contrite heart, O God, thou wilt not despise" (Ps.51:17).

c. There is the expectant, believing attitude. Note that the hopeless woman believed what "she had heard of Jesus." She believed the gospel, that Jesus loved and cared and would make her whole. Note the thoughts of her mind, "If I may touch but His clothes, I shall be whole" (v.28). She believed in her thoughts, in her heart. She believed two things: the gospel (what she had heard about Jesus) and the power of Jesus to make her whole.

Thought 1. The same expectant, believing attitude is essential for any person to come to Christ, whether hopeless or not. One must believe in the gospel and in the power of Jesus to make one whole.

"Repent ye and believe the gospel" (Mk.1:15).

"For I am not ashamed of the gospel of Christ: for it is the power of God unto salvation to every one that believeth" (Ro.1:16).

"If thou canst believe, all things are possible to him that believeth" (Mk.9:23).

d. There is the confessing attitude. Jesus had made the way easy for her. He had allowed her to be healed without embarrassment, but it was not enough to believe in secret. The secret disciple had to be brought to the point of confessing her faith.

1) The healing had cost Jesus. Spiritual virtue had flowed out from Him into the woman. The expenditure of virtue took its toll, sapping His physical strength. Jesus felt virtue drain from His body. He turned and asked the pressing throng surrounding Him, "Who touched my clothes?"

Thought 1. Imagine the enormous amounts of virtue that flowed out from Jesus from the day of His baptism to the cross! Imagine the fathomless flow of virtue that flowed from the cross, covering believers of all generations. It is incomprehensible! Yet it is a fact—a fact that proclaims the love of the Son of God. He poured out all the virtue within His eternal being for mankind.

2) The disciples were unaware of what it cost Jesus to minister. They were insensitive to the spiritual energy He was exerting. They were ignorant of what Jesus was doing:
   ⇒ "Himself took our infirmities, and bore our sicknesses" (Mt.8:17; see Is.53:4).
   ⇒ He was teaching that public confession of Him was essential.

The disciples were somewhat surprised at Jesus' question: "Who touched me?" He was completely surrounded by a mass of people. In their surprise, they asked Him why He was asking such a question in the midst of so many people. How could He possibly expect not to be touched?

3) The woman confessed. When Jesus asked the question, the woman came up to Jesus "fearing and trembling." She had approached Him *being unclean* and had not requested permission to touch Him. But she had still been healed. Now she felt that she must respond to His question and identify herself lest He rebuke her and reject her faith. She feared that somehow her healing might be reversed if she did not confess that she had touched Him. So "knowing what was done in her, [she] came and fell down before Him, and told Him all the truth." It was difficult and embarrassing, but she did it.

"Whosoever therefore shall confess me before men, him will I confess also before my Father which is in heaven" (Mt.10:32).

"Also I say unto you, Whosoever shall confess me before men, him shall the Son of man also confess before the angels of God" (Lu.12:8).

e. The result is glorious. Jesus granted the request of the hopeless. "Daughter, thy faith hath made thee whole, go in peace, and be whole" (v.34). The result was twofold. She received peace. The fear and trembling were taken away and she was flooded with peace. Second, she was made whole both physically and spiritually.

"Peace I leave with you, my peace I give unto you: not as the world giveth, give I unto you. Let not your heart be troubled, neither let it be afraid" (Jn.14:27).

"These things I have spoken unto you, that in me ye might have peace. In the world ye shall have tribulation: but be of good cheer; I have overcome the world" (Jn.16:33).

"And Jesus said unto the centurion, Go thy way; and as thou hast believed, so be it done unto thee. And his servant was healed in the selfsame hour" (Mt.8:13).

"Then touched he their eyes, saying, According to your faith be it unto you. And their eyes were opened; and Jesus straitly charged them, saying, See that no man know it" (Mt.9:29-30).

"Jesus said unto him, If thou canst believe, all things are possible to him that believeth" (Mk.9:23).

"Verily, verily, I say unto you, He that heareth my word, and believeth on him that sent me, hath everlasting life, and shall not come into condemnation; but is passed from death unto life" (Jn.5:24).

"That if thou shalt confess with thy mouth the Lord Jesus, and shalt believe in thine heart that God hath raised him from the dead, thou shalt be saved. For with the heart man believeth unto righteousness; and with the mouth confession is made unto salvation" (Ro.10:9-10).

4 (5:35-43) **Faith**: the third scene is that of a ruler's believing approach. This approach always lays hold of Jesus. Jesus knows when a person truly believes. A believing approach involves one simple attitude, but there are also several attitudes that it does not involve.

a. There is not a fearful, despairing attitude in faith. Believing has nothing to do with fear or despair.

1) Note the devastating circumstance that occurred. While Jesus was still talking with the woman, someone came from Jairus' home with terrible news: his daughter was dead. Imagine the trauma—how Jairus felt. How anxious he must have felt with the pushing and shoving and slow movement of the crowd. How nervous he must have become as Jesus stopped to handle the matter with the hemorrhaging woman. If Jesus had just hurried, He could have reached his daughter in time. Jairus was devastated, crushed, fearful, and despairing. Now it was too late. He was helpless; all hope was gone.

2) Note: the challenge of Jesus is the answer to all fear and despair: "Be not afraid, only believe." (See DEEPER STUDY # 2—Mk.5:36.)

b. There is not a wailing, whining attitude in faith. Believing has nothing to do with such an attitude. Society and others may engage in and encourage wailing and whining; they may feel and say that nothing can be done now, that all one can do is to bear up under the weight and tragedy of the loss.

However, the answer to any circumstance, mild or tragic, is not wailing and whining. The answer is Jesus' *comfort* and *assurance*. Even if the circumstance is death, Jesus comforts and assures: "Why make ye this ado, and weep? The damsel is not dead, but sleepeth" (v.39). There is hope of the resurrection, which is a living fact, a living event that is to take place soon. In addition, there is hope of eternal life, of never dying, of being transported into the very presence of God upon passing from this life (Jn.5:24-29; 11:25-26. See DEEPER STUDY # 1—2 Ti.4:18.)

"Verily, verily, I say unto you, He that heareth my word, and believeth on him that sent me, hath everlasting life, and shall not come into condemnation; but is passed from death unto life. Verily, verily, I say unto you, The hour is coming, and now is, when the dead shall hear the voice of the Son of God: and they that hear shall live" (Jn.5:24-25).

"Jesus said unto her, I am the resurrection, and the life: he that believeth in me shall never die. Believest thou this? She saith unto him, Yea, Lord: I believe that thou art the Christ, the Son of God, which should come into the world" (Jn.11:25-26).

"And the Lord shall deliver me from every evil work, and will preserve me [take me, transport me] unto his heavenly kingdom: to whom be glory for ever and ever" (2 Ti.4:18).

c. There is not a scornful, skeptical attitude. The mourners laughed Jesus to scorn (see note, pt.5—Mt.9:23-26 for a detailed discussion and thoughts).

d. There is an obedient attitude, an attitude that believes and follows Jesus. Note that the parents did exactly as Jesus said: they removed the guests and followed Jesus into the room where their dead daughter lay. They obeyed Him despite the scorn and skepticism of others.

Thought 1. A believing faith often requires bearing abuse, scorn, and persecution to follow Jesus. Conquering the impossible requires great faith, and often it requires standing all alone against everyone else.

e. Jesus granted the believer's request. Jesus demonstrated His great love and amazing power. He raised Jairus' daughter. He showed that He cared for the man and the family who approached Him in belief and trust.

The family, of course, was amazed, as anyone would be. But note the *thoughtfulness* of Jesus. He told the family to tell no one what had really happened in order to protect them from an immediate onrush of sightseers. And He showed a tenderness by telling them to give their daughter something to eat.

Thought 1. *Stubborn faith* is desperately needed by many parents in behalf of their children. However, note what must precede stubborn faith: a desperate faith that forgets and denies self and that seeks Jesus no matter the cost. Difficult cases require both a desperate faith and a stubborn faith. It is such faith that receives the *great* reward.

"Verily I say unto you, If ye have faith as a grain of mustard seed, ye shall say unto this mountain, Remove hence to yonder place; and it shall remove; and nothing shall be impossible unto you" (Mt.17:20; see Mt.21:21).

"And Jesus answering saith unto them, Have faith in God. For verily I say unto you, That whosoever shall say unto this mountain, Be thou removed, and be thou cast into the sea; and shall not doubt in his heart, but shall believe that those things which he saith shall come to pass; he shall have whatsoever he saith. Therefore I say unto you, What things soever ye desire, when ye pray, believe that ye receive them, and ye shall have them" (Mk.11:22-24).

"But when Jesus heard it, he answered him, saying, Fear not: believe only, and she shall be made whole" (Lu.8:50).

"And they rose early in the morning, and went forth into the wilderness of Tekoa: and as they went forth, Jehoshaphat stood and said, Hear me, O Judah, and ye inhabitants of Jerusalem; Believe in the LORD your God, so shall ye be established; believe his prophets, so shall ye prosper" (2 Chr.20:20).

DEEPER STUDY # 2

(5:36) **Faith—Fear**: fear is the opposite of belief. Believing God eliminates fear. Believing that God actually cares and will deliver one through any and all circumstances of life erases fear. If God does care, there is nothing to fear. However, if one does not believe that God cares, then fear is present. Why? Because there is no one beyond man to help, and man's help is limited—very limited. There are many times in life when man's help is not enough, or even close to being enough. Therefore for the unbelieving man, there are all kinds of things to fear: unfortunate circumstances, bad health, accident, loneliness, death, the loss of anything and everything—family, profession, friends, business, home.

Outline	Scripture	Scripture	Outline
	CHAPTER 6 **I. The Rejection of Jesus' Authority: Why Jesus Is Rejected,**[DS1] **6:1-6** *(Mt. 13:54-58; Lu. 4:16-30)*	are wrought by his hands? 3 Is not this the carpenter, the son of Mary, the brother of James, and Joses, and of Juda, and Simon? and are not his sisters here with us? And they were offended at him.	**3. Some were offended by Him: They thought of Him only as one of their own**
1. Jesus was in His hometown, Nazareth	And he went out from thence, and came into his own country; and his disciples follow him.	4 But Jesus said unto them, A prophet is not without honour, but in his own country, and among his own kin, and in his own house.	
a. He entered the synagogue b. He taught: The people were amazed **2. Some questioned His source of authority** a. He lacked proper credentials & education b. He was from human & humble beginnings[DS2]	2 And when the sabbath day was come, he began to teach in the synagogue: and many hearing him were astonished, saying, From whence hath this man these things? and what wisdom is this which is given unto him, that even such mighty works	5 And he could there do no mighty work, save that he laid his hands upon a few sick folk, and healed them. 6 And he marvelled because of their unbelief. And he went round about the villages, teaching.	**4. Some blocked God's power** **5. Some were gripped with unbelief—shockingly so**

DIVISION III

THE SON OF GOD'S CONTINUING MINISTRY: JESUS' PARABLES AND HIS AUTHORITY, 4:1-6:6

I. The Rejection of Jesus' Authority: Why Jesus Is Rejected, 6:1-6

(6:1-6) **Introduction—Jesus Christ, Rejected—Ministers**: Jesus' hometown was harsh with Him. Most of His neighbors could never accept the fact that He was the Messiah. The fact that a person from among their midst could really be the true Messiah, the Son of God, was beyond their comprehension. There were some who were envious and jealous of the prominence and esteem He had achieved. Unacceptance, unbelief, and rumors about Him were widespread among His own people; and their unbelief led them to do some terrible things.

⇒ Some in the city tried to kill Him.
⇒ Some friends and neighbors considered Him mad or insane, so they went after Him to take Him home (Mk.3:20-21; Lu.4:16-30).
⇒ His family was extremely embarrassed by His claims and the wild rumors surrounding Him (Mk.3:31-32).

The most severe critics of a man's life and work are, of course, those who have always known him.

1. Jesus was in His hometown, Nazareth (vv.1-2).
2. Some questioned His source of authority (vv.2-3).
3. Some were offended by Him: They thought of Him only as one of their own (vv.3-4).
4. Some blocked God's power (v.5).
5. Some were gripped with unbelief—shockingly so (v.6).

DEEPER STUDY # 1
(6:1-6) **Jesus Christ, Childhood and Early Life**: see note—Mt.2:12-23 for detailed discussion.

1 (6:1-2) **Jesus Christ, Hometown**: Jesus left Capernaum and returned to His hometown, Nazareth. Nazareth was the city where He had grown up as a child and young man. Note that the hometown folks did not flock to Him like they had everywhere else. From all indications, He had no opportunity to preach and teach until the Sabbath. When the Sabbath came, He entered the synagogue and began to teach. His teaching was powerful, extremely impressive—so much so that many were astonished and amazed at the ability and the force of what the *hometown boy* had to say.

Thought 1. Jesus was perfectly obedient to the Father (He.5:8). He lived and moved and had His being in the Father. This, of course, is the key to the believer's power in life and ministry. *Power living, power preaching*, and *power teaching* all come from the presence of God Himself.

"But ye shall receive power, after that the Holy Ghost is come upon you: and ye shall be witnesses unto me both in Jerusalem, and in all Judaea, and in Samaria, and unto the uttermost part of the earth" (Ac.1:8).

"[That ye may know] what is the exceeding greatness of his power to us-ward who believe, according to the working of his mighty power, which he wrought in Christ, when he raised him from the dead, and set him at his own right hand in the heavenly places" (Ep.1:19-20).

"Now unto him that is able to do exceeding abundantly above all that we ask or think, according to the power that worketh in us" (Ep.3:20).

"For God hath not given us the spirit of fear; but of power, and of love, and of a sound mind. Be not thou therefore ashamed of the testimony of our Lord, nor of me his prisoner: but be thou partaker of the afflictions of the gospel according to the power of God" (2 Ti.1:7-8).

2 (6:2-3) **Jesus Christ, Accusations Against**: some questioned Jesus' source of authority. There were two primary reasons for this.

a. Jesus did not have the right credentials and education. His wisdom could not be denied; neither could the mighty works which He had done elsewhere be denied. The people even recognized that His wisdom and power were a *given* wisdom and power (v.2), but they could not understand from where and from whom He had received these.

Their question was a good one; it was the right question to ask. It showed that they were thinking about Him, but they were making a mistake. Why? Because they were unwilling to acknowledge that He had personally come from God (Lu.4:16-21; Jn.10:30-38). (See note, pt.1—Mt.13:54-56 for more discussion and applications.)

b. Jesus was from human and humble beginnings. He was a mere working man, a carpenter. His family had offered him no social or educational advantage. They were just common, ordinary folk, none of whom had ever achieved anything significant; yet, here He was teaching as a great Rabbi. (See note, pt.2—Mt.13:54-56 for a detailed discussion.)

Thought 1. The basic problem with Jesus' homefolk was envy and jealousy. They begrudged Jesus the honor and esteem that was being given Him by so many. He had become far more famous than any of them, and most of them had held so much more advantage and promise as children. They were just unwilling to admit that Jesus was really who He claimed to be (see Lu.4:16-24). They resented His claims, resented them so much that they became stiffnecked, giving themselves over to obstinate unbelief.

"Then said they unto him, Where is thy Father? Jesus answered, Ye neither know me, nor my Father: if ye had known me, ye should have known my Father also" (Jn.8:19).

"Therefore I said, Surely these are poor; they are foolish: for they know not the way of the LORD, nor the judgment of their God" (Je.5:4).

"But they know not the thoughts of the LORD, neither understand they his counsel" (Mi.4:12).

DEEPER STUDY # 2

(6:3) **Jesus Christ—Accusations Against**: Jesus was not just being rejected—He was being sneered at and despised (Is.53:3). Contrary to their claims, He had not come *from* such a humble place as Nazareth, but He had come *to* Nazareth, come to seek and save those who had been His neighbors.

"For unto us a child is born, unto us a son is given: and the government shall be upon his shoulder: and his name shall be called Wonderful, Counselor, The mighty God, The everlasting Father, The Prince of Peace" (Is.9:6).

"But thou Bethlehem Ephratah, though thou be little among the thousands of Judah, yet out of thee shall he come forth unto me that is to be ruler in Israel; whose goings forth have been from of old, from everlasting" (Mi.5:2).

"Let this mind be in you, which was also in Christ Jesus: who, being in the form of God, thought it not robbery to be equal with God: but made himself of no reputation, and took upon him the form of a servant, and was made in the likeness of men: and being found in fashion as a man, he humbled himself, and became obedient unto death, even the death of the cross" (Ph.2:5-8).

3 (6:3-4) **Jesus Christ, Rejected**: some were offended by Him, offended because they thought of Him only as one of their own.

"He was in the world, and the world was made by him, and the world knew him not. He came unto his own, and his own received him not" (Jn.1:10-11).

"For they being ignorant of God's righteousness, and going about to establish their own righteousness, have not submitted themselves unto the righteousness of God" (Ro.10:3).

"Having the understanding darkened, being alienated from the life of God through the ignorance that is in them, because of the blindness of their heart" (Ep.4:18).

Note that Jesus identified three groups who were offended and doing dishonor to Him. (See note—Mt.13:57 for a detailed discussion.)

1. "His own country": who attempted to kill Him (see outline and notes—Lu.4:16-30).
2. "His own kin": friends and neighbors who thought Him insane (see outline, notes, and DEEPER STUDY # 1—Mk.3:20-21).
3. "His own house": family members who were embarrassed by His claims and the neighbors' talk (see outline and notes—Mk.3:31-32).

Thought 1. One thing that God abhors is envy, resenting the gifts given to others. God bestows gifts as He wills to help mankind in its desperate plight. He expects the gifts to be used, and He expects all to encourage one another in the use of those gifts.

"For who maketh thee to differ from another? and what hast thou that thou didst not receive? now if thou didst receive it, why dost thou glory, as if thou hadst not received it?" (1 Co.4:7).

"Charity suffereth long, and is kind; charity envieth not; charity vaunteth not itself, is not puffed up" (1 Co.13:4).

"Let us not be desirous of vain glory, provoking one another, envying one another" (Ga.5:26).

4 (6:5) **Jesus Christ, Rejected—Unbelief**: some blocked God's power for the whole community. Their obstinate unbelief, questioning, rumors, and repulsion toward Jesus kept most away. Only a few sick folk were healed.

Thought 1. A man's unbelief affects and influences others. It keeps others away from Christ. What an awful responsibility—a terrible accounting—for one's own family and neighbors and country.

"But whoso shall offend one of these little ones which believe in me, it were better for him that a millstone were hanged about his neck, and that he were drowned in the depth of the sea" (Mt.18:6).

"But woe unto you, scribes and Pharisees, hypocrites! for ye shut up the kingdom of heaven against men: for ye neither go in yourselves, neither suffer ye them that are entering to go in" (Mt.23:13).

"Let us not therefore judge one another any more: but judge this rather, that no man put a stumblingblock or an occasion to fall in his brother's way" (Ro.14:13).

"He that loveth his brother abideth in the light, and there is none occasion of stumbling in him" (1 Jn.2:10).

Thought 2. Note that Christ tried to reach all three segments of society during His lifetime. Every believer is responsible to reach out to the same three segments of society. We shall be held accountable for how faithfully we reach out.

5 (6:6) **Jesus Christ, Rejected—Unbelief**: some were gripped with unbelief—shockingly so (see note—Mt.13:58). Note the words, "He marvelled because of their unbelief." They had His presence, His wisdom, and the testimony of His mighty works. They had His power to help them in all their need, yet they stayed away from His meetings. They would not come to Him. In pride, they refused to trust and believe Him. The situation amazed Jesus. Their unbelief was just incredible, but He had to accept their rejection. He could not force Himself upon them, so He left town and travelled to all the villages surrounding Nazareth.

Thought 1. Unbelief is shocking. It is an amazing thing to think that any man would ever reject the salvation of Christ—the salvation that delivers man from sin, death, and judgment to come, and that Christ enriches and enhances life so much (see Ga.5:22-23. See DEEPER STUDY # 4,5—Mt.1:21; note—2 Co.3:17-18; DEEPER STUDY #1—Ep.1:7; see Ro.8:28-39.)

"For this people's heart is waxed gross, and their ears are dull of hearing, and their eyes they have closed; lest at any time they should see with their eyes, and hear with their ears, and should understand with their heart, and should be converted, and I should heal them" (Mt.13:15).

"Therefore they say unto God, Depart from us; for we desire not the knowledge of thy ways" (Jb.21:14).

	IV. THE SON OF GOD'S TRAINING MINISTRY: JESUS' INTENSIVE PREPARATION OF THE DISCIPLES, 6:7-8:26 **A. The Sending Out of the Disciples, 6:7-13** *(Mt. 9:35-10:42; Lu. 9:1-6)*	and not put on two coats. 10 And he said unto them, In what place soever ye enter into an house, there abide till ye depart from that place.	b. Were to show stability & settledness
		11 And whosoever shall not receive you, nor hear you, when ye depart thence, shake off the dust under your feet for a testimony against them. Verily I say unto you, It shall be more tolerable for Sodom and Gomorrha in the day of judgment, than for that city.	c. Were to reject any who were not hospitable & receptive 1) The reason: As a warning 2) The judgment: Terrible
1. The disciples were equipped a. Were called to Him b. Were sent two by two c. Were given authority	7 And he called unto him the twelve, and began to send them forth by two and two; and gave them power over unclean spirits;		
2. The disciples were instructed a. Were to live in utter simplicity & humility	8 And commanded them that they should take nothing for their journey, save a staff only; no scrip, no bread, no money in their purse: 9 But be shod with sandals;	12 And they went out, and preached that men should repent. 13 And they cast out many devils, and anointed with oil many that were sick, and healed them.	d. Were to preach repentance e. Were to minister to the demon-possessed & the sick

DIVISION IV

THE SON OF GOD'S TRAINING MINISTRY:JESUS' INTENSIVE PREPARATION OF THE DISCIPLES, 6:7-8:26

A. The Sending Out of the Disciples, 6:7-13

(6:7-13) **Introduction**: every man has to be equipped before He goes forth, no matter the project or endeavor. To a great degree success depends upon how well equipped a man is. This is certainly true of men in the business world. It is also true of God's servants and disciples. They must be equipped by God as they go forth to carry on their ministry for the Lord.

1. The disciples were equipped (v.7).
2. The disciples were instructed (vv.8-13).

1 (6:7) **Disciples—Ministers**: Christ equipped the disciples. He did not send them out unprepared and unequipped.

a. Christ called His disciples "unto Him" (Mk.3:13; 6:7). He called them "that they should be with Him, that He might [later] send them forth to preach" (Mk.3:14. See note—Mk.3:14-15 for a detailed discussion.)

This was the very method Christ used to equip His disciples: the method of *attachment* or the method of *discipleship.* Christ simply called men to *be with Him*: to walk and associate with Him, to follow and live in His presence. By being "*with Him,*" they would see how He walked with God and ministered to people. They would begin to absorb and assimilate His very character and behavior. They would begin to be like Him, and in becoming like Him, they would begin to follow Him and to serve Him more and more. (See note—Mt.28:19-20 for a detailed discussion on Christ's method of discipleship.)

b. Christ sent His disciples forth two by two. There are at least two reasons for doing this.

1) Every word was to be established (confirmed, upheld) in the mouth of two witnesses (Mt.18:16).
2) The two would provide company for each other and be able to more easily face trials together. They could encourage, support, and strengthen each other.

c. Christ gave His disciples great power. Note that power over unclean spirits is all that is mentioned (see Mk.3:15). However, the power "to heal all manner of sickness and all manner of disease" and "to preach the kingdom of God" was also given (see Mt.10:1; Lu.9:1-2). Why then does Mark concentrate only on the power over evil spirits? The reason seems to be twofold.

1) Mark is writing to the Gentiles, a people...
   - who did not glorify God as God.
   - who were not thankful to God.
   - who had become vain in their imaginations.
   - who had hearts that were foolish and darkened.
   - who professed themselves to be wise, but were fools.
   - who changed the glory of God into images such as corruptible man, and birds, and four-footed beasts, and creeping things.
   - who were unclean through the lusts of their own hearts.
   - who dishonored their own bodies between themselves.
   - who changed the truth of God into a lie.
   - who worshipped and served the creature more than the Creator.
   - who were given over to vile affections.
   - whose women changed the natural use into that which is against nature.
   - whose men left the natural use of the woman, and burned in their lust one toward another.
   - who did not like to retain God in their knowledge.
   - who had reprobate minds.
   - who did those things that are degrading and immoral (see Ro.1:21-28).

Very simply and clearly stated, Mark was writing to a people filled with all kinds of evil, a people who were *subject* to being controlled by all kinds of evil spirits. Gentile society needed to be aware of the unclean spirits among them and their need to be cleansed of such uncleanness and evil.

"Being filled with all unrighteousness, fornication, wickedness, covetousness, maliciousness; full of envy, murder, debate, deceit, malignity; whisperers, backbiters, haters of God, despiteful, proud, boasters, inventors of evil things, disobedient to parents, without understanding, covenantbreakers, without natural affection, implacable, unmerciful" (Ro.1:29-31).

2) Mark focuses upon the central purpose of Christ: to conquer the *spirit of evil* and to *destroy the works of the devil*, especially in the hearts and lives of men.

"Now is the judgment of this world: now shall the prince of this world be cast out" (Jn.12:31).

"And having spoiled principalities and powers, he made a show of them openly, triumphing over them in it" (Col.2:15).

"He that committeth sin is of the devil; for the devil sinneth from the beginning. For this purpose the Son of God was manifested, that he might destroy the works of the devil" (1 Jn.3:8).

2 (6:8-13) **Minister, Life of—Believers, Life-Style—Healing, Oil**: Christ instructed the disciples. He gave them five specific instructions.

a. The disciples were to live in utter simplicity and humility (v.8-9). Christ spelled out exactly what He meant by this.

⇒ They were to take a staff only, that is, a walking staff.
⇒ They were to take no scrip or wallet, no bread, and no money in their purse.
⇒ They were to wear sandals for protection and coolness and comfort of the feet.
⇒ They were not to wear two coats, for this would display extravagant and wasteful living.

Thought 1. The whole idea is that the servant of God is to live simply and humbly just as ordinary folk live. The servant is not to be extravagant and flamboyant, worldly and materialistic-minded, indulgent and fleshy. There are four critical reasons for this instruction.

1) The Lord's servant is to "seek...and set his affection on things above, not on things on the earth" (Col.3:1-2). He is to be *heavenly minded*, so that men will know there is a far better life and land than what this earth offers (see Heb.11:13-16, 24-26).

"For they that are after the flesh do mind the things of the flesh; but they that are after the Spirit the things of the Spirit. For to be carnally minded is death; but to be spiritually minded is life and peace" (Ro.8:5-6).

2) The Lord's servant is to have his mind centered on *preaching the gospel and ministering* to people, not on material things such as money, land, clothes, the best food, buying and selling, and accumulating.

"Preach the word; be instant in season, out of season; reprove, rebuke, exhort with all longsuffering and doctrine" (2 Ti.4:2).

3) The Lord's servant (as he labors and serves) is to demonstrate trust in God for his needs, so that others might learn to depend upon God (Mt.6:24-34).

"But seek ye first the kingdom of God, and his righteousness; and all these things shall be added unto you" (Mt.6:33).

4) The Lord's servant is to teach and depend upon God's people to provide for him (see Mt.10:9-10).

"Do ye not know that they which minister about holy things live of the things of the temple? and they which wait at the altar are partakers with the altar? Even so hath the Lord ordained that they which preach the gospel should live of the gospel" (1 Co.9:13-14).

b. The disciples were to show stability and settledness (v.10). When they entered a town and found a host, they were to remain with that host and not be moving about from place to place. They were not to seek more comfort and luxury as they came to know a place

Thought 1. There are several good reasons for this instruction. (See note—Mt.10:11 for the kind of host to seek.)
(1) Favoring some hosts over others would indicate favoritism and cause jealousy.
(2) Favoring some hosts over others would indicate a selfish, materialistic, and soft mind and would lead to the questioning of the disciple's commitment.
(3) Favoring some hosts over others would distract from the disciple's purpose and ministry.
(4) Favoring some hosts over others would hurt and often alienate the first host and others in the congregation.

c. The disciples were to reject any who were not hospitable and receptive (v.11). (See note, pts. 3, 4—Mt.10:12-15 for a detailed discussion.)

d. The disciples were to preach repentance (v.12). The disciples were not to preach their own message or ideas, not what they thought or believed. They were heralds...

- men who represented the King.
- men who were given the message of the King.
- men who were to proclaim the message of the King.

Thought 1. The message was that men should repent. Men should change their lives from the way they were living. (See DEEPER STUDY # 1, *Repentance*—Ac.17:29-30.)

> **"I tell you, Nay: but, except ye repent, ye shall all likewise perish" (Lu.13:3).**
> **"Then Peter said unto them, Repent, and be baptized every one of you in the name of Jesus Christ for the remission of sins, and ye shall receive the gift of the Holy Ghost" (Ac.2:38).**
> **"Repent ye therefore, and be converted, that your sins may be blotted out, when the times of refreshing shall come from the presence of the Lord" (Ac.3:19).**
> **"Repent therefore of this thy wickedness, and pray God, if perhaps the thought of thine heart may be forgiven thee" (Ac.8:22).**
> **"Let the wicked forsake his way, and the unrighteous man his thoughts: and let him return unto the LORD, and he will have mercy upon him; and to our God, for he will abundantly pardon" (Is.55:7).**
> **"But if the wicked will turn from all his sins that he hath committed, and keep all my statutes, and do that which is lawful and right, he shall surely live, he shall not die" (Eze.18:21).**
> **"Cast away from you all your transgressions, whereby ye have transgressed; and make you a new heart and a new spirit: for why will ye die?" (Eze.18:31).**

e. The disciples were to minister to the evil-possessed and the sick (v.13). Note they were to minister to both body and soul. They were to liberate the soul from evil spirits, delivering those who were so clearly gripped by the bondage of sin and shame. They were also to minister to those sick in body, those who were suffering and hurting.

Note: they "anointed with oil many that were sick." This is the anointing spoken of in James (see note—Js.5:14-15).

1) Oil is a symbol of the Holy Spirit, of His presence. The oil helps the sick person to focus and concentrate upon the presence of the Holy Spirit and His power. It is often difficult for a sick person to focus and concentrate. This is especially true with those who are hurting and suffering, racked with excruciating pain. It is also true of those with jerky and short attention spans. The oil—its presence and placement upon the body—helps the sick person focus and concentrate upon the Holy Spirit, His presence and power.
2) Oil is a symbol of God's care, comfort, and joy, of His mercy to us. It is the oil of gladness. Therefore, oil actually focuses the attention and stirs the sick person to believe in God's mercy. The focused attention and stirred faith helps to fill the person's heart with gladness.

> **"Thou lovest righteousness, and hatest wickedness: therefore God, thy God, hath anointed thee with the oil of gladness above thy fellows" (Ps.45:7).**
> **"Thou hast loved righteousness, and hated iniquity; therefore God, even thy God, hath anointed thee with the oil of gladness above thy fellows" (He.1:9).**

1. People's opinions about Jesus: Word spread as the disciples preached, vv.7, 30f
- a. Herod: Thought Jesus was John the Baptist risen from the dead
- b. Others: Thought Jesus was Elijah or a prophet

2. Herod's reaction to Jesus: He had a guilty conscience
- a. Because of several illegal acts
  - 1) Imprisoning a just man
  - 2) Stealing his half-brother's wife
  - 3) Committing adultery
- b. Because of an inadequate religion*DS1*
- c. Because of a partying, drunken spirit*DS2*

B. The Death of John the Baptist: The Immoral Vs. the Righteous, 6:14-29

(Mt. 14:1-14; Lu. 9:7-9)

14 And king Herod heard
of him; (for his name was
spread abroad:) and he said,
That John the Baptist was
risen from the dead, and
therefore mighty works do
show forth themselves in
him.
15 Others said, That it is
Elias. And others said, That it
is a prophet, or as one of the
prophets.
16 But when Herod heard
thereof, he said, It is John,
whom I beheaded: he is risen
from the dead.
17 For Herod himself had
sent forth and laid hold upon
John, and bound him in prison for Herodias' sake, his
brother Philip's wife: for he
had married her.
18 For John had said unto
Herod, It is not lawful for
thee to have thy brother's
wife.
19 Therefore Herodias had a
quarrel against him, and
would have killed him; but
she could not:
20 For Herod feared John,
knowing that he was a just
man and an holy, and ob-
served him; and when he
heard him, he did many
things, and heard him gladly.
21 And when a convenient
day was come, that Herod on
his birthday made a supper to
his lords, high captains, and
chief estates of Galilee;
22 And when the daughter
of the said Herodias came in,
and danced, and pleased
Herod and them that sat with
him, the king said unto the
damsel, Ask of me whatsoever thou wilt, and I will give it
thee.
23 And he sware unto her,
Whatsoever thou shalt ask of
me, I will give it thee, unto
the half of my kingdom.
24 And she went forth, and
said unto her mother, What
shall I ask? And she said,
The head of John the Bap-
tist.
25 And she came in straightway with haste unto the king,
and asked, saying, I will that
thou give me by and by in a
charger the head of John the
Baptist.
26 And the king was ex-
ceeding sorry; yet for his
oath's sake, and for their
sakes which sat with him, he
would not reject her.
27 And immediately the king
sent an executioner, and
commanded his head to be
brought: and he went and
beheaded him in the prison,
28 And brought his head in
a charger, and gave it to the
damsel: and the damsel gave
it to her mother.
29 And when his disciples
heard of it, they came and
took up his corpse, and laid it
in a tomb.

- d. Because of seeking social approval*DS3*
  - 1) Herod gave in to his fleshly desires
  - 2) Salome conformed to the world with her indecent apparel & lewd dancing
- e. Because of reckless oaths

3. Salome's reaction to Herod: Weakness & an immature dependence upon her mother

4. Herodias' reaction to John: A vengeful spirit, v.19
- a. Used Salome to strike back at John
- b. Requested the head of John the Baptist on a platter

5. Herod's reaction to Salome's request: The king regretted his foolish oath, but feared men more than God
- a. The executioner beheaded John immediately
- b. Herodias received what she asked for: She took a man's life to cover her sinful behavior

6. The disciple's reaction to John's death: He was a courageous martyr, loyal to the Messiah to the end

DIVISION IV

THE SON OF GOD'S TRAINING MINISTRY: JESUS' INTENSIVE PREPARATION OF THE DISCIPLES, 6:7-8:26

B. The Death of John the Baptist: The Immoral vs. the Righteous, 6:14-29

(6:14-29) **Introduction—Herod**: the preaching of the disciples throughout Galilee reached the ears of Herod. Herod heard about Jesus and the news troubled and disturbed him, apparently causing some spiritual conviction. Why? The reason is contained in this passage, a passage that pictures *The Immoral vs. the Righteous*.

1. People's opinions about Jesus: word spread as the disciples preached (vv.14-15).
2. Herod's reaction to Jesus: he had a guilty conscience (vv.16-23).
3. Salome's reaction to Herod: weakness and an immature dependence upon her mother (vv.24-25).
4. Herodias' reaction to John: a vengeful spirit (v.25).
5. Herod's reaction to Salome's request: the king regretted his foolish oath, but feared men more than God (vv.26-28).
6. The disciple's reaction to John's death: he was a courageous martyr, loyal to the Messiah to the end (v.29).

1 (6:14-15) **Jesus Christ, Opinions of**: the opinions about Jesus spread like wildfire as the disciples preached (see v.7, 30f). Herod heard all about what was going on. He heard about a man called Jesus who preached righteousness and who worked enormous miracles. Herod was again stricken in conscience. He was living such an immoral and murderous life that He could not escape the guilt, especially when a righteous person appeared on the scene. At first, when he heard about Jesus and His phenomenal works, he was perplexed. He had known only one man who was so righteous that he was able to do mighty works, and that was John. Therefore, Herod concluded that John the Baptist had "risen from the dead," that is, risen in the body of Jesus Christ. However, others believed and told Herod that it was not John, but Elijah or one of the other prophets (see note—Mk.8:28 for discussion). As will be seen, Herod refused to believe it was anyone other than John the Baptist.

2 (6:16-23) **Herod—Guilt**: Herod's reaction to Jesus was that of a guilty conscience. The man lived a life of gross sin, immorality, and murder—including the murder of God's prophet, John the Baptist.

Herod had a guilty conscience because of several illegal acts. He had imprisoned a just and innocent man, John the Baptist, because John had been preaching against the kind of life Herod was living. Herod had married the daughter of Aretas, King of the Nabataean Arabs. On a trip to Rome, he had visited his half-brother and was deeply attracted to his wife, Herodias. He seduced her and talked her into returning with him. Herod's own wife discovered his plans and fled to her father, King Aretas. Two serious sins were committed by Herod. He had put away his own wife (her life was probably threatened), and he had stolen the wife of his half-brother. It was against such immorality that John preached (see DEEPER STUDY # 1,2—Mt:14:1-14 for detailed discussion and thoughts).

DEEPER STUDY # 1
(6:20) **Herod—Religion, Inadequate**: Herod had a guilty conscience because of an inadequate religion. Herod had a sensitive conscience; he was not totally hardened against the truth of righteousness. He kept John alive for a little over a year. He recognized something in John, something that drew him and caused him to want to hear what John had to say, and apparently he even tried to observe and do some of the things John preached. (How many try to do some of the things the preacher says?) However, whatever religious works Herod did, they were inadequate. As every genuine believer knows, religion is never adequate. Only a personal relationship with God suffices and meets the need of the human soul. Herod was inconsistent, loving the world and its things more than God and His righteousness.

"Wherefore come out from among them, and be ye separate, saith the Lord, and touch not the unclean thing; and I will receive you, and will be a Father unto you, and ye shall be my sons and daughters, saith the Lord Almighty" (2 Co.6:17-18).

"Love not the world, neither the things that are in the world. If any man love the world, the love of the Father is not in him. For all that is in the world, the lust of the flesh, and lust of the eyes, and the pride of life, is not of the Father, but is of the world" (1 Jn.2:15-16).

DEEPER STUDY # 2
(6:21-22) **Herod—Partying**: Herod had a guilty conscience because of a partying, drunken spirit. An example of this is seen in the event recorded in this passage. He apparently followed the Greek custom of celebrating special events with lavish feasts, heavy drinking, and suggestive and passionate dancing. (See note—Mt.14:6-8 for detailed discussion.)

Thought 1. What a scene! So much like our day and time; in fact, so much like so many generations!

"Neither yield ye your members as instruments of unrighteousness unto sin: but yield yourselves unto God, as those that are alive from the dead, and your members as instruments of righteousness unto God" (Ro.6:13).

DEEPER STUDY # 3
(6:22) **Herod—Passion**: Herod had a guilty conscience because of seeking social approval above godly honor and respect. When he was full of drink, he was stirred with such lust and passion for his step-daughter that he offered her anything, even half his kingdom. Herod's marred judgment and foolishness were seen in the *reckless offer* to his step-daughter. He was foolish to think that he had to keep a wicked and dishonorable oath or else lose favor with his friends and associates. (See DEEPER STUDY # 1—Mt.14:1-14 for detailed discussion.)

Thought 1. How often people use parties and drinking events to seek social approval! How often social approval is sought by reckless and foolish behavior—ranging from too much drink, suggestive movement of the body in dance, suggestive conversation; and, as in Herod's case, all of these.

Thought 2. Why does so much irresponsible, loose, and sinful behavior take place at drinking and dancing events?
⇒ A person needs social approval and acceptance.
⇒ A person has low self-esteem and needs to fit in.
⇒ A person fears disapproval, unacceptance, and rejection.

"Ye adulterers and adulteresses, know ye not that the friendship of the world is enmity with God? whosoever therefore will be a friend of the world is the enemy of God" (Js.4:4).

"And take heed to yourselves, lest at any time your hearts be overcharged with surfeiting, and drunkenness, and cares of this life, and so that day come upon you unawares" (Lu.21:34).

3 (6:24-25) **Worldliness—Immaturity—Salome**: Salome's reaction to John was weakness of character. This is seen in two acts.

a. She sought social approval and conformity (v.22). Her dress apparel was bound to be what the dancing girls wore at dancing and drinking parties. Socially acceptable dress exposed certain parts of the body and was worn to attract attention and to cause the gaping of others. Salome's dance borders on the incredible because she was of the royal family. The fact that she would dance so suggestively is a sad picture of her character.

Thought 1. What a lesson on the effect of dress and dancing and drinking parties!

"In like manner also, that women adorn themselves in modest apparel, with shamefacedness and sobriety; not with broided hair, of gold, or pearls, or costly array" (1 Ti.2:9).

"Whose adorning let it not be that outward adorning of plaiting the hair, and of wearing of gold, or of putting on of apparel" (1 Pe.3:3; see Is.3:16-24).

b. She had an immature dependence upon her mother (v.24). Apparently, Salome's behavior was instigated by her mother, Herodias. Salome's age is not known, but she could not have been just a child; she could not have been underage. To have danced a solo dance at a social event indicates that she was at least a young woman. She was of age, personally responsible for her decisions. But note how heavily influenced she was by her mother, both in dancing and in seeking what to ask as a reward. She was immature in both spirit and personal responsibility. She did not have the ability to make right decisions. She was easily led into irresponsible and sinful behavior, lacking self-esteem and a strong spirit.

"And he [Ahaziah] did evil in the sight of the LORD, and walked in the way of his father, and in the way of his mother, and in the way of Jeroboam the son of Nebat, who made Israel to sin: for he served Baal, and worshipped him, and provoked to anger the LORD God of Israel, according to all that his father had done" (1 K.22:52-53).

"He [Ahaziah] also walked in the ways of the house of Ahab: for his mother was his counselor to do wickedly" (2 Chr.22:3).

"But have walked after the imagination of their own heart, and after Baalim, which their fathers taught them" (Je.9:14).

"I will not turn away the punishment thereof; because they have despised the law of the LORD, and have not kept his commandments, and their lies caused them to err, after the which their fathers have walked" (Am. 2:4).

"But I said unto their children in the wilderness, Walk ye not in the statutes of your fathers, neither observe their judgments, nor defile yourselves with their idols: I am the LORD your God; walk in my statutes, and keep my judgments, and do them" (Eze.20:18-19).

Thought 1. Salome is a picture of so many today who lack self-esteem and a strong spirit, of many who sense a great need to fit in. Therefore, they give in to the immoral and sinful suggestions and lusts of others.

"Wherefore come out from among them, and be ye separate, saith the Lord, and touch not the unclean thing; and I will receive you, and will be a Father unto you, and ye shall be my sons and daughters, saith the Lord Almighty" (2 Co.6:17-18).

"Thou shalt not follow a multitude to do evil; neither shalt thou speak in a cause to decline after many to wrest judgment" (Ex.23:2).

4 (6:24-25) **Vengeance—Sin, Love of—Herodias**: Herodias' reaction to John was a vengeful spirit (vv.19, 24). Her bitterness and her desire to humiliate John are clearly seen in verses 18-19. John's preaching against immorality angered her tremendously. She wanted him dead, and apparently she plotted this whole event hoping to trap Herod into executing John. Herodias' life is a picture of vengeance and its causes.

a. She *wanted to live as she wished* and not be told how to live by anyone else—not by the king nor by the righteous and certainly not by God.

b. She *wanted to sin without interference* and without being reminded of it. She wanted everything and everyone removed out of her presence that reminded her that she was sinning.

c. She *ignored God*, His law and demand for accountability. She ignored the message of God and His righteousness. She ignored the fact that she had to meet God after death.

"And as it is appointed unto men once to die, but after this the judgment" (He.9:27).

"He that saith he is in the light, and hateth his brother, is in darkness even until now" (1 Jn.2:9).

"Whosoever hateth his brother is a murderer: and ye know that no murderer hath eternal life abiding in him" (1 Jn.3:15).

5 (6:26-28) **Herod—Pride**: Herod's reaction to Salome's request was one of regret. He had a guilty conscience because of his fear of what men might say. This is seen in v.26: "For their sakes which sat with him, he would not reject her." Herod had made a foolish promise. Now he was faced with keeping a wicked oath or breaking one of God's major laws: "Thou shalt not kill." His pride prevented him from confessing his error. He feared being shamed and embarrassed by a woman's tantrums before his guests and being the object of ridicule in their jokes. He knew what he should do, but in *pride and weakness* before men, he buckled under to a terrible sin. (See DEEPER STUDY # 1—Mt.14:1-14 for a detailed discussion.)

> **"And be not conformed to this world: but be ye transformed by the renewing of your mind, that ye may prove what is that good, and acceptable, and perfect, will of God" (Ro.12:2).**

6 (6:29) **Faithfulness—Dedication**: the disciples' reaction to John's death was that he was courageous and loyal to the Messiah to the end. John stood firm for God. He preached righteousness while languishing in the rat- and roach-infested prison for a year and a half. He was savagely killed as a martyr for the cause of righteousness. (See notes—Mt.14:10-14 for detailed discussion and application.)

> **"And in nothing terrified by your adversaries: which is to them an evident token of perdition, but to you of salvation, and that of God" (Ph.1:28).**
>
> **"The LORD is on my side; I will not fear: what can man do unto me?" (Ps.118:6).**
>
> **"Behold, God is my salvation; I will trust, and not be afraid: for the Lord JEHOVAH is my strength and my song; he also is become my salvation" (Is.12:2).**
>
> **"Fear none of those things which thou shalt suffer: behold, the devil shall cast some of you into prison, that ye may be tried; and ye shall have tribulation ten days: be thou faithful unto death, and I will give thee a crown of life" (Re.2:10).**

C. The Need for Rest & Its Dangers, 6:30-34
(Lu. 9:10; Jn. 6:1-4)

1. The setting: The disciples returned from their mission
   a. Reported what they had done
   b. Reported what they had taught

30 And the apostles gathered themselves together unto Jesus, and told him all things, both what they had done, and what they had taught.

2. The 1st danger: Not taking time to rest
   a. The disciples were working long & hard
   b. The disciples were pressed by the crowds
   c. The disciples left to rest

31 And he said unto them, Come ye yourselves apart into a desert place, and rest a while: for there were many coming and going, and they had no leisure so much as to eat.
32 And they departed into a desert place by ship privately.

3. The 2nd danger: Taking too much time to rest when people are seeking help

33 And the people saw them departing, and many knew him, and ran afoot thither out of all cities, and outwent them, and came together unto him.

4. The 3rd danger: Losing sight of people who are as sheep without a shepherd
   a. Jesus saw the people & had compassion
   b. Jesus began to teach

34 And Jesus, when he came out, saw much people, and was moved with compassion toward them, because they were as sheep not having a shepherd: and he began to teach them many things.

DIVISION IV

THE SON OF GOD'S TRAINING MINISTRY:JESUS' INTENSIVE PREPARATION OF THE DISCIPLES, 6:7-8:26

C. The Need for Rest and Its Dangers, 6:30-34

(6:30-34) **Introduction—Rest**: every person needs rest, relaxation, and time alone with God. However, when the believer is seeking to rest, he must know there are some serious dangers that confront him. This passage shows three of the dangers.

1. The setting: the disciples returned from their mission (v.30).
2. The first danger: not taking time to rest (vv.31-32).
3. The second danger: taking too much time to rest when people are seeking help (v.33).
4. The third danger: losing sight of people who are as sheep without a shepherd (v.34).

[1] (6:30) **Disciples—Ministers**: the disciples returned from their mission and reported to Jesus. They reported two things: what they had done and what they had taught. How they had lived and what they had taught were both of vital interest to Christ. He had given them precise instructions in both areas. This report would reveal their obedience to Him, the degree of commitment and effectiveness of each disciple. Jesus needed to know, for the salvation of the world depended on their lives and teaching. He was soon to leave all in their hands.

> **Thought 1.** Believers are accountable both for how they live and for what they teach. They are to be obedient to Christ—living exactly as He has said and teaching exactly what He has said to teach. Every disciple is held accountable to God (2 Co.5:10; He.13:17).

> **Thought 2.** A disciple should live and teach so that he can share anything with the Lord. He should have nothing to hide or of which to be ashamed.

[2] (6:31-32) **Rest—Devotion**: the first danger is not taking time to rest. The disciples were extremely tired. They had gone forth for the Lord and carried out His mission, and it had exhausted them. Since returning, the demanding crowds surrounding Jesus were pressing in upon them. They barely had time to make their reports, much less rest and meditate. Therefore, Jesus suggested they go apart into a desert place and get alone with God for awhile. Note several things.

a. It was both the work of the ministry and the demands of the crowd that taxed the disciples' energy.

> **Thought 1.** It is not work alone that tires the body. Responsibility and the weight of it create pressure and tax one's energy. Just the presence of a demanding crowd is a reminder that one is responsible to work.

b. The disciples had bodies that naturally required some relief from pressure and rest from labor.

> **"And I said, Oh that I had wings like a dove! for then would I fly away, and be at rest. Lo, then would I wander far off, and remain in the wilderness" (Ps.55:6-7).**

c. The disciples had spirits that required some extended periods alone with God in meditation, study, and prayer. They had to receive from God in order to share the presence and message of God. They had to be still and listen, giving God opportunity to share with them. They had to be recharged before they could charge.

> **"Now therefore stand still, that I may reason with you before the Lord of all the righteous acts of the Lord, which he did to you and to your fathers" (1 S.12:7).**
> **"Hearken unto this, O Job: stand still, and consider the wondrous works of God" (Jb.37:14).**

"The LORD is my shepherd; I shall not want. He maketh me to lie down in green pastures: he leadeth me beside the still waters" (Ps.23:1-2).

"This is the rest wherewith ye may cause the weary to rest; and this is the refreshing: yet they would not hear" (Is.28:12).

d. The disciples needed a quiet, deserted place to get alone with God—not a place where others were, not a place of business, of commercialism, of fine accommodations.

e. The Lord cared about them; He cared about their exhaustion. They had poured themselves into His mission and into the lives of people. He knew they needed rest and rekindling, refuge and consoling, relaxation and worship. He had compassion upon them, so He said, "Come ye apart...and rest a while."

"Come unto me, all ye that labour and are heavy laden, and I will give you rest" (Mt.11:28).

"And he said, My presence shall go with thee, and I will give thee rest" (Ex.33:14).

"Six days thou shalt work, but on the seventh day thou shalt rest: in earing time and in harvest thou shalt rest" (Ex.34:21).

"Six days shall work be done: but the seventh day is the sabbath of rest, a holy convocation; ye shall do no work therein: it is the sabbath of the LORD in all your dwellings" (Le.23:3).

"Be still, and know that I am God: I will be exalted among the heathen, I will be exalted in the earth" (Ps.46:10).

"Surely I have behaved and quieted myself, as a child that is weaned of his mother: my soul is even as a weaned child" (Ps.131:2).

"But whoso hearkeneth unto me shall dwell safely, and shall be quiet from fear of evil" (Pr.1:33).

3 (6:33) **Rest**: the second danger is taking too much time to rest. People are desperately seeking help; therefore, the believer must take only the time needed to rest his body and spirit, no more, no less. The scene was dramatic. The people saw where Jesus and the disciples were heading. They began to run by foot around the lake. As they ran, they passed through the cities shouting excitedly the news that Jesus was nearby. Throngs of people joined in the streaming mass of humanity making its way around the lake. By the time they reached the place where Jesus' ship was to dock, the crowd had grown to five thousand men not counting women and children.

This is the crucial point: the disciples needed rest. They knew it and Jesus knew it, yet here was the demanding crowd. They were interfering and keeping the disciples from their much needed rest. The disciples became irritated and soon wanted the people sent away. (This is seen by their request in v.36 and the rude way they asked the question in v.37.) However, Jesus knew something. The disciples had rested some coming across the lake. The sea, their old stomping ground, had relaxed them a great deal. That was sufficient to carry the disciples through another session of ministry. It was a matter of just how exhausted the human body *really* was vs. the needs of the people. In this particular case, the disciples were ready to act selfishly and take too much rest, thereby neglecting the people.

Thought 1. There is a time to minister just as there is a time to spend alone with God. There is a time to work just as there is a time to pray. There is a time to get up and get to it just as there is a time to rest and relax.

"And the work of righteousness shall be peace; and the effect of righteousness, quietness and assurance for ever" (Is.32:17).

Thought 2. Unfortunately, many have the problem of resting and relaxing too much instead of working too much. Some even spend too much time in what they call Bible study, prayer, and fellowship with God and neglect being out among the people enough. While on this earth, fellowship with God is primarily to prepare us to go out and minister.

"I must work the works of him that sent me, while it is day: the night cometh, when no man can work" (Jn.9:4).

"For we cannot but speak the things which we have seen and heard" (Ac.4:20).

"Necessity is laid upon me; yea, woe is unto me, if I preach not the gospel!" (1 Co.9:16).

"For Zion's sake will I not hold my peace, and for Jerusalem's sake I will not rest, until the righteousness thereof go forth as brightness, and the salvation thereof as a lamp that burneth" (Is.62:1).

"Then I said, I will not make mention of him, nor speak any more in his name. But his word was in mine heart as a burning fire shut up in my bones, and I was weary with forbearing, and I could not stay" (Je.20:9).

4 (6:34) **Shepherd—Sheep**: the third danger is losing sight of people who are as sheep without a shepherd. Again the scene is descriptive. As the boat approached the shore, Jesus stood in the boat watching the multitude clamoring for space on the seashore. He needed rest, and the disciples needed rest even more. But He was not annoyed or irritated with the people. Contrariwise, He was moved with deep, intense compassion because the people were as sheep without a shepherd. He could not turn from them. He could not send them away despite the need for rest. He could do only one thing. He had to meet their need; He had to teach them, so He began "to teach them many things."

Note: when Jesus saw the multitude, He said, "They were as sheep without a shepherd." He meant at least three things by this statement. (See notes—Jn.10:1-6; 10:11-18. See Is.53:6.)

a. Sheep without a shepherd are bewildered and wander about, not knowing where they are or where they are going. They get lost ever so easily and cannot find their way back to the flock. So it is with people. People without the shepherd, the Lord Jesus Christ, are bewildered. They do not know where they have come from, where they are going, nor why they are where they are. They wander about, getting lost in place after place, never finding the way to true life (see note and DEEPER STUDY # 1—Lu.15:4).

> **"But when he saw the multitides, he was moved with compassion on them, because they fainted, and were scattered abroad, as sheep having no shepherd" (Mt.9:36).**
> **"Jesus saith unto him, I am the way, the truth, and the life: no man cometh unto the Father, but by me" (Jn.14:6).**
> **"For ye were as sheep going astray; but are now returned unto the Shepherd and Bishop of your souls" (1 Pe.2:25).**
> **"My people hath been lost sheep: their shepherds have caused them to go astray, they have turned them away on the mountains: they have forgotten their resting place" (Je.50:6).**
> **"My sheep wandered through all the mountains, and upon every high hill: yea, my flock was scattered upon all the face of the earth, and none did search or seek after them" (Eze.34:6).**

b. Sheep without a shepherd go hungry. They do not have adequate nourishment. They cannot find sufficient food to live. So it is with people. People without the Shepherd, the Lord Jesus Christ, go hungry. They do not have the Shepherd of God to feed and inspire their souls nor to satisfy their inner longings for peace, love, and joy (Ga.5:22-23). They have only themselves to depend upon as they seek to meet their craving for life. They have only themselves in seeking the answer to...

- purpose
- direction
- assurance
- loneliness
- emptiness
- disturbance
- depression
- sickness
- death

> **"And Jesus said unto them, I am the bread of life: he that cometh to me shall never hunger; and he that believeth on me shall never thirst" (Jn.6:35).**
> **"I am the living bread which came down from heaven: if any man eat of this bread, he shall live for ever: and the bread that I will give is my flesh, which I will give for the life of the world" (Jn.6:51).**

c. Sheep without a shepherd cannot find shelter or safety. The sheep are exposed to all the dangers of the wilderness (see note 3—Lu.15:4). So it is with people. People without the Shepherd, the Lord Jesus Christ, are exposed to all that is within the world, and they are doomed. They are doomed because the beasts, the temptations and trials of the world, attack at every opportunity and destroy all who wander about. (See outlines and notes—Jn.10:1-18; DEEPER STUDY # 3—10:27-29 for more discussion and application.)

> **"Be sober, be vigilant; because your adversary the devil, as a roaring lion, walketh about, seeking whom he may devour" (1 Pe.5:8).**
> **"Be merciful unto me, O God, be merciful unto me: for my soul trusteth in thee: yea, in the shadow of thy wings will I make my refuge, until these calamities be overpast" (Ps.57:1).**
> **"He that dwelleth in the secret place of the most High shall abide under the shadow of the Almighty" (Ps.91:1; see Ps.61:1-4; 91:1-6).**

	D. The Attitudes Toward Human Need & Resources, 6:35-44 *(Mt. 14:15-21; Lu. 9:11-17; Jn. 6:1-15)*	knew, they say, Five, and two fishes. 39 And he commanded them to make all sit down by companies upon the green grass.	c. Organizing to use what resources one has
1. Two attitudes toward human need a. Individual responsibility: The disciples wanted the people sent away, wanted to be responsible only for their own welfare	35 And when the day was now far spent, his disciples came unto him, and said, This is a desert place, and now the time is far passed: 36 Send them away, that they may go into the country round about, and into the villages, and buy themselves bread: for they have nothing to eat.	40 And they sat down in ranks, by hundreds, and by fifties. 41 And when he had taken the five loaves and the two fishes, he looked up to heaven, and blessed, and brake the loaves, and gave them to his disciples to set before them; and the two fishes divided he among them all.	d. Being thankful for what one has & can give e. Giving what one has
b. Corporate responsibility: Jesus wanted the disciples to feel responsible **2. Six attitudes toward resources** a. Questioning one's ability to give b. Checking to see what one can give	37 He answered and said unto them, Give ye them to eat. And they say unto him, Shall we go and buy two hundred pennyworth of bread, and give them to eat? 38 He saith unto them, How many loaves have ye? go and see. And when they	42 And they did all eat, and were filled. 43 And they took up twelve baskets full of the fragments, and of the fishes. 44 And they that did eat of the loaves were about five thousand men.	f. Being careful in the handling of resources

DIVISION IV

THE SON OF GOD'S TRAINING MINISTRY: JESUS' INTENSIVE PREPARATION OF THE DISCIPLES, 6:7-8:26

D. The Attitudes Toward Human Need and Resources, 6:35-44

(6:35-44) **Introduction**: this event is of critical importance. The feeding of five thousand is the *only miracle* recorded by all four gospel writers. The apostles were deeply affected by the miracle. It made a dramatic and lasting impact upon them.

The miracle has to do with what is so close to God's heart: human need. Christ deals with our attitudes toward human need. He is concerned with how we handle our resources, with how we go about meeting the needs that confront us. The lesson is powerful (see outline and notes—Mt.14:15-21; Lu.9:10-17; Jn.6:1-15).

1. Two attitudes toward human need (vv.35-37).
2. Six attitudes toward resources (vv.37-44).

(6:35-44) **Another Outline**: What Christ Does with What Is Given to Him.

1. He thanks God for it (v.41).
2. He blesses it (v.41).
3. He breaks it (v.41).
4. He multiplies it (v.41).
5. He feeds with it (v.42).
6. He supplies more than enough (v.43).

1 (6:35-37) **Needs, Attitudes Toward—Stewardship**: there are two attitudes toward human need. Christ had been teaching for many hours, and now it was late afternoon, probably after 3 p.m. The disciples were exhausted and still wanted some rest. They came to Jesus and reminded Him of the time because there was little time left in the day for them to rest. They suggested, "Send the multitude away so they can go and buy food *for themselves*. But Jesus said, "No. You give them food to eat." In these words are seen the two attitudes toward human need.

a. There is the attitude of individual or personal responsibility. It is true that neither the disciples nor Jesus had invited the crowd. In fact, the crowd was not even wanted. The disciples and Jesus had planned something else. The crowd was interfering; therefore, the disciples sensed no responsibility for the crowd. They wanted to get rid of the people so they could be free to do as they wished. Their attitude was: "They are responsible for themselves, so send them away to fend for themselves."

b. There is the attitude of corporate responsibility. Jesus said very simply, "You give them food. They are hungry, and they are your neighbors, part of your world. You are responsible for your world and the people in it. If you know of people who have need, then you are the one who is responsible to help them. They may be irresponsible. They may not have been invited, and they may be interfering with your plans; but they have need, and you know about their need. So meet it. Feed them."

> **Thought 1.** Too many try to escape their responsibility for the world. When looking at or hearing about the poor and hungry, lonely and depressed, problem-centered and burdened, too many say: "Send them away. They got themselves into this mess because they were too lazy or irresponsible or sinful. If they wanted to be straight and responsible, they could. I'm too busy to become involved with such shiftless and irresponsible people."

Such an attitude misses the whole point of Christ. Man is responsible for his world, no matter the condition. We are responsible for our neighbors. In fact, the worse off a neighbor is, the more we are responsible to help. The cause of his condition does not matter: whether sin and shame, or clear and understandable circumstances.

⇒ If his condition is sin and shame, then we are to share the gospel and teach him how to live and work responsibly.

⇒ If his condition is due to clear and understandable circumstances, then we are to help restore and replace him to a position of responsibility and self-worth.

"Brethren, if a man be overtaken in a fault, ye which are spiritual, restore such an one in the spirit of meekness; considering thyself, lest thou also be tempted" (Ga.6:1).

2 (6:37-44) **Resources**: there are six attitudes toward resources. It takes resources to meet human need. In consideration of this, there is a fact that needs to be acknowledged. Every person has something he can give. Every person can help and do something to meet a need when a need confronts him. The problem is not lack of resources nor a lack of ability or money or time. The problem is attitude—attitude toward the resources which one has.

a. There is the attitude of questioning one's ability to give (v.37). Jesus had just said, "Give them food." The disciples were shocked and even disturbed with the instructions, for the crowd was enormous and the task *impossible*. They were already upset over the presence and burden of the crowd. Irritated, the disciples fired back at Jesus, "Shall we go and buy two hundred pennyworth of bread, and give them to eat?" This amounted to about six months' labor for the disciples. They did not have the money, so the request by Jesus was ridiculous to them. There was no way they could give food to meet the need of the crowd. But note something: the disciples forgot two things.

1) They forgot that they did have something. The need of the crowd in this instance was for food, and the disciples had food for themselves (or at least enough money to buy food for themselves). Yet, they did not think to mention this fact. They were thinking only of what excess, what above their own needs they had to give.
2) They forgot the power of God. They forgot that God loved and cared for these people as well as for them. They forgot that God would meet the needs of any and all, if only they would put what they had at His disposal. They forgot that God's power could take little and multiply it.

Thought 1. The widow's mite is an excellent application for this point.

"And Jesus sat over against the treasury, and beheld how the people cast money into the treasury: and many that were rich cast in much. And there came a certain poor widow, and she threw in two mites, which make a farthing. And he called unto him his disciples, and saith unto them, Verily I say unto you, that this poor widow hath cast more in, than all they which have cast into the treasury: for all they did cast in of their abundance; but she of her want did cast in all that she had, even all her living" (Mk.12:41-44).

"Give, and it shall be given unto you; good measure, pressed down, and shaken together, and running over, shall men give into your bosom. For with the same measure that ye mete withal it shall be measured to you again" (Lu.6:38).

"Honor the LORD with thy substance, and with the first fruits of all thine increase" (Pr.3:9).

b. There is the attitude of checking to see what one can give (v.38). In response to the disciples' impatience, Jesus remained cool, asking rather forcefully, "How many loaves have you? Go and see." The disciples checked and reported that they had five loaves of bread and two fish. Note two facts.

1) They had resources that were *overlooked.* Why were they overlooked? Because the resources were so little. There was no possibility the resources could ever meet the need. In fact, two fish and five loaves of bread could not even make a dent in the hunger of five thousand men. In the eyes of the disciples, it was impossible for the resources to do any good whatsoever.
2) Jesus did not ask the disciples to check on how to feed all five thousand men. He asked them to check on *what resources they had* to give. They were to look at what they themselves could give, not at how the whole task could be done. Their eyes and perspective were to be on using what they had, not on the mammoth impossibility of the task. This is a critical point, and it should be carefully noted when looking at the vast needs of the world.

Thought 1. We need to check and to search out every resource, every single thing we can give, no matter how small and insignificant. Every single thing can be used by God to help meet the need.

Thought 2. The need may be overwhelming. It may swamp and easily discourage us. The answer is what Christ is teaching. Set your eyes on what you can give and do, not on the impossibility of the task. Check up on yourself. Find out what resources you have and can give to *help* meet the need.

"Then the disciples, every man according to his ability, determined to send relief unto the brethren which dwelt in Judaea" (Ac.11:29).

"Upon the first day of the week let every one of you lay by him in store, as God hath prospered him, that there be no gatherings when I come" (1 Co.16:2).

"Every man shall give as he is able, according to the blessing of the LORD thy God which he hath given thee" (De.16:17).

c. There is the attitude of organizing what resources one has so that they might be used (vv.39-40). This is an important step Christ takes, and it should be well noted. The hour was late. Darkness was rapidly approaching. Distribution could have easily become a problem. The people had to be organized into small circles or rows which left room for the disciples to walk between them to distribute the food.

Thought 1. Our resources, whatever we give and do, should be used in an organized fashion. Organization, arrangement, and orderliness were always God's will in the meeting of needs and the handling of resources.

"Let all things be done decently and in order" (1 Co.14:40).

d. There is the attitude of being thankful for what one has and can give (v.41). What Jesus did was impressive. He took into His hands what they had, and He looked up to heaven and gave thanks for it. It was small; it was insignificant. It looked like it would do little, like it would be insignificant; but He took it anyway and *looked up to heaven and blessed it.*

Thought 1. What a tremendous lesson on attitude toward resources! No resource, no gift, no ability is too small. God should be thanked for whatever resource(s) we have, no matter how insignificant, unimpressive, or unattractive.

"The earth is the LORD'S, and the fulness thereof; the world, and they that dwell therein" (Ps.24:1).

"For every beast of the forest is mine, and the cattle upon a thousand hills" (Ps.50:10).

"The silver is mine, and the gold is mine, saith the LORD of hosts" (Hag.2:8).

e. There is the attitude of giving what one has (vv.41-42). After giving thanks, Jesus took the food and gave it to the disciples to set before the people. And a miracle happened! The resource multiplied: all the people were fed and were filled (v.42).

Thought 1. At least two lessons are seen in this act of Christ.

(1) We are to give what we have, no matter how small. We *are* to take *all* of what we have and give it to meet the need.

"I have showed you all things, how that so labouring ye ought to support the weak, and to remember the words of the Lord Jesus, how he said, It is more blessed to give than to receive" (Ac.20:35).

"Then said Jesus unto his disciples, If any man will come after me, let him deny himself, and take up his cross, and follow me. For whosoever will save his life shall lose it: and whosoever will lose his life for my sake shall find it" (Mt.16:24-25).

"Jesus said unto him, If thou wilt be perfect, go and sell that thou hast, and give to the poor, and thou shalt have treasure in heaven: and come and follow me" (Mt.19:21).

"But rather give alms of such things as ye have; and, behold, all things are clean unto you" (Lu.11:41).

"Sell that ye have, and give alms; provide yourselves bags which wax not old, a treasure in the heavens that faileth not, where no thief approacheth, neither moth corrupteth" (Lu.12:33).

"Charge them that are rich in this world, that they be not highminded, nor trust in uncertain riches, but in the living God, who giveth us richly all things to enjoy; that they do good, that they be rich in good works, ready to distribute, willing to communicate; laying up in store for themselves a good foundation against the time to come, that they may lay hold on eternal life" (1 Ti.6:17-19).

(2) Christ is *The Perfect Provider, The Perfect Supplier.* He takes what we give and multiplies it to meet the need.

"But seek ye first the kingdom of God, and his righteousness; and all these things shall be added unto you" (Mt.6:33).

Thought 2. Christ takes whatever is given to Him, and He multiplies its purpose, meaning, and significance.

f. There is the attitude of being careful in the handling of resources (vv.43-44). Very simply, Christ teaches that resources are not to be wasted. They are to be used day after day. When there is more than enough to meet one need, what is left over is to be gathered up to use elsewhere.

Thought 1. Note three lessons.

(1) There is no room in Christ's economy for extravagance. When there is more than what is needed, the excess is to be saved for another need.
(2) There is no room for wasting. No resource is to be wasted; it is to be used elsewhere.
(3) There is no room for resources to be stored and banked; there is not any excuse for allowing resources to lie around unused. All resources—abilities or money—are to be used to meet needs as long as needs exist (see notes—Mt.19:21-22; 19:23-26).

	E. Five Wise Lessons for Service, 6:45-52 *(Mt. 14:22-33; Jn. 6:16-21)*	walking upon the sea, and would have passed by them.	
		49 But when they saw him walking upon the sea, they supposed it had been a spirit, and cried out:	b. Their fear was horrifying c. Their cry was desperate
1. Lesson 1: Crowd excitement is not always wise	45 And straightway he constrained his disciples to get into the ship, and to go to the other side before unto Bethsaida, while he sent away the people.	50 For they all saw him, and were troubled. And immediately he talked with them, and saith unto them, Be of good cheer: it is I; be not afraid.	**4. Lesson 4: Receiving the presence of Jesus is wise**DS2 a. His presence erases fear
2. Lesson 2: Prayer after service is wise	46 And when he had sent them away, he departed into a mountain to pray.		
3. Lesson 3: Crying for help in time of need is wise	47 And when even was come, the ship was in the midst of the sea, and he alone on the land.	51 And he went up unto them into the ship; and the wind ceased: and they were sore amazed in themselves beyond measure, and wondered.	b. His presence calms the storm
a. Their struggle was long*DS1*	48 And he saw them toiling in rowing; for the wind was contrary unto them: and about the fourth watch of the night he cometh unto them,	52 For they considered not the miracle of the loaves: for their heart was hardened.	**5. Lesson 5: Remembering & trusting the power of Jesus is wise**

DIVISION IV

THE SON OF GOD'S TRAINING MINISTRY: JESUS' INTENSIVE PREPARATION OF THE DISCIPLES, 6:7-8:26

E. Five Wise Lessons for Service, 6:45-52

(6:45-52) **Introduction—Jesus Christ, Messiahship**: Jesus had to constrain His disciples to leave and go to the other shore. They argued against going. There were several reasons why the use of constraint was necessary.

First, right after Jesus had fed the crowd, they wished to take Him by force and make Him King. The Gospel of John tells us this (Jn.6:15). Jesus knew the popular view of Messiahship. The Messiah was to lead Israel in revolt against the Roman conquerors and free the people, establishing the government of theocracy, that is, the rule and reign of God over all the earth (see notes—Mt.1:1; DEEPER STUDY # 1—1:18; DEEPER STUDY # 3—3:11; notes—11:1-6; 11:2-3; DEEPER STUDY #1—11:5; DEEPER STUDY #2—11:6; DEEPER STUDY #1—12:16; note—Lu.7:21-23). The disciples were caught up in the excitement. Christ had to send them across the lake and disperse the crowd in order to prevent an immediate uprising.

Having to strain against a storm and fight for survival would calm the disciples' excitement. His calming the storm would also prove His Messiahship and again show that He was in control of all things and knew the best way to proclaim His Messiahship.

Second, it was time for Jesus to move on. Others needed His ministry. He wanted the disciples to make use of what little daylight there was in crossing the lake.

Third, and so important to see, Jesus needed time alone for prayer.

Fourth, Christ wanted the disciples to learn five lessons for service—lessons that would prove invaluable in their ministry to the world (see outlines and notes—Mt.14:22-33; Jn.6:16-21).

1. Lesson 1: crowd excitement is not always wise (v.45).
2. Lesson 2: prayer after service is wise (v.46).
3. Lesson 3: crying for help in time of need is wise (vv.47-49).
4. Lesson 4: receiving the presence of Jesus is wise (vv.50-51).
5. Lesson 5: remembering and trusting the power of Jesus is wise (v.52).

1 (6:45) **Jesus Christ, Messiahship—Excitement—Crowd**: the first lesson is that crowd excitement is not always wise. The crowd had been fed miraculously. They were extremely excited, for Jesus was bound to be the Messiah. He could always feed them and meet their needs, no matter what their needs were. They wanted to take Him by force and make Him King (see note—Mk.6:45-52; see Jn.6:14-15). Of course, the authorities would never allow a revolt; they would crush the people. But the people were not thinking. They wanted to act now, whether wise or unwise.

⇒ Fleshy emotions were running wild.
⇒ Selfish desires were dominating.
⇒ Rationality and thoughtfulness were lacking.
⇒ Spiritual insight was completely absent.

Jesus could not allow the disciples to be caught up in the excitement and worldly desires of the crowd. God's will had to be done; and His will was the cross, an eternal kingdom, not a worldly kingdom that gives man a life span of only seventy or so years. God wants man to live now, yes, but He also wants man to live eternally. Jesus knew this. And He also knew that man could live forever *only by the cross, only by a spiritual rebirth* wrought by the death of the Son of God (Jn.3:16;

Ep.1:7; 1 Pe.2:24; 3:18). Jesus had to do God's will. He had to get the disciples away from the crowd and their carnal, fleshy excitement lest the disciples be ill-affected (see note—Jn.6:14-15).

Thought 1. Motive, objective, and personal control are what make the difference. Excitement due to wrong motives and desires can lead to several problems.
(1) Carnal and unwise action and behavior without thought or understanding.
(2) Stimulation or exaltation of the flesh.
(3) Ignoring thoughtful prayer and God's will.

When a crowd of people is excited, a person will often follow along with the crowd's emotional excitement. He goes ahead and does what the crowd does without thinking. His flesh is stimulated, excited, tingling and often craving. He gives way to his urge. He acts in his own flesh and strength. He ignores God, giving no consideration whatsoever to seeking God's will. This was the danger with the disciples. It is often the danger confronting us.

The answer, of course, is what Jesus did with the disciples: getting away from the crowd and its worldly and carnal motives and excitement.

"Wherefore come out from among them, and be ye separate, saith the Lord, and touch not the unclean thing; and I will receive you, and will be a Father unto you, and ye shall be my sons and daughters, saith the Lord Almighty" (2 Co.6:17-18).

"And have no fellowship with the unfruitful works of darkness, but rather reprove them" (Ep.5:11).

Thought 2. We must be surrendered to walk in God's will and way, not in the will and way of a worldly crowd.

"I beseech you therefore, brethren, by the mercies of God, that ye present your bodies a living sacrifice, holy, acceptable unto God, which is your reasonable service. And be not conformed to this world: but be ye transformed by the renewing of your mind, that ye may prove what is that good, and acceptable, and perfect, will of God" (Ro.12:1-2).

2 (6:46) **Prayer—Crowd**: the second lesson is that prayer after service is wise (see note—Mt.14:22-23 for discussion). Jesus had been teaching the crowd and ministering to them. In the eyes of the world, He could not have been more successful. The results of His service and ministry were phenomenal.

⇒ He had a large successful ministry. The crowds were huge, ranging in the thousands. They were literally running and clamoring to get to him (see Mk.6:33).
⇒ He had the recognition, esteem, praise, and honor of the crowd.
⇒ He had the excitement and motivation of the crowd. They were motivated enough to even make Him King.

But note what Jesus did. He dismissed the people, sent them away. Why? So He could get alone "to pray." God, not the crowds, was...

- His source
- His rest
- His excitement
- His deliverance
- His strength
- His motivation
- His object of worship
- His source of renewal

He had to get alone with God. The word for prayer (proseuchasthai) is a descriptive word. It means to pray fervently, to pour one's whole heart and total being out to God. Jesus was totally dependent upon God, not upon the crowds. The crowds could give Him nothing, whereas God could give Him everything.

⇒ He was exhausted. He needed God's presence and rest.
⇒ He was tempted. He needed God's strength and deliverance (see note—Mt.14:22-23).
⇒ He was drained spiritually. He needed to worship God and to be renewed.
⇒ He was weary of man's worldly excitement and motives. He needed God's excitement and motivation.

"Watch and pray, that ye enter not into temptation: the spirit indeed is willing, but the flesh is weak" (Mt.26:41).

"And he spake a parable unto them to this end, that men ought always to pray, and not to faint" (Lu.18:1).

"Pray without ceasing" (1 Th.5:17).

"Seek the LORD and his strength, seek his face continually" (1 Chr.16:11).

3 (6:47-49) **Fear**: the third lesson is that a cry for help in time of need is wise. A storm came up while the disciples were crossing the lake. Three things are stressed about the disciples in the storm.

a. Their toil was long. The Lake of Galilee was only four to six miles across. They had been rowing against a headwind for some six to nine hours and had progressed only about three miles.

b. Their fear was horrifying. The disciples were physically exhausted and mentally drained from using all the seaman's skills at their disposal. Their lives were at stake; they were struggling for survival. All of a sudden, out of nowhere, they saw a figure, an apparition (ghost) walking on the water. They were scared, frightened, perhaps bordering on going into shock—perhaps thinking that the death angel, or a premonition of their death, was at hand.

c. Their cry was desperate. They were all toiling and rowing to save their lives (v.48); and "they all saw Christ, and were troubled [agitated, terrorized]" (v.50).

Thought 1. Note two significant points.

(1) The disciples desperately needed help. They did exactly what they needed to do to get help: they cried out to Jesus.

> **"Casting all your care upon him; for he careth for you" (1 Pe.5:7).**
>
> **"Thou calledst in trouble, and I delivered thee; I answered thee in the secret place of thunder" (Ps.81:7).**
>
> **"Call unto me, and I will answer thee, and show thee great and mighty things, which thou knowest not" (Je.33:3).**

(2) The disciples were doing God's will when the storm came. They were doing exactly what Christ had told them to do, that is, cross the lake and get ready to minister there. The storm was part of God's will. They had to learn...

- to confess their need for Him before He could help.
- to endure against the storms of life.
- to trust through all, no matter how terrifying.

DEEPER STUDY # 1

(6:48) **A Day's Timetable**: Hebrew time was used in the Gospels of Matthew, Mark, and Luke, and the Book of Acts. Sunrise (6 a.m.) was the beginning of the day. The first hour was 7 a.m. and so on. Sometimes Scripture refers to a watch. Both the day and the night were divided into four watches each. A watch was three hours long. The first watch of the day was 6 a.m. to 9 a.m. The fourth watch of the night mentioned above was 3 a.m. to 6 a.m. The disciples had been rowing between six and nine hours and had advanced only three miles. The Gospel of John uses Roman time, with the hours beginning at twelve noon and twelve midnight. Note that twentieth century time is the same as Roman time.

4 (6:50-51) **Jesus Christ, Presence**: the fourth lesson is that receiving the presence of Jesus is wise. It was an eerie, stormy night. The disciples were terrified; they cried out for help. All of a sudden, a voice from the body walking out on the water shouted out: "Be of good cheer: it is I; be not afraid" (v.50). The authority and assurance of the voice made the disciples realize that it was Jesus. The disciples were encouraged. They knew they were safe and secure. He cared and He had the power to take care of them all. Note three results.

1. Their fear was erased.
2. The storm was calmed.
3. They stood amazed (beyond measure) in the presence of the Lord.

Thought 1. Receiving the presence of Jesus Christ takes care of all problems and trials. He gives the strength to row through all the storms of life, no matter their turbulence and severity.

Thought 2. Think: What if the disciples had been forced to face the storm alone? What if we had to face the storms of life alone? Which storm would drown the breath of life out of us? Which storm would send us reeling into eternity, having to meet God *unprepared*?

> **"But as many as received him, to them gave he power to become the sons of God, even to them that believe on his name" (Jn.1:12).**
>
> **"Peace I leave with you, my peace I give unto you: not as the world giveth, give I unto you. Let not your heart be troubled, neither let it be afraid" (Jn.14:27).**
>
> **"These things I have spoken unto you, that in me ye might have peace. In the world ye shall have tribulation: but be of good cheer; I have overcome the world" (Jn.16:33).**
>
> **"Be careful for nothing; but in every thing by prayer and supplication with thanksgiving let your requests be made known unto God. And the peace of God, which passeth all understanding, shall keep your hearts and minds through Christ Jesus" (Ph.4:6-7).**
>
> **"And the Lord shall deliver me from every evil work, and will preserve me unto his heavenly kingdom: to whom be glory for ever and ever. Amen" (2 Ti.4:18).**
>
> **"And deliver them who through fear of death were all their lifetime subject to bondage" (He.2:15).**
>
> **"So that we may boldly say, The Lord is my helper, and I will not fear what man shall do unto me" (He.13:6).**
>
> **"The Lord knoweth how to deliver the godly out of temptations, and to reserve the unjust unto the day of judgment to be punished" (2 Pe.2:9).**
>
> **"Surely he shall deliver thee from the snare of the fowler, and from the noisome pestilence" (Ps.91:3).**
>
> **"For thou hast delivered my soul from death, mine eyes from tears, and my feet from falling" (Ps.116:8).**
>
> **"Fear thou not; For I am with thee: be not dismayed; for I am thy God: I will strengthen thee; yea, I will help thee; yea, I will uphold thee with the right hand of my righteousness" (Is.41:10).**
>
> **"And even to your old age I am he; and even to hoar hairs will I carry you: I have made, and I will bear; even I will carry, and will deliver you" (Is.46:4).**

> **DEEPER STUDY # 2**
> (6:50) **"I Am"—Jesus Christ, Names - Titles**: this is the great name of God, the Self-Existent One, the Supreme One of the Universe (see note—Jn.6:20-21).

5 (6:52) **Jesus Christ, Power—Heart, Hard**: the fifth lesson is that remembering and trusting the power of Jesus is wise. The disciples had no reason to be so amazed at Jesus' calming the storm. They had just witnessed the miracle of the loaves and the feeding of five thousand men with just a little food. Christ was unquestionably God. And God not only cared about people, He could do anything for people—even control all of nature. How could they forget so easily? "Their heart was hardened" (v.52). A hardened heart is attached to the earth. It cannot break loose from the earth; it cannot see anything beyond the ordinary and explainable. It is slow to see anything beyond natural law controlling the world. The hardened heart may hope that God exists; it may even say that God exists, but to really believe there exists a true God who is actively controlling the world is difficult to accept and apply to everyday life. Profession is easy; living in complete trust upon God is difficult.

Thought 1. The disciples were as so many are: they had spiritual experience after experience, but they were attached to the earth. Therefore, they grew hard and callous, and they became dull to spiritual truth. Their spiritual understanding was always needing a boost.

"For the heart of this people is waxed gross, and their ears are dull of hearing, and their eyes have they closed; lest they should see with their eyes, and hear with their ears, and understand with their heart, and should be converted, and I should heal them" (Ac.28:27).

"There is none that understandeth, there is none that seeketh after God" (Ro.3:11).

"Ever learning, and never able to come to the knowledge of the truth" (2 Ti.3:7).

"They know not, neither will they understand; they walk on in darkness: all the foundations of the earth are out of course" (Ps.82:5).

"Thou dwellest in the midst of a rebellious house, which have eyes to see, and see not; they have ears to hear, and hear not: for they are a rebellious house" (Eze.12:2).

"But they know not the thoughts of the LORD, neither understand they his counsel" (Mi.4:12).

Thought 2. A spiritual mind and constant prayer are the answer to hardness of heart (see v.46).

"And be not conformed to this world: but be ye transformed by the renewing of your mind, that ye may prove what is that good, and acceptable, and perfect, will of God" (Ro.12:2).

"Casting down imaginations, and every high thing that exalteth itself against the knowledge of God, and bringing into captivity every thought to the obedience of Christ" (2 Co.10:5).

"That ye put off concerning the former conversation the old man, which is corrupt according to the deceitful lusts; and be renewed in the Spirit of your mind; and that ye put on the new man, which after God is created in righteousness and true holiness" (Ep.4:22-24).

"And have put on the new man, which is renewed in knowledge after the image of him that created him" (Col.3:10).

"Be careful for nothing; but in every thing by prayer and supplication with thanksgiving let your requests be made known unto God. And the peace of God, which passeth all understanding, shall keep your hearts and minds through Christ Jesus. Finally, brethren, whatsoever things are true, whatsoever things are honest, whatsoever things are just, whatsoever things are pure, whatsoever things are lovely, whatsoever things are of good report; if there be any virtue, and if there be any praise, think on these things" (Ph.4:6-8).

Outline	Scripture
	F. The Steps to Healing, 6:53-56 *(Mt. 14:34-36)*
1. Step 1: Recognizing Jesus	53 And when they had passed over, they came into the land of Gennesaret, and drew to the shore. 54 And when they were come out of the ship, straightway they knew him,
2. Step 2: Acknowledging one's need & believing that Jesus can help	55 And ran through that whole region round about, and began to carry about in beds those that were sick, where they heard he was.
3. Step 3: Asking unashamedly & unreservedly for Jesus' help	56 And whithersoever he entered, into villages, or cities, or country, they laid the sick in the streets, and besought him that they might touch if it were but the border of his garment: and as many as touched him were made whole.

DIVISION IV

THE SON OF GOD'S TRAINING MINISTRY: JESUS' INTENSIVE PREPARATION OF THE DISCIPLES, 6:7-8:26

F. The Steps to Healing, 6:53-56

(6:53-56) **Introduction**: a person can be healed spiritually and healed physically (see Ro.10:9-13). Here are the steps for both spiritual and physical healing. If a man wishes to be healed by Christ, he must take the same three steps. (See outline and notes—Mt.14:34-36 for a more detailed discussion.)

1. Step 1: recognizing Jesus (vv.53-54).
2. Step 2: acknowledging one's need and believing that Jesus can help (v.55).
3. Step 3: asking unashamedly and unreservedly for Jesus' help (v.56).

1 (6:53-54) **Jesus Christ, Mission—Healing**: the first step to healing is recognizing Jesus. The people *knew Him* (epiginosko); that is, they fully recognized, perceived, knew exactly who He was. The idea is that the people *knew Him by experience.* Some had been touched and healed by Jesus before; others had witnessed Him touch and heal members of their family, friends, and strangers. The people knew two things.

a. They knew that Jesus had come to their land. He was now present, at hand, reachable, available to make them and their loved ones whole.

b. They knew that Jesus cared about the sick and that He had the power to make them whole. There was just something different about Jesus. His interest and care in people and His power to help them were phenomenal. He was so humble and meek, yet authoritative and strong. The presence of God was unquestionably within Him in a most unique way.

Thought 1. Jesus has come to earth. He has come to our land, and He is available and able to make us whole.

> **"Even as the Son of man came not to be ministered unto, but to minister, and to give his life a ransom for many" (Mt.28:20).**
>
> **"For the Son of man is come to seek and to save that which was lost" (Lu.19:10).**
>
> **"For God so loved the world, that he gave his only begotten Son, that whosoever believeth in him should not perish, but have everlasting life. For God sent not his Son into the world to condemn the world; but that the world through him might be saved" (Jn.3:16-17).**
>
> **"I am come that they might have life, and that they might have it more abundantly" (Jn.10:10).**
>
> **"Seek ye the LORD while he may be found, call ye upon him while he is near: let the wicked forsake his way, and the unrighteous man his thoughts: and let him return unto the LORD, and he will have mercy upon him; and to our God, for he will abundantly pardon" (Is.55:6-7).**

2 (6:55) **Need, Acknowledging—Jesus, Seeking**: the second step to healing is acknowledging one's need and believing Jesus can help. Note a significant fact. The people not only came to Jesus themselves, they "ran through that whole region" and brought their families and friends. They even spread the word about Jesus to strangers. The picture is very descriptive. All who "knew Jesus" (v.54) cared deeply for all the people throughout their region. Their care and love were intense. No trouble was too great, no pain was too much to bear—they "ran through that whole region...and began to carry...those that were sick." They carried them wherever they heard Jesus was. The picture is that of running to and fro. If Jesus was not where they went, they picked the sick back up and rushed on to the next village or town, searching for Him until they found Him.

Two things would cause such intense seeking after Jesus.

a. The people knew they had great need. They were sick and needed to be made whole. They readily confessed their need. They did not try to hide their disease or injury.

b. The people believed Jesus could help; they believed He could make them whole. There was no chance they were going to miss this opportunity.

Thought 1. The same two things are true about us.
(1) We have the need to be made whole...

- spiritually
- mentally
- emotionally
- physically
- racially
- socially
- nationally
- internationally

"The whole world lieth in wickedness" (1 Jn.5:19; see Ro.3:10-18 for a descriptive picture of man's desperate need. Also see Ro.1:18-32.)

"As it is written, there is none righteous, no, not one: there is none that understandeth, there is none that seeketh after God. They are all gone out of the way, they are together become unprofitable; there is none that doeth good, no, not one. Their throat is an open sepulchre; with their tongues they have used deceit; the poison of asps is under their lips" (Ro.3:10-13).

"For the wages of sin is death; but the gift of God is eternal life through Jesus Christ our Lord" (Ro.6:23).

(2) We must believe Jesus can help us. He can, but we *must believe* that He can before the world will come to Him for help.

"When Jesus heard it, he saith unto them, They that are whole have no need of the physician, but they that are sick: I came not to call the righteous, but sinners to repentance" (Mk.2:17).

"If thou canst believe, all things are possible to him that believeth" (Mk.9:23).

"That if thou shalt confess with thy mouth the Lord Jesus, and shalt believe in thine heart that God hath raised him from the dead, thou shalt be saved. For with the heart man believeth unto righteousness; and with the mouth confession is made unto salvation" (Ro.10:9-10).

3 (6:56) **Salvation—Decision—Humility—Belief**: the third step to healing is asking unashamedly and unreservedly for Jesus' help. The people asked and begged Jesus to let them touch Him, to simply touch "the border of His garment" (see DEEPER STUDY # 1—Mt.14:36). Note the word "besought." It means to ask, to beg. The word points to three essential attitudes necessary to be made whole.

a. A sense of need: sensing our need for Christ's help so much that we beseech Him, asking and begging in desperation if needed.

b. A sense of humility: sensing that our need is really desperate and beyond man's cure. We must sense the desperation so deeply that we humble ourselves, beseeching Christ to make us whole. Spectators and curiosity seekers who might be looking on just do not matter. We are willing to humble ourselves, no matter what men may say, in order to have our need met.

c. A belief in Christ's power and willingness to make us whole: believing so much that we beseech and ask and beg Him to make us whole through and through.

Note that all who touched Jesus were made whole. Touching Jesus brought healing to their whole being (see note—Mt.14:36). Jesus did not shrink from anyone, no matter how deformed, abnormal, diseased, unattractive, dirty, immoral, or sinful the person was.

Thought 1. Jesus loves everyone, and He sees the need within everyone and longs to meet that need. Anyone who reaches out for Him is taken by the hand and pulled to His heart. The person is received and made whole through and through.

"But as many as received him, to them gave he power to become the sons of God, even to them that believe on his name" (Jn.1:12).

"Him that cometh to me I will in no wise cast out" (Jn.6:37).

"If ye shall ask any thing in my name, I will do it" (Jn.14:14).

"If my people, which are called by my name, shall humble themselves, and pray, and seek my face, and turn from their wicked ways; then will I hear from heaven, and will forgive their sin, and will heal their land" (2 Chr.7:14. Note how this verse includes all three points in this note.)

Outline	Scripture
	CHAPTER 7 **G. The Emptiness of (Man-Made) Tradition, Ritual, Ceremony, Works, 7:1-13** *(see Mt. 15:1-9)*
1. Tradition tragically can be placed before need	Then came together unto him the Pharisees, and certain of the scribes, which came from Jerusalem.
a. The religionists found fault with Jesus' disciples b. The fault: Eating with unwashed & unclean hands	2 And when they saw some of his disciples eat bread with defiled, that is to say, with unwashen, hands, they found fault.
1) The tradition of cleanliness explained	3 For the Pharisees, and all the Jews, except they wash their hands oft, eat not, holding the tradition of the elders.
2) The tradition illustrated	4 And when they come from the market, except they wash, they eat not. And many other things there be, which they have received to hold, as the washing of cups, and pots, brasen vessels, and of tables.
c. The charge against the disciples: Was brought to Jesus	5 Then the Pharisees and scribes asked him, Why walk not thy disciples according to the tradition of the elders, but eat bread with unwashen hands?
2. Tradition can be hypocritical honor	6 He answered and said unto them, Well hath Esaias prophesied of you hypocrites, as it is written, This people honoureth me with their lips, but their heart is far from me.
3. Tradition can be empty, worthless worship	7 Howbeit in vain do they worship me, teaching for doctrines the commandments of men.
4. Tradition can be man-made commands	8 For laying aside the commandment of God, ye hold the tradition of men, as the washing of pots and cups: and many other such like things ye do.
5. Tradition can be kept before the commands of God	9 And he said unto them, Full well ye reject the commandment of God, that ye may keep your own tradition. 10 For Moses said, Honour thy father and thy mother; and, Whoso curseth father or mother, let him die the death:
a. They twisted God's commands[DS1]	11 But ye say, If a man shall say to his father or mother, It is Corban, that is to say, a gift, by whatsoever thou mightest be profited by me, he shall be free.
b. They insisted on obedience to tradition	12 And ye suffer him no more to do ought for his father or his mother;
6. Tradition can nullify the Word of God or make the Word of God ineffective[DS2,3]	13 Making the word of God of none effect through your tradition, which ye have delivered: and many such like things do ye.

DIVISION IV

THE SON OF GOD'S TRAINING MINISTRY: JESUS' INTENSIVE PREPARATION OF THE DISCIPLES, 6:7–8:26

G. The Emptiness of (Man-Made) Tradition, Ritual, Ceremony, Works, 7:1-13

(7:1-13) **Introduction**: this passage is of critical importance for the destiny of both man and religion. Why is it so important? Because neither man nor religion can survive being institutionalized, that is, being based and focused upon tradition, ritual, ceremony, and works. Survival depends upon the hearts of man and of religion. The heart of both must be focused upon acceptance and reconciliation, approval and redemption, peace and love, humility and giving, joy and hope. Men can survive only when they...

- accept each other and are reconciled to God in Christ (together).
- approve each other and are redeemed.
- live in peace and love.
- experience the joy and hope of Christ.
- walk humbly and live a life of service.

1. Tradition, tragically, can be placed before need (vv.1-5).
2. Tradition can be hypocritical honor (v.6).
3. Tradition can be empty, worthless worship (v.7).
4. Tradition can be man-made commands (v.8).
5. Tradition can be kept before the commands of God (vv.9-12).
6. Tradition can nullify the Word of God or make the Word of God ineffective (v.13).

1 (7:1-5) **Religionists—Tradition**: the scene is that of religionists who found fault with Jesus' disciples. The religionists were a fact-finding commission from Jerusalem. They had come to investigate Jesus, to see exactly what was going on and happening. News of His preaching and healing and of His conflicts with local authorities were constantly being brought to the Jerusalem leaders. They had already sent one fact-finding commission to confront Jesus. Their report had not been good. They had accused Jesus of healing and casting out demons by Beelzebub. They had also accused Him of breaking the Sabbath law. There had also been a fact-finding commission sent to investigate John the Baptist, the man who was said to be the forerunner of Jesus. His preaching and baptism and his priesthood had been suspect (see notes—Mt.3:7-10; Jn.1:19).

The whole country was astir with news of Jesus' claims and unbelievable miracles. People were stirred up, dangerously so. All this necessitated another commission being sent out to investigate Jesus.

When the commission arrived, they immediately saw the disciples breaking one of their traditions. The disciples were eating with unwashed and unclean hands. Of course, what they meant was not that the disciples had bad manners, nor that they were practicing bad health. They meant the disciples were unclean in the eyes of God. Why? Because the disciples had not washed their hands as a sign to God that they were offering themselves and their food to God . The traditional ceremony of washing one's hands before meals (as a sign of thanksgiving to God) had been broken. The disciples were ceremonially unclean.

The Law of Moses prescribed washing before handling some items. The idea was to instill within the people the holiness of God and His temple, and the need for man to be *spiritually clean* before approaching Him or handling His affairs. But what had happened was that some religionists had added to God's Word. They had taken the Law of God, including the laws of cleansing, and had added thousands and thousands of rules and regulations. There was a rule governing practically every thing a person did, so many rules in fact that no one could conceivably keep them. Instead of pointing a person to God and to the need for the cleansing of the heart, the rules caused a person to concentrate on the rules and the keeping of them. The rules became the center and focus of attention, not God.

In the case at hand, the rule being broken was that of washing the hands before eating a meal. The disciples had violated the tradition of the church and had embarrassed the religious faithful of their day. In the eyes of the investigating committee, they were unclean in the sight of God. They had broken a tradition of the elders and there was no excuse for it, not if they were the disciples of a true Rabbi. A true Rabbi would be teaching his disciples the traditions of the elders, not ignoring and violating them. Thus, the commission brought their charge to Jesus (v.5).

2 (7:6) **Tradition—Hypocrites**: tradition can be hypocritical honor. Jesus took the charge of the religionists and turned it against them. He quoted from Scripture, applying Isaiah's words to their spiritual condition (Is.29:13; see 1 S.15:22; 16:7). His words were strong and forceful: He called them "hypocrites" (see DEEPER STUDY # 2—Mt.23:13). They honored God with their lips, but their heart was far from Him.

> **Thought 1.** A hypocrite gives lip service while keeping his heart far from God. He acknowledges God and attends worship, but this is about all he does. However, there are some who are *religiously deceived* (see the Pharisees and Scribes). They study the Scripture, pray, witness, help the needy, and keep the rules. They would even fight to maintain religious tradition. Yet, Jesus says they are hypocrites. Why? Because their heart is not God's. They refuse to personally accept Jesus as the Son of God, the Messiah and Savior of the world. They do not know God personally, not in the depths of their heart (Jn.14:6).
>
> > **"They profess that they know God; but in works they deny him, being abominable, and disobedient, and unto every good work reprobate" (Tit.1:16).**
> >
> > **"Forasmuch as ye know that ye were not redeemed with corruptible things, as silver and gold, from your vain conversation received by tradition from your fathers; but with the precious blood of Christ, as of a lamb without blemish and without spot" (1 Pe.1:18-19).**
> >
> > **"For when they [hypocrites] speak great swelling words of vanity, they allure through the lusts of the flesh, through much wantonness, those that were clean escaped from them who live in error. While they promise them liberty, they themselves are the servants of corruption: for of whom a man is overcome, of the same is he brought in bondage" (2 Pe.2:18-19).**
> >
> > **"Hereby know ye the Spirit of God: Every spirit that confesseth that Jesus Christ is come in the flesh is of God: and every spirit that confesseth not that Jesus Christ is come in the flesh is not of God: and this is that spirit of antichrist, whereof ye have heard that it should come; and even now already is it in the world" (1 Jn.4:2-3).**

3 (7:7) **Tradition—Worship**: tradition can be empty, worthless worship. Jesus accused the religionists of worshipping in vain. "Ye worship ye know not what" (Jn.4:22). A religionist worships, but with an empty heart. Jesus taught that true worship must be *in spirit and in truth*, not only *in spirit*, but *in truth* as well (Jn.4:24). A person who denies Christ or denies God's Word cannot truly worship God (Jn.14:6; 17:17). He may worship; but his worship is empty, worthless, unacceptable. The religionists of Jesus' day were professing religion with their lips, but denying Christ, God's Son, in their hearts (see vv.17-20).

4 (7:8) **Tradition**: tradition can be man-made commandments. A religionist teaches tradition as God's commandment. He teaches his tradition as he practices it or proclaims it. Tradition is man's *idea* of what should be or what should not be done. Some traditions are good; however, they are not to be taught as though they were the commandments of God. As important as some traditions may be, they are not as important as God's Word.

> **"Preach the word; be instant in season, out of season; reprove, rebuke, exhort with all longsuffering and doctrine" (2 Ti.4:2).**
>
> **"Beware lest any man spoil you through philosophy and vain deceit, after the tradition of men, after the rudiments of the world, and not after Christ" (Col.2:8).**

"Not giving heed to Jewish fables, and commandments of men, that turn from the truth" (Tit.1:14; see Jn.17:17).

5 (7:9-12) **Tradition—Commandments**: tradition can be kept before the commandments of God. Jesus made another serious charge. He said that the religionist broke God's law *in order to keep* the traditions of religion. And Jesus gave an example:

"Scripture says, 'Honor thy father and mother.' But your tradition says that once a person vows to give a gift to the temple, he can never back out of the vow, even if he later needs the gift to take care of his parents."

Jesus was saying, "I am not the law breaker, the hypocrite. You are. You are the ones who are breaking God's law. You put your own rule above the law of God." (Several notes should be read at this point to see the background of this conflict. See notes—Mt.12:1-8; note and DEEPER STUDY # 1—12:10; DEEPER STUDY # 1—Mk.7:11; DEEPER STUDY # 1—Lu.6:2.)

"For laying aside the commandment of God, ye hold the tradition of men" (Mk.7:8).
"And this is his commandment, That we should believe on the name of his Son Jesus Christ, and love one another, as he gave us commandment" (1 Jn.3:23).
"Little children, yet a little while I am with you. Ye shall seek me: and as I said unto the Jews, Whither I go, ye cannot come; so now I say to you. A new commandment I give unto you, That ye love one another; as I have loved you, that ye also love one another" (Jn.13:33-34).
"Wherefore the Lord said, Forasmuch as this people draw near me with their mouth, and with their lips do honor me, but have removed their heart far from me, and their fear toward me is taught by the precept of men" (Is.29:13).

DEEPER STUDY # 1
(7:11) **Corban**: a gift dedicated to God. When a person gave a gift or left an estate to God, he simply pronounced the words, "My goods are corban." It was an official statement that was legally binding. Once the statement was made, the goods belonged to the temple. The problem arose when the religious leaders went too far in encouraging such gifts and estates. They tried to secure the vow even from those who had parents or family members that needed help. In such cases, a person was evading the most basic duty: caring for his family members (see Ex.20:12; 21:17).

6 (7:13) **Tradition—Word of God**: tradition can make the Word of God ineffective. Jesus charged the religionists with setting aside God's Word for tradition. Religious traditions may be described as institutional or personal.

a. Institutional traditions are such things as rituals, rules, regulations, schedules, forms, services, procedures, organizations—anything that gives order and security to the persons involved.

b. Personal traditions are such things as church attendance, prayers, habits, ceremonies, objects which a person uses (somewhat superstitiously) to keep himself religiously secure.

Jesus was attacking the fact that so many religionists put their traditions first while neglecting and ignoring God's Word (see notes—Mt.12:1-8; note and DEEPER STUDY # 1—12:10).

"But he answered and said unto them, Why do ye also transgress the commandment of God by your tradition?" (Mt.15:3).
"Stand fast therefore in the liberty wherewith Christ hath made us free, and be not entangled again with the yoke of bondage" (Ga.5:1).
"Wherefore if ye be dead with Christ from the rudiments of the world, why, as though living in the world, are ye subject to ordinances" (Col.2:20).
"[Worship] which stood only in meats and drinks, and divers washings, and carnal ordinances, imposed on them until the time of reformation. But Christ being come an high priest of good things to come, by a greater and more perfect tabernacle, not made with hands, that is to say, not of this building; neither by the blood of goats and calves, but by his own blood he entered in once into the holy place, having obtained eternal redemption for us. For if the blood of bulls and of goats, and the ashes of an heifer sprinkling the unclean, sanctifieth to the purifying of the flesh: how much more shall the blood of Christ, who through the eternal Spirit offered himself without spot to God, purge your conscience from dead works to serve the living God?" (He.9:10-15).

DEEPER STUDY # 2
(7:13) **Making of none effect** (a kuruntes): to make void, ineffective; to annul; to deprive of authority and power; to invalidate.

DEEPER STUDY # 3
(7:13) **Word of God**: see notes and DEEPER STUDY # 1—1 Th.2:13; notes—2 Th.2:13; 2 Ti.3:16; note and DEEPER STUDY # 1,2—2 Pe.1:19-21. See Ac.17:11; 20:32; 1 Pe.2:2-3.

Outline	Scripture
	H. The Things That Defile, That Make a Person Unclean, 7:14-23 *(Mt. 15:10-20; Lu. 11:37-41)*
1. Jesus called the crowd together & shared a parable a. The importance stressed: Listen & understand	14 And when he had called all the people unto him, he said unto them, Hearken unto me every one of you, and understand:
b. The parable shared	15 There is nothing from without a man, that entering into him can defile him: but the things which come out of him, those are they that defile the man.
c. The disciples' dullness & request for the parable to be explained	16 If any man have ears to hear, let him hear. 17 And when he was entered into the house from the people, his disciples asked him concerning the parable.
2. Explanation 1: The thing that enters the body neither defiles it nor makes a person unclean	18 And he saith unto them, Are ye so without understanding also? Do ye not perceive, that whatsoever thing from without entereth into the man, it cannot defile him;
a. It does not enter the heart b. It enters the digestive tract	19 Because it entereth not into his heart, but into the belly, and goeth out into the draught, purging all meats?
3. Explanation 2: The thing that comes out from the heart does defile a person[DS1] a. The progression & growth of sin[DS2] b. The sins listed[DS3-15]	20 And he said, That which cometh out of the man, that defileth the man. 21 For from within, out of the heart of men, proceed evil thoughts, adulteries, fornications, murders, 22 Thefts, covetousness, wickedness, deceit, lasciviousness, an evil eye, blasphemy, pride, foolishness:
4. Explanation 3: The source of evil is the heart	23 All these evil things come from within, and defile the man.

DIVISION IV

THE SON OF GOD'S TRAINING MINISTRY: JESUS' INTENSIVE PREPARATION OF THE DISCIPLES, 6:7-8:26

H. The Things That Defile, That Make a Person Unclean 7:14-23

(7:14-23) **Introduction**: this is one of the most startling things Jesus ever taught. It shook the world of His day, and it has disturbed and gnawed at the minds and consciences of men ever since. It revolutionizes man's idea of evil and wrong-doing, of just what evil is and what causes it. It knocks the props out from under man's religion and morality. It lays man bare before God making him totally dependent upon God for salvation and life.

1. Jesus called the crowd together and shared a parable (vv.14-17).
2. Explanation 1: the thing that enters the body neither defiles it nor makes a person unclean (vv.18-19).
3. Explanation 2: the thing that comes out from the heart does defile a person (vv.20-22).
4. Explanation 3: the source of evil is the heart (v.23).

1 (7:14-17) **Heart—Defilement**: Jesus called the multitude to Him. Note verse fifteen where He says, "Hearken, hear and understand. Do not only hear what I am about to say, but understand it. It is of supreme importance."

> **"There is nothing from without a man, that entering into him can defile him: but the things which come out of him, those are they that defile the man" (v.15).**

Simply stated, a man is not defiled by what enters his body, but by what comes out of his heart. Now note verse sixteen. The importance of the point is again stressed: if any man has ears, let him hear. But the disciples were spiritually dull. They did not understand the parable. They asked Him to explain.

Thought 1. It is not enough for us to hear what Christ is saying, we must understand.

2 (7:18-19) **Sin, Source—Defilement**: the first explanation—the thing that enters the body does not defile. What defiles a man is not what he eats and drinks. What a man eats and drinks does not enter his heart; it enters his digestive tract and passes through his body. Therefore, food and drink, or eating with unwashed hands, or doing any other outward thing cannot defile a man—not *spiritually*.

There is no connection between what we eat and spirituality. That is not to say that excessive eating and intemperance are not wrong. Lustful and excessive appetites come *out of the heart*. But when it comes to the items themselves, the food and drink, there is no merit or value, no morality or virtue to them—not within themselves. It is *what we do with the things*, what our heart does, that makes us either good or bad, spiritual or carnal.

Thought 1. When *formal* or *outward religion* is outlined like Christ shares in this passage, the foolishness of holding such a position is really seen.

> **"The kingdom of God is not meat and drink" (Ro.14:17).**
> **"Circumcision is nothing, and uncircumcision is nothing" (1 Co.7:19).**

"But meat commendeth us not to God: for neither, if we eat, are we the better; neither, if we eat not, are we the worse" (1 Co.8:8).

"Ye observe days, and months, and times, and years. I am afraid of you, lest I have bestowed upon you labour in vain" (Ga.4:10-11).

"Having a form of godliness, but denying the power thereof: from such turn away" (2 Ti.3:5).

3 (7:20-22) **Sin, Source—Heart**: the second explanation—the thing that comes out from the heart does defile. Note exactly what Jesus was saying: "It is not things that defile a man. It is the heart that defiles a man. A man's heart is corrupt; therefore, he corrupts himself. Man is not *made unclean* by things; he is unclean because of his polluted heart. *It is he himself who takes things and does unclean things with them* (see DEEPER STUDIES # 3-15—Mk.7:21-22 for discussion).

DEEPER STUDY # 1
(7:19-20) **Heart** (kardia): in the Bible the word "heart" refers to both the major organ of the body (Le.17:11) and to the most important part of a person, that is, to man's innermost being. The heart is the central part, the very center of man's life. It is the most vital part of man's being.

The heart is man's inward life. It lies deep within, containing the *hidden man* or the real man (1 Pe.3:4); that is, the heart contains what a man really is, his true character. The heart determines what a man does, his behavior, whether good or depraved (Mt.15:18; Mk.7:21-23).

1. The heart is the source of man's rational being: reasoning (Mk.2:6), understanding (Mt.13:15), thinking (Mt.9:4).
2. The heart is the source of man's emotional being: joy (Jn.16:22; Ep.5:19), affections (Lu.24:32), desires (Mt.5:28).
3. The heart is the source of man's spiritual being: conscience (Ac.2:37), will (Ro.6:17), faith (Mk.11:23; Ro.10:10), evil (Mt.15:18; Mk.7:21-23; see Je.17:9).

DEEPER STUDY # 2
(7:21) **Sin**: note the progression of sin within man. (1) It begins in human nature: "within, out of the heart." (2) It develops in the human mind: in "evil thoughts." (3) It is expressed in human acts: "adulteries, fornications...."

DEEPER STUDY # 3
(7:21) **Evil Thoughts** (dialogismoi hoi kakoi): thoughts and imaginations and ideas and concepts that are base, wrong, wicked, immoral, unjust, reprehensible; thoughts that are not what they should be; thoughts that are not moral, clean and pure; thoughts that are not just and equitable; thoughts that are not uplifting and edifying; thoughts that are not spiritual, but carnal. (See Ro.8:6; 2 Co.10:5; Ph.4:8. See Mt.5:28.) Evil thoughts are a sin against all the commandments (Ex.20:1f).

"And Jesus knowing their thoughts said, Wherefore think ye evil in your hearts?" (Mt.9:4).

"Because that, when they knew God, they glorified him not as God, neither were thankful; but became vain in their imaginations, and their foolish heart was darkened" (Ro.1:21).

"And God saw that the wickedness of man was great in the earth, and that every imagination of the thoughts of his heart was only evil continually" (Ge.6:5).

"The Lord knoweth the thoughts of man, that they are vanity" (Ps.94:11).

"The thoughts of the wicked are an abomination to the Lord: but the words of the pure are pleasant words" (Pr.15:26).

"For as he thinketh in his heart, so is he: Eat and drink, saith he to thee; but his heart is not with thee" (Pr.23:7).

"The thought of foolishness is sin: and the scorner is an abomination to men" (Pr.24:9).

"Then said he unto me, Son of man, hast thou seen what the ancients of the house of Israel do in the dark, every man in the chambers of his imagery? for they say, The Lord seeth us not; the Lord hath forsaken the earth" (Eze.8:12).

DEEPER STUDY # 4
(7:21) **Adultery** (moicheiai): sexual unfaithfulness to husband or wife. It is also looking on a woman or a man to lust after her or him. Looking at and lusting after the oppposite sex, whether in person, magazines, books, on beaches, or anywhere else, is adultery. Imagining and lusting within the heart is the very same as committing the act. (See notes—Mt.5:28; DEEPER STUDY # 5—19:9 for discussion.) Adultery is a sin against the seventh commandment.

"Thou shalt not commit adultery" (Ex.20:14).

"Ye have heard that it was said by them of old time, Thou shalt not commit adultery: but I say unto you, That whosoever looketh on a woman to lust after her hath committed adultery with her already in his heart" (Mt.5:27-28).

"Know ye not that the unrighteous shall not inherit the kingdom of God? Be not deceived: neither fornicators, nor idolaters, nor adulterers, nor effeminate, nor abusers of themselves with mankind....shall inherit the kingdom of God" (1 Co.6:9-10).

"Having eyes full of adultery, and that cannot cease from sin; beguiling unstable souls" (2 Pe.2:14).

DEEPER STUDY # 5
(7:21) **Fornication** (porneiai): a broad word including all forms and kinds of immoral and sexual acts. It is premarital sex and adultery; it is abnormal sex, all kinds of sexual vice.

"Flee fornication. Every sin that a man doeth is without the body; but he that committeth fornication sinneth against his own body" (1 Co.6:18).
"But fornication, and all uncleanness, or covetousness, let it not be once named among you, as becometh saints" (Ep.5:3).
"Mortify therefore your members which are upon the earth; fornication, uncleanness, inordinate affection, evil concupiscence, and covetousness, which is idolatry" (Col.3:5).
"For this is the will of God, even your sanctification, that ye should abstain from fornication" (1 Th.4:3).

DEEPER STUDY # 6
(7:21) **Murder** (phonos): to kill, to take the life of another. Murder is a sin against the sixth commandment.

"Thou shalt not kill" (Ex.20:13).
"He saith unto him, Which? Jesus said, Thou shalt do no murder, Thou shalt not commit adultery, Thou shalt not steal, Thou shalt not bear false witness" (Mt.19:18).
"Owe no man any thing, but to love one another: for he that loveth another hath fulfilled the law. For this, Thou shalt not commit adultery, Thou shalt not kill, Thou shalt not steal, Thou shalt not bear false witness, Thou shalt not covet; and if there be any other commandment, it is briefly comprehended in this saying, namely, Thou shalt love thy neighbour as thyself. Love worketh no ill to his neighbour: therefore love is the fulfilling of the law" (Ro.13:8-10).
"Whosoever hateth his brother is a murderer: and ye know that no murderer hath eternal life abiding in him" (1 Jn.3:15).

DEEPER STUDY # 7
(7:22) **Thefts** (klopi): to cheat and steal; to take wrongfully from another person, either legally or illegally.

"Thou shalt not steal" (Ex.20:15).
"Ye shall not steal, neither deal falsely, neither lie one to another" (Le.19:11).
"Let him that stole steal no more: but rather let him labour, working with his hands the thing which is good, that he may have to give to him that needeth" (Ep.4:28).
"Not purloining [stealing], but showing all good fidelity; that they may adorn the doctrine of God our Saviour in all things" (Tit.2:10).

DEEPER STUDY # 8
(7:22) **Covetousness** (pleonexiai): to lust for more and more; to have a starving appetite for something; to have a love of possessing (2 Pe.2:14); to crave after and for. It means to crave and grasp after possessions, pleasure, power, fame. Covetousness lacks restraint. It lacks the ability to discriminate. It wants to have in order to spend in pleasure and luxury. Covetousness is an insatiable lust and craving of the flesh that cannot be satisfied. It is an intense appetite for gain, a passion for the pleasure that things can bring. It is a lust and craving so deep that a person finds his happiness in things instead of in God. It is idolatry (Ep.5:5).

"Thou shalt not covet thy neighbor's house, thou shalt not covet thy neighbor's wife, nor his manservant, nor his maidservant, nor his ox, nor his ass, nor any thing that is thy neighbor's" (Ex.20:17).
"And he said unto them, Take heed, and beware of covetousness: for a man's life consisteth not in the abundance of the things which he possesseth" (Lu.12:15).
"For this ye know, that no whoremonger, nor unclean person, nor covetous man, who is an idolater, hath any inheritance in the kingdom of Christ and of God" (Ep.5:5).
"Mortify therefore your members which are upon the earth; fornication, uncleanness, inordinate affection, evil concupiscence, and covetousness, which is idolatry" (Col.3:5).
"And they come unto thee as the people cometh, and they sit before thee as my people, and they hear thy words, but they will not do them: for with their mouth they show much love, but their heart goeth after their covetousness" (Eze.33:31).
"And they covet fields, and take them by violence; and houses, and take them away: so they oppress a man and his house, even a man and his heritage" (Mi.2:2).

DEEPER STUDY # 9
(7:22) **Wickedness** (poneria): to be depraved, to be actively evil, to do mischief, to trouble others and cause harm, to be malicious, to be dangerous and destructive. It is malice, hatred, and ill-will. It is an active wickedness, a desire within the heart to do harm and to corrupt people. It is actually pursuing others in order to seduce them or to harm them.

> **"For we ourselves also were sometimes foolish, disobedient, deceived, serving divers lusts and pleasures, living in malice and envy, hateful, and hating one another" (Tit.3:3).**
> **"For there is no faithfulness in their mouth; their inward part is very wickedness; their throat is an open sepulchre; they flatter with their tongue" (Ps.5:9).**
> **"The wicked plotteth against the just, and gnasheth upon him with his teeth" (Ps.37:12).**
> **"For they sleep not, except they have done mischief; and their sleep is taken away, unless they cause some to fall" (Pr.4:16).**
> **"Ah sinful nation, a people laden with iniquity, a seed of evildoers, children that are corrupters: they have forsaken the LORD, they have provoked the Holy One of Israel unto anger, they are gone away backward" (Is.1:4).**
> **"But the wicked are like the troubled sea, when it cannot rest, whose waters cast up mire and dirt" (Is.57:20).**

DEEPER STUDY # 10
(7:22) **Deceit** (dolos): to bait, to snare, to mislead, to beguile, to be crafty and deceitful, to mislead or give a false impression by word, act, or influence. It is conniving and twisting the truth to get one's own way. A man plots and deceives, doing whatever has to be done in order to get what he wants.

> **"Their throat is an open sepulchre; with their tongues they have used deceit; the poison of asps is under their lips" (Ro.3:13).**
> **"Lie not one to another, seeing that ye have put off the old man with his deeds" (Col.3:9).**
> **"Thou shalt destroy them that speak leasing: the Lord will abhor the bloody and deceitful man" (Ps.5:6).**
> **"He that worketh deceit shall not dwell within my house: he that telleth lies shall not tarry in my sight" (Ps.101:7).**
> **"Lying lips are abomination to the Lord: but they that deal truly are his delight" (Pr.12:22).**
> **"The getting of treasures by a lying tongue is a vanity tossed to and fro of them that seek death" (Pr.21:6).**
> **"And they will deceive every one his neighbor, and will not speak the truth: they have taught their tongue to speak lies, and weary themselves to commit iniquity" (Je.9:5).**
> **"The heart is deceitful above all things, and desperately wicked: who can know it?" (Je.17:9).**
> **"For the rich men thereof are full of violence, and the inhabitants thereof have spoken lies, and their tongue is deceitful in their mouth" (Mi.6:12).**

DEEPER STUDY # 11
(7:22) **Lasciviousness** (aselgeia): filthiness, indecency, shamelessness. A chief characteristic of the behavior is open and shameless indecency. It means unrestrained evil thoughts and behavior. It is giving in to brutish and lustful desires, a readiness for any pleasure. It is a man who knows no restraint, a man who has sinned so much that he no longer cares what people say or think. It is something far more distasteful than just doing wrong. The man who misbehaves usually tries to hide his wrong, but a lascivious man does not care who knows about his exploits or shame. He wants; therefore, he seeks to take and gratify. Decency and opinion do not matter. When he initially began to sin, he did as all men do: he misbehaved in secret. But eventually, the sin got the best of him—to the point that he no longer cared who saw or knew. He became the subject of a master—the master of habit, of the thing itself. Men become the slaves of such things as unbridled lust, wantonness, licentiousness, outrageousness, shamelessness, insolence (Mk.7:22), wanton manners, filthy words, indecent body movements, immoral handling of males and females (Ro.13:13), carnality, gluttony, and sexual immorality (1 Pe.4:3; 2 Pe.2:2, 18). (See 2 Co.12:21; Ga.5:19; Ep.4:19; 2 Pe.2:7.)

> **"And likewise also the men, leaving the natural use of the woman, burned in their lust one toward another; men with men working that which is unseemly, and receiving in themselves that recompence of their error which was meet" (Ro.1:27).**
> **"Who being past feeling have given themselves over unto lasciviousness, to work all uncleanness with greediness" (Ep.4:19).**
> **"For there are certain men crept in unawares, who were before of old ordained to this condemnation, ungodly men, turning the grace of our God into lasciviousness, and denying the only Lord God, and our Lord Jesus Christ....Even as Sodom and Gomorrha, and the cities about them in like manner, giving themselves over to fornication, and going after strange flesh, are set forth for an example, suffering the vengeance of eternal fire" (Jude 4, 7).**
> **"For the time past of our life may suffice us to have wrought the will of the Gentiles, when we walked in lasciviousness, lusts, excess of wine, revellings, banquetings, an abominable idolatries" (1 Pe.4:3).**

DEEPER STUDY # 12
(7:22) **Evil Eye** (aphthalmos poneros): to look where one should not; to lust after what one should not; to envy, covet, crave and desire by looking; to use the eye in an evil way; to satisfy one's lusts and desires by looking.

"The light of the body is the eye: therefore when thine eye is single, thy whole body also is full of light; but when thine eye is evil, thy body also is full of darkness" (Lu.11:34).
"So that the man that is tender among you, and very delicate, his eye shall be evil toward his brother, and toward the wife of his bosom, and the remnant of his children which he shall leave" (De.28:54).
"Eat thou not the bread of him that hath an evil eye, neither desire thou his dainty meats" (Pr.23:6).
"Ye have heard that it was said by them of old time, Thou shalt not commit adultery: but I say unto you, That whosoever looketh on a woman to lust after her hath committed adultery with her already in his heart" (Mt.5:27-28).

DEEPER STUDY # 13
(7:22) **Blasphemy** (blasphemia): to slander, insult, revile, speak evil of God or man (see DEEPER STUDY # 4—Mt.9:3).

"Verily I say unto you, All sins shall be forgiven unto the sons of men, and blasphemies wherewith soever they shall blaspheme: but he that shall blaspheme against the Holy Ghost hath never forgiveness, but is in danger of eternal damnation" (Mk.3:28-29).
"Of whom is Hymenaeus and Alexander; whom I have delivered unto Satan, that they may learn not to blaspheme" (1 Ti.1:20).
"Do not they blaspheme that worthy name by the which ye are called?" (Js.2:7).
"Thou makest us a strife unto our neighbours: and our enemies laugh among themselves" (Ps.80:6).
"Princes also did sit and speak against me: but thy servant did meditate in thy statutes" (Ps.119:23).

DEEPER STUDY # 14
(7:22) **Pride** (huperephania): self-exaltation, conceit, arrogance, haughtiness, putting oneself above others, looking down upon others, scorn, contempt. It means to lift one's head above another, to hold contempt for another, to compare oneself with others. Pride can be hidden in the heart as well as openly displayed. God resists the proud (Js.4:6; 1 Pe.5:5; Pr.3:24).

"Be of the same mind one toward another. Mind not high things, but condescend to men of low estate. Be not wise in your own conceits" (Ro.12:16).
"And if any man think that he knoweth any thing, he knoweth nothing yet as he ought to know" (1 Co.8:2).
"For all that is in the world, the lust of the flesh, and the lust of the eyes, and the pride of life, is not of the Father, but is of the world" (1 Jn.2:16).
"The wicked in his pride doth persecute the poor: let them be taken in the devices that they have imagined" (Ps.10:2).
"Be not wise in thine own eyes: fear the LORD, and depart from evil" (Pr.3:7).
"When pride cometh, then cometh shame" (Pr.11:2).
"Pride goeth before destruction, and a haughty spirit before a fall" (Pr.16:18).
"A high look, and a proud heart, and the plowing of the wicked, is sin" (Pr.21:4).
"Woe unto them that are wise in their own eyes, and prudent in their own sight!" (Is.5:21).

DEEPER STUDY # 15
(7:22) **Foolishness** (aphrosune): moral senselessness, folly, recklessness, thoughtlessness. It is a man who acts foolishly in morals and duty, behavior and thought.

"This their way is their folly: yet their posterity approve their sayings" (Ps.49:13).
"The folly of fools is deceit" (Pr.14:8).
"The heart of him that hath understanding seeketh knowledge: but the mouth of fools feedeth on foolishness" (Pr.15:14).
"He that answereth a matter before he heareth it, it is folly and shame unto him" (Pr.18:13).
"As a dog returneth to his vomit, so a fool returneth to his folly" (Pr.26:11).
"The fool hath said in his heart, There is no God. Corrupt are they, and have done abominable iniquity: there is none that doeth good" (Ps.53:1).
"Fools make a mock at sin: but among the righteous there is favour" (Pr.14:9).
"A fool despiseth his father's instruction: but he that regardeth reproof is prudent" (Pr.15:5).
"He that trusteth in his own heart is a fool: but whoso walketh wisely, he shall be delivered" (Pr.28:26).

> **"Dead flies cause the ointment of the apothecary [perfumer] to send forth a stinking savour: so doth a little folly him that is in reputation for wisdom and honour" (Ec.10:1).**
> **"As the partridge sitteth on eggs, and hatcheth them not; so he that getteth riches, and not by right, shall leave them in the midst of his days, and at his end shall be a fool" (Je.17:11).**
> **"And the Lord said unto him, Now do ye Pharisees make clean the outside of the cup and the platter; but your inward part is full of ravening and wickedness. Ye fools, did not he, that made that which is without, make that which is within also?" (Lu.11:39-40).**

4 (7:23) **Sin, Source—Evil**: the third explanation—the source of evil is the heart. The problem of evil is from within, not from without; it is internal, not external. Evil comes from man's heart (spirit), not his body. Consider the news report of any city on any given day. Notice the evil things reported and keep in mind—it is within one's own city that such evil is happening. Multiply that evil by every city of any size. Just think of all the evil that is being done every day, and that is only the reported evil, the *major* evil. Think of the evil words and evil treatment and evil thoughts—all the evil things done within all the cities (Mk.7:21-22)—and one has a picture of what Jesus meant. Man's heart is his problem. It is from the heart that *these evil things* come. Man knows better. He has more intelligence than to allow so much evil in his life and home and community and city and world. He just cannot control his heart.

Man makes three fatal mistakes when dealing with the problems of the law and evil, that is, with the problems of his heart.

a. Man judges evil to be external only. He judges only the sinful act, only the deed. In the eyes of society, a man would be considered perfect if he never did bad—never broke the law and never did the forbidden thing. A person is considered good if he *seldom* does bad—seldom breaks the law and seldom does the forbidden thing (for example, breaking the speed limit or taking a pencil from the office).

b. Man fails to see (or confess) that evil arises from the heart, from within. He does not consider that evil things come from an evil heart. Therefore, man puts little if any restraint upon the lust and inward thought. Man seldom thinks beyond the act; he seldom digs into the reason for the lust and thought; he seldom gives any attention to the heart. The result: man still grapples and always will have to grapple with the problem and tragedy of evil.

c. Man fails to see and acknowledge that the human heart needs to be changed, that is, converted. He refuses to face up to the fact that is so clearly seen: a new man is what is needed. Somehow man's heart needs to be reborn.

> **"Being born again, not of corruptible seed, but of incorruptible, by the word of God, which liveth and abideth for ever" (1 Pe.1:23).**
> **"And be renewed in the spirit of your mind; and that ye put on the new man, which after God is created in righteousness and true holiness" (Ep.4:23-24).**
> **"Put off the old man with his deeds; and have put on the new man, which is renewed in knowledge after the image of him that created him" (Col.3:9-10).**

Jesus revealed the problem so clearly in this passage. Note the progress of sin within man. (1) It begins in human nature: "within, out of the heart." (2) It develops in the human mind: in "evil thoughts." (3) It is expressed in human acts: "adulteries, fornications...."

	I. The Steps to Caring for the Rejected, 7:24-30 *(Mt. 15:21-28)*	he would cast forth the devil out of her daughter. 27 But Jesus said unto her, Let the children first be filled: for it is not meet to take the children's bread, and to cast it unto the dogs.	a. Listening to the cry of the rejected. b. Stressing to the rejected the need for humility: The Jews (children) were to receive the gospel first; the Gentiles (dogs) were to receive it later[DS1]
1. Step 1: Taking care of one's own body & spirit a. Jesus entered the land of the Gentiles b. Jesus needed rest & sought quiet in a house	24 And from thence he arose, and went into the borders of Tyre and Sidon, and entered into an house, and would have no man know it: but he could not be hid.	28 And she answered and said unto him, Yes, Lord: yet the dogs under the table eat of the children's crumbs.	c. Leading the rejected (a Gentile) to endure & believe
2. Step 2: Allowing interruptions of one's privacy or schedule by the rejected	25 For a certain woman, whose young daughter had an unclean spirit, heard of him, and came and fell at his feet:	29 And he said unto her, For this saying go thy way; the devil is gone out of thy daughter. 30 And when she was come to her house, she found the devil gone out, and her daughter laid upon the bed.	**4. Step 4: Meeting the needs of the rejected**
3. Step 3: Conversing with the rejected	26 The woman was a Greek, a Syrophenician by nation; and she besought him that		

DIVISION IV

THE SON OF GOD'S TRAINING MINISTRY: JESUS' INTENSIVE PREPARATION OF THE DISCIPLES, 6:7-8:26

I. The Steps to Caring for the Rejected, 7:24-30

(7:24-30) **Introduction**: prejudice and rejection are wrong. The rejected are to be reached out to and helped. The rejected are always *cut off* by society, excluded from walking in the midst of society. They are unacceptable and ostracized. Why? Because society wraps its acceptable behavior around itself and secludes itself from those who act differently. Society has little time to deal with those who differ, and sometimes even fears them, but this must not be. Society must allow its seclusion to be interrupted—face up to the differences and needs of the rejected; converse and discuss the differences with them; and then work to meet their needs. Note the steps that the rejected must take in order to receive help. The rejected woman approached Jesus humbly (v.25); discussed her need with Him (vv.26-28); persevered in asking for help (v.28); confessed her humble status or need (v.28); and then she received help (vv.29-30).

1. Step 1: taking care of one's own body and spirit (v.24).
2. Step 2: allowing interruptions of one's privacy or schedule by the rejected (v.25).
3. Step 3: conversing with the rejected (vv.26-28).
4. Step 4: meeting the needs of the rejected (vv.29-30).

1 (7:24) **Rest—Jesus Christ, Humanity**: Jesus needed rest. In this passage He is seen deliberately withdrawing to the borders of Gentile country. He needed quiet and time to prepare both Himself and His disciples for the end. The only place He could find freedom from the crowds and from His opponents was in the northern area, the area bordering Gentile territory. No Jew was likely to enter Gentile areas. It should be noted that this event foreshadowed the spread of the gospel worldwide and God's great desire for all barriers to be broken down (see outline and notes—Ep.2:11-18; 2:19-22).

Tyre was the capitol of Phoenicia. (See note, *Tyre*—Ac.21:1-3.) It was immediately north of Judaea, and Sidon was immediately north of its border. Apparently multitudes of people had flocked to Jesus from these Gentile areas. His fame had already spread as far away as Tyre and Sidon (Mk.3:8). Jesus sought quiet in a private house, but as Mark says, "He could not be hid."

> **Thought 1.** There is a time to labor, and there is a time to seek rest and God's presence. Note: Jesus wanted to be alone. "[He] would have no man know" where He was. Seeking rest and God's presence are essential if we are to serve in the power of God. Jesus' stay in Gentile country was apparently about six months long. Imagine being in God's presence on a spiritual retreat for much of a six-month period (see notes—Mk.7:31; see Mt.15:29).

2 (7:25) **Jew—Gentile**: the first step to caring for the rejected is to allow interruptions by the rejected. The woman had two strikes against her. First, she had a daughter with an unclean spirit. In the ancient world when a family member had an evil spirit, the whole family was shunned, sometimes feared and ostracized. Both the daughter and mother knew rejection and the deep emotions of it.

Second, the mother was a Greek, a Syrophenician or Canaanite by race. She was from one of the seven nations driven out of the land of Canaan in the Old Testament. They and the Jews were bitter enemies, ancestral enemies. They despised and hated each other. In approaching Jesus, she knew that she was coming to a Jew who was assumed to be her enemy.

But note a significant fact: Jesus let her come; He did not stop her. Others rejected her and her daughter, having nothing to do with them. She and her daughter stood alone in the world, rejected by all. Jesus needed rest and time alone with God, and the disciples objected to her (Mt.15:23). But Jesus allowed her to interrupt Him. She stood alone in the world as rejected as a person could be, but Jesus received her.

"Even as the Son of man came not to be ministered unto, but to minister, and to give his life a ransom for many" (Mt.20:28).

"Come unto me, all ye that labour and are heavy laden, and I will give you rest" (Mt.11:28).

"Then were there brought unto him little children [the needy], that he should put his hands on them, and pray: and the disciples rebuked them. But Jesus said, Suffer little children [the needy], and forbid them not, to come unto me: for of such is the kingdom of heaven" (Mt.19:13-14).

3 (7:26-28) **Care—Humility—Belief**: the second step to caring for the rejected is to converse with them. Note three things.

a. Jesus listened to the cry of the rejected. The rejected woman *besought* (erotao), asked, begged Christ to heal her demon-possessed daughter. The word *besought* is in the Greek imperfect tense which means she *kept on begging and begging*. Note that Jesus kept on listening and listening.

It is important to understand what was happening. The woman had only a *limited* concept of Jesus, of who He was. She had apparently heard that the Jews expected a Messiah, a son of the great King David who was to work miracles for them. And she had heard about Jesus, that He was delivering people from their sicknesses and healing them. But seeing Jesus only as a miracle worker and healer was an inadequate concept of Him. It prohibited Him from working. What the woman needed was to grow in her understanding of just who Jesus really was.

How gracious is our Lord! He listened to the cry of this rejected woman. He knew her heart, what was in it, every thought. He knew what she needed in order to be brought around to understanding His true Messiahship. So He began to lead her step by step to understand His Lordship and to confess her faith in a humble and worshipful spirit.

b. Jesus stressed the need for humility to the rejected. Jesus said two things to the woman—two things that are often thought to be harsh; therefore, what He said needs to be clearly understood.

1) Jesus said, "Let the children first be filled" (v.27). He was saying, "The Jews, the first children of God, must first be reached." There was no rejection whatsoever in this statement to the woman. It was merely a statement of fact. Jesus had come primarily to the house of Israel while on earth. He had to concentrate His ministry if He were to achieve His purpose. But why make this statement to the woman? There were apparently two reasons.
   - ⇒ The woman needed to learn persistence, humility, and trust.
   - ⇒ The woman needed to learn that there was only one true religion and one true Messiah. She was a Greek from a proud pagan society. She had been and probably was a worshipper of false gods; thereby she was undeserving of being heard by the true Messiah, the only living and true God of the universe. She had recognized Jesus as the Son of David, as the miracle worker of the Jews who was delivering them from their diseases. But she needed to recognize something else: that He was the *only Messiah* and the *only hope* for all people. No other religion, no other gods could do anything for her or for anyone else. He alone was her hope. He alone was to be the Lord and Master whom she was to worship. She had to learn the same lesson that the Samaritan woman at the well had to learn: salvation is of the Jews (Jn.4:22). (See note—Mt.15:21-28.)

2) Jesus also said, "It is not meet to take the children's bread, and to cast it unto the dogs" (v.27). These words could be interpreted as harsh except for one thing: Jesus never spoke harshly or rejected anyone who came to Him with a desperate need and had the potential of trusting Him as Lord. So, whatever happened, we know the words were not meant to be words of harshness or rejection.

   What, then, did they mean? Again, Jesus had to move the woman forward in faith and in understanding who He was: the Lord and Master of everyone's life, not just of the Jews. He was not just the Son of David. He had to teach her that salvation was of the Jews, and that He was that Salvation—the Master of all lives. He was telling her that "it was not right to take the bread of the gospel that belonged to the true worshippers of God and give it to the *dogs*, that is, the heathen.

   The woman was a Greek; she was of a proud people with a rich heritage, but the Greeks despised the Jews. She was a worshipper of false gods, a heathen, an outsider, a sinner; and He was the Messiah, the Master of all lives. Was she willing to humble herself, surrendering to Him as the Master of her life?

c. Jesus led the rejected woman to persist and believe. Incisively and with great spiritual insight, she saw and confessed that she was nothing spiritually: she was *a dog*. However, being a dog of the family, she had the right to eat the crumbs that fell from His table (see DEEPER STUDY # 1—Mk.7:27).

Note: the woman now called Jesus *Lord* and now worshipped Him as Lord. She called Him "Lord" before, but now she did the one essential thing: she worshipped Him as Lord (see v.22).

"Not every one that saith unto me, Lord, Lord, shall enter into the kingdom of heaven; but he that doeth the will of my Father which is in heaven" (Mt.7:21; see 7:21-23).

"That if thou shalt confess with thy mouth the Lord Jesus, and shalt believe in thine heart that God hath raised him from the dead, thou shalt be saved. For with the heart man believeth unto righteousness; and with the mouth confession is made unto salvation" (Ro.10:9-10).

"For whosoever shall call upon the name of the Lord shall be saved" (Ro.10:13).

"And that every tongue should confess that Jesus Christ is Lord, to the glory of God the Father" (Ph.2:11).

DEEPER STUDY # 1

(7:27) **Dog**: was usually a symbol of dishonor—referring to the wild scavenging dogs of the streets. Calling people *dogs* in the day of Jesus was a common practice. Paul called the Judaizers who hounded and persecuted believers *dogs* (Ph.3:2). Jews sometimes called Gentiles *dogs* as a term of contempt and insult. A Gentile was a *Gentile dog*, an *infidel dog*, or a *Christian dog*. However, note this: the word for dog used by Jesus is not the dog of the street, but of the house pet. This, as well as the tone of His voice, apparently took any contemptuous sting out of the word. This seems clear by the woman's persistence in seeking help. Jesus' use of the word was evidently to stir and test her sincerity and persistence (see notes—Mt.15:26-27; 15:28).

4 (7:29-30) **Ministering—Jesus Christ, Mission**: the fourth step to caring for the rejected is to meet their needs. Jesus answered her prayer. He cast the devil out of her daughter.

One things rises above all others in the experience of this mother. She believed Jesus could meet her need, and she would not let Him go until he had met her need. Her belief was so strong *she would not quit despite being met with silence, irritation, opposition, apparent rebuff, and being told that she was undeserving* (see notes—Mt.15:23-24; Mk.7:25). There is no way to say it except "O woman, great is thy faith."

> **"And I say unto you, Ask, and it shall be given you; seek, and ye shall find; knock, and it shall be opened unto you" (Lu.11:9).**

Imagine this also. She believed Jesus' power could overcome space and time. Her daughter was back home! What enormous faith!

But note a crucial point. Her faith in Jesus' power, as great as it was, was not enough. Her faith was not what caused Jesus to answer her prayer. What caused Jesus to answer her prayer was her personal humility (surrender) and worship of Him as Lord. Jesus answers the prayer and exercises His power in behalf of those who (1) surrender (humble) themselves to Him and (2) worship Him as Lord.

> **"Even as the Son of man came not to be ministered unto, but to minister, and to give his life a ransom for many" (Mt.20:28).**
>
> **"For we have not an high priest which cannot be touched with the feeling of our infirmities; but was in all points tempted like as we are, yet without sin. Let us therefore come boldly unto the throne of grace, that we may obtain mercy, and find grace to help in time of need" (He.4:15-16).**
>
> **"If ye shall ask any thing in my name, I will do it" (Jn.14:14).**

	J. The Verdict Sought For One's Service: Doing Everything Well, 7:31-37 *(Mt. 15:29-31)*	tongue; 34 And looking up to heaven, he sighed, and saith unto him, Ephphatha, that is, Be opened.	**4. He trusted God for power**
1. He looked after His own personal needs & the needs of His loved ones (the disciples)	31 And again, departing from the coasts of Tyre and Sidon, he came unto the sea of Galilee, through the midst of the coasts of Decapolis.	35 And straightway his ears were opened, and the string of his tongue was loosed, and he spake plain.	
2. He listened to the pleas of people for help	32 And they bring unto him one that was deaf, and had an impediment in his speech; and they beseech him to put his hand upon him.	36 And he charged them that they should tell no man: but the more he charged them, so much the more a great deal they published it;	**5. He sought no personal applause or praise**
3. He was considerate of the feelings & conditions of others: Took the man aside, alone	33 And he took him aside from the multitude, and put his fingers into his ears, and he spit, and touched his	37 And were beyond measure astonished, saying, He hath done all things well: he maketh both the deaf to hear, and the dumb to speak.	**6. He demanded a verdict: "He has done all things well"**

DIVISION IV

THE SON OF GOD'S TRAINING MINISTRY: JESUS' INTENSIVE PREPARATION OF THE DISCIPLES, 6:7-8:26

J. The Verdict Sought for One's Service: Doing Everything Well, 7:31-37

(7:31-37) **Introduction—Decision—Judgment**: this passage includes a phenomenal verdict about Jesus: "He has done all things well" (v.37). This was the verdict of this particular crowd, but it was not and never has been the verdict of every man. Yet every man has to make a decision about Jesus; he has to pass judgment upon Jesus. A verdict is required.

Note something else: the day is coming when God is going to pronounce His verdict, His judgment upon every man. Every man is determining exactly what God's verdict will be. How? By the way he lives.

The verdict Christ wants pronounced upon every man is, "He doeth all things well" (Mk.7:37). "Well done thou good and faithful servant" (Mt.25:21). How can we be assured of such a verdict by God? Jesus shows us how in this passage.

1. He looked after His own personal needs and the needs of His loved ones (the disciples) (v.31).
2. He listened to the pleas of people for help (v.32).
3. He was considerate of the feelings and conditions of others: took the man aside, alone (v.33).
4. He trusted God for power (vv.34-35).
5. He sought no personal applause or praise (v.36).
6. He demanded a verdict: "He hath done all things well" (v.37).

1 (7:31) **Disciples, Training of—Jesus Christ, Cross—Care**: Jesus looked after His own personal needs and the needs of His loved ones. This is a strange verse, for Jesus was in Tyre, and He wanted to go to Galilee which is south of Tyre. But note: the verse says He travelled north from Tyre to Sidon. Why would He go north to Sidon if He wished to go south to Galilee? Probably for two reasons. First, He needed a period of quietness before facing the opposition and storm that awaited Him in Galilee and beyond. Second, the disciples also needed a long period of quiet training.

The cross was lying immediately before Jesus. The end was at hand. The Gentile area was the only place He could be free from the crowds and have quiet with the disciples (see note—Mt.15:21-22). He and His disciples needed to be prepared for the end. Apparently the disciples had six months or more of uninterrupted and intensive training at the feet of Jesus. (See notes—Mt.15:21-22; 16:21-28; 17:22.) (See note—Mt.15:29 for more detailed discussion.)

Thought 1. Quiet is needed—freedom from crowds and from the hustle and bustle of daily responsibilities. However, rest does not mean inactivity. Even when resting, we should be meeting with God, preparing ourselves for what lies ahead.

> **"Now therefore stand still, that I may reason with you before the LORD of all the righteous acts of the LORD, which he did to you and to your fathers" (1 S.12:7).**
>
> **"Hearken unto this, O Job: stand still, and consider the wondrous works of God" (Jb.37:14).**
>
> **"Stand in awe, and sin not: commune with your own heart upon your bed, and be still" (Ps.4:4).**
>
> **"Be still, and know that I am God: I will be exalted among the heathen, I will be exalted in the earth" (Ps.46:10).**

Thought 2. Imagine six months of training on the death and resurrection of Christ. How supreme is its importance!

> **"For God so loved the world, that he gave his only begotten Son, that whosoever believeth in him should not perish, but have everlasting life" (Jn.3:16).**
>
> **"For I delivered unto you first of all that which I also received, how that Christ died for our sins according to the scriptures; and that he was buried, and that he rose again the third day according to the scriptures" (1 Co.15:3-4).**

"Who his own self bare our sins in his own body on the tree, that we, being dead to sins, should live unto righteousness: by whose stripes ye were healed" (1 Pe.2:24).

"Know ye not, that so many of us as were baptized into Jesus Christ were baptized into his death? Therefore we are buried with him by baptism into death: that like as Christ was raised up from the dead by the glory of the Father, even so we also should walk in newness of life. For if we have been planted together in the likeness of his death, we shall be also in the likeness of his resurrection: knowing this, that our old man is crucified with him, that the body of sin might be destroyed, that henceforth we should not serve sin" (Ro.6:3-6).

2 (7:32) **Listening—Compassion**: Jesus listened to the pleas of people for help. After six or so months, Jesus returned to the Sea of Galilee in the district of Decapolis. Some friends brought a deaf man to Him, and as is so often the case with deafness, the man's speech was affected. He "had an impediment in his speech"; he was tongue-tied.

The man could not hear. When the sounds of nature sang forth, he could not hear their beauty. When men carried on conversation, he could not participate. When strangers spoke loudly to help him hear, it only added to his embarrassment. He could only sit "as deaf," in stone silence.

The point is that Jesus felt compassion for the man; He listened to the plea for help. He was tender toward all men who had need. The man's friends "beseeched" Jesus to help by touching the man, and in compassion Jesus responded. He did exactly what He should do: "He did all things well" (v.37).

Thought 1. We should listen to the pleas of people for help. Listening is part of "doing all things well." Listening demonstrates a *Christ-centered heart*, a heart that belongs to a sensitive, godly servant of the Lord.

"For I was an hungred, and ye gave me meat: I was thirsty, and ye gave me drink: I was a stranger, and ye took me in: naked, and ye clothed me: I was sick, and ye visited me: I was in prison, and ye came unto me" (Mt.25:35-36).

"Be ye therefore merciful, as your Father also is merciful" (Lu.6:36).

"We then that are strong ought to bear the infirmities of the weak, and not to please ourselves" (Ro.15:1).

3 (7:33) **Consideration—Compassion—Care—Jesus Christ, Source**: Jesus was considerate of the feelings and condition of others. Note two things.

a. Jesus took the man aside, out of the presence of the others. There was tenderness in this act. The man had suffered embarrassment all his life because he could not participate in conversation or activities with others. Life was cruel to him. He knew what embarrassment really was. He was shy and reserved, perhaps even withdrawn. He had experienced embarrassment even standing there before Jesus. Jesus responded tenderly. He *considered* the man's feelings; therefore, He took him aside from the crowd.

Thought 1. Doing all things well requires consideration. Consideration, tenderly reacting to the feelings of others, is always to be the way of the believer.

"Bear ye one another's burdens, and so fulfil the law of Christ" (Ga.6:2).

"For we have not an high priest which cannot be touched with the feeling of our infirmities; but was in all points tempted like as we are, yet without sin. Let us therefore come boldly unto the throne of grace, that we may obtain mercy, and find grace to help in time of need" (He.4:15-16).

"Like as a father pitieth his children, so the LORD pitieth them that fear him" (Ps.103:13).

b. Jesus put His fingers into the man's ears and spat and touched the man's tongue. Why? The man could not hear what Jesus was saying. He needed to know that it was Jesus who alone had the power to heal him. The saliva and fingers were signs that the power came through Jesus' body, from within His very being. Jesus Christ, His power alone, was the man's source of healing, of being made whole. The man needed to know this beyond any question. He could not hear, so some symbolic act had to be used.

The scene must have been dramatic for the man. He saw it all; and his attention, standing there face to face with Jesus, must have been glued to every act of Jesus. The man's faith was bound to be stirred enormously when Jesus touched His stammering tongue and thrust His fingers into the man's ears. There was bound to be a tremendous sense of expectancy surging through the man's body.

Thought 1. The source of the man's healing was Jesus. Jesus used whatever was at His disposal to show this.
(1) Every man must be shown that the Source of healing, the Source of being made whole, is Jesus.
(2) Believers must use everything at their disposal to proclaim Jesus as the Source of man's deliverance (salvation).

"Wherefore in all things it behoved him to be made like unto his brethren, that he might be a merciful and faithful high priest in things pertaining to God, to make reconciliation for the sins of the people. For in that he himself hath suffered being tempted, he is able to succour them that are tempted" (He.2:17-18).

4 (7:34-35) **Jesus Christ, Power—Compassion**: Jesus trusted God for power. Note three acts.

a. Jesus looked up to heaven. (Remember the man could not hear.) Very simply, Jesus was demonstrating a point—a point that must always be made. The power to make a person whole comes from God above. The man must look up to heaven, to God, for deliverance.

Note a significant point: Jesus indicated in this act that He is *The Mediator* who stands between God and man. The source of power is God, and the power is brought to man by the Mediator, Jesus Christ.

b. Jesus *sighed* (stenazo); that is, He groaned. Jesus felt for the man; He was touched by the feeling of the man's infirmities. And He was probably thinking of all humanity, of the crowd in all its infirmity and sin (see Heb.4:15). He had just looked up to heaven and felt the great divergence between heaven and earth, the enormous difference between heaven's perfection and earth's sin and corruption. Jesus was bound to groan under the strain of such a spiritual ache—an ache for all men to be made whole.

c. Jesus exerted the power of God and healed the man. He said "ephphatha": be opened. He opened the man's ears and loosed his tongue, and the man was able to speak clearly.

Thought 1. The miracle was two things.

(1) It was proof that Jesus is the Messiah, the Son of God Himself. Isaiah had predicted such miracles of the Messiah (Is.35:5-6).

> **"The Spirit of the Lord is upon me, because he hath anointed me to preach the gospel to the poor; he hath sent me to heal the brokenhearted, to preach deliverance to the captives, and recovering of sight to the blind, to set at liberty them that are bruised, to preach the acceptable year of the Lord....And he began to say unto them, This day is this scripture fulfilled in your ears" (Lu.4:18-29, 21).**
>
> **"How God anointed Jesus of Nazareth with the Holy Ghost and with power: who went about doing good, and healing all that were oppressed of the devil; for God was with him" (Ac.10:38).**

(2) It was a demonstration of tender consideration for the needs and feelings of others—a strong lesson for every believer.

> **"Even as the Son of man came not to be ministered unto, but to minister, and to give his life a ransom for many" (Mt.20:28).**
>
> **"Then said Jesus to them again, Peace be unto you: as my Father hath sent me, even so send I you" (Jn.20:21).**
>
> **"Remember them that are in bonds, as bound with them; and them which suffer adversity, as being yourselves also in the body" (He.13:3).**

5 (7:36) **Humility—Witnessing**: Jesus sought no personal honor. He charged everyone to keep the miracle quiet, to tell no one. The word for *charge* (diestelleto) is strong. The order was clearly given. The reason is not known, but there is a lesson on humility in the charge. Jesus was not after the applause or praise of men. The miracles were not done for that reason. All that He was and all that He had done was to help men and point them to God. Men were lost, and He had come to seek and save the lost, not to win their applause (see Lu.19:10).

Thought 1. There are two lessons here.

(1) A lesson on humility.

> **"But it shall not be so among you: but whosoever will be great among you, let him be your minister; and whosoever will be chief among you, let him be your servant" (Mt.20:26-27).**
>
> **"Let nothing be done through strife or vainglory; but in lowliness of mind let each esteem other better than themselves. Look not every man on his own things, but every man also on the things of others" (Ph.2:3-4).**
>
> **"For if a man think himself to be something, when he is nothing, he deceiveth himself" (Ga.6:3).**

(2) A lesson on witnessing. The healed man and his friends were forbidden to share their godly experience, but they could not keep quiet. They were so full of the presence of God and His power, they just had to bear witness. How much more the disciples! They were bound to learn the importance of being filled with God and His power for witnessing.

> **"But ye shall receive power, after that the Holy Ghost is come upon you: and ye shall be witnesses unto me both in Jerusalem, and in all Judaea, and in Samaria, and unto the uttermost part of the earth" (Ac.1:8).**
>
> **"To wit, that God was in Christ, reconciling the world unto himself, not imputing their trespasses unto them; and hath committed unto us the word of reconciliation. Now then we are ambassadors for Christ, as though God did beseech you by us: we pray you in Christ's stead, be ye reconciled to God" (2 Co.5:19-20).**

6 (7:37) **Decision—Verdict**: Jesus demanded a verdict. Jesus healed a multitude of people at that time (Mt.15:30-31). The people were astonished *beyond measure* (huperperissos), overwhelmed. They pronounced the verdict: "He hath done all things well," the very verdict Christ was after. The people desperately needed to focus their attention upon *the Mediator and the power of God* to make men whole.

> **"For there is one God, and one mediator between God and men, the man Christ Jesus; who gave himself a ransom for all, to be testified in due time" (1 Ti.2:5-6).**
>
> **"Wherefore he is able also to save them to the uttermost that come unto God by him, seeing he ever liveth to make intercession for them" (He.7:25).**

	CHAPTER 8 **K. The Need for Spiritual Food, Compassion, & Evangelism, 8:1-9** *(Mt. 15:32-39)*	a man satisfy these men with bread here in the wilderness? 5 And he asked them, How many loaves have ye? And they said, Seven.	
1. The need for spiritual food a. Crowds followed Jesus b. Crowds hungered spiritually: Had gone without food	In those days the multitude being very great, and having nothing to eat, Jesus called his disciples unto him, and saith unto them,	6 And he commanded the people to sit down on the ground: and he took the seven loaves, and gave thanks, and brake, and gave to his disciples to set before them; and they did set them before the people.	c. Compassion involves orderly arrangement d. Compassion involves giving all & using all to meet needs e. Compassion involves giving thanks to God
2. The need for compassion[DS1] a. Compassion involves seeing needs	2 I have compassion on the multitude, because they have now been with me three days, and have nothing to eat:	7 And they had a few small fishes: and he blessed, and commanded to set them also before them.	
	3 And if I send them away fasting to their own houses, they will faint by the way: for divers of them came from far.	8 So they did eat, and were filled: and they took up of the broken meat that was left seven baskets.	f. Compassion involves saving & preserving
b. Compassion involves the use of resources	4 And his disciples answered him, From whence can	9 And they that had eaten were about four thousand: and he sent them away.	**3. The need for evangelism, for moving on to reach others**

DIVISION IV

THE SON OF GOD'S TRAINING MINISTRY: JESUS' INTENSIVE PREPARATION OF THE DISCIPLES, 6:7–8:26

K. The Need for Spiritual Food, Compassion, and Evangelism, 8:1-9

(8:1-9) **Introduction**: Jesus was doing two things in this event.

1. As always, He was demonstrating His Messiahship in order to drive the truth more and more deeply into the hearts and minds of the disciples.
2. In a most direct way, He was teaching His disciples that they were to minister to the needy, no matter who they were. In this event He was ministering primarily, if not totally, to Gentiles (see notes—Mt.15:21-22; 15:29). The Jews considered the Gentiles to be heathen, lost and despised by God. Jewish prejudice against the Gentiles ran deep. Jesus had come to save all men, not just the Jews. The disciples desperately needed to learn this truth, for they would need to minister to all men regardless of race after His return to the Father.

In a very simple yet forceful demonstration, Jesus revealed that the *whole world* has three great needs.

1. The need for spiritual food (v.1).
2. The need for compassion (vv.2-8).
3. The need for evangelism, for moving on to reach others (v.9).

1 (8:1) **Spiritual Hunger—Witnessing**: the people were hungry for spiritual food. Note two facts.

a. The crowd was large, "very great." Four thousand ate. This was an interesting number. The event occurred on the other side of the Sea of Galilee in Decapolis, a land heavily populated by Gentiles. These were the very people who had rejected Jesus earlier and had requested Him to leave their coasts after He had healed the demoniac (Mk.5:1-20). What brought about this significant change? The answer is probably found in Jesus' instructions to the healed demoniac. The demoniac had requested to follow Jesus, but Jesus had told him to remain in his own country to witness. Evidently his witness had borne great fruit and prepared the people for Jesus' return. (What a lesson to us on the importance of witnessing!)

b. The crowd hungered spiritually, so much so they had gone without food for three days. Some may have brought some provision, but by now all the food had been eaten. The people craved the Word of God. The word of Jesus was esteemed more highly than "necessary food" (Jb. 23:12).

> **"Blessed are they which do hunger and thirst after righteousness: for they shall be filled" (Mt.5:6).**
>
> **"As newborn babes, desire the sincere milk of the word, that ye may grow thereby: if so be ye have tasted that the Lord is gracious" (1 Pe.2:2-3).**
>
> **"And now, brethren, I commend you to God, and to the word of his grace, which is able to build you up, and to give you an inheritance among all them which are sanctified" (Ac.20:32).**
>
> **"And Jesus said unto them, I am the bread of life: he that cometh to me shall never hunger; and he that believeth on me shall never thirst" (Jn.6:35).**

2 (8:2-8) **Compassion**: the disciples needed to have compassion for the people. The disciples looked upon many of these people as outcasts. They were Gentiles, aliens from God's chosen race. They were even considered enemies by many of the Jews. There was nothing attractive or appealing about them in the eyes of the disciples. The disciples...

- had no compassion for them
- were not concerned for them
- did not observe them at all
- had no thought of helping them

Jesus had to teach His disciples compassion. He had already discussed the need for this with them (Mt.9:36-38). Now He tried to stir their compassion for the lost and outcast. He did this by showing just what compassion involves.

a. Compassion involves seeing needs (vv.2-3). Jesus had looked at and observed the people, and in doing so, He had seen their need. The disciples should have also looked and observed, but they had not. They were too prejudiced and too prideful. They felt the people were beneath them, not worthy of their time and effort. Therefore, the disciples never observed the people's needs. They should have, for Jesus had just taught the same lesson (Mk.6:35-44); but their prejudice and pride blinded their eyes and hearts, even from the truth that had just been taught. This shows the great need for Jesus to repeat the same truths over and over.

Thought 1. Looking at and observing people are essential in order to see need, and seeing need is essential to stir compassion. Compassion is aroused by seeing and observing or studying the needs of people. If we never expose ourselves to the needs of people, we will never experience compassion.

"Therefore said he unto them, The harvest truly is great, but the labourers are few: pray ye therefore the Lord of the harvest, that he would send forth labourers into his harvest" (Lu.10:2).

"Say not ye, There are yet four months, and then cometh harvest? behold, I say unto you, Lift up your eyes, and look on the fields; for they are white already to harvest" (Jn.4:35).

"Brethren, my heart's desire and prayer to God for Israel [all nations] is, that they might be saved" (Ro.10:1).

b. Compassion involves the use of resources (vv.4-5. See note—Mk.6:37-44.) Needs can never be met apart from resources. The disciples wondered about the resources, where enough bread could be secured to feed so many; and they asked Jesus about the matter, offering every objection and excuse.

⇒ The place was a wilderness, beyond reach (v.4).
⇒ Their resources were too meager (v.5).
⇒ The multitude and the need were too great (vv.1, 9).

Thought 1. Too many use the same excuses to keep from becoming involved. Too many needs go unmet because of such flimsy excuses.

Thought 2. Note two significant points.

(1) The disciples overlooked the resources they had.
(2) Jesus did not ask the disciples to discuss how they could meet so great a need. He told them to check on what resources *they had.* What resources others had and just how God was going to meet the need should not have been their concern. Their concern should have been seeing just what they could do.

"I have showed you all things, how that so labouring ye ought to support the weak, and to remember the words of the Lord Jesus, how he said, It is more blessed to give than to receive" (Ac.20:35).

"Distributing to the necessity of saints; given to hospitality" (Ro.12:13).

"As we have therefore opportunity, let us do good unto all men, especially unto them who are of the household of faith" (Ga.6:10).

"Charge them that are rich in this world, that they be not highminded, nor trust in uncertain riches, but in the living God, who giveth us richly all things to enjoy; that they do good, that they be rich in good works, ready to distribute, willing to communicate; laying up in store for themselves a good foundation against the time to come, that they may lay hold on eternal life" (1 Ti.6:17-19).

c. Compassion involves orderly arrangement (v.6). Note that meeting the people's needs was not done in a disorderly, haphazard way. The people were arranged to receive the provision (see note, pt.3—Mk.6:37-44 for discussion).

d. Compassion involves giving all, taking all, and using all that one has to meet the need (v.6). Note that all seven loaves were *given to Jesus*, then Jesus *took all* seven loaves and *used all* seven to meet the need. Nothing was held back. All the resources available were used to meet the need. Compassion will always give all, and then take all and use all to meet the need.

Thought 1. How often we hold back, store up, even deceive, lie and cheat about our resources just to keep from having to give. Christ teaches that we are to give all our resources to meet the needs of a desperate world. Then we are to make sure that all we gave is *taken and used* in meeting the needs. Such is *true compassion.*

"But lay up for yourselves treasures in heaven, where neither moth nor rust doth corrupt, and where thieves do not break through nor steal" (Mt.6:20).

"Sell that ye have, and give alms; provide yourselves bags which wax not old, a treasure in the heavens that faileth not, where no thief approacheth, neither moth corrupteth" (Lu.12:33).

"So likewise, whosoever he be of you that forsaketh not all that he hath, he cannot be my disciple" (Lu.14:33).

"Then the disciples, every man according to his ability, determined to send relief unto the brethren which dwelt in Judaea" (Ac.11:29).

e. Compassion involves thankfulness to God. Jesus "gave thanks" (v.6) and "blessed" (v.7) the resources. The point is striking. What the disciples had to give was small, really insignificant in meeting such a mammoth need, and what Jesus held in His hands was so meager it was impossible to meet the need. Yet Christ gave thanks for the meager resource, for what He held in His hands.

Thought 1. Note something. The resource had been given to be used; therefore, Jesus was able to use it despite its smallness. If it had not been given, it would not have been used. And most tragically, the need would not have been met. Christ is forever thankful for the resource given Him, no matter how small; and He is able to use the resource to meet the need—no matter how insignificant the resource and no matter how mammoth the need may seem.

f. Compassion involves saving and preserving whatever resource is left over (v.8). Resources are to be handled carefully. Nothing is to be wasted. Whatever is not used in meeting one need is to be used in meeting another need (see note, pt.6—Mk.6:37-44).

DEEPER STUDY # 1
(8:2) **Compassion**: see note 2 and DEEPER STUDY # 2—Mt.9:36.

3 (8:9) **Evangelism—Witnessing**: there was the need for evangelism, for moving on. Remember this crowd had hungered for the Word of God, hungered for spiritual food, even putting the spiritual before the physical. Now Jesus sent them away. The idea is that He sent them away as a group, as a body of people who had hungered spiritually and had been fed. As they went, they would certainly bear witness to their glorious experience of having been fed by Jesus, both spiritually and physically.

Thought 1. Christ has sent us, too, to proclaim that He alone can feed the soul of man.

Thought 2. There is a time to sit at the feet of Jesus and be fed, but there is also a time to be sent away, to go forth carrying the glorious message that He feeds the hungering heart.

"But they, when they were departed, spread abroad his fame in all that country" (Mt.9:31).
"Return to thine own house, and show how great things God hath done unto thee" (Lu.8:39).
"Then said Jesus to them again, Peace be unto you: as my Father hath sent me, even so send I you" (Jn.20:21).
"For we cannot but speak the things which we have seen and heard" (Ac.4:20).
"We having the same spirit of faith, according as it is written, I believed, and therefore have I spoken; we also believe, and therefore speak" (2 Co.4:13).
"And the things that thou hast heard of me among many witnesses, the same commit thou to faithful men, who shall be able to teach others also" (2 Ti.2:2).
"But sanctify the Lord God in your hearts: and be ready always to give an answer to every man that asketh you a reason of the hope that is in you with meekness and fear" (1 Pe.3:15).
"I will mention the lovingkindnesses of the LORD, and the praises of the LORD, according to all that the LORD hath bestowed on us, and the great goodness toward the house of Israel, which he hath bestowed on them according to his mercies, and according to the multitude of his lovingkindnesses" (Is.63:7).

	L. The Fault of the Spiritually Blind, 8:10-13 *(Mt. 16:1-4)*		
1. They confronted Jesus in disbelief a. Jesus crossed the lake b. Jesus entered Dalmanutha[DS1] c. The religionists confronted him	10 And straightway he entered into a ship with his disciples, and came into the parts of Dalmanutha. 11 And the Pharisees came forth, and began to question	sign from heaven, tempting him. 12 And he sighed deeply in his spirit, and saith, Why doth this generation seek after a sign? verily I say unto you, There shall no sign be given unto this generation. 13 And he left them, and entering into the ship again departed to the other side.	b. Their motive: To trick Him **3. They grieved the Lord[DS2]** **4. They received no sign from the Lord** **5. They were left behind by the Lord**
2. They sought a sign a. Their blindness: To His works	with him, seeking of him a		

DIVISION IV

THE SON OF GOD'S TRAINING MINISTRY: JESUS' INTENSIVE PREPARATION OF THE DISCIPLES, 6:7-8:26

L. The Fault of the Spiritually Blind, 8:10-13

(8:10-13) **Introduction**: spiritual blindness is a problem for every generation. Most men are spiritually blind (2 Co.4:4). They are blind to the "signs," to the presence, mercy, care, and gifts of God to men. God is easily seen by men who openly and honestly seek the truth. He is seen in the world and happenings of life, in the merciful actions that often occur in life, in the care and love often experienced, and in the gifts of goodness to help a person get along in an antagonistic world. Yet, so few look for God and give thanks to Him for all He is and does. Man chooses rather to reject a personal God and to attribute the happenings and things of life to his own efforts (humanism). Why? There is one clear reason: if man acknowledges a personal God, he has to surrender his life to that God. Therefore, man challenges: "If there be a God, prove yourself, show yourself, give us a sign." And all the while he expects no sign, and even if he saw one, he would deny it—all because he is spiritually blind to the truth.

What Jesus does in this passage is discuss the faults of the spiritually blind who want more signs.

1. They confronted Jesus in disbelief (vv.10-11).
2. They sought a sign (v.11).
3. They grieved the Lord (v.12).
4. They received no sign from the Lord (v.12).
5. They were left behind by the Lord (v.13).

1 (8:10) **Jesus Christ, Opposition to**: Jesus crossed the lake (Sea of Galilee) to the west side and to the lands close to Dalmanutha. As soon as He stepped off the boat, the religionists confronted Him. Note that Mark mentions only the Pharisees (v.11). Matthew says the Sadducees had joined forces with them in an attempt to discredit Jesus before the people (Mt.16:1). In so doing, they revealed their spiritual blindness (see note—Mt.12:1-8; note and DEEPER STUDY # 1—12:10; DEEPER STUDY # 4—12:24; notes—12:31-32; 15:1-20; DEEPER STUDY # 2—15:6-9).

DEEPER STUDY # 1

(8:10) **Dalmanutha**: this was a city sitting next to Magdala (Magadan) on the west coast of the lake or Sea of Galilee. Both cities were in the Decapolis district (see Mt.15:39).

2 (8:11) **Spiritual Blindness—Signs, Seeking**: the spiritually blind sought a sign. Note several things.

a. There is a sharp difference between man's natural and spiritual senses. Man's *natural senses can be very sharp and discerning*. He is skillful in drawing conclusions from his observations and experiences of the natural world. Weather is an example. However, *when it comes to the spiritual senses, man is dead and undiscerning*. He does not observe nor does he experience the spiritual world, not really. The signs of the times are an example.

The people of Jesus' day had signs. They lived in critical times, times that foretold the coming of the Messiah. A thoughtful and genuinely spiritual person could see the signs. Some did, such as Simeon and Anna (Lu.3:25f).

Some of the signs were as follows.

1) The scepter, that is, the lawgiver, had come from Judah (Mt.1:2).
2) The weeks or ages predicted by Daniel were closing out (see DEEPER STUDY # 1—Mt.24:15).
3) The predicted return of Elijah, who was fulfilled in the forerunner of the Messiah, John the Baptist, had come and proclaimed the Messiah to be Jesus (Mt.3:1-12).
4) The baby Jesus had been born in Bethlehem (Mt.2:1).
5) Many throughout the world were expecting the coming of some great person, some Messiah (Mt.1:18).
6) Many godly Jews were looking for the coming of the Messiah, God's great Deliverer of Israel (Lu.2:25f).
7) The message and works of Jesus were great evidence, phenomenal miracles given by God to substantiate His claims (see note and DEEPER STUDY # 1—Jn.14:11).

b. The people of our generation and every generation since Christ have had signs.

1) There are the signs of the natural world, the marvels of which are being revealed every day. But men refuse to acknowledge the Creator to whom creation points (see Ro.1:20; see Ro.1:18-32).

2) There are the privileges of life, the beauty of the world, and the experience of God's daily mercy. But men ascribe them all to natural happenings or to the laws of nature or to humanistic ability and evolution.
3) There is the Old Testament. But men, while perhaps appreciating some of its history, reject its prophetic promises of God's Messiah and salvation.
4) There is conscience or consciousness of sin (inner thought). But men deny sin. They deny it even while experiencing guilt and wondering deep within what the truth really is.
5) There is Jesus Christ and His claim to be the Messiah, the very Son of God. But men reject and deny His claim. They reject and deny while extolling the morality and value of all else He taught.
6) There is the death and resurrection of Christ, and its enormous effect upon so many down through the generations. But men deny a substitutionary death in behalf of men, and they deny the resurrection despite all the evidence validating it.
7) There are the changed lives of teeming thousands who proclaim that *the living Lord* has saved them from destruction and indwells their being. But men attribute such change to psychological causes.

c. The reason men are spiritually blind is because of their motive. The motive of the religionists was not open and honest, nor was it the motive of men's seeking the truth. They were out to *trick* Jesus, to disprove His claim and discredit Him before the people. They were out to show Him to be an imposter (see notes—Mt.12:1-8; DEEPER STUDY # 1—12:10; DEEPER STUDY # 3,4—12:24; notes—12:31-32; 15:1-20; DEEPER STUDY # 2—15:6-9).

Man can be very intelligent and discerning within the natural world, yet very ignorant and blind to the spiritual world. Too often the reason is his motive. His motive is to discredit the spiritual world, whether by denying and disproving its existence or by minimizing its influence and authority.

If man truly admits the existence of a spiritual world or of a Messiah, then he must surrender and follow the Messiah as Lord, or he must reject the Messiah and await his condemnation. Man does not want to be put into such a position. He does not want a sense, a constant nagging, of being condemned, nor does he want to change his life-style. So he closes his mind and says he will believe only if God gives him a personal sign, a miraculous sign, a sign from heaven. And all the while, he expects no sign, just knowing there will be none.

There are, of course, plenty of signs. It is a very simple matter to see God and the spiritual world behind the physical world. Any thinking man who is *open and honest and seeking the truth* will be touched by God. There is not a chance that God will not open the honest man's eyes and heart so that he can see and know. Such an honest and seeking man can clearly see that the world shows a Supreme Designer, a Supreme Intelligence and Force, an eternal purpose, a first cause. (See outlines and notes—Ro.1:19; 1:20; 1:21; 1:22-23.)

The problem is that natural man seeks justification for his worldly motives, desires, and life-style. He does not want to change his life and desires. He wants to do his own thing, to control his own destiny. In fact, man's morality, desires, motives, and life-style determine his beliefs. Natural man wants to justify himself, prove himself and his thoughts right. He does not want to discover a heavenly world and a spiritual Lord who would demand righteousness and love, total giving and sacrifice. He does not want to be under a Lord who requires all he is and has to meet the needs of a desperate world.

"And he said to them all, If any man will come after me, let him deny himself, and take up his cross daily, and follow me. For whosoever will save his life shall lose it: but whosoever will lose his life for my sake, the same shall save it" (Lu.9:23-24).

"So likewise, whosoever he be of you that forsaketh not all that he hath, he cannot be my disciple" (Lu.14:33).

"Therefore let all the house of Israel know assuredly, that God hath made that same Jesus, whom ye have crucified, both Lord and Christ" (Ac.2:36).

"Wherefore God also hath highly exalted him, and given him a name which is above every name: that at the name of Jesus every knee should bow, of things in heaven, and things in earth, and things under the earth" (Ph.2:9-10).

3 (8:12) **Spiritual Blindness**: the spiritually blind grieved the Lord. There is no excuse for spiritual blindness. Evidence after evidence, sign after sign, work after work can be clearly seen to the *honest, thinking* man. Yet man continues to deceive his own heart, and he does it knowingly. Man knows that God is; he knows down deep within the quiet recesses of his heart. Yet he outwardly denies, deceiving himself. Such is obstinate unbelief, and obstinate unbelief is both irrational and inexcusable.

Jesus faced a sad fact. The men who were standing before Him were spiritually blind, but they were not ordinary secular men. They were religionists who had the enormous evidence of His life and miracles before their very eyes. Yet even they chose to keep their lives in their own hands and to deny the Son of God who loved them and came to save them.

Thought 1. Obstinate unbelief grieves the Lord—terribly so.

"Grieve not the holy Spirit of God" (Ep.4:30).

"Quench not the Spirit" (1 Th.5:19).

"Wherefore I was grieved with that generation, and said, They do alway err in their heart; and they have not known my ways" (He.3:10).

Thought 2. There have always been unbelievers even among religious leaders. The acts of social justice—the care and ministry of enough food, clothing, housing, peace, security, happiness, health—have always attracted some to the service of Christ. Christ taught social justice and care, and what He taught is to be done. But He also taught that existence is eternal. He taught that man must be delivered from sin and corruption, born again spiritually so that he might inherit eternal life instead of dying and being separated from God eternally. (See DEEPER STUDY # 1—Heb.9:27.)

"Verily, verily, I say unto you, He that heareth my word, and believeth on him that sent me, hath everlasting life, and shall not come into condemnation; but is passed from death unto life" (Jn.5:24).

"Forasmuch then as the children are partakers of flesh and blood, he also himself likewise took part of the same; that through death he might destroy him that had the power of death, that is, the devil; and deliver them who through fear of death were all their lifetime subject to bondage" (He.2:14-15).

DEEPER STUDY # 2

(8:12) **Grieve** (anastenazas): means to groan, to sigh. Jesus felt both grief and indignation from the bottom of His heart. He was stirred to the depths, to the very core of His being. Grief and indignation were both aroused, and He groaned within His spirit (see notes—Ep.4:30; DEEPER STUDY # 1—1 Th.5:19; see DEEPER STUDY # 1—Mk.3:5; notes—Heb.3:10; Ps.95:10; Is.54:6).

4 (8:12) **Spiritual Blindness—Signs, Seeking**: the spiritually blind receive no sign from the Lord. There are seven reasons why "no sign shall be given this generation."

a. The Jews refused to look at the signs of the times (chose to be spiritually blind) because they were wicked and adulterous. There were never enough signs or evidences to convince them, to change their lives, nor to lead them to turn to God (see note—Mt.12:38-40).

"Light [Christ] is come into the world, and men loved darkness rather than light, because their deeds were evil" (Jn.3:19).

"Neither will they be persuaded, though one rose from the dead" (Lu.16:31).

b. The Jews were totally unjustified in seeking additional signs from Jesus. There had been sign after sign, miracle after miracle, work after work—enough to lead any man to the firm belief: "*Truly, this man is the Son of God*" (Mk.15:39; see Acts 2:22).

c. The Jews just did not believe. In fact, they did not want to believe. The result, of course, was what always happens to wilful unbelievers: they became obstinate in their unbelief (see DEEPER STUDY # 4—Mt.12:24; note—12:31-32).

d. The Jews did not understand the love and the faith of God, that is, the true religion of God. They failed to see what God was after: faith and love, not signs and works. God wants a man to simply believe and love Him because of who He is and because of what He has done and does do for man. The true religion of God is not a religion of works and signs, but of faith and love in Christ Jesus, His own Son (see DEEPER STUDY # 2—Jn.2:24; DEEPER STUDY # 1—4:22; note—4:48-49; DEEPER STUDY #1—Ro.4:1-25; note—4:5. See Acts 2:22.)

e. The Jews sought a sign because they were an evil and adulterous generation. The reason was simple. They were apostates, going after the false gods of works and signs instead of seeking the God of faith and love. In seeking signs and works, they were committing spiritual whoredom, turning from God and His Messiah to the false gods of signs and works. (Note: It is human reason that seeks signs and works and proofs. The spirit of man seeks belief and trust and love—the spiritual qualities that bind life together and make sense of life in all its facets.)

f. The Jews wanted signs of their own choosing, not the signs God had chosen to give. Men are always wanting God to deal with them through...

- some spectacular sign
- some brilliant sight
- some astounding truth
- some irrefutable argument
- some miraculous experience
- some unbelievable deliverance

g. God's great concern is not "signs from heaven," signs outside man. God's great concern is meeting people in their lives and hearts where they really need Him if they are to live abundantly and eternally. God wants to meet people in their sickness and sorrow, corruption and death. Meeting man in the areas of his need is an irrefutable sign given to every generation.

Thought 1. What is said of the religionists of Jesus' generation can be said of every generation of unbelievers. Unbelievers do not receive signs—not from the Lord. But believers do receive signs, the signs of having their needs met.

"Blessed are they which do hunger and thirst after righteousness: for they shall be filled" (Mt.5:6).

"But whosoever drinketh of the water that I shall give him shall never thirst; but the water that I shall give him shall be in him a well of water springing up into everlasting life" (Jn.4:14).

"In the last day, that great day of the feast, Jesus stood and cried, saying, If any man thirst, let him come unto me, and drink" (Jn.7:37).

"They shall be abundantly satisfied with the fatness of thy house; and thou shalt make them drink of the river of thy pleasures" (Ps.36:8; see Ps.23:1f).

"And the LORD shall guide thee continually, and satisfy thy soul in drought, and make fat thy bones: and thou shalt be like a watered garden, and like a spring of water, whose waters fail not" (Is.58:11).

5 (8:13) **Spiritual Blindness—Jesus Christ, Rejected**: the spiritually blind are left behind by the Lord. Note the force of the words, "He left them." They refused to believe despite all the evidence. Jesus had no choice. The decision was theirs. He had to turn and leave them.

> **"But whosoever shall deny me before men, him will I also deny before my Father which is in heaven" (Mt.10:33).**
>
> **"Whosoever therefore shall be ashamed of me and of my words in this adulterous and sinful generation; of him also shall the Son of man be ashamed, when he cometh in the glory of his Father with the holy angels" (Mk.8:38).**
>
> **"If we deny him, he also will deny us" (2 Ti.2:12).**
>
> **"Who is a liar but he that denieth that Jesus is the Christ? He is antichrist, that denieth the Father and the Son. Whosoever denieth the Son, the same hath not the Father: [but] he that acknowledgeth the Son hath the Father also" (1 Jn.2:22-23).**

	M. The Evil & Danger of Religionists & World Leaders, 8:14-21 *(Mt. 16:5-12)*	bread? perceive ye not yet, neither understand? have ye your heart yet hardened?	with the bread of this world
		18 Having eyes, see ye not? and having ears, hear ye not? and do ye not remember?	b. Danger 2: Not seeing & understanding the Lord's provision
1. The disciples' neglect a. They forgot to take bread b. Jesus used their forgetfulness to teach a needed lesson	14 Now the disciples had forgotten to take bread, neither had they in the ship with them more than one loaf.	19 When I brake the five loaves among five thousand, how many baskets full of fragments took ye up? They say unto him, Twelve.	1) The feeding of five thousand
2. The evil: Beware of the yeast of religionists & world leaders[DS1,2]	15 And he charged them, saying, Take heed, beware of the leaven of the Pharisees, and of the leaven of Herod.	20 And when the seven among four thousand, how many baskets full of fragments took ye up? And they said, Seven.	2) The feeding of four thousand
3. The danger in dealing with religionists & world leaders	16 And they reasoned among themselves, saying, It is because we have no bread.		
a. Danger 1: Being spiritually blinded & hard-hearted—a concern with material things,	17 And when Jesus knew it, he saith unto them, Why reason ye, because ye have no	21 And he said unto them, How is it that ye do not understand?	c. Danger 3: Grieving the Lord's heart

DIVISION IV

THE SON OF GOD'S TRAINING MINISTRY: JESUS' INTENSIVE PREPARATION OF THE DISCIPLES, 6:7-8:26

M. The Evil and Danger of Religionists and World Leaders, 8:14-21

(8:14-21) **Introduction**: some religionists and world leaders are a threat to most people, to every generation of men. Jesus taught this, and every man must take heed and beware of both. Just what Jesus meant is clearly seen and explained in this event.

1. The disciples neglect (v.14).
2. The evil: beware of the yeast of religionists and world leaders (v.15).
3. The danger in dealing with religionists and world leaders (vv.16-21).

1 (8:14) **Opportunity, Grasping**: all of a sudden the disciples remembered something. They had forgotten to bring food, and they had only one loaf of bread in the boat. Jesus saw in their forgetfulness the chance to teach a much needed lesson on the evil and dangers of religionists and world leaders.

2 (8:15) **Religionists—Leaven**: the evil of religionists and world leaders is leaven. Jesus said, "Take heed, beware of the leaven of the Pharisees, and of the leaven of Herod." The disciples completely misunderstood what Jesus was saying. Apparently they thought Jesus was saying one of three things.

⇒ They thought He was rebuking them for having forgotten to take bread.

⇒ They thought He was warning them not to eat the "bread" of the religionists or world leaders. The Pharisees were very strict in the kind of leaven that was to be used in bread. They used the rule governing leaven to stress ceremonial cleanliness. The disciples thought Jesus was saying they were not to become involved in the external stress of religion nor in the indulgence of the world.

⇒ They thought He meant they were not to sit down with the religionists and world leaders (fellowship) and eat their "leaven" and bread; that is, they were not to fellowship with them.

What did Jesus mean by the leaven of the Pharisees and of Herod or world leaders? (Matthew uses Sadducees instead of Herod. Most Herodians, followers of Herod, were Sadducees. See DEEPER STUDY # 2—Mt.22:16; DEEPER STUDY # 2—Ac.23:8.)

a. The leaven of the Pharisees (religionists) was their doctrine or teaching (Mt.16:12) and their hypocrisy, deception, and play-acting (Lu.12:1). The Pharisees *fermented and soured everyone they touched* (see DEEPER STUDY # 2—Acts 23:8; see DEEPER STUDY # 2—Mk.8:15).

The Pharisees believed in a personal God and in the Scripture as God's Word to man, but they added to God's Word (see DEEPER STUDY # 1—Lu.6:2). They added rules and regulations, rituals and ceremonies which put undue restrictions upon man's behavior. This led to three gross errors.

1) It led people to think that their good behavior and their religious rituals and ceremonies made them acceptable to God. A religion of good works was being depended upon for righteousness.
2) It led to a religion of social respectability, to an external religion. If one was socially respectable and did all the right things, then he was judged acceptable to God.
3) It led to an attitude and an air of self-righteousness. If one kept the rules and regulations, he naturally felt righteous and sometimes demonstrated it. There was a dependence upon oneself, upon keeping the right rules and thereby being righteous.

b. The Sadducees or Herodians were the liberal-minded of their day. Their leaven or false teaching was twofold.

1) They took away from God's Word, denying all Scripture except the Pentateuch, the first five books of the Old Testament.

2) They were free thinkers and rationalists who were secular and materialistic-minded. Therefore, they were willing to collaborate with the Romans in doing away with Jewish culture and instituting Roman and Greek culture. Because of this, Rome placed their leaders in the governing positions (the Sanhedrin) and gave them wealth. Their worldly-mindedness, secular philosophy, and liberal theology were always a threat to any man (see note—Mt.16:1-12).

Note the double warning that Jesus gave: "Take heed, beware." This stressed the supreme importance of guarding against the leaven of both religionists and world leaders (see DEEPER STUDY # 1,2—Mk.8:15).

"Beware of false prophets, which come to you in sheep's clothing, but inwardly they are ravening wolves" (Mt.7:15).

"Whosoever therefore shall break one of these least commandments, and shall teach men so, he shall be called the least in the kingdom of heaven: but whosoever shall do and teach them, the same shall be called great in the kingdom of heaven" (Mt.5:19).

"But in vain they do worship me, teaching for doctrines the commandments of men" (Mt.15:9).

"Also of your own selves shall men arise, speaking perverse things, to draw away disciples after them" (Ac.20:30).

"For they being ignorant of God's righteousness, and going about to establish their own righteousness, have not submitted themselves unto the righteousness of God" (Ro.10:3; see Ro.16:18).

"That we henceforth be no more children, tossed to and fro, and carried about with every wind of doctrine, by the sleight of men, and cunning craftiness, whereby they lie in wait to deceive" (Ep.4:14).

"Now the Spirit speaketh expressly, that in the latter times some shall depart from the faith, giving heed to seducing spirits, and doctrines of devils; speaking lies in hypocrisy; having their conscience seared with a hot iron" (1 Ti.4:1-2).

"For there are many unruly and vain talkers and deceivers, specially they of the circumcision [the doctrine of the law, of works]: whose mouths must be stopped, who subvert whole houses, teaching things which they ought not, for filthy lucre's sake" (Tit.1:10-11).

"But there were false prophets also among the people, even as there shall be false teachers among you, who privily shall bring in damnable heresies, even denying the Lord that bought them, and bring upon themselves swift destruction" (2 Pe.2:1).

"Little children, it is the last time: and as ye have heard that antichrist shall come, even now are there many antichrists; whereby we know that it is the last time. They went out from us, but they were not of us; for if they had been of us, they would no doubt have continued with us: but they went out, that they might be made manifest that they were not all of us" (1 Jn.2:18-19; see 2:22).

"For many deceivers are entered into the world, who confess not that Jesus Christ is come in the flesh. This is a deceiver and an antichrist" (2 Jn.7).

DEEPER STUDY # 1

(8:15) **Take Heed** (horao): to see, behold, discern, and acquaint oneself by closely observing and experiencing. Two things are needed for a person to *take heed*: active thought and a discerning mind. The thing to be heeded must be actively observed, thought through, and discerned.

In the present passage, the charge is a *present imperative*. The disciple is to *take heed* of leaven beginning right now, and he is to continue taking heed, always observing and discerning.

DEEPER STUDY # 2

(8:15) **Beware** (blepo): to see, perceive, grasp, and understand in order to watch out for something; to turn the mind upon an object and consider and keep a watchful eye upon it; to guard and protect against something.

Again, the charge is a *present imperative*. The person is to begin immediately to beware and to continue his watch, always looking out for the danger.

3 (8:16-21) **Religionists—World Leaders**: the danger in dealing with religionists and world leaders is threefold.

a. The first danger is spiritual blindness and hardness of heart, being concerned with material and earthly things (bread) (v.16). Note that Jesus does nothing but ask questions through the rest of this passage. His questions point out the failure of the disciples. They fail...

- to reason (v.17)
- to percieve (v.17)
- to understand (v.17)
- to have soft hearts (v.17)
- to see (v.18)
- to hear (v.18)
- to remember (v.18)

What Jesus is doing is rebuking such preoccupation with earthly matters. He calls it distrust: "O ye of little faith" (Mt.16:8). The Lord's followers are to be primarily concerned with spiritual matters, not with earthly affairs. Guarding one's mind and soul against the leaven of the Pharisees and world leaders is to be the believer's constant concern, not worrying and caring for earthly things. A person's thoughts must be dominated by the truth so that he may remain in the truth and not be misled spiritually (Mt.15:19; Ro.8:5-7; 2 Co.10:3-5; Ep.4:23-34). The leaven, the false teaching of religionists and world leaders, is the great threat to human survival. If believers are blind to this fact, then the world is doomed.

Thought 1. We face the same danger today: spiritual blindness and hardness. Too many are attached to the world and its things, its possessions and pleasures. The world and its god (the devil) blind the minds of men lest they see the truth (2 Co.4:4). As a result men are dying, and they are doomed to perish eternally.

"For the heart of this people is waxed gross, and their ears are dull of hearing, and their eyes have they closed; lest they should see with their eyes, and hear with their ears, and understand with their heart, and should be converted, and I should heal them" (Ac.28:27).

"For my people is foolish, they have not known me; they are sottish children, and they have none understanding: they are wise to do evil, but to do good they have no knowledge" (Je.4:22).

"Hear now this, O foolish people, and without understanding; which have eyes, and see not; which have ears, and hear not" (Je.5:21).

"Remember them that are in bonds, as bound with them; and them which suffer adversity, as being yourselves also in the body" (He.13:3).

"Wherefore come out from among them, and be ye separate, saith the Lord, and touch not the unclean thing; and I will receive you, and will be a Father unto you, and ye shall be my sons and daughters, saith the Lord Almighty" (2 Co.6:17-18).

"And be not conformed to this world: but be ye transformed by the renewing of your mind, that ye may prove what is that good, and acceptable, and perfect, will of God" (Ro.12:2).

b. The second danger is failing to see and understand the Lord's provision (vv.18-20). The disciples had just witnessed two phenomenal events. They had seen a crowd of people hungering for the Lord's Word, hungering so much that they had gone without food for three days. They had seen the Lord miraculously feed all four thousand of them with just seven loaves of bread (see outline and notes—Mk.8:1-9).

⇒ Yet, "having eyes, they did not see" what had really happened (v.18).
⇒ Yet, "having ears, they did not hear" what had really happened (v.18).
⇒ Yet, "they did not remember" (v.18).

The disciples had failed to make the connection between...

- the people's hunger for God's Word and the fact that Jesus alone could give them God's Word.
- the people's hunger for bread and the fact that Jesus alone could give them bread from heaven, the energy and power of His very being.

The disciples had failed to see and understand that Jesus Christ was "the Bread of Life," the only "Bread" that could satisfy the spiritual hunger of men. World and religious leaders could never satisfy their need (see note—Jn.6:1-71. See outline and notes—Jn.6:30-36 for application.)

"And Jesus said unto them, I am the bread of life: he that cometh to me shall never hunger; and he that believeth on me shall never thirst" (Jn.6:35).

"Verily, verily, I say unto you, He that believeth on me hath everlasting life. I am that bread of life. Your fathers did eat manna in the wilderness, and are dead. This is the bread which cometh down from heaven, that a man may eat thereof, and not die. I am the living bread which came down from heaven: if any man eat of this bread, he shall live for ever: and the bread that I will give is my flesh, which I will give for the life of the world" (Jn.6:47-51).

"Wherefore do ye spend money for that which is not bread? and your labor for that which satisfieth not? hearken diligently unto me, and eat ye that which is good, and let your soul delight itself in fatness" (Is.55:2).

c. The third danger is grieving the Lord's heart (v.21). All that the Lord had pointed out caused agony to the Lord's soul. He grieved deeply over...

- spiritual blindness
- hardness of heart
- materialistic and carnal minds
- not seeing and understanding His provision

The issues of leaven—true and false doctrine, real and hypocritical behavior—are of supreme importance. The issue of Jesus' being the Bread of Life—the real truth, the true doctrine, the only way to true satisfaction—is of supreme importance. At first the disciples failed to get the point and make the connection, and they grieved the Lord deeply. How many have grieved Him since that day? (See note—Ep.4:30; DEEPER STUDY # 1—1 Th.5:19.)

"Then he said unto them, O fools, and slow of heart to believe all that the prophets have spoken" (Lu.24:25).

"Jesus saith unto him, I am the way, the truth, and the life: no man cometh unto the Father, but by me. If ye had known me, ye should have known my Father also: and from henceforth ye know him, and have seen him. Philip saith unto him, Lord, show us the Father, and it sufficeth us. Jesus saith unto him, Have I been so long time with you, and yet hast thou not known me, Philip? he that hath seen me hath seen the Father; and how sayest thou then, Show us the Father?" (Jn.14:6-9).

"O Jerusalem, Jerusalem, which killest the prophets, and stonest them that are sent unto thee; how often would I have gathered thy children together, as a hen doth gather her brood under her wings, and ye would not!" (Lu.13:34).

	N. The Necessity for Caring, 8:22-26	him if he saw ought. 24 And he looked up, and said, I see men as trees, walking.	
1. Jesus cared for the man's friends: Did what they requested	22 And he cometh to Bethsaida; and they bring a blind man unto him, and besought him to touch him.	25 After that he put his hands again upon his eyes, and made him look up: and he was restored, and saw every man clearly.	**4. Jesus cared enough for the man's need to continue on: Healed in stages to strengthen the man's faith**
2. Jesus cared for the man's handicap **3. Jesus cared for the man's beliefs, that spit had some healing powers**	23 And he took the blind man by the hand, and led him out of the town; and when he had spit on his eyes, and put his hands upon him, he asked	26 And he sent him away to his house, saying, Neither go into the town, nor tell it to any in the town.	**5. Jesus cared for the man's family**

DIVISION IV

THE SON OF GOD'S TRAINING MINISTRY:JESUS' INTENSIVE PREPARATION OF THE DISCIPLES, 6:7-8:26

N. The Necessity for Caring, 8:22-26

(8:22-26) **Introduction**: the story of this blind man is told by Mark alone. The major thrust is care—caring for all involved. Jesus experienced deep feelings all throughout the event. His care and the intensity of it were seen at every turn. He was concerned and anguished over all the suffering and hurting of everyone involved. And through the whole experience, He was teaching His followers to care deeply.

1. Jesus cared for the man's friends: did what they requested (v.22).
2. Jesus cared for the man's handicap (v.23).
3. Jesus cared for the man's beliefs, that spit had some healing powers (vv.23-24).
4. Jesus cared enough for the man's need to continue on: healed in stages to strengthen the man's faith (v.25).
5. Jesus cared for the man's family (v.26).

1 (8:22) **Jesus Christ, Care—Service**: Jesus cared for the man's friends. Note two things.

a. It was friends who brought the blind man to Jesus, and they are the ones who begged Jesus to touch him. The friends cared for the man deeply. They cared enough to want him well. Apparently he had been blind all of his life, so the friends would have been accustomed to his blindness, to the daily routine year after year. However, here they were years later still caring, still hoping, still praying, and still wanting their friend made whole. Their care was deep and genuine, and Jesus saw their care.

b. The friends believed that Jesus could heal the blind man. It was primarily their faith and belief that led Jesus to act. They brought the man and begged Jesus to heal him.

Thought 1. This is a strong lesson on *intercession.* We are to care enough to bring people to Christ and to pray (beg) for Christ to heal them.

"Neither pray I for these alone, but for them also which shall believe on me through their word" (Jn.17:20).

"For God is my witness, whom I serve with my spirit in the gospel of his Son, that without ceasing I make mention of you always in my prayers" (Ro.1:9).

"Wherefore I also, after I heard of your faith in the Lord Jesus, and love unto all the saints, cease not to give thanks for you, making mention of you in my prayers" (Ep.1:15-16).

"For this cause I bow my knees unto the Father of our Lord Jesus Christ" (Ep.3:14).

"Praying always with all prayer and supplication in the Spirit, and watching thereunto with all perseverance and supplication for all saints; and for me, that utterance may be given unto me, that I may open my mouth boldly, to make known the mystery of the gospel" (Ep.6:18-19).

"I thank my God upon every remembrance of you, always in every prayer of mine for you all making request with joy" (Ph.1:3-4).

"We give thanks to God and the Father of our Lord Jesus Christ, praying always for you" (Col.1:3).

"Epaphras, who is one of you, a servant of Christ, saluteth you, always labouring fervently for you in prayers, that ye may stand perfect and complete in all the will of God" (Col.4:12).

"We give thanks to God always for you all, making mention of you in our prayers" (1 Th.1:2).

Thought 2. Jesus cares deeply for *friends* who care. He cares enough to receive and listen and act in their behalf. The caring person and the intercessor receive the care of Christ.

"Bear ye one another's burdens, and so fulfil the law of Christ" (Ga.6:2).

> **"As we have therefore opportunity, let us do good unto all men, especially unto them who are of the household of faith" (Ga.6:10).**
>
> **"But so shall it not be among you: but whosoever will be great among you, shall be your minister: and whosoever of you will be the chiefest, shall be servant of all" (Mk.10:43-44).**

2 (8:23) **Care—Handicap**: Jesus cared for the man's handicap. The man was blind. Imagine the scene. The blind man had never seen anything before. Surrounding him and Jesus was a throng of people with the noise that comes from such a massive crowd. The man was excited, nervous, and somewhat bewildered; and his concentration was weakened by it all. Jesus knew all that was within the man...

- that the man needed to be taken aside, away from the crowd so that he could more easily focus his attention and concentrate upon Jesus.
- that the man's eyes needed to be opened slowly, lest he be dazzled and bewildered with the sight of everything rushing in upon his mind.

Jesus knew all. He knew all the problems and difficulties that the man's blindness had caused, and He knew all that the man needed to be perfectly healed. Jesus cared for the man's handicap, so Jesus took the blind man by the hand and led him out of town. He was ever so sensitive to the blind man's needs.

Thought 1. We are to care for the people who are handicapped...

- understanding the problems and difficulties of the handicapped person.
- being sensitive to the special needs of the handicapped person.
- doing all we can to bring the handicapped person to Christ and to see that the handicapped person is helped or healed.

> **"Let love be without dissimulation. Abhor that which is evil; cleave to that which is good. Be kindly affectioned one to another with brotherly love; in honour preferring one another" (Ro.12:9-10).**
>
> **"We then that are strong ought to bear the infirmities of the weak, and not to please ourselves" (Ro.15:1).**
>
> **"I have showed you all things, how that so labouring ye ought to support the weak, and to remember the words of the Lord Jesus, how he said, It is more blessed to give than to receive" (Ac.20:35).**
>
> **"I was eyes to the blind, and feet was I to the lame. I was a father to the poor: and the cause which I knew not I searched out" (Jb. 29:15-16).**

3 (8:23) **Witnessing—Beliefs**: Jesus cared for the man's beliefs. People of that day believed spittle or saliva had some healing power. One of the first things usually done when a man burns or cuts his finger is put his finger into his mouth. The saliva seems to ease the pain. Note what Jesus did: He placed saliva on the man's eyes and put his hands upon the man. Jesus focused the man's attention upon the healing power of both the saliva and His hands. The touch of both would mean so much more than just spoken words, and the touch of both would stir the faith of the man more readily.

The point is this: Jesus cared for the man's belief in the healing power of saliva. Jesus began where the man was in his beliefs and led him on into the essential belief that healing comes through the Lord Himself, through His touch.

> **"For we have not an high priest which cannot be touched with the feeling of our infirmities; but was in all points tempted like as we are, yet without sin. Let us therefore come boldly unto the throne of grace, that we may obtain mercy, and find grace to help in time of need" (He.4:15-16).**
>
> **"Casting all your care upon him; for he careth for you" (1 Pe.5:7).**

Thought 1. Note three things involved in caring.

(1) We are to care for men even when their beliefs are wrong.
(2) We should begin where men are in dealing with them. We can begin with the faith men have and move them on to more belief in Christ.
(3) We must always lead men to the essential belief: the power to be made whole comes only through the Lord Himself.

4 (8:24-25) **Perseverance—Endurance—Witnessing—Training**: Jesus cared enough to keep after the man's need. So far as is known, this is the only miracle that took place in stages. Jesus had asked the man if "he saw anything." The man replied that he saw men as trees, walking. The man's sight was not completely healed. He saw only faintly, dimly. His eyes were foggy. He saw objects with bodies or trunks like trees, yet they were walking; so he reasoned and said they were bound to be men. The man was extremely excited and was bound to blurt out whatever crossed his mind first.

Note what Jesus did: He again put His hands upon the man's eyes and made him look up. The man's sight was restored, and he saw clearly. Why did Jesus heal the man in stages? Apparently, the man's faith was weak and needed to be strengthened step by step. Greater hope and desire needed to be stirred within the man. The man needed to grow more spiritually, grow more in faith, before he could be healed. This seems to be indicated by his silence in asking Jesus to touch him. His friends were the ones who asked, not him.

The point is this: Jesus cared enough to keep after the man's need. He did not ignore the man or turn from him just because his faith was weak. Jesus did not leave the man or let him go. He stayed right with him, doing all that was necessary to meet the man's need.

Thought 1. Note a critical point. A person grows by stages.
⇒ A person is not always led to Christ immediately.
⇒ A person is never *mature in Christ* immediately. There is no such thing as *instantaneous maturity.* A person grows in Christ step by step and stage by stage (2 Pe.3:18; 2 Th.1:3; 1 Pe.2:2-3).

The crucial point for believers and churches can be simply stated: we must *care enough* to keep after the person's need. We must care enough to keep after...

- witnessing
- visiting
- ministering
- feeding and clothing
- teaching and instructing
- loving

"And let us not be weary in well doing: for in due season we shall reap, if we faint not" (Ga.6:9).

"Therefore, my beloved brethren, be ye stedfast, unmoveable, always abounding in the work of the Lord, forasmuch as ye know that your labour is not in vain in the Lord" (1 Co.15:58).

"Remember them that are in bonds, as bound with them; and them which suffer adversity, as being yourselves also in the body" (He.13:3).

5 (8:26) **Family—Witnessing**: Jesus cared for the man's family. Jesus told the man not to go back into the town of Bethsaida. Apparently, he lived either in the countryside or in some surrounding town. Why did Jesus tell the man not to enter the town, but instead to go home? The reason seemed to be that Jesus cared for the whole family and was sensitive to their feelings and hopes. Since the man was from out of town, Jesus wanted the man to go home immediately to share the glorious news with his family. They all deserved to share in the joy.

Thought 1. Sensitivity to a person's family is essential. The feelings and hopes of family members matter greatly.

"So ought men to love their wives as their own bodies. He that loveth his wife loveth himself " (Ep.5:28).

"Only take heed to thyself, and keep thy soul diligently, lest thou forget the things which thine eyes have seen, and lest they depart from thy heart all the days of thy life: but teach them thy sons, and thy sons' sons" (De.4:9).

"And these words, which I command thee this day, shall be in thine heart: and thou shalt teach them diligently unto thy children, and shalt talk of them when thou sittest in thine house, and when thou walkest by the way, and when thou liest down, and when thou risest up....And thou shalt write them upon the posts of thy house, and on thy gates" (De.6:6-7, 9).

	V. THE SON OF GOD'S CLOSING MINISTRY: JESUS TEACHES THE IDEA OF GOD'S MESSIAHSHIP, NOT MAN'S MESSIAHSHIP, 8:27-9:50	the way he asked his disciples, saying unto them, Whom do men say that I am?	a. He visited the villages b. He questioned the people's belief about Himself
		28 And they answered, John the Baptist: but some say, Elias; and others, One of the prophets.	**2. The confession of men: He is a great man**
	A. The Great Confession of Peter: Who Jesus Is, 8:27-30 *(see Mt. 16:13-20; Lu. 9:18-21)*	29 And he saith unto them, But whom say ye that I am? And Peter answereth and saith unto him, Thou art the Christ.	**3. The confession of His disciples: He is the Christ**
1. The setting: Jesus in Caesarea Philippi*DS1*	27 And Jesus went out, and his disciples, into the towns of Caesarea Philippi: and by	30 And he charged them that they should tell no man of him.	**4. The need: To personally learn about God's Messiah before sharing the message**

DIVISION V

THE SON OF GOD'S CLOSING MINISTRY: JESUS TEACHES THE IDEA OF GOD'S MESSIAHSHIP, NOT MAN'S MESSIAHSHIP, 8:27-9:50

A. The Great Confession of Peter: Who Jesus Is, 8:27-30

(8:27-9:50) **DIVISION OVERVIEW: Jesus Christ, Savior—Messiah**: most men do not object to the idea of a Messiah, that is, a deliverer, savior, provider, and protector. Most men want a leader who is going to bring about a utopian society that will provide social justice and plenty for everyone. What men want is a Messiah who fits into the wants and passions and power structures of their world. Men want their bellies full, their bodies clothed and housed, and their urges satisfied. They want the *good things* of this world. If a Messiah can give these, then men are ready and willing to accept the Messiah. Jesus deliberately set out to make sure that the disciples saw Him as God's Messiah and not man's Messiah. He had to make sure they understood God's way of salvation and utopia, that God was after victory over death and a life that lasted eternally, not just for seventy or so years. God's Messiah and salvation was not man's way of power and pleasure; it was not leaving the future to take care of itself (see notes—Mt.1:1; DEEPER STUDY # 2—1:18; DEEPER STUDY # 3—3:11; notes—11:1-6; 11:2-3; DEEPER STUDY # 1—11:5; DEEPER STUDY # 2—11:6; DEEPER STUDY # 1—12:16; note—22:42).

(8:27-30) **Introduction**: Jesus was facing the end very, very soon and there was still much to teach the disciples. It was time for them to learn that He was building a church—an assembly of people who would be confessing Him to be the Messiah. The present passage is one of the most dramatic revelations ever made. It is also one of the most demanding questions ever asked. The answer given determines one's eternal destiny and requires a single answer: "Thou art the Christ." The importance of the question and its confession is clearly seen by glancing quickly at the points of the passage.

1. The setting: Jesus in Caesarea Philippi (v.27).
2. The confession of men: He is a great man (v.28).
3. The confession of His disciples: He is the Christ (v.29).
4. The need: to personally learn about God's Messiah before sharing the message (v.30).

1 (8:27) **Jesus Christ, Response to**: Jesus left Bethsaida and traveled into the villages of Caesarea Philippi (see DEEPER STUDY # 1—Mk.8:27). As He was traveling along the road between villages, He asked one of the key questions of life—the question whose answer determines a man's eternal fate: "Whom do men say that I am?"

DEEPER STUDY # 1

(8:27) **Caesarea Philippi**: the city had a rich religious history. It had once been the center of Baal worship with at least fourteen temples in and around the city. It was believed to have within its borders the cavern in which the Greek god of nature, Pan, was born. In the beginning of its history, the city was so identified with this god that it was named after the god, being called Panias. One of its most beautiful structures was the gleaming white marble temple built for the worship of Caesar. Herod the Great had built the temple in honor of Caesar when Caesar bestowed on him another country. But it was Herod's son Philip who adorned the temple with the magnificence for which it was known worldwide. It was also Philip who changed the name of the city from Panias to Caesarea, Caesar's town. He added his own name also, calling the city Caesarea Philippi.

The city proclaimed far and wide the worship of Caesar and of the gods of one's choice, that is, the worship of all except the One true and living God. It was against this dramatic yet terrible background that Jesus asked the pointed question, "But who do you say that I am?" (emphatic Greek translation). It was also against this background of religion that Peter made his great discovery and confession: Jesus is the Christ, the real Messiah.

2 (8:28) **Profession, False—Jesus Christ, Denial**: the confession of men shortchanged Jesus. Most men saw Jesus only as a great man, a man who was highly esteemed and respected. He was considered one of the greatest of men, but note a crucial point: these *professions* were not only untrue, they were dangerous. They contained only half-truths, and people were deceived and misled by them.

a. Some said Jesus was John the Baptist. They professed Jesus to be a great spirit of righteousness, a spirit that was willing to be martyred for its faith. Herod and others thought this (Mt.14:1-2). Upon hearing of Jesus' marvelous works, Herod fancied that either John had been revived or else his spirit indwelt the man Jesus.

The common people also saw some similarity between John and Jesus: both were doing a great work for God; both were divinely chosen and gifted by God; and both proclaimed the Kingdom of God and prepared men for it. Therefore, when some looked at Jesus and His ministry, they thought Jesus was not the Messiah Himself, but the promised forerunner of the Messiah (Mal.4:5).

b. Some said Jesus was Elijah. They professed Jesus to be the greatest prophet and teacher of all time, for Elijah was so considered. Elijah was predicted to be the forerunner of the coming Messiah (Mal.4:5). Even today the Jews expect Elijah to return before the Messiah. In the celebration of the Passover they always leave a chair vacant for him to occupy. Elijah had also been used by God to miraculously feed a widow woman and her son (1 K.17:14); therefore, the people connected Elijah's miracle and Jesus' feeding of the multitude.

c. Some said Jesus was one of the prophets. They professed Jesus to be a great prophet sent for their day and time. He was thought to be one of the great prophets brought back to life or one in whom the spirit of a great prophet dwelt (see De.18:15, 18).

Thought 1. The same false confessions about Christ exist in every generation.

(1) He was only a great man of righteousness who was martyred for His great faith. As such He leaves us a great example of how to live and stand up for what we believe.
(2) He was one of the greatest teachers and prophets of all time.
(3) He was only a great man who revealed some very important things to us about God and religion. As such He can make a significant contribution to every man in his search for God.
(4) He was only a great man, a prophet sent to the people (Jews) of His day from whom we can learn by studying His life.

"Is not this the carpenter, the son of Mary, the brother of James, and Joses, and of Juda, and Simon? and are not his sisters here with us? And they were offended at him" (Mk.6:3).

"He was in the world, and the world was made by him, and the world knew him not. He came unto his own, and his own received him not" (Jn.1:10-11).

"Then said they unto him, Where is thy Father? Jesus answered, Ye neither know me, nor my Father: if ye had known me, ye should have known my Father also" (Jn.8:19).

"Who is a liar but he that denieth that Jesus is the Christ? He is antichrist, that denieth the Father and the Son. Whosoever denieth the Son, the same hath not the Father" (1 Jn.2:22-23).

"Every spirit that confesseth not that Jesus Christ is come in the flesh is not of God: and this is that spirit of antichrist, whereof ye have heard that it should come; and even now already is it in the world" (1 Jn.4:3).

3 (8:29) **Confession—Jesus Christ, Names & Titles**: the confession of the disciples was that Jesus is the Christ, the Messiah. Note three facts that are stressed.

a. The word *saith* (eperotao) means to ask, to question. It is in the imperfect tense which means that Jesus kept on asking them. The question, "Whom say ye that I am?" was extremely critical. The answer required concentrated thought and correct belief and genuine confession.

b. The question asked is emphatic in the Greek: "But ye, whom do ye say that I am?" The answer to the question is critical; it is all important. It determines a person's destiny, his eternal destiny.

c. The answer given was immediate and terse: "Thou art the Christ," that is, the promised Messiah, the Son of the living God (see Mt.16:16 for the full confession. Remember Mark was Peter's disciple, and what Mark is writing shows the humility of Peter. He usually de-emphasizes the facts surrounding Peter.)

The confession is momentous, arising from a personal conviction. It is both the confession that saves the soul and the confession that lays the foundation for the church. The very life and survival of a man's soul and of the church as a whole rest upon this simple, yet profound conviction.

a. The Christ: the Messiah; the anointed One of God (see DEEPER STUDY # 1—Mt.1:18 for discussion).

b. The Son of God: of the same being, the same substance; One with the Father (see notes—Jn.1:1-2; 1:34; Ph.2:6).

c. Living: the source and being of life; possessing the source, energy, and power of life within Himself (see DEEPER STUDY #2—Jn.1:4; note—1:4-5; DEEPER STUDY # 1—17:2-3. See Jn.5:26; 1 Th.1:9 for discussion and application.)

4 (8:30) **Messiah—Messiahship—Study**: the disciples had a great need to learn about *God's Messiah.* Note: Jesus instructed the disciples not to share their confession with anyone else—not now. Why? Because they were just beginning to learn what God's idea of the Messiah really meant. They had to know the truth and be accurate in their preaching of the truth before they began to share. They could do irreparable harm by spreading a false concept of the Messiah. Jesus had to protect them against this error.

Thought 1. Confession is just the beginning of our spiritual journey. There is much to study and learn about Christ after coming to know Him personally. Note two things.

(1) We must be accurate in what we study. We must make sure we learn the truth and not error (see outline and notes—Mk.8:15).
(2) We must be accurate in what we share, making certain that we share the truth. This necessitates time to study and grow before we begin sharing.

"As newborn babes, desire the sincere milk of the word, that ye may grow thereby: if so be ye have tasted that the Lord is gracious" (1 Pe.2:2-3; see Ac.20:32; 2 Ti.2:15; 2 Pe.3:18).

"These were more noble than those in Thessalonica, in that they received the word with all readiness of mind, and searched the scriptures daily, whether those things were so" (Ac.17:11).

	B. The First Prediction of Death: God's Messiah Vs. Man's Messiah, 8:31-33 *(Mt. 16:21-23; Lu. 9:22)*	after three days rise again.	
		32 And he spake that saying openly. And Peter took him, and began to rebuke him.	**2. The way of man's messiah** a. Involves rejecting God's Messiah
1. The way of God's Messiah[DS1] a. Involves suffering & death b. Involves the resurrection from the dead	31 And he began to teach them, that the Son of man must suffer many things, and be rejected of the elders, and of the chief priests, and scribes, and be killed, and	33 But when he had turned about and looked on his disciples, he rebuked Peter, saying, Get thee behind me, Satan: for thou savourest not the things that be of God, but the things that be of men.	b. Involves following the way of Satan c. Involves setting the mind on material things, not on the things of God

DIVISION V

THE SON OF GOD'S CLOSING MINISTRY: JESUS TEACHES THE IDEA OF GOD'S MESSIAHSHIP, NOT MAN'S MESSIAHSHIP, 8:27-9:50

B. The First Prediction of Death: God's Messiah Vs. Man's Messiah, 8:31-33

(8:31-33) **Introduction—Utopia**: man aches and searches for utopia, for a messiah, for a savior who can bring utopia to earth. But there is a critical point to note. God's Messiah and man's messiah differ. (See outline and notes—Mk.8:27-9:50; 9:30-32; 10:32-34; Mt.16:21-23; 17:22-23; 20:17-19.)

1. The way of God's Messiah (v.31).
2. The way of man's messiah (vv.32-33).

1 (8:31) **Messiahship—Jesus Christ, Death; Resurrection**: the way of God's Messiah. The disciples had just made the profound confession that Jesus was the Christ, the Messiah, the Son of the living God. At this point Jesus launched a new stage. He began to indoctrinate them into the way of God's Messiah, for God's Messiah was not man's messiah (see note—Mk.8:27-9:50). Note several things.

a. The phrase "He began to teach them" is significant. Matthew says, "From that time forth"; that is, from the time of the profound confession that Jesus is the Messiah—beyond question the Messiah—something significant happened. A new stage was being launched. He revealed with a powerful thrust that the "Son of the living God" was going to be killed and raised again from the dead. Never before had this happened. Never again would it happen. History would be made. "Jerusalem...that killed the prophets" would now commit the ultimate crime: Jerusalem would kill God's own Son (see Mt.23:37).

b. Jesus had been telling His disciples about His death and resurrection for some time. But they had not understood. First, the idea of a suffering Messiah differed radically from their own idea of the Messiah (see notes—Mt.1:1; DEEPER STUDY # 2—1:18; DEEPER STUDY # 3—3:11; notes—11:1-6; 11:2-3; DEEPER STUDY # 1—11:5; DEEPER STUDY # 2—11:6; DEEPER STUDY #1—12:16; note—Lu.7:21-23). And second, the revelation had been hidden in pictures and symbols.

> **"Destroy this temple, and in three days I will raise it up" (Jn.2:19).**
>
> **"As Moses lifted up the serpent in the wilderness, even so must the Son of Man be lifted up" (Jn.3:14).**
>
> **"I am the living bread which came down from heaven: if any man eat of this bread, he shall live for ever: and the bread that I will give is my flesh, which I will give for the life of the world" (Jn.6:51).**

The difference now was that Jesus no longer spoke in pictures and symbols. He told them in simple and direct words (Mt.20:18-20; Lu.18:31-33). A new stage in the revelation of God's plan for the world was now to take place: God's Son was to die and be raised again for the sins of the world. God's plan for saving the world was to take place through a suffering Messiah, not a conquering Messiah. God's Messiah was not going to deliver a materialistic world into the hands of His followers. Contrariwise, He was to die, and His death was to usher in the Kingdom of God, making it possible for His followers to live eternally in the very presence of God Himself (see DEEPER STUDY # 3—Mt.19:23-24; see Jn.3:16; 5:24f).

c. The words "*must* [dei] suffer" are strong. *Must* is constraint, an utter necessity. (See DEEPER STUDY # 2, *Jesus Christ, Death*—Ac. 2:23 for more discussion.) It was absolutely necessary by the very nature of the case for Jesus to suffer. God is love and man is corruptible, so God, in love, must provide salvation for man. But God is also just, so He must provide salvation in such a way that justice will be done. The penalty must be paid; death must be carried out. Some *Ideal Man* must die for man so that His *Ideal Death* can stand for and cover all men (see notes, *Son of Man*—Jn.1:51; *Justification*—Ro.5:1). There is only One Ideal Man: Jesus, the Son of God. The Son of God must become the Son of Man, the Ideal Man:

⇒ He must live a perfect life providing for the world the Ideal Righteousness or Ideal Life.
⇒ He must die, providing for the world the Ideal Death.
⇒ He must arise from the dead, providing for the world the Ideal Resurrection.

d. The words "suffer many things" include much more than just the sufferings surrounding His death. This is often overlooked. Hebrews 5:8 makes this clear: "Though He were a Son, yet learned He obedience by the things which He suffered." However, the point is not seen unless one acknowledges the truth of the word *Son,* that is, Jesus' deity. Jesus is *the Son of God* who left the very presence of God. He left heaven with all the majesty and splendor, glory and worship, praise and honor due Him. He is *the Son of Heaven*, but He became the Son of a woman. He belonged in heaven, but He was present on earth. He had ruled in the perfect, incorruptible world, but He was now a servant in this imperfect and corruptible world.

Every sight, sound, touch, taste—every experience and awareness was a world of distance from what He had known. He suffered through every moment and through every experience. Every experience drained "virtue" out of Him, for He always had before His face the truth and glory of heaven and the sin and corruption of earth.

e. Jesus' prediction of His resurrection is clear to us because we can look back upon it. But it was never clear to His disciples. Why? Very simply, it was to be a new experience. No one had ever risen from the dead, not a person who was never again to die. It had never happened before; it was unprecedented. Perhaps the disciples believed somewhat like Martha, that there was to be a future resurrection of all men (Jn.11:24-26). Such a belief was an expression of the hope that is within every man, the hope to continue on in some form of existence. Such a belief is easy to hold. But to think of an immediate resurrection, to think of a person's arising from the dead today is difficult (just think about it). The idea of the Messiah's dying and arising from the dead would be almost unimaginable to those who had not been taught the truth.

Just what the disciples thought Jesus meant by "being raised again" is not known. The fact that they did not fully understand is clear from the fact that their spirits were crushed when He was killed. But some of His followers seemed to grasp more of a real bodily resurrection than others. This is clear by an immediate remembrance of His words after His resurrection. For example, there was John who did believe immediately (Jn.20:8-9); there was Mary Magdalene who was shown that He had risen (Mt.28:6). However, others were slower to understand and believe (Mk.16:11; Jn.20:24-25).

> **"Having therefore obtained help of God, I continue unto this day, witnessing both to small and great, saying none other things than those which the prophets and Moses did say should come: that Christ should suffer, and that he should be the first that should rise from the dead, and should show light unto the people, and to the Gentiles" (Ac.26:22-23).**
>
> **"For I delivered unto you first of all that which I also received, how that Christ died for our sins according to the Scriptures; and that he was buried, and that he rose again the third day according to the scriptures" (1 Co.15:3-4).**
>
> **"[Christ] died for all, that they which live should not henceforth live unto themselves, but unto him which died for them, and rose again" (2 Co.5:15).**
>
> **"For Christ also hath once suffered for sins, the just for the unjust, that he might bring us to God, being put to death in the flesh, but quickened by the Spirit" (1 Pe.3:18).**

DEEPER STUDY # 1
(8:31) **Jesus Christ, Opposition**: see note—Mt.8:31 for the three groups who opposed Christ.

2 (8:32-33) **Messiahship**: the way of man's messiah. Note the word *openly* (parresia). It means plainly, unmistakably, frankly, without hesitation (see note, pt.1—Mk.8:31). Jesus literally indoctrinated His disciples with the fact and meaning of His death. He talked about it so much that it shook the apostles, so much so that they had Peter to confront Christ. Note three points.

a. Natural man rejects God's Messiah. He rebels at the idea of the cross. He wants another way other than the cross. This is what Peter was doing: rebelling against the idea that *God's Son* was to die, that His blood was to be shed for the sins of the world (1 Pe.2:24). Peter could accept Jesus as *the Son of the living God*, but not as the Suffering Savior. Such an idea was repulsive and unacceptable to him. Therefore, he tried to stop the idea. Peter did two things.

1) Peter *took Him* (proslabomenos). The Greek is strong. It means *caught hold.* Peter took hold and grabbed Jesus. Peter bodily took Jesus aside for a conference.
2) Peter "began *to rebuke* [epitiman] Him." This again is strong. It is not just a wish, but a forcible attempt to stop the idea of the Suffering Savior: "This shall not be unto thee. This must not and cannot happen to you." *God forbid* is the equivalent idea. Peter was out to stop the cross. He was urging Jesus to be the Messiah of power, fame, and sensation that the Jews were expecting (see notes—Mk.8:27-9:50; 8:30; Mt.1:1; Deeper Study # 2—1:18; Deeper Study # 3—3:11; notes—11:1-6; 11:2-3; Deeper Study # 1—11:5; Deeper Study # 2—11:6; Deeper Study #1—12:16; note—Lu.7:21-23). Peter was urging Jesus to follow his own human schemes instead of God's way. And by such, he was tempting Jesus with the very same compromises that Satan used to tempt Jesus, the compromises of power, fame, and sensations (Mt.4:1-11). Peter was zealous for God, but He was mistaken and ignorant in his zeal. He did not understand that God was planning to save the world through the death of His Son (see note, pt.3—Mk.8:31).

   Peter's behavior is the way of the world. It is the natural, carnal mind. Man just rebels and recoils against the idea of a Suffering Savior who dies for the sins of the world, a Suffering Savior who demands the same sacrifice and denial of His followers. Such an idea is unacceptable and repulsive.

Thought 1. The natural man's idea of God and of God's plan for man is seen in three concepts.

(1) Some think the path of life is an indulgent love. God is seen as a giving, loving, indulgent *grandfather type* of person. He is seen as One who tolerates (and rewards by accepting) even the worst behavior, no matter how much human suffering and devastation is wrought by the hands of a person. To think of the cross and the blood of Christ as an emblem of suffering is repulsive. The cross is viewed only as an emblem of love, not of sin and shame. The way of love is thought to be the path of life that man is to follow.

(2) Some think that comfort and pleasure are the path of life and God's way. God again is viewed only as an indulgent *grandfather type*. His will for man is to have *the good life* of things: comfort and pleasure, ease and plenty, health and leisure. And again the cross is only an emblem of love and care for the world, not of suffering and sacrifice and self-denial. Its shame and pain and agony and its purpose of reconciling a world lost in sin and depravity are denied.

"And that which fell among thorns are they, which, when they have heard, go forth, and are choked with cares and riches and pleasures of this life; and bring no fruit to perfection" (Lu.8:14).

"And I will say to my soul, Soul, thou hast much goods laid up for many years; take thine ease, eat, drink, and be merry" (Lu.12:19).

"But she that liveth in pleasure is dead while she liveth" (1 Ti.5:6).

"[They] shall receive the reward of unrighteousness, as they that count it pleasure to riot [party] in the day time. Spots they are and blemishes, sporting themselves with their own deceivings while they feast with you" (2 Pe.2:13).

"Therefore hear now this, thou that art given to pleasures, that dwellest carelessly, that sayest in thine heart, I am, and none else beside me; I shall not sit as a widow, neither shall I know the loss of children: but these two things shall come to thee in a moment in one day, the loss of children, and widowhood: they shall come upon thee in their perfection for the multitude of thy sorceries, and for the great abundance of thine enchantments" (Is.47:8-9).

(3) Some feel that triumph, victory, power, and reigning supreme are God's way. This was the idea of most Jews in Christ's day. It was Peter's concept of the Messiah (see notes—Mt.1:1; DEEPER STUDY # 2—1:18; DEEPER STUDY # 3—3:11; notes—11:1-6; 11:2-3; DEEPER STUDY # 1—11:5; DEEPER STUDY # 2—11:6; DEEPER STUDY # 1—12:16; note—Lu.7:21-23). Applying man's ideas to his own emotional and mental state of being, as well as to his physical and material being, is revealing. The ideas show how some view the concepts of *Self-Image, Self-Improvement*, and *Personality Development* as being God's plan and path for man. Again, the idea of suffering and sacrifice and self-denial is rejected.

"They that are great exercise authority upon them. But it shall not be so among you: but whosoever will be great among you, let him be your minister; and whosoever will be chief among you, let him be your servant" (Mt.20:25-27).

"How can ye believe, which receive honour one of another, and seek not the honour that cometh from God only?" (Jn.5:44).

"And if any man think that he knoweth any thing, he knoweth nothing yet as he ought to know" (1 Co.8:2).

"For all that is in the world, the lust of the flesh, and the lust of the eyes, and the pride of life, is not of the Father, but is of the world" (1 Jn.2:16).

"Thou art wretched, and miserable, and poor, and blind, and naked" (Re.3:17).

"Nevertheless man being in honour abideth not: he is like the beasts that perish" (Ps.49:12).

"Pride goeth before destruction, and a haughty spirit before a fall" (Pr.16:18).

"Seest thou a man wise in his own conceit? There is more hope of a fool than of him" (Pr.26:12).

b. Natural man is of Satan. The literal meaning of the name Satan is *Adversary* (see DEEPER STUDY # 1—Rev.12:9). Calling Peter "Satan" was stern, yet such sternness was necessary. Peter was tempting Christ with the very same temptation Jesus had faced in the wilderness (see notes—Mt.4:8-10). All the world's glory that could be His flashed across His mind. The loyalty and allegiance of men without the cross was again being suggested to Him. How this must have cut the heart of Jesus! This time the temptation was coming from one of His own disciples. When a man refuses to accept God's plan for life, he becomes an adversary to God. He opposes God's will. In essence the man says that he knows what is best; he is *wiser* than God. Think! When a man does not accept God's plan for life, the crux of what he says to God is, "The cross is not necessary. Jesus' death to save the world is a useless plan. It is not needed."

This is what Peter was doing and saying. He was opposing God's plan for life, that is, opposing the salvation of the world through the death of God's Son. Peter was saying that he was wiser than God. Note: Jesus abruptly turned to Peter before Peter could say anything else and stopped him in his tracks. He charged Peter with being Satan, with being under the authority of Satan, with speaking for Satan. He had become as Satan, an adversary against God's plan for His Son and for the salvation of the world.

"And said, O full of all subtilty and all mischief, thou child of the devil, thou enemy of all righteousness, wilt thou not cease to pervert the right ways of the Lord?" (Ac.13:10).

"Ye are of your father the devil, and the lusts of your father ye will do" (Jn.8:44).

"In time past ye walked according to the course of this world, according to the prince of the power of the air, the spirit that now worketh in the children of disobedience" (Ep.2:2).

"In this the children of God are manifest, and the children of the devil: whosoever doeth not righteousness is not of God, neither he that loveth not his brother" (1 Jn.3:10).

c. Natural man sets his mind on material things, not on the things of God. The words *thou savorest not* (ou phroneis) mean to think, to mind. Peter did not have his mind, his thinking, in line with God's mind and thoughts. His tastes were different from God's tastes. Peter's thoughts and tastes were worldly and self-pleasing, not spiritual and not pleasing to God. He was using human reasoning, not God's reasoning. The death of God's Son by shedding His blood for the sins of the world was distasteful to Peter. In his mind such a concept was unfit for God.

Note Jesus' words to Peter and how true they are: "Thou savourest not the things that be of God, but those that be of men." The death of Jesus reveals man's true nature, a nature that uses natural and carnal reasoning instead of spiritual reasoning.

"For they that are after the flesh do mind the things of the flesh; but they that are after the Spirit the things of the Spirit. For to be carnally minded is death; but to be spiritually minded is life and peace. Because the carnal mind is enmity against God: for it is not subject to the law of God, neither indeed can be" (Ro.8:5-7).

"This I say therefore, and testify in the Lord, that ye henceforth walk not as other Gentiles walk, in the vanity of their mind" (Ep.4:17).

"For many walk, of whom I have told you often, and now tell you even weeping, that they are the enemies of the cross of Christ: whose end is destruction, whose God is their belly, and whose glory is in their shame, who mind earthly things" (Ph.3:18-19).

"And you, that were sometime alienated and enemies in your mind by wicked works, yet now hath he [God] reconciled in the body of his flesh through death, to present you holy and unblameable and unreproveable in his sight" (Col.1:21-22).

"Unto the pure all things are pure: but unto them that are defiled and unbelieving is nothing pure; but even their mind and conscience is defiled" (Tit.1:15).

"The LORD knoweth the thoughts of man, that they are vanity" (Ps.94:11).

"Wash thine heart from wickedness, that thou mayest be saved. How long shall thy vain thoughts lodge within thee?" (Je.4:14).

Thought 1. Jesus was tempted to bypass God's will for His life. And note: the temptation came from a disciple. We are often tempted to bypass God's will, and unfortunately, the temptation often comes from friends! They may mean well; they may want to save us from the difficult path of trouble, sorrow, and trials. Nevertheless, their suggestion to bypass the cross is not of God. It is of Satan.

Thought 2. Note Peter's testimony after Jesus' death and resurrection.

"Blessed be the God and Father of our Lord Jesus Christ, which according to his abundant mercy hath begotten us again unto a lively hope by the resurrection of Jesus Christ from the dead, to an inheritance incorruptible, and undefiled, and that fadeth not away, reserved in heaven for you" (1 Pe.1:3-4).

"Forasmuch as ye know that ye were not redeemed with corruptible things, as silver and gold, from your vain conversation received by tradition from your fathers; but with the precious blood of Christ, as of a lamb without blemish and without spot" (1 Pe.1:18-19).

"Who by him [you] do believe in God, that raised him up from the dead, and gave him glory; that your faith and hope might be in God" (1 Pe.1:21).

"Who his own self bare our sins in his own body on the tree, that we, being dead to sins, should live unto righteousness: by whose stripes ye were healed" (1 Pe.2:24).

"For Christ also hath once suffered for sins, the just for the unjust, that he might bring us to God, being put to death in the flesh, but quickened by the Spirit" (1 Pe.3:18).

"Forasmuch then as Christ hath suffered for us in the flesh, arm yourselves likewise with the same mind" (1 Pe.4:1).

	C. The Issues of God & the Issues of Men, 8:34-9:1 *(Mt. 16:24-28; Lu. 9:23-27)*	37 Or what shall a man give in exchange for his soul?	
		38 Whosoever therefore shall be ashamed of me and of my words in this adulterous and sinful generation; of him also shall the Son of man be ashamed, when he cometh in the glory of his Father with the holy angels.	**5. The issue of the Messiah: Being ashamed of Christ vs. confessing Christ**
1. Jesus spoke to all, to the people & to His disciples	34 And when he had called the people unto him with his disciples also, he said unto		
2. The issue of discipleship: Indulging self vs. denying self[DS1,2,3]	them, Whosoever will come after me, let him deny himself, and take up his cross, and follow me.		
3. The issue of life: Saving life vs. losing life	35 For whosoever will save his life shall lose it; but whosoever shall lose his life for my sake and the gospel's, the same shall save it.	**CHAPTER 9**	
		And he said unto them, Verily I say unto you, That there be some of them that stand here, which shall not taste of death, till they have seen the kingdom of God come with power.	**6. The issue of death: Tasting death vs. seeing God's kingdom**
4. The issue of value: Gaining the world vs. saving the soul	36 For what shall it profit a man, if he shall gain the whole world, and lose his own soul?		

DIVISION V

THE SON OF GOD'S CLOSING MINISTRY: JESUS TEACHES THE IDEA OF GOD'S MESSIAHSHIP, NOT MAN'S MESSIAHSHIP, 8:27-9:50

C. The Issues of God and the Issues of Men, 8:34-9:1

(8:34-9:1) **Introduction**: the issues of God and the issues of men differ radically. This passage shows just how much they differ, and as such it warns every man.

1. Jesus spoke to all, to the people and to His disciples (v.34).
2. The issue of discipleship: indulging self vs. denying self (v.34).
3. The issue of life: saving life vs. losing life (v.35).
4. The issue of value: gaining the world vs. saving the soul (vv.36-37).
5. The issue of the Messiah: being ashamed of Christ vs. confessing Christ (v.38).
6. The issue of death: tasting death vs. seeing God's kingdom (v.9:1).

1 (8:34) **Jesus Christ, Warns**: Jesus spoke to all, to the people and to His disciples. Note that Jesus "had called the people...with His disciples." What He now said was a warning to the whole crowd, to the whole world.

2 (8:34) **Discipleship—Indulgence—Denying Self**: there is the issue of discipleship, that is, indulging self vs. denying self. Jesus was very pointed: there is a life of self-indulgence and there is a life of self-denial (Ro.12:1-2; 2 Co.6:17-18; 1 Jn.2:15-16). A person has to make a choice between...

• loving comfort and ease	or	• commitment and discipline
• loving wealth and property	or	• work and compassion
• loving recognition and fame	or	• humility and sacrifice
• loving position and power	or	• service and ministry
• loving pleasure and indulgence	or	• righteousness and self-control

The question is: "How does a person go about making the right choice?" Jesus said four things.

1. A man must *will to come* after Him (see DEEPER STUDY # 1, *Wills*—Mk.8:34).
2. A man must *deny himself* (see DEEPER STUDY # 2, *Deny*,—Mk.8:34).
3. A man must *take up his cross* (see DEEPER STUDY # 1, *Cross*—Lu.9:23).
4. A man must *follow Christ* (see DEEPER STUDY # 3, *Follow*—Mk.8:34).

DEEPER STUDY # 1

(8:34) **Wills** (thelei): to desire, wish, design, purpose, resolve, determine. It is a deliberate willing, a deliberate choice, a determined resolve to follow Christ. If a person really wills and deliberately chooses to follow Christ, then he has to do the three things mentioned. Note, the choice is voluntary. It is not forced upon the person. It is the individual who wills and chooses; therefore, it is the individual who must act and do the three things mentioned.

DEEPER STUDY # 2

(8:34) **Deny** (aparneomai): to disown, disregard, forsake, renounce, reject, refuse, restrain, disclaim, do without. It means to subdue, to disregard oneself and one's interest. Very simply, it means to say "no." But note: the call is not to say "no" to some behavior or thing, but to *self.* A person is to *deny self.* This means much more than just being negative, that is, giving up something and doing without something. It means that we are to act positively, to say "yes" to Christ and "no" to self. It means to let Christ rule and reign in one's heart and life, to let Christ have His way completely. Of course, if a person allows Christ to rule in his life, all negative as well as positive behavior is taken care of (see outline note 2—Mk.8:34). In the Greek the word is an ingressive aorist, which means the person enters a new state or condition. It means *let him at once begin* to "deny self."

DEEPER STUDY # 3
(8:34) **Follow** (akolootheo): to be a follower or companion, to be a disciple. It has the idea of seeking to be in union with and in the likeness of. It is following Christ, seeking to be just like Him. Again, this is not passive behavior, but an active commitment and walk. It is energy and effort, action and work. It is going after Christ with zeal and energy, struggling and seeking to follow in His footsteps no matter the cost. Note that His steps lead to death before they lead to glory (Mt.16:21).

3 (8:35) **Life—Gospel**: there is the issue of life, that is, saving life vs. losing life. Jesus made a very surprising statement. If a man wished to save his life, he must lose it. What did He mean? The key is found in two phrases.

a. The first phrase is: "for my sake." "Whosoever shall lose his life *for my sake*...the same shall save it." The person who abandons this life, who sacrifices and gives all that he is and has for Christ, shall save his life. But the person who *keeps* his life, that is, what he has, and *seeks* more and more of this life shall lose his life completely and eternally.

The person who "saves his life, who..."

- seeks to avoid aging, decaying, and death and denies Christ, shall lose his life eternally.
- seeks to make his life more and more comfortable and secure beyond what is necessary and neglects Christ, shall lose his life eternally.
- seeks to gain wealth, power, and fame, and who compromises Christ, shall lose his life eternally.
- seeks the thrills, excitement, and stimulation of this world and ignores Christ, shall lose his life eternally.

As said above, the person who loses his life for Christ, who sacrifices and gives all he is and has for Christ, saves his life; and he saves it eternally. The person who keeps his life and what he has for himself shall lose his life, and he loses it eternally. The call of Christ is just what He says: a life of denial that takes up the cross and follows in His steps.

"And I will say to my soul, Soul, thou hast much goods laid up for many years; take thine ease, eat, drink, and be merry. But God said unto him, Thou fool, this night thy soul shall be required of thee: then whose shall those things be, which thou hast provided?" (Lu.12:19-20).

"Wherefore do ye spend money for that which is not bread? and your labor for that which satisfieth not? hearken diligently unto me, and eat ye that which is good, and let your soul delight itself in fatness" (Is.55:2).

"Treasures of wickedness profit nothing: but righteousness delivereth from death" (Pr.10:2).

b. The second phrase is: "and the gospel's [sake]." Whosoever shall lose his life for...the gospel's [sake], the same shall save it." The person who abandons this life, who sacrifices and gives all he is and has for the gospel shall save his life. But the person who keeps his life and all that he has and tries to keep himself and his family free from the suffering and needs of this world—that person shall lose his life.

The person who saves his life...	*The person who gives his life...*
• who lies around in the comforts of home... shall lose his life.	• who becomes an explorer and pioneer for Christ... shall save his life.
• who spends all he has on himself and his family... shall lose his life	• who sacrifices and gives all he is & has to the gospel... shall save his life.
• who takes all his time for his own affairs and desires... shall lose his life.	• who gives of his time for the gospel (visiting, teaching, sharing, witnessing, ministering)... shall save his life.

"And every one that hath forsaken houses, or brethren, or sisters, or father, or mother, or wife, or children, or lands, for my name's sake, shall receive an hundredfold, and shall inherit everlasting life" (Mt.19:29).

"I was a stranger, and ye took me not in: naked, and ye clothed me not: sick, and in prison, and ye visited me not" (Mt.25:43).

"For we which live are alway delivered unto death for Jesus' sake, that the life also of Jesus might be made manifest in our mortal flesh" (2 Co.4:11).

"For unto you it is given in the behalf of Christ, not only to believe on him, but also to suffer for his sake" (Ph.1:29).

"But whoso hath this world's good, and seeth his brother have need, and shutteth up his bowels of compassion from him, how dwelleth the love of God in him?" (1 Jn.3:17).

"And when ye did eat, and when ye did drink, did not ye eat for yourselves, and drink for yourselves?" (Zec.7:6).

4 (8:36-37) **Worldliness—Value—Soul**: there is the issue of value, that is, gaining the world vs. saving the soul. The Greek word translated *soul* is the same Greek word translated *life*. Jesus used the word *life* in two senses. There are *two stages, two beings, two existences to the same life*: the life that exists on this earth and the life that shall exist beyond this earth. Once a person (life) is born into this world, he will exist forever. It is just a matter of where he goes after life in this world: to be with God or to be apart from God.

No man can gain the whole world. But what if he could? All the pleasure and wealth and power and fame are nothing compared with his soul. There are four primary reasons why the soul is far superior to the things of this earth.

a. Everything fades and passes away. A person possesses something but for a short time...
- A man may choose money and property instead of helping to meet the needs of the world. But money and property can be held only for a short time.
- A man may choose position and power instead of giving his life where it would do the most good. But position and power are held only for a short time.
- A woman may choose freedom and pleasure instead of home and family. But freedom and pleasure last only for a short time.
- A person may choose the world and comfort instead of God and His church. But the world and comfort do not satisfy, and they last only for a short time.

"For we brought nothing into this world, and it is certain we can carry nothing out" (1 Ti.6:7).

"For all flesh is as grass, and all the glory of man as the flower of grass. The grass withereth, and the flower thereof falleth away" (1 Pe.1:24).

"The voice said, Cry. And he said, What shall I cry? All flesh is grass, and all the goodliness thereof is as the flower of the field" (Is.40:6).

b. Everything cannot be used all at once. Everything sits, is unused most of the time. Most of the time...
- clothes sit.
- a car sits.
- power goes unused.
- popularity and fame are not thought of.

c. The human soul is eternal; it never dies, never ceases to exist. It shall live forever, either with or apart from God.

"He that believeth on the Son hath everlasting life: and he that believeth not the Son shall not see life; but the wrath of God abideth on him" (Jn.3:36).

"He that loveth his life shall lose it; and he that hateth his life in this world shall keep it unto life eternal" (Jn.12:25).

"For he that soweth to his flesh shall of the flesh reap corruption; but he that soweth to the Spirit shall of the Spirit reap life everlasting" (Ga.6:8).

d. The human soul is of more value than the whole world.

"For what is a man profited, if he shall gain the whole world, and lose his own soul? or what shall a man give in exchange for his soul?" (Mt.16:26).

"Nevertheless man being in honour abideth not: he is like the beasts that perish" (Ps.49:12).

5 (8:38) **Confession**: there is the issue of the Messiah, that is, being ashamed of Christ vs. confessing Christ. At least five things are said in this verse (see note—Mt.10:32-33).

a. Christ is the true Messiah. *He and His words* determine a man's destiny. Note the words, "Me and my words."

b. A man can be ashamed of Christ, and some men are ashamed of Him. Some fear what others will say. They fear being ridiculed by peers: talked about, questioned, avoided, sneered at, abused, persecuted. Therefore, they deny Christ. They deny by word, act, and silence.

c. The world makes it difficult to confess Christ. Why? The world is an adulterous and sinful place. And every generation passes down its adulterous and sinful behavior. Few ever want to confess (follow) the true and living God. God's insistence on the denial of self and the giving of all one is and has is too high a price for most persons. Most persons want to keep some control over their lives and some wealth for themselves. Most are unwilling to give all they are and have to God (that is, to the gospel) and to the demanding love that *the needs of this desperate world require*.

d. The day of the Messiah's glory is coming, a day when His glory shall be revealed to all. It will be a day of glory and splendor, of triumph and victory, a day when all shall see Him as He really is: the true Messiah, the Son of the living God.

e. The day of judgment—of shame and of being ashamed—is coming. All who are ashamed of the Messiah in this world will be ashamed of their behavior where it really counts—before God Himself. The person will see Christ's standing with God, and Christ will be ashamed of the person and of the selfish life the person has lived. And then the *ashamed person* will hear those fateful and terrifying words, "I never knew you: depart from me, ye that work iniquity" (Mt.7:23; see Mt.25:41-46).

"And then will I profess unto them, I never knew you: depart from me, ye that work iniquity" (Mt.7:23).

"But he that denieth me before men shall be denied before the angels of God" (Lu.12:9).

"But he shall say, I tell you, I know you not whence ye are; depart from me, all ye workers of iniquity" (Lu.13:27).

6 (9:1) **Death, Spiritual—Salvation—God's Kingdom**: there is the issue of death, that is, tasting death vs. seeing God's kingdom. This is not a reference to the Lord's second coming. The disciples did die before Jesus' return. More than likely it refers to the Lord's victory over death and hell which took place upon the cross and in the resurrection. It refers to the rule and reign of God's kingdom that takes place within the heart of the believer, to the rule and reign of the Holy Spirit when the Holy Spirit comes to take residence within the believer (see notes—Mt.16:28, pt.4; DEEPER STUDY #3—19:23-24; see Jn.8:52; Heb.2:9).

Thought 1. A man either tastes death or sees God's kingdom with power.
(1) Most men walk in death.

"Then Jesus said unto them, Verily, verily, I say unto you, Except ye eat the flesh of the Son of man, and drink his blood, ye have no life in you" (Jn.6:53).
"Wherefore he saith, Awake thou that sleepest, and arise from the dead, and Christ shall give thee light" (Ep.5:14).
"But she that liveth in pleasure is dead while she liveth" (1 Ti.5:6).
"I know thy works, that thou hast a name that thou livest, and art dead" (Re.3:1).

(2) Some men experience the saving power of God's kingdom (see note, pt.1—Mt.19:23-24).

"It was meet that we should make merry, and be glad: for this thy brother was dead, and is alive again; and was lost, and is found" (Lu.15:32).
"And you hath he quickened, who were dead in trespasses and sins" (Ep.2:1).
"And you, being dead in your sins and the uncircumcision of your flesh, hath he quickened together with him, having forgiven you all trespasses" (Col.2:13).
"Then said the Jews unto him, Now we know that thou hast a devil. Abraham is dead, and the prophets; and thou sayest, If a man keep my saying, he shall never taste of death" (Jn.8:52).
"But we see Jesus, who was made a little lower than the angels for the suffering of death, crowned with glory and honour; that he by the grace of God should taste death for every man" (He.2:9).

D. The Transfiguration: A Glimpse of Heaven's Glory, 9:2-13
(Mt. 17:1-13; Lu. 9:28-36)

1. The setting: Jesus took three disciples up a high mountain—all alone[DS1]

2. The transfiguration strengthened Jesus[DS2]
- a. His transfiguration: His clothing began to shine
- b. His companions
  - 1) The great prophet
  - 2) The great lawgiver, Moses

3. The transfiguration strengthened the disciples
- a. Helped their shattered faith
- b. Gave them a taste of glory
- c. Struck them with awesome fear
- d. Made them witnesses of God's approval[DS3]

2 And after six days Jesus
taketh with him Peter, and
James, and John, and leadeth
them up into an high mountain apart by themselves: and he
was transfigured before them.
3 And his raiment became
shining, exceeding white as
snow; so as no fuller on earth
can white them.
4 And there appeared unto
them Elias with Moses: and
they were talking with
Jesus.
5 And Peter answered and
said to Jesus, Master, It is
good for us to be here: and
let us make three taber-
nacles; one for thee, and
one for Moses, and one for
Elias.
6 For he wist not what to
say; for they were sore afraid.
7 And there was a cloud
that overshadowed them: and
a voice came out of the
cloud, saying, This is my beloved Son: hear him.
8 And suddenly, when they
had looked round about, they
saw no man any more, save
Jesus only with themselves.
9 And as they came down
from the mountain, he
charged them that they
should tell no man what
things they had seen, till the
Son of man were risen from
the dead.
10 And they kept that saying with themselves, questioning one with another
what the rising from the dead
should mean.
11 And they asked him,
saying, Why say the scribes
that Elias must first come?
12 And he answered and
told them, Elias verily
cometh first, and restoreth all
things; and how it is written
of the Son of man, that he
must suffer many things,
and be set at nought.
13 But I say unto you, That
Elias is indeed come, and
they have done unto him
whatsoever they listed, as it
is written of him.

4. The transfiguration gave a unique opportunity to discuss God's Messiahship
- a. Jesus charged the disciples to tell no man about the experience until after His resurrection
- b. The disciples discussed the resurrection: Why must Elijah come first?
- c. Jesus revealed three facts to the disciples
  - 1) Elijah was to come first
  - 2) Scripture said that the Messiah must suffer & die
  - 3) Elijah had already come: He was John the Baptist

DIVISION V

THE SON OF GOD'S CLOSING MINISTRY: JESUS TEACHES THE IDEA OF GOD'S MESSIAHSHIP, NOT MAN'S MESSIAHSHIP, 8:27-9:50

D. The Transfiguration: A Glimpse of Heaven's Glory, 9:2-13

(9:2-13) **Introduction**: the purpose of the transfiguration was to reveal heaven's glory. Heaven's glory would strengthen Jesus to bear the cross and strengthen the disciples in their belief that Jesus was God's Messiah (see note—Mt.17:1-13; Lu.9:28-36). A close study of the transfiguration will strengthen the faith of any believer in his Lord. And a strengthened faith will enable the believer to bear the cross of his own call.

1. The setting: Jesus took three disciples up a high mountain—all alone (v.2).
2. The transfiguration strengthened Jesus (vv.2-4).
3. The transfiguration strengthened the disciples (vv.5-7).
4. The transfiguration gave a unique opportunity to discuss God's Messiahship (vv.8-13).

(9:2-13) **Another Outline**: The Transfiguration—Some Strange Events.

1. There was Jesus transfigured (v.3).
2. There were Elijah and Moses talking with Jesus (v.4).
3. There was the ecstatic exhilaration of the experience (vv.5-6).
4. There was God's voice (v.7).
5. There was the sudden silence (v.8).
6. There was the restriction: "Tell no man" (v.9).
7. There was the statement: Jesus was to arise from the dead (vv.9b-10).
8. There was the discussion of Messiahship (vv.11-13).

1 (9:2) **Disciples, Inner Circle**: Jesus took three disciples all alone up into a high mountain. Why did He not take the other disciples with them? The answer is not given. It is only speculation to guess. (See DEEPER STUDY # 1, *Inner Circle*—Mk.9:2.)

DEEPER STUDY # 1

(9:2) **Disciples, Inner Circle**: Peter, James, and John apparently formed an inner circle around Jesus. Jesus revealed more to these three men than to the other disciples. They were with Him when He raised Jairus' daughter, when He was in the Garden of Gethsemane, and here on the mount of transfiguration. Why were these three chosen to receive these additional revelations?

What is known is this. Each was being chosen for a very special ministry role or call. They were not aware of it yet, but they were to fill unique positions in the ministry.

1. Peter was to be the leader of the early church, the one who was to open the door of the gospel to both Jew and Gentile after Pentecost (Ac.2:1f; 10:1f).
2. James was called to be an apostle and to be martyred for his faith in Christ (Ac.12:2).
3. John was to receive *The Revelation* from God to close out the Scripture.

2 (9:2-4) **Jesus Christ, Transfiguration—Glory**: the transfiguration strengthened Jesus. Jesus needed to be strengthened. He was about to face the cross and the full weight of all that was involved in dying for the sins of the world. The pressure of bearing God's judgment for *all* the sins of the world was beginning to press in upon Him. He needed God's strength, encouragement, and assurance in a very special way. Therefore, God gave Jesus two very special experiences.

a. Jesus "was transfigured...His raiment became shining" (see DEEPER STUDY # 2, *Transfigured*—Mk.9:2-3).

b. Jesus was visited by two saints from heaven: Moses, the great lawgiver, and Elijah, the great prophet. Why did Moses and Elijah appear with Jesus? There seem to be two reasons.

1) To discuss His death (Lu.17:31). Jesus needed to be strengthened to bear the weight and pressure of the cross. See the Garden of Gethsemane experience and His cry on the cross (Lu.22:39-46; see note—Mt.27:46-49.)
2) They show that Jesus is the true Messiah, the Son of God, the One who is superior to the law and the prophets. Moses represented the law; and Elijah, who was considered the greatest of the prophets, represented the prophets. These two men were honoring and ministering to Jesus. They were symbolizing that the law and the prophets found their fulfillment in Jesus. Jesus is the One of whom the law and the prophets spoke; He is the One to whom the law and the prophets pointed. The old covenant was now to be fulfilled and superseded by Jesus who was to usher in the new covenant (see outline and notes—2 Co.3:6-18; He.9:15-22; see Mt.9:16-17.)

DEEPER STUDY # 2

(9:2-3) **Transfigured** (metamorphoo): a change into another form; a transformation; a change of countenance; a complete change. Luke says, "the fashion of His countenance was altered" (Lu.9:29). Note how the gospel writers describe what happened.

> **"His face did shine as the sun and His raiment was white as the light" (Mt.17:2).**
> **"His raiment became shining, exceeding white as snow; so as no fuller on earth can white them" (Mk.9:3).**
> **"The fashion of His countenance was altered, and His raiment was white and glistening" (Lu.9:29).**

Apparently, *the glory* of His Godly nature was allowed to shine through His body. "The glory which [He] had with the Father before the world was" emanated through His body right on through His clothes (Jn.17:5). Peter says, "We were eyewitnesses of His majesty." In John's vision of Jesus in *The Revelation*, he describes the glory of Christ as the sun which "shineth in its strength" (Re.1:16). The Scripture says:

> **"God is light" (1 Jn.1:5).**
> **"[God]...*dwelling* in the light which no man can approach" (1 Ti.6:16).**
> **"[God] who *coverest* thyself with light as with a garment" (Ps.104:2).**

Two things need to be noted.

1. The word *shining* (stilbo) is a Greek participle which means the shining is active. The transfiguration was a real, active experience. It was no illusion, no dream; it was not of the imagination. It was not a reflection of the sun's shining off some rock, glass, or lake. "His [own] face did shine." The "shining" was the glory of the Lord's inner nature, of His Godly nature actively shining right through His being.
2. The full glory of the Godhead was not shining through Jesus. No man could ever stand in the full glory of the Lord's presence, not in man's present physical body. As Scripture says, "Our Lord Jesus Christ...the King of kings, and Lord of lords; who only hath immortality, dwelling in the light *which no man can approach unto*; whom no man hath seen, nor can see" (1 Ti.6:14-16). Apparently God allowed only a small degree of the glory, only what the three disciples could bear to shine through the body and clothing of Jesus.

The transfiguration is, of course, a mystery to man. But it should be remembered that it is a mystery cloaked in the fullness of the Godhead. And God's glory is so brilliant there is no need for a sun (Re.21:23; 22:5). The glory of the Supreme Being who stands behind the universe in His unlimited presence and power is bound to be beyond description and thought (see Ep.3:20).

3 (9:5-7) **Jesus Christ, Transfiguration—Shattered Faith—Disciples**: the transfiguration strengthened the disciples. They were strengthened in at least four ways.

a. The transfiguration helped the disciples' shattered faith (v.5). The disciples were shattered because Jesus said that He was going to Jerusalem to die (Mk.8:31). They began to interpret His words symbolically (Mk.8:10). The transfiguration made them eyewitnesses to the brilliant splendor and radiance of the Messiah's glory and to God's voice of approval. They also saw that the law and the prophets found their fulfillment in Him as represented in Moses and Elijah. Therefore, their spirits were bolstered in the firm conviction that Jesus was God's Messiah.

b. The transfiguration gave the disciples a taste of glory (v.5). The three disciples were tasting some of heaven's joy, peace, security, fulfillment, and perfection. They did not want to leave this hallowed ground.

Note what Peter did.

1) He offered to build three *shelters* (skenas) for Jesus and the two prophets. By this act, he hoped to extend the stay of the heavenly guests and the glorious experience. The shelters which Peter offered to build were

the booths made of branches and grass which could be quickly built, the kind often built by travelers on their stops along the road night by night.

2) He said, "If thou wilt." Peter, even in a moment as glorious as this, would not act against his Lord's will. Imagine the devotion and loyalty.

c. The transfiguration struck the disciples with awesome fear (v.6). The disciples' experience can be applied to the future, to the believer's appearance before God in the great Day of Redemption. In fact, that is just what happened to Peter, James, and John. They found themselves in God's presence. The believer's experience in the Day of Redemption will undoubtedly be very much like what they experienced.

1) The believer will experience the Shekinah glory, see its full manifestation upon Christ.
2) The believer will hear the voice of God proclaiming Christ to be His Son, expressing perfect approval of His redemptive work, and rejoicing that He has been heard and is to be heard throughout all eternity.
3) The believer will fall upon his face, prostrate before Christ in awe and adoration and worship.
4) The believer will experience the Lord's intercessory work. He will feel the Lord's hand reaching out to touch him and to lift him up. And the believer will stand in the Lord's righteousness and perfection, living in a state of glory forever.
5) The believer will witness and experience the Lord's preeminence throughout all eternity.

d. The transfiguration made the disciples witnesses of God's approval (v.7. See DEEPER STUDY # 3, *Cloud*—Mk.9:7. Also see note—Mt.17:8.)

Thought 1. The believer must often get alone with Christ in order to have his strength renewed.

"But they that wait upon the LORD shall renew their strength; they shall mount up with wings as eagles; they shall run, and not be weary; and they shall walk and not faint" (Is.40:31).

"Fear thou not; For I am with thee: be not dismayed; for I am thy God: I will strengthen thee; yea, I will help thee; yea, I will uphold thee with the right hand of my righteousness" (Is.41:10).

"Keep silence before me...and let the people renew their strength: let them come near" (Is.41:1).

"For which cause we faint not; but though our outward man perish, yet the inward man is renewed [strengthened] day by day" (2 Co.4:16).

DEEPER STUDY # 3

(9:7) **Cloud**: the cloud enveloped both Jesus and the three disciples. The cloud and the voice of God terrified the disciples and caused them to fall immediately upon their faces, prostrate and unable to look up. As mortal men they were paralyzed in fear. Note three facts.

1. The cloud was "a bright cloud." This was the Shekinah glory, the cloud that symbolized God's presence. It was the cloud that guided Israel out of Egypt and that rested upon the tabernacle (Ex.40:34-38) and above the Mercy Seat in the Most Holy Place. God "only hath immortality, dwelling in the light which *no man can approach unto*" (1 Ti.6:16). God dwells in unapproachable light upon which no man can look. Peter later called it "the excellent glory" (2 Pe.1:17).

2. The "bright cloud" overshadowing Jesus is in contrast to the dark and threatening cloud that overshadowed the giving of the old covenant to Moses, that is, the law (Ex.19:18; 20:21). There is a point to be made here. The law (old covenant) was dark and threatening (see DEEPER STUDY # 2—Gal.3:10); the new covenant (the love of Christ) is bright and is given to save and bless, not to threaten and condemn (He.12:18-24. See Heb.8:6-13.)

3. The voice speaking actually says in the Greek, "This is My Son, the Beloved One." Note the two facts stressed. Jesus is God's Son, and He is the Beloved One. The idea is that Jesus is the "only begotten Son" who was to be given for the world (Jn.3:16).

4 (9:8-13) **Jesus Christ, Transfiguration**: the transfiguration gave a unique opportunity to discuss God's Messiahship. Jesus charged the disciples to tell no one about their experience until after He had "risen from the dead." The mentioning of *rising from the dead* stirred them to question what He meant. They had just witnessed His glory and seen Moses and Elijah with Him. They thought that He was going to set up His kingdom *now* and that He would now reign in glory. Why, then, did Elijah leave? The Scribes said that Elijah had to come before the Messiah would set up His kingdom. Christ answered the disciples and corrected the view that the Scribes had always taught.

First, Scripture does teach that Elijah must come first and restore or prepare all things.

Second, Scripture also teaches that the Messiah must die. And it is this fact that they were overlooking (Jn.10:11, 15, 17-18).

Third, Elijah had already come. He was John the Baptist.

Thought 1. Jesus Christ is the Messiah, the Son of God. Belief in Him is absolutely essential.

"I said therefore unto you, that ye shall die in your sins: for if ye believe not that I am he, ye shall die in your sins" (Jn.8:24).

"The woman saith unto him, I know that Messias cometh, which is called Christ: when he is come, he will tell us all things. Jesus saith unto her, I that speak unto thee am he" (Jn.4:25-26).

"And we believe and are sure that thou art that Christ, the Son of the living God" (Jn.6:69; see Jn.11:25-27).

"But Saul [Paul the apostle] increased the more in strength, and confounded the Jews which dwelt at Damascus, proving that this is very Christ" (Ac.9:22; see Ac.17:2-3).

"Whosoever believeth that Jesus is the Christ is born of God: and every one that loveth him that begat loveth him also that is begotten of him" (1 Jn.5:1).

E. The Problem of Spiritual Immaturity & Powerlessness, 9:14-29
(Mt. 17:14-21; Lu. 9:37-42)

1. Spiritual immaturity belittles & shames
   a. The crowds gathered
   b. The Scribes or teachers of the law questioned
   c. The crowds rushed up to Jesus—overwhelmed with wonder[DS1]
   d. Jesus drew attention from the humiliated disciples
   e. The cause of the embarrassment
      1) The need—a sick child[DS2]
      2) The weak faith—of a concerned father, 23
      3) The powerless ministry—of the disciples[DS3]

2. Spiritual immaturity grieves the Lord
   a. The faithlessness of men
   b. The pitiful condition of a person's need
   c. The desperate plight of loved ones

14 And when he came to his
disciples, he saw a great multitude about them, and the
scribes questioning with
them.
15 And straightway all the
people, when they beheld
him, were greatly amazed,
and running to him saluted
him.
16 And he asked the
scribes, What question ye
with them?
17 And one of the multi-
tude answered and said, Master, I have brought unto thee
my son, which hath a dumb
spirit;
18 And wheresoever he taketh him, he teareth him: and
he foameth, and gnasheth
with his teeth, and pineth
away: and I spake to thy
disciples that they should
cast him out; and they could
not.
19 He answereth him, and
saith, O faithless generation,
how long shall I be with you?
how long shall I suffer you?
bring him unto me.
20 And they brought him
unto him: and when he saw
him, straightway the spirit
tare him; and he fell on
the ground, and wallowed
foaming.
21 And he asked his father,
How long is it ago since this
came unto him? And he said,
Of a child.
22 And ofttimes it hath cast
him into the fire, and into the
waters, to destroy him: but if
thou canst do any thing, have
compassion on us, and help
us.
23 Jesus said unto him, If
thou canst believe, all things
are possible to him that believeth.
24 And straightway the
father of the child cried out,
and said with tears, Lord, I
believe; help thou mine unbelief.
25 When Jesus saw that the
people came running to-
gether, he rebuked the foul
spirit, saying unto him, Thou
dumb and deaf spirit, I
charge thee, come out of him,
and enter no more into him.
26 And the spirit cried, and
rent him sore, and came out
of him: and he was as one
dead; insomuch that many
said, He is dead.
27 But Jesus took him by
the hand, and lifted him up;
and he arose.
28 And when he was come
into the house, his disciples
asked him privately, Why
could not we cast him out?
29 And he said unto them,
This kind can come forth by
nothing, but by prayer and
fasting.

3. Spiritual immaturity must be acknowledged to receive God's blessings
   a. Acknowledged by faith
   b. Acknowledged by humility & by crying for help
   c. Result: Spiritual blessings are secured by Jesus' word & power

4. Spiritual immaturity can be conquered: Spiritual power is available
   a. By seeking the Lord
   b. By prayer & fasting[DS4,5]

DIVISION V

THE SON OF GOD'S CLOSING MINISTRY: JESUS TEACHES THE IDEA OF GOD'S MESSIAHSHIP, NOT MAN'S MESSIAHSHIP, 8:27–9:50

E. The Problem of Spiritual Immaturity and Powerlessness, 9:14-29

(9:14-29) **Introduction**: the Scripture and outline above point out a chronic problem among believers—spiritual immaturity and a powerless life and ministry.

1. Spiritual immaturity belittles and shames (vv.14-18).
2. Spiritual immaturity grieves the Lord (vv.19-22).
3. Spiritual immaturity must be acknowledged to receive God's blessings (vv.23-27).
4. Spiritual immaturity can be conquered; spiritual power is available (vv.28-29).

1 (9:14-18) **Spiritual Immaturity**: spiritual immaturity belittles and shames. As Jesus descended from the mountain, He saw that a great crowd had gathered at the foot awaiting His return. As He drew closer, He noticed that the Scribes were ridiculing and shaming the disciples. The Scribes were, of course, questioning and belittling their credentials to minister. By discrediting the disciples, they hoped to discredit Jesus in the eyes of the people (see notes—Mt.12:1-8; note and DEEPER STUDY #1—12:10). When Jesus was seen approaching, the crowds were "greatly amazed" and ran to meet Him (see DEEPER STUDY #1—Mk.9:15).

When Jesus reached the Scribes and the disciples, He asked the Scribes what it was they were questioning. Note how Jesus had stepped into the scene. He drew attention from the disciples' humiliation. He delivered them.

Note also who it was that answered Jesus. It was not the Scribes, but the desperate father of a needy child. The cause of the embarrassment was threefold.

a. There was the sickness that caused embarrassment (v.17. See DEEPER STUDY # 2, *Evil Spirits*—Mk.9:17-18.) Demon possession and epilepsy were cursed diseases, diseases that caused isolation and rejection by society. Because of society's reaction, families were often embarrassed when a member was afflicted. Just imagine this scene. The child and father were right in the midst of a shameful experience. They were the subject of the questioning and ridicule. Imagine their embarrassment in being the focus of the crowd's attention, their problem of demon possession, and their having sought help from apparent frauds.

"And said, O my God, I am ashamed and blush to lift up my face to thee, my God: for our iniquities are increased over our head, and our trespass is grown up unto the heavens" (Ezr.9:6).
"But Zion said, The LORD hath forsaken me, and my Lord hath forgotten me" (Is.49:14).
"My confusion is continually before me, and the shame of my face hath covered me" (Ps.44:15).

b. There was the presence of weak faith. The father's faith was weak.

⇒ He was part of the "faithless generation" (v.19).
⇒ He was told "if thou canst believe" (v.23).
⇒ He had to cry, "help thou mine unbelief" (v.24).

The child had not been healed because of weak faith. But it was not just the weak faith of the disciples; no one had faith enough to heal the child—not the father, not the disciples, not the religionists (Scribes).

"And he did not many mighty works there because of their unbelief" (Mt.13:58).
"And immediately Jesus stretched forth his hand, and caught him, and said unto him, O thou of little faith, wherefore didst thou doubt?" (Mt.14:31).
"Then Jesus answered and said, O faithless and perverse generation, how long shall I be with you? how long shall I suffer you? bring him hither to me" (Mt.17:17).
"And he said unto them, Why are ye so fearful: how is that ye have no faith?" (Mk.4:40).

c. There was a powerless ministry (v.18). The very persons who should have been able to help were the disciples. Nine disciples were there when the man first came for help, yet not a single one of them was able to help. They all lacked the power (see DEEPER STUDY # 3—Mk.9:18).

Thought 1. *No power* affects the testimony of believers (see DEEPER STUDY # 3—Mk.9:18).

Thought 2. Remember this critical fact: the world uses the lives of believers to judge not only their testimonies but also Christ Himself. The world tries to discredit Christ because of the powerlessness of believers.

Thought 3. Note the three causes of embarrassment in this passage: a weak faith, a powerless ministry, and the boy's illness. Some illnesses (whether due to natural causes or brought on by immorality, drunkenness, or some other sinful behavior that destroys or brings injury to the body) will always cause embarrassment. There is no excuse for a believer's living a sinful life, a life so sinful that his faith becomes weak, his ministry becomes powerless, or his body contracts a disease.

"O LORD, I know that the way of man is not in himself: it is not in man that walketh to direct his steps" (Je.10:23).
"John...said, A man can receive nothing, except it be given him from heaven" (Jn.3:27).
"I am the vine, ye are the branches: He that abideth in me, and I in him, the same bringeth forth much fruit: for without me ye can do nothing" (Jn.15:5).
"Not that we are sufficient of ourselves to think any thing [power] as of ourselves; but our sufficiency is of God" (2 Co.3:5).

DEEPER STUDY # 1
(9:15) **Greatly Amazed** (ekethambethe): to be filled with wonder. What amazed the people when they "beheld" Jesus?

1. Perhaps Jesus retained some of the glory of the transfiguration (see Ex.34:29 when Moses came down from the mountain after having been with God). The people may have seen a glow, a majestic countenance, about Jesus.
2. Perhaps Jesus came at such an opportune time that the people were amazed to see Him, as though His timing was destined. He arrived just when His disciples needed help.
3. Perhaps Jesus walked with a renewed aire, a more authoritative and decisive countenance than before. Just coming from the transfiguration was bound to instill a renewed confidence and authority within Him.

DEEPER STUDY # 2
(9:17-18) **Evil Spirits**: the son's illness seems to have been both physical and spiritual. The description of the illness in Mark points toward what is known today as epilepsy and demon possession (Mt.17:15; Mk.9:17-18; Lu.9:39). The demon possession in particular seems to have heightened and aggravated the condition, perhaps causing some suicidal tendencies (Mt.17:15; Mk.9:22). Throughout the gospels this seems to be one of the major works of evil spirits: to *heighten and aggravate* existing conditions.

Note the description of the three gospels. Luke's description is especially interesting because it is the description of a physician.

Mark 9:17-18	*Luke 9:39*	*Mt.17:15*
A dumb spirit	A spirit (evil)	A devil (v.18)
It takes Him (seizes hold)	Takes him	Lunatick
It tears him (strikes down)	Cries out	Sore vexed
He foams	Tears him	Falls into the fire
He gnashes with his teeth	Foams	Falls into the water
He pines away (wastes away)	Bruises him	

DEEPER STUDY # 3
(9:18) **Power, Lack of**: Why do the servants of God fail? Why do they often lack power? Why does their faith weaken? This experience of the disciples reveals much about spiritual failure and lack of power.

1. A sense that Christ is far away and out of reach makes one ineffective. The indwelling presence and power of Christ are just not felt—not to the extent that they need to be available. In the above situation Christ was absent, but His power was still available. The disciples were just not all that aware of His power.
2. The lack of leadership causes the faith and loyalty of some to weaken. The nine disciples apparently had no leader to stand forth as a champion of faith and power.
3. Uncompromising unbelief can weaken one's trust (v.16). This was true of the Scribes' unbelief and questioning. They distracted and sapped the disciples' faith and power.
4. An atmosphere of questioning and unbelief often affects the faith and power of a person's life. A terrible atmosphere of unbelief and distrust in God was created by everyone present: the man's questionable belief (v.22), the Scribes' questioning (v.16), the disciples' lack of faith and power, and the people's disturbance over the whole affair.

What happens when the servants of God have *no power*? What are the results of a powerless life and ministry?

⇒ No power causes embarrassment and shame.
⇒ No power causes the world to question and ridicule and belittle.
⇒ No power questions the deity (validity) of Christ and God.
⇒ No power causes the questioning of God and His ability to deliver.

The answer to no power is given by Christ. Power comes (1) by seeking and (2) by prayer and fasting (vv.28-29).

2 (9:19-22) **Spiritual Immaturity**: spiritual immaturity grieves the Lord in three areas.

a. The faithlessness of men grieves Christ. Christ rebuked the generation standing before Him; but in all honesty, every generation was rebuked, for every generation has proven to be faithless. Having no faith saddened and brought sorrow to the Lord's heart, and He expressed that sorrow: "How long shall I be with you? How long shall I suffer [bear with] you?"

Who is being rebuked? Who is faithless? To whom is Christ speaking? The answer is clearly seen. There was not a single person present who helped the desperate child: not the father, not the crowd, not the disciples, and not even the questioning religionists.

⇒ The father was unbelieving.
⇒ The crowd was unspiritual and worldly.
⇒ The disciples were ineffective and powerless.
⇒ The religionists were self-centered and critical.

> **"And when he had looked round about on them with anger, being grieved for the hardness of their hearts, he saith unto the man, Stretch forth thine hand. And he stretched it out: and his hand was restored whole as the other" (Mk.3:5).**
>
> **"Wherefore I was grieved with that generation, and said, They do alway err in their heart; and they have not known my ways" (He.3:10).**
>
> **"I [was] grieved with this generation, and said, It is a people that do err in their heart, and they have not known my ways" (Ps.95:10).**

b. The pitiful condition of a person's need grieves Christ. The son was helpless, under the power of an evil spirit that tore (convulsed) him and caused him to wallow around, foaming at the mouth (see notes—Mk.1:23-24; 5:6-7). The sight of the boy in such a pitiful condition touched and grieved the heart of Christ.

c. The desperate plight of loved ones grieves the Lord. Jesus cared for the father just as much as He cared for the son. The father was hurting in his heart. It was his love for the son that drove him to seek Jesus in the first place. Jesus knew this, and Jesus knew something else. The father's faith was weak and needed strengthening, so Jesus asked the father about the history of the boy's illness. But note: Jesus was not interested so much in the boy's case history as He was in getting the father...

- to focus on his desperate need.
- to focus on Jesus who stood before him.
- to focus on Jesus who alone could meet his need.
- to focus on Jesus so much that his faith would be stirred.

Jesus' purpose worked: the man's attention was focused upon Jesus and upon his son's case history. The man said two significant things to Jesus.

1. "If thou canst do anything...help us."
2. "Have compassion on us, and help us."

The man lacked personal knowledge and faith in Jesus' power, but He cried for the compassion of Jesus—if Jesus really did have the power to help. There was no way Jesus would turn away from the man's cry for mercy (see Lu.18:13).

Thought 1. Note two significant statements. It is not so much our faith as it is our cry for mercy and compassion that arouses God to help us. It is not so much our faith as the object of our faith (God Himself) that saves us (see note—Mk.11:22-23).

"The LORD is nigh unto them that are of a broken heart; and saveth such as be of a contrite spirit" (Ps.34:18).

"Because he hath set his love upon me, therefore will I deliver him: I will set him on high, because he hath known my name. He shall call upon me, and I will answer him: I will be with him in trouble; I will deliver him, and honour him" (Ps.91:14-15).

Thought 2. The same three things that grieved Christ should grieve the heart of every believer. We should be grieved to the point that we act and minister just as Christ did.

[3] (9:23-27) **Spiritual Blessings**: spiritual immaturity must be acknowledged to receive God's blessings.

a. Spiritual immaturity must be acknowledged by *faith*. The father's faith was immature. Jesus threw the father's words back to him: "It is not a question, If I can, but 'If thou canst believe. All things are possible to him that believeth.'"

1) All things are possible to the Son of God. The power of God is available, but a person must trust in God's power.
2) The great principle of prayer and faith was being taught to the man.

"And all things, whatsoever ye shall ask in prayer, believing, ye shall receive" (Mt.21:22). (See note—Mk.11:22-23.)

"But without faith it is impossible to please him: for he that cometh to God must believe that he is, and that he is a rewarder of them that diligently seek him" (He.11:6).

b. Spiritual immaturity must be acknowledged by *humility and crying for help*. The man was weak, but his need was desperate. He *accepted* the Lord's Word...

- about his being weak (sinful) and needing help personally.
- about his lack of faith being the problem.

The man responded in humility and cried out with tears, "Lord I believe; help thou mine unbelief." Note that he cried out for Jesus to help him *even* in his faith. He needed help even in believing; but he did the one essential, he cried out with all his heart and being, *confessing* that he needed help.

"For we have not an high priest which cannot be touched with the feeling of our infirmities; but was in all points tempted like as we are, yet without sin. Let us therefore come boldly unto the throne of grace, that we may obtain mercy, and find grace to help in time of need" (He.4:15-16).

"For thus saith the high and lofty One that inhabiteth eternity, whose name is Holy; I dwell in the high and holy place, with him also that is of a contrite and humble spirit, to revive the spirit of the humble, and to revive the heart of the contrite ones" (Is.57:15).

"For godly sorrow worketh repentance to salvation not to be repented of: but the sorrow of the world worketh death" (2 Co.7:10).

"Like as a father pitieth his children, so the LORD pitieth them that fear him" (Ps.103:13).

c. Spiritual blessings are secured by Jesus' Word and power. Note several things.

1) Jesus healed the boy when He saw the crowd running toward them. He had apparently pulled the father and boy to the side to help the father's concentration (see v.25. See note, pt.1—Lu.9:14-18.)
2) It was the word of Jesus that healed the boy. It was His Word that broke the devil's power. The word *rebuked* (epetimese) is strong, authoritative, even severe. Satan cannot stand before God's Word. Christ has spoiled the principalities and powers of evil (Col.2:15).
3) The evil spirit made one last effort to disrupt and discredit the power of Christ. The evil spirit (as so often happens) apparently attempted to destroy the boy.
4) Jesus took the boy by the hand and lifted him up, and the boy arose, being healed.

[4] (9:28-29) **Spiritual Immaturity—Power—Prayer—Fasting**: spiritual immaturity can be conquered; spiritual power is available.

a. Immaturity can be conquered by *seeking spiritual power*. The disciples sought to know why they failed. They wanted to know the cause. Remember: Jesus had already given them power over evil spirits, and they had already exercised such power. They could not understand why they had failed when they had been successful before (Mk.3:14-15; see Lu.9:1; 10:17).

b. Immaturity can be conquered by *prayer and fasting*. Jesus pointed to one thing: the disciples were not living close enough to God. They were not praying and fasting enough, not seeking Him enough, not putting Him before food and other things. They were taking time for other things, taking time to eat, but not taking time for God.

Thought 1. God must be depended upon so much that food and everything else are set aside in order to seek Him. A man's heart must sometimes crave God so much that food and all else are set aside to seek Him.

"And I say unto you, Ask, and it shall be given you; seek, and ye shall find; knock, and it shall be opened unto you" (Lu.11:9).

"If ye shall ask any thing in my name, I will do it" (Jn.14:14).

"But if from thence thou shalt seek the LORD thy God, thou shalt find him, if thou seek him with all thy heart and with all thy soul" (De.4:29).

"And ye shall seek me, and find me, when ye shall search for me with all your heart" (Je.29:13).

"I love them that love me; and those that seek me early shall find me" (Pr.8:17).

DEEPER STUDY # 4
(9:29) **Prayer**: see note—Mt.7:7-11; see Ep.6:18.

DEEPER STUDY # 5
(9:29) **Fasting**: see note—Mt.6:16-18.

	F. The Second Prediction of Death: Intensive Training on the Death of Christ, 9:30-32 *(Mt. 17:22-23; Lu. 9:43-45)*	31 For he taught his disciples, and said unto them, The Son of man is delivered into the hands of men, and they shall kill him; and after that he is killed, he shall rise the third day.	**2. The lesson: Jesus taught His disciples that He was to die & arise***DS1,2*
1. The preparation: Jesus got alone with His disciples	30 And they departed thence, and passed through Galilee; and he would not that any man should know it.	32 But they understood not that saying, and were afraid to ask him.	**3. The response: The disciples rejected what they did not wish to see**

DIVISION V

THE SON OF GOD'S CLOSING MINISTRY: JESUS TEACHES THE IDEA OF GOD'S MESSIAHSHIP, NOT MAN'S MESSIAHSHIP, 8:27–9:50

F. The Second Prediction of Death: Intensive Training on the Death of Christ, 9:30-32

(9:30-32) **Introduction**: the thrust of this passage is the death and resurrection of Jesus Christ (see outline and notes—Mk.8:31-33; 10:32-34; Mt.16:21-23; 17:22-23; 20:17-19). Because of its enormous importance, Jesus drilled the truth of His death and resurrection into His disciples. It is absolutely essential that every man grasp the death and resurrection of Jesus.

⇒ A man's eternal destiny depends upon his grasping the truth.
⇒ The fate of the Christian message depends upon believing the truth.
⇒ The fate of the world, moral truth and justice, depends upon men's grasping and believing the truth.

1. The preparation: Jesus got alone with His disciples (v.30).
2. The lesson: Jesus taught His disciples that He was to die and arise (v.31).
3. The response: the disciples rejected what they did not wish to see (v.32).

1 (9:30) **Jesus Christ, Teaching**: the preparation—Jesus got alone with His disciples. This was a pivotal point in Jesus' ministry. He left the area of Caesarea Philippi in the north country where He was safe and headed toward Galilee from where He was to go into Jerusalem. The cross was sitting right before His face (see Mk.8:31-33). But note: He was still moving about quietly. Matthew says that Jesus "moved to and fro" Galilee. The idea is that Jesus moved about in order to avoid the crowds, yet He was moving ever so much closer to Jerusalem and the cross. Jesus needed to concentrate on His disciples, to drill into them the fact that He had to die and arise from the dead. He had to continue repeating and reiterating His death and resurrection because it was contrary to all their hopes and expectations. It was different from all they had ever heard or been taught. The Messiah was thought to be a Messiah of power and sovereign rule, not a Messiah who had to suffer and die in order to save man. (See notes—Mt.1:1; DEEPER STUDY # 2—1:18; DEEPER STUDY # 3—3:11; notes—11:1-6; 11:2-3; DEEPER STUDY #1—11:5; DEEPER STUDY # 2—11:6; DEEPER STUDY # 1—12:16; notes—22:42; Lu.7:21-23.)

2 (9:31) **Jesus Christ, Death; Resurrection**: the lesson. Jesus taught His disciples that He was to die and arise from the dead. Note three things.

1. Jesus *taught* (edidaske) His disciples. The Greek tense is imperfect; that is, He continued to teach them, kept right on teaching them. It was a continuous process, pulling one to the side, then another, then two, then four or five, then the whole group. He taught and taught, drilling the fact of His death and resurrection into them.

2. The word *delivered* (paradidotai) means to be delivered over and into death. It means that His death was determined, ordained, set in the plan and counsel of God. Note that Jesus said, "The Son of Man *is* delivered." His death is right before His face.

1) God delivered Christ up to be betrayed.

> **"Him, being delivered by the determinate counsel and foreknowledge of God, ye have taken, and by wicked hands have crucified and slain" (Ac.2:23).**
> **"He that spared not his own Son, but delivered him up for us all, how shall he not with him also freely give us all things?" (Ro.8:32).**

2) Christ delivered Himself up to be crucified.

> **"Who gave himself for our sins, that he might deliver us from this present evil world, according to the will of God and our Father" (Ga.1:4).**
> **"And walk in love, as Christ also hath loved us, and hath given himself for us an offering and a sacrifice to God for a sweetsmelling savour" (Ep.5:2).**
> **"Husbands, love your wives, even as Christ also loved the church, and gave himself for it" (Ep.5:25).**
> **"Who gave himself for us, that he might redeem us from all iniquity, and purify unto himself a peculiar people, zealous of good works" (Tit.2:14).**

"Hereby perceive we the love of God, because he laid down his life for us: and we ought to lay down our lives for the brethren" (1 Jn.3:16).

3) Judas betrayed Him (see notes—Mt.26:20-25; 27:3-5; Mk.14:10-11; Lu.22:4-6; Jn.13:18; 13:21-26).

Jesus named the man who would kill Him (see DEEPER STUDY # 1-Mt.16:21). The betrayal would be by *Judas* who identified Him for the *elders*, *chief priests*, and *Scribes*; they in turn would deliver Him to the *Gentiles* (or Romans) for execution (Mt.20:19).

In preaching to the Jews right after Pentecost, Peter accused the Jews: "Ye have taken [Him] and by wicked hands [the hands of the lawless Gentiles or Romans] have crucified and slain" (Ac.2:23).

c. There are several reasons why Jesus repeated and repeated the fact of His death (also see DEEPER STUDY # 1—Mk.9:31).

1) To enforce that He was *dying as a willing sacrifice* and not as a hopeless martyr or as a mistaken man who thought He was the Messiah.

"I am the good shepherd: the good shepherd giveth his life for the sheep" (Jn.10:11).

"As the Father knoweth me, even so know I the Father: and I lay down my life for the sheep" (Jn.10:15).

"Therefore doth my Father love me, because I lay down my life, that I might take it again. No man taketh it from me, but I lay it down of myself. I have power to lay it down, and I have power to take it again. This commandment have I received of my Father" (Jn.10:17-18).

2) To stress that He was *dying to redeem man* just as God willed.

"Being justified freely by his grace through the redemption that is in Christ Jesus: whom God hath set forth to be a propitiation through faith in his blood, to declare his righteousness for the remission of sins that are past, through the forbearance of God" (Ro.3:24-25).

"Christ hath redeemed us from the curse of the law, being made a curse for us: for it is written, Cursed is every one that hangeth on a tree" (Ga.3:13).

"In whom we have redemption through his blood, the forgiveness of sins, according to the riches of his grace" (Ep.1:7).

"And walk in love, as Christ also hath loved us, and hath given himself for us an offering and a sacrifice to God for a sweetsmelling savour" (Ep.5:2).

"In whom we have redemption through his blood, even the forgiveness of sins" (Col.1:14).

"Who gave himself for us, that he might redeem us from all iniquity, and purify unto himself a peculiar people, zealous of good works" (Tit.2:14).

"Neither by the blood of goats and calves, but by his own blood he entered in once into the holy place, having obtained eternal redemption for us" (He.9:12).

"Forasmuch as ye know that ye were not redeemed with corruptible things, as silver and gold, from your vain conversation received by tradition from your fathers; but with the precious blood of Christ, as of a lamb without blemish and without spot" (1 Pe.1:18-19).

"And they sung a new song, saying, Thou art worthy to take the book, and to open the seals thereof: for thou wast slain, and hast redeemed us to God by thy blood out of every kindred, and tongue, and people, and nation" (Re.5:9).

3) To assure that His death was deliberately planned in the purposes of God and that He was willingly dying to fulfill that purpose.

"Him, being delivered by the determinate counsel and foreknowledge of God, ye have taken, and by wicked hands have crucified and slain" (Ac.2:23).

"He that spared not his own Son, but delivered him up for us all, how shall he not with him also freely give us all things?" (Ro.8:32).

4) To keep the disciples from thinking that the Messiah, the Son of God, could never die (see note, pt.2—Mk.9:31).

5) To drill His death into the disciples so that they could better understand the truth after His resurrection.

DEEPER STUDY # 1

(9:31) **Jesus Christ, Death**: Jesus Christ was killed for two reasons (see note, *Death*—Mt.17:23 for discussion. This note includes most of the New Testament passages dealing with the death of Christ. See note and DEEPER STUDY # 1—Acts 1:3; DEEPER STUDY # 2,3—2:23; DEEPER STUDY # 2—Ro.3:24; notes—5:1; 5:6-7; 5:6-11; 6:1-10; 7:4; DEEPER STUDY # 2—8:3; note—8:31-33.)

DEEPER STUDY # 2

(9:31) **Jesus Christ, Resurrection**: God raised Christ for several reasons (see note, *Resurrection*—Mt.17:23 for discussion. This note includes most of the New Testament passages dealing with the resurrection of Christ. See note and DEEPER STUDY #1—Acts 1:3; DEEPER STUDY # 4—2:24.)

3 (9:32) **Jesus Christ, Death**: the response. The disciples rejected what they did not wish to see. Jesus stressed and stressed His death and resurrection to the disciples. He meant what He said: He was to die, and He was to arise from the dead. The disciples were just not able to accept the literal facts. Their confusion and rejection were understandable.

⇒ They had been taught all their lives that the Messiah was coming to free them from all oppression and suffering (see notes—Lu.3:24-31).

⇒ Jesus had taught them that the kingdom was at hand, ready to be established now. How could it be established if He were to literally die? They failed to see the various stages of the kingdom (see DEEPER STUDY # 3—Mt.19:23-24).

⇒ They had been with Jesus for only a few months. *A complete reversal and unlearning of beliefs takes time.* They had not had enough time to sit at Jesus' feet, not enough time to accept and understand the literal truth of His death and resurrection.

Apparently, the disciples spiritualized His death and resurrection. They clearly saw a new air about Him as He quickened His pace and set His face toward Jerusalem. They could tell that something was pending, something that seemed to draw Christ forward with more determination than ever before. They knew that for many months now, He had been concentrating upon teaching them and sharing the truth of His death and resurrection. However, it was all a mystery to them; it was a puzzle (see notes—Mt.17:22; Mk.9:30, outline note 1). By death and resurrection did He mean...

- that He had to *die to self*, being shamed and discredited by the leaders, before He would become riled enough to *rise up and establish the kingdom*?
- that He had to die to self, rejecting the present order of things (present religion and government), before He could *rise up* and restore things to some higher level or state?
- that the conflict of freeing Israel from her enemies would be so severe that it would be like a death and the victory which would take three days would be like a resurrection from the dead?

The disciples just did not understand. They certainly did not want to accept the fact that their Lord would be literally killed. So they went along with the desire of their flesh and spiritualized what He said.

"Then he said unto them, O fools, and slow of heart to believe all that the prophets have spoken" (Lu.24:25).

"And Jesus said, Are ye also yet without understanding?" (Mt.15:16).

"For the heart of this people is waxed gross, and their ears are dull of hearing, and their eyes have they closed; lest they should see with their eyes, and hear with their ears, and understand with their heart, and should be converted, and I should heal them" (Ac.28:27).

"They know not, neither will they understand; they walk on in darkness: all the foundations of the earth are out of course" (Ps.82:5).

"But they know not the thoughts of the LORD, neither understand they his counsel: for he shall gather them as the sheaves into the floor" (Mi.4:12).

	G. The Disciples' Terrible Ignorance of Messiahship: A Problem of Ambition, 9:33-37 *(Mt. 18:1-4; Lu. 9:46-48)*	35 And he sat down, and called the twelve, and saith unto them, If any man desire to be first, the same shall be last of all, and servant of all.	**3. Ambition needs instruction** **4. Ambition is a virtue, but it must be directed toward the right goal: To serve**
1. Ambition can cause disputes, arguments a. The disciples argued b. Jesus questioned what they were arguing about **2. Ambition can shame**	33 And he came to Capernaum: and being in the house he asked them, What was it that ye disputed among yourselves by the way? 34 But they held their peace: for by the way they had disputed among themselves, who should be the greatest.	36 And he took a child, and set him in the midst of them: and when he had taken him in his arms, he said unto them, 37 Whosoever shall receive one of such children in my name, receiveth me: and whosoever shall receive me, receiveth not me, but him that sent me.	**5. Ambition for service proves a person's discipleship** a. The illustration: Welcoming a child b. The lesson: Proves one's discipleship 1) Proves one has received Christ 2) Proves one has received God

DIVISION V

THE SON OF GOD'S CLOSING MINISTRY: JESUS TEACHES THE IDEA OF GOD'S MESSIAHSHIP, NOT MAN'S MESSIAHSHIP, 8:27-9:50

G. The Disciples' Terrible Ignorance of Messiahship: A Problem of Ambition, 9:33-37

(9:33-37) **Greatness**: the disciples, on more than one occasion, argued over who should hold the highest position in the kingdom (see outlines and notes—Mt.18:1-2; 20:20-28; Lu.22:24-30). Their desire was for recognition and honor in an earthly kingdom. Jesus had to reeducate their thinking.

The same reeducation is needed by all men. All men have the same needs for...

- some recognition
- some position
- some prestige
- some money
- some authority
- some esteem
- some challenge
- some physical satisfaction

There is nothing wrong with these needs. They are human and legitimate and must be met, but men allow their hearts to be overtaken with selfishness. Men begin to want more and more to the point of lusting and consuming and hoarding. They become prideful, covetous, worldly, ambitious, envious, and hurtful even to the point of destroying and killing in order to fulfill their lusts (see Js.4:1-3).

What Christ sets out to do is change lives and reeducate man's concept of greatness.

1. Ambition can cause disputes, arguments (v.33).
2. Ambition can shame (v.34).
3. Ambition needs instruction (v.35).
4. Ambition is a virtue, but it must be directed toward the right goal: to serve (v.35).
5. Ambition for service proves a person's discipleship (vv.36-37).

[1] (9:33) **Ambition—Divisiveness**: ambition can cause disputes, arguments. Jesus had returned to Capernaum, His headquarters, and entered the home which was so often opened to Him. Along the way there, the disciples had been disputing among themselves and were probably continuing to argue after entering the house. The word *disputed* (dialogizomai) means arguing and bickering as well as reasoning. And they were definitely arguing.

Imagine how Jesus' heart must have been cut to the core. How often He had told them about the cross. And here He was about to stand face-to-face with the cross, yet the disciples were arguing over who should be the greatest.

He could do only one thing: continue to teach them. He knew about the dispute, but they were not aware that He knew. He very simply turned and asked, "What were you arguing about along the way?"

Thought 1. How often we have heard about the cross, and yet how easily we forget.
(1) Many have heard time after time and have never responded. This deeply cuts the heart of Christ.
(2) Many have heard and have responded, yet they continue to seek the things of the world: power, position, wealth, property, fame. This also cuts the heart of Christ.

Thought 2. A man who pursues the world soon forgets the cross. He forgets that he "was purged from his old sins" (2 Pe.1:9).

[2] (9:34) **Ambition—Ashamed—Shame**: ambition can shame. The disciples had been arguing over who should be the greatest in Jesus' government. Note several things about their argument.

a. They did not mean who would be the greatest in quality or character, but in name and position. They were thinking in terms of power, fame, wealth, position, and name (see notes—Mt.1:1; DEEPER STUDY # 1—1:18; DEEPER STUDY # 3—3:11; notes—11:1-6; 11:2-3; DEEPER STUDY # 1—11:5; DEEPER STUDY # 2—11:6; DEEPER STUDY # 1—12:16; note—Lu.7:21-23 for a picture of their concept of the Messiah).

1) They sensed that Jesus was about to set up His kingdom, about to assume His throne. They were looking forward to becoming chiefs of state in His kingdom.
2) They had seen three men among them honored in special ways (Peter, James, and John, Mt.17:1-13). And one of them in particular had been distinguished (Peter, Mt.16:17-19). Who were to be the leaders in the Lord's kingdom? They were apparently gripped with jealousy, envy, ambition, and some rivalry.
3) They misinterpreted Jesus' words that He must die and arise again. They spiritualized His words instead of taking them at face value (see notes—Mk.9:32; Mt.17:22). Apparently they connected the thought of "rising from the dead" with the setting up of His kingdom and began to argue over the top positions of leadership.

b. They did not yet understand what the kingdom was. They still saw an earthly, temporal kingdom and not a spiritual, eternal kingdom. This passage shows just how far away they were from understanding God's idea of the Messiah (see points above. See note—Mk.10:35-37.)

Note that the disciples "held their peace." They kept quiet and said nothing in response to Jesus. They knew they had done wrong and were ashamed and embarrassed. Their ambition had led them to quarrel and divide. Their ambition shamed them.

Thought 1. Ambition that leads to argument and division is wrong. The person who seeks and secures by dispute and division shall soon stand before Christ ashamed and embarrassed.

Thought 2. All men shall be asked what they were reasoning and disputing about as they walked through life.

"For we must all appear before the judgment seat of Christ; that every one may receive the things done in his body, according to that he hath done, whether it be good or bad" (2 Co.5:10).

"And as it is appointed unto men once to die, but after this the judgment" (He.9:27).

Thought 3. Each man will be called to give an account for his disputes. He shall give an account both for his words and his life.

"For by thy words thou shalt be justified, and by thy words thou shalt be condemned" (Mt.12:37).

"And whosoever shall exalt himself shall be abased; and he that shall humble himself shall be exalted" (Mt.23:12).

"So then because thou art lukewarm, and neither cold nor hot, I will spue thee out of my mouth. Because thou sayest, I am rich, and increased with goods, and have need of nothing; and knowest not that thou art wretched, and miserable, and poor, and blind, and naked" (Re.3:16-17).

"They that trust in their wealth, and boast themselves in the multitude of their riches; none of them can be any means redeem his brother, nor give to God a ransom for him" (Ps.49:6-7).

"Though thou exalt thyself as the eagle, and though thou set thy nest among the stars, thence will I bring thee down, saith the LORD" (Ob.4).

3 (9:35) **Ambition**: ambition needs instruction. Note that Jesus "*sat down* and called the twelve." In Jesus' day, when a Rabbi was ready to give a profound lesson, he sat down before his pupils. The disciples had slipped into a gross error and committed a serious sin. They must be corrected and taught the truth. Their ambition needed to be instructed and guided in the right direction.

"Study to show thyself approved unto God, a workman that needeth not to be ashamed, rightly dividing the word of truth. But shun profane and vain babblings: for they will increase unto more ungodliness" (2 Ti.2:15-16).

4 (9:35) **Ambition**: ambition is a virtue, but it must be directed toward the right goal. Note the points made by Jesus.

a. Ambition is a virtue. It is not wrong to desire greatness, to desire to make a contribution. Jesus did not rebuke the disciples' ambition. What He did was to direct their ambition, their energy and motive and efforts, in the right direction.

b. The way to greatness is service, humble service. If a man wishes to be great, then he must actively seek to serve others. No matter his position or authority, he is to serve; he is to actively work for the sake and benefit of others. A man's ambition must not be to rule for the sake of holding position and authority and receiving honor from men.

To be great, a man's ambition must be to use his gifts and abilities to serve others, helping and ministering to them in every way possible. A great man does not build his own prestige. A great man builds the lives and betters the welfare of others.

"For I say, through the grace given unto me, to every man that is among you, not to think of himself more highly than he ought to think; but think soberly, according as God hath dealt to every man the measure of faith" (Ro.12:3).

"Be of the same mind one toward another. Mind not high things, but condescend to men of low estate. Be not wise in your own conceits" (Ro.12:16).

"Let nothing be done through strife or vainglory; but in lowliness of mind let each esteem other better than themselves. Look not every man on his own things, but every man also on the things of others" (Ph.2:3-4).

"For the wicked boasteth of his heart's desire, and blesseth the covetous, whom the LORD abhorreth" (Ps.10:3).

"Whoso boasteth himself of a false gift is like clouds and wind without rain" (Pr.25:14).

5 (9:36-37) **Discipleship—Salvation—Child**: ambition for service proves one's discipleship. Jesus illustrated His point. He took a child into His arms, receiving and gathering the child unto Himself. And then He drove His point home. He said that the very qualities that are necessary to *receive* a child are the qualities that are to characterize the believer's life. The believer is to treat all men as he treats a child when he receives a child into his arms.

Note the qualities present when a man receives and gathers up a child into his arms.

a. Receiving a child requires humility. In the matters of adult life, many consider the child useless, unable to contribute. They overlook and fail to consider the great contributions a child makes to an adult. A child requires and teaches the spirit of love, caring, forgiveness, courage, trust, and on and on. A person who serves a child must be humble.

b. Receiving a child requires courage. A child is a great responsibility. When a man receives a child, he undertakes the child's care and welfare. A person who serves a child must be courageous.

c. Receiving a child requires faith and trust. A person has to believe the child will respond and learn, not rebel and reject. A person who serves a child must believe and trust.

d. Receiving a child requires patience and endurance. A person has to be patient and persevering in teaching and training. The child is sometimes slow. A person who serves a child must be patient.

e. Receiving a child requires forgiveness. A child falls and fails often, making the same mistake time and again. A person who serves a child must be forgiving.

Jesus was teaching that a child has needs. Thus it is with society. All men have needs. Just as we receive a little child, so we must receive all men. Just as we serve and treat a little child, so we must serve and treat all men. Note that Jesus made a wonderful promise. If we receive a child, a man in need, we receive Him; and if we receive Him, we receive God (see Mt.25:34f).

"For thus saith the high and lofty One that inhabiteth eternity, whose name is Holy; I dwell in the high and holy place, with him also that is of a contrite and humble spirit, to revive the spirit of the humble, and to revive the heart of the contrite ones" (Is.57:15).

"Humble yourselves in the sight of the Lord, and he shall lift you up" (Js.4:10).

"Even as the Son of man came not to be ministered unto, but to minister, and to give his life a ransom for many" (Mt.20:28).

"Then said Jesus to them again, Peace be unto you: as my Father hath sent me, even so send I you" (Jn.20:21).

"I have showed you all things, how that so labouring ye ought to support the weak, and to remember the words of the Lord Jesus, how he said, It is more blessed to give than to receive" (Ac.20:35).

"We then that are strong ought to bear the infirmities of the weak, and not to please ourselves" (Ro.15:1).

"Bear ye one another's burdens, and so fulfil the law of Christ" (Ga.6:2).

	H. The Conditions of Tolerance, 9:38-41 *(Lu. 9:49-50)*	not: for there is no man which shall do a miracle in my name, that can lightly speak evil of me.	**Receive him** a. Condition 1: If he does not say anything bad about Christ
1. The setting: The disciples felt guilt for rejecting a man a. A man who was ministering in Jesus' name b. A man who was not following them	38 And John answered him, saying, Master, we saw one casting out devils in thy name, and he followeth not us: and we forbad him, because he followeth not us.	40 For he that is not against us is on our part. 41 For whosoever shall give you a cup of water to drink in my name, because ye belong to Christ, verily I say unto you, he shall not lose his reward.	b. Condition 2: If he is not against Christ c. Condition 3: If he shows kindness to the followers of Christ
2. The instruction of Jesus:	39 But Jesus said, Forbid him		

DIVISION V

THE SON OF GOD'S CLOSING MINISTRY: JESUS TEACHES THE IDEA OF GOD'S MESSIAHSHIP, NOT MAN'S MESSIAHSHIP, 8:27-9:50

H. The Conditions of Tolerance, 9:38-41

(9:38-41) **Introduction**: Jesus had just taught a lesson on ambition and service. Now He teaches a lesson on tolerance. The lesson is greatly needed, for tolerance is often misunderstood. Some believe that every person should be received and accepted no matter their beliefs or behavior. Others are convinced that beliefs and behavior matter; that is, if a person's beliefs and behavior are damaging to the welfare of others, then that person should not be received and accepted (for example Hitler, agnosticism, humanism, atheism).

Jesus' words in v.37 stirred John to share about a man's ministering in Jesus' name. John saw immediately that Jesus seemed to be saying that people were to be accepted and cared for in His name—no matter who they were. Jesus took John's account of rejection and laid down the conditions of tolerance.

1. The setting: the disciples felt guilt for rejecting a man (vv.38-39).
2. The instruction of Jesus: receive Him (vv.39-41).

1 (9:38-39) **Tolerance**: John felt guilt because he had rejected a man. Jesus had just said that His followers were to be open-armed in receiving people (v.37). These words aroused guilty feelings within John. He and the other apostles had seen a man ministering in Jesus' name, and they had stopped him. Why? Note John's words: "He *followeth not us*: and we forbad him, because he *followeth not us*." The disciples stopped him because he...

- was not one of them, of their group.
- was not of their inner circle.
- was unattached, had not been called and ordained by their Leader (Christ).
- had not been taught by their Teacher (Christ).
- could not have been as strong and firm in his beliefs as they were.
- did not stand with them. In their minds their way was the only way.

However, note this about the man.

⇒ He had somehow been influenced by the Lord. He knew about the Lord.

⇒ He had a strong faith in the Lord's name. He had given himself to the ministry and was ministering to people. In fact, he was ministering to the most difficult cases, to the demon-possessed. And note: ministering to the demon-possessed was the ministry which was difficult for the disciples to perform (see Mk.9:14-29).

There are several reasons why men oppose others, why men are not tolerant.

1. Loyalty to an organization or to a leader can cause intolerance. If a person does not stand for our organization or leader, he is often unacceptable.

2. Conviction of our own position and belief can cause intolerance. If a person does not agree with our position or belief, he is often unacceptable.

3. The need for unity can cause intolerance. If a person questions or opposes us or our organization and its acts, he is often unacceptable.

4. A sense of authority and self-exaltation can cause intolerance. We can think too highly of ourselves, feeling that we are *the great defenders* of the truth. Therefore, if a person questions or opposes our position or acts, he is often unacceptable.

5. Jealousy and envy can cause intolerance. Who a person *is* (spiritually, physically, mentally) and what he *has* (position, gifts, recognition) are often secretly desired or coveted. Therefore, the person is often unacceptable.

6. A sense of pride and arrogance, of being better than others, can cause intolerance. A person who is poor, disadvantaged, unemployed, uneducated, single, and a myriad of other *conditions* can be unacceptable.

This man, although professing and ministering *in the name of Christ*, was rebuked and stopped by the apostles. What he was doing was unacceptable to them. But note: John sensed guilt over the matter, and he was honest enough to confess his intolerance and ask Jesus about the matter.

What did Jesus say? Very simply, "Forbid him not. Receive him. Let him minister." Then Jesus laid down the conditions of tolerance.

Thought 1. The disciples made several gross errors.
(1) They set themselves up as judges of others.
(2) They were too narrow, too exclusive.
(3) They denied another the right to serve.
(4) They wrecked a servant's ministry.
(5) They kept many from ever being helped.
(6) They taught intolerance.

Thought 2. Intolerance has wrecked many lives and churches. Intolerance causes strife and division, hurt and pain. It shames and ruins and paralyzes both individuals and churches.

2 (9:39-41) **Tolerance—Kindness—Jesus Christ, Speaking Evil Against—Ministers**: Jesus Christ Himself gave these instructions: receive the person. But he is to be received only if he meets certain conditions, three in particular.

a. The first condition is, receive a person and be tolerant of him if he does not speak evil of Christ. The emphasis of this point seems to be on the phrase "speaking evil of Christ." A man who truly ministers "in the name of Christ" *will most likely* not speak evil of Christ. If he ever does speak evil of Christ, it will not be while he is ministering and sharing about Christ, but sometime later, after he ministers "in Christ's name."

Therefore, the man who does not speak evil of Christ shows that he is ministering "in the name of Christ." But the opposite is also true. The man who speaks evil of Christ shows that he is an enemy of Christ. The first man is to be accepted. The last man who speaks evil of Christ is not to be accepted.

> **"Some indeed preach Christ even of envy and strife; and some also of good will: the one preach Christ of contention, not sincerely, supposing to add affliction to my bonds: but the other of love, knowing that I am set for the defence of the gospel. What then? notwithstanding, every way, whether in pretence, or in truth, Christ is preached; and I therein do rejoice, yea, and will rejoice" (Ph.1:15-18).**
>
> **"We then that are strong ought to bear the infirmities of the weak, and not to please ourselves" (Ro.15:1).**
>
> **"And why beholdest thou the mote that is in thy brother's eye, but considerest not the beam that is in thine own eye?" (Mt.7:3).**

b. The second condition is, be tolerant if a man is not against Christ and His disciples (v.40). Note two things.

1) Jesus used the word "us." "He that is not against us is on our part [for us]." (See Mt.12:30.) A person's attitude toward both Christ *and His disciples* (church) is to be observed. Man's attitude toward believers reveals his attitude toward Christ. In Christ's eyes He and His people are one. To stand against His followers is to stand against Him. To mistreat His followers is to mistreat Him. To speak evil of His followers is to speak evil of Him.

> **"And other sheep I have, which are not of this fold: them also I must bring, and they shall hear my voice; and there shall be one fold, and one shepherd" (Jn.10:16).**
>
> **"That they all may be one; as thou, Father, art in me, and I in thee, that they also may be one in us: that the world may believe that thou hast sent me" (Jn.17:21).**
>
> **"He that receiveth you receiveth me, and he that receiveth me receiveth him that sent me" (Mt.10:40).**
>
> **"He that heareth you heareth me; and he that despiseth you despiseth me; and he that despiseth me despiseth him that sent me" (Lu.10:16).**

2) A man's actions are to be looked at—nothing else: not his appearance, education, credentials, group, or label. If a man has a spirit of faith, love, joy, peace, forgiveness, oneness, and worship, he is to be accepted. He does not stand against Christ. But if a man has a spirit of unbelief, disturbance, unforgiveness, or divisiveness, he is against Christ and His followers. This man's behavior should not be accepted. He is "against us."

> **"He that is not with me is against me: and he that gathereth not with me scattereth" (Lu.11:23).**
>
> **"No servant can serve two masters: for either he will hate the one, and love the other; or else he will hold to the one, and despise the other. Ye cannot serve God and mammon" (Lu.16:13).**
>
> **"But when ye sin so against the brethren, and wound their weak conscience, ye sin against Christ" (1 Co.8:12).**

c. The third condition is, be tolerant if a man shows kindness to the followers of Christ (v.41). Giving a cup of water in a hot country like Palestine was a common sight. But note: Christ is talking about giving "in His name." If a person does something for a believer "because he belongs to Christ," then that person shall be rewarded. And the idea is that he will be rewarded greatly. The whole point is helping, giving to a person "because he belongs to Christ." Note three points.

1) Many people help and give to others. They help and give because...
- it is the custom and practice
- it is the respectable thing to do
- they wish recognition and honor
- they would be embarrassed not to give
- they are touched by the need

2) The reward is promised for a specific act, the act of helping a person because he "belongs to Christ."

3) The reward is given for the most simple and humble of acts, the giving of water to a thirsty believer. Anyone would give a drink of water, yet so simple an act done for one of Christ's followers will be greatly rewarded.

Thought 1. No gift, no service is too small. God notices all. What an encouragement! What a challenge to use what we have and all we have for Christ and His followers! "We shall not lose our reward" (1 Co.15:58; 2 Co.5:10). Our reward is sure; it is guaranteed!

"And every one that hath forsaken houses, or brethren, or sisters, or father, or mother, or wife, or children, or lands, for my name's sake, shall receive an hundredfold, and shall inherit everlasting life" (Mt.19:29).

"Then shall the King say unto them on his right hand, Come, ye blessed of my Father, inherit the kingdom prepared for you from the foundation of the world: for I was an hungred, and ye gave me meat: I was thirsty, and ye gave me drink: I was a stranger, and ye took me in: naked, and ye clothed me: I was sick, and ye visited me: I was in prison, and ye came unto me....Verily I say unto you, Inasmuch as ye have done it unto one of the least of these my brethren, ye have done it unto me" (Mt.25:34-36, 40).

Outline	Scripture
	I. The Terribleness of Sin, 9:42-50
1. The terrible sin of causing others to sin a. Especially causing little ones to sin b. The better alternative: To drown one's self[DS1,2]	42 And whosoever shall offend one of these little ones that believe in me, it is better for him that a millstone were hanged about his neck, and he were cast into the sea.
2. The terrible sins of the hands a. The better alternative: To cut off one's hand b. The reason: Sins of the hand condemn one to hell c. Hell is punishment & it is forever	43 And if thy hand offend thee, cut it off: it is better for thee to enter into life maimed, than having two hands to go into hell, into the fire that never shall be quenched: 44 Where their worm dieth not, and the fire is not quenched.
3. The terrible sins of the feet a. The better alternative: To cut off one's foot b. The reason: Sins of the feet condemn one to hell c. Hell is punishment & it is forever	45 And if thy foot offend thee, cut it off: it is better for thee to enter halt into life, than having two feet to be cast into hell, into the fire that never shall be quenched: 46 Where their worm dieth not, and the fire is not quenched.
4. The terrible sins of the eyes a. The better alternative: To pluck out one's eye b. The reason: Sins of the eye condemn one to hell c. Hell is punishment & it is forever	47 And if thine eye offend thee, pluck it out: it is better for thee to enter into the kingdom of God with one eye, than having two eyes to be cast into hell fire: 48 Where their worm dieth not, and the fire is not quenched.
5. The terrible surety of judgment upon everyone	49 For every one shall be salted with fire, and every sacrifice shall be salted with salt.
6. The challenge to save oneself from sin a. Search oneself b. Be salted: Be pure & useful	50 Salt is good: but if the salt have lost his saltness, wherewith will ye season it? Have salt in yourselves, and have peace one with another.

DIVISION V

THE SON OF GOD'S CLOSING MINISTRY: JESUS TEACHES THE IDEA OF GOD'S MESSIAHSHIP, NOT MAN'S MESSIAHSHIP, 8:27-9:50

I. The Terribleness of Sin, 9:42-50

(9:42-50) **Introduction**: this is a sinful world, full of terrible evil and behavior. No one can walk out into the world without facing temptation after temptation and pull after pull to look, touch, taste—to experience the *good life* of physical gratification and earthly comfort and personal fulfillment. We are tempted, seduced, and influenced at every turn. There is no escape (see Ro.3:9-18).

> **"The whole world lieth in wickedness" (1 Jn.5:19).**
> **"For all have sinned and come short of the glory of God" (Ro.3:23).**

In this passage Christ stressed just how terrible sin is, and He warned the sinner. Every man is personally responsible for his sin. The fact of a sinful world does not lessen a man's personal responsibility. He cannot blame the world, society, or others, for he has a free will. In addition, he has the knowledge of much good, and he has the pull to do good (at least initially). He also has examples of goodness, and he can choose to do good. Man can even work to overcome and strengthen his weaknesses. And most of all he has God, who provides a way to escape temptation (1 Co.10:13). Woe to the sinner—he is *personally* responsible. Every sin becomes a stumbling block to others! Woe to the man who sins and places the stumbling block for others to fall over.

1. The terrible sin of causing others to sin (v.42).
2. The terrible sins of the hands (vv.43-44).
3. The terrible sins of the feet (vv.45-46).
4. The terrible sins of the eyes (vv.47-48).
5. The terrible surety of judgment upon everyone (v.49).
6. The challenge to save oneself from sin (v.50).

1 (9:42) **Sin—Stumbling Block**: Christ mentioned the terrible sin of offending others, that is, of causing others to stumble, of actually leading others to sin (see note—Mt.18:5-10 for more discussion).

Note several things. (See outlines and notes—Mt.18:6 for more discussion.)

a. The word *offend* (skandalizo) means to cause a person to stumble, to lead a person to sin (see notes—Mt.5:29; outline note 4—17:27).

b. The *little ones* are identified by Christ. They are those who "believe in me." Christ often called the believers little ones and referred to the believer as a little child (see note—Mt.18:5-10). Believers are children of God. A little one is any little child, any *new beginner* in the faith, and any person who has a *child-like faith and spirit in Christ.*

c. Christ seemed to be saying, "The most terrible sin of all is leading another person to sin. There is no sin any worse than leading another person astray. It is the worst conceivable sin."

There are several ways we cause others to sin.

1) By leading them into sin and teaching them to sin. "Oh, come on, no one will know. It's not going to hurt you."

2) By example, things that we do. Example is not a direct vocal suggestion. We are not necessarily aware that "the child" sees or is observing us; nevertheless, he sees and learns from what we do. He thinks to himself: "If it's all right for him, then it is bound to be all right for me."
3) By overlooking or passing over wrong; by giving soft names to it; by considering some sins to be merely minor sins. "Oh, that's all right. There's not that much to it. It isn't going to hurt anyone. Don't pay any attention to it. Just forget it."
4) By ridiculing or poking fun at, or by joking and sneering at a person's attempt to do right. "Oh, don't be a fuddy-duddy, a square; you're acting like a fanatic. You and your religion."
5) By looking at, touching, and tasting some things that are socially acceptable; but that are sinful to God. They are harmful, habit forming, and physically stimulating when they should not be. "Wow, look at that." "Taste that." "What a turn on!"
6) By persecuting and threatening "a child" or a believer. The threat can range all the way from loss of promotion, job, friendship, or acceptance to imprisonment and death.

d. The terribleness of this sin is stressed by the better alternative Christ gives. A person would be better off to hang a huge stone about his neck and cast himself into the sea than to lead another person to sin (see DEEPER STUDY # 1,2—Mk.9:42).

> **"Then said he unto the disciples, It is impossible but that offences will come: but woe unto him, through whom they come! It were better for him that a millstone were hanged about his neck, and he cast into the sea, than that he should offend one of these little ones" (Lu.17:1-2).**
>
> **"Let us not therefore judge one another any more: but judge this rather, that no man put a stumblingblock or an occasion to fall in his brother's way" (Ro.14:13).**
>
> **"But if thy brother be grieved with thy meat, now walkest thou not charitably. Destroy not him with thy meat, for whom Christ died" (Ro.14:15).**
>
> **"It is good neither to eat flesh, nor to drink wine, nor any thing whereby thy brother stumbleth, or is offended, or is made weak" (Ro.14:21).**
>
> **"Give none offence, neither to the Jews, nor to the Gentiles, nor to the church of God" (1 Co.10:32).**
>
> **"Giving no offence in any thing, that the ministry be not blamed" (2 Co.6:3).**
>
> **"He that loveth his brother abideth in the light, and there is none occasion of stumbling in him" (1 Jn.2:10).**

DEEPER STUDY # 1

(9:42) **Millstone** (mulos/onikos): the word *onos* is the word for an ass or a donkey. The word *mulos* is the word for the millstone that the donkey pulled around to grind the grain. Thus, the millstone Christ spoke of is the huge millstone, not the small hand millstone used by the women to grind a little grain at a time. Note: The very fact that Christ chose the huge millstone to demonstrate His point shows how great this sin is. The person would be held to the bottom by the most awful and terrible weight. The sin of leading a child astray is the worst possible sin; therefore, its condemnation shall be awful and terrible.

DEEPER STUDY # 2

(9:42) **Death—Drowning**: drowning was a form of criminal punishment used by the Romans, but never by the Jews. The Jews saw drowning as a symbol of *utter destruction and annihilation*, of being in the very depths of death. They feared it. Even the Romans reserved it only for the worst criminals.

Note something: Christ *added to the fear* of His audience. He painted the picture of a stone around the offender's neck. Why? So that the body could never rise to the top and be properly buried. But He went even further to add to the fear—He pictured the huge millstone, not the small one. Why did He want to strike fear into the heart of His hearers, laying additional stress upon the fear? The answer is clear: the sin of leading another person astray is terrible, and the offender must know the fate that is awaiting him.

2 (9:43-44) **Sin—Hands—Hell—Life**: Christ mentioned the terrible sins of the hand. He made five significant points about the sins of the hand (see note—Mt.18:7-9).

a. The hand can offend and be a stumbling block. If something is *forbidden or unwise* or if it should be *given or let go*, the hand can sin...

- by touching
- by clutching
- by holding
- by grabbing
- by pointing
- by stroking
- by striking

b. There is a better alternative than sinning with one's hand: cutting it off. This is strong language, very descriptive, and radical in its point. But honesty and thought are called for in seeing the point of Christ. What is more horrible than taking one's hand and leading "a little one" to sin and being a stumbling block to his life and salvation? What is more horrible than dooming him to what Christ calls *hell fire*? What is more horrible than doing the same with one's self? If God really loves man and hell fire is real, then descriptive and radical language is needed to awaken man to the truth.

c. Sinning with one's hand condemns one to hell. Christ said very plainly: "If thy hand offend...it [shall]...go into hell, into the fire that shall never be quenched" (see DEEPER STUDY # 2, *Hell*—Mt.5:22).

d. Hell is punishment and it is forever (v.44). Christ said, "Their worm dieth not, and the fire is not quenched." The point of this verse is both punishment and duration. The punishment shall be just like the punishment inflicted by a worm and fire, and the punishment shall be forever.

By "worm" Christ meant one of two things.

1) There is a "worm" in hell that afflicts man; therefore, it can be called "their worm." This is, of course, a picture of something within hell that would prey upon man, wound him, and inflict a biting, gnawing, and consuming pain. And note, it "dies not"; it never ends.
2) There is a "worm" within man in hell. It is a "worm" within, a worm created by his own sinful hands, a worm within that bites, gnaws, and consumes him. Perhaps the worm is memory and conscience that never leaves the man alone. It disturbs and reminds him of what he has missed and lost. (See *The Rich Man and Lazarus*—Lu.16:19-31.) Note that the punishment is forever. Both worm and fire are forever.

e. Life can be lived abundantly even if one is maimed in the eyes of the world. Abundance of life does not depend upon physical wholeness. A person can have life and be without a hand. The abundance and wholeness of life depend upon righteousness, upon living for Christ and not allowing one's hand to sin (see Jn.10:10).

Thought 1. The hand determines our destiny.

"Wherefore come out from among them, and be ye separate, saith the Lord, and touch not the unclean thing; and I will receive you, and will be a Father unto you, and ye shall be my sons and daughters, saith the Lord Almighty" (2 Co.6:17-18).

3 (9:45-46) **Sin—Foot—Hell—Life**: Christ mentioned the terrible sins of the foot. He made five significant points about sins of the foot (see note—Mt.18:7-9).

a. The foot can offend and be a stumbling block. If something is *forbidden or unwise* or if it should be *avoided or attended*, the foot can sin...

- by standing
- by running
- by jumping
- by walking
- by pointing
- by dancing
- by turning
- by kicking

b. There is a better alternative than sinning with the foot: cutting it off (see note, pt.2—Mk.9:43-44 for discussion).

c. Sinning with one's foot condemns one to hell. Again Christ said, "If thy foot offend...it [shall]...be cast into hell, into the fire that never shall be quenched." (See DEEPER STUDY # 2, *Hell*—Mt.5:22.)

d. Hell is punishment and it is forever (v.45-46). (See note, pt.4—Mk.9:43-44.)

e. Life can be lived abundantly even if one is maimed in the eyes of the world (see note, pt.5—Mk.9:43-44).

Thought 1. The believer is to walk even as Christ walked.

"See then that ye walk circumspectly, not as fools, but as wise" (Ep.5:15).
"As ye have therefore received Christ Jesus the Lord, so walk ye in him" (Col.2:6).
"He that saith he abideth in him ought himself also so to walk, even as he walked" (1 Jn.2:6).

4 (9:47-48) **Sin—Eyes—Hell—Kingdom of God**: Christ mentioned the terrible sins of the eye. He made five significant points about the sins of the eye (see note—Mt.18:7-9).

a. The eye can offend and be a stumbling block. If something is *forbidden or unwise* or if it should be *avoided or observed*, the eye can sin...

- by looking
- by staring
- by focusing
- by glancing
- by winking
- by opening
- by blinking
- by scanning
- by closing

b. There is a better alternative to sinning with one's eye: plucking it out. Note that the alternative in this case is the Kingdom of God instead of life. The eye is one of *the doors* into the mind and heart of man. What a man looks at and focuses upon is of extreme importance. Sight can lead to a spirit of lust quicker than any other single thing: the lust...

- for the world and excitement.
- for material goods and possessions.
- for illicit affairs and relationships.
- for recognition and fame.
- for money and wealth.

Every man knows the importance of sight, of being able to see. Most people would rather lose any other sense than to lose the sense of sight. Because of the enormous need for sight and the power of the eye, Christ stacked it up against the Kingdom of God. It would be better to enter the kingdom of God with one eye, than to allow an eye to sin and doom one to hell.

c. Sinning with one's eye condemns one to hell. For a third time, Christ has said the very same thing, "If thine eye offend...it [shall]...be cast into hell fire" (see DEEPER STUDY # 2, *Hell*—Mt.5:22).

d. Hell is punishment and it is forever (v.48). (See note, pt.4—Mk.9:43-44.)

e. The Kingdom of God can be entered even if one is without an eye (see note—Mt.19:23-24).

Thought 1. Scripture's warning about the eye is pointed.

"Whosoever looketh on a woman to lust after her hath committed adultery with her already in his heart" (Mt.5:28).

"All that is in the world, the lust of the flesh, and the lust of the eyes, and the pride of life, is not of the Father, but is of the world" (1 Jn.2:16).

"He that winketh with the eye causeth sorrow" (Pr.10:10).
"The eye is not satisfied with seeing, nor the ear filled with hearing" (Ec.1:8).
"Neither is his eye satisfied with riches" (Ec.4:8).

5 (9:49) **Judgment**: the terrible surety of judgment. Everyone shall be judged: every sacrifice a person has made and every work a person has done shall be judged.

a. "Salted with fire" probably means everyone will be tried with fire. A man's works and sacrifices will be set afire. The wood, hay, and stubble will be burned. Why? Because they...
- are impure.
- are worthless and cannot be used.
- are unpleasing.

But the gold, silver, and precious stones shall last and be proven incorruptible. Why? Because they...
- are pure.
- are beneficial and can be used.
- are pleasing.

b. "Salted with salt" probably means that every sacrifice and work will be preserved, no matter what sort they are. If the sacrifice and work are good, they will be preserved forever in the Kingdom of God. But if the sacrifice and work are bad, they will be preserved forever in hell. There will be no end to the new world that is coming.

"For the Son of man shall come in the glory of his Father with his angels; and then he shall reward every man according to his works" (Mt.16:27).

"Whosoever cometh to me, and heareth my sayings, and doeth them, I will show you to whom he is like: he is like a man which built an house, and digged deep, and laid the foundation on a rock: and when the flood arose, the stream beat vehemently upon that house, and could not shake it: for it was founded upon a rock. But he that heareth, and doeth not, is like a man that without a foundation built an house upon the earth; against which the stream did beat vehemently, and immediately it fell; and the ruin of that house was great" (Lu.6:47-49).

"Every man's work shall be made manifest: for the day shall declare it, because it shall be revealed by fire; and the fire shall try every man's work of what sort it is" (1 Co.3:13).

"And if ye call on the Father, who without respect of persons judgeth according to every man's work, pass the time of your sojourning here in fear" (1 Pe.1:17).

"And I saw the dead, small and great, stand before God; and the books were opened: and another book was opened, which is the book of life: and the dead were judged out of those things which were written in the books, according to their works" (Re.20:12).

"And, behold, I come quickly; and my reward is with me, to give every man according as his work shall be" (Re.22:12).

"I the Lord search the heart, I try the reins, even to give every man according to his ways, and according to the fruit of his doings" (Je.17:10).

6 (9:50) **Salt—Sin, Deliverance from**: the wonderful challenge is to save oneself from sin. Salt is good, beneficial, and useful (see note, *Salt*—Mt.5:13 for a detailed discussion of this point). Christ said three things are necessary to save oneself from the terribleness of sin.

a. Search oneself and labor. Evaluate one's "*saltiness*," one's purity and usefulness.
b. Be sure to be salted, to have salt. One must be pure and useful.
c. Live in peace one with another. This is essential.

"A new commandment I give unto you, That ye love one another; as I have loved you, that ye also love one another. By this shall all men know that ye are my disciples, if ye have love one to another" (Jn.13:34-35).

"Let all bitterness, and wrath, and anger, and clamour, and evil speaking, be put away from you, with all malice: and be ye kind one to another, tenderhearted, forgiving one another, even as God for Christ's sake hath forgiven you" (Ep.4:31-32).

Note what brought about this great lesson from Christ: the arguing among the disciples (Mk.9:33-37), and the intolerance shown toward a man's ministering in the Lord's name (Mk.9:38-41).

CHAPTER 10

VI. THE SON OF GOD'S LAST PUBLIC MINISTRY: JESUS DEALS WITH SOME SPECIAL PROBLEMS, 10:1-52

A. The Problem of Divorce, 10:1-12

(Mt. 19:1-12. See Mt. 5:31-32; Lu. 16:18; 1 Co. 7:10-16)

1. Jesus began to minister in Judea
   a. The crowds gathered & Jesus taught
   b. The Pharisees gathered & asked a trick question: Is divorce legal?*DS1*
      1) Jesus asked what their law said
      2) The Pharisees replied: The law grants divorce

And he arose from thence,
and cometh into the coasts of
Judaea by the farther side of
Jordan: and the people resort
unto him again; and, as he
was wont, he taught them
again.
2 And the Pharisees came
to him, and asked him, Is it
lawful for a man to put away
his wife? tempting him.
3 And he answered and said
unto them, What did Moses
command you?
4 And they said, Moses suffered to write a bill of divorce-
ment, and to put her away.
5 And Jesus answered and
said unto them, For the hardness of your heart he wrote
you this precept.
6 But from the beginning of
the creation God made them
male and female.
7 For this cause shall a man
leave his father and mother,
and cleave to his wife;
8 And they twain shall be one
flesh: so then they are no
more twain, but one flesh.
9 What therefore God hath
joined together, let not man
put asunder.
10 And in the house his disciples asked him again of the
same matter.
11 And he saith unto them,
Whosoever shall put away
his wife, and marry another,
committeth adultery against
her.
12 And if a woman shall put
away her husband, and be
married to another, she committeth adultery.

2. Jesus saw divorce as hardness of heart
3. Jesus saw marriage as God's way—since creation
4. Jesus saw marriage as the most precious bond, a bond that cleaves & unites
5. Jesus saw marriage as the closest human bond—as two becoming one flesh
6. Jesus saw true marriage as a divine, spiritual bond wrought by God
7. Jesus saw divorce & remarriage as adultery*DS2*

DIVISION VI

THE SON OF GOD'S LAST PUBLIC MINISTRY: JESUS DEALS WITH SOME SPECIAL PROBLEMS, 10:1-52

A. The Problem of Divorce, 10:1-12

(10:1-12) **Marriage—Divorce**: marriage and divorce are always burning questions, extremely controversial within societies heavily influenced by Christian teaching. Opinions vary and interpretations differ. There is always the closed view that says divorce is never allowed by God no matter the cruelty and meanness that may exist within the marriage. And there is always the more open view that says divorce is allowed if the rift between a couple is not reconciled and causes more damage than good.

The former says Jesus gave a complete exposition on marriage and divorce; the latter says He gave guidelines. The former sometimes treats divorce in such a spirit that it appears to be the unpardonable sin; the latter sometimes treats it in such a spirit that it appears to be the escape route to do as one likes (ranging from minor selfish ends to licentious pleasures).

In Jesus' day the two schools of thought were the Shammai School (conservative) and the Hillel School (liberal). (See DEEPER STUDY # 1—Mt.19:1-12 for discussion.) As in every generation, there were those within each school that would have nothing to do with anyone who held another opinion. A man's view was made a matter of fellowship.

It was because of these strong feelings that the religionists (Pharisees) thought they could entrap and discredit Jesus. No matter what He said, a great number of people would differ, and they would stop supporting His ministry. He would be discredited and His ministry destroyed.

Note several things.

a. There is always a reluctance to express a different opinion when a great number hold a particular position. Compare for example: slavery, prejudice, smoking, overeating, drinking, mixed bathing, gambling, playing cards, movies, television, and divorce.

b. It is wrong not to face the issues of marriage and divorce, no matter the different opinions and practices of society. Why?

1) There are always a large number of divorced people. Many of these desperately need help. Their faith, hope, security, children—their whole lives have been drastically affected. If God's people do not open their hearts to them, then a great opportunity to reach them and help them grow in Christ is missed.

2) There are always a large number of marriages (perhaps most) experiencing some serious difficulty. Hardness and cruelty, ranging from mild withdrawal to physical abuse, just tear and tear away at the marriage commitment. Sometimes it is the fault of one; sometimes it is the fault of both. In either case, great need exists. Again, if God's people do not reach out to help, a great opportunity is lost for Christ.

Note what Jesus did. He did not hesitate to speak up and teach, and the issue was as controversial in His day as it has been in most generations. (Also see outlines and notes—Mt.5:31-32; 1 Co.7:1-16; Ep.5:22-33.)

1. Jesus began to minister in Judea (vv.1-4).
2. Jesus saw divorce as hardness of heart (v.5).
3. Jesus saw marriage as God's way—since creation (v.6).
4. Jesus saw marriage as the most precious bond, a bond that cleaves and unites (v.7).
5. Jesus saw marriage as the closest of human bond—as two becoming one flesh (v.8).
6. Jesus saw true marriage as a divine, spiritual bond wrought by God (v.9).
7. Jesus saw divorce and remarriage as adultery (vv.10-12).

1 (10:1-4) **Judean Ministry**: Jesus began to minister in Judea. Chapters 1-9 of Mark have covered the Galilean ministry of Jesus; now, Chapters 10-15 cover Jesus' Judean ministry. It should be noted that a great deal took place between these two ministries that is omitted by Mark. The omitted section is usually called the Travel-Narrative or Travel-Ministry. It is covered in detail by Luke, chapters 9-18. Matthew also gives isolated events of the Travel-Ministry.

Note that the crowds flocked to Jesus, and "He taught them again" and healed them (Mt.19:2). The success of the Lord's ministry was phenomenal. During the few months of His ministry, it seemed the whole country was flocking to Him. This, of course, aroused the leaders, both civil and religious (see notes—Mt.12:1-8; note and DEEPER STUDY # 1—12:10; DEEPER STUDY #2—Mk.3:22). Again the leaders of Jerusalem sent an investigating committee to discredit Him before the people. The Jewish leaders (Sanhedrin) were convinced they must break the people away from Jesus. He seemed to be undermining Jewish religion and leading the people astray. And there was always the danger that the Roman authorities would clamp down on the apparent disturbance caused by this so-called Messiah. They feared the Romans would remove them from power and replace them with more capable leaders.

It is this background that caused the investigating committee to confront Jesus. They questioned Him about divorce, and they were thoroughly convinced that Jesus could not answer without entrapping Himself (see DEEPER STUDY # 1—Mk.10:2-4).

DEEPER STUDY # 1

(10:2-4) **Marriage—Divorce—Schools of Thought—Shammai—Hillel**: the Pharisees came to Jesus tempting Him, trying to discredit Him. They asked, "Is it lawful for a man to put away his wife?" Matthew adds, "for every cause" (Mt.19:3).

There was a background to this question. The society of Jesus' day was very loose morally—even Jewish society. Marriage was considered nothing more than a piece of paper: if it worked, fine; if it did not work, fine. One could always divorce (see notes—Mt.5:31).

There were two positions or schools of thought on divorce. Moses had said that any man could divorce his wife if "she find no favor in his eyes, because he has found some uncleanness in her" (De.24:1).

1. The school of Shammai said that the words "some uncleanness" meant adultery only. A wife could be as loose and as mean as Jezebel, but she was not to be divorced unless she committed adultery.
2. The school of Hillel said that the words "some uncleanness" meant anything that was not pleasing to the man. A person should remember that women were counted as nothing but *property* to be possessed by men. They had no rights whatsoever, except as a man might wish to give. Of course, the position followed by society was the position that allowed human nature to run loose. Women were abused: neglected, used, discarded, and violated. They had no rights whatsoever and were seldom given any. They were nothing but chattel property of men, very often considered of less value than property (whether animals or things). Therefore, divorce ran rampant in Jesus' day.

The Pharisees wished to embroil Jesus in the controversy between the conservative (Shammai) and liberal view (Hillel). They were simply asking Him if He agreed with the school of Hillel: "Is it lawful for a man to put away his wife for *every* cause?" No matter which position Jesus took, He would offend and stir up a large number of people, becoming embroiled in a mean controversy. He answered as follows.

1. "God made them [Adam and Eve] male and female." He did not make them male*s* and female*s* as He did animals. But He made *one male* and *one female*. Each one was made for the other. They were not made for anyone else, for there was no one else.
2. "A man [shall] leave father and mother, and shall cleave to his wife." One man shall cleave to his wife and create a new family distinct from the family of his parents. He says "a man," not men, and "his wife," not wives. Note that a man leaves his father and mother. The union between husband and wife is to gain primacy over the union between parent and child. The union, cleaving, is wrought by God and appointed by God; therefore, marriage is a divine institution. Just as parents and children are not to divorce one another, neither are the husband and wife to divorce each other.
3. "A man...shall cleave to his wife and they twain [two] shall be one flesh." There is the molding into one person. The man and the wife cleave: "wherefore they are no more twain, but one flesh." What is it that makes them one flesh? Cleaving. They are one body, one flesh, one person. They are not joined to two or three or four other persons, but they cleave only to one other person.
4. "What therefore God hath joined together, let not man put asunder." "A man...shall cleave to his wife...wherefore [cleaving] they are no more twain, but one flesh [joined together by God]. What therefore God hath joined together, let not man put asunder."

The points are clear.

a. The cleaving man and wife are joined together by God.
b. No one is to cut asunder what God joins together. Neither one of them nor anyone else is to step in between the two and cause separation.

2 (10:5) **Divorce—Heart, Harden**: Jesus saw divorce as hardness of heart. The Old Testament (Moses) *did not command* divorce if two people were not compatible and did not get along. The Old Testament *only permitted divorce*. Note four things.

a. The ancient world treated women as nothing more than chattel property. A man could secure as many wives as he wished (polygamy), and he could discard them *whenever*, *wherever*, and *however* he wished. He could *kick a wife out* and dispose of her as he wished. Man's heart was hard in his treatment of women and in his attitude toward marriage and divorce. There was...

- a total disdain for morality
- a total defiance against marital law
- a total disregard of God's will for marriage
- a total insensitivity to women's rights in marriage

b. The Old Testament (Moses) law was not a loose law, not in the ancient world. It required a *written contract of divorce*, which was unpracticed and unheard of in most societies. It required some time and some thought before a divorce could be issued, and a man could no longer get rid of his wife without involving a third party in the matter. Some official had to approve and write up *the bill of divorce.*

c. The law of the Old Testament (Moses) taught that "A Written Contract of Divorce"...

- could check the breakdown of the family to some degree.
- would give time for a person to think about the consequences of divorce.
- did proclaim that there was a higher law than a man's own whims, urges, and desires. If nothing else, a man had to seek "A Contract of Divorce" from a higher authority.

d. Jesus *saw divorce as hardness of heart.* He said, "For the *hardness of your heart he* [Moses] wrote you this precept." Note that Jesus was saying three things about the Old Testament law on divorce.

1) Divorce was a concession, *not the will of God.*
2) Divorce was allowed *only because man's heart was hard, that is, sinful.*
3) Divorce *was never willed and was not the purpose of God.* (See DEEPER STUDY # 4, *Hardness of Heart*—Mt.19:8 for detailed discussion and application of this point.)

3 (10:6) **Divorce—Marriage—Creation—Adam—Eve**: Jesus saw marriage as God's way—since creation. Jesus said, "From the beginning of the creation God made them [Adam and Eve] male and female." What Jesus was saying is that creation is the root basis, the very foundation for marriage. He pointed out three truths in His simple statement.

a. The creative truth. Jesus said that God did not make man and woman plural. He did not make them male*s* and female*s*. He made one male and one female—each made for the other. They were not made for *any* other, for there was no one else—just Adam and Eve.

b. The spiritual truth. Jesus was saying that male and female were created distinctively from animals. Animals were created en masse, to be together with any and many. But male and female were created differently and distinctively. They were created one male and one female, created as spiritual beings, created for a much higher purpose than animals. Since there were not others like them, they were sharing their purpose together in constant fellowship with God. Note: they were sharing their purpose with no other, for there was no other.

c. The logical truth. Reason alone says that if God created all other animals en masse, and then turned around and created one male and one female, then the male and female belonged to each other. They were created to be together, one with one, even as animals were created to be together en masse.

4 (10:7) **Marriage—Divorce—Cleaving**: Jesus saw marriage as the most precious bond, a bond that cleaves. "For this cause shall a man *leave* his father and mother, and *cleave* to his wife." Note several truths.

a. A man (one) shall cleave to his wife and create a new family distinct from the family of his parents. Jesus said "a man," not men, and "his wife," not wives.

b. A man leaves his father and mother. The union between husband and wife is to gain primacy over the union between parent and child. *Leaving* is a permanent act; *cleaving* is also a permanent act.

c. *Cleaving* means more than being close and intimate. It is more than the closeness that exists between parent and child, for it causes a husband and wife to leave parents. By *cleaving,* Jesus meant a spiritual union that could be wrought and given only by God (see DEEPER STUDY # 2, *Cleave*—Mt.19:5). Therefore, marriage becomes the most precious bond that can be known between human beings. Marriage becomes a divine institution.

d. Just as parents and children are not to divorce one another, so husband and wife are not to divorce one another. Note that father, mother, and child comprise a unit, a family. Jesus said father and mother are there when the child leaves, and the child (man) leaves to "cleave to his wife." There is no thought, not even a hint of separation in this statement. It is unquestionably a statement of God's purpose for father, mother, and child. The structure of the family is the means by which man is to carry out the purposes of God on earth. Divorce, tearing down the structure of the family, is not the purpose of God. Father, mother, and child—the structure of a family—is the purpose of God.

e. The relation between father and mother is to be closer, more intimate, and longer than that between parent and child. The day comes when the child (man) leaves the parent and the parents are left with each other—alone. This says much to husband and wife: they must not neglect their life together. The day comes when they are alone, by themselves.

5 (10:8) **Marriage—Divorce**: Jesus saw marriage as the closest of human bonds—as two becoming one flesh. Jesus had just said that a man shall "cleave to his wife." Now he adds, "And they twain [two] shall be one flesh: so then they are no more twain, but one flesh." Jesus was pointing out at least three facts.

a. *Cleaving*, when spiritually wrought by God, molds two people into one person. As the husband and wife cleave, as they become more and more spiritually united by God, they become more and more meshed into one being. Each grows into the very being of the other spouse. They become one body, one flesh, one person.

b. The husband and wife are not joined to two or three or four other persons. They can *cleave* only under God and only to one other person.

c. The power of God is enormous to a couple who will obey Him. God can cause their cleaving to bind them so close together that they are as one person.

6 (10:9) **Marriage—Divorce**: Jesus saw true marriage as a divine, spiritual bond wrought by God. Jesus said: "What therefore God hath joined together, let not man put asunder" (v.9).

a. God joins together "a man [who] leaves his father and mother and *cleaves* to his wife" (v.7). It is the *cleaving* husband and wife who are joined together by God. But note something of critical importance. By *cleaving,* Christ does not mean what is often thought or pictured: cleaving does not mean taking hold of a wife by civil contract, embracing, or sexual union.

Note the words...

- "cleaving"
- "one flesh" (physical union)
- "what God hath joined together" (spiritual union)

Spouses who are *obedient* to Christ by cleaving to each other (not only physically, but spiritually—in all of their life and being as God intended) are the ones who become one flesh and the ones who God joins together. A civil contract does not bind people together—neither does embracing—neither does sex. Only God can bind a couple together spiritually, and He does so because a couple is obedient to Him. He rewards and blesses obedience, not disobedience.

b. No one is to cut asunder what God joins together. Neither wife nor husband nor anyone else is to step in between the two and cause separation.

c. Marriage is to be a bond so closely and spiritually bound together that it can match the spiritual union between Christ and His church (Ep.5:32) and Christ and the believer. (See outline and notes—Ep.5:22-33; Col.3:18-21; 1 Co.6:19.)

> **"Husbands, love your wives, even as Christ also loved the church, and gave himself for it" (Ep.5:25).**

7 (10:10-12) **Marriage—Remarriage—Divorce—Adultery**: Jesus saw divorce and remarriage as adultery. In a discussion of this point, Matthew is much more thorough in what he covers. For this reason, Matthew should always be studied in looking at divorce and remarriage (see outline and notes—Mt.19:9-12).

DEEPER STUDY # 2

(10:10-12) **Fornication—Adultery**: a person, especially a Christian believer, needs to think about the real meaning of adultery. Adultery is the turning away from a spouse to another person. Many a person would never think of turning away from their spouse to a third person, yet they readily and willingly turn toward self and toward other things. As God said of the nation Israel, "I saw, when for all the *causes* whereby backsliding Israel committed adultery I had put her away, and given her a bill of divorce" (Je.3:8). Many a person has done just as Israel did. They have refused to surrender to God; they have lived in a backslidden state, and day by day they have turned more and more away from their spouse and in many cases from their children.

Day by day a person can take a spouse and children and...

- be mean and ugly.
- be nagging and mentally cruel.
- be neglectful and unthoughtful.
- be physically abusive and life-threatening.
- be deliberately withdrawn and separated.

And the truth of the matter is that many are selfishly that way.

⇒ Some are cruel; others sadistic.
⇒ Some are critical; others sarcastic; still others demonic and hellish.
⇒ Some are mentally abusive; others physically abusive, even to the point of murdering spouse and children—the unthinkable.

The truth of a marriage is known only to God. A husband or a wife can use his or her personality to present a front to the world. Yet within the heart there can be such a hardness toward his or her spouse, such an unwillingness to truly cleave that God just cannot join them together as one flesh. Hardness, very simply, wrecks a marriage by causing one spouse to turn away and separate from the other spouse. If the spouses are not together, then they are separate, not cleaving. There can be no cleaving if the two are not together. And as pointed out earlier, cleaving is the blessing and the gift of God. Cleaving is only possible as each allows God to *join them together* into the spiritual union of marriage.

Outline	Scripture	Scripture (cont.)	Outline (cont.)
	B. The Problem of Children & the Truth About Children, 10:13-16 *(Mt. 19:13-15; Lu. 18:15-17)*	little children to come unto me, and forbid them not: for of such is the kingdom of God.	b. They are citizens of God's kingdom[DS4]
1. The problem with children[DS1] a. Totally dependent b. Cause frivolous pride c. Interfere with work	13 And they brought young children to him, that he should touch them: and his disciples rebuked those that brought them.	15 Verily I say unto you, Whosoever shall not receive the kingdom of God as a little child, he shall not enter therein.	c. They illustrate how one receives the kingdom[DS5]
2. The truth about children[DS2] a. They are invited to Jesus[DS3]	14 But when Jesus saw it, he was much displeased, and said unto them, Suffer the	16 And he took them up in his arms, put his hands upon them, and blessed them.	d. They are received & blessed by Jesus[DS6] e. They respond to Jesus[DS7]

DIVISION VI

THE SON OF GOD'S LAST PUBLIC MINISTRY: JESUS DEALS WITH SOME SPECIAL PROBLEMS, 10:1-52

B. The Problem of Children and the Truth About Children, 10:13-16

(10:13-16) **Children—Jesus Christ, Anger**: note that this event with children followed right after the matter of divorce (also see Mt.19:13). The family as a whole was being discussed: the husband, wife, and children.

Children are a joy, but many are also looked upon as problems. And tragically, children are sometimes neglected, ignored, oppressed, and even abused.

In this passage, Jesus pulled no punches. It was one of the times He became violently angry, filled and moved with indignation. Jesus is the great defender of children, and every man and woman must heed His words.

1. The problem with children (v.13).
2. The truth about children (vv.14-16).

1 (10:13) **Children**: the problem with children. The scene was both touching and tragic. Some parents, tenderly and with hope, were bringing their children to Jesus. Why? That He might simply *touch them*. The parents were hoping that Jesus would simply touch their children, and in touching, their children would be blessed. But this was not the only scene. The disciples were rebuking the parents for bringing the children. The word *rebuke* (epitimao) is a strong word: it means actively hindering and reproving. The disciples were actually holding the parents and pushing them back, trying to stop them from bringing their children to Jesus. Why? Very simply, the disciples saw a problem with children. They looked upon children just as many others look upon them: they felt the children could contribute nothing to the adult world. In adult affairs, children were useless, unimportant; therefore, they should not disturb the adults when they were busy at work. They felt Jesus was too busy and His work was too important to be disturbed. The disciples, just like so many adults, saw the following problems with children.

a. Children are totally dependent. These children were so young they had to be brought to Jesus. The disciples felt they could contribute nothing significant. They were too young, too helpless, too dependent. Therefore, their place was off to the side someplace. They should not be bothering the Lord right now. Their parents should have known this and should have been more respectful.

b. Children cause frivolous pride. Parents often have a frivolous pride over their children. The disciples may have thought the parents just wanted to show off their children and have Jesus make over them. The frivolous pride of parents is often felt undeserving of interruption. Frivolous pride often aggravates busy men, especially when they are interrupted by parents who merely want to show off their children. The disciples felt that the children were not important enough to be allowed to interfere, certainly not right now.

c. Children interfere with work. The disciples knew that this was one of the major problems with children. They do interrupt work, sometimes important work. They distract, causing a person to lose his thought; they require attention and help. The disciples felt the children were not important enough to be allowed to interrupt at this time.

DEEPER STUDY # 1

(10:13) **Brought** (prosphero): to bring to; to bring unto. It is the word used in connection with offerings. The idea is that whatever is brought is being brought as an offering. It is a dedication to God (see Mt.5:23-24).

2 (10:14-16) **Children**: the truth about children. Jesus saw the children's being mistreated, and the Scripture literally says, "He was displeased [moved with indignation]." (See note, Displeased—Mk.10:14.) Children are not a problem—not to Jesus, not ever. He wanted His disciples to learn this, so He began to teach them five truths about children.

a. Children are invited to Jesus.
b. Children are citizens of the kingdom.
c. Children illustrate how one receives the kingdom.
d. Children are received and blessed by Jesus.
e. Children respond to Jesus.

DEEPER STUDY # 2

(10:14) **Displeased—Indignation** (aganaktese): to be indignant; to be moved with indignation; to feel pain; to grieve; to be displeased, sore displeased, and much displeased (see 2 Co.7:11).

The word is very strong, expressing deep, even violent emotion. The Lord was moved with indignation toward the disciples for what they were doing. Note two facts indicated by this experience.

1. Strong indignation against sin and injustice is sometimes justified.
2. Not being moved with indignation toward sin and injustice is sometimes a gross wrong.

DEEPER STUDY # 3

(10:14) **Children**: children are to be invited to Jesus. Jesus said let the children come and forbid them not. The word *forbid* (koluo) means to hinder, to prevent. The tense is a *present imperative*, a continuous command: stop hindering, stop preventing the children from coming to Me. In this case His own disciples were hindering the children, continuously preventing their coming to Jesus. No wonder He was moved with indignation. Note four points.

1. Jesus called for and received children. They were welcome, even when they were so little they had to be brought. They may have been too little to understand, but He was big enough to bless them and see to it that the blessing remained all through eternity. He is, after all, God; and as God He is omnipotent, all-powerful, and able to exercise His power as He wills. Children will in no way be rejected.
2. Jesus rebuked those who stopped and disregarded the children. He said that such action was wrong. We are not to stop little children from coming to Christ. Contrariwise, we are to bring them to Him. He is God; and as God He is providential, doing as He wills; therefore, He is the One who determines whom He will bless. No man determines it for Him. Despite the tender age and lack of reason, children are not to be kept from coming to Him. No obstacle is to be put in their way.
3. The benefits of bringing children to Christ are innumerable. Just a few major ones are as follows:
    a. A child learns love: that he is loved by God and by all who trust God, no matter how evil some in the world may act. He is even taught to love those who do wrong.
    b. A child grows, learning power and triumph: that God will help His followers through all trials and temptations. He learns there is a supernatural power available to help, a power to help when mother and dad and loved ones have done all they can.
    c A child grows, learning hope and faith: that no matter what happens, no matter how great a trial, he can still trust God and hope in Him. God has provided a very special strength to carry him through the trials of life (no matter how painful); and He has provided a very special place called heaven where He will carry him and his loved ones when he faces death.
    d. A child grows, learning the truth of life and endurance (service): that God has given him the privilege of life and of living in a beautiful earth and universe. The evil and bad that exist in the world are caused by evil and bad people. But despite such evil, he is to appreciate and to serve life and the beautiful earth. He is to continue to work, making the greatest contribution he can to both life and the earth.
    e. A child grows, learning trust and endurance: that life is full of temptations and pitfalls which can easily rob him of joy, destroying his life and the fulfillment of his purpose. The way to escape the temptations and pitfalls is to follow Christ and cling to Him, enduring in his work and purpose.
    f. A child grows, learning peace: that there is an inner peace despite the turbulent waters of this world, and that peace is knowing and trusting Christ.
4. There are several reasons why parents do not bring their children to Christ.
    a. Some parents (in civilized as well as uncivilized parts of the world) are not aware of the only living and true God. Therefore, they are blind; they just do not know. Christians have failed to take the gospel to the whole world.
    b. Some parents have heard the truth, but they have rejected Christ. They are agnostics or atheists, or else they love the world and the things of the world more than they love the news of the living God who gives eternal life. They do not care about anything beyond the comfort of self and the benefits of this world.
    c. Some parents do believe, at least mentally, but they are complacent and lethargic. They are not concerned enough to come to Christ nor to bring their child to Christ.
    d. Some parents are believers, but unfortunately they are immature and inconsistent in their Christian life. Their own Christian life and worship are weak and neglected, so their child is taught that Christ is not really all that important.
    e. Some parents are liberal-minded. They are not willing to influence and mold their child's thinking spiritually. They want their child to make his own choices. They are willing to teach him what foods to eat and books to read and anything else that will teach him how to care for himself physically and materially. But they leave the care of the spiritual up to him after he becomes an adult.

There are two great errors with all five of the above reasons.

a. The philosophy underlying every one of the reasons is false. Any parent who does not bring his child to Christ is following a false philosophy of life and is not facing reality.

> **"I said therefore unto you, that ye shall die in your sins: for if ye believe not that I am [he], ye shall die in your sins" (Jn.8:24).**
>
> **"Jesus saith unto him, I am the way, the truth, and the life: no man cometh unto the Father, but by me" (Jn.14:6).**
>
> **"For there is one God, and one mediator between God and men, the man Christ Jesus" (1 Ti.2:5).**

"But without faith it is impossible to please him: for he that cometh to God must believe that he is, and that he is a rewarder of them that diligently seek him" (He.11:6).

b. A child's mind is molded by those he is with, whether the loose and immoral or the disciplined and moral. If the child's mind is not molded by *godly parents*, it will be molded by the worldliness of the parents and the carnality of those who walk in selfish and corrupt ways.

"And he did evil in the sight of the LORD, and walked in the way of his father, and in the way of his mother, and in the way of Jeroboam the son of Nebat, who made Israel to sin" (1 K.22:52).

"And the LORD was with Jehoshaphat, because he walked in the first ways of his father David, and sought not unto Baalim" (2 Chr.17:3).

"And he walked in the way of Asa his father, and departed not from it, doing that which was right in the sight of the LORD" (2 Chr.20:32).

"He also walked in the ways of the house of Ahab: for his mother was his counsellor to do wickedly" (2 Chr.22:3).

"And he did that which was right in the sight of the LORD, according to all that his father Amaziah did" (2 Chr.26:4).

"But have walked after the imagination of their own heart, and after Baalim, which their fathers taught them" (Je.9:14).

"But I said unto their children in the wilderness, Walk ye not in the statutes of your fathers, neither observe their judgments, nor defile yourselves with their idols" (Eze.20:18).

"And she, being before instructed of her mother, said, Give me here John Baptist's head in a charger" (Mt.14:8).

"When I call to remembrance the unfeigned faith that is in thee, which dwelt first in thy grandmother Lois, and thy mother Eunice; and I am persuaded that in thee also" (2 Ti.1:5).

DEEPER STUDY # 4

(10:14) **Children**: children are citizens of God's kingdom. Jesus said, "of such [little children] is the kingdom of God." What Jesus meant was at least two things.

1. Little children are citizens of God's kingdom, at least until they are able to reason and make decisions between right and wrong, that is, the age of accountability.

2. Little children show what a man must be like to enter the Kingdom of God. The nature, character, and traits that are essential to get into heaven are seen in little children.

a. A little child is dependent and trusting. He is totally dependent. He knows little and can do little in taking care of himself. *Big people,* especially mommy and daddy, know everything and can do everything. The child is also trusting. He trusts everyone. Anyone can take the child into his arms. The child has not learned to suspect the world. Everyone is a friend; no one is an enemy, and few are strangers.

b. A little child is responsive and submissive. A child responds to an adult. He will come, go, pick up, do whatever is suggested to him. He will drop whatever he is doing, surrender whatever is occupying his thoughts and behavior, and respond.

c. A little child is obedient and learning. He will do exactly what he is asked to do, and he will learn by it. He is ever learning what he sees and is told, whether good or bad.

d. A little child is humble and forgiving. He is not interested in prominence, fame, power, wealth, or position. He does not push himself forward. He does not want to sit around in the midst of a group of adults. He has not been taught to think in terms of self-importance, not yet. The child also forgives and forgets (unless, of course, it is extreme abuse. We must remember Christ is talking about the child in a normal, healthy environment.)

DEEPER STUDY # 5

(10:15) **Children**: children illustrate exactly how one receives the Kingdom of God. Note the strong words of Jesus—the terrible end of the man who does not come to God as a child. A man has to approach God and receive God's kingdom (His rule, reign, and authority) into his life just like a little child, or else "he shall not enter the eternal Kingdom of God" (see DEEPER STUDY # 5—Mt.19:23-24).

What did Jesus mean by receiving the kingdom as a little child? (See note, *Conversion*—Mt.18:3 for a clear illustration of this.)

1. The child trusts and depends upon Jesus: (a) He senses the warmth, tenderness, care, and love of Jesus; and (b) he listens to the call (message, gospel) of Jesus. He trusts what He hears and depends upon Jesus to take care of him now and forever.

"Surely I have behaved and quieted myself, as a child that is weaned of his mother: my soul is even as a weaned child" (Ps.131:2).

"Verily, verily, I say unto you, He that heareth my word, and believeth on him that sent me, hath everlasting life, and shall not come into condemnation; but is passed from death unto life" (Jn.5:24).

2. The child responds and surrenders to Jesus. He is ready and willing to respond to Jesus. He is willing to give up what he is doing, to surrender whatever is occupying his thoughts, behavior, and time, in order to receive Jesus. He wants the Kingdom of God in his heart (God's rule and reign), and he wants to enter the eternal Kingdom of God someday out in the future.

"The Spirit itself beareth witness with our spirit, that we are the children of God: And if children, then heirs; heirs of God, and joint-heirs with Christ; if so be that we suffer with him, that we may be also glorified together" (Ro.8:16-17).

"But when the fulness of the time was come, God sent forth his Son, made of a woman, made under the law, To redeem them that were under the law, that we might receive the adoption of sons. And because ye are sons, God hath sent forth the Spirit of his Son into your hearts, crying, Abba, Father. Wherefore thou art no more a servant, but a son; and if a son, then an heir of God through Christ" (Ga.4:4-7).

3. The child is obedient to Jesus and is ever learning of Him. He listens and does exactly what Jesus says, even if it is difficult and requires self-denial. He does it simply because Jesus asks him to do it. He does not act independently or behave selfishly.

"If ye keep my commandments, ye shall abide in my love; even as I have kept my Father's commandments, and abide in his love....Ye are my friends, if ye do whatsoever I command you" (Jn.15:10, 14).

"Be ye therefore followers of God, as dear children" (Ep.5:1).

"And ye have forgotten the exhortation which speaketh unto you as unto children, My son, despise not thou the chastening of the Lord, nor faint when thou art rebuked of him: For whom the Lord loveth he chasteneth, and scourgeth every son whom he receiveth" (He.12:5-6; see v.5-10).

4. The child is humble and forgiving (see note, pt.2—Mk.10:14).

"He hath showed thee, O man, what is good; and what doth the LORD require of thee, but to do justly, and to love mercy, and to walk humbly with thy God?" (Mi.6:8).

"Blessed [are] the peacemakers: for they shall be called the children of God" (Mt.5:9).

"But ye [shall] not [be] so: but he that is greatest among you, let him be as the younger; and he that is chief, as he that doth serve" (Lu.22:26).

"Let all bitterness, and wrath, and anger, and clamour, and evil speaking, be put away from you, with all malice: And be ye kind one to another, tenderhearted, forgiving one another, even as God for Christ's sake hath forgiven you" (Ep.4:31-32).

"Likewise, ye younger, submit yourselves unto the elder. Yea, all of you be subject one to another, and be clothed with humility: for God resisteth the proud, and giveth grace to the humble. Humble yourselves therefore under the mighty hand of God, that he may exalt you in due time" (1 Pe.5:5-6).

DEEPER STUDY # 6

(10:16) **Children**: children are received and blessed by Jesus. Note how Jesus took the children "up in His arms, put His hands upon them, and blessed them." The scene is warm, full of genuine care and truth that we often overlook. It is not so much that we come and touch God as it is that He comes and touches us. It is not so much that we apprehend God as it is that we are apprehended by Him (Ph.3:12-13).

"I love them that love me; and those that seek me early shall find me" (Pr.8:17).

"But as many as received him, to them gave he power to become the sons of God, even to them that believe on his name: Which were born, not of blood, nor of the will of the flesh, nor of the will of man, but of God" (Jn.1:12-13).

"All that the Father giveth me shall come to me; and him that cometh to me I will in no wise cast out" (Jn.6:37).

God's blessing is not so much due to how rational and capable *we are* as it is to *His purpose and will.* God can choose to touch and bless whom He wills, and He demonstrates beyond all question that He chooses to touch and bless the children brought to Him.

DEEPER STUDY # 7

(10:16) **Children**: children respond to Jesus. They have nothing to give but themselves, and they are ready to give themselves. Their little hearts are tender and responsive to authority. They look to others to provide, teach, protect, and care for them. They are ready to respond; all they need is for someone to present the warmth and tenderness and love of Jesus.

"And when the chief priests and scribes saw the wonderful things that he did, and the children crying in the temple, and saying, Hosanna to the Son of David; they were sore displeased" (Mt.21:15. See note—Mt.21:15-16 for an excellent example of this point.)

"And he said unto them, How is it that ye sought me? wist ye not that I must be about my Father's business?" (Lu.2:49).

"When I call to remembrance the unfeigned faith that is in thee, which dwelt first in thy grandmother Lois, and thy mother Eunice; and I am persuaded that in thee also" (2 Ti.1:5).

"And that from a child thou hast known the holy scriptures, which are able to make thee wise unto salvation through faith which is in Christ Jesus" (2 Ti.3:15).

"And the child Samuel grew on, and was in favour both with the LORD, and also with men" (1 S.2:26).

"And the child Samuel ministered unto the LORD before Eli. And the word of the LORD was precious in those days; there was no open vision" (1 S.3:1).

"Joash was seven years old when he began to reign, and he reigned forty years in Jerusalem. His mother's name also was Zibiah of Beersheba. And Joash did that which was right in the sight of the LORD all the days of Jehoiada the priest" (2 Chr.24:1-2).

"Josiah was eight years old when he began to reign, and he reigned in Jerusalem one and thirty years. And he did that which was right in the sight of the LORD, and walked in the ways of David his father, and declined neither to the right hand, nor to the left. For in the eighth year of his reign, while he was yet young, he began to seek after the God of David his father: and in the twelfth year he began to purge Judah and Jerusalem from the high places, and the groves, and the carved images, and the molten images" (2 Chr.34:1-3).

	C. The Rich Young Ruler: The Problem of Eternal Life, 10:17-22 *(Mt. 19:16-22; Lu. 18:18-23)*	ness, Defraud not, Honour thy father and mother. 20 And he answered and said unto him, Master, all these have I observed from my youth.	a. Laws of respectability b. His respectable character
1. Fact 1: Seeking Christ is not enough to receive eternal life a. A rich young man eagerly sought Christ b. His concern: Sought eternal life	17 And when he was gone forth into the way, there came one running, and kneeled to him, and asked him, Good Master, what shall I do that I may inherit eternal life?	21 Then Jesus beholding him loved him, and said unto him, One thing thou lackest: go thy way, sell whatsoever thou hast, and give to the poor, and thou shalt have treasure in heaven: and come, take up the cross, and follow me.	**4. Fact 4: To be loved by Jesus is not enough to receive eternal life** **5. Fact 5: To give everything is required to receive eternal life** a. The meaning: Total & sacrificial giving, the abandonment of all
2. Fact 2: To praise Christ is not enough to receive eternal life	18 And Jesus said unto him, Why callest thou me good? there is none good but one, that is, God.		
3. Fact 3: To be respectable is not enough to receive eternal life	19 Thou knowest the com- mandments, Do not commit adultery, Do not kill, Do not steal, Do not bear false wit-	22 And he was sad at that saying, and went away grieved: for he had great pos- sesssions.	b. The result: The requirement was too heavy—he went away sad & grieved

DIVISION VI

THE SON OF GOD'S LAST PUBLIC MINISTRY: JESUS DEALS WITH SOME SPECIAL PROBLEMS, 10:1-52

C. The Rich Young Ruler: The Problem of Eternal Life, 10:17-22

(10:17-22) **Introduction**: this man is known as "the rich young ruler." He is so called because of the combined picture gleaned from all three gospels.

⇒ He was rich (Mt.19:22; Mk.10:22; Lu.18:23).
⇒ He was young (Mt.19:20).
⇒ He was a ruler (Lu.18:18).

He was a rare young man among the people of his day. This is seen in two facts.

1. He was conscientious, responsible, dependable—traits so often lacking in youth. He had already been placed into a position of leadership.
2. He was eagerly seeking eternal life—a spiritual matter often shunned by young people.

The dominant theme of the young man's experience is his sincerity, his desperate search for eternal life. Jesus takes the man's desperation and shocks the world. Desperation, sincerity, eagerness, and seeking eternal life are not enough. To inherit eternal life takes much more than just being desperate to possess it. Man has a problem in seeking eternal life.

1. Fact 1: seeking Christ is not enough to receive eternal life (v.17).
2. Fact 2: to praise Christ is not enough to receive eternal life (v.18).
3. Fact 3: to be respectable is not enough to receive eternal life (vv.19-20).
4. Fact 4: to be loved by Jesus is not enough to receive eternal life (v.21).
5. Fact 5: to give everything is required to receive eternal life (vv.21-22).

1 (10:17) **Seeking Jesus**: the scene was striking. A rich young man sought Jesus—sought Him with a sense of urgency and desperation seldom seen.

a. The man was *eager*, ever so eager: he was *running* to Jesus.

b. The man was *humble*: he cast himself to the ground, kneeling before Jesus, showing extreme reverence. He esteemed Jesus ever so highly. He bowed the knee to Him.

c. The man was *respectful*: he addressed Jesus as "Good Master," which was the proper and courteous address to a revered Rabbi or Teacher.

d. The man was *concerned* about his spiritual welfare. He asked what he should do to inherit eternal life.

The young man demonstrated how we should seek eternal life. He did exactly what we should do when we wish anything: seek it. We are to *seek* eternal life as the rich young ruler did. But in seeking, there is something critical. We must go to the right *source*. This is exactly what the rich young man did: (a) he approached Jesus, the Source of eternal life; and (b) he asked, confessing his need.

Note two things about the young man's seeking eternal life.

1. He believed that eternal life existed, that there was such a thing as eternal life. He believed there was life in another world, and he was sincere and eager (perhaps desperate) to receive it. He "came running and kneeled" before Jesus.

2. He did a rare thing. He openly confessed his eager concern for eternal life. Few of the rich would ever confess an open concern as he did, and few of the young would ever consider it important enough at their young stage of life. He lacked and had need, and he knew it and openly confessed it. He was seeking for inner peace and a sense of completeness and fulfillment and satisfaction.

2 (10:18) **Eternal Life**: the first fact to know about eternal life is this: to praise Jesus is not enough to receive eternal life. The young man had praised and honored Jesus as much as a person could. He had eagerly sought and reverenced Jesus, not only kneeling before Him but also casting himself into the dust of the ground before Jesus. He addressed Jesus with as high a title as a man could address a revered teacher. He could not praise Jesus more. But note: the man's praise and honor of Jesus were not enough.

He called Jesus "Good Master," but by Master he meant *good teacher, good Rabbi.* He was acknowledging that Jesus was an honorable person to be highly regarded. But he conceived Jesus to be *only* a highly regarded teacher. He did not consider Jesus to be the divine Son of God. He conceived Jesus to be but a mere man, not God. He thought Jesus was a man who had achieved unusual moral goodness and by such had become a *good Master*, one capable of teaching the great truths of God and life. (See note, pt.1—Lu.18:18-23 for another idea and more discussion.)

Jesus had to correct this gross error. He attempted to correct it by simply saying, "Why callest thou me good? There is none good, but one, that is, God." He was saying to the young man, "God alone is good. No man is good, not in comparison to God, not good enough to ever stand before God in righteousness. *If I am but a mere man*, a good teacher, then I am not 'good' and do not have the words to eternal life. *But if I am God*, then you can address me as 'good,' and I do have the words to eternal life."

Note two things.

1. Jesus told the young man how to enter life, that is, how to receive eternal life. Therefore, Jesus was claiming to be God.
2. Jesus was correcting the young man. He was speaking these words forcefully: "Why callest thou me good? there is none good but one, that is God." Jesus would not have the young man thinking of Him only as a man, no matter how preeminent a teacher the young man thought Him to be. He is God, God's very own Son; and He is to be known and called the Son of God. Therefore, Jesus tried to lead the young man to acknowledge and honor Him as God. It was the only way the young man could ever receive eternal life.

> **"For God so loved the world, that he gave his only begotten Son, that whosoever believeth in him should not perish, but have everlasting life" (Jn.3:16).**
>
> **"Then Simon Peter answered him, Lord, to whom shall we go? thou hast the words of eternal life" (Jn.6:68).**
>
> **"I said therefore unto you, that ye shall die in your sins: for if ye believe not that I am he, ye shall die in your sins" (Jn.8:24).**
>
> **"Jesus saith unto him, I am the way, the truth, and the life: no man cometh unto the Father, but by me. If ye had known me, ye should have known my Father also: and from henceforth ye know him, and have seen him" (Jn.14:6-7).**
>
> **"Neither is there salvation in any other: for there is none other name under heaven given among men, whereby we must be saved" (Ac.4:12).**
>
> **"For there is one God, and one mediator between God and men, the man Christ Jesus; who gave himself a ransom for all, to be testified in due time" (1 Ti.2:5-6).**

3 (10:19-20) **Eternal Life—Self Righteousness—Respectability**: the second fact to know about eternal life is this: to be respectable is not enough to receive eternal life. Note a crucial point: the young man had asked, "What *good thing* shall I do?" He had a religion of works, not of faith. He thought man himself could secure eternal life by being good. He felt that if he could just keep some great rule or law and live a moral, clean life, then God would accept him. He believed that his acts of morality and good works just piled up a balance sheet and made him acceptable to God.

This was the man's second major error. Again Jesus had to correct the man; He had to strike right at the root of the problem. The man was failing to love his neighbor as himself, and Jesus knew it (this will be brought out later). So Jesus told the young man very simply, "Thou knowest the commandments"; and He proceeded to quote five of the ten commandments, the five laws of respectability that had to do with his duty toward his neighbor (Ex.20:12-16).

The man made the phenomenal claim that he had kept all five of the commandments that Jesus quoted. He, of course, had not kept them perfectly, not in God's eyes, not in the spirit in which God intended them to be kept. He was not generous enough with others, not giving and helping like he should. Jesus was now ready to show him and lead him to do this. In summary, here is what Jesus had said to the rich young ruler: keep the commandments dealing with your neighbor—the ones especially needed by rulers and the rich—the ones so often misunderstood and neglected by rulers and the rich.

But the rich young ruler misunderstood God's law: he had a tragic sense of self-righteousness.

1. He thought some commandments were more important than others.
2. He thought man could keep God's law and build up a balance sheet with God, securing God's acceptance.

> **Thought 1.** "*What shall I do*" to inherit eternal life? It is not the *good thing* that I do nor is it all the *good things* that I do that give me eternal life.
>
> > **"For I say unto you, That except your righteousness shall exceed the righteousness of the scribes and Pharisees [religionists], ye shall in no case enter into the kingdom of heaven" (Mt.5:20).**
> >
> > **"Many will say to me in that day, Lord, Lord, have we not prophesied in thy name? and in thy name have cast out devils? and in thy name done many wonderful works? And then will I profess unto them, I never knew you: depart from me, ye that work iniquity" (Mt.7:22-23).**
> >
> > **"Knowing that a man is not justified by the works of the law, but by the faith of Jesus Christ, even we have believed in Jesus Christ, that we might be justified by the faith of Christ,**

and not by the works of the law: for by the works of the law shall no flesh be justified" (Ga.2:16).

"For by grace are ye saved through faith; and that not of yourselves: it is the gift of God: not of works, lest any man should boast" (Ep.2:8-9).

"Who hath saved us, and called us with an holy calling, not according to our works, but according to his own purpose and grace, which was given us in Christ Jesus before the world began" (2 Ti.1:9).

"But after that the kindness and love of God our Saviour toward man appeared, not by works of righteousness which we have done, but according to his mercy he saved us, by the washing of regeneration, and renewing of the Holy Ghost" (Tit.3:4-5).

4 (10:21) **Eternal Life—Jesus Christ, Love of**: the third fact to know about eternal life is this: to be loved by Jesus is not enough to receive eternal life. Note the exact words, "Jesus beholding him, *loved* him." Jesus' eyes penetrated into the man's innermost being and sensed a deep, deep longing and earnestness. The man's longing and ache for eternal life touched Jesus deeply. Jesus was drawn to the man and loved him in a very, very special sense.

But note the crucial point: the love of Jesus for a man's soul—even the very, very special love of Jesus for a man—was not enough to save the man. The man still lacked one thing.

Thought 1. The love of Christ is great, and it is touching and encouraging. But it is not enough. The Lord's love cannot save us, not by itself, not against our will, not if we refuse to *surrender all*—all we are and all we have.

"O Jerusalem, Jerusalem, thou that killest the prophets, and stonest them which are sent unto thee, how often would I have gathered thy children together, even as a hen gathereth her chickens under her wings, and ye would not!" (Mt.23:37).

"Because I have called, and ye refused; I have stretched out my hand, and no man regarded" (Pr.1:24).

"Cast away from you all your transgressions, whereby ye have transgressed; and make you a new heart and a new spirit: for why will ye die?" (Eze.18:31).

5 (10:21-22) **Eternal Life—Self-Denial—Cross**: the fourth fact to know about eternal life is this: to give everything is required to receive eternal life. *Giving everything* is the one thing lacking, the one thing that causes so many to lose eternal life.

Jesus knew exactly what the young man needed. His rejection of Jesus showed this. He was hoarding wealth instead of distributing it. God had given wealth to him that he might be able to help others, but he was failing to love and help his neighbor as he should (Ep.4:28).

What the young man needed to hear was just what Jesus said: "If thou wilt be perfect [receive heaven, really keep the commandments, as you say you have], then demonstrate to all publicly and without question that you love your neighbor. Go and sell all you have, and give to the poor...and come *follow me*."

In our struggle to protect the glorious truth that man is saved by grace and grace alone, we often forget and neglect another great truth: *to follow Christ is to serve and minister to our neighbor*. To follow Christ is to deny self completely—*all that we are and all that we have* (see DEEPER STUDY # 1—Lu.9:23). When we love our neighbor as ourselves, then we show that we truly love God. If we do not love and minister to our neighbor (above self), then we do not love God.

When we deny self and give all we are and have (1 Jn.4:20), then and only then do we receive heaven; but more importantly, we receive treasure in heaven. To deny self, *to give all we are and have,* is a hard saying, but Christ demands it. Our attempt to soften it does not annul His demand (see DEEPER STUDY # 1—Ro.3:3).

The young man rejected Jesus for three reasons.

a. Unbelief: he was not willing to entrust his life to Jesus. There was some lack of belief that the Man Jesus standing before him was really God.

b. Self-righteousness and pride: his concept of religion was keeping laws and doing good in order to secure God's acceptance. He felt that he, as well as other men, had the power and goodness to make God approve and accept him.

c. Love of the world: he was rich and was unwilling to give up the comfort and possessions he had obtained. He made the fatal mistake that so many make with wealth, power, and fame.

1) He loved the things of the world more than he loved people. He preferred hoarding and extravagance, living sumptuously and comfortably to helping those who were so desperately needful.
2) He loved the things of the world more than he loved the hope of eternal life.
3) He loved the position, recognition, esteem, and power of the earth more than he loved Christ.

Now, note a critical point: the subject of *giving all* is a sensitive subject, so sensitive that the words of Christ are seldom taken or preached at face value. The words of the Lord are *watered down* to mean no more than an ideal in the mind of a man—an ideal that is left up to every man to decide within his own selfish, deceptive, and corrupt heart. Is the man *willing to give all*? Then his willingness is said to be acceptable to God. The fact that he does not give all is said not to matter. However, the critical point seldom crosses the mind of men: the God of all men *can never justify keeping and storing and banking and hoarding and even holding back as long as a single need exists and is going unmet.*

If all men are truly God's by creation, then God is bound to expect all needs to be met; and He is bound to hold accountable the man who has and keeps, stores and banks, hoards and holds back. The point is easily understood by the honest and thinking person when he thinks about the issue. The thinking and honest person sees both the single person and the masses...

- who are starving
- who are without clothes, housing, medicine, treatment, education, and skills
- who are lost from God and doomed eternally because they have never heard the gospel

Imagine the millions who have never heard about Christ even once. When the thinking person sees the picture and is honest, he can no longer refuse to accept Jesus' words at face value. Yet, so many do not think and so many refuse to be honest. So they continue to *spiritualize and idealize what Jesus was saying* to this young man. Why? Do we fear the strictness of what Christ says? Do we fear the reaction of people? Do we fear what we will have to give up? Do we lack the faith within to trust God? (See outline, notes, and DEEPER STUDY # 1—Mt.10:28; note—Mk.10:23-27 for more discussion.)

Thought 1. God expects us to work so that we can have enough to help others (Ep.4:28). We are to help as we are able, but we are to be *honest* about our ability to help.

Thought 2. Note a crucial point. God gives us *a talent* to use in taking care of our own needs, but after our needs are met, the talent entrusted to us is to be used to help others in their need.

Thought 3. The young man had a serious flaw—the very same flaw that exists within so many today: he did not believe heaven was glorious enough to *merit the giving up* of his possessions.

"And he said to them all, If any man will come after me, let him deny himself, and take up his cross daily, and follow me" (Lu.9:23).

"But rather give alms of such things as ye have; and, behold, all things are clean unto you" (Lu.11:41).

"Sell that ye have, and give alms; provide yourselves bags which wax not old, a treasure in the heavens that faileth not, where no thief approacheth, neither moth corrupteth" (Lu.12:33).

"And Zacchaeus stood, and said unto the Lord; Behold, Lord, the half of my goods I give to the poor; and if I have taken any thing from any man by false accusation, I restore him fourfold" (Lu.19:8).

"Give, and it shall be given unto you; good measure, pressed down, and shaken together, and running over, shall men give into your bosom. For with the same measure that ye mete withal it shall be measured to you again" (Lu.6:38).

"I have showed you all things, how that so labouring ye ought to support the weak, and to remember the words of the Lord Jesus, how he said, It is more blessed to give than to receive" (Ac.20:35).

"Distributing [giving] to the necessity of saints" (Ro.12:13).

"And though I bestow all my goods to feed the poor, and though I give my body to be burned, and have not charity, it profiteth me nothing" (1 Co.13:3).

"For if there be first a willing mind, it is accepted according to that a man hath, and not according to that he hath not" (2 Co.8:12).

"But this I say, He which soweth sparingly shall reap also sparingly; and he which soweth bountifully shall reap also bountifully" (2 Co.9:6).

"As we have therefore opportunity, let us do good [give] unto all men, especially unto them who are of the household of faith" (Ga.6:10).

"Let him that stole steal no more: but rather let him labour, working with his hands the thing which is good, that he may have to give to him that needeth" (Ep.4:28).

"Charge them that are rich in this world, that they be not highminded, nor trust in uncertain riches, but in the living God, who giveth us richly all things to enjoy; that they do good, that they be rich in good works, ready to distribute, willing to communicate" (1 Ti.6:17-18).

"But to do good and to communicate [give] forget not: for with such sacrifices God is well pleased" (He.13:16).

"The liberal soul shall be made fat: and he that watereth shall be watered also himself" (Pr.11:25).

"He that hath a bountiful eye shall be blessed; for he giveth of his bread to the poor" (Pr.22:9).

	D. The Problem of Wealth & Its Dangers, 10:23-27 *(Mt. 19:23-26; Lu. 18:24-27)*	in riches to enter into the kingdom of God!	b. Their trust is not in the truly valuable, not in God
		25 It is easier for a camel to go through the eye of a needle, than for a rich man to enter into the kingdom of God.	**3. Rich men face great difficulty—spiritually**
1. Rich men face the peril of wealth[DS1] a. The shocking statement[DS2] b. The peril of wealth: Can bar a person from God's kingdom	23 And Jesus looked round about, and saith unto his disciples, How hardly shall they that have riches enter into the kingdom of God!	26 And they were astonished out of measure, saying among themselves, Who then can be saved?	**4. Rich men are set on a pedestal by the world**
2. Rich men tend to trust in riches a. Their trust is in riches, the world	24 And the disciples were astonished at his words. But Jesus answereth again, and saith unto them, Children, how hard is it for them that trust	27 And Jesus looking upon them saith, With men it is impossible, but not with God: for with God all things are possible.	**5. Rich men have only one hope—God alone** a. God alone can save b. God alone judges

DIVISION VI

THE SON OF GOD'S LAST PUBLIC MINISTRY: JESUS DEALS WITH SOME SPECIAL PROBLEMS, 10:1-52

D. The Problem of Wealth and Its Dangers, 10:23-27

(10:23-27) **Introduction**: Jesus took the rich young ruler's rejection of heaven and warned all men about the problem and dangers of wealth. Wealth is fraught with dangers and pitfalls, both for the man who is seeking to be rich and for the man who is already rich. The dangers are many, and they are entangling and enslaving, so much so that Jesus made the shocking statement, "It is difficult, extremely difficult, for a rich man to be saved."

The words are strong; the idea is shocking. Yet Jesus must be truthful, for He loves and cares for all men. He must warn all men: it is extremely difficult for a rich man to enter heaven. The dangers which face the rich are real and terrible, so the warning must be real and truthful.

1. Rich men face the peril of wealth (v.23).
2. Rich men tend to trust in riches (v.24).
3. Rich men face great difficulty—spiritually (v.25).
4. Rich men are set on a pedestal by the world (v.26).
5. Rich men have only one hope—God alone (v.27).

1 (10:23) **Wealth, Danger of**: this passage is tied to the rich young ruler. The picture is this: as the rich young ruler turned and walked away from Jesus, Jesus stood for the longest of times watching the young man fade into the distance. Jesus was heart-broken and thoughtful, for the young man had so much potential. Quickly, full of energy and authority, perhaps even bordering on anger (against the enslaving power of wealth), Jesus "looked around about" and made an earth-shaking statement: "How hardly [difficult] shall they that have riches enter into the kingdom of God."

The terrible peril of wealth is that it so easily bars a person from the Kingdom of God. Wealth, riches, and possessions (such as property, money, televisions, cars, recreational equipment) all pose a serious problem and an eternal danger for man.

DEEPER STUDY # 1

(10:23) **Riches** (chremata): money, things, gadgets—what one has and uses—material things or goods. It means all the things which a person has, all the things that have value and are worth something. Jesus chose a word that is applicable to every generation and every man who has possessions or has things of value.

DEEPER STUDY # 2

(10:23) **Riches—Wealth**: Who are the rich? Realistically, in comparison to what the vast majority of the world has, *the rich person is anyone who has anything to put back beyond meeting the true needs of his own family.*

This is exactly what Christ and the Bible say time and again (see also Mk.12:41-44; Lu.21:1-4; Ac.4:34-35; etc.).

In a summary statement, who is rich? *The rich person is any person who has anything beyond what he needs.* What Christ demands is that we give *all that we are and have* to meet the needs of those in such desperate need, holding back nothing. This is often the great complaint against Christians, that we do not believe what Christ says. The evidence of our unbelief is seen in Christ's insistence that we give all we have to feed the starving and to meet the desperate needs of the world, and yet we refuse to obey Him. Gandhi, the great leader of India's independence, is said to have never embraced Christianity for this very reason: because Christians live lives of hypocrisy. Christians do not follow the teachings of Christ; they do not give all they are and have to meet the desperate needs of the world. How many others have rejected Christ because of our hypocrisy?

"Go and sell that thou hast, and give to the poor, and thou shalt have treasure in heaven: and come and follow me" (Mt.19:21).

"And every one that hath forsaken houses, or brethren, or sisters, or father, or mother, or wife, or children, or lands, for my name's sake, shall receive an hundredfold, and shall inherit everlasting life" (Mt.19:29).

"For where your treasure is, there will your heart be also" (Mt.6:21).

"And the second is like unto it, Thou shalt love thy neighbor as thyself" (Mt.22:39).

"But rather seek ye the kingdom of God; and all these things shall be added unto you. Fear not, little flock; for it is your Father's good pleasure to give you the kingdom. Sell that ye have, and give alms; provide yourselves bags which wax not old, a treasure in the heavens that faileth not, where no thief approacheth, neither moth corrupteth. For where your treasure is, there will your heart be also" (Lu.12:31-34).

"And Zacchaeus stood, and said unto the Lord; Behold, Lord, the half of my goods I give to the poor; and if I have taken any thing from any man by false accusation, I restore him fourfold" (Lu.19:8).

"By this shall all men know that ye are my disciples, if ye have love one to another" (Jn.13:35).

"If ye keep my commandments, ye shall abide in my love; even as I have kept my Father's commandments, and abide in his love" (Jn.15:10).

"Let love be without dissimulation. Abhor that which is evil; cleave to that which is good" (Ro.12:9).

"Even as I please all men in all things, not seeking mine own profit, but the profit of many, that they may be saved" (1 Co.10:33).

"For ye know the grace of our Lord Jesus Christ, that, though he was rich, yet for your sakes he became poor, that ye through his poverty might be rich" (2 Co.8:9).

"Let him that stole steal no more: but rather let him labour, working with his hands the thing which is good, that he may have to give to him that needeth" (Ep.4:28).

"And the Lord make you to increase and abound in love one toward another, and toward all men, even as we do toward you" (1 Th.3:12).

"Let your conversation be without covetousness; and be content with such things as ye have: for he hath said, I will never leave thee, nor forsake thee" (He.13:5).

2 (10:24) **Wealth—Materialism—Worldliness**: rich men tend to trust in riches (money and things). Jesus made this statement because of the things that *pulled* the rich young ruler away. Wealth does pull a person away from heaven. There is a lure, an attraction, a force, a power, a pull that reaches out to draw any person who looks at or possesses wealth. There are pulls so forceful that they will enslave and doom any rich man that fails to turn and embrace God. There are three reasons given by Christ for this.

a. A man tends to trust in the world and in his riches. His wealth attaches him to the world. Wealth enables him to buy things that...

- make him comfortable
- please his taste
- stir his ego
- expand his experience
- challenge his mental pursuit
- stimulate his flesh
- stretch his self image

If a man centers his life upon the things of the world, his attention is on the world, not on God. He tends to become wrapped up in securing more and in protecting what he has. He gives little time and thought to heavenly matters. Wealth and the things it can provide can and usually do consume the rich.

b. A rich man's trust will more than likely not be in the most valuable, that is, in God. Wealth leads a man to trust himself, his abilities, his energy and efforts. Wealth creates the *big I* (see vv.17, 20). The wealthy are usually looked up to, esteemed, honored, envied. Wealth brings position, power, recognition. It boosts *ego*, making a person self-sufficient and independent in this world. As a result there is a tendency for the rich man to feel that he is truly independent and self-sufficient, that he needs nothing. And in such an atmosphere and world of thought, God is forgotten. Man forgets that there are things that money cannot buy and events from which money cannot save. Peace, love, joy—all that really matters within the spirit of man can never be bought. Neither can money save a person from disaster, disease, accident, death, and on and on.

c. A rich man tends to hoard, to be selfish with *most* of his money. He trusts in his riches, keeping *most* of everything for himself (see note, pt.2—Mt.19:23).

"But they that will be rich fall into temptation and a snare, and into many foolish and hurtful lusts, which drown men in destruction and perdition. For the love of money is the root of all evil: which while some coveted after, they have erred from the faith, and pierced themselves through with many sorrows" (1 Ti.6:9-10).

"Charge them that are rich in this world, that they be not highminded, nor trust in uncertain riches, but in the living God, who giveth us richly all things to enjoy" (1 Ti.6:17).

"And I will say to my soul, Soul, thou hast much goods laid up for many years; take thine ease, eat, drink, and be merry. But God said unto him, Thou fool, this night thy soul shall be required of thee: then whose shall those things be, which thou hast provided?" (Lu.12:19-20).

"If I have made gold my hope, or have said to the fine gold, Thou art my confidence; if I rejoiced because my wealth was great, and because mine hand had gotten much....this also were an iniquity to be punished by the judge: for I should have denied the God that is above" (Jb. 31:24-25, 28).

"Lo, this is the man that made not God his strength; but trusted in the abundance of his riches, and strengthened himself in his wickedness" (Ps.52:7).

"He that trusteth in his riches shall fall: but the righteous shall flourish as a branch" (Pr.11:28).

3 (10:25) **Wealth—Camel—Needle**: rich men face great difficulty—spiritually. It is extremely difficult for a rich man to enter into the Kingdom of God. It is so difficult that Jesus said, "It is easier for a camel to pass through the eye of a needle, than for a rich man to enter into the kingdom of God."

There have been various interpretations of "camel" and "needle" in an attempt to soften the words of Jesus. For example, some have said that the needle was a small gate in the wall surrounding Jerusalem. It sat right beside the large gate. At night the large gate was closed to protect the city from marauders and enemies, and the small gate was used. The small gate is said to have been called "The Needle's Eye" because it was so small that it was difficult for even a single person to pass through. Others have said that the Greek word Jesus used was *Kamilos* (a ship's rope or cable) not *Kamelos* (camel). Note the only difference between the two words is the second vowel.

Three things need to be noted about these interpretations.

a. There is no doubt that Jesus meant a literal needle. He as much as said so: "With men this is impossible" in v.27. What He did was use a proverbial saying for an *impossibility*. Most if not all countries have proverbs that express the impossibility of some things. The camel was the largest animal among the Jews, so Jesus simply used a well-known proverb among the Jews or else created one. There is also the point that when Jesus chose to speak in parables, He chose the most common and ordinary thing to express His meaning.

b. Attempts to soften the Lord's point are just that: attempts to soften. But nothing can be softened with v.27: "With men this is impossible." No man, not even the rich man himself, can save a rich man. The danger of riches is very real and terrible. Wealth entangles and enslaves a man so much that it is extremely difficult for a rich man to let go and give his wealth to help the desperate needs of the world. He just cannot accept the fact that he is to "labor...[so] that he may have to give to others" (Ep.4:28). It is so difficult not to live in personal luxury and build large estates. Heavy and fancy meals, full and fashionable wardrobes, a fine and large house, the largest and latest automobile—so much is so difficult to let go. It is the ego that refuses to let go.

c. It is just as difficult for the softening interpretations to be performed as it is for the literal interpretation. How does a camel trying to get through a gate made only for a man soften anything? It would be impossible. And how does threading a needle with a ship's cable soften anything? Again, it is impossible.

Thought 1. Few rich men will enter the Kingdom of God. Why? Scripture spells out the reasons in clear terms.

(1) Riches and worldliness choke the Word of God.

> **"And the cares of this world, and the deceitfulness of riches, and the lusts of other things entering in, choke the word, and it becometh unfruitful" (Mk.4:19).**

(2) Riches give men a sense of false security.

> **"And I will say to my soul, Soul, thou hast much goods laid up for many years; take thine ease, eat, drink, and be merry. But God said unto him, Thou fool, this night thy soul shall be required of thee: then whose shall those things be, which thou hast provided?" (Lu.12:19-20).**

(3) Riches bring a flood of temptations and snares upon a person.

> **"But they that will be rich fall into temptation and a snare, and into many foolish and hurtful lusts, which drown men in destruction and perdition" (1 Ti.6:9).**

(4) Riches cause men to be highminded (conceited, proud, arrogant, haughty).

> **"Charge them that are rich in this world, that they be not highminded, nor trust in uncertain riches, but in the living God, who giveth us richly all things to enjoy" (1 Ti.6:17).**
> **"The rich man's wealth is his strong city, and as a high wall in his own conceit" (Pr.18:11).**

(5) Riches tend to make a man forget God.

> **"And when thy herds and thy flocks multiply, and thy silver and thy gold is multiplied, and all that thou hast is multiplied; then thine heart be lifted up, and thou forget the LORD thy God...." (De.8:13-14).**

(6) Riches strengthen a man in his wickedness.

> **"Lo, this is the man that made not God his strength; but trusted in the abundance of his riches, and strengthened himself in his wickedness" (Ps.52:7).**

4 (10:26) **Wealth—Salvation**: rich men are set on a pedestal by the world. The Jews considered wealth a special blessing from God. It was the measure of a man's spiritual standing with God. This is the concept of *natural religion*. Throughout history a person who has been rich in wealth, intellect, talents, or personality has been thought to be especially blessed by God and to have all things easier.

Note: the disciples were astonished twice—beyond imagination (vv.24, 26). Why? Because they failed to see that riches are two things to a man: an acid test from God, and a responsibility for man to prove just how responsible he will be to God and to his fellow men in meeting their desperate needs. (See note—Js.1:9-11.)

Jesus was saying something diametrically opposed to what they and everyone else had always thought. They had always been taught (as have succeeding generations, even the church):

⇒ that prosperity (wealth, comfort, and things) is God's blessing.
⇒ that a person receives and has because God is blessing him.
⇒ that prosperity is the reward of righteousness and obedience.
⇒ that God blesses a person with the things of this earth if they are righteous and obedient.

But in this passage, Jesus was saying the very opposite: a prosperous person would most likely never enter heaven; prosperity posed such a dangerous threat to a person that his eternal doom was almost assured. The disciples knew that God would never put a person in such a precarious, dangerous position. They knew that Jesus was attacking the world's most cherished and ardent belief: be good (righteous) and you will be blessed by God (and the thought of blessing was always of material blessings. See note—Ep.1:3 for a discussion of God's blessings.)

They were shocked, thoroughly dismayed: Who then can be saved? The vast majority of people were threatening their own eternal destiny. They were dooming themselves. Since prosperity was not the reward (sign) for righteousness, and the rich were barred from heaven, that meant that the poor, too, were barred; for they were spending most of their time in dreaming and seeking prosperity.

The idea that prosperity is the reward for righteousness, that God blesses a person with the things of this earth if they are righteous and obedient, is so prevalent a view that a comment is needed at this point.

a. God's concern is spiritual blessings, not material blessings. God does promise a man the necessities of life (food, clothing, shelter) if he seeks Him first (Mt.6:33; see 6:25-34). And God can, if He chooses, bless any of us with whatever He wishes so that we may "have to give to him that needeth." But just because a man is prosperous does not mean he is righteous, and just because a person is righteous does not mean he is going to be blessed materially. Righteousness and prosperity have nothing to do with each other. In fact, "a rich man shall hardly enter into the kingdom of heaven."

b. Wealth is *seldom* a good thing. As Jesus teaches in this passage, wealth is fraught with dangers that make it extremely difficult for the rich to enter heaven. Yet the whole world, rich and poor alike, believer and non-believer, puts its primary attention upon dreaming and getting more and more.

c. Wealth is secured by man himself, by his own energy and effort. Man secures wealth by dreaming how to make it (a clear vision, perspective), and by having the initiative to make it (acting and timing). A man may trust God to help him secure wealth, but a man may also have nothing to do with God and secure wealth on his own. There is a sense in which a man's strength and mind are from God, but that has nothing to do with a personal, active relationship with God. Most rich men control their own lives and go about securing their treasure on this earth *without God* (Mt.6:21).

On the other hand, a man may trust God to bless him so that he may help others, and God may choose to bless him. But God's choosing to bless him is for the purpose of helping others, not to hoard and live above what is needed (extravagantly and sumptuously). In fact, what Jesus teaches is that *the rich are to live just as sacrificially as the poor in order to meet the desperate needs of a starving, doomed, and dying world. May God grant that we never forget this*! Our eternal destiny depends upon our living it, upon our living sacrificially. Because of this, the truth bears repeating: what Jesus teaches is that *the rich are to live just as sacrificially as the poor in order to meet the desperate needs of a starving, doomed, and dying world.* (See notes and DEEPER STUDY # 1,2—Mt.19:23; note—Mk.12:42. See outline—Lu.21:1-4.)

Thought 1. One of the most tragic and dangerous tendencies of men is to set the rich (the powerful, the athletic, the gifted) up on a pedestal. Scripture is clear: a person's hope and security must not be placed in other men.

> **"It is better to trust in the LORD than to put confidence in princes" (Ps.118:9).**
> **"Cease ye from man, whose breath is in his nostrils: for wherein is he to be accounted of?" (Is.2:22).**
> **"Thus saith the LORD; Cursed be the man that trusteth in man, and maketh flesh his arm, and whose heart departeth from the LORD" (Je.17:5).**

5 (10:27) **Wealth—Salvation—Repentance**: rich men face the possibility of God alone. Christ said two things.

a. God alone can save. A rich man must turn to God and away from the world. No man can save him, not himself nor any other man.

1) No man has the strength or know-how to break the power of *seeking things* that holds sway over him. The natural urge within man is to seek more and more comfort and ease and possessions. No man has the power to break that *natural urge*. The entanglements are too pleasing and enslaving.
2) No man can re-create the soul of a man; no man can change the soul of another man so that he seeks "those things which are above" and sets his "affection on things above, *not on things on the earth*" (Col.3:1-2). No philosophy, no psychology, no medicine, no education, no politics, no social movement can change the soul of a man.

> **"A rich man shall hardly enter into the kingdom of heaven...Who then can be saved [for even the poor dream and seek]?...With men this [salvation] is impossible" (Mt.19:23, 25-26).**

A rich man must turn to God and His power. God is the only hope for a rich man. Only God can break a rich man's enslavement to this earth—only God can convert, change, turn, and save the rich man from the danger and doom of wealth. How? Very simply. The words of Jesus to the rich young ruler tell the rich man what to do:

"Go and sell that thou hast, and give to the poor, and thou shalt have treasure in heaven: and come and follow me" (Mt.19:21).

This is a hard saying, a difficult thing for any of us to do—so difficult we try to escape from its stringent demand, and soften and explain it away. But *it is what Jesus said.* The disciples understood it perfectly (vv.25-27). In very practical terms, to receive eternal life we must give *all we are and have.* This is, naturally, more difficult for the rich; for "he has great possessions" (v.22).

b. God alone judges. God shall judge rich men on the basis of how they got their wealth and how they used their wealth. There are four practical steps that will help a rich man be saved.

1) Listen and heed immediately the inner voice, the pricking of conscience to give one's life and possessions to God. Turn immediately to God. Never turn away.
2) Study God's Word for direction—every day—and talk to and trust God to keep one's heart free from the lure and deception of possessions.
3) Use one's wealth to help the desperate needs of others. *Realize, know, and acknowledge that the vast majority* of the world is hungry, hurting, and needing help—desperately so; and that God expects us to use all we have *to meet those needs, not to hoard and live extravagantly in the midst of so much need.*
4) Develop a strong desire for heaven, knowing that our sojourn on earth is ever so short, as brief as the lily of the field.

Thought 1. If the righteous scarcely be saved, where shall the ungodly and the sinner (the rich) appear (1 Pe.4:18)?

Thought 2. Christ is forced to let every rich person make his own decision. He had to let the rich young ruler walk away to his own eternal doom. He has to let us walk away if we choose. He cannot violate our free will. He cannot make us robots.

Thought 3. Money and possessions cannot take care of us. Money and gadgets have no life. They are material. They cannot look after us. We have to look after them. But not so with God. God can take care of and look after our welfare, both now and eternally.

"For with God nothing shall be impossible" (Lu.1:37).

"I know that thou canst do every thing, and that no thought can be withholden from thee" (Jb. 42:2).

"Charge them that are rich in this world, that they be not highminded, nor trust in uncertain riches, but in the living God, who giveth us richly all things to enjoy; that they do good, that they be rich in good works, ready to distribute, willing to communicate; laying up in store for themselves a good foundation against the time to come, that they may lay hold on eternal life" (1 Ti.6:17-19).

"For other foundation can no man lay than that is laid, which is Jesus Christ" (1 Co.3:11).

	E. The Problem of Re-	house, or brethren, or sisters,	
	wards: What One Re-	or father, or mother, or wife,	
	ceives for Following	or children, or lands, for my	b. Whether property or wealth
	Christ, 10:28-31	sake, and the gospel's,	
	(Mt. 19:27-30; Lu. 18:28-30)	30 But he shall receive an	
		hundredfold now in this time,	
1. Peter asked about rewards	28 Then Peter began to say	houses, and brethren, and sis-	
	unto him, Lo, we have left	ters, and mothers, and chil-	
	all, and have followed	dren, and lands, with perse-	
	thee.	cutions; and in the world to	**3. A person receives persecution**
2. A person receives a hundred	29 And Jesus answered and	come eternal life.	**4. A person receives eternal life**
times what he gives up	said, Verily I say unto you,	31 But many that are first	**5. A person receives an immedi-**
a. Whether housing or family	There is no man that hath left	shall be last; and the last first.	**ate assurance & warning**

DIVISION VI

THE SON OF GOD'S LAST PUBLIC MINISTRY: JESUS DEALS WITH SOME SPECIAL PROBLEMS, 10:1-52

E. The Problem of Rewards: What One Receives for Following Christ, 10:28-31

(10:28-31) **Introduction**: the idea of rewards in heaven is foreign to many; it is rejected by others, feeling the idea of God's rewarding people is mercenary. They feel rewards of rank and position, of possession and levels of responsibility have no place in a perfect world. However, Christ Himself endured the cross "*for the joy* that was set before Him" (He.12:2). And it is said of Moses that he esteemed "the reproach of Christ greater riches than the treasures in Egypt" (He.11:26; see Heb.11:1-40). Scripture abounds with the teaching of rewards "in the world to come" (v.30).

Reward is the point of this passage. Jesus deals with the problem of rewards, of just what a true disciple shall receive both in this world and in the world to come. (See notes—Lu.16:10-12; Jn.4:36-38.)

1. Peter asked about rewards (v.28).
2. A person receives a hundred times what he gives up (vv.29-30).
3. A person receives persecution (v.30).
4. A person receives eternal life (v.30).
5. A person receives an immediate assurance and warning (v.31).

1 (10:28) **Rewards**: Peter asked about rewards, for he had just been shocked. He had seen a rich young man with enormous potential turn and walk away from Jesus. The man had rejected Jesus because he was unwilling to forsake all he had, unwilling to forsake his wealth and use it to meet the needs of the world. Then Peter had heard Jesus give an earth-shaking discussion on riches—just how difficult it is for people with riches to enter heaven. Why? Because they are unwilling to give their wealth to meet the needs of the world. A person must forsake all to enter heaven; he must give all he is and has to save a desperate world.

The demand sounded hard and stringent. Peter was shocked and stunned. He felt he and the disciples had given all. He was *almost sure they were holding nothing back, but he wanted to make absolutely sure.* Anyone would need assurance after what Jesus had just said. Few sell everything and give it all away, and few (rich or poor) control their dreams and urges to have more (see note—Mt.19:25). The disciples, as all honest men, knew this. They also knew the extreme demands Jesus was making to be a true follower of His. *They, unlike so many of us in our attempts to soften His words, understood exactly what He was saying.* The extremity of His words was shocking. They could not see how anyone could be saved. And the answer Jesus gave to their question about salvation said nothing to give them personal assurance: "With men this is impossible; but with God all things are possible" (Mt.19:26).

The disciples sensed a deep need for assurance. Had they done enough, given up enough? They thought so, were almost sure they had, but had they? Peter, somewhat meekly, said, "Lord, behold [look] we have forsaken all, and followed thee. We have surrendered all to you. What shall we have therefore? Shall we receive eternal life...?" (See Mt.19:27.)

Jesus used Peter's question to teach a wonderful truth. They, His own dear apostles, and all who follow Him thereafter, can rest assured—they shall all be enormously rewarded.

a. "We have left all." What a glorious testimony! Just think about these men. They had "left all" for Christ's sake and the gospel's (v.29). They had left family, friends, businesses, professions, wealth—left all in order to meet the needs of a desperate world. It should be noted that they readily met the needs of their family (see Mt.8:14). Even Jesus saw to the care of His mother (Jn.19:26-27). *Leaving all does not mean the desertion or shirking of one's responsibility. It means centering one's life and possessions upon Christ and using all one is and has to serve Him and to meet the needs of the world.* It means putting Christ first (Mt.6:33).

b. "We...have followed thee." They had followed Jesus and His gospel; they had not followed some other self-proclaimed Messiah or false message (see Gal.1:6-9). They knew Him to be the true Messiah, the Son of the living God; and they had committed their lives and possessions, all they were and had to Him and His gospel.

Leaving all and following Christ are the two bases for reward. Any person who leaves all and follows Christ can expect reward. This is the wonderful truth Jesus was about to teach His disciples. They were uneasy because of what had just happened to the rich young ruler and because of Jesus' comments about the incident. Jesus wanted to assure them. They were very dear to Him because they had left all and were following Him. He wanted them to know they would be rewarded and rewarded abundantly.

2 (10:29-30) **Reward—Fellowship—Blessings**: Jesus made an astounding promise. The *true disciple* will be abundantly rewarded; in fact, he will receive a hundred times what he gives up and sacrifices. But note the crucial point: what is given is given *"for Christ's sake, and the gospel's."* The person's motive has to be that he is giving for Christ and the spread of the gospel. He is sacrificing and giving what he has for the Lord and His cause. He is doing his part, all that he can, to accomplish the mission of redemption and the helping of mankind. Note what Jesus mentioned.

a. The giving of housing and family. There are two ideas here.

1) Some have been rejected by family and lost their home. When they turned to Jesus for salvation or set out to serve Jesus, their family rejected them and turned them out.
2) All *true disciples* serve Jesus, putting Him first. They take all they are and have, including family and house, and use it "for Christ's sake, and the gospel's." The house and family are sacrificed for Him, that is, centered around Him and used for Him. The house and family are known...
   - as a place where He is honored.
   - as a place that is used to spread the gospel.

There is also the fact that a true disciple serves Jesus away from the house and family. The disciple has to sacrifice, to leave his house and family to serve Jesus out in the world through visiting, ministering, preaching, doing whatever his missionary call is. This often involves being away from home and family for extended periods of time (for example: evangelists, missionaries, even ministers who are on call day and night).

Now, note the glorious promise of Christ. The true disciple who gives up his house and family for Christ's sake and the gospel's will receive a hundredfold. He will receive...

- a spiritual bond and kinship with a much larger family, the family of God throughout both heaven and earth. (See outline and notes, *Brotherhood*—Mt.12:46-50; Lu.8:19-21.)
- a fellowship and communion, a very present and practical help when needed through the local church, the fellowship of believers within his own community (see notes and DEEPER STUDY # 1-5—Acts 2:42).
- the presence of the Spirit of God who communes with and directs him day by day.

Thought 1. A true believer needs to make sure that he is in a local church or fellowship that is truly centered on Christ and His gospel. Not every church is.

Thought 2. Every church needs to search its heart and make sure that it honors Christ and His gospel, that it does have the warm heart and spiritual bond, the open arms and strong fellowship, that are needed among God's people.

> **"That which we have seen and heard declare we unto you, that ye also may have fellowship with us: and truly our fellowship is with the Father, and with his Son Jesus Christ" (1 Jn.1:3).**
>
> **"But if we walk in the light, as he is in the light, we have fellowship one with another, and the blood of Jesus Christ his Son cleanseth us from all sin" (1 Jn.1:7).**
>
> **"And they continued stedfastly in the apostles' doctrine and fellowship, and in breaking of bread, and in prayers" (Ac.2:42).**
>
> **"For where two or three are gathered together in my name, there am I in the midst of them" (Mt.18:20).**
>
> **"So we, being many, are one body in Christ, and every one members one of another" (Ro.12:5).**
>
> **"I am a companion of all them that fear thee, and of them that keep thy precepts" (Ps.119:63).**
>
> **"Then they that feared the LORD spake often one to another: and the LORD hearkened, and heard it, and a book of remembrance was written before him for them that feared the LORD, and that thought upon his name" (Mal.3:16).**

b. The giving of property and wealth. The promise of being *blessed materially*, of receiving a hundredfold is astounding to the world, but not to the believer. The believer understands what Jesus is saying. Jesus is laying down God's principle of money, of finances, of riches, of possessions, of material goods, of giving, of stewardship—whatever we wish to call the *mammon* and *things* of this world that we value (see DEEPER STUDY # 1, *Riches*—Mk.10:23). The principle is simple. It can be stated several ways.

⇒ The true believer seeks the Kingdom of God and His righteousness first, and then all the necessities of life are given to him (Mt.6:33). He simply gives all he is and has to the Kingdom of God, and God sees to it that he has what is needed to take care of his necessities. The idea is a present experience, a continuous process. The believer keeps on giving of himself and what he has, and God keeps on giving to the believer.

⇒ The true believer works so that he may have enough to give to others. His very purpose for working is not only to take care of his own needs but also to earn enough to help others. Again the idea is a continuous process. The believer works and earns and gives to others, so God continues to give to him so that he can continue to spread the gospel and help others.

⇒ A true disciple gives all he is and has to meet the needs of a desperate world. God sees to it that the believer receives more. But what the believer receives is not given to keep and store up. God replenishes the believer so that the believer can continue to reach and help the world. The true believer keeps on giving, and God keeps on giving to him, so that the believer, as long as he lives, can continue to spread the gospel and meet the needs of the world.

The whole idea is that the believer never sees an end to what he receives from God. The giving and receiving goes on and on, never ending. The resource is unending, never ceasing.

There is another idea behind what Jesus was saying: the idea of security and confidence and assurance. The man who seeks God first, who gives all he is and has, is assured of being taken care of—always. God promises the true believer that he will always have food, clothing, and shelter—if he truly seeks God first. A price tag cannot be put upon such assurance, confidence, and security. It is invaluable, more than a hundredfold. As long as the true believer is to remain on earth, until God is ready to take him home to heaven, the believer is assured of God's taking care of him. And then on top of all this, there is life eternal, the glorious experience of living forever in all the majesty and glory of God and serving Him forever.

> **"But seek ye first the kingdom of God, and his righteousness; and all these things shall be added unto you" (Mt.6:33; see Mt.6:25-34).**
> **"The thief cometh not, but for to steal, and to kill, and to destroy: I am come that they might have life, and that they might have it more abundantly" (Jn.10:10).**
> **"And God is able to make all grace abound toward you; that ye, always having all sufficiency in all things, may abound to every good work" (2 Co.9:8).**
> **"Now unto him that is able to do exceeding abundantly above all that we ask or think, according to the power that worketh in us" (Ep.3:20).**
> **"But my God shall supply all your need according to his riches in glory by Christ Jesus" (Ph.4:19).**
> **"For so an entrance shall be ministered unto you abundantly into the everlasting kingdom of our Lord and Saviour Jesus Christ" (2 Pe.1:11).**
> **"And ye shall serve the LORD your God, and he shall bless thy bread, and thy water; and I will take sickness away from the midst of thee" (Ex.23:25).**
> **"Thou preparest a table before me in the presence of mine enemies: thou anointest my head with oil; my cup runneth over" (Ps.23:5).**
> **"They shall be abundantly satisfied with the fatness of thy house; and thou shalt make them drink of the river of thy pleasures" (Ps.36:8).**
> **"Blessed be the Lord, who daily loadeth us with benefits, even the God of our salvation" (Ps.68:19).**
> **"Then shall he give the rain of thy seed, that thou shalt sow the ground withal; and bread of the increase of the earth, and it shall be fat and plenteous: in that day shall thy cattle feed in large pastures" (Is.30:23).**
> **"And ye shall eat in plenty, and be satisfied, and praise the name of the Lord your God, that hath dealt wondrously with you: and my people shall never be ashamed" (Joel 2:26).**
> **"Bring ye all the tithes into the storehouse, that there may be meat in mine house, and prove me now herewith, saith the LORD of hosts, if I will not open you the windows of heaven, and pour you out a blessing, that there shall not be room enough to receive it" (Mal.3:10).**

3 (10:30) **Reward—Persecution**: the true disciple also receives the reward of persecution. This statement is shocking. How can persecution be considered a reward? Peter tells us.

> **"If ye be reproached for the name of Christ, happy are ye; for the spirit of glory and of God resteth upon you: on their part he is evil spoken of, but on your part he is glorified" (1 Pe.4:14).**

The words "reproached for...Christ" mean that a believer suffers for righteousness; that is, he is persecuted or abused or ridiculed for Christ. When a disciple suffers for Christ, "the Spirit of glory and of God rests upon [him]." He is given a very *special closeness*, a oneness with Christ that is beyond imagination, unexplainable (Ac.7:54-60). The Holy Spirit infuses him with a deep, *intense consciousness* of the Lord's presence, a consciousness so deep that it cannot be experienced apart from some severe experience of suffering.

In suffering for Christ, the disciple also experiences a very special identification with Christ. For as the Lord suffered on behalf of the disciple, so now the disciple suffers on behalf of the Lord. There is a sense in which the disciple's sufferings "fill up the sufferings of Christ" and complete the sufferings of Christ for the church (see note—Col.1:24).

These two experiences, gaining a deeper consciousness of the Lord's presence and being used to complete the sufferings for the church, are gained only through suffering. They make suffering a privilege and a joy for the disciple, for the disciple suffers even as his Lord suffered (Mt.10:24-25; Acts 5:41).

> **"Blessed are ye, when men shall revile you, and persecute you, and shall say all manner of evil against you falsely, for my sake. Rejoice, and be exceeding glad: for great is your reward in heaven: for so persecuted they the prophets which were before you" (Mt.5:11-12).**
> **"For unto you it is given in the behalf of Christ, not only to believe on him, but also to suffer for his sake" (Ph.1:29).**
> **"Yea, and all that will live godly in Christ Jesus shall suffer persecution" (2 Ti.3:12).**
> **"For even hereunto were ye called: because Christ also suffered for us, leaving us an example, that ye should follow his steps" (1 Pe.2:21).**
> **"But and if ye suffer for righteousness' sake, happy are ye: and be not afraid of their terror, neither be troubled" (1 Pe.3:14).**

4 (10:30) **Reward—Eternal Life**: the true disciple receives eternal life. Christ not only promises to reward the disciple in this life, He promises to reward him "in the world to come [with] eternal life." Imagine the reward: to *live forever in a perfect state of being*. Imagine the heavens and earth's being made into "a new heavens and earth," being made perfect and eternal. Living forever in that *perfect world* is what Christ promises to the true disciple, the man who gives all he is and has for Christ's sake, and the gospel's (see notes and DEEPER STUDY # 1—Mt.19:28; DEEPER STUDY # 2—Jn.1:4; DEEPER STUDY # 1—17:2-3).

"One thing thou lackest: go thy way, sell whatsoever thou hast, and give to the poor, and thou shalt have treasure in heaven: and come, take up the cross, and follow me" (Mk.10:21).

"Verily, verily, I say unto you, He that heareth my word, and believeth on him that sent me, hath everlasting life, and shall not come into condemnation; but is passed from death unto life" (Jn.5:24).

5 (10:31) **Reward—Judgment**: Jesus both assured and warned the disciples. God is going to switch and change and reverse the order of men in heaven. Many who are first in this world are going to be placed last, and they are going to be last forever, for all eternity. But many who are last are going to be placed *first* by God forever.

God is going to place every man exactly where he belongs. He is going to rectify injustices. No matter what the esteem and rank are on earth, if a man belongs last, God is going to place him last. If he belongs first, God is going to place him first. And Christ actually says that "many" changes are coming. The idea is that the majority of people will be switched. In God's eyes, some of the dearest, most repentant, heart-broken, and diligent people are now last; but He is going to exalt them to be ever so near and close to Him.

"For we must all appear before the judgment seat of Christ; that every one may receive the things done in his body, according to that he hath done, whether it be good or bad" (2 Co.5:10).

"Every man's work shall be made manifest: for the day shall declare it, because it shall be revealed by fire; and the fire shall try every man's work of what sort it is. If any man's work abide which he hath built thereupon, he shall receive a reward. If any man's work shall be burned, he shall suffer loss: but he himself shall be saved; yet so as by fire" (1 Co.3:13-15).

"He hath put down the mighty from their seats, and exalted them of low degree" (Lu.1:52).

"Woe unto you that are full! for ye shall hunger. Woe unto you that laugh now! for ye shall mourn and weep" (Lu.6:25).

"Son, remember that thou in thy lifetime receivedst thy good things, and likewise Lazarus evil things: but now he is comforted, and thou art tormented" (Lu.16:25).

"But God is the judge: he putteth down one, and setteth up another" (Ps.75:7).

Outline	Heading / Verse	Verse	Outline
	F. The Third Prediction of Death: The Problem of Christ's Death, 10:32-34 *(Mt. 20:17-19; Lu. 18:31-34)*	pen unto him,	
		33 Saying, Behold, we go up to Jerusalem; and the Son of man shall be delivered unto the chief priests, and unto the	**4. Jesus' magnificent love & courage** a. He will be betrayed to the Jews & condemned
1. Jesus' iron determination: Was set on His purpose—to die	32 And they were in the way going up to Jerusalem; and Jesus went before them:	scribes; and they shall condemn him to death, and shall deliver him to the Gentiles:	b. He will be handed over to the Gentiles, tortured & killed
2. Jesus' amazing drawing power: Many followed	and they were amazed; and as they followed, they were	34 And they shall mock him, and shall scourge him,	**5. Jesus' great purpose** a. To die
3. Jesus' thoughtful consideration: Took the disciples aside to explain His death	afraid. And he took again the twelve, and began to tell them what things should hap-	and shall spit upon him, and shall kill him: and the third day he shall rise again.	b. To arise

DIVISION VI

THE SON OF GOD'S LAST PUBLIC MINISTRY: JESUS DEALS WITH SOME SPECIAL PROBLEMS, 10:1-52

F. The Third Prediction of Death: The Problem of Christ's Death, 10:32-34

(10:32-34) **Introduction**: this is the third time that Mark stresses the death and resurrection of Christ. Christ was constantly drilling the fact into His disciples. (See outline and notes—Mk.8:31-33; 9:30-32; Mt.16:21-23; 17:22-23; 20:17-19. These passages should be studied along with this passage. Mt.17:22-23 includes most of the New Testament passages on the death and resurrection of Christ.) This passage gives a striking portrait of Jesus and deals very straightforwardly with the problem of His death.

1. Jesus' iron determination: was set on His purpose—to die (v.32).
2. Jesus' amazing drawing power: many followed (v.32).
3. Jesus' thoughtful consideration: took the disciples aside to explain His death (v.32).
4. Jesus' magnificent love and courage (v.33).
5. Jesus' great purpose (v.34).

[1] (10:32) **Jesus Christ, Death**: there was the iron determination of Jesus. The picture was graphic. Jesus had set the course for Jerusalem. As He walked along, He became engrossed in thought—the thought of the cross that lay ahead. As He had said earlier, "I have a baptism to be baptized with; and how am I straightened [constrained] till it be accomplished" (Lu.12:50). The time had now come. He was to go up to Jerusalem for the last time, go up to receive the baptism, the immersing of the cross. As He walked along thinking about the cross, He became so engrossed He lost consciousness of all around Him. God gave Him a spirit of determination, a determination so strong that He unconsciously quickened His pace and moved out far ahead of the disciples, so far that it perplexed the apostles. However, the point to see is the iron determination of Jesus. He was determined to face the cross. The cross lay right ahead of Him, yet it held so much meaning that He set His course to bear it. He was driven, constrained, pressed, compelled, determined (an iron determination) to bear the sufferings of the cross. Why?

a. The cross was the way to save the world.

> **"For God so loved the world, that he gave his only begotten Son, that whosoever believeth in him should not perish, but have everlasting life" (Jn.3:16).**
> **"And I, if I be lifted up from the earth, will draw all men unto me" (Jn.12:32).**
> **"Who his own self bare our sins in his own body on the tree, that we, being dead to sins, should live unto righteousness; by whose stripes ye were healed" (1 Pe.2:24).**
> **"For Christ also hath once suffered for sins, the just for the unjust, that he might bring us to God, being put to death in the flesh, but quickened by the Spirit" (1 Pe.3:18).**

b. The cross was the way to please God His Father (see note—Ep.5:2).

> **"I can of mine own self do nothing: as I hear, I judge: and my judgment is just; because I seek not mine own will, but the will of the Father which hath sent me" (Jn.5:30).**
> **"Now is my soul troubled; and what shall I say? Father, save me from this hour: but for this cause came I unto this hour. Father, glorify thy name. Then came there a voice from heaven, saying, I have both glorified it, and will glorify it again" (Jn.12:27-28).**
> **"But that the world may know that I love the Father; and as the Father gave me commandment, even so I do. Arise, let us go hence [to the cross]" (Jn.14:31).**
> **"I have glorified thee on the earth: I have finished the work which thou gavest me to do [die]" (Jn.17:4).**

c. The cross was the way to assure His own joy.

> **"Looking unto Jesus the author and finisher of our faith; who for the joy that was set before him endured the cross, despising the shame, and is set down at the right hand of the throne of God" (He.12:2).**

2 (10:32) **Jesus Christ, Death**: there was the amazing *drawing power* of Jesus. Note the two words used to describe the people's reaction to Jesus: amazed and afraid. We cannot be sure if the ones who were "afraid" were His apostles or some other disciples following Him. In either case, the reaction was amazement and fear. There were at least two reasons for these reactions.

a. Jesus' behavior was unusual. He usually walked along with the disciples, utilizing every moment as a teaching opportunity. It was His practice not to lose a moment, other than when He needed to be alone for meditation. When the disciples saw His striding out ahead of them, they knew something serious and unusual was occupying His mind. His pace and His preoccupation amazed and perplexed them.

b. Jesus' depth of thought and serious, foreboding countenance amazed and perplexed them. They marvelled that He could be so lost in thought that He would become unconscious of all around Him. He seemed to be focused on some happening that lay right before Him in Jerusalem. Whatever it was, He had to get there.

The point is this: Jesus' unusual behavior and foreboding countenance caused amazement and fear in the disciples. They could tell by Jesus' unusual actions that apparently something dreadful was about to happen. They had no idea what it was. Therefore, they were *bewildered, apprehensive, and hesitant* to move on. They were gripped with both amazement and fear. Yet note something: despite their not understanding and their fear, they followed right behind Jesus. They did not withdraw nor forsake Him. Why? Because they were drawn to Him through love. Jesus was their life. He had done so much for them, He was their all—all there was worth following. And they were thoroughly convinced that He was the true Messiah. They knew that to follow Him would be well worthwhile.

Thought 1. Many do not understand the behavior (sinless nature) or the depth of thought (teachings) of Christ. In such cases Christ demands the same response He demanded of the disciples: faith. He expects us to follow Him even when we may not understand.

Thought 2. The love of Jesus drew the disciples to Him. They loved Him because He loved them. It was love that kept them following after Him, even when they feared and did not understand.

"For the love of Christ constraineth us; because we thus judge, that if one died for all, then were all dead: and that he died for all, that they which live should not henceforth live unto themselves, but unto him which died for them, and rose again" (2 Co.5:14-15).

"Perfect love casts out fear" (1 Jn.4:18).

3 (10:32) **Jesus Christ, Death**: there was the thoughtful consideration of Jesus. This can be stated very simply. Jesus became aware of the disciples' bewilderment and fear. They were distressed, caught in the dark and unable to see what lay ahead. They needed His help. They needed to be prepared for the onrushing tragedy. They were hard to teach and slow to learn. Jesus had already informed them of His impending death and of God's concept of the Messiah. Of necessity, He had to consider the disciples and their slowness and dullness of heart and continue to teach them until they grasped God's Messiahship. As always, He took them aside to meet their need. (See notes—Lu.18:31-34.)

Thought 1. Note three important lessons.
(1) Jesus will always meet our need, no matter how small or large.
(2) It is not Jesus' will for us to be bewildered or gripped by fear.
(3) We must, however, remember that we are to walk by faith. Therefore, it is not God's purpose for us to know all things.

"For God hath not given us the spirit of fear; but of power, and of love, and of a sound mind" (2 Ti.1:7).

"Now the just shall live by faith: but if any man draw back, my soul shall have no pleasure in him. But we are not of them who draw back unto perdition; but of them that believe to the saving of the soul" (He.10:38-39).

"Yea, though I walk through the valley of the shadow of death, I will fear no evil: for thou art with me; thy rod and thy staff they comfort me" (Ps.23:4).

"Oh how great is thy goodness, which thou hast laid up for them that fear thee; which thou hast wrought for them that trust in thee before the sons of men!" (Ps.31:19).

"Therefore will not we fear, though the earth be removed, and though the mountains be carried into the midst of the sea" (Ps.46:2).

"Behold, God is my salvation; I will trust, and not be afraid: for the Lord JEHOVAH is my strength and my song; he also is become my salvation" (Is.12:2).

"For since the beginning of the world men have not heard, nor perceived by the ear, neither hath the eye seen, O God, beside thee, what he hath prepared for him that waiteth for him" (Is.64:4).

4 (10:33) **Jesus Christ, Death; Love**: there was the magnificent love and courage of Jesus. The great love of Jesus is seen in many things, but the epitomy of His love is seen in one supreme act: the *willingness* of Jesus to be sacrificed for man.

Note that Jesus knew what lay ahead of Him in Jerusalem. He made two points.

a. He would be delivered to the Jews and condemned. The word *delivered* (paradothesetai) means to be delivered over into. It means that His death was determined, ordained, set in the plan and counsel of God. Note that Jesus said, "The

Son of Man shall be delivered." His death was *right before His face*, ready to take place.

Jesus had already named the men who would kill Him (see DEEPER STUDY # 1—Mt.16:21). The betrayal would be by *Judas* who would identify Him for the *elders*, *chief priests*, and *Scribes*; and they in turn would deliver Him to the *Gentiles* (or Romans) for execution (Mt.20:19).

Peter, in preaching to the Jews right after Pentecost, accused the Jews: "Ye have taken [Him] and by wicked hands [the hands of the lawless Gentiles and Romans] have crucified and slain" (Ac.2:23).

The fact that Jesus was being condemned by the Jews, the people who had been chosen to bring salvation to the world, must have cut Him deeply. "He came unto His own [the Jews] and His own received Him not" (Jn.1:11).

b. He would be delivered to the Gentiles and tortured and killed. Note that the prosecutors of Jesus were named. They were to be the Jews, in particular the leaders among the Jews: the chief priests and Scribes and elders (see DEEPER STUDY #1—Mt.16:21; note—1 Th.2:15-16). But note, they were to be only the prosecutors, not the executioners. They were forbidden by law to execute anyone (Jn.18:31). They had to deliver Jesus over to the Gentiles for execution.

There is symbolism seen in this fact: (1) both Jew and Gentile (the world) are guilty of the death of God's Son, and (2) Jesus was to bear the sins of both Jew and Gentile (the world) in His death. He was to reconcile both to God. (See outline and notes—Ep.2:14-15; 2:16-17.)

Jesus was to be delivered to the Gentiles for torture and execution. Note the four forms of torture mentioned.

1. Mockery: to ridicule, scorn, insult, humiliate, defy, jeer.
2. Scourge: to beat with a rod or a whip weighted with either jagged metal or bone chips. Thirty-nine or forty lashes were inflicted. The whole purpose of scourging was to inflict severe pain.
3. Spitting: a sign of utter contempt (see DEEPER STUDY # 1—Mk.14:65).
4. Crucifixion: see DEEPER STUDY # 1—Mt.27:26-44 for the terrible suffering of the cross.

Jesus bore the sins of man, suffering the ultimate degree of pain. He suffered pain in an absolute sense.

⇒ Mentally, while He was being tortured, His mind was bound to be upon why He was suffering. He was thinking about the sin of man and the problem sin had caused God. Imagine the world's sin—all of it, the enormity and awfulness of it—consuming His mind. He was suffering mentally to the ultimate degree.

⇒ Spiritually, His heart was being broken. Those whom He loved so much were committing a sin so horrendous it defied imagination. They were rebelling against God so much that they were killing God's own Son.

In addition, and more terrible, His own Father was to turn His back upon Him. He was to be separated from God, bearing the condemnation of sin for man (see notes—Mt.27:46-49; Mk.15:34). He was beginning to bear and was going to bear spiritual pain in an absolute sense (1 Pe.2:24; 2 Co.5:21. See Is.53:4-7 for a descriptive account of His bearing our sin.)

⇒ Physically, His pain was to be more severe because of the mental and spiritual pressure He was having to bear at the same time. There is also truth to the fact that the more ridicule within a persecutor's heart, the more he tortures his victim (see the crown of thorns, royal robe, and excessive mockery of the soldiers). The fact that Jesus claimed to be the Son of God aroused the hearts of the persecutors to inflict more scorn and torture.

Thought 1. Magnificent is the glorious love of Christ—His *willingness* to bear so much for us!

"I am the good shepherd: the good shepherd giveth his life for the sheep" (Jn.10:11).

"As the Father knoweth me, even so know I the Father: and I lay down my life for the sheep" (Jn.10:15).

"Therefore doth my Father love me, because I lay down my life, that I might take it again. No man taketh it from me, but I lay it down of myself. I have power to lay it down, and I have power to take it again. This commandment have I received of my Father" (Jn.10:17-18).

"Who gave himself for our sins, that he might deliver us from this present evil world, according to the will of God and our Father" (Ga.1:4).

"And walk in love, as Christ also hath loved us, and hath given himself for us an offering and a sacrifice to God for a sweetsmelling savour" (Ep.5:2).

"Who gave himself for us, that he might redeem us from all iniquity, and purify unto himself a peculiar people, zealous of good works" (Tit.2:14).

"Hereby perceive we the love of God, because he laid down his life for us: and we ought to lay down our lives for the brethren" (1 Jn.3:16).

"And from Jesus Christ, who is the faithful witness, and the first begotten of the dead, and the prince of the kings of the earth. Unto him that loved us, and washed us from our sins in his own blood" (Re.1:5).

5 (10:34) **Jesus Christ, Death**: there was the great purpose of Jesus. He was to die and rise again.

"Who his own self bare our sins in his own body on the tree, that we, being dead to sins, should live unto righteousness: by whose stripes ye were healed" (1 Pe.2:24).

The summit of pain was experienced in the sufferings and death of Jesus Christ. He suffered pain to the ultimate degree, in an absolute sense. Yet in the midst of such terrible suffering, there is something that is very precious—a thought, a truth that should be very, very precious to us. It is this: *Jesus' death was dear to his heart*—dear despite the terrible suffering He was to endure. In a way unknown to man and which can never be understood by man, Jesus set His heart and face toward the cross. He was consumed and obsessed with the cross. Why? Because the cross was the focus of God's purpose throughout all eternity.

a. The cross was dear to His heart because it was His Father's will. In dying, He could please His Father, and pleasing His Father was the supreme objective of His life (see note—Ep.5:2).

> **"No man taketh it from me, but I lay it down of myself. I have power to lay it down, and I have power to take it again. This commandment have I received of my Father" (Jn.10:18).**
>
> **"And walk in love, as Christ also hath loved us, and hath given himself for us an offering and a sacrifice to God for a sweetsmelling savour" (Ep.5:2).**

b. The cross was dear to His heart because it was the means by which He was to gain many brothers (see note—Ro.8:28-39).

> **"But when the fulness of the time was come, God sent forth his Son, made of a woman, made under the law, to redeem them that were under the law, that we might receive the adoption of sons. And because ye are sons, God hath sent forth the Spirit of his Son into your hearts, crying, Abba, Father" (Ga.4:4-6).**
>
> **"For whom he did foreknow, he also did predestinate to be conformed to the image of his Son, that he might be the firstborn among many brethren" (Ro.8:29).**

c. The cross was dear to His heart because through death He was to be made "the captain" of man's salvation.

> **"But we see Jesus, who was made a little lower than the angels for the suffering of death, crowned with glory and honour; that he by the grace of God should taste death for every man. For it became him, for whom are all things, and by whom are all things, in bringing many sons unto glory, to make the captain of their salvation perfect through sufferings" (He.2:9-10).**

d. The cross was dear to His heart because by His death He was to destroy the power of the devil over man, that is, death.

> **"Forasmuch then as the children are partakers of flesh and blood, he also himself likewise took part of the same; that through death he might destroy him that had the power of death, that is, the devil; and deliver them who through fear of death were all their lifetime subject to bondage" (He.2:14-15).**

e. The cross was dear to His heart because by the cross He was to reconcile all men, reconcile them both to God and to one another (see outline and notes—Ep.2:13-18).

> **"But now in Christ Jesus ye who sometimes were far off are made nigh by the blood of Christ. For he is our peace, who hath made both one, and hath broken down the middle wall of partition between us....And that he might reconcile both unto God in one body by the cross, having slain the enmity thereby" (Ep.2:13-14, 16).**

f. The cross was dear to His heart because through death He was to arise and return to His former glory which He had with the Father before the foundation of the world (Jn.17:1-5). (See notes, *Resurrection*—Mt.17:23; note and DEEPER STUDY #1—Acts 1:3; DEEPER STUDY #4—2:24.)

> **"I have glorified thee on the earth: I have finished the work which thou gavest me to do. And now, O Father, glorify thou me with thine own self with the glory which I had with thee before the world was....Father, I will that they also, whom thou hast given me, be with me where I am; that they may behold my glory, which thou hast given me: for thou lovedst me before the foundation of the world" (Jn.17:4-5, 24).**

	G. The Problem of Ambition, 10:35-45 *(Mt. 20:20-28; Lu. 22:24-47)*
1. The deceitfulness of wrong ambition a. A secret approach, v.41 b. An unlimited request	35 And James and John, the sons of Zebedee, come unto him, saying, Master, we would that thou shouldest do for us whatsoever we shall desire.
2. The possible motives for ambition a. Favoritism & wealth	36 And he said unto them, What would ye that I should do for you?
b. Power & social status c. Love, faith, loyalty	37 They said unto him, Grant unto us that we may sit, one on thy right hand, and the other on thy left hand, in thy glory.
3. The great price of ambition[DS1] a. The cup: Sacrifice & suffering b. The baptism: Immersed, dying to self	38 But Jesus said unto them, Ye know not what ye ask: can ye drink of the cup that I drink of? and be baptized with the baptism that I am baptized with?
c. The prophecy: The certainty of paying the price[DS2,3]	39 And they said unto him, We can. And Jesus said unto them, Ye shall indeed drink of the cup that I drink of; and with the baptism that I am baptized withal shall ye be

baptized:	
40 But to sit on my right hand and on my left hand is not mine to give; but it shall be given to them for whom it is prepared.	**4. The exclusive right of God regarding ambition**
41 And when the ten heard it, they began to be much displeased with James and John.	**5. The potential conflict among men with ambition**
42 But Jesus called them to him, and saith unto them, Ye know that they which are accounted to rule over the Gentiles exercise lordship over them; and their great ones exercise authority upon them.	**6. The meaning & greatness of good ambition** a. Not to rule, not to exercise authority
43 But so shall it not be among you: but whosoever will be great among you, shall be your minister:	b. To be a servant
44 And whosoever of you will be the chiefest, shall be servant of all.	c. To be a slave, a bond-slave
45 For even the Son of man came not to be ministered unto, but to minister, and to give his life a ransom for many.	**7. The supreme example of ambition** a. Supreme humiliation b. Supreme mission c. Supreme price[DS4]

DIVISION VI

THE SON OF GOD'S LAST PUBLIC MINISTRY: JESUS DEALS WITH SOME SPECIAL PROBLEMS, 10:1-52

G. The Problem of Ambition, 10:35-45

(10:35-45) **Introduction**: Jesus was on His way to Jerusalem. This was to be a momentous visit to the capital. This was the visit when the crises of His death and resurrection were to take place. He had just shared the fact of the crisis again (v.17-19). For months it had consumed His attention and private messages to the disciples (Mt.16:13-20; 16:21-28; 17:1-13; 17:22; 17:24-27; 20:17). There was no question in the disciples' minds: this visit to Jerusalem was the momentous event for which they had long looked. Jesus was about to free Israel and set up His kingdom on earth.

We, who live today, know what Jesus meant by His death and resurrection. He was to die for our sins and be raised again to impart new life to us. But the disciples did not know this. Jesus had not yet died and been raised from the dead. To them He was speaking of an earthly and material kingdom. Therefore, if He was about to set up His kingdom, now was the time to seize the positions of power in His kingdom. Now was the time to secure the positions of rule and authority. (See notes—Mt.1:1; DEEPER STUDY # 1—1:18; DEEPER STUDY # 3—3:11; notes—11:1-6; 11:2-3; DEEPER STUDY # 1—11:5; DEEPER STUDY # 2—11:6; DEEPER STUDY # 1—12:16; note—Lu.7:21-23.)

This is what James and John were doing. They were assuring themselves of key positions in Jesus' government. (See outlines and notes—Mt.18:1-4; Lu.22:24-30.)

1. The deceitfulness of wrong ambition (v.35).
2. The possible motives for ambition (vv.36-37).
3. The great price of ambition (vv.38-39).
4. The exclusive right of God regarding ambition (v.40).
5. The potential conflict among men with ambition (v.41).
6. The meaning and greatness of good ambition (vv.42-44).
7. The supreme example of ambition (v.45).

1 (10:35) **Ambition**: the deceitfulness of wrong ambition. Note what James and John did.

a. They made a secret approach to Jesus. They wanted to get the upper hand on the other disciples; they were aware that the other disciples were also ambitious for position (see Lu.9:46). They knew that they must get some kind of inside track. They persuaded their mother to go with them, and they approached Jesus when He was off by Himself (Mt.20:20-21). Remember that Salome was probably the sister of Mary, the aunt of Jesus. Most likely James and John felt she would add weight to their request. Therefore, they made a secret approach to Jesus. The ambition that was gripping their heart was not healthy ambition; it was evil ambition. And evil ambition is sneaky. It tries to get an inside track, the upper hand, by hook or crook. It uses any means whatsoever, including the use and misuse of people, even loved ones (see Salome).

b. They made an unlimited appeal. Note their words, "Do for us whatsoever we shall desire." Again, they were being sneaky. They tried to get a commitment before they revealed their request. They sensed their desire might be wrong and evil; but they subdued the sense of conscience, blinded by the lust for honor, position, power, wealth, and recognition.

Thought 1. Wrong or evil ambition is *always deceitful* and *sneaky*. When a man wants something he should not have and he is determined to get it anyway, he becomes sneaky.

⇒ He will sneak to get things of the world.
⇒ He will sneak to get things of the flesh.
⇒ He will sneak to use and misuse people.

"And whosoever shall exalt himself shall be abased; and he that shall humble himself shall be exalted" (Mt.23:12).

"How can ye believe, which receive honour one of another, and seek not the honour that cometh from God only?" (Jn.5:44).

"Though thou exalt thyself as the eagle, and though thou set thy nest among the stars, thence will I bring thee down, saith the LORD" (Ob.4).

2 (10:36-37) **Ambition—Motive**: the possible motives for ambition. Jesus asked the two men what their request was. They answered straight to the point, wasting no time, as any conscientious leader would: "Grant us the top positions in your kingdom [glory, government] which you are going to set up when we get to Jerusalem." The men were extremely ambitious. They wanted to be the top ministers of state in Christ's government.

What needs to be noted is that ambition can be good or bad. The determining factor is motive. One's motive makes ambition either good or bad. The ambition of James and John exposes several possible motives. Each one touches a sensitive spot within every man and urges every man to examine the motives of his heart (see note, *Ambition*—Mt.20:20-21).

a. There was the motive of favoritism. James and John, along with Peter, formed an inner circle around Christ (see DEEPER STUDY #1—Mk.9:2). They apparently had some feeling that they were special, the favorites of Christ; therefore, they were due the top positions.

Thought 1. Feeling special, as though one is a favorite of God, is a common sin—a sin of pride. How many of us have felt we are one of God's specials or favorites? How often have we felt this way?

Thought 2. The inner circle, or the multi-gifted, often feel as though they are the special ones of God or of the church. Some often feel as though they are due special favors.

"God is no respecter of persons" (Ac.10:34).

"Pride goeth before destruction, and a haughty spirit before a fall" (Pr.16:18). (Remember James' and John's desertion of Christ at the cross.)

b. There was the motive of wealth. Zebedee, the father of James and John, was apparently wealthy. He owned a fishing business large enough to furnish fish for the palace (see note—Mk.1:20; Jn.18:15-18). They were better off financially than some of the other disciples. There was the possibility that the two men were acting as selfish, pampered young men seeking more. Wealth did carry weight with monarchs of their day, and they knew it.

Thought 1. Note two points.

(1) Wealth can make a man self-centered. It can pamper and make one selfish. It can cause one to expect more attention, more honor, more recognition, more favor.
(2) Those who have wealth often want more. And they set out to get more, whether wise or unwise, whether right or wrong. The wisdom and righteousness of having wealth are determined by a person's motive and true need.

"And the cares of this world, and the deceitfulness of riches, and the lusts of other things entering in, choke the word, and it becometh unfruitful" (Mk.4:19).

"But they that will be rich fall into temptation and a snare, and into many foolish and hurtful lusts, which drown men in destruction and perdition" (1 Ti.6:9).

c. There was the motive of power, position, influence, and authority. This was clearly one of the motives of James and John. They wanted to be right next to Jesus in position and influence, power and authority. It is the very thing they asked.

Thought 1. Men want position. Men think in terms of position and influence. Within the business world, men want a position that assures influence and reward. Within the church, some want a position of leadership and of influence. Men seldom think in terms of service or in terms of how they can help the company or the church. Too often their thoughts are on the honor, the reward, the influence, the position they will receive.

Thought 2. How many seek to be next to the boss, the pastor, the leader, or the teacher, seeking to curry his favor; seeking to be recognized by him or by others as knowing him well and as being favored by him?

"Let no man seek his own, but every man another's wealth" (1 Co.10:24).

"Even as I please all men in all things, not seeking mine own profit, but the profit of many, that they may be saved" (1 Co.10:33).

"For ye know the grace of our Lord Jesus Christ, that, though he was rich, yet for your sakes he became poor, that ye through his poverty might be rich" (2 Co.8:9).

"Be of the same mind one toward another. Mind not high things, but condescend to men of low estate. Be not wise in your own conceits" (Ro.12:16).

"Look not every man on his own things, but every man also on the things of others" (Ph.2:4).

d. There was the motive of social status. James and John did have some social standing. They were somewhat wealthy and were accepted within the palace and were personally known by the High Priest (see notes—Mk.1:20; Jn.18:15-18. See Jn.18:16.)

Social standing often makes a person feel that he is entitled to more—more position, more recognition, a higher seat. Social standing can also make one feel he is better or above others. Perhaps James and John had a tinge of both feelings.

e. There was the motive of love, faith, and loyalty. When ambition is rooted in the Lord and steeped in love and loyalty, it is *always right and healthy*. There is the possibility that James and John wanted to be next to Jesus because they were sensing some degree of love and loyalty to Him. Their love and loyalty to Him would not be the dominant force in their ambition right now, but it was definitely present.

⇒ They definitely believed Jesus: His Word, His promises, His kingdom, His power. They were showing loyalty to Christ by expressing confidence in His power to usher in the Kingdom of God. They were asking for positions in His kingdom. They knew He was the true Messiah, the Son of the living God who was to become the King of kings and Lord of lords.

⇒ They definitely wanted the positions because they wanted to be next to Him. To them He *deserved* the kingdom and the honor. He deserved it because He had done so much and was going to do so much for them and for the people of God.

"For the Father himself loveth you, because ye have loved me, and have believed that I came out from God. I came forth from the Father, and am come into the world: again, I leave the world, and go to the Father. His disciples said unto him, Lo, now speakest thou plainly, and speakest no proverb. Now are we sure that thou knowest all things, and needest not that any man should ask thee: by this we believe that thou camest forth from God" (Jn.16:27-30).

"Grace be with all them that love our Lord Jesus Christ in sincerity" (Ep.6:24).

"Whom having not seen, ye love; in whom, though now ye see him not, yet believing, ye rejoice with joy unspeakable and full of glory" (1 Pe.1:8).

[3] (10:38-39) **Ambition—Cup—Baptism**: the great price of ambition. Jesus was straightforward, pulling no punches with these two ambitious men. "Ye know not what ye ask. Can you drink of the cup that I drink of? and be baptized with the baptism that I am baptized with?" Jesus was asking the ambitious believer, "Can you go through the terrible experience I have to suffer? Can you drink the cup of my terrible agony, of my inward agony and pain? Can you bear the baptism of my terrible sufferings?" (See DEEPER STUDY # 1, *Cup—Baptism*—Mk.10:38-39 for discussion.)

Note: the two men accepted the Lord's challenge, and they responded immediately, very positively: "We can." Of course, they did not know what they were doing, not fully. Nevertheless, at this particular moment they were willing to die for Christ in Jerusalem if necessary.

Note also that Jesus foretold them that they would pay the price for their ambition (see DEEPER STUDY # 2,3—Mk.10:39 for discussion).

Thought 1. The same challenge is issued to every man. We are to drink the Lord's cup and be baptized with His baptism.

(1) We are to suffer for His sake, to labor and serve to the point of exhaustion in getting the gospel out and in ministering to a lost world.

(2) We are to bear persecution if necessary to fulfill His mission. In essence, we are to deny self, do whatever is necessary (see notes and DEEPER STUDY # 1—Lu.9:23; DEEPER STUDY # 1—Mk.10:38-39).

Thought 2. We should follow the example of James and John. We should accept the Lord's challenge...

- accept it immediately, not hesitating at all.
- accept it even though we may not fully understand what it involves.

"So likewise, whosoever he be of you that forsaketh not all that he hath, he cannot be my disciple" (Lu.14:33).

Thought 3. There is a price to pay for ambition. If a man really wants to achieve, he must get to it, and getting to it takes time and work. It involves sacrifice and pain, sweat and tears, isolation and loneliness, and often involves sacrificing his social life. In all honesty, few are willing to pay such a price.

"And he said to them all, If any man will come after me, let him deny himself, and take up his cross daily, and follow me. For whosoever will save his life shall lose it: but whosoever will lose his life for my sake, the same shall save it" (Lu.9:23-24).

"If any man come to me, and hate not his father, and mother, and wife, and children, and brethren, and sisters, yea, and his own life also, he cannot be my disciple. And whosoever doth not bear his cross, and come after me, cannot be my disciple" (Lu.14:26-27).

"For if ye live after the flesh, ye shall die: but if ye through the Spirit do mortify the deeds of the body, ye shall live" (Ro.8:13).

"And they that are Christ's have crucified the flesh with the affections and lusts" (Ga.5:24).

"Yea doubtless, and I count all things but loss for the excellency of the knowledge of Christ Jesus my Lord: for whom I have suffered the loss of all things, and do count them but dung, that I may win Christ" (Ph.3:8).

DEEPER STUDY # 1

(10:38-39) **Cup—Baptism**: there is a difference between drinking the cup of suffering and being baptized with suffering. The cup refers more to what one takes into himself and bears within himself. It is more internal suffering, inward agony. The baptism refers more to what is put upon one from the outside. It is more external suffering.

The cup means drinking the bitterness and agony of trials, pain, hurt, sorrow, heartbreak, suffering, disappointment, and tears (see Christ's experience in the Garden of Gethsemane, Mt.26:36-46; His sufferings, Mt.20:19; 27:46-49; and John's experience on Patmos, Rev.1:9; see Introduction—Date).

The baptism of suffering means being immersed in the rapids of affliction, rejection, abuse, ridicule, opposition, persecution, and martyrdom.

The Christian believer who truly lives and witnesses for Christ will drink His cup and be baptized with His baptism. Just think for a moment. Christ demands *all we are and have* in order to help people and to carry the message of salvation to a lost world. If we should be serious and give *all we are and have*, just imagine the cost to us. That is how different we would be from the world. Imagine the world's reaction to us. That is the reason Jesus and the apostles met with so much opposition so often. They gave *all they were and had* and lived so differently. They lived for God instead of living for self and the world. Therefore, the world could not understand them. Some ignored and others ridiculed, abused, persecuted, and even killed them. They had the Lord's cup and baptism of suffering and sacrifice to bear. And so do all who truly follow Christ. (See outlines and notes—Mt.10:16-23; 10:24-33; 10:34-42; 19:23-26; 19:27-30. See Mt.10:22; Ph.1:28; 2 Ti.3:12; 1 Pe.2:21; 4:1-5; 5:10; Mt.19:29; Ro.8:16-17.)

DEEPER STUDY # 2

(10:39) **James**: was killed by Herod. He was the first apostle to drink the cup of martyrdom.

DEEPER STUDY # 3

(10:39) **John**: lived to be around one hundred years old. Just how John died is unknown; however, he drank the cup and was baptized with suffering in a most distressful way.

1. He witnessed the sufferings of Jesus' death.
2. He lived through the murder and deaths of all the other apostles.
3. He lived a long life of banishment and exile on the island of Patmos (see Introduction, Revelation—Date).

4 (10:40) **Ambition**: the prerogative of God in ambition. Note the exact words of Jesus: "To sit...is not mine to give; but it shall be given to them for whom it is prepared." Two things are being said.

a. Jesus said that some *will sit* on His right and some on His left hand. God is preparing to bestow such honor upon some. This points toward degrees of glory in heaven.

b. Jesus said that the right to reign with Him is to be determined by God alone (that is, His absolute justice). He also makes a distinction between the *great*, who only commit themselves to minister and the *chief* (greatest), who commit themselves to be *bond-slaves*. (See note—Mt.20:23-28.)

"What I tell you in darkness, that speak ye in light: and what ye hear in the ear, that preach ye upon the housetops" (Mt.10:27).

"If any man serve me, let him follow me; and where I am, there shall also my servant be: if any man serve me, him will my Father honour" (Jn.12:26).

"If I then, your Lord and Master, have washed your feet; ye also ought to wash one another's feet" (Jn.13:14).

"He saith to him again the second time, Simon, son of Jonas, lovest thou me? He saith unto him, Yea, Lord; thou knowest that I love thee. He saith unto him, Feed my sheep" (Jn.21:16).

"For ye are bought with a price [Christ's blood]: therefore glorify God in your body, and in your spirit, which are God's" (1 Co.6:20).

"For he that is called in the Lord, being a servant, is the Lord's freeman: likewise also he that is called, being free, is Christ's servant" (1 Co.7:22).

"Knowing that of the Lord ye shall receive the reward of the inheritance: for ye serve the Lord Christ" (Col.3:24).

5 (10:41) **Ambition**: the potential conflict among men with ambition. How did the other ten disciples hear what James and John had done? They probably saw the two approach Jesus off in the distance. They saw them bow before Him

(Mt.20:20). Such was most unusual because of their daily association with Him. They knew something unusual was happening. When James and John returned, the ten asked what was going on. Of course, James and John were hesitant to reveal the truth. But, as would be expected, this only aroused the disciples' curiosity and cross-examination more. They pressed and pressed the issue until James and John had to tell their evil and ugly plot.

⇒ Anger was aroused.
⇒ Tempers flared.
⇒ Arguments became inflamed.

The ten were indignant with James and John. What right did they have to do such a thing? Why did they deserve a higher position than any of them? Jealousy, envy, pride, self-centeredness, and bitterness bred within the heart of each against the two. Perhaps even hatred was being expressed. One thing is certain. The band of disciples was threatened; their cohesiveness and the very work of the Lord was at stake. A divisiveness beyond repair was possible.

Thought 1. Selfish ambition can cause some terrible things among men. It can cause...

- jealousy
- envy
- bitterness
- anger
- hatred
- sneakiness
- conflict
- self-centeredness
- suffering
- divisiveness
- death
- destruction

"He loveth transgression that loveth strife: and he that exalteth his gate seeketh destruction" (Pr.17:19).

"It is not good to eat much honey: so for men to search their own glory is not glory" (Pr.25:27).

"And whosoever shall exalt himself shall be abased; and he that shall humble himself shall be exalted" (Mt.23:12).

"How can ye believe, which receive honour one of another, and seek not the honour that cometh from God only?" (Jn.5:44).

6 (10:42-44) **Ambition**: the greatness of good ambition. Jesus did not find fault with ambition on the whole. There is good and true ambition just as there is bad and false ambition. But Jesus was quite clear about the difference between the two. One is of the world, the other of God. Note exactly what He said. True ambition, ambition that is good and healthy, is an ambition that does not seek to rule and to exercise authority.

a. The world's view of ambition is twofold. Most men are caught up to some degree in worldly ambition, seeking more and more. Few are void of worldly ambition.

"Hear this, all ye people; give ear, all ye inhabitants of the world" (Ps.49:11).

1) There is the internal view of ambition. A man should have some degree of freedom to seek what he wishes. A man should be allowed some recognition, some position, some influence, some fame, some wealth, some gadgets, some vehicles, some machines. A man should be allowed to fulfill his ambition, seeking and securing whatever he wishes.
2) There is the external view of ambition. A man's ambition (greatness) is judged successful by...
   - his wealth
   - his influence
   - his home
   - his recognition
   - his vehicles
   - his social standing
   - his gadgets
   - his fame
   - his position
   - his authority

b. The Lord's view of ambition is fourfold.

1) True ambition or greatness is not exercising lordship and authority over people. It is not desiring the chief positions. True ambition is not self-centered and selfish, not worldly-minded.
2) True ambition does desire greatness. Note Jesus' exact words: "Whosoever will be great among you." But there is a crucial point to note: the greatness desired must focus upon Christ if it is to be true ambition. A man becomes great by doing what Christ says. The greatness sought *must not* be greatness for oneself, but in doing what the Son of God says. It is greatness due to obedience, due to doing what Christ has revealed.
3) True ambition (greatness) seeks to minister, not to be ministered unto (see Mk.10:45). It looks for people to help and for ways to help them, whether at work, home, play, or church. It is always seeking those who need a visit, care, attention, company, food, clothing, shelter, money. It seeks for the sake of ministering (see Mt.25:34-40).
4) True ambition (greatness) becomes the *servant of all.* The word *servant* (doulos) means a *bond-slave* (see note—Ro.1:1). Christ made a significant distinction between the terms *great* and *chief.* Note the difference.
   ⇒ The "great" are they who "minister."
   ⇒ The "chiefest" are they who are "servants" or *bond-slaves.*

What Jesus was saying is that among His disciples, *they who minister are great*, but they who are *bond-slaves are the chief.* The idea of ministering is that of occasional service, whereas the bond-slave is a person who is bound to the Lord every moment of life, always serving—regardless of hour or call or difficulty.

The idea of degrees of service is unquestionably in mind. Not every believer serves with the same fervor or commitment. The idea of degrees of reward for works is also conveyed by our Lord's teaching.

What Christ means is this: a person is to be a minister and a servant. True greatness is not found in being a lord or a master, but in ministering and serving others. True ambition and greatness is a person's becoming a *minister and a servant by nature*. He assumes the role of a servant, of a bond-slave (see notes, *Servant*—Ro.1:1).

"And whosoever shall give to drink unto one of these little ones a cup of cold water only in the name of a disciple, verily I say unto you, he shall in no wise lose his reward" (Mt.10:42).

"Even so it is not the will of your Father which is in heaven, that one of these little ones should perish" (Mt.18:14).

"But ye shall not be so: but he that is greatest among you, let him be as the younger; and he that is chief, as he that doth serve" (Lu.22:26).

"If I then, your Lord and Master, have washed your feet; ye also ought to wash one another's feet" (Jn.13:14).

"With good will doing service, as to the Lord, and not to men" (Ep.6:7).

"Wherefore we receiving a kingdom which cannot be moved, let us have grace, whereby we may serve God acceptably with reverence and godly fear" (He.12:28).

"By humility and the fear of the LORD are riches, and honor, and life" (Pr.22:4).

"He hath showed thee, O man, what is good; and what doth the LORD require of thee, but to do justly, and to love mercy, and to walk humbly with thy God?" (Mi.6:8).

7 (10:45) **Ambition—Jesus Christ, Purpose**: the supreme act of ambition is seen in Jesus Christ. He set His face like a flint to accomplish His purpose. This is seen in three supreme acts.

a. The supreme humiliation. This is the act of coming to earth: "The Son of Man *came*." The incarnation is the Son of God becoming man. To most men, mankind is the summit of creation on this earth. But within the span and scope of the universe and before God, man is nothing—not to an honest and thinking man. He is as a microbe on a speck of sand floating through what seems to be infinite space and lasting only about seventy years if he can.

In all reality, for God to become a member of so low a race of beings is unimaginable. It is the most humiliating act possible.

b. The supreme mission. There is the act of ministering: "[He] came not to be ministered unto, but to minister." He was treated as the lowest by the men to whom He came. Impossible, yet true! They gave Him no place to lay His head (Mt.8:20; Lu.9:58), and only three years after publicly announcing that He had come to save them, they killed Him. Now note: Jesus is the King of kings and Lord of lords, yet He secured his kingdom by becoming a minister and a servant to all. He did not "lord it" over men. He ministered to and served men. Because He became the servant to all, God has now highly exalted Him (Ph.2:8).

c. The supreme price. This is the act of giving His life "a ransom for many" (see DEEPER STUDY # 4—Mk.10:45 for discussion and verses).

DEEPER STUDY # 4

(10:45) **Ransom for many** (lutron anti pollon): a ransom in *exchange* (pollon) for many, a ransom for many, a ransom instead of many.

Ransom (lutron) is a means of setting loose in the Old Testament. It is the setting loose (ransom) of a life (Ex.21:30); it is the ransom price, the redemptive price for something, for example: a slave (Le.19:20), some land (Le.25:24), a captive (Is.45:13).

The Greek word for *ransom* (lutron) is significant. There is no question that the idea of *exchange* is present. Christ gave His life in *exchange*, as a substitute for many. The word is used two other times in the New Testament, in the equivalent passage in Mt.20:28 and in 1 Ti.2:6. In 1 Ti.2:6 the words are a *substitutionary ransom for all* (antilutron huper panton). In the Greek *huper* is the preposition for the idea of substitution. It is a substitution in behalf of all.

"And that he died for all, that they which live should not henceforth live unto themselves, but unto him which died for [huper] them, and rose again" (2 Co.5:15).

"For he hath made him to be sin for [huper] us, who knew no sin; that we might be made the righteousness of God in him" (2 Co.5:21).

"Who needeth not daily, as those high priests, to offer up sacrifice, first for his own sins, and then for [huper] the people's: for this he did once, when he offered up himself" (He.7:27).

"For if the blood of bulls and of goats, and the ashes of an heifer sprinkling the unclean, sanctifieth to the purifying of the flesh: how much more shall the blood of Christ, who through the eternal Spirit offered himself without spot to God, purge your conscience from dead works to serve the living God?" (He.9:13-14).

"Nor yet that he should offer himself often, as the high priest entereth into the holy place every year with blood of others; for then must he often have suffered since the foundation of the world: but now once in the end of the world hath he appeared to put away sin by the sacrifice of himself " (He.9:25-26).

"By the which will we are sanctified through the offering of the body of Jesus Christ once for all" (He.10:10).

"But this man, after he had offered one sacrifice for sins for ever, sat down on the right hand of God....For by one offering he hath perfected for ever them that are sanctified" (He.10:12, 14).

"Who his own self bare our sins in his own body on the tree, that we, being dead to sins, should live unto righteousness" (1 Pe.2:24; see 1 Co.5:7; Ep.5:2).

	H. The Steps for Getting Help: Blind Bartimaeus, 10:46-52 *(Mt. 20:29-34; Lu. 18:35-43)*	mercy on me.	
		49 And Jesus stood still, and commanded him to be called. And they call the blind man, saying unto him, Be of good comfort, rise; he calleth thee.	**5. Step 5: Eagerly expecting to receive Jesus' help** a. Jesus stopped & then called to the man
1. Step 1: Having Jesus available to help a. Jesus came to Jericho b. Jesus was followed by the disciples & the crowd c. A blind man sat by the road begging	46 And they came to Jericho: and as he went out of Jericho with his disciples and a great number of people, blind Bartimaeus, the son of Timaeus, sat by the highway side begging.	50 And he, casting away his garment, rose, and came to Jesus.	b. The man threw aside his impeding cloak
2. Step 2: Believing the reports about Jesus **3. Step 3: Acknowledging personal need**[DS1]	47 And when he heard that it was Jesus of Nazareth, he began to cry out, and say, Jesus, thou Son of David, have mercy on me.	51 And Jesus answered and said unto him, What wilt thou that I should do unto thee? The blind man said unto him, Lord, that I might receive my sight.	**6. Step 6: Requesting precisely what is needed**
4. Step 4: Enduring, persevering after Jesus[DS2]	48 And many charged him that he should hold his peace: but he cried the more a great deal, Thou Son of David, have	52 And Jesus said unto him, Go thy way; thy faith hath made thee whole. And immediately he received his sight, and followed Jesus in the way.	**7. Step 7: Experiencing the power of Jesus & following Him**

DIVISION VI

THE SON OF GOD'S LAST PUBLIC MINISTRY: JESUS DEALS WITH SOME SPECIAL PROBLEMS, 10:1-52

H. The Steps for Getting Help: Blind Bartimaeus, 10:46-52

(10:46-52) **Introduction**: this is the picture of a man's needing help and needing it desperately. As we read the story, there is no question but that the man's blindness is a picture of the blindness, darkness, and needs of a world that reels in desperation for help. The need may be physical, mental, emotional, or spiritual; it may be some problem with the mind, some desperate loneliness, or some tragic sin. Whatever it is, this passage spells out the steps for getting help.

1. Step 1: having Jesus available to help (v.46).
2. Step 2: believing the reports about Jesus (v.47).
3. Step 3: acknowledging personal need (v.47).
4. Step 4: enduring, persevering after Jesus (v.48).
5. Step 5: eagerly expecting to receive Jesus' help (vv.49-50).
6. Step 6: requesting precisely what is needed (vv.51-52).
7. Step 7: experiencing the power of Jesus and following Him (v.52).

1 (10:46) **Jericho—Bartimaeus**: Jesus had been in Jericho (how long we do not know). In the days of Jesus, Jericho was one of the most important cities of Palestine. One of the world's main commercial roads ran right through the city, north to south. The city was only about seventeen miles from Jerusalem, and it is thought to be the oldest city in the world.

It was the Passover season, which means that thousands of pilgrims were making their way to Jerusalem. The pilgrims were passing right through Jericho. Blind Bartimaeus knew this, and he also knew that religious people were more sensitive to the needs of helpless people who had to beg for a living. It is also possible that Bartimaeus had heard that Jesus was in Jericho (see Lu.18:35-43). If so, he knew that his best chance to find Jesus would be to station himself at the city limits where Jesus would be passing as He left the city. Whatever the case, Bartimaeus had to beg for a living, so he "sat by the [main] highway...begging."

> **Thought 1.** A man must go where he knows Jesus is, where Jesus "passes by." A man must go where he can hear Jesus, or he may miss the chance of eternal life.
>
> **"Seek ye the LORD while he may be found, call ye upon him while he is near" (Is.55:6).**
>
> **"For every one that asketh receiveth; and he that seeketh findeth; and to him that knocketh it shall be opened" (Lu.11:10).**

2 (10:47) **Belief**: the first step to getting help is believing the reports about Jesus. Sitting there, Bartimaeus heard all kinds of noises coming from the people passing by—the noise of individuals, of groups, of whole caravans. He heard the noise of feet tramping along, of animals, of conversation, of laughter, of play among children. He heard all kinds of talking: serious, jovial, commercial, vain, rude, off-colored, religious. But then something happened: the size of the crowd and the noise and talk changed. The passers-by became a throng, a multitude of people; and the noise and talk were about Jesus, the One for whom he had hoped and longed.

Bartimaeus had been blind for years, maybe for life, with no hope of ever seeing. Apparently he was a beggar with no one to care for him. But then the most glorious event of his life happened. He heard about One called Jesus of Nazareth who was claiming to be the true Messiah. For the first time in his life, hope swelled up in him. He knew there was a possibility that he might be healed and enabled to see. From the very first day that he had heard about Jesus, he had hoped and longed for the chance when Jesus might pass by. Why? Because he *believed the testimonies* about Jesus.

Note another fact. Sitting there by the road as Jesus passed by, he had no way to know it was Jesus. He could not see Him. He could only hear people walking and talking. When he heard people talking about Jesus, he believed it was He. He believed and trusted what he was hearing.

Thought 1. A man must believe the report, the testimony about Jesus. All Bartimaeus ever had was what he heard. He had never seen or been around Jesus. He only knew the testimony people were sharing: Jesus is the Messiah, the Son of David. And he believed the testimony.

"Verily, verily, I say unto you, The hour is coming, and now is, when the dead shall hear the voice of the Son of God: and they that hear shall live" (Jn.5:24).

"But these are written, that ye might believe that Jesus is the Christ, the Son of God; and that believing ye might have life through his name" (Jn.20:31).

"That if thou shalt confess with thy mouth the Lord Jesus, and shalt believe in thine heart that God hath raised him from the dead, thou shalt be saved. For with the heart man believeth unto righteousness; and with the mouth confession is made unto salvation" (Ro.10:9-10).

"Who hath believed our report? and to whom is the arm of the LORD revealed?" (Is.53:1).

"The spirit of the Lord GOD is upon me; because the LORD hath anointed me to preach good tidings unto the meek; he hath sent me to bind up the brokenhearted, to proclaim liberty to the captives, and the opening of the prison to them that are bound; to proclaim the acceptable year of the LORD, and the day of vengeance of our God; to comfort all that mourn" (Is.61:1-2).

3 (10:47) **Decision, Public—Profession—Mercy—Messiahship**: the second step to getting help is acknowledging personal need. As soon as Bartimaeus heard that it was Jesus, he instantly began shouting out to attract Jesus, creating as much fuss and noise as he could above the crowd and its noise.

The point is this: Bartimaeus acknowledged his need, and he confessed it publicly. He did not approach Jesus secretly or quietly by asking someone close by to appeal to Jesus in his behalf. He had a desperate need and he accepted the fact. He wanted the help of Jesus no matter what. Note two facts.

a. He cried to the "Son of David." This was an inadequate concept of Jesus. But Bartimaeus approached Jesus as his hope, his savior, his deliverer, his leader. He used what knowledge he had of Jesus and cried out to Him.

Thought 1. No man has an adequate concept of Jesus when he first comes to Jesus. No man understands Jesus until after he is saved and has received the Holy Spirit into his life and learned of Christ.

b. He cried out for mercy, not for anything else. He was blind and he was a beggar, yet he did not cry for housing or clothing or food. He cried for his most basic need to be met—for mercy.

"And the publican, standing afar off, would not lift up so much as his eyes unto heaven, but smote upon his breast, saying, God be merciful to me a sinner. I tell you, this man went down to his house justified" (Lu.18:13-14).

"For godly sorrow worketh repentance to salvation not to be repented of: but the sorrow of the world worketh death" (2 Co.7:10).

"This poor man cried, and the LORD heard him, and saved him out of all his troubles" (Ps.34:6).

"The LORD is nigh unto them that are of a broken heart; and saveth such as be of a contrite spirit" (Ps.34:18).

"Lord, all my desire is before thee; and my groaning is not hid from thee" (Ps.38:9).

"The sacrifices of God are a broken spirit: a broken and a contrite heart, O God, thou wilt not despise" (Ps.51:17).

"From the end of the earth will I cry unto thee, when my heart is overwhelmed: lead me to the rock that is higher than I" (Ps.61:2).

"For all those things hath mine hand made, and all those things have been, saith the LORD: but to this man will I look, even to him that is poor and of a contrite spirit, and trembleth at my word" (Is.66:2).

"And rend your heart, and not your garments, and turn unto the LORD your God: for he is gracious and merciful, slow to anger, and of great kindness, and repenteth him of the evil" (Joel 2:13).

DEEPER STUDY # 1

(10:47) **Son of David**: see notes—Mt.1:1; DEEPER STUDY # 1—1:18; DEEPER STUDY #3—3:11; notes—11:1-6; 11:2-3; DEEPER STUDY #1—11:5; DEEPER STUDY # 2—11:6; DEEPER STUDY # 1—12:16; note—Lu.7:21-23.

4 (10:48) **Persistence**: the third step to getting help is persisting and persevering after Jesus. Many among the crowd tried to hush Bartimaeus, but he was desperate and determined and in dead earnest. He would not be discouraged, silenced or stopped. He repeatedly cried to the top of his lungs: "Thou Son of David, have mercy on me."

The point is that Bartimaeus persevered. He had need, and he would not stop seeking to have his need met. Note the voices raised against him, and they were "many." His faith in Jesus was strong. He believed Jesus could really help him. His faith stood against all the voices of *discouragement* and against the feelings of so many that it was *useless*.

Thought 1. Perseverance is the answer to desperate need—persevering prayer and persevering faith (see note and DEEPER STUDY # 1—Mt.7:7; note and DEEPER STUDY #1—Lu.11:5-10 for discussion).

> **"For every one that asketh receiveth; and he that seeketh findeth; and to him that knocketh it shall be opened" (Mt.7:8).**
>
> **"But if from thence thou shalt seek the LORD thy God, thou shalt find him, if thou seek him with all thy heart and with all thy soul" (De.4:29).**
>
> **"And ye shall seek me, and find me, when ye shall search for me with all your heart" (Je.29:13).**

Thought 2. Worldly voices will rise up against us, attempting...

- to pull us away
- to tell us all is useless
- to convince us that our need is too desperate to be met
- to encourage us to try the world's way

DEEPER STUDY # 2

(10:48) **Persistence—Perseverance**: persistence always grabs the Lord's attention (see outline and notes—Mt.7:7-11. See Lu.18:1.) Note Jesus' question. He already knew what the blind man wanted. He had probably heard him as well, but He wanted the blind man to experience persistence. Why does Christ teach perseverance instead of just meeting our needs immediately? There are at least five reasons.

1. Having to persevere sharpens, increases, and grows our faith. It teaches endurance, experience (victorious living), and hope (Ro.5:2-4).
2. Having to persevere sharpens and makes us more aware of our minds. It gives us more time for thought and meditation and for the searching of the truth about ourselves and our needs. It focuses in on real needs.
3. Having to persevere teaches us to pray and to seek God more. It creates more awareness of our helplessness and our need for His presence and help. It necessitates more fellowship and deep communion with Him.
4. Having to persevere gives us more part in His work and worship. It creates a sense within us of having a greater part. This is not a need on God's part, but a need on our part. Serving Him is a great privilege which He allows us.
5. Having to persevere allows more time for a greater number of people to be reached with God's power. Perseverance is a greater witness for God. When God answers and moves, more people are aroused to observe God's working.

5 (10:49-50) **Expectation**: the fourth step to getting help is eagerly expecting to receive Jesus' help. There are two significant acts in this point.

a. "Jesus *stood still*." The crowd must have been huge. Jesus had to send for the man. Jesus *stood still...*

- because of the man's need. He could not reach Jesus by himself.
- because the man had persisted in crying despite many's opposing him (see DEEPER STUDY # 2—Mk.10:48).
- because Jesus never turned away from a man who cried for help.

> **"All that the Father giveth me shall come to me; and him that cometh to me I will in no wise cast out" (Jn.6:37).**
>
> **"The Lord is not slack concerning his promise, as some men count slackness; but is longsuffering to us-ward, not willing that any should perish, but that all should come to repentance" (2 Pe.3:9).**

b. The man cast aside his coat, cast aside all impediments. This was an interesting act. Bartimaeus wanted nothing to hinder him from reaching Jesus as quickly as he could. All in one motion, he cast aside the hindrances, sprang to his feet (ana pedesas), and moved toward Jesus. The stress is on his eagerness to reach Jesus and allowing nothing to hinder him.

Thought 1. What a lesson for us! How few are so eager! How many hang on to that which hinders and hampers and keeps them from reaching Christ?

> **"That ye put off concerning the former conversation the old man, which is corrupt according to the deceitful lusts" (Ep.4:22).**
>
> **"Wherefore seeing we also are compassed about with so great a cloud of witnesses, let us lay aside every weight, and the sin which doth so easily beset us, and let us run with patience the race that is set before us" (He.12:1).**
>
> **"Dearly beloved, I beseech you as strangers and pilgrims, abstain from fleshly lusts, which war against the soul" (1 Pe.2:11).**
>
> **"If iniquity be in thine hand, put it far away, and let not wickedness dwell in thy tabernacles" (Jb. 11:14).**
>
> **"Let the wicked forsake his way, and the unrighteous man his thoughts: and let him return unto the LORD, and he will have mercy upon him; and to our God, for he will abundantly pardon" (Is.55:7).**

6 (10:51-52) **Conversion**: the fifth step to getting help is requesting precisely what is needed. Note several facts.

a. Bartimaeus knew exactly what he needed and had no difficulty stating his need. He did not waver at all. He was not like many who are vague in their prayers and requests. He had examined himself and knew precisely what he needed.

> **"And all things, whatsoever ye shall ask in prayer, believing, ye shall receive" (Mt.21:22).**

"And whatsoever ye shall ask in my name, that will I do, that the Father may be glorified in the Son. If ye shall ask any thing in my name, I will do it" (Jn.14:13-14).

"Hitherto have ye asked nothing in my name: ask, and ye shall receive, that your joy may be full" (Jn.16:24).

"And it shall come to pass, that before they call, I will answer; and while they are yet speaking, I will hear" (Is.65:24).

"Call unto me, and I will answer thee, and show thee great and mighty things, which thou knowest not" (Je.33:3).

b. Bartimaeus needed, however, to make a personal confession to Jesus. Jesus, of course, knew what Bartimaeus needed; but the Lord's knowing about the man's need was not enough. The man had to make a personal confession to Jesus.

"Whosoever therefore shall confess me before men, him will I confess also before my Father which is in heaven. But whosoever shall deny me before men, him will I also deny before my Father which is in heaven" (Mt.10:32-33).

c. Bartimaeus needed to confess his faith in Jesus' power for the sake of the others standing there. They needed to know that it was faith in Jesus that saved a man.

"That if thou shalt confess with thy mouth the Lord Jesus, and shalt believe in thine heart that God hath raised him from the dead, thou shalt be saved. For with the heart man believeth unto righteousness; and with the mouth confession is made unto salvation" (Ro.10:9-10).

"For whosoever shall call upon the name of the Lord shall be saved" (Ro.10:13).

d. The word for Lord (Rabboni) means *my Master*. It is a title of reverent respect. Note the possessive "my." Bartimaeus' heart reached out to Jesus, desiring to belong to Him.

"And he said to them all, If any man will come after me, let him deny himself, and take up his cross daily, and follow me" (Lu.9:23).

e. A specific request got a specific answer: "Thy faith hath made thee whole" (see notes—Mk.11:22-23; DEEPER STUDY # 1—Jn.2:24; notes—Ro.10:16-17; Heb.11:1; DEEPER STUDY # 1—11:6).

"Wherefore he is able also to save them to the uttermost that come unto God by him, seeing he ever liveth to make intercession for them" (He.7:25).

"But without faith it is impossible to please him: for he that cometh to God must believe that he is, and that he is a rewarder of them that diligently seek him" (He.11:6).

"Commit thy way unto the Lord; trust also in him; and he shall bring it to pass" (Ps.37:5).

"Trust in the Lord with all thine heart; and lean not unto thine own understanding" (Pr.3:5).

"Trust ye in the LORD for ever: for in the LORD JEHOVAH is everlasting strength" (Is.26:4).

7 (10:52) **Discipleship—Following Jesus**: the sixth step to getting help is following Jesus. This was a very tender scene. Note what Jesus had told Bartimaeus, "Go thy way." But Bartimaeus did not go, not after his Master had touched him. Bartimaeus clung to Jesus. Nothing was going to pry him away. He "followed Jesus in the way."

Thought 1. There are several lessons here.

(1) There is a heart of appreciation, of being grateful and thankful.

"Giving thanks unto the Father, which hath made us meet to be partakers of the inheritance of the saints in light" (Col.1:12).

"And let the peace of God rule in your hearts, to the which also ye are called in one body; and be ye thankful" (Col.3:15).

"When thou hast eaten and art full, then thou shalt bless the LORD thy God for the good land which he hath given thee" (De.8:10).

(2) There is the idea of genuineness of conversion. He followed through.

"And he said to them all, If any man will come after me, let him deny himself, and take up his cross daily, and follow me" (Lu.9:23).

(3) There is the idea of growing, wanting to learn more and more about this Savior of men.

"Come unto me, all ye that labour and are heavy laden, and I will give you rest. Take my yoke [service and discipleship] upon you, and learn of me; for I am meek and lowly in heart: and ye shall find rest unto your souls" (Mt.11:28-30).

(4) There is the testimony of loyalty and faithfulness.

"Therefore, my beloved brethren, be ye stedfast, unmoveable, always abounding in the work of the Lord, forasmuch as ye know that your labour is not in vain in the Lord" (1 Co.15:58).

CHAPTER 11

VII. THE SON OF GOD'S LAST JERUSALEM MINISTRY: JESUS' WARNING & CONFLICT WITH RELIGIONISTS, 11:1-12:44

A. The Triumphal Entry: A Dramatic Warning, Jesus is the Messiah,[DS1] 11:1-11

(Mt. 21:1-11; Lu. 19:28-40; Jn. 12:12-19)

1. Scene 1: The colt—Christ came in peace[DS2]

And when they came nigh to
Jerusalem, unto Bethphage
and Bethany, at the mount of
Olives, he sendeth forth two
of his disciples,

a. The painstaking details that had to be followed

2 And saith unto them, Go
your way into the village
over against you: and as soon
as ye be entered into it, ye

1) The securing of the colt that had never been sat upon

shall find a colt tied, whereon
never man sat; loose him, and
bring him.

2) The owner & his question[DS3]

3 And if any man say unto
you, Why do ye this? say ye
that the Lord hath need of
him; and straightway he will
send him hither.

b. The details minutely followed

4 And they went their way,
and found the colt tied by the
door without in a place where
two ways met; and they loose
him.
5 And certain of them that
stood there said unto them,
What do ye, loosing the colt?
6 And they said unto them
even as Jesus had commanded: and they let them go.

c. The homage of the disciples[DS4]

7 And they brought the colt
to Jesus, and cast their garments on him; and he sat upon him.

2. Scene 2: The triumphal entry—Christ came to save now (Hosanna)

8 And many spread their
garments in the way: and
others cut down branches off
the trees, and strawed them in
the way.

a. The people's concept: A national hero—Hosanna, save now[DS5,6]

9 And they that went be-
fore, and they that followed,
cried, saying, Hosanna; Blessed is he that cometh in the
name of the Lord:

b. The Lord's meaning: He came to bring spiritual peace[DS7,8]

10 Blessed be the kingdom
of our father David, that
cometh in the name of the
Lord: Hosanna in the highest.

3. Scene 3: The investigation of the situation—Christ came obediently

11 And Jesus entered into
Jerusalem, and into the temple: and when he had looked
round about upon all things,

4. Scene 4: The seclusion at Bethany—Christ prepared spiritually

and now the eventide was
come, he went out unto
Bethany with the twelve.

DIVISION VII

THE SON OF GOD'S LAST JERUSALEM MINISTRY: JESUS' WARNING AND CONFLICT WITH RELIGIONISTS, 11:1-12:44

A. The Triumphal Entry: A Dramatic Warning, Jesus Is the Messiah, 11:1-11

(11:1-12:44) **DIVISION OVERVIEW: Jesus Christ, Ministry—Jerusalem**: three significant points needs to be made about Jesus' ministry in Jerusalem.

a. The first three gospels (*Matthew, Mark, Luke*) say little about Jesus' ministry in Jerusalem. The present passage is the first mention of a specific visit. The three synoptic gospels give only a hint that Jesus was ever in Jerusalem, hints such as...

- "O Jerusalem, Jerusalem...how often would I have gathered thy children" (Mt.23:37). This indicates He had been in the city and made appeal after appeal to the people.
- His warm family-like relationship with Martha and her sister and brother, Mary and Lazarus. Their home was His home when in Jerusalem (see note—Jn.11:1-3).
- His friendship with Nicodemus and Joseph of Arimathaea. They were both involved in His burial, indicating a close friendship probably developed in several meetings (see note—Mt.27:57-60. See Jn.19:38-42.)

The first three gospels concentrate on Jesus' ministry in Galilee. It is the fourth gospel, the Gospel of *John*, that covers Jesus' ministry in Judea and Jerusalem. John tells us that Jesus was in Jerusalem quite often, especially during the great feasts. (See Jn.2:13f; 5:1f; 7:1-10f; esp. v.10 to get an idea of His ministry in Jerusalem.)

b. When Jesus visited Jerusalem, His ministry differed entirely from His Galilean ministry. In Galilee Jesus taught many subjects, but in Jerusalem He focused only upon one theme: His Messiahship. He spent His time proclaiming strongly that He was beyond any question the Messiah. There was a reason for this. Jerusalem was the capital of Palestine, and the temple itself was there. Jerusalem was the hub and center of Jewish life and worship. The population of Jerusalem and the surrounding suburbs and cities ranged in the hundreds of thousands (for example, Bethphage and Bethany. Even Jericho, a city of sizeable population, was only about seventeen miles away.) The temple required over twenty thousand priests alone, not counting the Levite helpers who must have numbered even more. If there was any place where Jesus would proclaim His Messiahship, it would be in Jerusalem. Jerusalem was a city that held every sort of man who had been born and who was yet to be born. Jerusalem was to hear the truth of God's Son and of God's great love for the world. The men of Jerusalem and all men born thereafter were to be left without excuse.

"O Jerusalem, Jerusalem [world, world], thou that killest the prophets, and stonest them which are sent unto thee, how often would I have gathered thy children together, even as a hen gathereth her chickens under her wings, and ye would not!" (Mt.23:37).

c. Note the following visits to Jerusalem.
1) John 2:13f: Jesus cleansed the temple proclaiming it to be "My Father's house" (Jn.2:16); He proclaimed that He was the Son of Man (Jn.3:14); and God's only begotten Son (Jn.3:16).
2) John 5:1f: Jesus healed a man on the Sabbath, a man who had been sick for thirty-eight years. Then He proclaimed that He had the right to break the Sabbath law because He was the Son of the Father. He was equal with God in every sense of the word (Jn.5:1-16; 5:17-30).
3) Jn.7:1-10f: He declared that He was sent of God (Jn.7:16-17, 28-29; 8:18, 26, 29, 42); the Source of life (Jn.7:37-39); the Light of the World (Jn.8:12; 9:5); the Messiah (Jn.8:24, 28); the Spokesman of God (Jn.8:26-28, 40); the Son of Man (Jn.8:28); that God was His Father (Jn.9:28, 36, 38, 49, 54); that He had come from God (Jn.8:42); that He was the great "I Am" (Jn.8:58); the Son of God (Jn.9:35-37); the Great Shepherd of Life (Jn.10:1-42); and on and on (see the verses in Jn.10-21 and the Master Index).

(11:1-11) **Introduction**: there is no louder declaration of our Lord's Messiahship than the triumphal entry. He was picturing that He was *the Messiah*, deliberately proclaiming that He was "the Son of the living God" (Mt.16:16). But the triumphal entry was something else as well. Jesus was *dramatically warning* the people. They must change their concept of Messiahship. He was not coming as the *national hero* to save the world physically and materially by overthrowing the Roman and Gentile governments of the world. He was coming as the *King of Peace* to save the world spiritually and eternally. Spiritual and eternal salvation must occur first, then He would *return* to bring peace and national salvation to all men everywhere. He had to come first as the King of Peace; then He would come as the King of Conquest.

1. Scene 1: the colt—Christ came in peace (vv.1-7).
2. Scene 2: the triumphal entry—Christ came to save now (Hosanna) (vv.8-10).
3. Scene 3: the investigation of the situation—Christ came obediently (v.11).
4. Scene 4: the seclusion at Bethany—Christ prepared spiritually (v.11).

DEEPER STUDY # 1
(11:1-11) **Jesus Christ, Last Week—Holy Week—Palm Sunday**: this was the beginning of Jesus' last week on earth. He had spent the night before (the Sabbath evening) in Bethany with Martha, Mary, and Lazarus (Jn.12:1f). The last week of our Lord's life has been known as Holy Week from the earliest times by Christians everywhere. The triumphal entry was the first event of the week, taking place on the first day. It is called Palm Sunday.

1 (11:1-7) **Jesus Christ, King; Purpose**: the first scene involved the colt, which symbolized that Christ came in peace. Note an important fact. The stress of these verses is the painstaking details that must be followed, and they were followed to the most minute detail. Christ had a reason for making such detailed preparations to enter Jerusalem. He was deliberately fulfilling the prophecy of Zec.9:9. The prophecy said four things.

a. "Tell ye the daughter of Sion [that is, Jerusalem]": Jerusalem was to be told, given a threefold warning. Why must she be warned? Because what she expected was not going to happen, not like she anticipated.

b. "Behold, thy King cometh unto thee": this was the first warning. Jerusalem's King was coming, just as Jerusalem had expected. The people were correct in this part of their expectation. But there was danger in their expectation, the danger of being so fervent in their own expectancy and ideas that they missed what really happened. "Thy King cometh," but He came somewhat differently than expected.

Thought 1. What a lesson for us! We must guard against reading into Scripture what is not there, especially in looking toward the return of our Lord. We must not dictate *how* Jesus is to return; we must not add to what God has revealed in His Word.

c. "Thy King cometh...*meek*": this was the second warning. The Messiah was coming in meekness, not as a reigning monarch. He was coming to win men's hearts and lives spiritually and eternally, not physically and materially (see notes—Mk.11:1-11; Ep.1:3. See Mt.11:29.)

d. "Thy King cometh...sitting upon an ass, and a colt": this was the third warning. The Messiah was coming not as a conqueror riding a white stallion, but as a King of peace riding a young colt. He was coming to save the world peacefully, to reconcile the world to the God of love and reconciliation, not to the God of hate and retaliation and war. He was not going to kill men and overthrow their governments (the Romans and Gentiles). He was coming to win men's hearts and lives through the glorious news (gospel) that God loves and reconciles (see outline and notes—Ep.2:13-18).

Again, note the prophecy and the careful preparation Christ made to fulfill the prophecy. This says something: Christ was dramatizing His Messiahship so clearly that men could not fail to see and understand that He was God's Messiah. This was God's will, prophesied generations before Christ came. God wanted His Son to proclaim His Messiahship so clearly that the people could not mistake what He was doing. God wanted the world to know that He was bringing peace to earth through His Son Jesus Christ.

"Through the tender mercy of our God; whereby the dayspring from on high hath visited us, to give light to them that sit in darkness and in the shadow of death, to guide our feet into the way of peace" (Lu.1:78-79).

"And suddenly there was with the angel a multitude of the heavenly hosts praising God, and saying, Glory to God in the highest, and on earth peace, good will toward men" (Lu.2:13-14).

"Peace I leave with you, my peace I give unto you: not as the world giveth, give I unto you. Let not your heart be troubled, neither let it be afraid" (Jn.14:27).

These things I have spoken unto you, that in me ye might have peace. In the world ye shall have tribulation: but be of good cheer; I have overcome the world" (Jn.16:33).

"The word which God sent unto the children of Israel, preaching peace by Jesus Christ: (he is Lord of all:)" (Ac.10:36).

"Therefore being justified by faith, we have peace with God through our Lord Jesus Christ" (Ro.5:1).

"For the kingdom of God is not meat and drink; but righteousness, and peace, and joy in the Holy Ghost" (Ro.14:17).

"For he is our peace, who hath made both one, and hath broken down the middle wall of partition between us" (Ep.2:14).

"And, having made peace through the blood of his cross, by him to reconcile all things unto himself; by him, I say, whether they be things in earth, or things in heaven" (Col.1:20).

"The LORD will give strength unto his people; the LORD will bless his people with peace" (Ps.29:11).

DEEPER STUDY # 2

(11:1-7) **Ass—Colt**: in ancient days the colt was a noble animal. It was used as a beast of service to carry the burdens of men. But more significantly, it was used by kings and their emissaries. When they entered a city in peace, they rode a colt to symbolize their peaceful intentions (see the judges of Israel and the chieftains throughout the land, Jud.5:10; 10:4). This differed dramatically from a conquering king. When a king entered a city as a conqueror, he rode a stallion.

Jesus was dramatically demonstrating two things for the people. First, He was unquestionably the promised King, the Savior of the people; but secondly, He was not coming as the conquering king. He was not coming as a worldly potentate, in pomp and ceremony; not coming as the leader of an army to kill, injure, and maim. The people must change their concept of the Messiah. He was coming as the Savior of Peace, the Savior of all men. He was coming to show men that God is the God of love and reconciliation.

1. The colt was a symbol of peace. Jesus came to bring peace, as pointed out in the above discussion.
2. The colt symbolized service. It was a noble animal, an animal used in the service of men to carry their burdens. Jesus came upon the colt symbolizing that He came to serve men, to bear their burdens for them.
3. The colt symbolized sacredness. It had never been ridden before (v.2). Animals and things used for sacred or religious purposes had to be animals and things that had never been used before (Nu.19:2; De.21:3; 1 S.6:7). This detail points to the sacredness of the event. It pictured for everyone that Jesus was deliberately proclaiming that *He is the sacred hope*, the promised Messiah of the people.

DEEPER STUDY # 3

(11:3-6) **The Owner of the Colt**: see note, *Prophecy*—Mt.21:2-5.

DEEPER STUDY # 4

(11:7) **Disciples, Homage to Jesus—Obedience**: Christ deliberately received the homage of the disciples (reverence, recognition). They did exactly what He asked despite the uncertainty of the matter. They probably had no money to buy or rent the animals, and they were to be questioned about why they wanted the animals; yet they obeyed, not questioning or doubting.

Note the other act of homage. There was no saddle for their Lord. They cared about Him and His comfort, so they took their own outer garments and threw them across the animal. The two men, by following Christ, would have accepted a life of poverty, so they would have little clothing. It cost them to use their clothing for such a humble act. The clothing would become soiled and smelly. Nevertheless, they cared and they worshipped through this act.

The point is that Christ was now unmistakably claiming the dignity and rights of a king. He was not washing feet now, nor portraying Himself as the servant of men; He was deliberately accepting the people's homage and reverence.

But note something of critical importance. In claiming the dignity and rights of a king, He was doing it in the most humble practice of His day: entering the city as a king of peace riding a young colt instead of the conqueror's stallion. He was disclaiming all ideas of an earthly and material kingdom. He had come to save Jerusalem and the world through peace, not war.

2 (11:8-10) **Jesus Christ, Purpose**: the second scene was the triumphal entry itself. This symbolized that Christ came to save now (Hosanna). Note the word "many" (v.8). There was a "very great multitude" (Mt.21:8). They were proclaiming Jesus to be the Messiah, the Son of David, who had come to deliver them from the bondage of Roman and Gentile rule (see DEEPER STUDIES # 5-8—Mk.11:9-10). Of course by riding the colt, Jesus was proclaiming that *He had come to save now*, but to save by bringing peace spiritually, not militarily (see notes—Mk.11:1-11; 11:1-7).

Note, however, that Jesus deliberately received the homage of the people. Apparently what happened was this. The multitude had begun to gather since early morning, excitedly looking for Him who had raised Lazarus from the dead. John tells us this. In fact, he says there were so many people that the Pharisees said "the world is gone after Him" (Jn.12:17-19). There was the crowd of disciples already accompanying Him, the pilgrims on their way to the Passover Feast who had joined His caravan, the residents of Bethany and Bethphage who had heard of His presence and the miracles, and those who were already in Jerusalem, citizens and pilgrims who rushed out searching for Him.

We are led to imagine an enormous crowd of teeming thousands lining the roadway as Christ was helped atop the colt to begin His triumphal entry into Jerusalem. There are several facts that point toward this conclusion.

a. Two million pilgrims or more gathered in Jerusalem every year for the Passover Feast (see DEEPER STUDY # 1—Mt.26:2). Thousands upon thousands were strict religionists, believing in the Jewish Messiah.

b. The news being spread throughout the city and surrounding area concerned the miracles Christ had performed—a concentration of miracles for some days now which included the raising of Lazarus from the dead (Jn.11:1f; 11:55-56). The very atmosphere was electric with the exciting news that Jesus was God's promised Messiah. Multitudes had heard that He was in Bethany and Bethphage (Mk.14:1-9). As is said above, there was the multitude who turned around from Jerusalem to meet Him (Jn.12:17-19). There was the multitude already travelling with Him (Mt.21:29). And there was the multitude of citizens in Bethany and Bethphage who had begun gathering around Him (Mk.14:1-9; Jn.12:1f). The whole thrust of the picture points to teeming thousands searching for Him and rushing out to welcome Him when they heard He was coming. (Note the words of Matthew: "the multitudes that went before, and that followed," v.9.)

The multitudes did two things.

1. They received Him as King. This was shown by two acts that were always done for kings when they entered a city. They stripped off their cloaks and cut down tree branches, and they spread both out on the roadway before Him. They wished to honor and pay Him the homage of a King. They wished to show Him that they received Him as the promised King of Israel.

2. They received Him as Messiah (see notes—Mt.21:8-9).

> **"Nathanael answered and saith unto him, Rabbi, thou art the Son of God; thou art the King of Israel" (Jn.1:49).**
>
> **"For God so loved the world, that he gave his only begotten Son, that whosoever believeth in him should not perish, but have everlasting life" (Jn.3:16).**
>
> **"Pilate therefore said unto him, Art thou a king then? Jesus answered, Thou sayest that I am a king. To this end was I born, and for this cause came I into the world, that I should bear witness unto the truth. Every one that is of the truth heareth my voice" (Jn.18:37).**
>
> **"For he saith, I have heard thee in a time accepted, and in the day of salvation have I succoured thee: behold, now is the accepted time; behold, now is the day of salvation" (2 Co.6:2).**
>
> **"Which in his times he shall show, who is the blessed and only Potentate, the King of kings, and Lord of lords" (1 Ti.6:15).**
>
> **"For the grace of God that bringeth salvation hath appeared to all men, teaching us that, denying ungodliness and worldly lusts, we should live soberly, righteously, and godly, in this present world" (Tit.2:11-12).**

DEEPER STUDY # 5
(11:9) **Hosanna**: means save now, or save, we pray.

DEEPER STUDY # 6
(11:9) **Blessed...of the Lord**: means blessed is He who is sent by God to save His people; blessed is He who is sent with the authority of God.

DEEPER STUDY # 7
(11:10) **Kingdom of David**: see notes—Mt.1:1; DEEPER STUDY # 1—2:18; DEEPER STUDY # 3—3:11; notes—11:1-6; 11:2-3; DEEPER STUDY # 1—11:5; DEEPER STUDY # 2—11:6; DEEPER STUDY # 1—12:16; note—Lu.7:21-23.

DEEPER STUDY # 8
(11:10) **In the Highest**: means God save, we pray; thou who art in the Highest, save now through Him whom You have sent.

3 (11:11) **Obedience**: the third scene was the investigation of the temple, of the situation. This symbolized that Jesus came obediently. The scene was descriptive. Jesus "entered into the temple: and...looked round about upon *all things*." He stood there, off to the side someplace where He had the vantage point of seeing all that was happening. Evening was approaching and He was tired. He stood all alone. The point to see is that He was doing God's will. It took great courage to stand there. The Jewish authorities were seeking some opportunity to take His life, and they were upset more than ever now, for He had not discouraged the homage of the people (see Lu.19:39).

⇒ The Romans sensed that a popular uprising might be boiling.
⇒ The Jewish Herodians (ruling party) feared being blamed and replaced by the Romans.
⇒ The Pharisees were stirred to new depths of envy and malice.

But despite all, He had to be courageous; He had to stand there. It was God's will. He had to investigate the situation, investigate God's house. He had to prepare all things for the salvation of God's people. He had come obediently; He had come to obey God.

> **"Jesus saith unto them, My meat is to do the will of him that sent me, and to finish his work" (Jn.4:34).**

"I seek not mine own will, but the will of the Father which hath sent me" (Jn.5:30).

"But that the world may know that I love the Father; and as the Father gave me commandment, even so I do. Arise, let us go hence" (Jn.14:31).

"Though he were a Son, yet learned he obedience by the things which he suffered" (He.5:8).

Thought 1. There are two lessons in this point.
(1) We are to obey, no matter the threat and opposition.
(2) We should investigate before entering into any situation that is threatening or involves corruption (see note—Mk.11:15-19).

4 (11:11) **Preparation—Prayer**: the fourth scene was the seclusion at Bethany. This symbolized that Christ prepared spiritually. Jesus retired for the night in the surrounding area of Bethany. No doubt He spent a good deal of time alone in prayer. Much lay ahead of Him in this last week of His life. He knew it, sensing every detail and emotion He was to experience. He needed the strong hand of His Father upholding Him. He needed to prepare spiritually. (See note, *Preparation*—Lu.21:37, where we are told that Jesus spent the nights of His last week in prayer on the Mount of Olives.)

"And he withdrew himself into the wilderness, and prayed" (Lu.5:16).

"And it came to pass in those days, that he went out into a mountain to pray, and continued all night in prayer to God" (Lu.6:12).

	B. The Fig Tree Cursed: A Warning Against a Fruitless Life, 11:12-14 *(Mt. 21:17-20)*	haply he might find any thing thereon: and when he came to it, he found nothing but leaves; for the time of figs was not yet.	**3. Jesus examined the fruit**
1. Jesus had need	12 And on the morrow, when they were come from Bethany, he was hungry:	14 And Jesus answered and said unto it, No man eat fruit of thee hereafter for ever. And his disciples heard it.	**4. Jesus condemned profession that does not bear fruit**
2. Jesus saw potential	13 And seeing a fig tree afar off having leaves, he came, if		

DIVISION VII

THE SON OF GOD'S LAST JERUSALEM MINISTRY: JESUS' WARNING AND CONFLICT WITH RELIGIONISTS, 11:1-12:44

B. The Fig Tree Cursed: A Warning Against a Fruitless Life, 11:12-14

(11:12-14) **Introduction—Fig Tree—Judgment—God, Severity**: Why did Jesus destroy the fig tree? Many say that such destruction was contrary to His character. They say He would never lash out at a tree just for not bearing fruit, especially when it was not even time for the figs to be ripe (v.13). But two things always need to be remembered.

First, God is both good and severe. As Paul says, "Behold therefore the goodness and severity of God" (Ro.11:22). We are to stress both the goodness and severity of God, not just His goodness. God is love, but He is also pure and just. He demonstrates care and forgiveness, but He also holds men responsible and accountable. God is not an indulgent Father who is never severe. He is not weak and foolish in dealing with men, winking at and never punishing their unfruitfulness. Unfruitfulness and sin lead to destruction, and God is not *a bad Father* who is going to allow the whole human race to destroy itself. God is good to men. He punishes unfruitfulness so that others will bear fruit.

Second, Jesus always acted either to teach men or to save and help men. In the destruction of the fig tree, Jesus was teaching men a much needed lesson—a lesson that shouts loudly, "*Be fruitful*! Guard against profession without bearing fruit."

1. Jesus had need (v.12).
2. Jesus saw potential (v.13).
3. Jesus examined the fruit (v.13).
4. Jesus condemned profession that does not bear fruit (v.14).

1 (11:12) **Jesus Christ, Purpose**: Jesus had need. Mark says very simply, "He was hungry." Jesus had spent the night in Bethany. Matthew says He was walking into Jerusalem "in the morning." It was early morning before most had arisen from bed (see DEEPER STUDY # 1—Mt.21:18). Most likely, Jesus had been up praying for some time. He needed to be spiritually prepared; He needed very special strength in this final week of His life upon earth.

He left Bethany before breakfast. The point is He was hungry; He had need. And His need painted a picture of His craving for fruit—much fruit in the lives of men. Christ wants men, and He wants fruitful men. This is His hunger, His craving, His longing. This is the very purpose of His being.

> **"The thief cometh not, but for to steal, and to kill, and to destroy: I am come that they might have life, and that they might have it more abundantly" (Jn.10:10).**
>
> **"I am the vine, ye are the branches: He that abideth in me, and I in him, the same bringeth forth much fruit: for without me ye can do nothing...Herein is my Father glorified, that ye bear much fruit; so shall ye be my disciples" (Jn.15:5, 8).**
>
> **"For the Son of man is come to seek and to save that which was lost [unfruitful]" (Lu.19:10).**
>
> **"What fruit had ye then in those things whereof ye are now ashamed? for the end of those things is death. But now being made free from sin, and become servants to God, ye have your fruit unto holiness, and the end everlasting life" (Ro.6:21-22).**
>
> **"Ye also are become dead...by the body of Christ...that [ye] should bring forth fruit unto God" (Ro.7:4).**
>
> **"By him therefore let us offer the sacrifice of praise to God continually, that is, the fruit of our lips giving thanks to his name" (He.13:15).**

2 (11:13) **Hypocrisy—Unfruitfulness**: Jesus saw potential. Jesus saw the tree "afar off," a great distance away. The tree was so full of foliage (despite the early date) that it appeared to be fully developed. This, of course, meant that there were figs on the tree; for the fig tree puts forth its buds before its leaves (see note 3 —Mk.11:13). One would at least expect the tree to have fruit even if not ripe. It was a natural expectation. The full foliage, fruitful appearance was openly professed. Note four things. (See outline and notes—Mk.4:3-20.)

a. The leafy appearance indicated fruit. So it is with men who profess: their profession indicates fruit.

b. The leafy appearance indicated healthiness, the lack of disease. Profession indicates that the disease of sin has been taken care of, sprayed, and destroyed.

c. The leafy appearance, full foliage stirred expectation. Jesus expected fruit to be present. He expected His hunger to be satisfied by the fruit of the tree. Profession stirs expectation among all who observe, especially among those who are close.

d. The leafy appearance, full foliage necessitates fruit. Profession necessitates that fruitfulness follow. If there is no fruit, then profession is empty and good for nothing. It may as well not exist (see Mt.5:13; Jn.15:6).

"Even so ye also outwardly appear righteous unto men, but within ye are full of hypocrisy and iniquity" (Mt.23:28).

"Having a form of godliness, but denying the power thereof: from such turn away" (2 Ti.3:5).

"They profess that they know God; but in works they deny him, being abominable, and disobedient, and unto every good work reprobate" (Tit.1:16).

3 (11:13) **Judgment—False Profession—Unfruitfulness**: Jesus examined. When Jesus came to the fig tree, He looked, inspected, and examined; but He found *nothing*—no fruit whatsoever. Despite its foliage and appearance, the tree was barren and destitute. It *appeared fruitful*, declared itself to be fruitful; but after inspection, the tree had nothing *but leaves* (appearance). Note two warnings.

a. The appearance of full foliage attracted attention. It was the very appearance of the tree that drew Jesus. Thus it is with profession. Christ is definitely attracted to any man who professes Him. He comes to the man desiring to love, help, and fellowship with him.

b. The appearance of full foliage invited inspection. Jesus was hungry for the fruit. When He arrived, He looked and looked, but found no fruit. So it is with man. Christ craves fruit from man. If He sees a man profess Him, Christ is going to draw near and inspect. A man who professes Christ is inviting Christ to inspect him, and Christ will inspect; in fact, He will inspect a man who professes much quicker than the man who does not profess. The professing hypocrite is much more accountable than the non-professor.

"Every man's work shall be made manifest: for the day shall declare it, because it shall be revealed by fire; and the fire shall try every man's work of what sort it is" (1 Co.3:13).

"So then every one of us shall give account of himself to God" (Ro.14:12).

"For there is nothing hid, which shall not be manifested; neither was any thing kept secret, but that it should come abroad" (Mk.4:22).

"For God shall bring every work into judgment, with every secret thing, whether it be good, or whether it be evil" (Ec.12:14).

4 (11:14) **False Profession—Unfruitfulness**: Jesus condemned profession without fruit. Standing there, Jesus saw no fruit. The tree had life; it was existing. It had the sap to produce a rich foliage of leaves; but the sad fact was, despite all the appearance of fruit-bearing, the tree had none. Its very purpose for existing was to bear fruit, but it did not. It failed at three points.

a. The tree had an empty profession. So do men. Men profess, but their profession is empty. Their lives do not match their profession. They lack life, behavior, works, purity, holiness, faith, love, and on and on. There is no distinction between them and the world.

b. The tree had an unfulfilled purpose. So do men. They profess Christ, but they continue in their own worldly pursuits, forgetting God's purpose entirely. Many who profess Christ spend their time, energy, and money to pursue their own desires and ambitions instead of God's will and purpose.

c. The tree deceived instead of serving. So do men. They profess to serve, and perhaps do show a little service; but their commitment is to self, family, business, property, society—to an innumerable list of things. Service to God is only an *addition* to everything else. God is not the true Lord of the professor. The professor has no intention of serving the Lord. He looks upon God as merely *being there*, along with everything else.

"And now also the axe is laid unto the root of the trees: therefore every tree which bringeth not forth good fruit is hewn down, and cast into the fire" (Mt.3:10).

"Even so every good tree bringeth forth good fruit; but a corrupt tree bringeth forth evil fruit" (Mt.7:17).

"But that which beareth thorns and briers is rejected, and is nigh unto cursing: whose end is to be burned" (He.6:8).

"For their vine is of the vine of Sodom, and of the fields of Gomorrah: their grapes are grapes of gall, their clusters are bitter" (De.32:32).

C. The Temple Cleansed: A Warning to Those Who Abuse God's Temple, 11:15-19
(Mt. 21:12-16; Lu. 19:45-46; Jn. 2:13-16)

Outline	Scripture	Scripture	Outline
1. Jesus entered the temple **2. Jesus drove some out of the temple** a. Those who commercialized or secularized religion b. Those who desecrated God's house	15 And they come to Jeru- salem: and Jesus went into the temple, and began to cast out them that sold and bought in the temple, and overthrew the tables of the moneychangers, and the seats of them that sold doves; 16 And would not suffer	that any man should carry any vessel through the temple. 17 And he taught, saying unto them, Is it not writ- ten, My house shall be called of all nations the house of prayer? but ye have made it a den of thieves. 18 And the scribes and chief priests heard it, and sought how they might de- stroy him: for they feared him, because all the people was astonished at his doc- trine. 19 And when even was come, he went out of the city.	c. Those who affected the atmosphere of prayer d. Those who shut people out e. Those who changed the purpose of the temple **3. Jesus caused a reaction when the truth of the temple was proclaimed** a. Some sought to persecute & kill Him b. Some were amazed **4. Jesus left when the truth was rejected**

DIVISION VII

THE SON OF GOD'S LAST JERUSALEM MINISTRY: JESUS' WARNING AND CONFLICT WITH RELIGIONISTS, 11:1-12:44

C. The Temple Cleansed: A Warning to Those Who Abuse God's Temple, 11:15-19

(11:15-19) **Introduction—Temple, Cleansing**: the cleansing of the temple took place on Monday, the day after the triumphal entry into Jerusalem. The scene was this: teeming thousands had lined the roadway for Jesus' triumphal entry. As He rode along to the shouts of welcome from the multitudes, He was led right up to the steps of the temple. He entered the temple and "looked round about upon all things" (v.11), observing all that was going on. He stood off to the side observing all the corruption. After some time, heartbroken and weary, He left, returning to Bethany to spend Sunday night. When He arose on Monday morning, He returned to the temple and cleansed it of those who profaned its sacredness.

Four things should be noted about the temple during this last week of our Lord's life.

1. Jesus was ending His ministry in the temple, His Father's house of prayer, the place where God's presence dwells in a very special way. He was about to complete His life upon earth—a glorious ministry fulfilling the will of God perfectly. The night before, as He had stood off by Himself in the temple observing all that was taking place, His thoughts must have been very contemplative: meditating upon His Father, His life now about completed, the great sacrifice He was to pay for man's sins, the corruption of the temple taking place all around Him, the worshipping that should be taking place, and so much more. His heart was probably drawn ever so close to God, yet broken and weeping within. Right before Him was a picture of the terrible sin for which He was to die. The temple itself, the place where men should be able to draw close to God, was corrupted by men. It had become anything but a house of prayer. It was a place for commercialism, for man's greed.
2. Jesus was revealing who He was by cleansing the temple. He was proclaiming to all generations that He had the right to determine how the temple was to be used and to purge it of corruptions. As God's Son, the temple was His dwelling place, the place where the worship of God was to be especially known.
3. In cleansing the temple, Jesus was revealing how men were to treat and use the temple of God.
4. Jesus began and ended His ministry by cleansing the temple. The two cleansings were separate events which marked the opening and closing of His ministry. The importance of the temple as God's house of prayer and worship was thereby demonstrated.

When our Lord entered Jerusalem, He did not go up to the palace of a King, nor to the courts of the rulers; but He went up to the temple, to the House of God. His kingdom was not of this world; it was not a physical kingdom. It was of heaven; it was a spiritual kingdom. His authority and rule were in the temple of God and in the hearts of men. Therefore, He went up to the temple of God to cleanse it and to teach us how the temple is to be used.

1. Jesus entered the temple (v.15).
2. Jesus drove some out of the temple (vv.15-17).
3. Jesus caused a reaction when the truth of the temple was proclaimed (v.18).
4. Jesus left when the truth was rejected (v.19).

[1] (11:15) **Temple**: Jesus entered the temple. A person must understand the layout of the temple in order to see what was happening in this event. It sat on top of Mt. Zion, and it is thought to have covered about thirty acres of land. The temple consisted of two parts, the temple building itself and the temple precincts or courtyards. The Greek language has two different words to distinguish which is meant.

a. *The temple building* (naos) was a small, ornate structure which sat in the center of the temple property. It was called the Holy Place or Holy of Holies, and only the High Priest could enter its walls; but even he could enter only once during the year, on the Day of Atonement.

b. *The temple precincts* (hieron) were four courtyards which surrounded the temple building, each decreasing in their importance to the Jewish mind. It is critical to remember that great walls separated the courts from each other.

1) The Court of the Priests was first. Only the priests were allowed to enter this court. Within the courtyard stood the great furnishings of worship: the Altar of Burnt Offering, The Brazen Laver, the Seven Branched Lampstand, the Altar of Incense, and the Table of Showbread.
2) The Court of the Israelites was next. This was a huge courtyard where Jewish worshippers met together for joint services on the great feast days. It was also where worshippers handed over their sacrifices to the priests.
3) The Court of the Women was the third courtyard. Women were usually limited to this area except for worship. They could, however, enter the Court of the Israelites when they came to make sacrifice or worship in a joint assembly on a great feast day.
4) The Court of the Gentiles was the last courtyard. It covered a vast space, surrounding all the other courtyards, and was the place of worship for all Gentile converts to Judaism.

When Jesus entered the temple, it was the Court of the Gentiles that He entered. It is this court, the outer court, that is the center of Jesus' anger.

Thought 1. Note two significant points.
(1) Great barriers are built between people in their worship. Imagine the huge walls (barriers) separating people from God and the various courtyards favoring Jewish men before women and all Jews before any Gentile. Imagine the self-righteousness, pride, self-centeredness, prejudice, envy, and jealousy. Where is love, care, ministry, evangelism, social consciousness, and a sense of human need in such a scheme of religion? Every generation of believers must search their hearts for any sign of prejudice and division and purge their hearts of such sins.
(2) Christ cleansed the *outer court*, not the *inner court*. It was not just the worship center that was *set apart* to God; it was the worship precincts as well. All thirty acres were hallowed ground and were to be treated as such. This is a warning to the church that must be heeded (see note—1 Co.3:17).

2 (11:15-17) **Temple—Church**: Jesus drove some out of the temple. This whole scene took place in the court of the Gentiles. There were five offenses, five defilements or corruptions, that caused Jesus to cast men out of the temple.

a. Jesus cast out those who commercialized and secularized religion. The outer court of the temple, the court of the Gentiles, was the place where Gentiles worshipped. But it was tragically abused. It had become nothing more than a commercial marketplace owned, and in many cases operated, by the priests. It was used for the selling and buying of sacrificial animals which included oxen and sheep as well as smaller doves and pigeons. It was used for the inspection of the animals' purity, and it was also used for the exchanging of foreign currencies. Every Passover season found thousands of pilgrims from all nations traveling great distances to come to the temple. It was usually impossible for a pilgrim to bring his own animal for sacrifice; but if he did, he had to get it by the inspector, which often cost a fee. The bickering back and forth created an atmosphere of utter chaos that apparently gave off the sound of a human volcanic uproar (see note, pt.2—Ep.2:14-15).

Hundreds of thousands of animals were sold at the great feasts; and, unfortunately, the High Priest and other priests were often in the middle of the commercialism. It was this commercialism and secularism of religion that Jesus struck out against. (See DEEPER STUDY # 1—Mt.21:12-16 for detailed discussion and thoughts.)

"Ye shall keep my sabbaths, and reverence my sanctuary: I am the LORD" (Le.19:30).
"But the LORD is in his holy temple: let all the earth keep silence before him" (Hab.2:20).

b. Jesus cast out those who desecrated God's house. Note that people were using the temple grounds as a thoroughfare (v.16). The temple and its grounds were so large that the entrances had become a shortcut from one section of town to another, especially if one were carrying a heavy load. Jesus was forbidding such disrespect and desecration of God's house.

Thought 1. Note how hallowed the temple was to Jesus. He forbade people to walk across its outer courtyard, even if they were carrying a heavy load and had to travel a much longer route. This should speak loudly and clearly to the church in every generation. God expects His church and its grounds or courtyards to be held in the highest respect and esteem.

"God is greatly to be feared in the assembly of the saints, and to be had in reverence of all them that are about him" (Ps.89:7).
"And he said, Draw not nigh hither: put off thy shoes from off thy feet, for the place whereon thou standest is holy ground" (Ex.3:5).

c. Jesus cast out those who affected the atmosphere of prayer within the temple. The temple was more than just a building and grounds. It was a "house of prayer." In fact, note Jesus' exact words. He said three things about the temple.

1) The temple is "My house." "My" is possessive. Christ possesses the temple. He is the Lord, the Owner of it. Any who are within its walls are either His guests or His servants. No one has the right to mistreat someone else's house. The guest and servant are to respect the property of the Owner.
2) "My house shall be called...the house of prayer." The purpose of the Lord's house is prayer. It is to be used for prayer *so much* that it becomes known as and called "the house of prayer." Prayer is to be its distinctiveness, its function, the very thing for which it is known (communion, sharing, praising, requesting, giving thanks, listening, and worship).
3) "My house shall be called *of all nations* the house of prayer." The temple is to be the same in all nations: a house of prayer. No nation, no people is to use it for any other purpose. Within all nations, the temple is to be used for prayer and to be known and called "the house of prayer."

Thought 1. The atmosphere for prayer is hindered by...

- noise
- other religious activities
- secular activities
- personal barriers
- disturbed spirits
- divisive spirits
- spiritual unpreparedness
- religious barriers

"God is a Spirit: and they that worship him must worship him in spirit and in truth" (Jn.4:24).

"Give unto the LORD the glory due unto his name: bring an offering, and come before him: worship the LORD in the beauty of holiness" (1 Chr.16:29).

"O come, let us worship and bow down: let us kneel before the LORD our maker" (Ps.95:6).

"Exalt ye the LORD our God, and worship at his footstool; for he is holy" (Ps.99:5).

d. Jesus cast out those who shut people out. The temple was to be a house of prayer for *all* nations. Note two things.

1) Neither the Gentiles nor anyone else were to be excluded. The women and Gentiles were to have as much *access* to the inner court of worship as the Jewish men (see Is.56:7).

2) The Court of the Gentiles was to have an atmosphere of prayer as much as any other court of the temple. There were no *sections for worship* within the temple, not in the Lord's mind. All the temple and its courtyards were for prayer and worship.

Thought 1. This is a critical lesson—a lesson that God has tried and tried to teach men and nations down through the years. There is no caste system, social crust, superior race, or inferior race. There is not even a *better person or worse person or favorite person or special person,* not in God's eyes.

"God is no respecter of persons" (Ac.10:34).

"For God so loved the world [every nation, every man equally], that he gave his only begotten Son, that whosoever believeth in him should not perish, but have everlasting life" (Jn.3:16).

Thought 2. Every person is to have access to the temple of God. No one is to be barred, not even ignored in the temple. The temple (church) is to be opened wide for all, and all are to know that it is *God's house of prayer* for each one. Each one is to know that he can pray therein, being welcomed, comforted, and put at ease. This includes...

- the poor
- the destitute
- the widower
- the widow
- the dirty
- the smelly
- the divorced
- the sick
- the ragged
- the sinner
- the child
- the retarded
- the hungry
- the orphan
- the elderly

e. Jesus cast out those who changed the purpose of the temple. Tragically, it was the priests themselves who altered the purpose of the temple. It is not known just when, but at some point in history the priests decided to take advantage of the worshippers' need for sacrificial animals and supplies. The priests saw how they could reap some of the profit for the welfare of the temple and for themselves. They began to set up booths within the Court of the Gentiles for the convenience of the pilgrims and to help defray the cost of the temple and to meet their own needs.

Note a crucial point that issues a severe warning to God's people. The people were sold items that were necessary for their worship. They were not just items that would *help them* in their spiritual growth and their worship, but they were items that were absolutely necessary. They had to have the items.

Now think for a moment. If the items were necessary for their worship and growth, what was wrong with what the priests did? The words of v.15 tell us: "Jesus...cast out all them that sold and bought in the temple." The buying and selling of the items for worship and growth was necessary and good, *but not within the temple.* It was to be done outside the temple walls, off the temple grounds. The temple and church were not the place for commercialism.

"And said unto them that sold doves, Take these things hence; make not my Father's house an house of merchandise" (Jn.2:16).

"What? have ye not houses to eat and to drink in? or despise ye the church of God, and shame them that have not? What shall I say to you? shall I praise you in this? I praise you not" (1 Co.11:22).

"Keep thy foot when thou goest to the house of God, and be more ready to hear, than to give the sacrifice of fools: for they consider not that they do evil" (Ec.5:1).

"For the children of Judah have done evil in my sight, saith the LORD: they have set their abominations in the house which is called by my name, to pollute it" (Je.7:30).

"Her [the temple, the churches] prophets are light and treacherous persons: her priests have polluted the sanctuary, they have done violence to the law" (Zep.3:4).

3 (11:18) **Temple—Jesus Christ, Reaction Against**: Jesus caused a reaction when the truth of the temple was proclaimed. There were three reactions against Him.

a. Some were so angered they began to persecute Jesus. In fact, they sought to destroy Him. The Greek word *destroy* (apolesousin) means to completely overthrow, to disable. This violent reaction was, of course, from those who were abusing and desecrating the temple. They wanted to immediately stamp out His influence. They feared lest what He was doing would catch on, forcing them to stop their secular activities within the temple. The only way they saw to stamp out His influence was to get rid of Him.

Thought 1. How many today would be *gotten rid of* if they really sought to cleanse the church of the abusers and secular activities often allowed and promoted within its walls?

"For the love of money is the root of all evil: which while some coveted after, they have erred from the faith, and pierced themselves through with many sorrows" (1 Ti.6:10).

"Your gold and silver is cankered; and the rust of them shall be a witness against you, and shall eat your flesh as it were fire. Ye have heaped treasure together for the last days" (Js.5:3).

"Better is a little with righteousness, than great revenues without right" (Pr.16:8).

"As the partridge sitteth on eggs, and hatcheth them not; so he that getteth riches, and not by right, shall leave them in the midst of his days, and at his end shall be a fool" (Je.17:11).

b. Some were astonished at Jesus' doctrine, at what He was teaching by His action.

"Blessed are they which do hunger and thirst after righteousness: for they shall be filled" (Mt.5:6).

"Lord, all my desire is before thee; and my groaning is not hid from thee" (Ps.38:9).

"With my soul have I desired thee in the night; yea, with my spirit within me will I seek thee early: for when thy judgments are in the earth, the inhabitants of the world will learn righteousness" (Is.26:9).

4 (11:19) **Jesus Christ, Response to**: Jesus left when the truth was rejected by the leaders. His life was being threatened; it was dangerous to stay overnight in the city. He could not foolishly expose Himself—He still had some things to do for God. His hour had not yet arrived, so He returned to the Mount of Olives which was safer during the night hours. (See note 2 and DEEPER STUDY # 1, *Mount of Olives*—Lu.21:37.)

Thought 1. In doing things for God and in carrying out His will, we are not to foolishly expose ourselves to danger and threats.

D. The Conditions of Prayer, 11:20-26
(Mt. 21:21-22)

1. The setting: The fig tree was noticed, 12-14
   a. The tree had been cursed by Jesus
   b. Peter was surprised at the answer to Jesus' prayer

2. The 1st condition of prayer: Have faith in God
   a. The object of faith: God
   b. The purpose of faith: To remove mountains
   c. The way to possess faith: Prayer
      1) Not doubting—in your heart
      2) Believing—in God's authority
   d. The results of faith

20 And in the morning, as they passed by, they saw the fig tree dried up from the roots.
21 And Peter calling to remembrance saith unto him, Master, behold, the fig tree which thou cursedst is withered away.
22 And Jesus answering saith unto them, Have faith in God.
23 For verily I say unto you, That whosoever shall say unto this mountain, Be thou removed, and be thou cast into the sea; and shall not doubt in his heart, but shall believe that those things which he saith shall come to pass; he shall have whatsoever he saith.
24 Therefore I say unto you, What things soever ye desire, when ye pray, believe that ye receive them, and ye shall have them.
25 And when ye stand praying, forgive, if ye have ought against any: that your Father also which is in heaven may forgive you your trespasses.
26 But if ye do not forgive, neither will your Father which is in heaven forgive your trespasses.

3. The 2nd condition of prayer: Desire, expect—ask & believe
   a. Emotions: Desire
   b. Will: Ask
   c. Spirit: Believe

4. The 3rd condition of prayer: Forgive others—while praying, forgive
   a. If forgive, will be forgiven
   b. If do not forgive, will not be forgiven

DIVISION VII

THE SON OF GOD'S LAST JERUSALEM MINISTRY: JESUS' WARNING AND CONFLICT WITH RELIGIONISTS, 11:1-12:44

D. The Conditions of Prayer, 11:20-26

(11:20-26) **Introduction**: prayer has its conditions. Jesus used the fig tree to teach what the conditions of prayer are.
1. The setting: the fig tree was noticed (vv.20-21).
2. The first condition of prayer: have faith in God (vv.22-23).
3. The second condition of prayer: desire, expect—ask and believe (v.24).
4. The third condition of prayer: forgive others—while praying, forgive (vv.25-26).

1 (11:20-21) **Prayer**: the fig tree was noticed as the disciples returned to the temple on Tuesday morning. It had not been noticed the evening before because they either took a different route out of the city to Bethany or it was too dark to notice when they passed by.

There are those who say the fig tree represented Israel. The fig tree was full of leaves, appearing fruitful, but it had no fruit. Israel appeared to be full, to be religious, professing spiritual fruit; but the nation bore no fruit. Its religion was barren, legalistic, and fruitless. Thus, the tree was a sign of disappointment and of coming justice and punishment.

We must note, however, this was not the lesson drawn by Jesus. There may be many lessons drawn from the event, including Israel's experience; but the application made by Jesus was clearly power, power that comes through faith and prayer (see outline and notes—Mt.21:17-22). Mark approaches the subject from a slightly different angle, an angle that can be titled "*The Conditions of Prayer*."

Peter was *surprised* at the answer to Jesus' prayer or pronouncement in cursing the fig tree. His surprise was both at the *effectiveness and the quickness of the answer*.

> **Thought 1.** The man who meets the conditions of prayer will be more effective and be more likely to have quick answers to his prayers.

2 (11:22-23) **Faith—Prayer**: the first condition to prayer is faith in God. But note four significant facts.

a. The object of faith is God Himself. The critical words are "in God." There are three significant things that need to be noted about the object of faith.

1) Jesus did not say, "Have faith," but "Have faith *in God*." Faith has to have an object. "In God" is where one is to have faith, where one is to place his faith. Faith has no value by itself; only the object (God) has value.

   The Bible never says to have faith in faith, yet this is the experience of many. Too often, a great difficulty or problem arises, and the believer feels he has to *arouse* his faith. He feels that if he can just *stir up* enough faith, he will whip the problem. But in reality he has had faith in faith. His mind, his attention, and his heart have been focused upon faith—not upon God.

2) Faith has no power; it is the object that has power. A man's faith is not going to remove the mountain. God is going to remove the mountain. The strength of faith is not faith, but God. In the Bible practically everyone who came to God had weak faith. Only a few had strong faith, yet God saved them and granted their requests (see Mt.14:22-33).

3) Faith requires knowing the object. The more one knows the object of faith, the more one believes in the object (see He.11:6). For example, consider two men who want to go out on a frozen lake to fish. One man is told to go ahead and cross the lake. He is assured by his friend that the ice will hold him up. Yet, when he begins to step out on the ice, he cautiously and tremblingly takes step after step—usually until he can stand

it no more and returns. But the other man walks out courageously and boldly, cuts a hole in the ice, sits down, and begins to fish.
Note three important questions.

⇒ What supported the man sitting out on the ice? Not his faith, but the ice—the object of his faith.
⇒ Who had the strongest faith? Of course the man out on the ice. The one with the weak faith is the man who slowly inched his way back.
⇒ What made the difference between the faith of the two? One thing. One man *knew* the ice, and the other man *did not know* the ice.

b. A second fact to note about faith is its purpose. The purpose of faith is to remove mountains. Jesus' teaching says, "Have faith in God...[and then] say unto this mountain, Be thou removed." Mountains represent the immovable, the impossible. It is something almost too steep to climb, almost too high to cross, almost too awesome to see beyond.

This is the reason Jesus discussed prayer and communion along with faith. One learns to have faith in God as He prays and communes with God. And the more he prays and communes with God, the more he will know God; and the more he knows God, the more he can experience faith in God and experience the removal of mountains that slow his progress through life. (See note and DEEPER STUDY # 3—Mt.17:20 for more discussion.)

c. A third fact to note about faith is the way to possess faith. The way is prayer. Jesus explicitly says, "Whosoever...shall not doubt...but shall believe that those things which he saith shall come to pass; he shall have whatsoever he saith." There are two crucial points in this promise.

1) Not doubting at all. This means never having a thought whether a thing can be done or not. It means not hesitating, not wondering, not questioning, not considering, not being concerned at all. Realistically, only God Himself can know if a thing will happen or not—know so perfectly that no wondering thought would ever cross His mind. What Christ is after is that we grow in belief and trust. He wants us to believe that all things are possible through Christ who strengthens us (Ph.4:13). (See outlines and notes—Mt.17:15-16; 17:17-18; 17:19-20; DEEPER STUDY # 3—Mk.9:18.)
2) Believing in God's authority. Note the words "shall say" (see note and DEEPER STUDY # 3—Mt.17:20). The power of Christ came from the authority of God. All He had to do was *say*, that is, speak the word and it was done. That is the very point He was making to us. If we believe, doubting not, then we stand in the authority of God. We may *say*, speak the word, and it shall be done.

d. A fourth fact to note about faith is the result of faith. A man who prays having faith, truly "having faith *in God,*...has whatsoever he saith." The mountains which confront him will be removed, *effectively and quickly* (see note—Mk.11:20-21).

"And all things, whatsoever ye shall ask in prayer, believing, ye shall receive" (Mt.21:22).

"Jesus said unto him, If thou canst believe, all things are possible to him that believeth" (Mk.9:23).

"Verily, verily, I say unto you, He that believeth on me, the works that I do shall he do also; and greater works than these shall he do; because I go unto my Father. And whatsoever ye shall ask in my name, that will I do, that the Father may be glorified in the Son. If ye shall ask any thing in my name, I will do it" (Jn.14:12-14).

"He shall call upon me, and I will answer him: I will be with him in trouble; I will deliver him, and honour him" (Ps.91:15).

"When the poor and needy seek water, and there is none, and their tongue faileth for thirst, I the LORD will hear them, I the God of Israel will not forsake them" (Is.41:17).

3 (11:24) **Prayer**: the second condition to prayer is expectancy. A man must believe and expect the answer to his prayer. He must be confident and assured, must anticipate and look for the answer (see note—Mt.21:22). The exact words of Jesus' promise are interesting (glance at the verse). Expectancy involves all of man's being. The spirit of expectancy...

- involves a man's emotions: he desires.
- involves a man's will (volition): he asks.
- involves a man's spirit: he believes.

"And this is the confidence that we have in him, that, if we ask any thing according to his will, he heareth us: and if we know that he hear us, whatsoever we ask, we know that we have the petitions that we desired of him" (1 Jn.5:14-15).

"But let him ask in faith, nothing wavering. For he that wavereth is like a wave of the sea driven with the wind and tossed" (Js.1:6).

"And it shall come to pass, that before they call, I will answer; and while they are yet speaking, I will hear" (Is.65:24).

4 (11:25-26) **Prayer—Forgiveness**: the third condition to prayer is forgiveness. This is a critical condition in prayer, a condition that is stressed time and again by Jesus (Mt.6:14-15; 5:23-24; 18:32-33). Note, it is while a person is *actually praying*, "when ye stand praying," that he must forgive. It does no good to pray unless he does forgive. When praying, there must always be forgiveness of those who have wronged us. Hard feelings or anger against a person is sin. It is evidence that we have not truly turned from our sins and are not really sincere in seeking forgiveness. (See outline and notes—Mt.6:14-15 for detailed discussion.) Note the stress Jesus puts upon the condition of receiving forgiveness in prayer. No request for forgiveness is granted unless a man has completely forgiven all others.

"And forgive us our debts, as we forgive our debtors" (Mt.6:12).

"For if ye forgive men their trespasses, your heavenly Father will also forgive you: but if ye forgive not men their trespasses, neither will your Father forgive your trespasses" (Mt.6:14-15).

"Blessed are the merciful: for they shall obtain mercy" (Mt.5:7).

"Be ye therefore merciful, as your Father also is merciful. Judge not, and ye shall not be judged: condemn not, and ye shall not be condemned: forgive, and ye shall be forgiven" (Lu.6:36-37).

	E. The Authority of Jesus Questioned: Two Choices Concerning Jesus, 11:27-33 *(Mt. 21:23-27; Lu. 20:1-8)*	by what authority I do these things. 30 The baptism of John, was it from heaven, or of men? answer me.	
1. The setting: Jesus was in the temple a. He was walking b. The religionists approached & questioned Him	27 And they come again to Jerusalem: and as he was walking in the temple, there come to him the chief priests, and the scribes, and the elders,	31 And they reasoned with themselves, saying, If we shall say, From heaven; he will say, Why then did ye not believe him?	a. Choice one: He was from God
2. The question of Jesus' authority a. The authority of His works b. The authority of His person	28 And say unto him, By what authority doest thou these things? and who gave thee this authority to do these things?	32 But if we shall say, Of men; they feared the people: for all men counted John, that he was a prophet indeed.	b. Choice two: He was a mere man
3. The choices for man: Illustrated by John the Baptist	29 And Jesus answered and said unto them, I will also ask of you one question, and answer me, and I will tell you	33 And they answered and said unto Jesus, We cannot tell. And Jesus answering saith unto them, Neither do I tell you by what authority I do these things.	**4. The tragic answer: No decision**

DIVISION VII

THE SON OF GOD'S LAST JERUSALEM MINISTRY:JESUS' WARNING AND CONFLICT WITH RELIGIONISTS, 11:1-12:44

E. The Authority of Jesus Questioned: Two Choices Concerning Jesus, 11:27-33

(11:27-33) **Introduction**: this is an important event. It began a series of six combative situations for Jesus. Both religionists and civil leaders confronted Jesus head-on, doing all they could to trap and discredit Jesus before the people so they could arrest Him and have Him killed. All the events of this section as well as the Olivet discourse (Mt.24-25) seem to have taken place on Tuesday (see Mt.22:23; 25:1; 26:1-2). A quick reading of this section is an eye-opener into the great tragedy and problem with self-righteousness and unbelief. Jesus was very forceful in attacking self-righteousness and unbelief. He delivered a *sustained attack*, leaving no doubt that a person, even a religionist, who continued in self-righteousness was unworthy of God's kingdom. Obstinate unbelief would doom any man.

1. The setting: Jesus in the temple (v.27).
2. The question of Jesus' authority (v.28).
3. The choices for man: illustrated by John the Baptist (vv.29-32).
4. The tragic answer: no decision (v.33).

1 (11:27) **Temple—Solomon's Porch—Jesus Christ, Opposition**: Jesus was in the temple, apparently walking through one of the arcades meditating and praying. He seems to have been alone. The scene was dramatic when one pictures the background.

The temple actually had two arcades surrounding the Court of the Gentiles. They were just as films picture the arcades of the Greek and Roman eras: stately, magnificent, and awe-inspiring. There was an east arcade and a south arcade. The east arcade was known as Solomon's porch. Several Biblical events took place in this magnificent arcade (Jn.10:23; Acts 3:11; 5:12). It was an arcade for teaching, and Rabbis often strolled among the colonnades while teaching their pupils. The arcades were also large enough to allow large crowds to gather for classroom type instructions. Their magnificence can be imagined by picturing the stately columns which towered thirty-five feet above the ground. The arcades provided both shelter from rain and sun and an inspiring setting.

Jesus was apparently walking along in one of the two arcades when the religionists approached Him. Again, they were an official delegation from the ruling body of the Jews, that is, from the Sanhedrin. Representatives from the three major groups were there: the chief priests, the Scribes, and the elders (see DEEPER STUDY #1—Mt.16:21). They were upset, infuriated, enraged. All that had happened—the triumphal entry, Jesus' acceptance of the people's homage and the title of Messiah, the cleansing of the temple and the disruption of the priests' profits from those who sold and bought, the healing of the blind and lame, the worship of the children—naturally created a crisis for the ruling body. What Jesus was doing simply infuriated them, sending them into a rage. It aroused them to question: "Who does this Jesus of Nazareth think He is?" (Mt.21:10-11).

Note that the question they asked was one of contempt, not of seeking. The question was an attempt to discredit, not to learn the truth. The question was aroused because their own position, esteem, and gain were disturbed; not because they really wanted to know if He were the Messiah. Their minds were closed and shut to His claims. They had many claims and many proofs of His Messiahship, but they willfully ignored and denied His divine mission. They had plenty of opportunity to learn the truth (see note—Jn.3:1-2), yet they would allow nothing to change them. They were gripped by obstinate unbelief (see DEEPER STUDY # 1—Mt.12:1-8; note and DEEPER STUDY # 1—12:10; note—15:1-20; DEEPER STUDY # 2—15:6-9. These notes will give some background to the opposition against Jesus.)

2 (11:28) **Jesus Christ, Opposition; Authority Questioned; Deity—Man, Basic Question**: the question of authority. This was the basic question that should have been asked, a question that probed into the very nature of Jesus: What was

His authority? Who sent Him? Who empowered Him? Who gave Him the right to do as He was doing? Where had He come from?

The leaders wanted to know what right He had to interfere with their lives and area of responsibility. They were the authorized guardians and rulers of the temple and of the people. He was interfering with their management and had no right to interfere. Note, they asked Him two questions.

a. What was the authority for His works? "By what authority doest thou *these things*?" He marched triumphantly into the city of Jerusalem as a King, receiving the homage of the Messianic King from the people; He cast the market traders out of the temple; He healed the blind and lame (Mt.21:14); and He accepted the homage of small children's proclaiming Him to be the Messiah. What authority did He have to do these things?

The leaders were asking the basic question that needed to be asked. Perhaps they were unaware of it, but they were asking the question that would determine their eternal fate. Every man needs to ask, "What is the authority, the explanation, for the works of Christ?" There are the works of...

- ministry
- raising the dead
- healing
- ascending into heaven
- preaching
- teaching
- rising again
- foretelling the future
- calming the storms of nature
- dying and fulfilling Scripture

b. What was the authority of His person: "*Who gave thee* this authority?" He *was claiming...*

- to be the promised Messianic King by entering the city as He did.
- to be the Head, the God of the Temple: "My house."
- to be the Light of the world to the blind and the Messianic Healer to the lame (Mt.21:14).
- to be the Messianic fulfillment of Scripture by receiving the praise of the children.

The authorities knew who He was claiming to be. They just rejected His claims and refused to believe. They chose the course of obstinate unbelief. They had proof upon proof, but still refused to believe.

There are two possible answers to the question about who Jesus is.

1) Jesus could have claimed to act by His own authority, could have said the power was His own. This would have made Him an ego-maniac or a great imposter, the greatest in history. Of course, if He had claimed to act of His own authority, the authorities would have been able to discredit Him immediately and to arrest Him for causing so much havoc.
2) Jesus could have claimed to act by the authority of God, to be of and from God. Now note: Jesus did make such a claim time and again. But if He had made it in the face of the authorities, they would have arrested Him immediately for blasphemy. They would have claimed that God would never have given orders to cause such turmoil in the temple.

   Again the leaders were asking the basic question that needs to be asked by every man: *Who gave Jesus His authority*? Who is He: a mere man or truly the Son of God? Is He of man or of God? Is His authority of men or from within, of His very own nature as God?

3 (11:29-32) **Decision—Jesus Christ, Deity; Opposition—Messiah**: the choices for man—illustrated by John the Baptist. Jesus knew what the authorities were plotting. Note what He did.

First, He met them on their own ground. He said He would answer them, but they must first answer a question, then He would answer them.

Second, He formulated and asked a question that was astounding in its effect.

⇒ It actually answered their question.
⇒ It silenced them, for if they answered they would indict themselves.
⇒ It ended the discussion and their questioning of Christ and immediate threat to Him.
⇒ It revealed their obstinate unbelief and made them even more inexcusable before God (heaping wrath upon themselves).

Jesus simply asked them, "The baptism of John, was it from heaven [of God], or of men?" The question posed two choices to man.

a. The first choice: Was John from God? If so, then Jesus was from God. Why? Because being from God, John would not lie, and John testified:

> **"Behold the Lamb of God, which taketh away the sin of the world....And I saw, and bare record that this is the Son of God" (Jn.1:29, 34).**

b. The second choice: Was John a mere man? If so, then Jesus could be a mere man. But how could this ever be? If John's and Jesus' ministry were really of men, then how could so many *changed lives* and *marvelous works* be accounted for? This one question alone shows the absurdity and sin of unbelief, not only of unbelievers in Jesus' day but also of unbelievers in our day as well (see outline and notes—Mt.3:1-17).

> **"And all the people that heard him [John] and the publicans, justified God, being baptized of John" (Lu.7:29).**
>
> **"Jesus answered them, I told you, and ye believed not: the works that I do in my Father's name, they bear witness of me" (Jn.10:25).**
>
> **"Say ye of him, whom the Father hath sanctified, and sent into the world, Thou blasphemest; because I said, I am the Son of God? If I do not the works of my Father, believe me not. But if I do, though**

ye believe not me, believe the works: that ye may know, and believe, that the Father is in me, and I in him" (Jn.10:36-38).

"And many resorted unto him, and said, John did no miracles: but all things that John spake of this man were true. And many believed on him there" (Jn.10:41-42).

"Believest thou not that I am in the Father, and the Father in me? the words that I speak unto you I speak not of myself: but the Father that dwelleth in me, he doeth the works" (Jn.14:10).

Note the words, "They reasoned *with themselves*" (par eantois). This means they discussed their answer among themselves. They did not just *in* (en) themselves, with each left to his own thoughts. This was a planned attack against Jesus, a deliberate rejection of Jesus.

The Lord's questioners immediately knew their predicament. If they replied that John's ministry was of God, then Jesus would ask them why they did not believe John's testimony about the Messiah. If they replied that John's ministry was of men, they would arouse the people against themselves, for the people believed strongly that John was a true prophet from God.

Note how the questioners reasoned with themselves. Their concern was not to discover the truth; but to save face and protect their position, esteem, and security. They, therefore, committed a threefold sin.

a. They deliberately denied Jesus. To confess that John was of God would force them to acknowledge Jesus. And they were not willing to confess Him. They feared the loss of all they possessed (position, power, wealth, esteem, image, security).

b. They feared men; they were deliberately cowardly. They feared the reactions of men (abuse, ridicule, persecution).

c. They chose expediency, to deliberately be ignorant. They feared being shamed, embarrassed, ridiculed. To confess Jesus would mean confessing *they* had been wrong all along. It would mean denying self completely and doing so publicly. Most men...

- choose expediency rather than principle.
- choose to play it safe rather than to stand for the truth.
- choose to say I don't know rather than to speak the truth.

Thought 1. We have the same two choices that the authorities did. Christ is either a mere man (ego-maniac or imposter) or He is as John declared, "the Lamb of God...the Son of God" (Jn.1:29, 34). Every man has to choose and make a decision.

"Jesus answered them, I told you, and ye believed not: the works that I do in my Father's name, they bear witness of me" (Jn.10:25).

"Say ye of him, whom the Father hath sanctified, and sent into the world, Thou blasphemest; because I said, I am the Son of God? If I do not the works of my Father, believe me not. But if I do, though ye believe not me, believe the works: that ye may know, and believe, that the Father is in me, and I in him" (Jn.10:36-38).

"Believest thou not that I am in the Father, and the Father in me? the words that I speak unto you I speak not of myself: but the Father that dwelleth in me, he doeth the works" (Jn.14:10).

4 (11:33) **Decision**: the tragic answer—no decision (see notes and DEEPER STUDY #5—Mt.8:21-22). The authorities said, "We cannot tell." They lied. They knew perfectly well that John's baptism was of God. They just were not willing to run the risk of losing their position, prosperity, and security. They loved the world more than they loved God and the hope He extended toward them. Therefore, they denied, acted cowardly, and chose the route of expediency.

These unbelievers made no decision. It was tragic. Indecision and agnosticism are always tragic. They just would not be convinced of the truth. It was not that they *could not* be convinced, but they *would not*. Such obstinate unbelief seldom, if ever, sees the truth of Christ. Even if Christ openly revealed the truth to them, they would reject.

"If they hear not Moses and the prophets, neither will they be persuaded though one rose from the dead" (Lu.16:31).

"And ye will not come to me, that ye might have life" (Jn.5:40).

"[God] sent forth his servants to call them that were bidden to the wedding: and they would not come" (Mt.22:3).

"And now, because ye have done all these works, saith the LORD, and I spake unto you, rising up early and speaking, but ye heard not; and I called you, but ye answered not....And I will cast you out of my sight" (Je.7:13, 15).

"I call heaven and earth to record this day against you, that I have set before you life and death, blessing and cursing: therefore choose life, that both thou and thy seed may live: that thou mayest love the LORD thy God, and that thou mayest obey his voice, and that thou mayest cleave unto him: for he is thy life, and the length of thy days" (De.30:19-20).

"For he saith, I have heard thee in a time accepted, and in the day of salvation have I succoured thee: behold, now is the accepted time; behold, now is the day of salvation" (2 Co.6:2).

CHAPTER 12

F. The Parable of the Wicked Tenants: God & Israel or God & Man, 12:1-12

(Mt. 21:33-46; Lu. 20:9-19; Is. 5:1-7)

1. God is generous: He gives man everything needed

2. God is trusting: He gives man the responsibility & freedom to govern life

And he began to speak unto them by parables. A certain man planted a vineyard, and set an hedge about it, and digged a place for the winefat, and built a tower, and let it out to husbandmen, and went into a far country.

3. God is exacting: He expects payment

4. God is patient: He sends messengers to receive payment

2 And at the season he sent to the husbandmen a servant, that he might receive from the husbandmen of the fruit of the vineyard.

a. One suffers mild abuse

3 And they caught him, and beat him, and sent him away empty.

b. Another suffers severe abuse

4 And again he sent unto them another servant; and at him they cast stones, and wounded him in the head, and sent him away shamefully handled.

c. Still another suffers capital abuse

5 And again he sent another; and him they killed, and many others; beating some, and killing some.

5. God is love: He sends His very own Son to the world

6 Having yet therefore one son, his well-beloved, he sent him also last unto them, saying, They will reverence my son.

a. Man's plot: To kill the Son*DS1*

b. Man's reason: To steal the inheritance

7 But those husbandmen said among themselves, This is the heir; come, let us kill him, and the inheritance shall be ours.

c. Man's crime: They killed the Son

8 And they took him, and killed him, and cast him out of the vineyard.

6. God is just: He will come to destroy the evil keepers (Israel or man)

9 What shall therefore the lord of the vineyard do? he will come and destroy the husbandmen, and will give the vineyard unto others.

7. God is trustworthy: He fulfills His promises*DS1*

a. The promise of the Messiah—the stone

b. The exaltation of the Messiah

10 And have ye not read this scripture; The stone which the builders rejected is become the head of the corner:

11 This was the Lord's doing, and it is marvellous in our eyes?

8. Conclusion: The great tragedy

a. Reacting instead of repenting

b. Holding the wrong view of Messiah

c. Leaving Him & going their own way

12 And they sought to lay hold on him, but feared the people: for they knew that he had spoken the parable against them: and they left him, and went their way.

DIVISION VII

THE SON OF GOD'S LAST JERUSALEM MINISTRY: JESUS' WARNING AND CONFLICT WITH RELIGIONISTS, 11:1-12:44

F. The Parable of the Wicked Tenants: God and Israel or God and Man, 12:1-12

(12:1-12) **Introduction**: this is one of the most interesting parables ever told by Jesus. It is interesting because it is both historical and predictive. Jesus covered the history of Israel from God's perspective, just as God sees it (vv.1-5). And then He predicted or revealed exactly what was going to happen to Israel: they were going to reject God's own Son (v.6), and because of their rejection and cruelty, God was going to reject them by giving the Kingdom of God to another people (v.9).

What is said throughout this passage is applicable to all people as well as to Israel. God has entrusted the vineyard of the church and of the world to us (Mt.28:19-20), the new nation, the new creation of God (see notes—Ep.2:11-18; pt.4—Ep.2:14-15; 4:17-19). Every point covered in Israel's history should, therefore, be a dynamic message speaking to our hearts.

1. God is generous: He gives man everything needed (v.1).
2. God is trusting: He gives man the responsibility and freedom to govern life (v.1).
3. God is exacting: He expects payment (v.2).
4. God is patient: He sends messengers to receive payment (vv.2-5).
5. God is love: He sends His very own Son to the world (vv.6-8).
6. God is just: He will come to destroy the evil keepers (Israel or man) (v.9).
7. God is trustworthy: He fulfills His promises (vv.10-11).
8. Conclusion: the great tragedy (v.12).

1 (12:1) **God, Provision—Care—World—Israel**: God is generous. He gives everything needed. Note three marvelous, generous things that God did for His vineyard. He provided every conceivable thing to take care of His vineyard and the cultivators. Everything was provided to assure growth and fruitfulness. The cultivators have no excuse for not producing.

a. God "hedged it round about." This was a wall built around the vineyard to keep the animals away from the grapes. The hedge or wall *assured* growth and fruitfulness.

b. God dug a winepress. This was a trough or vat into which the wine was pressed. The trough was sometimes dug in rock, sometime built out of wood. The trough stands for the equipment which God provides to get His work done.

c. God built a tower. It was a watchtower used to guard and protect the vineyard from thieves. The tower stands for the assurance and security of God's care which He gives to His cultivators (see Mt.6:25-34).

Thought 1. God is generous to every man.

(1) God has given every man the world and his space in it to look after. (See note—Mk.12:1 for discussion and verses.)

(2) God has hedged His followers and the church round about. He protects them and assures growth and fruitfulness (Jn.15:1-8).

> **"Ye have not chosen me, but I have chosen you, and ordained you, that ye should go and bring forth fruit, and that your fruit should remain: that whatsoever ye shall ask of the Father in my name, he may give it you" (Jn.15:16).**
>
> **"Being filled with the fruits of righteousness, which are by Jesus Christ, unto the glory and praise of God" (Ph.1:11).**
>
> **"That ye might walk worthy of the Lord unto all pleasing, being fruitful in every good work, and increasing in the knowledge of God; strengthened with all might, according to his glorious power, unto all patience and longsuffering with joyfulness" (Col.1:10-11).**

(3) God gives His followers the gifts, the equipment they need to carry out their task on earth (1 Co.12:4-11).

> **"And unto one he gave five talents, to another two, and to another one; to every man according to his several ability; and straightway took his journey" (Mt.25:15).**
>
> **"But ye shall receive power, after that the Holy Ghost is come upon you: and ye shall be witnesses unto me both in Jerusalem, and in all Judaea, and in Samaria, and unto the uttermost part of the earth" (Ac.1:8).**
>
> **"Having then gifts differing according to the grace that is given to us" (Ro.12:6).**
>
> **"Now there are diversities of gifts, but the same Spirit" (1 Co.12:4).**

(4) God gives His followers the assurance and security of His care (Mt.6:25-34).

> **"Therefore take no thought, saying, What shall we eat? or, What shall we drink? or, Wherewithal shall we be clothed? (For after all these things do the Gentiles seek:) for your heavenly Father knoweth that ye have need of all these things" (Mt.6:31-32).**
>
> **"But even the very hairs of your head are all numbered. Fear not therefore: ye are of more value than many sparrows" (Lu.12:7).**
>
> **"Casting all your care upon him; for he careth for you" (1 Pe.5:7).**
>
> **"But my God shall supply all your need according to his riches in glory by Christ Jesus" (Ph.4:19).**

2 (12:1) **Freedom of Will—Responsibility—Trust**: God is trusting. He gives responsibility and freedom to govern life. God entrusted His vineyard to cultivators. The cultivators were the nation and people of Israel, in particular the leaders (both religious and civil). Everyone was to take care of the whole body of people. Everyone was responsible, thereby contributing to the welfare and provision of all. (See the whole body of the church and every member's responsibility to labor in the vineyard doing his part.)

Note two things.

a. God trusts men. Think what a glorious privilege it is to be trusted by God. Imagine how dear God's vineyard is to Him, and then think about how He entrusts its care to us and not to angels or some other higher form of being. What a wonderful and marvelous thing that God would trust us with His most precious vineyard!

b. God gives man freedom. God left the cultivators to care for His vineyard as they wished. They were to exercise their will, their choice, their drive to care for the vineyard. They had the glorious privilege of freedom, of not having someone looking over their shoulder forcing behavior.

Thought 1. Two of the greatest gifts God has given men are *trust* and *freedom*. The very fact of being trusted by God is one of the most glorious privileges of life. And being given the freedom to care for God's immense creation is beyond comprehension. How marvelous are these two glorious gifts! Yet, note how men have neglected, abused, violated, and even worked to destroy these great gifts.

> **"So God created man in his own image, in the image of God created he him; male and female created he them. And God blessed them, and God said unto them, Be fruitful, and multiply, and replenish the earth, and subdue it: and have dominion over the fish of the sea, and over the fowl of the air, and over every living thing that moveth upon the earth" (Ge.1:27-28).**
>
> **"Thou madest him to have dominion over the works of thy hands; thou hast put all things under his feet" (Ps.8:6).**
>
> **"For the kingdom of heaven is as a man travelling into a far country, who called his own servants, and delivered unto them his goods" (Mt.25:14).**
>
> **"Moreover it is required in stewards, that a man be found faithful" (1 Co.4:2).**
>
> **"Keep that which is committed to thy trust, avoiding profane and vain babblings, and oppositions of science falsely so called" (1 Ti.6:20).**
>
> **"And he called his ten servants, and delivered them ten pounds, and said unto them, Occupy till I come" (Lu.19:13).**

3 (12:2) **Accountability**: God is exacting—He expects payment. He is businesslike; He holds men accountable. God sent messengers to gather the fruits of His vineyard. The messengers would be the prophets and the good and godly leaders throughout Israel's history (judges, kings, and priests).

Note two things.

a. Fruit was expected. Every cultivator, that is, every person responsible for the vineyard, was expected to labor and produce.

b. A day of accountability did come. Every man was expected to pay his dues, to make his contribution for the wonderful privilege of living in the beautiful vineyard and being blessed by it. (The Kingdom of God, the world, the church—however one applies this passage—all are wonderful vineyards for which we are responsible to contribute what fruit we can.)

> **"He spake also this parable; A certain man had a fig tree planted in his vineyard; and he came and sought fruit thereon, and found none" (Lu.13:6).**
>
> **"Every branch in me that beareth not fruit he taketh away: and every branch that beareth fruit, he purgeth it, that it may bring forth more fruit" (Jn.15:2).**
>
> **"I am the vine, ye are the branches: He that abideth in me, and I in him, the same bringeth forth much fruit: for without me ye can do nothing. If a man abide not in me, he is cast forth as a branch, and is withered; and men gather them, and cast them into the fire, and they are burned" (Jn.15:5-6).**

4 (12:2-5) **God, Patience of—Long-Suffering**: God is patient—He sends messengers to receive payment. All through Israel's history, God loved and showed His loving-kindness by not reacting and rejecting the nation. God gives man chance after chance. He sends messengers across our path time after time. He loves and aches for us to pay our dues, to bear fruit by living as we should.

Tragically, most cultivators continue as always: rebelling and claiming all rights to the vineyard and to their own lives. Therefore, they continue to react against God's messengers. This was true of Israel. They rebelled and refused to pay the Master. In fact, their rebellion led to the persecution and murder of God's servants.

a. Men do deliberately rebel against God. Men want to rule the vineyard themselves. They want to be the kings of the kingdom, the rulers of the earth, and even the heads of the church. They want things to go their way and to rule and reign as they desire and will. They want no authority above themselves. They want to live and do things as they wish, and they want to claim the fruits for themselves.

b. Men want their own way so much that they ridicule, slander, persecute, and even murder the true servants of God.

> **"Which of the prophets have not your fathers persecuted? and they have slain them which showed before of the coming of the Just One; of whom ye have been now the betrayers and murderers" (Ac.7:52. See Mt.23:34-37; Heb.11:36-38.)**

c. The servant of God must understand that he is called to suffer (see DEEPER STUDY # 2—Mt.20:22-23). Note the detailed description of the world's treatment of God's messengers.

⇒ They *beat and gave no fruit* to the first messenger.
⇒ They cast stones, wounded, and shamefully handled the second messenger.
⇒ They killed the third messenger.
⇒ They beat "many others."
⇒ They killed "many others."

> **"Then said he unto the dresser of his vineyard, Behold, these three years I come seeking fruit on this fig tree, and find none: cut it down; why cumbereth it the ground? And he answering said unto him, Lord, let it alone this year also, till I shall dig about it, and dung it: and if it bear fruit, well: and if not, then after that thou shalt cut it down" (Lu.13:7-9).**
>
> **"The Lord is not slack concerning his promise, as some men count slackness; but is longsuffering to us-ward, not willing that any should perish, but that all should come to repentance" (2 Pe.3:9).**
>
> **"For my name's sake will I defer mine anger, and for my praise will I refrain for thee, that I cut thee not off" (Is.48:9).**

Thought 1. How many believers, laymen and ministers alike, are mistreated by the world!

> **"For unto you it is given in the behalf of Christ, not only to believe on him, but also to suffer for his sake" (Ph.1:29).**
>
> **"Yea, and all that will live godly in Christ Jesus shall suffer persecution" (2 Ti.3:12).**
>
> **"Beloved, think it not strange concerning the fiery trial which is to try you, as though some strange thing happened unto you: but rejoice, inasmuch as ye are partakers of Christ's sufferings; that, when his glory shall be revealed, ye may be glad also with exceeding joy" (1 Pe.4:12-13; see 1 Pe.2:21; 4:5-6; Mt.19:29; Ro.8:16-17).**

5 (12:6-8) **God, Love of**: God is love. Therefore, God sent His very own Son to the world, wanting to speak personally to men. He condescended and asked His Son to leave the glory of eternity and to bring His Word to earth, speaking face to face with man. Perhaps they would listen to His voice and reverence His rights.

Note five facts.

a. Jesus claimed to be God's Son. He was different from all the servants sent before. He was more than another man-servant; He was God's very own Son. There is no question that Jesus was clearly making this unique claim for Himself.

b. The cultivators saw God's Son. There were all kinds of evidence: Old Testament prophecies, the testimony of John the Baptist, Jesus' own claim and the miraculous works to prove His deity, the fulness or signs of the times (Ga.4:4). There was a feeling that He was the promised Messiah even among those who opposed Him (see note—Jn.3:1-2; see Jn.11:47-53). This is the tragic indictment against the Jews. Down deep within, they had a sense that Jesus really was the Messiah; but sin and greed for position, esteem, power, and security kept them from acknowledging Him. Their unbelief was deliberate and obstinate (see outline and notes—Mt.21:23-27).

c. The cultivators plotted His death (see Mt.12:14; Jn.11:53).

d. The cultivators planned to seize His inheritance. Men wanted to possess the kingdom, the nation, the property, the power, the rule, the reign, the position, the esteem, the fame, the recognition, the wealth. Whatever the possession is, men want the possession themselves. And they will deny, deceive, lie, cheat, steal, and even kill to get it. (See notes—Mt.12:1-8; note and DEEPER STUDY # 1—12:10; note—15:1-20; DEEPER STUDY # 2—15:6-9.)

e. The cultivators murdered the Son. They committed the worst crime of human history: they killed the Son of God Himself. Note two things: (1) Jesus' death was being prophesied. He was predicting His death Himself. And (2) Jesus' death was a willing act on His part. He knew death lay ahead, so He could have escaped. But He chose to die. It was in "the determinate counsel of God" (Ac.2:23).

> **"For God so loved the world, that he gave his only begotten Son, that whosoever believeth in him should not perish, but have everlasting life" (Jn.3:16).**
>
> **"But God commendeth his love toward us, in that, while we were yet sinners, Christ died for us" (Ro.5:8).**
>
> **"But God, who is rich in mercy, for his great love wherewith he loved us, even when we were dead in sins, hath quickened us together with Christ, (by grace ye are saved)" (Ep.2:4-5).**

DEEPER STUDY # 1

(12:7) **Man, Error**: man feels God is too far away to do anything about his rejection. He feels God is too inactive and irrelevant. This is known by the "far country" (v.1), and the continuous rejection (vv.3-5), and the final denial of God's Son (vv.6-8).

6 (12:9) **God, Justice of**: God is just—He shall come and destroy evil keepers. There are three important points here.

a. Jesus said the Lord of the vineyard is coming. He is coming to revenge the death of His only Son.

b. God is coming to destroy the wicked. The destruction is to be *miserable* (kakos), terrible. Note that it was both the rulers and the people who said that justice would be executed. Man, by his very nature, expects injustice to be punished.

c. God is going to trust His vineyard to others. Again, it was the crowd who said this. Even man knows that a vineyard will not lie unkept. It will be cultivated by someone. God will raise up a new people to care for it (the church, the new creation of God. See DEEPER STUDY # 8—Mt.21:43; notes—Ro.9:25-33; Ep.2:11-18; pt.4—Ep.2:14-15; 4:17-19 for more discussion.)

> **"And now also the axe is laid unto the root of the trees: therefore every tree which bringeth not forth good fruit is hewn down, and cast into the fire" (Mt.3:10).**
>
> **"But that which beareth thorns and briers is rejected, and is nigh unto cursing: whose end is to be burned" (He.6:8).**

7 (12:10-11) **Jesus Christ, the Stone—Promise Fulfilled**: God is trustworthy—He fulfills His promises. Christ is the Head cornerstone (see note—Lu.2:34). This is a quotation from Ps.118:22-23. It was recognized as a Messianic prophecy. The Messiah was to be the head cornerstone who was to begin building the Kingdom of God and who was to support all other stones or leaders who came later. The religious leaders standing around Christ knew that Christ was referring to the Messiah (Is.28:16; Da.2:34; Zec.3:9).

But note the promises. The stone was to be rejected at first. It was to be considered unsuitable and useless for the building. The builders would not allow the stone to be a part of the building; they would cast it aside and treat it as unusable.

However, the great Architect overruled the builders. He raised the stone from the graveyard of rejected stones and exalted it to the position of head cornerstone, the stone which supports all other stones and which holds the building of God's kingdom both up and together (see Ph.2:9-11. See notes—Ep.2:20.)

The symbolism of the head cornerstone says at least two significant things to us.

a. The cornerstone is the first stone laid. All other stones are placed after it. It is the preeminent stone in time. So it is with Christ. He is *the first* of God's new movement.

⇒ Christ is the captain of our salvation. All others are crew members or soldiers who follow Him.

> **"For it became him, for whom are all things, and by whom are all things, in bringing many sons unto glory, to make the captain of their salvation perfect through sufferings" (He.2:10).**

⇒ Christ is the author of eternal salvation and of our faith. All others are the readers of the story.

> **"And being made perfect, he became the author of eternal salvation unto all them that obey him" (He.5:9).**

"Looking unto Jesus the author and finisher of our faith; who for the joy that was set before him endured the cross, despising the shame, and is set down at the right hand of the throne of God" (He.12:2).

⇒ Christ is the beginning and the end. All others come after Him.

"I am Alpha and Omega, the beginning and the ending, saith the Lord, which is, and which was, and which is to come, the Almighty" (Re.1:8; see 21:6; 22:13).

⇒ Christ is the forerunner into the very presence of God. All others enter God's presence after Him.

"Which hope we have as an anchor of the soul, both sure and stedfast, and which entereth into that within the veil; whither the forerunner is for us entered, even Jesus, made an high priest for ever after the order of Melchisedec" (He.6:19-20).

b. The cornerstone is the supportive stone. All other stones are placed upon it and held up by it. They all rest upon it. It is the preeminent stone in position and power. So it is with Christ. He is the support and power, the Foundation of God's new movement.

⇒ Christ is *the head cornerstone*, the only true foundation upon which man can build. All crumble who are not laid upon Him.

"For other foundation can no man lay than that is laid, which is Jesus Christ" (1 Co.3:11).

⇒ Christ is *the chief cornerstone* upon which all others are fitly formed together. All who wish to be fitly formed together have to be laid upon Him.

"And are built upon the foundation of the apostles and prophets, Jesus Christ himself being the chief corner stone; in whom all the building fitly framed together groweth unto an holy temple in the Lord: in whom ye also are builded together for an habitation of God through the Spirit" (Ep.2:20-22).

⇒ Christ is *the living stone* upon which all others are built up a spiritual house. All others have to be built upon Him if they wish to live and have their spiritual sacrifice accepted by God.

"To whom coming, as unto a living stone, disallowed indeed of men, but chosen of God, and precious, ye also, as lively stones, are built up a spiritual house, an holy priesthood, to offer up spiritual sacrifices, acceptable to God by Jesus Christ" (1 Pe.2:4-5).

Note it is all God's work. He is the One who raises up the Savior. Note also, the Savior is the object of marvel and wonder.

8 (12:12) **Jesus Christ, Response—Decision**: the conclusion of the parable was a great tragedy, a tragedy that has been seen in so many people down through the years.

a. There was the tragedy of reacting instead of repenting. The leaders saw that Jesus was speaking to them. But their consciences were seared by obstinate unbelief (1 Ti.4:2). They were insensitive to His warnings (v.9). Therefore, they reacted instead of repenting. They should have heeded His warnings, but they did not. They were set against Him, seeking to destroy Him and thereby silencing His claim.

b. There was the tragedy of holding the wrong view of the Messiah. This is seen in the people. The leaders were afraid to arrest Jesus because of the people. The people saw Jesus as some great prophet (a great Teacher) and not as the Messiah, the Son of the Living God. This, too, was tragic; but God was able to use their respect to protect Christ until the appointed time for His death.

c. There was the tragedy of leaving Jesus and going their own way. Note this was exactly what they did. (See note, *Decision*—Mk.11:33 for Scripture application.)

Outline	Scripture	Scripture (cont.)	Outline (cont.)
	G. The Question of Civil & Religious Power: The State & God, 12:13-17 *(Mt. 22:15-22; Lu. 20:20-26)*	not?	
		15 Shall we give, or shall we not give? But he, knowing their hypocrisy, said unto them, Why tempt ye me? bring me a penny, that I may see it.	**3. Life within the state depends upon God, not money: Jesus does not have even a coin**
1. The false views a. Religion is supreme*DS1* b. The state is supreme*DS2* (Herodians)	13 And they send unto him certain of the Pharisees and of the Herodians, to catch him in his words.	16 And they brought it. And he saith unto them, Whose is this image and superscription? And they said unto him, Caesar's.	**4. The state is ordained by God: Some things belong to the state**
2. The sins common to false views of the state*DS3* a. Selfish ambition: Selfish ambition: Leads to compromise b. Deception: Leads to false flattery & destruction c. Obstinate unbelief: Leads to denial of truth, condemnation	14 And when they were come, they say unto him, Master, we know that thou art true, and carest for no man: for thou regardest not the person of men, but teachest the way of God in truth: Is it lawful to give tribute to Caesar, or	17 And Jesus answering said unto them, Render to Caesar the things that are Caesar's, and to God the things that are God's. And they marvelled at him.	**5. The state is limited in its power: God is due the things that are God's**

DIVISION VII

THE SON OF GOD'S LAST JERUSALEM MINISTRY: JESUS' WARNING AND CONFLICT WITH RELIGIONISTS, 11:1-12:44

G. The Question of Civil and Religious Power: The State and God, 12:13-17

(12:13-17) **Introduction**: this was the second challenge of the leaders against Jesus. The Sanhedrin, the ruling body of the Jews, had met officially and plotted how they might "catch [Jesus] in his words" (v.13). They devised a question dealing with taxes and a person's citizenship in the state: "Is it lawful to give tribute [taxes] to Caesar, or not?" A *yes* answer would discredit Jesus with the people because they opposed paying taxes to a foreign conqueror (Rome). A *no* answer would cause Him to be arrested by the Roman authorities for opposing the law and threatening a revolt.

Jesus, being the Messiah, the Son of God Himself, saw through their plot. And Jesus used the occasion to teach the truth about citizenship, a truth which was both astounding and earth-shaking to the people of that day. It was earth-shaking because the Jews had always believed that the loyalty of a citizen belonged only to God, and the rest of the world believed that their loyalty belonged to the ruling monarch of their territory. Jesus astounded the world of His day by declaring that there is an earthly citizenship to which some things are to be given, and there is a spiritual, heavenly citizenship to which some things are to be given.

1. The false views (v.13).
2. The sins common to false views of the state (v.14).
3. Life within the state depends upon God, not money: Jesus does not have even a coin (v.15).
4. The state is ordained by God: some things belong to the state (vv.16-17).
5. The state is limited in its power: God is due the things that are God's (v.17).

1 (12:13) **State—Citizenship**: the false views of the state are seen in the Pharisees and Herodians. But it must be remembered that the world did not know the concepts were false until this experience.

a. The first false concept is that religion is supreme. This is seen in the view of the Pharisees (see DEEPER STUDY # 3—Acts 23:8). They believed strongly in the heavenly, spiritual world, so much so that they believed all obedience and loyalty were due God and God alone. In fact, all things on earth were due God. The state and all other power and authority were to be subject to religious rule. Therefore, they were strongly against paying taxes to a foreign king. Paying taxes to a secular government was an infringement upon God's right.

b. The second false concept is that the state is supreme. This is seen in the view of the Herodians (see DEEPER STUDY #2—Mk.12:13 for discussion).

Picture the scene, how strange it was. The Pharisees held that religion was dominant over government. They despised Roman authority and taxation. The Herodians held that government was dominant over religion. They would agree that taxes must be paid to Caesar rather than to God. They and the Pharisees were bitter enemies. To find them together was strange indeed. But their hatred of Jesus had brought them together against One whom they considered a common enemy. (See notes—Mk.3:6; DEEPER STUDY # 3—Ac.23:8.)

DEEPER STUDY # 1
(12:13) **Pharisees**: see DEEPER STUDY # 3—Ac.23:8.

DEEPER STUDY # 2
(12:13) **Herodians**: the Herodians were not a religious party, but a political party of Herod, the King of Galilee. They were supportive of Rome, compromising wherever they could in order to preserve their own power and influence. They had compromised to such a point that they gave some degree of consent to pagan temples. Religiously, they were mainly Sadducees who gave their first loyalty to the state (see DEEPER STUDY # 3—Ac.23:8). Therefore, they opposed all Messianic claims because of the disturbance such claims caused among the people. They would agree that taxes must be paid to Caesar rather than to God.

2 (12:14) **Citizenship—Sins**: there are the sins common to false views of the state. On the surface the question which these men asked was innocent. It was a question asked by some in every generation: "Is it lawful to give tribute to Caesar [the state] or not?" But the answer was dangerous. If Jesus had said taxes were due Caesar, the people would have called Him a traitor and turned against Him as a Roman stooge. If He had said it was unlawful to pay taxes, the religionists would have reported Him to the Romans and accused Him of insurrection.

There was something even more repulsive and horrible than their trickery. It was the camouflage of their trickery with flattery. Note how the flattery flowed on and on, distastefully so. They hoped the flattery would make Jesus think they were sincere and do away with any suspicions He had.

There are sins that are often committed by those who hold false concepts of citizenship. Some of these sins are seen in the plot of the Pharisees and Herodians against Jesus.

a. There is *selfish ambition*, which often leads to compromise and intrigue. Nothing could be more surprising than to see the Pharisees and Herodians working together. They stood diametrically opposed to one another. The Pharisees thought the Herodians were no better than the heathen doomed to hell. Yet they are seen working with the Herodians against Jesus. What was it that brought them together? Selfish ambition. They feared the loss of their position, influence, power, wealth, and security (see notes—Mt.12:1-8; note and DEEPER STUDY # 1—12:10; note—15:1-20; DEEPER STUDY # 2—15:6-9. These notes will help considerably in understanding why the rulers feared Jesus so much.)

The depth of sin in selfish ambition is seen in that the primary plotters were religious leaders. They were not only willing to plot evil, they were trying to put a man to death. Just *how evil* selfish ambition can be, in both government and religion, is clearly seen in this passage.

> **"How can ye believe, which receive honour one of another, and seek not the honour that cometh from God only?" (Jn.5:44).**

Thought 1. A man who lives for this world will become a bedfellow with almost anyone to protect his security. The degree or strange appearance of the compromise will seldom matter.

b. There is *deception*, which usually leads to flattery and destruction. The deception is seen in two facts.

1) Deception is seen in that the Pharisees themselves did not go to Jesus. They sent "their disciples with the Herodians." The disciples were learners, students who would actually be seeking the answer to such a question. The Herodians were along to give the appearance that the disciples had asked them first but were not satisfied with their answer. It would seem they wanted to know what He (One who claimed to be the Messiah) would answer. Thus, Jesus would think the question was the legitimate question of a student, never suspecting a plot to entrap Him.
2) Deception, the lowest kind of deception, is seen in the words of flattery which are used in approaching Jesus.
   - ⇒ "Master...
   - ⇒ "we know that thou art true...
   - ⇒ "and carest for no man:...
   - ⇒ "for thou regardest not the person of men...
   - ⇒ "but teachest the way of God in truth...."

Note that everything they said about Jesus was true.

- ⇒ He was Master: a rabbi, a teacher. He was even more: He was the Master and Lord of the universe.
- ⇒ He was true and truthful: a teacher from God. (Contrast their hypocritical approach with the sincerity of Nicodemus, Jn.3:2.)
- ⇒ He did teach the way of God: how a man was to live and behave if he wished to please God.
- ⇒ He did not care what men said about Him: it did not influence Him or His action.
- ⇒ He did not regard man's person: He did not show partiality or favoritism.

The problem was that they did not mean what they were professing, not in their hearts. What they were professing about Him was coming from an evil motive. They wanted to use Him to secure their own selfish purposes. In the end they were successful; they were able to do what they were plotting. They were able to have Him destroyed.

Thought 1. Deception always destroys that which is truthful and strong and lovely.

> **"For thy mouth uttereth thine iniquity, and thou choosest the tongue of the crafty" (Jb.15:5).**
> **"For there is no faithfulness in their mouth; their inward part is very wickedness; their throat is an open sepulcher; they flatter with their tongue" (Ps.5:9).**
> **"A man shall not be established by wickedness: but the root of the righteous shall not be moved" (Pr.12:3).**
> **"A man that flattereth his neighbor spreadeth a net for his feet" (Pr.29:5).**

c. There are *close-mindedness and obstinate unbelief* which lead to denial of the truth and self-condemnation. The question asked of Jesus was simple: "Is it lawful to give tribute to Caesar, or not?"

- ⇒ The Pharisees, sincere Jewish religionists, would shout, "No!"
- ⇒ The Herodians (and those securing position and wealth by Roman rule) would say, "Yes!"

Standing there, the questioners thought they had entrapped Jesus. If He said, "No, taxes should not be paid to Caesar," then the authorities would arrest and remove Him; and the people would soon know that His claim to be the Messiah was false.

If He said, "Yes, taxes should be paid to Caesar," then He would be denying the Sovereignty of God; and the people, who strongly opposed Roman rule and taxes, would rise up against Him. Both the Pharisees and Herodians were close-minded. They would see nothing beyond themselves and the threat to their position and wealth. They were steeped in obstinate unbelief. Therefore, they rejected the truth; and, as results from all rejection of the truth, they condemned themselves (see Jn.3:18-21).

DEEPER STUDY # 3
(12:14) **Tribute—Tax**: the tax asked about was the poll tax. It was a tax that had to be paid by every person between the ages of twelve or fourteen and sixty-five. The poll tax amounted to about one days wage in that time (see DEEPER STUDY # 1—Ro.13:6).

3 (12:15) **Citizenship—Needs—Necessities**: life within the state depends upon God, not money. This is seen in the fact that Jesus did not have a penny. He was living in the state of Israel and living under the rule of another state, the rule of Rome. He was, theoretically, a citizen of two states, yet He did not have a penny. His sustenance and existence did not rest in the state nor in the things of the state. It rested in God's hands. His trust was in God, not in the state.

Thought 1. The state is not necessary for life, but God is. The state can be and should be helpful, but it is not necessary. However, God is necessary, for man does not live by bread alone. He cannot live an abundant life apart from God. With God man has purpose, fulfillment, and life—eternally. But without God he has none of these life-giving qualities, not permanently. The state can offer some liberties that allow some opportunities to pursue life; but God can make life free, completely free, instilling within the human heart a perfect assurance that one shall live forever.

"But seek ye first the kingdom of God, and his righteousness; and all these things shall be added unto you" (Mt.6:33).
"And ye shall serve the LORD your God, and he shall bless thy bread, and thy water; and I will take sickness away from the midst of thee" (Ex.23:25).
"But thou shalt remember the LORD thy God: for it is he that giveth thee power to get wealth, that he may establish his covenant which he sware unto thy fathers, as it is this day" (De.8:18).
"And it shall come to pass, if ye shall hearken diligently unto my commandments which I command you this day, to love the LORD your God, and to serve him with all your heart and with all your soul, that I will give you the rain of your land in his due season, the first rain and the latter rain, that thou mayest gather in thy corn, and thy wine, and thine oil. And I will send grass in thy fields for thy cattle, that thou mayest eat and be full" (De.11:13-15).
"And I have also given thee [Solomon] that which thou hast not asked, both riches, and honor: so that there shall not be any among the kings like unto thee all thy days" (1 K.3:13).
"Who giveth food to all flesh: for his mercy endureth for ever" (Ps.136:25).

4 (12:16-17) **Citizenship**: the state is ordained by God. Jesus confirmed this fact in two points. He clearly demonstrated that there are some things which *belong* to the state. Therefore, there are some responsibilities *due* the state. What belongs to Caesar belongs to Caesar. He is responsible primarily for three functions: law and order, community services, and protection. No man is an island within a state. He owes the state for the services and goods the state provides. Citizenship carries with it responsibility.

Jesus was brilliant and brief as He dealt with the Pharisees and their false concept of citizenship. "Bring me a penny...whose is this image?" He simply asked.

Note two things.

a. He forced the Pharisees (religion is supreme concept) to admit that some things belong to an earthly power. There is an *earthly citizenship*. The image was Caesar's; the superscription was Caesar's; and the coin had been made or coined by Caesar's government. Therefore, the coin was Caesar's if Caesar said it was due him. The point was clear. Since the religionists *used what was owned and provided by Caesar*, they owed to Caesar what was due him. He strikingly said, "Render therefore unto Caesar the things that are Caesar's."

b. He revealed a very important truth for believers of all time. They *have a double citizenship*. They are citizens of heaven, yes, but they are also citizens of this world. Therefore, they have an obligation to the government under which they live. They receive the benefits of government just as the worldly-minded do (for example, roads, sewage, water, protection, and public transportation). Therefore, believers are to pay their due share. (See note—Ro.13:1-7. This note is a thorough discussion of citizenship.)

"Let every soul be subject unto the higher powers. For there is no power but of God: the powers that be are ordained of God" (Ro.13:1).
"Notwithstanding, lest we should offend them, go thou to the sea, and cast an hook, and take up the fish that first cometh up; and when thou hast opened his mouth, thou shalt find a piece of money: that take, and give unto them for me and thee" (Mt.17:27).
"Put them in mind to be subject to principalities and powers, to obey magistrates, to be ready to every good work" (Tit.3:1).
"Submit yourselves to every ordinance of man for the Lord's sake: whether it be to the king, as supreme; or unto governors, as unto them that are sent by him for the punishment of evildoers, and for the

praise of them that do well. For so is the will of God, that with well doing ye may put to silence the ignorance of foolish men" (1 Pe.2:13-15).

"Honour all men. Love the brotherhood. Fear God. Honour the king" (1 Pe.2:17).

"And whosoever will not do the law of thy God, and the law of the king, let judgment be executed speedily upon him, whether it be unto death, or to banishment, or to confiscation of goods, or to imprisonment" (Ezr. 7:26).

"I counsel thee to keep the king's commandment, and that in regard of the oath of God" (Ec.8:2).

5 (12:17) **Citizenship**: the state is limited in its power. God is due the things that are God's. A heavenly citizenship belongs to God. Jesus was just as brilliant in dealing with the Herodians and their false concept of citizenship. The Herodians not only subjected religion to the state, but they were worldly-minded and denied much of the supernatural, including life after death and the spiritual world or dimension of being.

Note two things.

1) Jesus declared unequivocally to the Herodians: there is a spiritual world. God is; He does exist; therefore, there are some things which belong to God. "Render therefore...unto God the things that are God's." Again, the point is clear. Since the Herodians (the state is supreme concept), as citizens of the world and of life itself, used what was owned and provided by God, they owed God what was due Him.
2) Jesus revealed a very important truth to all generations of men. They are beings of God as well as of this world, spiritual as well as physical beings. Therefore, they are responsible to live as citizens of God as well as citizens of this world. All men have received so much from God...
    - life that was made to exist with God forever; therefore man owes God his life.
    - a spirit that can be *born again* and live a self-denying life of love and joy and peace for the sake of all men everywhere (Ga.5:22-23).
    - a mind and body that have the power to enjoy the aesthetic beauty of the earth and to learn, reason, and produce for the betterment and service of all mankind.

Thought 1. All men receive these benefits and many more from God. Therefore, men are to pay their due share to God.

(1) They are to love God supremely.

"And Jesus answered him, The first of all the commandments is, Hear, O Israel; The Lord our God is one Lord" (Mk.12:29-30).

(2) They are to seek the Lord.

"God that made the world and all things therein, seeing that he is Lord of heaven and earth, dwelleth not in temples made with hands; neither is worshipped with men's hands, as though he needed any thing, seeing he giveth to all life, and breath, and all things; and hath made of one blood all nations of men for to dwell on all the face of the earth, and hath determined the times before appointed, and the bounds of their habitation; that they should seek the Lord, if haply they might feel after him, and find him, though he be not far from every one of us" (Ac.17:24-27).

(3) They are to know that the Lord is God, and He alone is to be worshipped.

"Know ye that the LORD he is God: it is he that hath made us, and not we ourselves; we are his people, and the sheep of his pasture. Enter into his gates with thanksgiving, and into his courts with praise: be thankful unto him, and bless his name" (Ps.100:3-4).

(4) They are not to forget the Lord.

"And forgettest the LORD thy maker, that hath stretched forth the heavens, and laid the foundations of the earth; and hast feared continually every day because of the fury of the oppressor, as if he were ready to destroy? and where is the fury of the oppressor?" (Is.51:13).

(5) They are not to profane God's covenant.

"Have we not all one father? hath not one God created us? why do we deal treacherously every man against his brother, by profaning the covenant of our fathers?" (Mal.2:10).

Outline	Scripture
	H. The Question & Proof of the Resurrection, 12:18-27 *(Mt. 22:23-33; Lu. 20:27-38)*
1. The Sadducees attempted to discredit Jesus	18 Then come unto him the Sadducees, which say there is no resurrection; and they asked him, saying,
2. The resurrection is denied & scoffed at: The unbelieving Sadducees posed a sarcastic question about an unlikely situation	19 Master, Moses wrote unto us, If a man's brother die, and leave his wife behind him, and leave no children, that his brother should take his wife, and raise up seed unto his brother.
a. The first of seven brothers married a woman then died, leaving no children	20 Now there were seven brethren: and the first took a wife, and dying left no seed.
b. The remaining six brothers, in turn, married the same woman; each man died leaving no children	21 And the second took her, and died, neither left he any seed: and the third likewise.
c. The woman died	22 And the seven had her, and left no seed: last of all the woman died also.
d. The question: Whose wife will she be in heaven?	23 In the resurrection therefore, when they shall rise, whose wife shall she be of them? for the seven had her to wife.
3. The resurrection is based on the Scriptures & the power of God	24 And Jesus answering said unto them, Do ye not therefore err, because ye know not the scriptures, neither the power of God?
4. The resurrection is different from any earthly experience: It is of another world, another dimension	25 For when they shall rise from the dead, they neither marry, nor are given in marriage; but are as the angels which are in heaven.
5. The resurrection is a living relationship that cannot be broken a. God is the living God of past saints who are present with Him	26 And as touching the dead, that they rise: have ye not read in the book of Moses, how in the bush God spake unto him, saying, I am the God of Abraham, and the God of Isaac, and the God of Jacob?
b. God is the God of the living c. Any other belief is a great error	27 He is not the God of the dead, but the God of the living: ye therefore do greatly err.

DIVISION VII

THE SON OF GOD'S LAST JERUSALEM MINISTRY: JESUS' WARNING AND CONFLICT WITH RELIGIONISTS, 11:1-12:44

H. The Question and Proof of the Resurrection, 12:18-27

(12:18-27) **Introduction**: it was still Tuesday of the Lord's last week. On this day the challenges to His authority had been pressing in ever so heavily upon Him. The chief priests and lay leaders (elders) had challenged His authority (see outline and notes—Mt.21:23-27). Jesus had met the challengers head-on and routed them. But in so doing, His mind had been focused upon His death and Israel's rejection. The very thought that Israel, in whom God had put so much trust, was failing God by putting His Son to death was bound to be ripping out Jesus' heart (see outline and notes—Mt.21:33-46; 22:1-14).

The Pharisees and Herodians (Herod's political party) had attempted to discredit Jesus by pitting Him either against the government or the people (see outlines and notes—Mt.22:15-22). Again, Jesus had met and routed His challengers. But the struggle had been tiring and pressuring, hard and heavy.

Now, for a third time, the Lord was confronted and challenged. And again it was a different group who tried to out-argue and discredit Him. His challengers were the Sadducees, the religious and political liberals of the day. As Matthew points out, "[They] say that there is no resurrection" (Mt.22:23). Luke adds, "The Sadducees say there is no resurrection, neither angel, nor spirit" (Ac.23:8) (see DEEPER STUDY # 3—Mt.16:12; DEEPER STUDY # 2—Ac.23:8). Their liberal position caused two things: It caused them to stumble at the spiritual and supernatural. They ridiculed and scorned both. Therefore, in their minds, the teachings of Jesus were those of an unthinking and illogical man, teachings lacking philosophical analysis and natural proof.

It also caused them to feel threatened and to oppose Jesus. The people were flocking to Jesus and soaking up His teachings. This meant the Sadducees were losing their grip on the people. Their position and wealth were being jeopardized; therefore, they were compelled to attack and discredit Him before the people.

1. The Sadducees attempted to discredit Jesus (v.18).
2. The resurrection is denied and scoffed at: the unbelieving Sadducees posed a sarcastic question about an unlikely situation (vv.19-23).
3. The resurrection is based on the Scriptures and the power of God (v.24).
4. The resurrection is different from any earthly experience: it is of another world, another dimension (v.25).
5. The resurrection is a living relationship that cannot be broken (vv.26-27).

1 (12:18) **Sadducees**: see DEEPER STUDY # 2—Ac.23:8 for discussion.

2 (12:19-23) **Resurrection—Sadducees**: the resurrection is denied and scoffed at. Down through the centuries many liberal-minded people have laughed at the resurrection (see 1 Co.15:12-58; 2 Pe.3:3-18). Note the argument of the Sadducees.

a. They used Moses' law, the Levrite law, as the basis of their argument (De.25:5-6). When a husband died without a son, the Levrite law said that his brother was to marry his wife and bear a son. By law, the son was considered the first-born son of the deceased brother. This assured two things: (1) that the family name continued, and (2) that the property holdings were kept in the family. This was a law that had been given to help preserve and to enlarge the nation of Israel (see Ru.4:5).

b. The Sadducees then suggested a logical situation that could have or actually had arisen. Note that there were seven brothers. The first brother married and died before bearing children. Each of the other brothers obeyed the law, but each died before bearing a child. Finally, the woman died also.

c. The logical question was now asked, the question which in the Sadducees' mind showed the absurdity of the resurrection. They asked, "Whose wife shall she be in eternity?" Note three things by reading through verses 23-28 several times.

1) The spirit of the questioning was mocking. The situation was logical; but the spirit was cold and coarse, egotistical and unbelieving, regrettable and revolting. The unbeliever's spirit is often self-incriminating and self-condemning.
2) The argument was thought to be irrefutable by the Sadducees. They believed it pointed out just how foolish the idea of another world, of a spiritual world, was to the thinking person.
3) The Sadducees were thinking that the spiritual world would be just like the physical world, that it would be nothing more than a continuation of this world, both in *its nature and in its relationships.*

Thought 1. A picture of what the Scripture says about the natural man is clearly seen in this event.

> **"But the natural man receiveth not the things of the Spirit of God: for they are foolishness unto him: neither can he know them, because they are spiritually discerned" (1 Co.2:14).**

Thought 2. The resurrection and return of the Lord are often questioned.

> **"Now if Christ be preached that he rose from the dead, how say some among you that there is no resurrection of the dead?" (1 Co.15:12. See v.13-34 for a full discussion.)**
> **"But some man will say, How are the dead raised up? and with what body do they come?" (1 Co.15:35. See v.36-58 for a full discussion.)**
> **"Knowing this first, that there shall come in the last days scoffers, walking after their own lusts, and saying, Where is the promise of his coming? for since the fathers fell asleep, all things continue as they were from the beginning of the creation" (2 Pe.3:3-4. See v.5-15 for a full discussion.)**

3 (12:24) **Resurrection—Scriptures—God, Power of—Spiritual World**: the resurrection is based on the Scriptures and the power of God. Jesus said very pointedly to the Sadducees and to all who follow their liberal position: "You are in error. The resurrection is denied for two erroneous reasons."

a. "You do not know the Scriptures." The Scriptures are plain and clear. They leave no doubt that there is a spiritual world and that a resurrection into the spiritual world and dimension of being will take place.

> **"For I know that my Redeemer liveth, and that he shall stand at the latter day upon the earth: and though after my skin worms destroy this body, yet in my flesh shall I see God: whom I shall see for my self, and mine eyes shall behold, and not another; though my reins be consumed within me" (Jb.19:25-27).**
> **"Thy dead men shall live; together with my dead body shall they arise. Awake and sing, ye that dwell in dust: for thy dew is as the dew of herbs, and the earth shall cast out the dead" (Is.26:19).**
> **"And many of them that sleep in the dust of the earth shall awake, some to everlasting life, and some to shame and everlasting contempt" (Da.12:2).**
> **"Verily, verily, I say unto you, The hour is coming, and now is, when the dead shall hear the voice of the Son of God: and they that hear shall live" (Jn.5:25).**
> **"Marvel not at this: for the hour is coming, in the which all that are in the graves shall hear his voice, and shall come forth; they that have done good, unto the resurrection of life; and they that have done evil, unto the resurrection of damnation" (Jn.5:28-29).**
> **"And this is the will of him that sent me, that every one which seeth the Son, and believeth on him, may have everlasting life: and I will raise him up at the last day" (Jn.6:40).**
> **"Jesus said unto her, I am the resurrection, and the life: he that believeth in me, though he were dead, yet shall he live" (Jn.11:25).**
> **"And have hope toward God, which they themselves also allow, that there shall be a resurrection of the dead, both of the just and unjust" (Ac.24:15).**
> **"But if the Spirit of him that raised up Jesus from the dead dwell in you, he that raised up Christ from the dead shall also quicken your mortal bodies by his Spirit that dwelleth in you" (Ro.8:11).**
> **"For as in Adam all die, even so in Christ shall all be made alive" (1 Co.15:22).**
> **"Knowing that he which raised up the Lord Jesus shall raise up us also by Jesus, and shall present us with you" (2 Co.4:14).**
> **"For the Lord himself shall descend from heaven with a shout, with the voice of the archangel, and with the trump of God: and the dead in Christ shall rise first" (1 Th.4:16).**
> **"But God will redeem my soul from the power of the grave: for he shall receive me" (Ps.49:15; see Ps.71:20; Ho.13:14).**

Thought 1. There are three reasons why a person may not know the Scriptures.
(1) He has not *really studied* the Scriptures.
(2) He does not believe the Scriptures. He rejects the Scripture as God's Word.
(3) He does not take the Scriptures literally for what they say. He spiritualizes and allegorizes them.

b. "You do not know the power of God."

Thought 1. There are three reasons why a person does not know the power of God.

(1) He is ignorant of God. He knows nothing about God and seldom, if ever, gives any thought to God and His power.

(2) He does not believe in God nor in His power. He prefers to acknowledge God's eternal power and Godhead seen in creation and to go about *creating* (mentally and physically) gods of his own (Ro.1:20-32). He just refuses to acknowledge the facts of nature:

> **"Thou fool, that which thou sowest is not quickened, except it die: and that which thou sowest, thou sowest not that body that shall be, but bare grain, it may chance of wheat, or of some other grain: but God giveth it a body as it hath pleased him" (1 Co.15:36-38).**

(3) He believes, but his belief in God and His power is weak. He cannot picture much happening beyond the physical world and the power of natural laws.

Thought 2. The idea of a spiritual world is perplexing to the natural man. Just imagine! While we are sitting here surrounded by all that we see...

- there is another world, an unseen spiritual dimension of being, that actually exists.
- there is a spirit, the real life within our bodies, that is destined to exist forever.
- there is to be a resurrection of all the dead bodies that have been lying and decaying in the graves for ages and ages. And the bodies of believers shall be perfected and glorified to live and work again—forever and ever in the new heavens and earth.

Thought 3. When really thinking about the facts of the resurrection, two confessions have to be made by every man, believer and unbeliever.

(1) The natural man, that is, man within himself and his world, *can never know* about a spiritual world. He is bound by the physical and material world of which he is a part. He can only think and guess and hypothesize that a spiritual world exists and speculate on details such as a resurrection. Man cannot, while living in this world, penetrate the spiritual world with his body to scientifically prove the existence of the spiritual world.

(2) God alone could reveal the reality of the spiritual dimension and the fact of a resurrection yet to take place. Such could be known and experienced only by the power of God. No man has the power to bring it about. If a resurrection is to take place, God's power will have to do it.

Thought 4. Two things will keep a person from error.

(1) Knowing the Scriptures.

(2) Trusting the power of God.

4 (12:25) **Resurrection—Spiritual Dimension**: the resurrection is different from any earthly experience. It is of another dimension of being. Jesus said that the resurrection exceeds earthly relationships. The Sadducees did not know the Scriptures nor the power of God. Therefore, when they thought of the resurrection into another world, they saw life simply as continuing on as it does now. They pictured heaven as being a continuation of this world. Very simply, they could not conceive that God would change the qualities of life and give man a totally new environment in which to live.

Jesus said two things.

a. Future life and relationships will exceed earthly relationships, even the bond of marital relationships. The strong union and bond of marriage will not be less, it will be greater and stronger.

b. Future life and relationships will be equal to that experienced by the angels and God. This means at least two things. (Note: Jesus had just admitted the existence of angels, refuting the disbelief of the liberal-minded Sadducces.)

1) Heavenly life and relationships will be perfected. Our relationships as they are known on earth will cease to be in heaven. They will be changed in that they will be perfected; selfishness and sin will not affect our love and lives. Our love will be perfected; therefore, we will love everyone perfectly. A wife on this earth will not be loved as she was on this earth, imperfectly. She will be loved more, loved perfectly. Everyone will love everyone else perfectly. God will change all relationships into perfection, even as the relationships between angels and God are perfected.

2) Heavenly life and relationships will be eternal. There will be no ending of relationships. A man and wife will always have the other to love. One will not cease to be (die) before the other (as is the case now). Everyone will always have everyone else to love. God will change the brief time that we now have with each other into an eternal relationship. We will enjoy the presence of each other eternally, even as the relationship between angels and God is enjoyed eternally.

Thought 1. Two warnings must always be issued when thinking of heaven and eternal life.

(1) A person can *materialize heaven* and *humanize eternal life*. That is, we can conceive heaven to be nothing more than a glorified world, and we can conceive eternal life to be nothing more than physical life, plus a little more. This was the mistake of the Sadducees, and it is often the concept pictured by liberal thinkers when they hear about the resurrection.

(2) A person can *idealize heaven* and *allegorize eternal life*. We can think of heaven as little more than an ideal land for which we should seek and toward which we should direct our lives. And we can think of eternal life

as little more than a utopian dream of an indefinite quality, or we can think of it as floating around and being free of trouble and trials, or we can think of it as simply a place to which we go after our departure from this world.

The teaching of Scripture, of God's revelation, must always be kept in mind when thinking of heaven and eternal life. Scripture teaches that the very nature of things will be changed.

⇒ Heaven is said to be a spiritual dimension, a real world of being. And Scripture declares that the heavens and earth that now are will one day be transformed into that spiritual dimension of being (2 Pe.3:3-13; Re.21:1, 5).

⇒ Eternal life is said to be life that will exist forever in the spiritual world and dimension of being. The Scripture says:

> **"So also is the resurrection of the dead. It is sown in corruption; it is raised in incorruption: it is sown in dishonour; it is raised in glory: it is sown in weakness; it is raised in power: it is sown a natural body: it is raised a spiritual body. There is a natural body, and there is a spiritual body" (1 Co.15:42-44. See 1 Th.5:13-18.)**
>
> **"As we have borne the image of the earthy, we shall also bear the image of the heavenly. Now this I say, brethren, that flesh and blood cannot inherit the kingdom of God; neither doth corruption inherit incorruption. Behold, I show you a mystery; we shall not all sleep, but we shall all be changed, in a moment, in the twinkling of an eye, at the last trump: for the trumpet shall sound, and the dead shall be raised incorruptible, and we shall be changed. For this corruptible must put on incorruption, and this mortal must put on immortality. So when this corruptible shall have put on incorruption, and this mortal shall have put on immortality, then shall be brought to pass the saying that is written, Death is swallowed up in victory" (1 Co.15:49-54).**

(See notes and DEEPER STUDY # 1—Mt.19:28; DEEPER STUDY # 1—Jn.17:2-3; DEEPER STUDY # 1—2 Ti.4:18. See DEEPER STUDY # 2—Jn.1:4 for discussion.)

5 (12:26-27) **Resurrection, Proofs**: the resurrection is a living relationship that cannot be broken. Two major points show this.

a. God is the God of past saints, believers who have passed on. God is the God of Abraham, Isaac, and Jacob. Jesus means at least two things in this point.

1) God's relationships are active relationships, not inactive. God says, "I am the God of...." not, "I was the God of...." His relationships with His subjects are continuous. They are maintained. God is eternal; therefore, He creates and maintains eternal, active relationships. God's subjects do enter into the spiritual realm of His presence and actively relate to Him. The resurrection is a fact.
2) God's relationships are good and rewarding. The patriarchs of old were promised rewards, personal rewards (see Heb.11:13-16). There has to be a resurrection if our relationship with God is good and rewarding. To die and be left dead as a decayed corpse is not good or rewarding. Abraham, Isaac, and Jacob have a good and rewarding relationship with God. They are alive, more alive than they were while on earth, for they are perfected and eternal. They are with God Himself. And so shall we be. The resurrection is a fact.

b. God is the God of the living, not of the dead. God is the God of Abraham, Isaac, and Jacob, not the God of dead decayed corpses. When Moses wrote these words, the three patriarchs had been dead for many years. If they were dead, God was not their God. Since He was their God, they were alive, living in God's presence in relationship to Him, perfect and eternal. There is to be a resurrection.

> **"For none of us liveth to himself, and no man dieth to himself. For whether we live, we live unto the Lord; and whether we die, we die unto the Lord: whether we live therefore, or die, we are the Lord's. For to this end Christ both died, and rose, and revived, that he might be Lord both of the dead and living" (Ro.14:7-9).**

One simple fact clearly comes to the forefront in these points made by Christ: *since God is*, God is not the God of the dead, but of the living.

> **"Why should it be thought a thing incredible with you, that God should raise the dead?" (Ac.26:8).**
> **"There shall be a resurrection of the dead, both of the just and unjust" (Ac.24:15).**

(See note—Mt.22:31-32 for more detailed discussion and for Scriptures dealing with the resurrection.)

	I. The Question About the Greatest Commandment, 12:28-34 *(Mt. 22:34-40; Lu. 10:25-37)*	31 And the second is like, namely this, Thou shalt love thy neighbor as thyself. There is none other commandment greater than these.	c. The Lord our God demands that we love our neighbors as ourselves[DS3,4]
1. The setting: A teacher of the law approached Jesus[DS1] a. Observed Jesus' arguments b. Posed a test question: Which is the most important commandment?	28 And one of the scribes came, and having heard them reasoning together, and perceiving that he had answered them well, asked him, Which is the first commandment of all?	32 And the scribe said unto him, Well, Master, thou hast said the truth: for there is one God; and there is none other but he:	**3. The great scope of the commandment** a. So great it causes honest & thinking men to agree
2. The greatest commandment a. The Lord our God, the Lord is one[DS2]	29 And Jesus answered him, The first of all the commandments is, Hear, O Israel; The Lord our God is one Lord:	33 And to love him with all the heart, and with all the understanding, and with all the soul, and with all the strength, and to love his neighbour as himself, is more than all whole burnt offerings and sacrifices.	b. So great it exceeds all offerings & sacrifices
b. The Lord our God is to be loved	30 And thou shalt love the Lord thy God with all thy heart, and with all thy soul, and with all thy mind, and with all thy strength: this is the first commandment.	34 And when Jesus saw that he answered discreetly, he said unto him, Thou art not far from the kingdom of God. And no man after that durst ask him any question.	c. So great it almost assures salvation to those who understand it

DIVISION VII

THE SON OF GOD'S LAST JERUSALEM MINISTRY: JESUS' WARNING AND CONFLICT WITH RELIGIONISTS, 11:1-12:44

I. The Question About the Greatest Commandment, 12:28-34

(12:28-34) **Introduction**: Jesus had met His third group of challengers, the Sadducees. He had silenced and routed them. The Pharisees, the strict religionists of that day, heard about Jesus' conquering His challengers again. In their minds, His threat to their security remained. All three attempts to discredit Him had failed. Somehow, they felt they must discredit Him before the people in order to break His hold on them. There was the very dangerous possibility that the people might follow through with their proclaiming Him to be the Messiah, that they might rise up against the Roman authorities. The responsibility for such action, of course, would lie at their feet as Jewish leaders; and they would be replaced as the ruling body of the Sanhedrin, losing their position, authority, esteem, and wealth.

They met together to plan and plot against Jesus again (see Mt.22:34). This time they took a different approach. Earlier they had challenged Him as a body of questioners. Now they chose only one member from among their body to attack Jesus. He was a lawyer or a Scribe who was most brilliant and versed in the law.

Jesus used the occasion to teach man the greatest *provision* and *duty* of human life: love. Love will provide for every need man has; therefore, love is the greatest duty of man.

1. The setting: A teacher of the law approached Jesus (v.28).
2. The greatest commandment (vv.29-31).
3. The great scope of the commandment (vv.32-34).

1 (12:28) **Commandments, Supreme**: this man was a lawyer (Mt.22:35). Apparently his heart had been touched by Jesus. There were two indications of this. First, Mark tells us that the man was present when Jesus was "reasoning together" with the Sadducees (Mt.12:28), and he perceived "that [Christ] had answered them well." Second, at the conclusion of his own discussion with Jesus, Jesus said to the man, "Thou art not far from the kingdom of God" (Mk.12:34).

Something about Jesus struck a chord within this man. His heart had been touched and stirred rather deeply. True, he was being put forward by the official body to challenge Jesus. But personally there was something about Jesus when Jesus was answering the Sadducees—the spirit, the wisdom, the self-confidence, the authority—that had stirred the lawyer's heart to wonder and to want to learn more about Jesus.

Note the question: "Which is the first commandment of all?" Through the years, Jewish teachers had set up six hundred commandments. There were so many commandments that in day-to-day life no person could keep them all. So the question was often discussed: Which commandments must be absolutely obeyed? Which ones are important and which ones are not? Can the failure to obey some be condoned or not? Which commandments are heavy and which are light? If a person keeps the greatest of the precepts, can he be excused for his failure to keep the others (see Mt.19:16f)? Note two quick points.

a. This is the sin which James attacks.

"For whosoever shall keep the whole law, and yet offend in one point, he is guilty of all" (Js.2:10).

b. Christ teaches that some laws are all inclusive and broader than others.

> **"Woe unto you, scribes and Pharisees, hypocrites! for ye pay tithe of mint and anise and cummin, and have omitted the *weightier matters* of the law, judgment, mercy, and faith: these ought ye to have done, and not to leave the other undone" (Mt.23:23).**

What the Pharisees were trying to do was this. Various groups believed the greatest commandment to be different things such as circumcision, sacrifices, and the Sabbath. They hoped that by stating His opinion, Jesus would disturb the people who held a position different from His. He would thereby lose their following. There was the strong possibility that a man giving his judgment would seem to be lessening the weight of other very important commandments.

DEEPER STUDY # 1
(12:28) **Lawyer** (nomikos): a profession of laymen who studied, taught, interpreted, and dealt with the practical questions of Jewish law. They were a specialization within the profession commonly called Scribes (see Mt.22:35). They functioned both in the court and synagogues (see Lu.7:30; 10:25; 11:45, 46, 52; 14:3; Tit.3:13). They were apparently a specialization dealing more with the study and interpretation of the law.

2 (12:29-31) **Commandments—God, Nature—Man, Responsibility—Brotherhood**: What was the greatest commandment in the law? Note that Jesus answered without hesitation or equivocation. He answered with all the authority of God Himself, and what He said was an eye-opener to people steeped in man-made religions.

a. Know that "the Lord our God is one Lord." (See note, *God, Nature*—Ro.3:29-30 for more discussion.)

1) He is *the Lord*, Jehovah, Yahweh. There is no other. Monotheism (one God) is the true belief. Polytheism (many gods) is a false belief.
2) He is *our God*. This is a personal relationship between a worshipper and his God. It is a daily experience. We are related to Him; we are His people, the sheep of His pasture. Therefore, we should love, adore, and worship Him.
3) He is *one Lord*. He is the focus and concentration of our life, attention, worship, love, and praise. He is the only Subject of our devotion. There is no reason, no excuse for distraction by any other subject. He is *the One Lord, the only Subject.*

> **"There is none other God but one" (1 Co.8:4).**
> **"One God and Father of all, who is above all, and through all, and in you all" (Ep.4:6).**
> **"For there is one God, and one mediator between God and men, the man Christ Jesus" (1 Ti.2:5).**
> **"For there are three that bear record in heaven, the Father, the Word, and the Holy Ghost: and these three are one" (1 Jn.5:7).**
> **"Wherefore thou art great, O LORD God: for there is none like thee, neither is there any God besides thee, according to all that we have heard with our ears" (2 S.7:22).**
> **"For thou art great, and doest wondrous things: thou art God alone" (Ps.86:10).**
> **"Ye are my witnesses, saith the LORD, and my servant whom I have chosen: that ye may know and believe me, and understand that I am he: before me there was no God formed, neither shall there be after me. I, even I, am the LORD; and beside me there is no savior" (Is.43:10-11).**
> **"Thus saith the LORD the King of Israel, and his Redeemer the LORD of hosts; I am the first, and I am the last; and beside me there is no God" (Is.44:6).**
> **"For thus saith the LORD that created the heavens; God himself that formed the earth and made it; he hath established it, he created it not in vain, he formed it to be inhabited: I am the LORD and there is none else" (Is.45:18).**

b. The Lord our God is to be loved. "Thou shalt love the Lord thy God." Love God as *your* very own God. This is a personal relationship, not a distant relationship. God is not impersonal, far out in space someplace, distant and removed. God is personal, ever so close, and we are to be personally involved with God on a face-to-face basis. The command is to "*love the Lord thy God.*" Loving God is alive and active, not dead and inactive. We are, therefore, to maintain a personal relationship with God that is alive and active.

Note that Jesus says to love God with all your being. Jesus breaks our being down into three parts: the heart, the soul, and the mind (see DEEPER STUDY # 4,5,6—Mt.22:37 for discussion).

Note also that Jesus adds "with all thy strength." Love is man's chief duty. Man is responsible to maintain a loving relationship with God. Very practically, loving God involves the very same factors that loving a person involves (see outlines and notes—Ep.5:22-33).

1) A loving relationship involves *commitment and loyalty*. True love does not allow lustful behavior with others. True love does not covet and does not care for a carnal definition that allows fleshly acts and sensual relationships with others.

   True love is commitment and loyalty to one person. It is very significant that the very first commandment God gives deals with commitment and loyalty. God strikes out at the very core of man's carnal behavior and tendency to define love in terms that allow him to satisfy his lust. "Thou shalt have no other gods" (Ex.20:3).

2) A loving relationship involves *trust and respect* for the person loved. It is loving the person for who he is. We love God because of Himself, because He is who He is.
   ⇒ He is the Creator and Sustainer of life; therefore we love Him.
   ⇒ He is the Savior and Redeemer; therefore we love Him.
   ⇒ He is the Lord and Owner of life; therefore we love Him.

3) A loving relationship involves the *giving and surrendering* of oneself. The drive is to give oneself, to surrender oneself to the other, not to get.
4) A loving relationship involves *knowing and sharing*. The desire is to know and to share, to be learning, growing, working, and serving ever so closely together.

Thought 1. Man is to love God supremely.

> **"Keep yourselves in the love of God, looking for the mercy of our Lord Jesus Christ unto eternal life" (Jude 21).**
> **"And the Lord direct your hearts into the love of God, and into the patient waiting for Christ" (2 Th.3:5).**
> **"And now, Israel, what doth the LORD thy God require of thee, but to fear the LORD thy God, to walk in all his ways, and to love him, and to serve the LORD thy God with all thy heart and with all thy soul" (De.10:12).**
> **"Therefore thou shalt love the LORD thy God, and keep his charge, and his statutes, and his judgments, and his commandments, always" (De.11:1).**
> **"But take diligent heed to do the commandment and the law, which Moses the servant of the LORD charged you, to love the LORD your God, and to walk in all his ways, and to keep his commandments, and to cleave unto him, and to serve him with all your heart and with all your soul" (Jos.22:5).**
> **"O love the LORD, all ye his saints: for the LORD preserveth the faithful, and plentifully rewardeth the proud doer" (Ps.31:23).**

c. The Lord our God demands that we love our neighbors as ourselves. Because of the length of this discussion, it is handled in a separate footnote (see DEEPER STUDY # 3—Mk.12:31).

DEEPER STUDY # 2
(12:29) **God—Monotheism**: see De.6:4. (See note—Ro.3:29-30.)

DEEPER STUDY # 3
(12:31) **Love—Brotherhood**: the Lord our God demands that we love our neighbors as ourselves. This is actually a second commandment. Jesus said so. The lawyer had not asked for it, but the first commandment is abstract; it cannot be seen or understood standing by itself. There has to be a *demonstration, an act, something done* for love to be seen and understood. A profession of love without demonstration is empty. It is only profession. Love is not known without showing it.

Several important things need to be said about love at this point.

1. Love is an active experience, not inactive and dormant. That is what Christ was pointing out. Love for God *acts*. Love acts by showing and demonstrating itself. It is inaccurate and foolish for a man to say, "I love God"; and then be inactive, dormant, doing nothing for God. If he truly loves God, he will *do things* for God. Any person who loves does things for the one loved.

2. The primary thing God wants from us is to love our neighbor, *not the doing of religious things*. Doing religious things is good; but it only deals with things such as rituals, observances, ordinances, laws. Such things are lifeless, unfeeling, unresponsive. They are immaterial. They are not helped by our doing them. Only we are helped. They make us feel good and religious, which is beneficial to our growth, but religious things are not what demonstrate our love for God. Loving our neighbor is what proves our love for God. A man may say he loves God, but if he hates and acts unkindly toward his neighbor, everyone knows his religion is only profession.

> **"A new commandment I give unto you, That ye love one another; as I have loved you, that ye also love one another. By this shall all men know that ye are my disciples, if ye have love one to another" (Jn.13:34-35).**
> **"If a man say, I love God, and hateth his brother, he is a liar: for he that loveth not his brother whom he hath seen, how can he love God whom he hath not seen? And this commandment have we from him, That he who loveth God love his brother also" (1 Jn.4:20-21).**

3. The great commandment to love God flows downward into another great commandment: to love our neighbor as ourselves. The fact is inescapable.

> **"God commendeth [demonstrated] His love toward us, in that, while we were yet sinners, Christ died for us" (Ro.5:8).**

When a man really sees the love of God, he cannot help but love God and share the love of God with his neighbors. It is the love of Christ for us, His death and sacrifice, that compels us to go and love all men everywhere.

"We love him, because he first loved us...and this commandment have we from him, That he who loveth God love his brother also" (1 Jn.4:19, 21).

"For the love of Christ constraineth us; because we thus judge, that if one died for all, then were all dead: and that he died for all, that they which live should not henceforth live unto themselves, but unto him which died for them, and rose again" (2 Co.5:14-15).

4. We are to love self.
   a. There is a corrupt love of self that feels the world should center around oneself. This self-love...
      - wants all attention centered around oneself.
      - pushes self forward.
      - insists on one's own way.
      - demands and revels in recognition.
      - shows conceit and ignores others.

   b. However, there is a godly love for self that is natural and pleasing to God. It is a love that stirs a strong self-image, confidence and assurance, and even helps in preventing some diseases and illnesses such as ulcers, tension, and high blood pressure. The right love of self or the godly love of self comes from knowing three things.
      ⇒ That one is actually the creation of God: the highest creation possible.
      ⇒ That one is actually the object of God's love: the most supreme love possible.
      ⇒ That one is actually the trustee of God's gifts: the greatest gifts possible.

   c. The godly love of self has three traits that are clearly seen.
      ⇒ It esteems others better than itself. It does esteem self ever so highly as God's glorious creation, but it esteems others more highly.

      "Let nothing be done through strife or vainglory; but in lowliness of mind let each esteem other better than themselves" (Ph.2:3).

      ⇒ It looks on the things of others. It does look on one's own things as a trustee of God's gifts, but it also looks on the things of others.

      "Look not every man on his own things, but every man also on the things of others" (Ph.2:4).

      ⇒ It walks humbly before others.

      "But he that is greatest among you shall be your servant. And whosoever shall exalt himself shall be abased; and he that shall humble himself shall be exalted" (Mt.23:11-12).

      "...all of you be subject one to another, and be clothed with humility: for God resisteth the proud, and giveth grace to the humble" (1 Pe.5:5).

5. We are to love our neighbor as ourselves. Note three very specific things about this second great commandment.
   a. To love our neighbor is a command, not an option. If the commandment is not obeyed, God is displeased, and we stand guilty of having broken the law of God.
   b. To love our neighbor arouses the question: Who is our neighbor? Jesus answered the question Himself in the Parable of the Good Samaritan. A good neighbor is "he that shows mercy on any who need mercy," even if the needy person is socially despised (Lu.10:25-37, esp. 36-37). Everyone in the world needs mercy; therefore, our neighbor is everyone in the world, no matter his status, condition, or circumstance. Every man is to be esteemed ever so highly and helped no matter who he is. No man is to be injured or wronged. Every man is always to be esteemed better than oneself (Ph.2:3).
   c. To love our neighbor is a very practical command. It involves some very practical acts that are spelled out in Scripture (see 1 Co.13:4-7).
      ⇒ Love suffers long (endures long, is patient).
      ⇒ Love is kind.
      ⇒ Love envies not (is not jealous).
      ⇒ Love vaunts not itself (brags, boasts not).
      ⇒ Love is not puffed up (vainglorious, arrogant, prideful).
      ⇒ Love does not behave itself unseemly (unbecomingly, rudely, indecently, unmannerly).
      ⇒ Love seeks not her own (is not selfish, self-seeking, insisting on a person's own rights and way).
      ⇒ Love is not easily provoked (not touchy, angry, fretful, resentful).
      ⇒ Love thinks no evil (harbors no evil or immoral thoughts, takes no account of a wrong done it).
      ⇒ Love rejoices not in iniquity (not in wrong, sin, evil, injustice); but rejoices in the truth (what is right, just, righteous).
      ⇒ Love bears all things.
      ⇒ Love believes all things (exercises faith in everything; is ready to believe the best in everyone).
      ⇒ Love hopes all things (keeps up hope in everything, under all circumstances).
      ⇒ Love endures all things (keeps a person from weakening; gives the power to endure).

DEEPER STUDY # 4
(12:31) **Love—Brotherhood**: see Le.19:18.

3 (12:32-34) **Love, Law of—Almost Persuaded**: the great scope of the commandment is threefold.

a. The commandment of love is so great that it causes thinking and honest men to agree. This lawyer was a thinking man, and he was open and honest. Imagine the bitter hatred of this man's peers against Jesus, yet he was open and honest enough to listen to Jesus and face the truth of what Jesus said. (How many are as open and honest today?)

b. The commandment of love is so great that it exceeds all offerings and sacrifices. The man had been wrapped up in offerings and sacrifices all his life. His life as a Scribe was literally dedicated to and possessed by a religion that was steeped in offerings and sacrifices.

He had come a long way in making this statement (vv.32-33). He was beginning to see that life and religion were not ritual and ceremony and rules and regulations. Life is love—loving God with all of one's being and loving one's neighbor as oneself.

c. The commandment of love is so great that it almost assures salvation to those who understand it. Jesus said so: "Thou art not far from the kingdom of God."

> **Thought 1.** How many people really think and are at the same time open and honest? Some do think through the deeper issues of life, but there are fewer who are open and honest.

> **Thought 2.** How many are not "far from the kingdom of God?" Some are not far away, but note: they are still away. They are not in the kingdom.

    1. Jesus questioned men: About the Messiah **2. The entangled idea of the Messiah: He is David's son—a mere man** **3. The correct idea of the**	**J. The Entangled Idea of the Messiah, 12:35-37** *(Mt. 22:41-46; Lu. 20:39-44)* 35 And Jesus answered and said, while he taught in the temple, How say the scribes that Christ is the Son of Da- vid? 36 For David himself said	by the Holy Ghost, The Lord said to my Lord, Sit thou on my right hand, till I make thine enemies thy foot- stool. 37 David therefore himself calleth him Lord; and whence is he then his son? And the common people heard him gladly.	**Messiah: He is the Lord of David—God Himself**[DS1] **4. The crowds listened to Jesus: With delight**

DIVISION VII

THE SON OF GOD'S LAST JERUSALEM MINISTRY: JESUS' WARNING AND CONFLICT WITH RELIGIONISTS, 11:1-12:44

J. The Entangled Idea of the Messiah, 12:35-37

(12:35-37) **Introduction**: it was still Tuesday of the Lord's last week on earth. He had just been challenged four different times by four different opponents. He had met each group, each questioner head-on by turning the questions around to teach much needed truths (see Mt.21:23f; 22:15f; 22:23f; 22:34f). Jesus had silenced those who opposed His claim to be the Messiah.

Now it was His turn to question His opponents. But note: Jesus did not stand against them as an opponent. He questioned them as men who were in error and needed to see the truth. He was reaching out to them in the hope that some would receive the truth of His Messiahship and accept Him as the Son of God. The spirit of His questioning is seen in the brief discussion He had with them. The question He asked of them is the all important question which He asks of every man: "What think ye of Christ, the Messiah?"

1. Jesus questioned men: about the Messiah (v.35).
2. The entangled idea of the Messiah: He is David's son—a mere man (v.35).
3. The correct idea of the Messiah: He is the Lord of David—God Himself (vv.36-37).
4. The crowds listened to Jesus: with delight (v.37).

1 (12:35) **Jesus Christ, Questions**: Jesus questions men—and there are reasons He questions them. These are clearly seen in His dealing with these men.

a. Jesus is long-suffering and tender. These men had challenged Jesus time and again trying to discredit and embarrass Him before the crowd. Yet He never reacted once. He answered their questions honestly, opening up new truths which they desperately needed to know. He questioned them because He was patient and long-suffering. He wanted to open up further truths to them. He longed for them to see and know and surrender to His Messiahship.

b. Jesus continues to question in order to reach out to man over and over. In the case of these men, Jesus was making a last-ditch effort, a last appeal to them. They had rejected and rejected until there was little hope. But Jesus was still hoping, still reaching out to them. He questioned in order to lead them to see that He was the Messiah, the Lord, the Son of God Himself.

While considering the Lord's questioning, there is another fact to consider—a critical fact. There is an end to His questioning, a time when He knows there is no hope and no chance that a man will repent and believe. There is a time when He begins to pronounce judgment. This was Jesus' last question. Once it was answered, He began to pronounce judgment. Jesus discussed and questioned repeatedly, but after these men had rejected so many times, they became steeped in their unbelief. Therefore, Jesus ceased the discussion and pronounced judgment (see Mt.23:1-39).

2 (12:35) **Messiah**: the entangled idea of the Messiah was that He was David's son, *a mere man.* Jesus' question was one of the most important questions that can be asked of a man: "How say the scribes that Christ is the Son of David?" Matthew says that Jesus had first asked the Scribes, "What think ye of Christ [Messiah]? Whose Son is He?" (Mt.22:42). Note four points.

a. The Greek uses the definite article "*the* Messiah" (tou Christou). Jesus was trying to stir them to think about the Messiah. He did not ask these men what they thought of Him, but what they thought about *the Messiah.*

b. Jesus asked a specific question about the Messiah: "Whose Son is He?" Think about the Messiah. What is His origin? Who gave birth to Him? In practical day-to-day living, Jesus was asking three things.

1) Where does your deliverance come from? The Messiah is to deliver man from all the evil and enslavements of the world. Where will such a Person come from?
2) Where does your Lord come from—the Person you are to follow? The Messiah is to be the Lord who is to rule and reign and govern all lives, executing perfect justice and care.
3) Where does your utopia come from—the Person who is to bring about the perfect world and all that is good and beneficial? Where does the Person come from who is to bring utopia and the Kingdom of God to earth?

c. The common title for the Messiah was "the Son of David." The Old Testament definitely said the Messiah was to come from the line of David. It was from such passages as these that the Messiah was known as "the Son of David." (See note, *Jesus Christ, Son of David*—Lu.3:24-31; DEEPER STUDY # 3—Jn.1:45 for verses and fulfillment.)

"Once have I sworn by my holiness that I will not lie unto David. His seed shall endure for ever, and his throne as the sun before me" (Ps.89:35-36).

"For unto us a child is born, unto us a son is given: and the government shall be upon his shoulder: and his name shall be called Wonderful, Counselor, The mighty God, The everlasting Father, The Prince of Peace. Of the increase of his government and peace there shall be no end, upon the throne of David, and upon his kingdom, to order it, and to establish it with judgment and with justice from henceforth even for ever. The zeal of the Lord of hosts will perform this" (Is.9:6-7).

"And there shall come forth a rod out of the stem of Jesse, and a Branch shall grow out of his roots: the spirit of the Lord shall rest upon him, the spirit of wisdom and understanding, the spirit of counsel and might, the spirit of knowledge and of the fear of the Lord; and shall make him of quick understanding in the fear of the Lord: and he shall not judge after the sight of his eyes, neither reprove after the hearing of his ears: but with righteousness shall he judge the poor, and reprove with equity for the meek of the earth: and he shall smite the earth with the rod of his mouth, and with the breath of his lips shall he slay the wicked. And righteousness shall be the girdle of his loins, and faithfulness the girdle of his reins" (Is.11:1-5).

The Messiah was to do four specific things. (See notes—Mt.1:1; DEEPER STUDY # 2—1:18; DEEPER STUDY # 3—3:11; notes—11:1-6; 11:2-3; DEEPER STUDY # 1—11:5; DEEPER STUDY # 2—11:6; DEEPER STUDY # 1—12:16; notes—Lu.7:21-23. These notes are important for the full concept of the Messiah.)

1) He was to free Israel from all enslavement. Enslavement was to be abolished and all men were to be set free under God's domain.
2) He was to give victory over all enemies. Israel was to be established as the seat of His rule. This, of course, meant Israel was to be the leading nation of the world.
3) He was to bring peace to earth. All were to serve God under the government established by the Messiah.
4) He was to provide plenty for all. The Messiah was to see that all men had the benefits of God's rule and care.

d. The common idea of the Messiah's origin was that He was to be human, of a man. The idea that He might be of divine origin, of God Himself was just unacceptable to them.

3 (12:36-37) **Messiah**: the correct idea of the Messiah is that He is the Lord of David, God Himself. Jesus now pointed out the claim of Scripture: the Messiah is Lord, the Lord of David. Scripture does not only say that the Messiah is the Son of David, it also says that He is the *Lord* of David.

The Scripture is strong in its statement.

a. The fact is this: David called the Messiah "Lord" *in the Spirit.* That is, David's words were spoken under the inspiration of the Holy Spirit. God was directing Him (see 2 Pe.1:21 and 1 Co.12:3).

b. The fact is this: David said that "the Lord [Jehovah God] said to *my* Lord [the Messiah]." David unquestionably called the Messiah, "*My Lord.*"

c. The fact is this: David said that *my* Lord "sits on God's right hand." The Messiah is *Lord*, for He is *exalted* by God.

"Which he wrought in Christ, when he raised him from the dead, and set him at his own right hand in the heavenly places" (Ep.1:20).

"Wherefore God also hath highly exalted him, and given him a name which is above every name" (Ph.2:9).

"Now of the things which we have spoken this is the sum: We have such an high priest, who is set on the right hand of the throne of the Majesty in the heavens" (He.8:1).

d. The fact is this: David said that my Lord's "enemies are to be made His footstool." The Messiah is Lord, for all His enemies are to be subjected under Him.

"That at the name of Jesus every knee should bow, of things in heaven, and things in earth, and things under the earth; and that every tongue should confess that Jesus Christ is Lord, to the glory of God the Father" (Ph.2:10-11).

After quoting the Scripture, Jesus asked the key question: How can the Messiah be both David's Lord and Son? Jesus was doing at least two things.

First, Jesus was saying that to think of the Messiah only in human terms was inadequate—totally inadequate. It is not enough to think in terms of earthly power, of national, political, military, and institutional leaders. There is no way a *mere man* can bring perfect deliverance, leadership, and utopia to this earth. The Messiah is not only man; He is the Lord from heaven.

Second, Jesus was claiming to be the Son of God Himself. Man's concept has to go beyond the mere human and physical. Man's idea has to stretch upward into God's very own heart. God loves this earth; therefore, God sent His Son to earth, sacrificing Him in order to save it.

"For God so loved the world, that he gave his only begotten Son, that whosoever believeth in him should not perish, but have everlasting life" (Jn.3:16).

"And Simon Peter answered and said, Thou art the Christ, the Son of the living God" (Mt.16:16).

"The woman saith unto him, I know that Messias cometh, which is called Christ: when he is come, he will tell us all things. Jesus saith unto her, I that speak unto thee am he" (Jn.4:25-26).

"Then said Jesus unto the twelve, Will ye also go away? Then Simon Peter answered him, Lord, to whom shall we go? thou hast the words of eternal life. And we believe and are sure that thou art that Christ, the Son of the living God" (Jn.6:67-69).

"I said therefore unto you, that ye shall die in your sins: for if ye believe not that I am he, ye shall die in your sins" (Jn.8:24).

"Then said Jesus unto them, When ye have lifted up the Son of man, then shall ye know that I am he, and that I do nothing of myself; but as my Father hath taught me, I speak these things" (Jn.8:28).

"Jesus said unto her, I am the resurrection, and the life: he that believeth in me, though he were dead, yet shall he live: and whosoever liveth and believeth in me shall never die. Believest thou this? She saith unto him, Yea, Lord: I believe that thou art the Christ, the Son of God, which should come into the world" (Jn.11:25-27).

"But Saul increased the more in strength, and confounded the Jews which dwelt at Damascus, proving that this is very Christ" (Ac.9:22).

"And Paul, as his manner was, went in unto them, and three sabbath days reasoned with them out of the scriptures, opening and alleging, that Christ must needs have suffered, and risen again from the dead; and that this Jesus, whom I preach unto you, is Christ" (Ac.17:2-3).

"Whosoever believeth that Jesus is the Christ is born of God: and every one that loveth him that begat loveth him also that is begotten of him" (1 Jn.5:1).

Thought 1. Note a terrible tragedy: the religionists missed the truth of the Messiah because...
- they misread the Scripture, not letting the Scripture speak for itself.
- they did not pay close enough attention to the exact words of the Scripture. (Note how Christ takes a simple statement and shows how its exact words predicted the Messiah.)
- they studied their teachers and authorities more than the Scripture itself.
- they were dogmatic about their own ideas and notions about the future and how events would actually take place. Prophecies concerning the coming of the Messiah were made a matter of fellowship.

DEEPER STUDY # 1
(12:36) **Prophecy, of Messiah**: see Ps.110:1. The Pharisees recognized these Scriptures as being Messianic.

4 (12:37) **Jesus Christ, Response to**: the crowds, that is, the common people, listened to Jesus with delight. As seen before, they were amazed and stricken with awe at such profoundness of character and ability. Jesus was such an able teacher, and He was equally able in refuting those who were His avowed enemies.

Thought 1. The people heard Him gladly. Why? Because of the debating? Argument and dissension attract interest in a worldly and fleshly sense. Many enjoy seeing a heated argument and fight, especially when an underdog is getting the upper hand. Yet, there is no mention of the people's trusting Christ and becoming His followers. Some may have, but there is no mention of the fact.

1. **Dressing: To draw attention**	**K. The Warning to the Crowds & Religionists: Some Things to Guard Against, 12:38-40** *(Mt. 23:5-6, 14; Lu. 20:45-47)* 38 And he said unto them in his doctrine, Beware of the scribes, which love to go in long clothing, and love	salutations in the marketplaces, 39 And the chief seats in the synagogues, and the uppermost rooms at feasts: 40 Which devour widows' houses, and for a pretence make long prayers: these shall receive greater damnation.	**2. Greetings & titles: To exalt man** **3. Front seats & high places: To be seen, admired, & honored** **4. Devouring widows: To use widows for gain** **5. Long prayers: To show piety**

DIVISION VII

THE SON OF GOD'S LAST JERUSALEM MINISTRY: JESUS' WARNING AND CONFLICT WITH RELIGIONISTS, 11:1-12:44

K. The Warning to the Crowds and Religionists: Some Things to Guard Against, 12:38-40

(12:38-40) **Introduction**: men need to be warned. There are some things that especially disturb and arouse anger in Jesus, some things that will result in terrible judgment. This passage discusses six of these sins. Note that all six have to do with pride or flaunting oneself, either by elevating oneself above others or by misusing others.

1. Dressing: to draw attention (v.38).
2. Greetings and titles: to exalt man (v.38).
3. Front seats and high places: to be seen, admired, and honored (v.39).
4. Devouring widows: to use widows for gain (v.40).
5. Long prayers: to show piety (v.40).

1 (12:38) **Dress—Clothing—Appearance**: beware of dressing to draw attention. There are three ways a person can dress to draw attention.

a. A person can desire and love to wear the clothing of the extravagant and wasteful. The long robe was the dress of the nobility, the rich, the well-known, the person of style. It was a long robe reaching to the ground. A man was unable to work in it; therefore, it was the sign of *higher society* or of a man of leisure. Jesus was not speaking against fine clothing. What He said was, "Beware of [those] who *love* to go in long clothing" (fine clothing). He condemned the person who was extravagant and wasteful, whose mind was on attracting attention, on self, on appearance. A person's mind is not to be on clothing, but on ...

> **"Whatsoever things are true, whatsoever things are honest, whatsoever things are just, whatsoever things are pure, whatsoever things are lovely, whatsoever things are of good report; if there be any virtue, and if there be any praise, think on these things" (Ph.4:8).**

A man's life consists not in the things he has, but in the service he renders to others. The world is desperate, swamped with enormous needs. God's will is for all persons to be wrapped up in meeting the needs of the world and not in clothing. This is especially God's wish for the Christian. The Christian's concern is to be righteousness. He is to work for Christ and His kingdom, not for expensive, stylish, ostentatious clothing.

> **"Let him that stole steal no more: but rather let him labour, working with his hands the thing which is good, that he may have to give to him that needeth" (Ep.4:28).**

b. A person can change his dress, his clothing, and his appearance *in order to attract attention.* A person often desires attention, so he seeks to attract by being different and making himself stand out. This was a sin of the religionists in Christ's day.

1) They wore phylacteries. These were little leather type boxes which contained a piece of parchment with four passages of Scripture written on it. The Scriptures were Ex.13:1-10; 13:11-16; De.6:4-9; and 11:13-21.
   The use of the phylacteries apparently arose from a literal translation of Ex.13:9 and Pr.7:3. The true meaning of these two passages seems to be that we are to have the Word of God in our minds just as clearly as if we had them before our eyes. The great fault of the religionists was that they not only interpreted the passages literally and wore little leather boxes on their forehead, but they enlarged the little leather boxes to draw attention to themselves as being religious.
2) They also enlarged the borders of their garments; that is, they wore outside tassels. God had instructed the Jews to make fringes or tassels on the borders of their outer robe. When a person noticed them, he was to be reminded to keep God's commandments. Again, the error was that the religionist changed his appearance from others; he enlarged the tassels, drawing attention to his being more religious than others.

c. A person can wear clothes that expose the body, that actually attract attention to certain parts of the body. A person can wear clothes that are too tight, too low cut, too high cut, too thin. A person can wear too little clothing, clothing that fails to cover enough of the body.

Jesus very simply said to beware of dressing to attract attention. The religionists did it to appear righteous. Others do it to appear worldly (appealing).

"Neither yield ye your members [bodily parts] as instruments of unrighteousness unto sin: but yield yourselves unto God, as those that are alive from the dead, and your members as instruments of righteousness unto God" (Ro.6:13).

"In like manner also, that women adorn themselves in modest apparel, with shamefacedness and sobriety; not with broided hair, or gold, or pearls, or costly array; but (which becometh women professing godliness) with good works" (1 Ti.2:9-10).

"[Women] whose adorning let it not be that outward adorning of plaiting the hair, and of wearing of gold, or of putting on of apparel; but let it be the hidden man of the heart, in that which is not corruptible, even the ornament of a meek and quiet spirit, which is in the sight of God of great price" (1 Pe.3:3-5).

2 (12:38) **Honor, Worldly—Titles—Marketplace**: beware of greetings and titles that exalt man. The religionists loved the *titles* that greeted and exalted them with honor. Note the title was "Rabbi," meaning teacher or master. It was only a simple title, yet some loved and reveled in the recognition above other men. It took a man who was supposed to be God's messenger and said, "Here I am; look at me." It honored the man and not the Lord.

Thought 1. Men exalt one another with titles: Reverend, Doctor, Director, Executive, Chairman—all to elevate self above the masses below.

"And whosoever shall exalt himself shall be abased; and he that shall humble himself shall be exalted" (Mt.23:12).

"Though thou exalt thyself as the eagle, and though thou set thy nest among the stars, thence will I bring thee down, saith the LORD" (Ob.4).

"For when he dieth he shall carry nothing away: his glory shall not descend after him" (Ps.49:17).

The leaders were also to beware of showing themselves in the marketplace. Displaying oneself in the marketplace was and still is a sin. The marketplace is wherever the people are. It is the center of traffic, the place where a person is seen and can attract attention. It is the streets, the office, the club, the school, the beach, and so on. Neither dress nor title is to be used to attract attention or elevate oneself above others.

Thought 1. What Christ is after is love—love among all men and women, boys and girls. And the only way love will ever rule upon earth is for all to begin serving and *lifting up others* instead of self. Dressing and using titles to draw attention to oneself do not lend themselves to love. They tend to elevate self and to destroy the morals and stability of both families and the nation.

"For all flesh is as grass, and all the glory of man as the flower of grass. The grass withereth, and the flower thereof falleth away" (1 Pe.1:24).

3 (12:39) **Self-Seeking—Honor, Worldly—Pride**: beware of front seats and high places, seats and places to be seen, admired, and to show one's prominence. In the synagogue the leaders and distinguished men sat on a bench in front of the ark (where the Scripture was kept), and they sat facing the congregation. No leader could be missed.

On social occasions the most honored sat at the right hand of the host, then the next honored at his left hand, and so on, alternating from the right to the left down the table. Position and recognition were set.

Some loved the positions of honor, special seats, and places of recognition. There are those who love the restricted neighborhoods and clubs, the preferred lists. They love the preeminence (3 Jn.9). Note what is condemned: not being in these positions and places, but the *love* of them. Someone has to hold the upper positions and fill the major places. It is the *love* of such, the love and the feeling of pride because of the place and position that is wrong.

"How can ye believe, which receive honour one of another, and seek not the honour that cometh from God only?" (Jn.5:44).

"Nevertheless man being in honour abideth not: he is like the beasts that perish" (Ps.49:12).

4 (12:40) **Widows—Stealing—Motive, Evil**: beware of devouring widows, of using widows for gain. Many commit this sin, and Jesus is most severe in His warning against it. He says that the man who devours (takes advantage of) a widow "shall receive *greater damnation*." Note who these men were.

a. They were lawyers (Scribes). Of course others were guilty as well, but the ones who stood before Jesus were lawyers. They used their legal position to manage the wills and other legal business for the widows, and they cheated, devouring the widows by skimming too much out of their estates.

b. They were religionists, professing to believe in God. Some used the guise of religion to steal from widows.

There are some today—lawyers, religionists, preachers, and institutional, civic, and Christian leaders (all professing hypocrites)—who court the attention and favor of people, especially widows, for the purpose of securing money. They seek large donations, endowments, trusts, investments, and gifts *to promote themselves* and their institution. And the great tragedy is, such false and hypocritical hearts use the guise of religion to promote themselves and their false ideas. Their call to people is to institutional religion, not to the honor of God and the spirit of self-denial. Vain men, of course, are susceptible to such appeals, but widows in particular are exposed to those who seem to be so devoted to God.

Note that Jesus said the damnation of these shall be greater. There are some sins more horrible than others. Using religion for selfish ends is one of them. Such will receive a greater damnation. Something should be noted here. Widows hold a special place in God's heart. He has always instructed His people to care for them in a very special way.

> **"He doth execute the judgment of the fatherless and widow, and loveth the stranger, in giving him food and raiment" (De.10:18).**
>
> **"Cursed be he that perverteth the judgment of the stranger, fatherless, and widow" (De.27:19).**
>
> **"A father of the fatherless, and a judge of the widows, is God in his holy habitation" (Ps.68:5).**
>
> **"Learn to do well; seek judgment, relieve the oppressed, judge the fatherless, plead for the widow" (Is.1:17).**
>
> **"And there was a widow in that city; and she came unto him, saying, Avenge me of mine adversary. And he would not for a while: but afterward he said within himself, Though I fear not God, nor regard man; yet because this widow troubleth me I will avenge her, lest by her continual coming she weary me" (Lu.18:3-7).**
>
> **"Let him that stole steal no more: but rather let him labour, working with his hands the thing which is good, that he may have to give to him that needeth" (Ep.4:28).**

5 (12:40) **Prayers**: beware of long prayers to show piety. There are two prominent sins and dangers with long prayers.

a. There is the *danger of praying publicly for attention.* The problem in Jesus' day dealt with *long public prayers*; however, in our day short public prayers are just as big a problem. Men too often pray publicly...

- to sound good.
- to demonstrate their ability at language.
- to show their devotion to God.
- to simply impress people.

Again, some use long prayers while others use short prayers to show their piety.

b. There is *the danger of sharing one's private prayer* life with others, in particular when one has spent a long time in prayer (all night or for hours) or is consistent in daily prayer. Sharing such a personal matter as prayer, even with one's closest friend, causes a *surge* of spiritual pride, of *super-spirituality*, of being a little bit better than a Christian brother.

Again, the sin of pretence in praying, of sharing one's times with God, is a gross sin. It shall receive greater condemnation.

> **"But when ye pray, use not vain repetitions, as the heathen do: for they think that they shall be heard for their much speaking" (Mt.6:7).**

	L. The Widow's Offerings: Real Giving, 12:41-44 *(Lu. 21:1-4)*		
1. Real giving was demonstrated: Jesus observed some people giving a. Saw the wealthy give much b. Saw a widow give little	41 And Jesus sat over against the treasury, and beheld how the people cast money into the treasury: and many that were rich cast in much. 42 And there came a certain poor widow, and she threw in	two mites, which make a farthing. 43 And he called unto him his disciples, and saith unto them, Verily I say unto you, That this poor widow hath cast more in, than all they which have cast into the treasury: 44 For all they did cast in of their abundance; but she of her want did cast in all that she had, even all her living.	**2. Real giving is sacrificial giving** **3. Real giving is measured by how much a person has left—not by how much a person gives** **4. Real giving seeks to have a need met** **5. Real giving is giving all a person has**

DIVISION VII

THE SON OF GOD'S LAST JERUSALEM MINISTRY:JESUS' WARNING AND CONFLICT WITH RELIGIONISTS, 11:1-12:44

L. The Widow's Offerings: Real Giving, 12:41-44

(12:41-44) **Introduction**: this is a touching story with a powerful message often ignored. It is a story that...
- shows how God's heart reaches out to those in need—reaches out in tenderness and compassion and love.
- shows how much devotion and commitment and boldness mean to Him.
- shows how deeply God is moved by those who give all they are and have to Him (contrast the Rich Young Ruler, Mk.10:17-22).
- shows what real giving is.

1. Real giving was demonstrated: Jesus observed some people giving (vv.41-42).
2. Real giving is sacrificial giving (v.42).
3. Real giving is measured by how much a person has left—not by how much a person gives (v.43).
4. Real giving seeks to have a need met (v.44).
5. Real giving is giving all a person has (v.44).

1 (12:41-42) **Stewardship**: Jesus observed people giving. Following all the plotting and argument in the Court of the Gentiles (Mk.11:27-12:40), Jesus walked into the Court of the Women over by the treasury. The treasury was an area in which there were thirteen trumpet shaped collection boxes where the worshippers dropped their offerings. He sat down, apparently all alone, to get some relief and rest from the tension of the past hours. While resting, He "beheld how the people cast money into the treasury" The word *beheld* (etheorei) means He was deliberately observing, discerning the motives of the people as they made their offerings. He saw many walk by and drop in sizeable offerings. Some were apparently quite large contributions. He could see the handfuls of coins and hear them clang against the sides as they slid down the funnel shaped trumpets. But none attracted His admiration. Finally a poor widow came along and threw in two mites, which were the smallest of coins, coins of very little value. Christ took what he saw and taught what true giving really is.

2 (12:42) **Stewardship**: real giving is sacrificial giving. The word *poor* (ptoches) means pauper. She was not just poor, she was destitute, in deep poverty. Her poor dress and plain appearance showed her desperate plight. The coins were all she had, yet she gave them despite her own desperate need.

Now note the point: what she gave was a *sacrifice*. What the others gave was not a sacrifice. It did not cost them nor hurt them. They still had plenty left, for they gave only what they could spare. But not the widow. Her gift cost her. It hurt to give, for she gave what she could not spare. She gave what Christ called a *sacrificial gift*. She sacrificed; she went without a meal or gave up something else so that she could give.

> **Thought 1.** There is a great difference between giving what one can spare and giving sacrificially, actually giving up something in order to give. Sacrificial giving costs something. Sacrificial giving is giving when it hurts, when a person has nothing left, nothing to spare. The difference needs to be stressed, for God expects sacrificial giving. If the world and its desperate needs are ever to be reached for Christ, then every believer must give sacrificially.
>
> > **"Upon the first day of the week let every one of you lay by him in store, as God hath prospered him, that there be no gatherings when I come" (1 Co.16:2).**
> >
> > **"Every man according as he purposeth in his heart, so let him give; not grudgingly, or of necessity: for God loveth a cheerful giver....For the administration of this service not only supplieth the want of the saints, but...they glorify God for your professed subjection unto the gospel of Christ, and for your liberal distribution unto them, and unto all men....Thanks be unto God for his unspeakable gift" (2 Co.9:7, 12-13, 15).**
> >
> > **"Every man shall give as he is able, according to the blessing of the LORD thy God which he hath given thee" (De.16:17).**

3 (12:43) **Stewardship:** real giving is measured by how much a person has left, not by how much a person gives. Jesus called His disciples to him and used the great sacrifice that the widow made to teach a much needed lesson. Note several facts.

a. They all gave an offering to God: both "the people" (v.41) who had and the poor widow who did not have.
b. The ones who had plenty gave more money, much more than the widow. Their contributions were generous. Their incomes were dazzling, so their offerings were large.
c. But in God's eyes the widow gave more. Why? Because God measures what was *kept*, not what was given.
⇒ The widow had less remaining; the others still had much.
⇒ The widow had given more of what she had; the others had given less of what they had.
⇒ The widow had sacrificed more; the others had sacrificed less.

In proportion to what she had, the widow gave a larger percent. The others gave a much smaller percent. After they had given, they still had 85 percent or 90 percent or 95 percent to spend on themselves.

This is the lesson Jesus was teaching, a critical lesson. God counts what we have left, not what we give. He counts the amount of sacrifice, not the amount of money. The gift that matters is the gift that costs the giver to give. To the thoughtful recipient it is not the size of the gift that impresses, but the sacrifice the giver had to make in order to give the gift. The greater the sacrifice, the more appreciative the recipient. (See Related Subjects—Subject Index for more discussion.)

"For where your treasure is, there will your heart be also" (Mt.6:21).

"And Zacchaeus stood, and said unto the Lord; Behold, Lord, the half of my goods I give to the poor; and if I have taken any thing from any man by false accusation, I restore him fourfold" (Lu.19:8).

"For ye know the grace of our Lord Jesus Christ, that, though he was rich, yet for your sakes he became poor, that ye through his poverty might be rich" (2 Co.8:9).

4 (12:44) **Stewardship**: real giving seeks to have a need met. Note the words, "She *of her want* [out of her need] did cast in all that she had." She had great need for food, clothing, and shelter. She had so little; she was the kind of person who would have had to wander about seeking odd jobs just to survive in a depressed economy. Looking at her, a person could tell she never knew where she would get her next meal. She had no one to care for her and no one to help her. The weight of the world seemed to lie upon her shoulders. There was no man who cared or expressed care. This was evident in her appearance, but she knew something. Men may not care, but God cares; so she came to God for help. And what she did is a crucial lesson for men to learn.

She took her need and gave it to God. Her need was financial, so she took what money she had and gave it all to God. She simply said, "God, I have need, the need for money. I do not even have enough money to buy food. If I am to eat, you have to provide somehow, some way. I have worked as hard as I can at the jobs I have been able to find. Here is all I have. Take it; use it in your kingdom. You now take care of me."

She knew the great principle that God will take care of those who give all they are and have to Him. She knew that if she were to be *assured* of God's care, she had to give *all* to God. If she gave *all*, God would not deny her anything. He would provide all the necessities of life (Mt.6:33). She took her need and all that was involved in it and gave it to God. She sought God to meet her need by giving *all that she had* to God.

Note something else. Two needs are present and being met.
a. God's temple (church) had need. The widow, though poor, gave to help carry on the ministry of God.
b. The poor widow had need. She gave, believing God would see to it that she had food, clothing, and shelter.

"Give, and it shall be given unto you; good measure, pressed down, and shaken together, and running over, shall men give into your bosom. For with the same measure that ye mete withal it shall be measured to you again" (Lu.6:38).

"But this I say, He which soweth sparingly shall reap also sparingly; and he which soweth bountifully shall reap also bountifully" (2 Co.9:6).

"The liberal soul shall be made fat: and he that watereth shall be watered also himself" (Pr.11:25).

"He that hath a bountiful eye shall be blessed; for he giveth of his bread to the poor" (Pr.22:9).

"And if thou draw out thy soul to the hungry, and satisfy the afflicted soul; then shall thy light rise in obscurity, and thy darkness be as the noonday" (Is.58:10).

5 (12:44) **Stewardship**: real giving is giving all a person has. "She...did cast in all that she had, even all her living." Just imagine! *She gave her living*—not just part—not just a sacrifice—but *all*! She could have easily said what so many often feel:
⇒ "My gift doesn't matter. It's so little."
⇒ "I have so little. God will understand. He doesn't expect me to give it when I can't even buy food."

Thought 1. The lesson is twofold.
(1) We lack devotion and dedication in our commitment to God, whether commitment of life, time, gifts, or money.
(2) We lack boldness in giving and using what we have for God.

"Jesus said unto him, If thou wilt be perfect, go and sell that thou hast, and give to the poor, and thou shalt have treasure in heaven: and come and follow me" (Mt.19:21).

"And every one that hath forsaken houses, or brethren, or sisters, or father, or mother, or wife, or children, or lands, for my name's sake, shall receive an hundredfold, and shall inherit everlasting life" (Mt.19:29).

"Even as I please all men in all things, not seeking mine own profit, but the profit of many, that they may be saved" (1 Co.10:33).

"Let him that stole steal no more: but rather let him labour, working with his hands the thing which is good, that he may have to give to him that needeth" (Ep.4:28).

1. Events that led to the great prophecies
a. The disciples admired the buildings of the temple
b. Jesus predicted the destruction of the buildings
c. The disciples asked two questions
1) When is the destruction to come?
2) What is the sign of the destruction?
d. Jesus warned: Watch out for deceivers

2. Sign 1: Spiritual deception & false messiahs

3. Sign 2: Wars & rumors of war, international disturbances

CHAPTER 13

VIII. THE SON OF GOD'S OLIVET MINISTRY: JESUS' PROPHECY OF HIS RETURN & THE END TIME,[DS1,2,3] 13:1-37

A. The Signs of the End Time, 13:1-13

(Mt. 24:1-14; Lu. 21:5-19)

And as he went out of the
temple, one of his disciples
saith unto him, Master, see
what manner of stones and
what buildings are here!
2 And Jesus answering said
unto him, Seest thou these
great buildings? there shall
not be left one stone upon
another, that shall not be
thrown down.
3 And as he sat upon the
mount of Olives over against
the temple, Peter and James
and John and Andrew asked
him privately,
4 Tell us, when shall these
things be? and what shall be
the sign when all these things
shall be fulfilled?
5 And Jesus answering them
began to say, Take heed lest
any man deceive you:
6 For many shall come in
my name, saying, I am Christ;
and shall deceive many.
7 And when ye shall hear
of wars and rumours of wars,
be ye not troubled: for such
things must needs be; but the
end shall not be yet.
8 For nation shall rise
against nation, and kingdom
against kingdom: and there
shall be earthquakes in divers
places, and there shall be
famines and troubles: these
are the beginnings of sorrows.
9 But take heed to yourselves:
for they shall deliver
you up to councils; and in the
synagogues ye shall be beaten:
and ye shall be brought
before rulers and kings for
my sake, for a testimony
against them.
10 And the gospel must first
be published among all nations.
11 But when they shall lead
you, and deliver you up, take
no thought beforehand what
ye shall speak, neither do ye
premeditate: but whatsoever
shall be given you in that
hour, that speak ye: for it is
not ye that speak, but the Holy Ghost.
12 Now the brother shall
betray the brother to death,
and the father the son; and
children shall rise up against
their parents, and shall cause
them to be put to death.
13 And ye shall be hated of
all men for my name's sake:
but he that shall endure unto
the end, the same shall be
saved.

4. Sign 3: Natural disasters
(Note: these signs are the beginning of sorrows)[DS4]

5. Sign 4: Persecution by civil & religious authorities

6. Sign 5: Worldwide evangelization

7. Sign 6: A supernatural witness

8. Sign 7: Divided families
a. Betrayal
b. Hatred & persecution

9. Sign 8: Some enduring & being saved

DIVISION VIII

THE SON OF GOD'S OLIVET MINISTRY: JESUS' PROPHECY OF HIS RETURN AND THE END TIME, 13:1-37

A. The Signs of the End Time, 13:1-13

(13:1-37) **DIVISION OVERVIEW***:* **End Time***:* noting the exact words of Jesus will help in understanding this chapter.

a. Jesus said "These are the beginnings of sorrows" (v.8). The words "the beginnings of sorrows" indicate that Jesus was dealing with the beginning of a terrible period of trial for the believer ("you," v.9). He was not *just* referring to the normal trials that occur upon earth or the regular persecutions that are launched against believers over the centuries (see DEEPER STUDY # 2—Mt.24:1-31). World trouble and persecutions against God's people have always existed, even from the beginning of time. The great sorrow He spoke about refers to some period of time which is to be terrible, so terrible that it can be said to be "*the beginnings of sorrows" or woes*. It is to be a period that is to be distinguished from all the other trouble the world and believers will suffer throughout history.

b. Jesus said, "When ye shall see the abomination of desolation...standing where it ought not...then let them that be in Judea flee" (v.14). Matthew words the warning this way: "Then...flee...for then shall be great tribulation, such as was not since the beginning of the world" (Mt.24:15-16, 21). There is no question about this sign. It launches the worst period of tribulation the world has ever seen. This sign definitely points to a specific period of human history. As to what the period should be called, it is probably best to title it as Matthew does: "great tribulation" (Mt.24:21).

c. Now, note what Jesus has said in the above verses.

> **"These are the beginnings of sorrows" (v.8).**
> **"When ye therefore shall see the abomination of desolation...standing where it ought not...then let them...flee" (v.14); or as Matthew says, "then...flee...*for then* shall be great tribulation such as was not since the beginning of the world" (Mt.24:15-16, 21).**

Jesus seemed to be giving a list of signs, one of which was the abomination of desolation. In verses 6-13 He gave eight signs, the eighth saying "He that shall endure to the end shall be saved" (v.13). But note in verse 14, how He seemed to pick up the signs again, giving what seems to be the most visible and terrible sign for which to watch. Note His words, reading verses 13 and 14 together, "He that shall endure to the end shall be saved. But when ye shall see the abomination of desolation...standing where it ought not...then let them...flee."

Jesus was saying there will be a difference between the signs that precede the abomination and the unparalleled trials that follow. When *the abomination of desolation* stands where it ought not (in the holy place), the trials that follow are much, much worse—unparalleled in human history.

The abomination of desolation will be the sign that launches the worst tribulations the world has ever known. Just when this abomination would appear Jesus did not say, but His appearance would be one of the nine signs Jesus gave; and His appearance would signal the worst devastation ever known by the world.

A chart diagramming Jesus' own words will perhaps help in understanding what He said.

1. His words were: "These [signs] are the beginnings of sorrows" (v.8).
2. "But when ye *shall see* the abomination of desolation...then let them...flee" (v.14); or as Matthew says, "*then shall be great tribulation*" (Mt.24:15, 21).
3. "But in those days, *after that tribulation*...shall they see the Son of Man coming" (vv.24-27).

THE END OF THE WORLD

	Seeing the Sign of the Abomination of Desolation *In the Middle of the Time or Years* (v.14)	Seeing the Son of *Man Coming* (v.26)
3 1/2 years Signs which are "The beginnings of sorrow" (v.8).	3 1/2 years Unparalleled trials of "the great tribulation" (v.19; see Mt.24:21)	"His angels... gather together His elect" (v.27)

(13:1-13) **Introduction—End Time**: in understanding what Jesus was saying, we have to be very careful not to add to or take away from what He said. Both mistakes were made by religionists concerning Jesus' first coming (Mt.2:4-6).

A major fact to keep in mind is this. The disciples did think that all three events (Jerusalem's destruction, the Lord's return, and the world's end) would happen at about the same time. They did think in terms of the Messianic Kingdom of God (Ac.1:6 compared with the Jewish concept of the Messiah show this). (See notes—Mt.1:1; DEEPER STUDY # 2—1:18; DEEPER STUDY # 3—3:11; notes—11:1-6; 11:2-3; DEEPER STUDY # 1—11:5; DEEPER STUDY # 2—11:6; DEEPER STUDY # 1—12:16; notes—22:42; Lu.7:21-23.) When Jesus said that the temple would be destroyed, the disciples assumed it would happen at the same time that He returned and ended the world, thereby restoring the kingdom to Israel.

Jesus, however, gave no timetable. He did not say when the three events would occur. What He did was give signs that would occur before the events, signs that pointed toward His return and toward the end of Jerusalem and the end of the world.

It is important to keep in mind that most of the signs happen throughout history, but there is this difference: the signs increase and intensify right before the end of Jerusalem and the end of the world. There will be a period known as "*the beginnings of sorrows*" (v.8), and a period launched by the abomination of desolation known as *the great tribulation*, such as was not since the beginning of the world" (Mt.24:21).

1. Events that led to the great prophecies (vv.1-5).
2. Sign 1: spiritual deception and false messiahs (v.6).
3. Sign 2: wars and rumors of war, international disturbances (vv.7-8).
4. Sign 3: natural disasters (v.8).
5. Sign 4: persecution by civil and religious authorities (v.9).
6. Sign 5: worldwide evangelization (v.10).
7. Sign 6: a supernatural witness (v.11).
8. Sign 7: divided families (vv.12-13).
9. Sign 8: some enduring and being saved (v.13).

DEEPER STUDY # 1

(13:1-37) **End Time—Daniel**: Jesus made another statement that helps in understanding this chapter. He said that the abomination of desolation was "spoken of by Daniel the prophet" (Mt.24:15). There are three passages in Daniel that refer to the abomination of desolation.

> **"Know therefore and understand, that from the going forth of the commandment to restore and to build Jerusalem unto the Messiah the Prince shall be seven weeks, and threescore and two weeks: the street shall be built again, and the wall, even in troublous times. And after threescore and two weeks shall Messiah be cut off, but not for himself: and the people of the prince that shall come shall destroy the city and the sanctuary; and the end thereof shall be with a flood, and unto the end of the war desolations are determined. And he shall confirm the covenant with many for one week: and in the midst of the week he shall cause the sacrifice and the oblation to cease, and for the overspreading**

of abominations he shall make it desolate, even until the consummation, and that determined shall be poured upon the desolate" (Da.9:25-27).

"And arms shall stand on his part, and they shall pollute the sanctuary of strength, and shall take away the daily sacrifice, and they shall place the abomination that maketh desolate" (Da.11:31).

"And from the time that the daily sacrifice shall be taken away, and the abomination that maketh desolate set up, there shall be a thousand two hundred and ninety days" (Da.12:11).

Several things can be said about Daniel's prophecy.

1. The prophecy had a past fulfillment in Antiochus Epiphanes (see DEEPER STUDY # 1—Mk.13:14).

2. Jesus said the prophecy of Daniel also had a future fulfillment. Note the words, "When ye shall see." The future fulfillment refers both to the fall of Jerusalem (vv.14-20) and to the end of the world, right before the Lord returns (vv.14, 24-27).

3. The words of Daniel give a division of time even as Jesus divided the signs into two periods. Daniel says, "In the midst of the week he [the prince] shall cause...." Note two facts.

   a. The words "in the midst of the week" definitely point to a separation of the week into two periods of time.
   b. "The week" is the seventieth week, the last week of Daniel's vision of history. This indicates that the end of time is being dealt with.

In discussing the end of time, Jesus was saying that He was discussing what Daniel prophesied. Now note what begins the second half of Daniel's week. It is the abomination of desolation or the prince's causing abomination of desolation in the holy place. Mark 13:14 actually uses the masculine participle which indicates that the abomination of desolation is a person, the prince himself. Note something else. What Jesus called the "great [unparalleled] tribulation" begins with the abomination of desolation (Mt.24:15-16, 21).

The indication again is that the beginning of sorrows and the great tribulation are one period of time, but the period includes two parts. (See Division Overview—Mk.13:1-37 for chart of the two periods.)

4. The length of the last part or half is actually given by Scripture (see notes—Re.11:2; 12:6; 13:4-8).

"Times, times, and half a time" (Da.7:25; 12:7).
"1260 days" (Re.12:6).
"42 months" (Re.11:2; 13:5-6).

Based upon this timetable, the tribulation of which Jesus spoke can be said to be seven years, divided into two parts:

"The beginning of sorrows," or the first half of the tribulation.
"The great tribulation," or the second half of the tribulation.

Again, seeing these two periods of time as discussed by Jesus (and referred to by Daniel) helps in understanding Jesus' answer to the disciples' two questions.

5. Jesus said that it would be after Daniel's prince that He would return: "after that tribulation...shall they see the Son of Man coming in the clouds with great power and glory. And then shall He send His angels, and shall gather together His elect..." (Mk.13:24-27). In these words, our Lord answered the two questions: "When shall the temple be destroyed? And what shall be the sign of thy coming and of the end of the world?" (Mt.24:3).

DEEPER STUDY # 2

(13:1-37) **End Time**: several other facts need to be kept in mind as a person studies this section of *Mark*.

1. Jesus was preparing His disciples for His death and departure from this world and preparing them to carry on after He was gone. His immediate disciples were to face some terrible times, ranging all the way from personal trials brought on by their witness for Jesus, to national trials involving the utter destruction of their nation. It would be generations stretching into centuries before He returned to earth. No one knew this at that time, but He did; so He needed to prepare His future disciples as well. They, too, were going to face all kinds of trials. There was always the danger that His disciples might tire waiting for His return. They were to see and experience so much trouble in the world that their faith might falter.

What Jesus did was use this occasion to reveal some of the events that were to take place upon the earth during "these last days," the days of the church (Ac.2:16-17; 1 Jn.2:18). By knowing some of the events, His disciples would be better prepared to endure and to keep their hope for His return alive.

2. Jesus was dealing with two questions throughout this passage. He was answering the questions: When will the temple be destroyed, and what shall be the sign of His return and of the end of the world?

Note something: Jesus was dealing with the end of the temple and with the end of the world, the destruction of the temple and the destruction of the world. He was covering the signs, the events that were to cause the judgment and to occur during the judgment of both the temple and the world. What is the point? Simply this. The Scripture teaches that the same signs and events cause the judgment of anything. That is, the events (sins) that cause judgment upon one thing are the same events that will bring judgment upon everything else. Therefore, the signs that surrounded the destruction of Jerusalem are much the same as the signs that shall surround the end of the world. Therefore, what Jesus was saying had a double meaning and application (see DEEPER STUDY # 3—Mt.24:1-14; 24:15-28. Both notes will help to see the double application.)

The Lord's words applied both to the disciples of His day and to all disciples who were to follow in succeeding generations. As long as the earth stands, the disciples of *the last days* (or ages) will face many of the same signs faced by those who experienced the destruction of Jerusalem. But there is to be one difference: at the end of the world, the signs will increase and intensify. The day is coming, so terrible, that it can be called *the beginnings of sorrows* (v.8), and *the great tribulation* (v.21). (See DEEPER STUDY # 1,2—Mt.24:1-31; note—24:15-28.)

3. A quick outline of the passage helps one understand what Jesus was doing.
    a. The eight signs of the last days (that is, the last days before both Jerusalem's destruction and the world's end) (Mk.13:1-13).
    b. The ninth and most terrible sign: the abomination of desolation and the great tribulation (Mk.13:14-23; see Mt.24:15, 21).
    c. The coming of the Son of Man (Mk.14:24-27).

The rest of what Jesus covered dealt with the actual time of the Lord's return (Mt.24:32-41) and the believer's duty to watch and be prepared (Mt.24:42-25:46 for discussion).

DEEPER STUDY # 3
(13:1-37) **End Time**: the great similarities between what Jesus said about the end time and sections of *Revelation* need to be noted (see DEEPER STUDY # 1,2—Mt.24:1-31 for discussion).

1 (13:1-5) **End Time**: a quick glance at the first four verses will show the events that led Jesus to deal with great prophecies covered by these chapters.

a. The disciples admired the temple's magnificence and drew Jesus' attention to its beauty. The temple was magnificent. It sat upon the towering summit of Mount Sion, and it was built of white marble plated with gold. The temple had several porches that were supported by huge, towering pillars, each one so large that it took three to four men reaching arm to arm to reach around it. The disciples apparently stood someplace where the temple in all its magnificent beauty struck them with awe, and they wanted Jesus to see the beautiful sight.

b. Jesus used the occasion to arouse the disciples' interest in coming events. He predicted the temple's utter destruction.

c. The disciples were aroused to ask two questions of the Lord: When will the temple be destroyed and what will be the sign of destruction? By these questions, Mark clearly shows that the disciples were thinking about the signs of Jesus' return and of the end of the world (Mt.24:3. See note—Lu.21:5-8.)

d. Jesus warned His disciples: they must guard against being deceived. This can mean one or two things. A person can be easily deceived when dealing with end-time prophecies, or a person can be easily deceived when facing the end-time events. He can be deceived into thinking that certain cataclysmic events are infallible signs that the end is at hand (v.7). Such too often results...

- in wild guesses about the end time
- in universal predictions
- in the deceiving of others
- in discouragement of a person's faith when the end does not come

2 (13:6) **Messiah, False—Deception**: the first sign of the end time is spiritual deception by false messiahs. Note three facts stated.

a. Many false messiahs shall come. There will not be just a few, but many.

b. They shall claim to be the Christ, the Messiah; that is, each one will claim to *the one* who can lead men into the utopian state. They will claim that they can solve man's problems and see to it that man has plenty of everything. He will claim that he is *the one* who can fulfill the dreams of people, delivering them from conflict and war into a state of peace and freedom, plenty and comfort, equality or supremacy. The false messiahs are sometimes politicians and sometimes religionists, but in either case, they wield power and proclaim themselves to be the hope of mankind.

> **Thought 1.** Think of the promises so often made by some politicians and religionists, promises that point toward them as the *personal answer* to man's hopes, dreams, and problems.

c. They "deceive many." They are *deceivers, imposters, seducers, pretenders.* They are not able to fulfill the dreams and hopes of men nor to solve the problems of men. They are not able to bring about the utopian state for men, for they do not have such power. They are mere men. They are not the true Messiah, not the Messiah of God. But despite this, many will follow them, believing their false promises and entrusting their lives and welfare into their keeping. Many will follow them as though they are the true deliverer of mankind.

> **"For they that are such serve not our Lord Jesus Christ, but their own belly; and by good words and fair speeches deceive the hearts of the simple" (Ro.16:18).**
>
> **"For such are false apostles, deceitful workers, transforming themselves into the apostles of Christ" (2 Co.11:13).**
>
> **"That we henceforth be no more children, tossed to and fro, and carried about with every wind of doctrine, by the sleight of men, and cunning craftiness, whereby they lie in wait to deceive" (Ep.4:14).**
>
> **"But evil men and seducers shall wax worse and worse, deceiving, and being deceived" (2 Ti.3:13).**
>
> **"For many deceivers are entered into the world, who confess not that Jesus Christ is come in the flesh. This is a deceiver and an antichrist" (2 Jn.7).**

3 (13:7-8) **War—World, Violence**: the second sign of the end time is national and international disturbances, wars and rumors of war.

a. Believers will hear of upheavals, nationally and internationally. Some, as citizens of a warring nation, will even be caught up in the conflict. The news will be bad and bleak, always filled with *wars and rumors of war—always plural, always referring to many.*

b. The believer is not to be troubled. The word *troubled* (throeo) means to be terrified, frightened, disturbed, alarmed, crying out within one's inner being. Three things can happen to the believer in looking at worldwide trouble.

1) The believer can become overly affected by the news of world affairs and turmoil. Such news can become so interesting and captivating that it can dominate the believer's life. He begins to live and thrive on the news.
2) The believer can become overly apprehensive about the personal safety of himself and his family. He can begin to fear so much that he forgets that his security is in God, not in this world. Fear over world affairs tends to emphasize the importance of the earth over the importance of God; it tends to emphasize the worldly over the spiritual. The world, of course, is important; but what needs to be stressed is the spiritual. And it is the believer's responsibility to stress the spiritual, the security and peace of heart that is found in Christ.
3) The believer can become so troubled over world affairs that he neglects his spiritual duties. The believer is naturally concerned over the world, as all men should be. But he is not to allow world affairs to interfere with his witnessing for Christ. He is to be at peace and to be secure with God, and he is to demonstrate the peace and security of God, going about his daily duties as much as possible within a turbulent world. The point is, the believer is to be witnessing for Christ no matter the turbulence of the world.

c. Jesus said that world disturbance and upheavals "must needs be." They exist because of *selfishness* and *greed*, the sinful and depraved nature of man. The dark side of man is and always will be revealed and exposed by...

- assaults
- attacks
- fighting
- arguments
- killing
- maiming
- cheating
- lying
- stealing
- abuse
- neglect
- hoarding
- storing up
- lusting
- unbelief (Ph.4:6-7)
- negative thinking (Ph.4:8)
- asking not (Js.4:2-3)

d. World disturbance does not mean the end is at hand. Note that Christ was specific about this fact: "The end is not yet." He had just said, "Take heed lest any man deceive you" (v.5).

"And nation was destroyed of nation, and city of city: for God did vex them with all adversity. Be ye strong therefore, and let not your hands be weak: for your work shall be rewarded" (2 Chr.15:6-7).

"My people, go ye out of the midst of her, and deliver ye every man his soul from the fierce anger of the LORD. And lest your heart faint, and ye fear for the rumor that shall be heard in the land; a rumor shall both come one year, and after that in another year shall come a rumor, and violence in the land, ruler against ruler" (Je.51:45-46).

"And take heed to yourselves, lest at any time your hearts be overcharged with surfeiting, and drunkenness, and cares of this life, and so that day come upon you unawares" (Lu.21:34).

"Be careful for nothing; but in every thing by prayer and supplication with thanksgiving let your requests be made known unto God" (Ph.4:6).

"Casting all your care upon him; for he careth for you" (1 Pe.5:7).

4 (13:8) **Earthquake—Famine**: the fourth sign of the end time is natural disasters. Two disasters of nature are mentioned in particular.

a. Earthquakes in *many places*. Unbelievable destruction and death are sometimes caused by earthquakes. Josephus records the fulfillment of Jesus' prophecy. He even hints that the natural disasters which happened were a sign of coming destruction.

> "...there broke out a prodigious storm in the night, with the utmost violence, and very strong winds, with the largest showers of rain, and continual lightnings, terrible thunderings, and amazing concussions and bellowings of the earth, that was in an earthquake. These things were a manifest indication that some destruction was coming upon men, when the system of the world was put into this disorder; and any one would guess that these wonders foreshowed some grand calamities that were coming."[1]

Earthquakes will occur in many places during the last days of the earth (Re.6:12; 11:12-13, 19; 16:17-19).

b. Famines. Scripture speaks of a "great famine" throughout all the world "which came to pass in the days of Claudius Caesar" (Ac.11:28-30). Josephus describes the famine as being so terrible that when flour "was brought into the temple...not one of the priests was so hardy as to eat one crumb of it...while so great a distress was upon the land."[2] He says in another place, "A famine did oppress them [Jerusalem]...and many people died for want of what was necessary to procure food."[3]

In the very last days before Jerusalem's fall, Josephus speaks of another terrible famine:

> "It was now a miserable case, and a sight that would justly bring tears into our eyes, how men stood to their food, while the more powerful had more than enough, and the weaker were lamenting (for want of it)."[4]
>
> "Then did the famine widen its progress, and devoured the people by whole houses and families; the upper rooms were full of women and children that were dying by famine; and the lanes of the city were full of the dead bodies of the aged; the children also and the young men wandered about the marketplaces like shadows, all swelled with famine, and fell down dead wheresoever their misery seized them"[5]

There is evidently to be terrible famine in the last days. The black horse of the four horsemen of the Apocalypse indicates terrible famine (see note—Re.6:5-6). The unbearable pain and terrible evil that hunger can cause is graphically described by Scripture.

---

1 Flavius Josephus. *Wars*. 4. 4:5. Josephus Complete Works, translated by William Whiston. Grand Rapids, MI: Kregel, 1960.
2 Josephus, *Ant*. 3. 15:3
3 Josephus, *Ant*. 20. 2:5
4 Josephus, *Wars*. 5. 10:3
5 Josephus, Wars. 5. 12:3

"They that be slain with the sword are better than they that be slain with hunger: for these pine away, stricken through for want of the fruits of the field. The hands of the pitiful women have sodden [boiled] their own children: they were their meat [food] in the destruction of the daughter of my people" (Lam.4:9-10).

Matthew adds a third disaster of nature: pestilence. Earthquakes and famines, of course, cause disease and pestilence (see note—Mt.24:7).

DEEPER STUDY # 4
(13:8) **Sorrows** (odinon): birth-pains; labor-pains; travailings; intolerable anguish; quick, sharp, violent travailing pain.

5 (13:9) **Persecution**: the fourth sign of the end time is persecution by civil and religious authorities. Jesus said several significant things about this sign.

a. "Take heed to yourselves." The believer is to take heed, to guard himself. The emphasis is upon the pronoun "yourselves," in order to stress the need to guard oneself. The believer must guard *himself*; he himself must take heed. He will face not only the deceptions and normal conflicts of a selfish world, not only the terrible disasters of nature, but he will face persecution by his fellow men.

b. "They [civil and religious men] shall deliver you up." Believers shall be abused, neglected, ignored, arrested, and tried before the courts of the world and of religion. Why? "For my sake, for a testimony [to] them." (In the Greek the word is "to," not "against." It is a simple dative case in the Greek.) Believers will stand before all *for the purpose of demonstrating loyalty to Christ*. Standing fast through the persecution is *a way of witnessing*. A believer shows that Christ and eternity are real when he suffers for Christ.

"But beware of men: for they will deliver you up to the councils, and they will scourge you in their synagogues" (Mt.10:17).

"Then shall they deliver you up to be afflicted, and shall kill you: and ye shall be hated of all nations for my name's sake" (Mt.24:9; see Lu.21:12-13).

"Remember the word that I said unto you, The servant is not greater than his lord. If they have persecuted me, they will also persecute you; if they have kept my saying, they will keep yours also" (Jn.15:20).

"These things have I spoken unto you, that ye should not be offended. They shall put you out of the synagogues: yea, the time cometh, that whosoever killeth you will think that he doeth God service. And these things will they do unto you, because they have not known the Father, nor me" (Jn.16:1-3).

"Yea, and all that will live godly in Christ Jesus shall suffer persecution" (2 Ti.3:12).

"Fear none of those things which thou shalt suffer: behold, the devil shall cast some of you into prison, that ye may be tried; and ye shall have tribulation ten days: be thou faithful unto death, and I will give thee a crown of life" (Re.2:10).

"O LORD my God, in thee do I put my trust: save me from all them that persecute me, and deliver me" (Ps.7:1).

"My times are in thy hand: deliver me from the hand of mine enemies, and from them that persecute me" (Ps.31:15).

"All thy commandments are faithful: they persecute me wrongfully; help thou me" (Ps.119:86).

"For the enemy hath persecuted my soul; he hath smitten my life down to the ground; he hath made me to dwell in darkness, as those that have been long dead" (Ps.143:3).

6 (13:10) **Evangelism**: the fifth sign of the end time is world evangelization. Note the exact words of Christ: "The gospel *must first* be published among all nations" before the end can come. Note three things.

a. The word "must" assures the fact. The fact is set in God's plan for the world. It cannot be changed. The gospel will be preached among all nations before the end of the world.

b. The promise was fulfilled in the first century. The gospel was carried to all the known world at that time (Ro.10:18; Col.1:23. See note—Mt.24:14 for detailed discussion.)

c. The promise of world evangelization is to be fulfilled in the end time. All nations of the world will hear the gospel before the end comes. Christ's promise was unrestricted. He said "among all nations." There is to be a proclamation of the gospel to the whole world before time ceases.

"And this gospel of the kingdom shall be preached in all the world for a witness unto *all nations*; and then shall the end come" (Mt.24:14).

"Go ye therefore, and teach all nations, baptizing them in the name of the Father, and of the Son, and of the Holy Ghost: teaching them to observe all things whatsoever I have commanded you: and, lo, I am with you alway, even unto the end of the world" (Mt.28:19-20).

"And he said unto them, Go ye into the all the world, and preach the gospel to every creature" (Mk.16:15).

"And that repentance and remission of sins should be preached in his name among all nations, beginning at Jerusalem" (Lu.24:47).

"Ask of me, and I shall give thee the heathen for thine inheritance, and the uttermost parts of the earth for thy possession" (Ps.2:8).

"All the ends of the world shall remember and turn unto the LORD: and all the kindreds of the nations shall worship before thee" (Ps.22:27).

"Declare his glory among the heathen, his wonders among all people" (Ps.96:3).

"And it shall come to pass in the last days, that the mountain of the LORD's house shall be established in the top of the mountains, and shall be exalted above the hills; and all nations shall flow unto it" (Is.2:2).

"They shall not hurt nor destroy in all my holy mountain: for the earth shall be full of the knowledge of the LORD, as the waters cover the sea" (Is.11:9).

"He shall not fail nor be discouraged, till he have set judgment in the earth: and the isles shall wait for his law" (Is.42:4).

"For from the rising of the sun even unto the going down of the same my name shall be great among the Gentiles; and in every place incense shall be offered unto my name, and a pure offering: for my name shall be great among the heathen, saith the LORD of hosts" (Mal.1:11).

7 (13:11) **Persecution—Holy Spirit—Witnessing**: the sixth sign of the end time is a supernatural witness (see note—Mt.10:19-20). There is going to be a strong surge of Spirit-led witnessing in the end time. Multitudes of believers are going to be called upon to give an answer for the hope that is within them. Note two things.

a. The words "take no thought" mean to worry not, be not anxious. The believer is not to be *overly* concerned about what he is to say, either in defense of himself or as a testimony to his persecutors.

b. The Holy Spirit will speak through the believer. The believer will not be left alone in defending himself in persecution. God will speak through the believer, standing right with him (see Ac.4:8f; 2 Ti.4:16-18).

"At my first answer no man stood with me, but all men forsook me: I pray God that it may not be laid to their charge. Notwithstanding the Lord stood with me, and strengthened me; that by me the preaching might be fully known, and that all the Gentiles might hear: and I was delivered out of the mouth of the lion. And the Lord shall deliver me from every evil work, and will preserve me unto his heavenly kingdom: to whom be glory for ever and ever" (2 Ti.4:16-18).

"So that we may boldly say, The Lord is my helper, and I will not fear what man shall do unto me" (He.13:6).

"Fear thou not; For I am with thee: be not dismayed; for I am thy God: I will strengthen thee; yea, I will help thee; yea, I will uphold thee with the right hand of my righteousness" (Is.41:10).

"Behold, the Lord GOD will help me; who is he that shall condemn me? lo, they all shall wax old as a garment; the moth shall eat them up" (Is.50:9).

8 (13:12-13) **Persecution—Family**: the seventh sign of the end time is divided families (see note—Mt.10:21). Two characteristics will be especially evident.

a. There will be betrayal—betrayal that leads to death (v.12). The practice will seep into the family and be widely practiced, so much so that Christ says it will be a common trait of the end time.

b. There will be intense hatred among all (the emphasis is, even within the family). Note why: because the believer stands for the name of Christ. His own family, as well as the world, will hate, persecute, and betray him because of his testimony for the Lord.

"And the brother shall deliver up the brother to death, and the father the child: and the children shall rise up against their parents, and cause them to be put to death" (Mt.10:21).

9 (13:13) **Endurance—Salvation**: the eighth sign of the end time is the scene of some enduring and being saved despite the terrible persecution. Note two points.

a. The word *endure* (upomeinas) means to bear up under suffering, to be courageous in suffering, to persevere and withstand patiently—but actively, not passively. It is enduring, actively bearing intense suffering. The believer is now called upon and will be called upon to stand firm through all forms of persecution and abuse, even if it leads to inhuman torture and death.

b. Jesus was talking to His disciples. Therefore, His promise of *being saved* was bound to mean the *soul's salvation in the last days*. It could not mean the safety of human life. He had just said some (many) would be killed (v.12; see Mt.24:9). Thus, the believer who stands firm is the one who proves that he is a genuine believer.

"Fear none of those things which thou shalt suffer: behold, the devil shall cast some of you into prison, that ye may be tried; and ye shall have tribulation ten days: be thou faithful unto death, and I will give thee a crown of life" (Re.2:10).

"To them who by patient continuance in well doing seek for glory and honour and immortality, eternal life: but unto them that are contentious, and do not obey the truth, but obey unrighteousness, indignation and wrath, tribulation and anguish, upon every soul of man that doeth evil, of the Jew first, and also of the Gentile" (Ro.2:7-9).

"Blessed is the man that endureth temptation [trial]: for when he is tried, he shall receive the crown of life, which the Lord hath promised to them that love him" (Js.1:12).

"Behold, we count them happy which endure. Ye have heard of the patience of Job, and have seen the end of the Lord; that the Lord is very pitiful, and of tender mercy" (Js.5:11).

"But ye are a chosen generation, a royal priesthood, an holy nation, a peculiar people; that ye should show forth the praises of him who hath called you out of darkness into this marvellous light" (1 Pe.2:9).

Outline	Scripture
	B. The Most Terrible Sign: The Abomination That Causes Desolation, 13:14-23 *(Mt. 24:15-28; Lu. 21:20-24)*
1. So terrible, it is named the abomination that causes desolation: The reason is that it stands where it does not belong (that is, in the temple)[DS1] **2. So terrible, it is to be fled from immediately**	14 But when ye shall see the abomination of desolation, spoken of by Daniel the prophet, standing where it ought not, (let him that readeth understand,) then let them that be in Judaea flee to the mountains:
a. To forget all comfort of home[DS2]	15 And let him that is on the housetop not go down into the house, neither enter therein, to take any thing out of his house:
b. To forget all personal possessions	16 And let him that is in the field not turn back again for to take up his garment.
c. To grieve for those who cannot flee rapidly	17 But woe to them that are with child, and to them that give suck in those days!
d. To pray for good conditions in fleeing	18 And pray ye that your flight be not in the winter.
3. So terrible, it causes horrifying, unparalleled affliction (the great distress or tribulation, see Mt. 24:21)	19 For in those days shall be affliction, such as was not from the beginning of the creation which God created unto this time, neither shall be.
4. So terrible, God has to intervene & shorten the days of affliction	20 And except that the Lord had shortened those days, no flesh should be saved: but for the elect's sake, whom he hath chosen, he hath shortened the days.
5. So terrible, it causes a frantic search for false messiahs (deliverers)	21 And then if any man shall say to you, Lo, here is Christ; or, lo, he is there; believe him not: 22 For false christs and false prophets shall rise, and shall show signs and wonders, to seduce, if it were possible, even the elect.
6. So terrible, it requires being foretold	23 But take ye heed: behold, I have foretold you all things.

DIVISION VIII

THE SON OF GOD'S OLIVET MINISTRY: JESUS' PROPHECY OF HIS RETURN AND THE END TIME, 13:1-37

B. The Most Terrible Sign: The Abomination of Desolation, 13:14-23

(13:14-23) **Abomination of Desolation**: this is a reference to the fall of Jerusalem in A.D. 70. However, it is also a reference to the antichrist (see notes and DEEPER STUDY # 1, *Antichrist*—Mk.13:14; note—2 Th.2:4-9; DEEPER STUDY # 1—Re.11:7; notes—13:1-10; 13:11-18; 17:7-14; see Da.9:20-27, esp. 27; 12:11). The antichrist himself will be a sign that the end time has come. Jesus pointed this out in answer to the double question of the disciples (see note—Mt.24:15-28). Note v.23 where Jesus said He had foretold all things. This statement and the wording of v.24, "But in those days, after that tribulation," clearly show that Jesus was continuing His discussion of the signs that pointed to the end time. (See note—Mt.24:15-28. This is an important note for the background to this passage.)

1. So terrible, it is named the abomination that causes desolation: the reason is that it stands where it does not belong (that is, in the temple) (v.14).
2. So terrible, it is to be fled from immediately (vv.14-18).
3. So terrible, it causes horrifying, unparalleled affliction (the great distress or tribulation) (v.19).
4. So terrible, God has to intervene and shorten the days of affliction (v.20).
5. So terrible, it causes a frantic search for false messiahs (deliverers) (vv.21-22).
6. So terrible, it requires being foretold (v.23).

1 (13:14) **Antichrist—Abomination of Desolation**: this sign is so terrible it is named the abomination that causes desolation (see note—Mt.24:15). The reason is because it stands "where it ought not," that is, in the temple of God. In fact, it stands in the holy place where the very presence of God is symbolized as filling the very atmosphere. The words "where it ought not" mean that it *stands as God, as a replacement for God.* It assumes the position of God within the temple of God. The picture is exactly what Paul described in speaking of this sign in the end time:

> **"Let no man deceive you by any means: for that day shall not come, except there come a falling away first, and that man of sin be revealed, the son of perdition; who opposeth and exalteth himself above all that is called God, or that is worshipped; so that he as God sitteth in the temple of God, showing himself that he is God" (2 Th.2:3-4).**

There is no greater crime than usurping the place of God in a human life. Every man who rejects God usurps God. He replaces God with someone or something else in his life. But the picture here includes much more than personal unbelief, even more than the corporate unbelief of false messiahs and their limited followings. It is a universal, worldwide attempt to replace God Himself in His own temple, so that *all believers* will actually see the event (v.14).

Some hold that the sign will be repeated in the end time and literally fulfilled within the temple. It has been literally fulfilled twice in the past when Antiochus Epiphanes and Titus stood within the temple. Others believe the words "the temple" refer to all religion. They believe the abomination will be the desolating of all religion, in particular genuine Christianity.

Note: the act of corrupting the temple of God is so terrible that God has given it the name of abomination—*the abomination of desolation.* How repulsive unbelief and rejection are to Him!

DEEPER STUDY # 1

(13:14) **Abomination of Desolation—Antichrist** (To Bdelugma Tes eremoseos): the abomination that makes desolate. Note Jesus' words, "the abomination of desolation, spoken of by *Daniel the prophet*" (Mt.24:15) There are three passages in Daniel that speak of the abomination of desolation.

> **"Seventy weeks are determined upon thy people and upon thy holy city....Know therefore and understand...." (Da.9:24-27).**
>
> **"And arms shall stand on his part, and they shall pollute the sanctuary of strength, and shall take away the daily sacrifice, and they shall place the abomination that maketh desolate" (Da.11:31).**
>
> **"And from the time that the daily sacrifice shall be taken away, and the abomination that maketh desolate set up, there shall be a thousand two hundred and ninety days" (Da.12:11).**

In Daniel 9:27, the term is *Bdelugma ton eremoseon.* The Hebrew says, "upon the wing [or pinnacle] of abominations [shall come] the desolater" or "upon wings as a desolater [shall come] abomination."

In Daniel 11:31, the Hebrew says, "they shall put [place] the abomination that desolates."

In Daniel 12:11, the Hebrew says, "and from the time the daily [sacrifice] shall be taken away, and the abomination that makes desolate set up, [shall be]...."

Several matters need to be discussed about the abomination of desolation spoken of by Jesus and Daniel.

1. The first matter that needs to be considered is *when Daniel's prophecy was fulfilled.*
   a. There was a past fulfillment; that is, there was a fulfillment before the time of Jesus about 178 B.C. This is clear. Antiochus Epiphanes, the King of Syria, conquered Jerusalem and tried to force Grecian culture upon the Jews. He wanted the Jews to become full-fledged Greeks both in custom and religion. He knew that to be successful he had to destroy the Jewish religion. Therefore, He did three of the most horrible things that could ever be done in the minds of the Jewish people. He desecrated the temple by (1) building an altar in the courtyard to the Grecian god Zeus, (2) by sacrificing swines' flesh upon it, and (3) by setting up a trade of prostitution in the temple chambers (see 1 Maccabees 1:20-62; see also Josephus, *Ant.* 12. 5: 3-4; *Wars.* 1. 1:2).
   b. Jesus said there is to be a future fulfillment: "When ye therefore *shall see* the abomination of desolation, spoken of by Daniel the prophet...." There are four primary views of the future fulfillment of Daniel's prophecy. (1) One view says there is no future fulfillment, that all the signs were fulfilled in the destruction of Jerusalem in A.D. 70 by Titus. (2) Others see Jesus referring to the church age and the trials the church has to go through before Christ returns. (3) Still others view the prophecy as referring exclusively to the end time, having nothing to do with the destruction of Jerusalem in A.D. 70 by Titus. (4) Others believe Jesus was answering the very questions the disciples asked; the prophecy refers to both the destruction of Jerusalem and to the end of the world.

In looking at what Jesus was saying, it is best to let Him speak for Himself without *adding to or taking away* from what He says. An attempt at this has been made in former notes (see DEEPER STUDY # 1,2—Mk.13:1-37; DEEPER STUDY # 1,2—Mt.24:1-31). The conclusion of the notes is that the prophecy is *fulfilled* in both Jerusalem's destruction and the end of the world. The Lord is answering the disciples' question.

Jesus was saying that the same thing that happened under Antiochus Epiphanes would happen again to the holy place; in fact, the temple would be so destroyed that not one stone would be left upon another. And it did happen. What Jesus said took place in a most literal sense under Titus in A.D. 70. (See outline, notes, and DEEPER STUDY # 3—Mt.24:1-14, especially the notes that quote Josephus, the Jewish historian. Reading Josephus' record of Jerusalem's desolation reveals just how terribly the temple, the city, and the people were devastated.)

However, as discussed in the former notes, Jesus was not only answering the disciples' question about when the destruction of Jerusalem would take place; He was *also answering* their question about His return and the end of the world. Daniel's prophecy, and the Lord's elaboration on Daniel's prophecy, are to have a double fulfillment. The signs that point toward one who had sinned so terribly (Jerusalem) are much the same as the signs that point toward another who is guilty of terrible sin (the world in the end time). There is one critical difference, however. The sin of Jerusalem was the most heinous sin that could be committed: the killing of God's own Son. However, the sin of the world at the end of time will be just as terrible by following the abomination of desolation. Therefore, the world will witness an increase and intensification of the signs at the end of time. As a result there will be great trial such as the world has never seen (v.19). (Again, see the outline and notes—Mt.24:1f for detailed discussion.)

2. A second matter that needs to be discussed about the abomination of desolation is *the division of time* that both Jesus and Daniel seem to give. Jesus did say that the abomination of desolation would launch the worst tribulation the world has ever known (Mk.13:14, 19; Mt:24:15, 21). In His own words, the signs that will occur up until the abomination of desolation are called "the beginning of sorrows" (Mt.24:8); and the trials that will occur after the abomination of desolation takes place are called "great tribulations." The tribulations will be unparalleled in history (Mt.24:21). Daniel also gave a division of time just as Jesus did.

> **"And he [the prince] shall confirm the covenant with many for *one week: and in the midst of the week* he shall cause...the overspreading of abominations" (Da.9:27).**

"In the midst of the week" (Daniel's seventieth week) definitely points to a period of time (one week) that is divided into two parts. Now note these factors.

a. Daniel is dealing with the "seventieth week," the end of his prophecy. The fact that Jesus was dealing with the end of Jerusalem and the end of the world and the fact that Jesus said He was elaborating on Daniel's prophecy tells us that Daniel is dealing with the end time just as Jesus was.

b. Daniel says that what begins the second half of his seventieth week is "the abomination of desolation" or the prince who causes "abominable idols" (H.C. Leupold. *Exposition of Daniel.* Grand Rapids, MI: Baker, 1969, p.434).

The words of Jesus should be carefully noted: "When ye therefore shall see the abomination of desolation, spoken of by Daniel the prophet...." (Mk.13:14; Mt.24:15). Jesus is about to explain in more detail what Daniel prophesied. Jesus explained that the first half of Daniel's week would consist of signs which are "*the beginnings of sorrows*" (Mk.13:8; see 13:5-13; Mt.24:8; 24:5-14), and the last half of Daniel's week would consist of unparalleled trials of "*great tribulations*." The second half of the week would be launched by "the abomination of desolation standing in the holy place" (Mk.13:14, 19; Mt:24:15, 21).

3. A third matter that needs to be looked at is *the time frame of the end time* (the seventieth week) as predicted by Jesus and Daniel. Scripture refers to the length in these words (see notes—Rev.11:2; 12:6).

"Time, times, and half a time" (Da.7:25; 12:7).
"1260 days" (Re.12:6).
"42 months" (Re.11:2; 13:5-6).

Based upon the days and months given in The Book of Revelation, if Daniel's time equals one year, then his words, "Time (1 year), times (2 years), and half a time (1/2 year)" are equal to 3 ½ years. Daniel stated that the abomination of desolation shall be executed "in the midst of the week," that is, after three and one half years. It is assumed that Christ's words "the beginning of sorrows" (that is, the first half of the week) are also three and one half years. Therefore, in combining the two periods of time (3 ½ years each) the length of the last days or end time is said to be a literal seven years. Based upon the words of Revelation, the prophecy of Christ can be charted as follows.

THE END OF THE WORLD

Seeing the Sign of the Abomination of Desolation In the Middle of the Time or Years (v.14)		*Seeing the Son of Man Coming* (v.26)
3 ½ years	3 ½ years	
Signs which are "The beginnings of sorrow" (v.8)	Unparalleled trials of "The great tribulation" (v.19)	"His angels...gather together His elect" (v.27)

However, it should be noted that many Biblical scholars say that the words "times" in Daniel and "days" and "months" in Revelation (in fact, throughout all Scripture) are often used to refer to blocks of time, that is, longer periods or indefinite periods of time.

4. A fourth matter that needs to be looked at is this: *What or who is meant by "the abomination of desolation"*? As has already been discussed, many excellent commentators hold that the prophecy refers to the destruction of Jerusalem under both Antiochus Epiphenes (B.C. 170) and under Titus (A.D. 70). There is strong historical evidence, as well as the fact that Jesus was answering a specific question of the disciples (Mk.13:4; Mt.24:3), to support a past fulfillment of the prophecy. But what about the future fulfillment? What or who is meant by "the abomination of desolation" at the end of the world? (See DEEPER STUDY # 1—Rev.11:7; see notes—2 Th.2:3-4; Rev.13:1; 13:3; 13:5-6. See General Subject Index.)

a. Some indication is perhaps given by the phrase itself. In the Old Testament the word *abomination* is connected with idolatry or sacrilege. *Of desolation* means the same as *causes desolation.* In this case it is *the abomination* that causes *desolations*. That is, the abomination acts upon the holy place and personally causes the desolation. This, of course points toward a person's fulfilling the prophecy in the future just as there were two literal persons who fulfilled it in the past, Antiochus and Titus.

b. Mark 13:14 actually uses the *masculine* participle which indicates strongly that the abomination of desolation is a person.

c. Daniel 9:25-27 speaks of a prince who causes the desolation. Leupold, the great Lutheran theologian, translates the prince as "the destroyer." (Leupold. *Exposition of Daniel*, p.433. Because of extraordinary scholarship and simplicity of writing, Leupold should be referred to in studying Daniel.)

d. Second Thessalonians and Revelation identify an *antichrist* who is to arise in the last days and cause unparalleled havoc upon the world and upon God's people.

> "That man of sin [shall] be revealed, the son of perdition; who opposeth and exalteth himself above all that is called God, or that is worshipped; so that he as God sitteth in the temple of God, showing himself that he is God. Remember ye not, that, when I was yet with you, I told you these things?" (2 Th.2:3-5). (See notes—Mk.13:14; 2 Th. 2:4-9; Re.6:2-7; DEEPER STUDY # 1—11:7; notes—13:1-10; 13:11-18; 17:7-14. See Da.9:20-27; 11:31; 12:11.)

2 (13:14-18) **Antichrist—Abomination of Desolation**: this sign is so terrible it is to be fled from immediately. The idea Jesus conveyed is that the abomination (he who makes desolate) will swoop upon the earth suddenly, unexpectedly. His rise and the war He launches against God's temple will be so quick that he takes people by surprise. He poses an immediate danger for believers. Jesus warned, "When *ye* [believers] see...flee" (v.14). The imminent danger and urgency was stressed by Christ in four statements.

a. A person is to forget all comfort of home: pictured by his arising from his roof and immediately fleeing (see note—Mt.24:17).

b. A person is to forget all personal possessions: pictured by his not returning from work to get his clothes (or possessions).

c. A person is to grieve for those who cannot flee rapidly: pictured by pregnant women and small children.

d. A person is to pray for good conditions in fleeing: pictured by both winter and the Sabbath day. Travel would be more difficult in winter. The Sabbath day represents certain religious rules that would forbid fleeing (travel) for the religiously strong.

> **"O generation of vipers, who hath warned you to flee from the wrath to come? Bring forth therefore fruits meet for repentance" (Mt.3:7-8).**

DEEPER STUDY # 2
(13:15) **House—Rooftop**: see DEEPER STUDY # 2—Mt.24:17.

3 (13:19) **Great Tribulation, The—Antichrist**: this sign is so terrible it causes horrifying, unparalleled affliction (the great distress or tribulation). Matthew actually uses the words "great tribulation." He says:

> **"For then shall be *great tribulation*, such as was not since the beginning of the world to this time, no, nor ever shall be" (Mt.24:21).**

It is from this that the term "the great tribulation" has come. It should be noted that it is the term Christ Himself used to describe the unbelievable afflictions of the end time. No better term could be chosen. "The great tribulation" (or period of unparalleled affliction) is an accurate term, a term chosen by our Lord to strike the truth home to the human heart.

The great tribulation is to be a period of affliction unparalleled in history.

a. In A.D. 66-70, Jerusalem experienced one of the most terrible sieges in all of history. In A.D. 66 the Jews revolted and the Roman army was swift to attack. But the city was difficult to take, primarily for two reasons: it sat upon a hill, well protected by the terrain, and the leaders of the revolt were religious fanatics. Well over a million people had fled into the city behind its protective walls.

As the siege wore on, the predictions of Jesus were literally fulfilled. Outside the walls was the Roman army and all the maiming and killing of war. Inside the walls neighbor after neighbor faced famine, pestilence, false deliverers (messiahs), betrayal, murder, revolt, rebellion, hatred. And all took their toll. Josephus says over 1,000,000 people died and 97,000 were taken captive. The horrors of the siege were well described by him (see notes—Mt.24:7; 24:10; 24:11. See Josephus, *Wars*. 5. 12:3; 6. 3:4; 6. 8:5).

> "It appears to me that the misfortunes of all men, from the beginning of the world, if they be compared to these of the Jews, are not so considerable as they were"[1]

b. In the end time, the world will experience great tribulations—unparalleled in history. Note that Jesus did not describe the great trials beyond what He had already said in vv.5-12. A quick glance at the great tribulation period covered in Revelation will give some idea of the trials (see outlines and notes—all of the following. See Da.12:1-2.)

⇒ Thunderings, lightnings, and an earthquake (Re.8:5; see 8:1-5).
⇒ Natural catastrophes (Re.8:6-12).
⇒ Demonic-like locust or plagues (Re.8:13-9:11).
⇒ Demonic-like army (Re.9:12-21).
⇒ Nations angry, destroying the earth (Re.11:18; see 11:14-19).
⇒ An evil political ruler (Re.13:1-10).
⇒ A false religious ruler (Re.13:11-18).
⇒ Terrible destruction and suffering both upon nature and men (Re.16:1-21).
⇒ An evil, deceptive world power (Re.17:1-18:24).

4 (13:20) **Great Tribulation, The**: this sign is so terrible God has to intervene and shorten the days of affliction. This was a promise to the believers of Jesus' day, and it is a promise to the believers of the end time. Note: Jesus said two things.

a. The days of the great tribulation shall be shortened. What is meant by shortened?

⇒ Shorter than what God would usually allow for such great sinfulness.
⇒ Shorter than what the enemy expected.
⇒ Shorter than what others would expect of a ruling government against such revolting fanatics.

---

1 Josephus, *Wars*. Preface 4.

God in His providence used His power to shorten the days for Israel's sake. In the midst of judgment, He was merciful. Israel was not totally annihilated. The siege was shorter than expected. Many have listed *the natural causes* that led to the shorter siege.

⇒ Division and factions. The Jewish leaders were divided from the first. They never could form a cohesive policy.
⇒ A disastrous fire. The fire destroyed many weapons and provisions.
⇒ Rampaging gangs. These were set on self-preservation, stealing, assaulting, and killing. They are well documented by Josephus.
⇒ Treason and betrayal. Some surrendered even their fortifications without a fight.
⇒ The quick attack by Rome. Rome sent the armed force under Titus much quicker than expected.
⇒ Weak fortifications. Herod Agrippa had intended to strengthen the walls, but he never did.

The believer, of course, sees God's hand in these natural causes. God *worked all things out for good in order to shorten the days and to fulfill His Word.* Despite the terrible tribulation, some lives were saved—saved because God was compassionate (2 Pe.3:9). The tribulations of the end time will also be shortened.

"Woe to the inhabiters of the earth and of the sea! for the devil is come down unto you, having great wrath...[but note]...because he knoweth that he hath but a short time" (Re.12:12).

"When he [antichrist] cometh, he *must* continue [but note] a short time" (Re.17:10).

"And then shall that Wicked be revealed, whom the Lord shall consume with the spirit of his mouth, and shall destroy with the brightness of his coming" (2 Th.2:8).

God shall shorten the days for the elect's sake. Apparently the Christians remembered the Lord's warning and fled Jerusalem before the attack, sometime around A.D. 66. They fled to a smaller town called Pella in the district of Decapolis. These believers prayed for their neighbors and their beloved city, and God heard their intercessions. He shortened the days of terrible trial—shortened them because of the prayers of the elect.

God's mercy toward the lost, even toward civilizations and cities, and His willingness to save these in answer to the believers' intercessory prayer is clearly illustrated in Scripture. Abraham's prayer for Sodom and Gomorrah is an example. If just ten righteous men could have been found, the cities would have been spared, despite terrible sin (Ge.18:23f). Lot's prayer for Zoar is another example (Ge.19:20-22).

"Confess your faults one to another, and pray one for another, that ye may be healed. The effectual fervent prayer of a righteous man availeth much" (Js.5:16).

"Run ye to and fro through the streets of Jerusalem, and see now, and know, and seek in the broad places thereof, if ye can find a man, if there be any that executeth judgment, that seeketh the truth; and I will pardon it" (Je.5:1).

"For there stood by me this night the angel of God, whose I am, and who I serve, saying, Fear not, Paul; thou must be brought before Caesar: and, lo, God hath given thee all them that sail with thee....And we were in all in the ship two hundred threescore and sixteen souls....But the centurion, willing to save Paul, kept them from their purpose; and commanded that they which could swim should cast themselves first into the sea, and get to land: and the rest, some on boards, and some on broken pieces of the ship. And so it came to pass, that they escaped all safe to land" (Ac.27:23-24, 37, 43-44).

5 (13:21-22) **False Messiahs**: this sign is so terrible it causes a frantic search for false messiahs (deliverers). Jesus said three things.

a. False messiahs and prophets will arise. When men are oppressed and oppressed, witnessing scene after scene of death by hunger, pestilence, murder and war, they cry for deliverance. They are ever so open to a deliverer arising on the scene. And some are always ready to assume the power and leadership for which men cry. Such men (deliverers who promised deliverance from both the Romans and the natural disasters) arose in the siege of Jerusalem. Apparently there was the constant belief and rumors that the Messiah had come, that He was either out in the desert or in some secret room within the city. He was just awaiting the hour to strike. The scene in Jerusalem was somewhat like Jeremiah's day.

"Then said I, Ah, Lord God! behold, the prophets say unto them, Ye shall not see the sword, neither shall ye have famine; but I will give you assured peace in this place. Then the Lord said unto me, The prophets prophesy lies in my name: I sent them not, neither have I commanded them, neither spake unto them: they prophesy unto you a false vision and divination, and a thing of nought, and the deceit of their heart" (Je.14:13-14).

The same kind of scene will repeat itself in the last days. The great false deliverer of the earth, the antichrist and his false prophet, shall arise to deceive the whole earth (see outlines and notes—Rev.13:1-18 and related passages). Note that Jesus very simply said, "Believe it not"—believe neither the rumors nor the false deliverer.

b. False deliverers will show great signs and wonders. Deliverers, local and national, always feel and lay claim to being destined. They point to signs and wonders. The end time will witness an increase and an intensification of signs and wonders that will stretch across the whole world.

"Then shall that Wicked [one] be revealed...even him...and with all deceivableness" (2 Th.2:8-10).

"And he doeth great wonders, so that he maketh fire come down from heaven on the earth in the sight of men, and deceiveth them that dwell on the earth by the means of those miracles which he had

power to do in the sight of the beast; saying to them that dwell on the earth, that they should make an image to the beast, which had the wound by a sword, and did live" (Re.13:13-14).

c. False deliverers will be so convincing they will threaten even the elect. The elect, of course, are genuine believers. They endure for Jesus regardless of the circumstance or trial. An excellent passage that describes much of the same picture is seen in 2 Th.2:1-17. The way the elect are able to stand is clearly stated.

"Therefore, brethren, stand fast, and hold the traditions which ye have been taught, whether by word, or our epistle. Now our Lord Jesus Christ himself, and God, even our Father, which hath loved us, and hath given us everlasting consolation and good hope through grace, comfort your hearts, and stablish you in every good word and work" (2 Th.2:15-17).

6 (13:23) **End Time—Great Tribulation**: this sign is so terrible it requires being foretold. The great tribulation is to be shattering to one's spirit—so crushing and threatening that man must be foretold. He must take heed and prepare in case the event occurs in his lifetime.

Note: Jesus said, "I have foretold you all things." He has not left us unprepared and in the dark. He wants us to know that God is still on the throne; God will not be taken by surprise when the abomination of desolation arises. We can have confidence and be assured of eternal deliverance, no matter the terrible affliction coming upon the earth.

Thought 1. Imagine the horror and suffering that would be caused by atomic warfare. The picture of such terrible affliction gives some idea of what Christ said about the great tribulation.

	C. The Coming of the Son of Man, 13:24-27 *(Mt. 24:29-31; Lu. 21:25-28)*	shaken.	
		26 And then shall they see the Son of man coming in the clouds with great power and glory.	**3. Event 2: There will be the return of the Son of Man in the clouds**
1. The setting: After the distress or tribulation	24 But in those days, after that tribulation, the sun shall		
2. Event 1: There will be astronomical happenings	be darkened, and the moon shall not give her light, 25 And the stars of heaven shall fall, and the powers that are in heaven shall be	27 And then shall he send his angels, and shall gather together his elect from the four winds, from the uttermost part of the earth to the uttermost part of heaven.	**4. Event 3: There will be the gathering of the elect**

DIVISION VIII

THE SON OF GOD'S OLIVET MINISTRY: JESUS' PROPHECY OF HIS RETURN AND THE END TIME, 13:1-37

C. The Coming of the Son of Man, 13:24-27

(13:24-27) **Introduction**: the greatest event yet to happen in the history of the world will be the return of Jesus Christ. The disciples wanted to know, "When shall these things be?" (Mk.13:4), and "What shall be the sign of thy coming?" (Mt.24:4). Jesus began to answer the second question about His return in this passage.

1. The setting: After the distress or tribulation (v.24).
2. Event 1: there will be astronomical happenings (v.24-25).
3. Event 2: there will be the return of the Son of Man in the clouds (v.26).
4. Event 3: there will be the gathering of the elect (v.27).

1 (13:24) **Jesus Christ, Return**: When will Jesus return? Right "after that tribulation" (see note—Mt.24:29-31). The disciples had asked two questions (Mk.13:4; see Mt.24:4).

a. When would the temple be destroyed?
b. What are the signs of the Lord's coming and of the end of the world?

Jesus was now dealing with His coming again (v.26); He was answering the disciples' questions. He revealed exactly when He was going to return. He will return "in those days, after that tribulation." The idea is immediately after the great tribulation. In fact, Matthew uses the word *immediately* (Mt.24:29). Jesus even said that the days of the great tribulation have to be shortened in order to save mankind (Mk.13:20). Apparently, it will be shortened by Jesus' return. Note a significant point.

Jesus did not return "after that tribulation" of Jerusalem in A.D. 70. (See note—Mt.24:29-31 for detailed discussion.) This is clearly evident as we stand here centuries later. Therefore, what Jesus says in this passage is bound to refer to His coming again. This also indicates that the tribulation just discussed will be the great tribulation lying out in the future. Jesus will return...

- "in those days, after that tribulation" (Mk.13:24).
- "immediately after the tribulation of those days" (Mt.24:29).

Both the great tribulation and the Lord's return will be tied together. The Lord's return will follow immediately upon the heels of the great tribulation. It is "in those days, after that tribulation," that He will return.

It must be remembered that the terrible afflictions predicted by our Lord referred both to Jerusalem's fall in A.D. 70 and to the great tribulation "such as was not from the beginning of the creation" (Mk.13:19; see Mt.24:21). The fact that Jesus said He would return "in those days, after that tribulation" tells us there are some terrible days of suffering and trouble coming upon the earth. But His return also tells us some glorious news.

1. He is definitely God. He is omniscient. He knows the future of the earth (evidenced by Jerusalem's destruction about forty years after His death, and the great trial yet to come upon the earth).
2. He is in control. He will return to shorten the day of trial and redeem mankind and the world. There will be an end to all trials (Mk.13:20).

2 (13:24-25) **End Times—Jesus Christ, Return—Heavenly Bodies—Outer Space**: the first event when Jesus returns will be astronomical happenings. The language is very descriptive.

⇒ "The sun shall be darkened."
⇒ "The moon shall not give her light."
⇒ "The stars of heaven shall fall."
⇒ "The powers that are in heaven shall be shaken."

Very practically, such astronomical happenings occur now. The earth is sometimes darkened by dust from earthly catastrophes such as volcanic eruptions, wind storms, and smoke from huge fires. Of course, whatever darkens the sun hides the light of the moon from earth. The stars, that is, meteorites of varying sizes, fall throughout space often. "The powers of the heavens" being shaken could be the heavenly bodies outside our solar system that are called by the Bible "the host of heaven" (De.4:19).

Something should be mentioned here about the power of the atom. Of course, an atom bomb exploding on earth is powerful enough to darken the sun and moon from earth's view. Worldwide atomic warfare would cause so much dust and pollution it would be difficult for any man to see anything in outer space. But as the atom is known today, it could not affect the axis or rotation (the falling or shaking) of the sun and moon and stars unless there is to be an intergalactical war of some sort way out in the future. Of course, there is always the possibility that there is a power much greater than what we know today. This is not to say that atomic warfare will never happen. There will be wars and rumors of war as long as the earth stands. But what the Bible teaches is that God is going to end all things, not man. When the world ends, it will be God's ending it by His own will and act and power.

An extreme literalism needs to be avoided when interpreting these verses, for there is just so much we do not know about the laws (powers) of nature and the forces God has put in motion throughout the universe. However, there is no reason for not understanding the Lord's words as actual or literal events.

What the present passage seems to mean is that the whole universe is going to be affected by Jesus' coming to earth. The sun and moon and the stars and powers (laws) of heaven will be affected in the sense that they will *open up and receive Him*. They will serve notice that this is the Creator, the Son of Man, God's very own Son, who is now coming to earth in great power and glory. Imagine a spectacular fireworks display, and perhaps it will give us a little glimpse of what Christ is saying. A simple question is: Why would not everything, including the heavenly bodies, put on a display (that would be terrifying to man) when its Creator, the Son of God, returns?

Note in the verses below that the astronomical bodies are affected because of *the evil of men and the wrath of God* that is being shown. That is, the scene of falling stars (meteorites) is not for the purpose of man's witnessing a spectacular event; it is to point to the Son of God, to His judgment's falling upon the earth. Every man is going to know beyond any doubt that Jesus is coming in all the power and the glory of God Himself. As Jesus said, "with power and great glory" He is coming. He is coming that "every knee should bow, of things in heaven, and things in earth, and things under the earth; and that every tongue should confess that Jesus Christ is Lord, to the glory of God the Father" (Ph.2:10-11).

The words "great power and glory" indicate that He is coming to subject all men to His rule and reign and to execute judgment upon the earth. Scripture definitely reveals that astronomical happenings will precede and accompany the coming of the Lord.

"For the stars of heaven and the constellations thereof shall not give their light: the sun shall be darkened in his going forth, and the moon shall not cause her light to shine. And I will punish the world for their evil, and the wicked for their iniquity; and I will cause the arrogancy of the proud to cease, and will lay low the haughtiness of the terrible. I will make a man more precious than fine gold; even a man than the golden wedge of Ophir. Therefore I will shake the heavens, and the earth shall remove out of her place, in the wrath of the Lord of hosts, and in the day of his fierce anger" (Is.13:10-13).

"Fear, and the pit, and the snare, are upon thee, O inhabitant of the earth. And it shall come to pass, that he who fleeth from the noise of the fear shall fall into the pit; and he that cometh up out of the midst of the pit shall be taken in the snare: for the windows from on high are open, and the foundations of the earth do shake. The earth is utterly broken down, the earth is clean dissolved, the earth is moved exceedingly. The earth shall reel to and fro like a drunkard, and shall be removed like a cottage; and the transgression thereof shall be heavy upon it; and it shall fall, and not rise again. And it shall come to pass in that day, that the Lord shall punish the host of the high ones that are on high, and the kings of the earth upon the earth. And they shall be gathered together, as prisoners are gathered in the pit, and shall be shut up in the prison...." (Is.24:17-22).

"And I will show wonders in the heavens and in the earth, blood, and fire, and pillars of smoke. The sun shall be turned into darkness, and the moon into blood, before the great and the terrible day of the Lord come" (Joel 2:30-31).

"The sun and the moon shall be darkened, and the stars shall withdraw their shining. The Lord also shall roar out of Zion, and utter his voice from Jerusalem; and the heavens and the earth shall shake: but the Lord will be the hope of his people, and the strength of the children of Israel" (Joel 3:15-16).

"But in those days, after that tribulation, the sun shall be darkened, and the moon shall not give her light, and the stars of heaven shall fall, and the powers that are in heaven shall be shaken" (Mk.13:24-25).

"But the same day that Lot went out of Sodom it rained fire and brimstone from heaven, and destroyed them all. Even thus shall it be in the day when the Son of man is revealed" (Lu.17:29-30).

"And there shall be signs in the sun, and in the moon, and in the stars; and upon the earth distress of nations, with perplexity; the sea and the waves roaring; men's hearts failing them for fear, and for looking after those things which are coming on the earth: for the powers of heaven shall be shaken" (Lu.21:25-26).

"And I will show wonders in heaven above, and signs in the earth beneath; blood, and fire, and vapor of smoke: the sun shall be turned into darkness, and the moon into blood, before that great and notable day of the Lord come" (Ac.2:19-20).

"And I beheld when he had opened the sixth seal, and, lo, there was a great earthquake; and the sun became black as sackcloth of hair, and the moon became as blood; and the stars of heaven fell unto the earth, even as a fig tree casteth her untimely figs, when she is shaken of a mighty wind. And the heaven departed as a scroll when it is rolled together; and every mountain and island were moved out of their places. And the kings of the earth, and the great men, and the rich men, and the chief captains, and the mighty men, and every bondman, and every free man, hid themselves in the dens and in the rocks of the mountains; and said to the mountains and rocks, Fall on us, and hide us from the face of him that sitteth on the throne, and from the wrath of the Lamb: for the great day of his wrath is come; and who shall be able to stand?" (Re.6:12-17). (See outline and notes—Rev.6:12-17.)

Note the exact words of the verses of Revelation above since they are referring to the same event as Jesus (v.30; see Rev.6:17). The coming of Christ will trigger a great earthquake on earth and astronomical happenings in the heavens above (v.12-14). Men, great and small, will be terrified and hide themselves (v.15) and cry for immediate death instead of having to face Jesus (v.16). Why? Because they will know something: "The great day of God's wrath is come; and who shall be able to stand?" (v.17).

The disciples had asked, "What shall be the sign of thy coming, and of the end of the world?" Jesus is answering them: terrifying astronomical happenings will be a sign.

3 (13:26) **Jesus Christ, Return**: the second event is the actual return of Jesus, the Son of Man Himself. Note three significant points.

a. It is the Son of Man who comes. Jesus claimed that He is the Son of Man, the Son of God incarnate in human flesh as the Perfect Man (see DEEPER STUDY # 3—Mt.8:20). In that day, there will be no doubt about who He is (see Mk.14:61-62). Right now, He is recognized only by believers, but then it will be unmistakable: He is the Son of Man.

b. All men and every eye shall see Him return. This is what is meant by "they." Matthew actually says, "All the tribes of the earth mourn, and they shall see the Son of Man coming" (Mt.24:30). His return will be visible to every man on earth, and every man shall then acknowledge Him to be Lord, God's very own Son (Ph.2:9-11; see Rev.1:7).

c. He is coming "in the clouds with great power and glory." Picture the scene: the backdrop of heaven is pitch dark, without any major light from the sun and moon. And then, suddenly, as quickly as the flash of lightning, the most brilliant focus of light ever known to man appears. The Shekinah glory of God shines in the person of Jesus Christ as He appears to the world. The Son of Man is there, in the clouds, having returned in great power and glory just as He said He would.

> **"Which also said, Ye men of Galilee, why stand ye gazing up into heaven? this same Jesus, which is taken up from you into heaven, shall so come in like manner as ye have seen him go into heaven" (Ac.1:11).**
>
> **"And to you who are troubled rest with us, when the Lord Jesus shall be revealed from heaven with his mighty angels, in flaming fire taking vengeance on them that know not God, and that obey not the gospel of our Lord Jesus Christ: who shall be punished with everlasting destruction from the presence of the Lord, and from the glory of his power; when he shall come to be glorified in his saints, and to be admired in all them that believe (because our testimony among you was believed) in that day" (2 Th.1:7-10).**
>
> **"And then shall that Wicked be revealed, whom the Lord shall consume with the spirit of his mouth, and shall destroy with the brightness of his coming" (2 Th.2:8).**
>
> **"Behold, he cometh with clouds; and every eye shall see him, and they also which pierced him: and all kindreds of the earth shall wail because of him. Even so, Amen" (Re.1:7).**
>
> **"And I saw heaven opened, and behold a white horse; and he that sat upon him was called Faithful and True, and in righteousness he doth judge and make war. His eyes were as a flame of fire, and on his head were many crowns; and he had a name written, that no man knew, but he himself. And he was clothed with a vesture dipped in blood: and his name is called The Word of God. And the armies which were in heaven followed him upon white horses, clothed in fine linen, white and clean. And out of his mouth goeth a sharp sword, that with it he should smite the nations: and he shall rule them with a rod of iron: and he treadeth the winepress of the fierceness and wrath of Almighty God. And he hath on his vesture and on his thigh a name written, KING OF KINGS, AND LORD OF LORDS" (Re.19:11-16).**

4 (13:27) **Jesus Christ, Return**: the third event when Jesus returns is the gathering of the elect. There are two significant points made in this verse.

a. The angels of God "gather together His elect." Who are the elect?

⇒ They are the people who cry (pray, converse, share) day and night unto God (Lu.18:7).
⇒ They are the people who are justified by God (Ro.8:33).
⇒ They are the people who are "holy and beloved," who "put on...bowels of mercies, kindness, humbleness of mind, meekness, longsuffering" (Col.3:12).

b. The elect are gathered from all over the earth. They shall be gathered from the most remote spot on earth and carried to "*the uttermost part of heaven.*"

> **"When the Son of man shall come in his glory, and all the holy angels with him, then shall he sit upon the throne of his glory: and before him shall be gathered all nations: and he shall separate them one from another, as a shepherd divideth his sheep from the goats" (Mt.25:31-32).**

Outline	Scripture	Scripture (cont.)	Outline (cont.)
	D. The End Time & Its Warning to Believers, 13:28-37 *(Mt. 24:32-51; Lu. 21:29-36)*	hour knoweth no man, no, not the angels which are in heaven, neither the Son, but the Father.	**neither the day nor the hour is known**
		33 Take ye heed, watch and pray: for ye know not when the time is.	**5. The need is to be on guard—stay alert** a. Because the time is unknown
1. The signs point to the end & are discernable a. Even as a fig tree b. Even as a cause has its effect	28 Now learn a parable of the fig tree; When her branch is yet tender, and putteth forth leaves, ye know that summer is near:	34 For the Son of man is as a man taking a far journey, who left his house, and gave authority to his servants, and to every man his work, and commanded the porter to watch.	b. Because believers must focus upon their assigned responsibilities & work
c. Even to the point of being immediate—near, right at hand, v.32	29 So ye in like manner, when ye shall see these things come to pass, know that it is nigh, even at the doors.		
2. The events occur rapidly—in one generation	30 Verily I say unto you, that this generation shall not pass, till all these things be done.	35 Watch ye therefore: for ye know not when the master of the house cometh, at even, or at midnight, or at the cock-crowing, or in the morning:	c. Because Christ is returning unexpectedly—suddenly
3. The events are a surety—irrevocable	31 Heaven and earth shall pass away: but my words shall not pass away.	36 Lest coming suddenly he find you sleeping.	d. Because a believer can be caught sleeping
4. The exact time is unknown—	32 But of that day and that	37 And what I say unto you I say unto all, Watch.	**6. The warning is to all—watch**[DS1]

DIVISION VIII

THE SON OF GOD'S OLIVET MINISTRY: JESUS' PROPHECY OF HIS RETURN AND THE END TIME, 13:1-37

D. The End Time and Its Warning to Believers, 13:28-37

(13:28-37) **Introduction**: Christ had just covered the signs of the end time and of His return. The truth is glorious, for it stirs hope and gives a picture of the future glory that can be man's. But one thing is needful: man must turn his life over to God or else he will be banished from the presence and glory of Christ forever. Christ gives six critical warnings to man.

1. The signs point to the end and are discernable (vv.28-29).
2. The events occur rapidly—in one generation (v.30).
3. The events are a surety—irrevocable (v.31).
4. The exact time is unknown—neither the day nor the hour is known (v.32).
5. The need is to be on guard—stay alert (v.33-36).
6. The need to all—watch (v.37).

1 (13:28-29) **End Time—Jesus Christ, Return**: Christ warned—the signs point to the end. The end and the return of Christ will be discernable. The fig tree illustrates what Christ meant. When the fig tree begins to put forth leaves, we know that summer is near. So when we see "these things," the signs He had been sharing, "know that it [His return] is nigh, even at the doors." Note two significant points.

a. Christ said, "*Know* that [His return] is near." We are to know; He does not leave us an option. It is a command: we are to stay alert, looking for the signs of the time so that we *can know* when His return is near. This is the whole point of this passage. We are to be looking for His return *lest* it catch us unexpectedly.

b. Christ was speaking of cause and effect: every cause has its effect. The signs covered by Christ are second causes (vv.6-27). Christ was saying when the signs are seen, expect the result (effect): the coming again of the Son of Man. When believers see...

- an unusual number of wars and natural disasters, they can know "the beginning of sorrows" has begun.
- "many" false messiahs and prophets arise, they can know an enormous number of the lost and carnal will be tragically deceived.
- bitter persecution, they can know that God will tolerate only so much against His people.
- iniquity's abounding and love's waxing cold, they can know that God will judge and stop such apostasy.
- the earth about to be destroyed, they can know that God will not wait much longer.

3. Christ says when the signs appear His return is immediate—near—at the door. The signs point to the *immediacy* of His return.

2 (13:30) **End Time—Jesus Christ, Return**: Christ warned—the events occur rapidly. They happen in one generation. Just what is meant by "generation" is often disputed. However, it must always be kept in mind that the disciples had asked two questions, one about Jerusalem's destruction and the other about the end of the world. In answering their questions, Christ did not draw a definite line between the two questions. The signs and events that precede one shall precede the other. Therefore, just as the signs and destruction of Jerusalem took place within a generation, the signs and destruction of the world will also occur within a generation. (See DEEPER STUDY # 2, pt.2—Mk.13:1-37 for more discussion.)

3 (13:31) **End Time—Jesus Christ, Return**: Christ warned—the events are a surety. They are irrevocable. Christ is definite about what He has said. "Heaven and earth *shall* pass away, but my words shall not pass away."

Note two things.

a. Heaven and earth shall pass away. Christ is saying they are actually going to be done away with and cease to exist in their present condition (2 Pe.3:10-11).

b. All that Christ has said—all about the great tribulation and His return—*will* happen. The great tribulation and His return are more sure than heaven and earth.

In the eyes of some men, it has been a long, long time since Christ spoke these words; and an innumerable list of events have happened. Therefore, they assume the whole idea of the second coming is a fable, the figment of hopeful imagination. God knew this would happen.

> **"Knowing this first, that there shall come in the last days scoffers, walking after their own lusts, and saying, Where is the promise of his coming? for since the fathers fell asleep, all things continue as they were from the beginning of the creation....But, beloved, be not ignorant of this one thing, that one day is with the Lord as a thousand years, and a thousand years as one day. The Lord is not slack concerning his promise, as some men count slackness; but is longsuffering to us-ward, not willing that any should perish, but that all should come to repentance. But the day of the Lord will come as a thief in the night; in the which the heavens shall pass away with a great noise, and the elements shall melt with fervent heat, the earth also and the works that are therein shall be burned up. Seeing then that all these things shall be dissolved, what manner of persons ought ye to be in all holy conversation and godliness, looking for and hasting unto the coming of the day of God, wherein the heavens being on fire shall be dissolved, and the elements shall melt with fervent heat? Nevertheless we, according to his promise, look for new heavens and a new earth, wherein dwelleth righteousness" (2 Pe.3:3-4, 8-13).**

Three things are certain in human history: "the beginning of sorrows" (v.8); the "great tribulation, such as was not since the beginning of the world" (v.24; Mt.24:21); and "the Son of Man coming in the clouds of heaven with power and great glory" (v.26; Mt.24:21). Heaven and earth shall pass away, but not the words Christ has spoken, not what He said would happen. What He said would happen will happen. The three events are certain.

4 (13:32) **End Time—Jesus Christ, Return—Humiliation**: Christ warned—the exact time is unknown. The day and hour are not known to anyone. God alone knows when Christ is to return. The general time will be seen by expectant believers, but the exact day and hour are known only by God.

a. The second coming is an actual event that is yet to happen. There is "that [fixed] day and hour" when Christ shall return.

b. The second coming is secret. "No man knoweth...but the Father." Throughout history some have thought they knew when Christ was to return. (See 2 Th.2:1-2.) But Christ is explicit: "Of that day and that hour knoweth no man...."

c. Some things are to be left entirely in God's hands. The exact day and hour of the Lord's return is one of those things. The *watchful* believer will be sensitive to the season (fig tree, v.28-29) and know the generation (v.30), but the exact hour and day are hid from men, even from the wisest and most spiritual men. *Only* God Himself knows the day. If a man claims to know the hour and day, he is a man from whom we should flee. That man's word is not of the Lord.

d. What did Christ mean when He said that even He did not know when He was to return to earth? If He is the Son of God, possessing the divine (omniscient) nature of God, how could He not know? When Christ came to earth, He "emptied Himself" (Ph.2:7, NASB). This means at least the following.

1) He took on the nature of man; He became flesh and blood (Ph.2:7; Heb.2:14).
2) He voluntarily surrendered and limited Himself to the nature of man *in some respects*. For example, men do not know the future. Christ limited Himself in knowing the future except when and where a demonstration of His divine omniscience was needed.
3) While man, Christ willed not to know some things and not to be able to do some things (for example, to be present everywhere, His omnipresence, see Jn.16:7). This enabled Him more effectively to identify with man in his limitations and needs.
4) While man, Christ subjected Himself completely to the Father. This means, of course, that He had to *live in* the Father and *be taught* by the Father (just as we are to live in and be taught by God, except Christ did so perfectly). This is a phenomenal truth. It means that God took His Son and pioneered the Ideal, Perfect life, teaching Him exactly how to live and what to say. Christ had "emptied Himself" in order to cast Himself *perfectly* upon God, trusting God to teach Him how to live and what to say day by day. He was Man, but there was one difference. He was living a perfect life, trusting and depending upon God completely. Therefore, God was able to fill Him completely and teach Him perfectly. Very simply stated, God was able to take Christ day-by-day and teach Him how to live and what to say and to do it *perfectly*. This is what Scripture proclaims and what Christ emphasized time and again.

> **"Though he were a Son, yet learned he obedience by the things which he suffered" (He.5:8).**
>
> **"I have many things to say and to judge of you: but he that sent me is true; and I speak to the world those things which I have heard of him....Then said Jesus unto them, When ye have lifted up the Son of man, then shall ye know that I am he, and that I do nothing of myself; but as my Father hath taught me, I speak these things. And he that sent me is with me: the Father hath not left me alone; for I do always those things that please him" (Jn.8:26, 28-29).**

"For I have not spoken of myself; but the Father which sent me, he gave me a commandment, what I should say, and what I should speak. And I know that his commandment is life everlasting: whatsoever I speak therefore, even as the Father said unto me, so I speak" (Jn.12:49-50).

"Believest thou not that I am in the Father, and the Father in me? the words that I speak unto you I speak not of myself: but the Father that dwelleth in me, he doeth the works" (Jn.14:10).

"He that loveth me not keepeth not my sayings: and the word which ye hear is not mine, but the Father's which sent me" (Jn.14:24).

"For I have given unto them the words which thou gavest me; and they have received them, and have known surely that I came out from thee, and they have believed that thou didst send me" (Jn.17:8).

Christ was God-Man, perfectly God, perfectly Man in one Person. There is no question about the teaching of Scripture on the Lord's two natures. How did the two natures interwork? There is no way to know. We can never understand the two natures of Christ *beyond what Scripture says*. And this is the point: we are to live by faith, live by the revelation of Scripture. We either accept the record (message, testimony, news) about Christ's becoming Man, or we reject it. That is exactly what God is after: belief in Him and in His Word—that He "so loved the world that He *gave* His only begotten Son, that whosoever believeth in Him should not perish, but have everlasting life" (Jn.3:16).

5 (13:33-36) **End Time—Jesus Christ, Return:** Christ warned—the need is to take heed—to watch and pray. (See outline and notes—Mt.24:42-51; note and DEEPER STUDY # 1,*2*—25:1-13; 25:14-30.) There are four reasons the believer must watch.

a. The believer must watch because the time of the Lord's return is unknown (see note—Mk.13:32).

b. The believer must watch because he has been given a specific task to do, and the job must be completed when Christ returns. The greatest of tragedies would be for a believer not to have finished the job Christ gave him to do. (See outline and notes—Mt.24:42-51; note and DEEPER STUDY # 1,*2*—25:1-13.)

c. The believer must watch because Christ is returning unexpectedly, suddenly. It may be any day, any hour.

d. The believer must watch because he can be caught napping and sleeping.

Thought 1. Four tragic things can happen to a believer while he is waiting for the Lord to return.

(1) A believer may fail to wait *long enough.* As the days, weeks, and years wear on and on, he may grow more and more drowsy, nodding more and more. Note the parable Jesus told. The owner simply failed...
- to stay awake *long enough.*
- to keep his mind alert *long enough.*
- to look and listen to the noises (signs) *long enough.*
- to stand guard *long enough.*

(2) A believer may delay or postpone or slack up in his work for the Lord. He may figure he has time to do it later; therefore, he feels that he can set it aside for a while. He feels that a little sidetrack here and there will not hurt that much.

(3) A believer may think he can go ahead and do what he wishes and cover it with the Lord later. He may think he will have time to correct the matter before the Lord returns.

(4) A believer may begin *to think* like the world. However, God knows how the world thinks, and He has described it clearly for the sake of His dear followers (see 2 Pe.3:3-4, 8-15).

"And I will say to my soul, Soul, thou hast much goods laid up for many years; take thine ease, eat, drink, and be merry. But God said unto him, Thou fool, this night thy soul shall be required of thee: then whose shall those things be, which thou hast provided?" (Lu.12:19-20).

"Go to now, ye that say, To day or to morrow we will go into such a city, and continue there a year, and buy and sell, and get gain: whereas ye know not what shall be on the morrow. For what is your life? It is even a vapour, that appeareth for a little time, and then vanisheth away" (Js.4:13-14).

"Come ye, say they, I will fetch wine, and we will fill ourselves with strong drink; and tomorrow shall be as this day, and much more abundant" (Is.56:12).

6 (13:37) **End Time—Jesus Christ, Return**: Christ warned—the warning is to *all*—watch. No one is exempt: no believer, no unbeliever. Every man...
- is "to take heed, watch and pray" (v.33).
- is "commanded...to watch" (v.34).
- is to "watch ye therefore" (v.35).
- is not to be caught "sleeping" (v.36).
- is to hear the warning: "what I say unto you I say unto *all, Watch*" (v.37).

DEEPER STUDY # 1

(13:37) **Watch** (gregoreo): to keep awake, to stay alert, to be watchful and sleepless, to be vigilant. It also includes the idea of being motivated, that is, of desiring, of holding and keeping one's attention (mind) upon a thing. Watching also has the idea of being alert at the right time. It is at night that one really needs to stay awake and watch for the thief (see 1 Th.5:4-9). The Lord said, "Watch." What does it mean for a believer to "watch" (see Mt.26:41; Mk.13:33, 34, 36; 14:38)?

"Watch ye, stand fast in the faith, quit you like men, be strong" (1 Co.16:13).
"Therefore let us not sleep, as do others; but let us watch and be sober" (1 Th.5:6).
"But watch thou in all things, endure afflictions, do the work of an evangelist, make full proof of thy ministry" (2 Ti.4:5).
"But the end of all things is at hand: be ye therefore sober, and watch unto prayer" (1 Pe.4:7).

	CHAPTER 14 **IX. THE SON OF GOD'S PASSION MINISTRY: JESUS' SUPREME SACRIFICE—REJECTED & CRUCIFIED, 14:1-15:47** **A. Jesus' Death Plotted: A Picture of the Passover & Jesus' Death, 14:1-2** *(Mt. 26:1-5; Lu. 22:1-2)*
1. Picture 1: The Passover celebrated Israel's deliverance, Ex. 12:1-51 **2. Picture 2: The religionists plotted Jesus' death**[DS1] a. Plotted by all the leaders b. Plotted by deception: To arrest Jesus on false charges after the pilgrims had left the feast	After two days was the feast of the Passover, and of unleavened bread: and the chief priests and the scribes sought how they might take him by craft, and put him to death. 2 But they said, Not on the feast day, lest there be an uproar of the people.

DIVISION IX

THE SON OF GOD'S PASSION MINISTRY: JESUS' SUPREME SACRIFICE—REJECTED AND CRUCIFIED, 14:1-15:47

A. Jesus' Death Is Plotted: A Picture of the Passover and Jesus' Death, 14:1-2

(14:1-2) **Introduction**: this passage begins the final stage of Jesus' life before He was killed. In dramatic fashion Mark sets the stage for what is coming. In two short verses he mentions the Passover, and then he mentions the religionists' plotting Jesus' death—two scenes as opposite from one another as can be imagined. The Passover was a feast, a joyous and festive occasion. It was a celebration of God's glorious deliverance of Israel from the bondage of Egypt. Yet during the very days of this joyous celebration, Jesus' murder was being plotted. And tragically, it was being plotted by religionists, the very people who should have been taking the lead in the Passover. On the one hand, there was the celebration of deliverance, the saving of life; on the other hand, there was the plotting of death, the taking of life. This passage deliberately sets the stage for what is to come.

1. Picture 1: the Passover celebrated Israel's deliverance (v.1).
2. Picture 2: the religionists plotted Jesus' death (vv.1-2).

1 (14:1) **Passover**: the first picture is that of the Passover. For months Jesus had been drilling into His disciples that He was to die. Mark points to two brief facts.

a. The Passover was to be celebrated in just two days.
b. While preparations were being made for the Passover, preparations were also being made to kill Jesus.

In these two simple statements, Mark ties the death of Jesus to the Passover (see outline and notes—Mt.26:17-19). Throughout history, the Passover had pictured Jesus' death. Jesus was fulfilling the Passover with the shedding of His own blood upon the cross.

a. Historically, the Passover refers back to the time when God delivered Israel from Egyptian bondage (Ex.11:1f). God had pronounced judgment (the taking of the firstborn) upon the people of Egypt for their injustices. As He prepared to execute the final judgment, those who believed God were instructed to slay a pure lamb and sprinkle its blood over the door posts of their homes. The blood of the innocent lamb would then serve as a sign that the coming judgment had already been carried out. When seeing the blood, God would *pass over* that house.

b. Symbolically, the Passover pictured the coming of Jesus Christ as the Savior. The *lamb without blemish* pictured His sinless life, and the *blood sprinkled on the door posts* pictured His blood shed for the believer (Ex.12:5; see Jn.1:29). It was a sign that the life and blood of the innocent lamb had been substituted for the firstborn (believers). The *eating of the lamb* pictured the need for spiritual nourishment gained by feeding on Christ, the Bread of Life. The *unleavened bread* (bread without yeast) pictured the need for putting evil out of one's life and household (see DEEPER STUDY # 1, *Feast of Unleavened Bread*—Mt.26:17).

2 (14:1-2) **Religionists—Jesus Christ, Death**: the scene was dramatic, yet tragic. While the people were in the streets openly preparing to praise God for His delivering power and the saving of life, the religionists were behind closed doors preparing to arrest and murder Jesus. Just imagine! The religionists themselves were plotting to take the life of God's very own Son. (See DEEPER STUDY # 1, *Religionists*—Mk.14:1-2.)

a. Jesus' death was *plotted by all the leaders*: the chief priests and the Scribes. Matthew adds that the elders or lay leaders were also in on the plot. Matthew also shows the secretiveness of the plot by stating that the leaders met in the home (palace) of the High Priest instead of meeting in the official court (see note—Mt.26:3-5).

b. Jesus' death was to be *wrought by deception and lies.*

1) He was to be arrested on false charges and killed (see outline, notes, and DEEPER STUDY # 2—Lu.22:2. See Mt.26:60-66.)

2) He was to be arrested quietly, after all the pilgrims had left the feast to return home. The *feast day* refers to all eight days of the feast. The danger of an uprising would not have passed until all the pilgrims had left the city. Of course the threat of an uprising was removed by Judas' willingness to betray Jesus. In the crowded mass of about two million people within the city, Judas was able to show them where Jesus was and to quietly identify Him. Judas was able to show them how Jesus could be secretly taken in the dark of the night (see Mt.26:47-50).

Thought 1. When men are set on doing something wrong (stealing, sexual acts, etc.), they plot and maneuver to do it. And, too often, they are willing to pay any price to sneak around to do it. This was the case with the religionists plotting Jesus' death. They were willing to pay any price to get rid of Him, even the price of becoming murderers.

Thought 2. Just think! These men were religionists, men who professed to know God. Think how deceived they were—how much they had to deceive themselves in order to carry out their evil plan.

> **"Their throat is an open sepulchre; with their tongues they have used deceit; the poison of asps is under their lips" (Ro.3:13).**
>
> **"Know ye not that the unrighteous shall not inherit the kingdom of God? Be not deceived" (1 Co.6:9).**
>
> **"Be not deceived; God is not mocked: for whatsoever a man soweth, that shall he also reap" (Ga.6:7).**
>
> **"Let no man deceive you with vain words: for because of these things cometh the wrath of God upon the children of disobedience" (Ep.5:6).**
>
> **"Little children, let no man deceive you: he that doeth righteousness is righteous, even as he is righteous. He that committeth sin is of the devil; for the devil sinneth from the beginning. For this purpose the Son of God was manifested, that he might destroy the works of the devil" (1 Jn.3:7-8).**
>
> **"But be ye doers of the word, and not hearers only, deceiving your own selves" (Js.1:22).**
>
> **"For he flattereth himself in his own eyes, until his iniquity be found to be hateful" (Ps.36:2).**
>
> **"All the ways of a man are clean in his own eyes; but the LORD weigheth the spirits" (Pr.16:2).**
>
> **"Every way of a man is right in his own eyes: but the Lord pondereth the hearts" (Pr.21:2).**
>
> **"There is a generation that are pure in their own eyes, and yet is not washed from their filthiness" (Pr.30:12).**
>
> **"Most men will proclaim every one his own goodness: but a faithful man who can find?" (Pr.20:6).**
>
> **"And they will deceive every one his neighbor, and will not speak the truth: they have taught their tongue to speak lies, and weary themselves to commit iniquity" (Je.9:5).**
>
> **"The heart is deceitful above all things, and desperately wicked: who can know it?" (Je.17:9).**

DEEPER STUDY # 1

(14:1-2) **Religionists, Plot to Kill Jesus**: the religionists' conflict with Jesus is often misunderstood. This is because so much of the conflict had to do with *rules and regulations* that seem petty and meaningless to *modern* minds (see Mk.2:23-28; 3:1-6; 3:22-30. See notes—Mt.12:1-8; note and DEEPER STUDY # 1—12:10; note—15:1-20; DEEPER STUDY # 2—15:6-9.) Four facts will help in understanding why the conflicts happened and were life-threatening, ending in the murder of Jesus Christ.

1. The Jewish nation had been held together by their religious beliefs. Through the centuries the Jewish people had been conquered by army after army, and by the millions they had been deported and scattered all over the world. Even in the day of Jesus, they were enslaved by Rome. Their religion was the *binding force* that kept Jews together—in particular their religious rules governing the Sabbath and the temple, and their religious belief that God had called them to be a distinctive people. It was they who worshipped the only true and living God. These rules and this belief protected them from alien beliefs and from being swallowed up by other nations through intermarriage. Their religion was what maintained their distinctiveness as a people and as a nation.

Jewish leaders knew this. They knew that their religion was the *binding force* that held their nation together. Therefore, they opposed anyone or anything that threatened to break the laws of their religion.

2. The religionists were men of deep conviction. They were strong in their beliefs; therefore, they became steeped in religious belief and practice, law and custom, tradition and ritual, ceremony and liturgy, rules and regulations. To break any law or rule governing any practice was a serious offense, for it taught *loose behavior*. And *loose behavior*, once it had spread enough, would weaken their religion, the binding force that held their people together. Therefore, Jesus was committing a great offense by breaking their law. He was weakening the binding force of their nation, their religion.

3. The religionists were men who had profession, position, recognition, esteem, livelihood, and security. Anyone who went contrary to what they believed and taught was a threat to all they had. Some religionists undoubtedly felt that Jesus was a threat to them. Every time Jesus broke their law, He was undermining their very position and security.

4. The religionists were exposed by Jesus. In order for people to know the truth, Jesus had to point out where they were wrong and what they needed to do to get right with God. Both the sin of men and the truth of God had to be proclaimed. The religionists just could not take it. They refused to accept the fact that they were unacceptable to God. They were, after all, the religionists of the day, the very ones who professed God. In their minds, they had no sin, at least not enough sin to bar them from God. Anyone who accused them of being so wrong and so depraved could not conceivably be of God. He must be of Beelzebub (see outline and note—Mk.3:22-30).

There were at least four responses to Jesus by the religionists.

1. Some were sincere men of deep conviction. They actually thought Jesus was an imposter, a deceiver, a false messiah. Saul of Tarsus, who was later to become Paul the apostle, would be an example of this position.

2. Some were open-minded enough to seek the truth about Jesus. They observed and reasoned, being honest enough to consider what He was saying, and they sought Him out to discover the truth. Nicodemus would be an example of this response.

3. Some did believe and trust Jesus (see Lu.13:31; Acts 6:7; 15:5; 18:8, 17).

4. Some were *professional* priests and ministers who looked upon Christ as a threat. They held their positions because of the prestige, comfort, livelihood, and security they received from them. Therefore, they opposed Christ rather vehemently. Caiaphas and Annas would be examples of this response.

The error of the religionists was fourfold.

1. They misinterpreted and corrupted God's Word (see notes—Mt.12:1-3; DEEPER STUDY # 1—Jn.4:22; see DEEPER STUDY # 6—Ro.9:4).

2. They committed serious sin after serious sin in God's eyes (see notes—1 Th.2:15-16; see note and DEEPER STUDY # 1—Ro.2:17-29).

3. They rejected God's way of righteousness—God's Messiah, which is Jesus Christ (see notes—Ro.10:4; 1 Co.1:30; Ph.3:9.)

4. They allowed religion in its tradition and ritual, ceremony and rules to become more important than meeting the basic needs of human life: religion was more important than a man's need for God and for spiritual, mental, and physical health. Jesus, being the true Messiah, was bound to expose such error. Therefore the battle lines were drawn.

The Messiah had to liberate people from this enslaving behavior. He had to liberate them so they could be saved and worship God in freedom of spirit.

The religionists had to oppose anyone who broke their law. They had to oppose Jesus because He was a threat to their nation and to their own personal position and security.

Outline	Scripture	Scripture	Outline
	B. Jesus' Anointing at Bethany: A Study of Love,[DS1] **14:3-9** *(Mt. 26:6-13; Jn. 12:1-8)*	been given to the poor. And they murmured against her.	
		6 And Jesus said, Let her alone; why trouble ye her? she hath wrought a good work on me.	**3. The woman's love was a good & lovely thing**
1. The woman's love was selfless & costly[DS2,3]	3 And being in Bethany in the house of Simon the leper, as he sat at meat, there came a woman having an alabaster box of ointment of spikenard very precious; and she brake the box, and poured it on his head.	7 For ye have the poor with you always, and whensoever ye will ye may do them good: but me ye have not always.	**4. The woman's love grasped the opportune time**
		8 She hath done what she could: she is come aforehand to anoint my body to the burying.	**5. The woman's love did all it could**
2. The woman's love was questioned & murmured against	4 And there were some that had indignation within themselves, and said, Why was this waste of the ointment made?	9 Verily I say unto you, Wheresoever this gospel shall be preached throughout the whole world, this also that she hath done shall be spoken of for a memorial of her.	**6. The woman's love was rewarded**
	5 For it might have been sold for more than three hundred pence, and have		

DIVISION IX

THE SON OF GOD'S PASSION MINISTRY: JESUS' SUPREME SACRIFICE—REJECTED AND CRUCIFIED, 14:1-15:47

B. Jesus' Anointing at Bethany: A Study of Love, 14:3-9

(14:3-9) **Introduction—Sacrifice—Sacrificial Love**: John tells us that the woman was Mary, the sister of Lazarus, who anointed Jesus (Jn.12:1f). The title of this passage could easily be, *A Study of Sacrifice*. The result is a strong lesson on sacrifice or sacrificial giving.

1. The woman's love was selfless and costly (v.3).
2. The woman's love was questioned and murmured against (vv.4-5).
3. The woman's love was a good and lovely thing (v.6).
4. The woman's love grasped the opportune time (v.7).
5. The woman's love did all it could (v.8).
6. The woman's love was rewarded (v.9).

DEEPER STUDY # 1

(14:3-9) **Mary, Sister of Martha and Lazarus**: multitudes were flowing into the city and the excitement of the Passover was filling the air. There was a sense that something significant was about to happen. Of course, Mary had no idea of the events that were to take place in the last week of Jesus' life, events which were to begin the very next morning with the triumphal entry. But Mary, along with everyone else, sensed that the time for the kingdom to be established was at hand. Mary, who was always sitting at Jesus' feet, sat there again gazing into His eyes. As she gazed she sensed two things. She sensed the need to repent of her recent criticism of Jesus (see Jn.12:3; see note—Jn.12:3), and she sensed a foreboding of trouble surrounding Him. She saw within His eyes a weight so heavy that she was *drawn* to express the most profound faith and appreciation in Him possible. She took the most precious thing she had, a valuable bottle of perfume, and anointed Him as the Messiah, the anointed One of her life.

Mary's act was one of the most loving and precious acts ever shown to Jesus. It was an act of supreme love and adoration. What He had to say about it shows this (vv.6-9). Just how loving an act it was can be seen by picturing all that was going on throughout the city at this time and all that was yet to happen: the plotting, the intrigue, the hostility, the attacks, the planned murder, the crowds' streaming into the city by the teeming thousands—crowds who created a worldly, carnival atmosphere. Even Simon's own household had an enormous crowd in it with all the disciples present. Just imagine the noise from the conversation alone. Yet, there sat Mary at Jesus' feet, once again soaking up all He said, loving and adoring Him. He had done so much for her family. Simon the leper was apparently her brother-in-law (husband to Martha). He had probably been healed by her Lord. Her brother, Lazarus, had been raised from the dead. They had all been saved by Him. How she loved Him! How she wished to express her love and faith in Him! He seemed so tired, so weary; there was something in His eyes that was foreboding as she gazed into them. She wanted to help Him, to encourage Him, to show Him that she cared for Him and loved Him. So she arose and went to get the most precious thing she had to give Him. And she gave it in the most precious way she knew: she anointed her Lord, even as David and all the kings of Israel had been anointed in the past. She anointed Him not from any official position, but from her heart. It is for this reason that her memory lives on in Scripture. In behalf of all, she anointed the Lord to be the One to experience death for all. In behalf of everyone, she anointed Him as the Lord and Savior, the true Messiah of all hearts and lives who worship and serve Him as the anointed One of God.

1 (14:3) **Love—Sacrifice—Stewardship—Giving**: Mary's love was selfless and costly. Because of the hot and dry climate, it was the custom of the day to anoint the head with oil, especially the heads of guests. But this was not Mary's purpose.

a. Mary anointed Jesus *herself.* A servant would ordinarily do the anointing; and Simon, owning a home large enough to entertain so many guests, would certainly have had servants. Mary was not a servant; she was one of the heads of the household. Mary was not just anointing to fulfill a custom of the day. Her purpose was much greater than that.

b. Mary took the most precious thing she had and *gave* it to Jesus in the most significant way, in an act of anointing. The oil used for anointing the head cost only a mite, the smallest coin in circulation (amounting to only a penny). But not the oil Mary used. She took a priceless oil which cost about 300 denarii per flask or bottle. It was the oil used by kings, and they used it only drop by drop. A denarii was the average pay for a day's work. Therefore, the bottle was worth about a whole year's wage.

Note how Mary gave the gift to Jesus. She did not just hand it to Him; she broke the neck of the flask and poured the whole bottle on His head and feet (see Jn.12:3). Why? What was Mary doing?

Mary's anointing of Jesus was a selfless act, a costly act, an act of love and faith in the Lord Jesus. Very simply put, Mary anointed Jesus to show Him how deeply she loved Him and believed Him to be the true Messiah, *the anointed One of God* (see DEEPER STUDY # 1—Mk.14:3-9; see DEEPER STUDY # 2—Mt.1:18). He was her Savior, Lord, and King. He had done so much for her and her family. She wanted Him to know how much she appreciated, loved, and believed Him.

Something else needs to be noted as well. Mary sensed something within Jesus: a foreboding, a preoccupation of mind, a heaviness of heart, a weight of tremendous pressure. Her heart reached out to Him and wanted to encourage and help Him. Being a young woman in the presence of so many men, she was not allowed to vocally express herself that much. Such privilege was not allowed women of that day, so she did all that she could: she acted. She arose and went for the most precious gift she could think of—a most costly bottle of perfume. And she gave it to Him in such a way that He would know that at least one person truly loved Him and believed Him to be the Messiah. Her hope was that such worship and such faith and love would boost His spirits.

Thought 1. True love is selfless and costly. True love forgets self and pays whatever price is necessary to demonstrate one's love. True love gives its most precious possession. True love is...

- being all that one should be, changing (repenting) to become that person.
- giving one's most prized possession, surrendering all that one is and has.
- going wherever one can best share his love.
- serving wherever one's love will be most effective.

"Grace be with all them that love our Lord Jesus Christ in sincerity" (Ep.6:24).

"Whom having not seen, ye love; in whom, though now ye see him not, yet believing, ye rejoice with joy unspeakable and full of glory" (1 Pe.1:8).

"Keep yourselves in the love of God, looking for the mercy of our Lord Jesus Christ unto eternal life" (Jude 21).

"O love the LORD, all ye his saints: for the LORD preserveth the faithful" (Ps.31:23).

DEEPER STUDY # 2
(14:3) **Anoint**: see DEEPER STUDY # 1—Acts 10:38.

DEEPER STUDY # 3
(14:3) **Simon the Leper**: see DEEPER STUDY # 1—Mt.26:6.

2 (14:4-5) **Love—Sacrifice—Giving**: Mary's love was questioned and murmured against. The word *indignation* (aganaktountes) means to ache within, to be vexed and disturbed. The word *murmured* (eneboimonto) means to growl, rebuke, scold. It indicates strong emotions. But note: only some of the disciples felt this way; all did not.

What disturbed the disciples was *not* the fact that Mary anointed Jesus. Anointing Him was easy enough to understand since it was a common custom of the day. What disturbed them was the gift she gave. The gift...

- seemed too valuable and priceless
- seemed too costly and sacrificial
- seemed unnecessary and thoughtless
- seemed to be a foolish and senseless act
- seemed misplaced and wasted

Very simply, the disciples questioned the act, and even murmured against it. They became rather emotional about the matter. They felt a cheaper oil should have been used for the anointing, and the more expensive oil should have been sold and the money given to the poor.

Thought 1. There are always those who question the believer's love and sacrifices for the Lord. Some even murmur against believers who make significant sacrifices. They do not understand the believer's love and commitment (sacrifice) for his Lord. They question the sacrifice of...

- money, possessions, comfort
- position, recognition, prestige
- pleasure, partying, popularity
- profession, promotion, security

Thought 2. There are always those who feel the believer's love and sacrifice go too far. They feel...

- commitment of life is not necessary, not to the extent of total sacrifice (see Lu.9:23).
- commitment of money is not necessary, not to the extent of tithing (see 1 Co.16:2; Mal.3:10).
- commitment of behavior is not necessary, not to the extent of *separation from the world* (see 2 Co.6:17-18).
- commitment of tongue is not necessary, not to the extent of cleaning up one's speech completely and witnessing courageously (see Ex.20:7; Mt.12:36-37).

3 (14:6) **Love—Sacrifice—Giving**: Mary's love was a good and lovely thing. Jesus knew the disciples were questioning and murmuring against Mary. He reacted strongly: "Let her alone...she hath wrought a good work on me." The word Christ used for good is not *agathos* which speaks of moral goodness. He chose to use the word *kalos* which means both good and lovely. It means something so good that it is striking, appealing, attractive, and pleasant.

Mary was driven to express her faith and love for Him in the most meaningful way she could. She did this by anointing Him as her Lord with the most expensive perfume she possessed.

The most significant person in Mary's life was the Lord. He was the Messiah, the Savior and Lord of her life and family. She wished to show Him that He was deserving of all she was and had. Therefore, Mary's love and sacrifice was *a good work*, a *lovely work*, and it struck the attention of the Lord. There was no way such love and sacrifice could ever escape His sight.

Thought 1. The love and sacrifice that leads a person to do *good works* and *lovely works* for Christ attract His attention. His eyes do not miss the good and lovely works of those devoted to Him. He is *struck* by their sacrifice of life, money, time, and whatever else they commit to Him.

"I know thy works, and charity, and service, and faith, and thy patience, and thy works" (Re.2:19; see Mt.25:34-40 for a descriptive picture of Jesus' knowledge about us).

"Let your light so shine before men, that they may see your good works, and glorify your Father which is in heaven" (Mt.5:16).

"In all things showing thyself a pattern of good works: in doctrine showing uncorruptness, gravity, sincerity" (Tit.2:7).

"And let us consider one another to provoke unto love and to good works" (He.10:24).

4 (14:7) **Love—Sacrifice—Initiative—Timing**: Mary's love grasped the opportune time. Jesus made a significant point that is often missed by men. Opportunities come and go—and once they are gone, they are gone for good. Mary demonstrated the difference. The poor would always be present for believers to help, but the privilege of ministering to Jesus would not always be available. If the disciples were to minister to Him, they had to grasp the opportunity while Jesus was with them.

Thought 1. What a lesson for mankind! The presence of Jesus, that is, a sense of His presence and of His Word, is not always pounding away at the mind and heart of man. Man must grasp the opportunity to show his love and sacrifice for Christ when it presents itself. The opportunity will pass. In fact, the opportunity and privilege of life itself will soon pass. The servant of the Lord must love and act while it is still day. The night cometh when no man can work.

"I must work the works of him that sent me, while it is day: the night cometh, when no man can work" (Jn.9:4).

"Redeeming the time, because the days are evil" (Ep.5:16).

5 (14:8) **Love—Sacrifice—Jesus Christ, Death**: Mary's love did all it could. Note two very special things.

a. Jesus said, "She hath done what she could." She took all she had, symbolized in her most precious and priceless possession, and sacrificed it for Jesus. She could do no more. Her heart reached out toward Jesus, and she acted sacrificially with the deepest devotion.

"But lay up for yourselves treasures in heaven, where neither moth nor rust doth corrupt, and where thieves do not break through nor steal" (Mt.6:20).

"For whosoever will save his life shall lose it; but whosoever shall lose his life for my sake and the gospel's, the same shall save it. For what shall it profit a man, if he shall gain the whole world, and lose his own soul?" (Mk.8:35-36).

"Yea doubtless, and I count all things but loss for the excellency of the knowledge of Christ Jesus my Lord: for whom I have suffered the loss of all things, and do count them but dung, that I may win Christ" (Ph.3:8).

b. The anointing of Jesus pointed toward His burial, His death. This is exactly what Jesus said: "She did it for my burial." Some commentators think Mary knew what she was doing, having grasped what Jesus had been saying—that He was soon to die. They feel Mary grasped the fact when others did not. But this is unlikely. The atmosphere surrounding everyone was that the kingdom was about to be set up. However, whether she knew what she was doing or not, Jesus took her act and applied it to His death. He said that her love and faith, the anointing of His body, pointed toward His death. In simple terms,

Mary's love and faith, gift and anointing *were a witness of anticipation.* She was witnessing to the Lord's death by looking ahead to it.

Today, the believer's love and faith, gift and anointing *are a witness of fact.* The believer is to witness to the Lord's death by looking back to it. It is a fact: He did die for the sins of the world.

> **"But God commendeth his love toward us, in that, while we were yet sinners, Christ died for us" (Ro.5:8).**
>
> **"Who his own self bare our sins in his own body on the tree, that we, being dead to sins, should live unto righteousness: by whose stripes ye were healed" (1 Pe.2:24).**

6 (14:9) **Love—Sacrifice**: Mary's love was rewarded. Jesus honored Mary because she had so greatly honored Him. Several things about Mary stand as an ideal for all: her deep love and faith in Jesus, her sacrificial gift, her courage in proclaiming her strong love and faith by anointing Jesus before a room full of men. Such devotion and love could not be allowed to fade from history. Jesus memorialized it, and He will memorialize the faith and love of any believer who sacrifices for Him.

> **"Charge them that are rich in this world, that they be not highminded, nor trust in uncertain riches, but in the living God, who giveth us richly all things to enjoy; that they do good, that they be rich in good works, ready to distribute, willing to communicate; laying up in store for themselves a good foundation against the time to come, that they may lay hold on eternal life" (1 Ti.6:17-19).**

	C. Jesus' Betrayal: Why a Disciple Failed, 14:10-11 *(Mt. 26:14-16; Lu. 22:3-6)*
1. Judas was personally irresponsible a. Was full of jealousy b. Was full of ambition c. Was full of greed d. Was devil-possessed, Jn. 13:27	10 And Judas Iscariot, one of the twelve, went unto the chief priests, to betray him unto them. 11 And when they heard it, they were glad, and promised to give him money.
2. Judas forsook Christ: Deceived & betrayed Him	And he sought how he might conveniently betray him.

DIVISION IX

THE SON OF GOD'S PASSION MINISTRY: JESUS' SUPREME SACRIFICE—REJECTED AND CRUCIFIED, 14:1-15:47

C. Jesus' Betrayal: Why a Disciple Failed, 14:10-11

(14:10-11) **Introduction**: Judas Iscariot denied and betrayed Jesus—two terrible sins that doomed him eternally. This is most tragic, for Judas had known Jesus personally. He had walked with Jesus during the Lord's earthly ministry, professing to be one of the close followers of the Lord. The fact that he could know Jesus so well and still end up failing and being doomed is a warning to all of us. All of us must heed why Judas failed so miserably.

1. Judas was personally irresponsible (vv.10-11).
2. Judas forsook Christ: deceived and betrayed Him (v.11).

1 (14:10-11) **Judas**: Judas was personally irresponsible. He forsook Jesus, denied and betrayed Him, and Judas is to be blamed. No one made him do it; he personally took the initiative. But why would Judas deny and betray Jesus? Several things are suggested in this passage.

a. Jealousy. Judas seems to have been jealous of the other apostles. The exact words, "Judas Iscariot, one of the twelve" are significant. The Greek actually reads, "Judas Iscariot, *the one* of the twelve." The word "the" is inserted. There seems to be some kind of priority and importance suggested. At first, Jesus had noticed some great potential, some unusual qualities about Judas. Judas was not only called by Jesus, he was elevated and given a position of authority among the apostles. He had been appointed the treasurer of the group, an extremely important function. He was in charge of the Lord's funds and the purchasing of whatever was needed (Jn.12:6; 13:29; see Lu.8:2-3). Such a high position and responsibility indicated the high esteem with which he was held by Jesus and the others. But something happened. Judas was never seen as one of the inner circle of three (Peter, James, and John).

He apparently began to turn sour at some point (see pt.3 of this note—Mk.14:11). Jesus, of course, knew what was happening to his heart and character; therefore, Judas saw himself excluded more and more from intimacy with Jesus. He saw himself, who had been one of the first, becoming one of the last.

Apparently, jealousy and envy began to fill his heart, and he refused to deal with it. The result was inevitable: he became even more unreachable to Jesus, less and less important. Judas could not take it. He began to be consumed with jealousy and envy and the urge to retaliate. He who *had been one* of the twelve denied Jesus and reacted against Him.

> **"Let us not be desirous of vain glory, provoking one another, envying one another" (Ga.5:26).**
> **"A sound heart is the life of the flesh: but envy the rottenness of the bones" (Pr.14:30).**

b. Ambition. Judas was definitely ambitious. He approached the chief priests thinking they were the *winning* side. Right along with the other disciples, Judas was seen seeking after the higher positions in the government Jesus was to set up. (See outline and notes—Mk.9:33-37; Mt.18:1-4; Lu.9:46-48.)

There was one difference, however, between Judas and the others. They never lost faith in Jesus' *Person*, that He was the true Messiah, but Judas did. They all thought that wealth, power, and position would be theirs when Jesus set up His kingdom. They simply misunderstood the Messiah's *method* for saving the world, not His *Person*, but Judas mistook both Jesus' method and Person. As the days passed, the fact that Jesus was not going to set up His kingdom became more and more apparent. The authorities were mobilizing against Jesus to kill Him, and it seemed as though they were going to be successful. Jesus had even been teaching that they were to be successful; He had predicted that He was to be killed by their hands.

Judas became convinced that he had been mistaken about Jesus. Jesus was not the real Messiah. He was just another mistaken self-proclaimed messiah. He was doomed and there was no way out. Judas experienced his dreams of wealth and power and position with Jesus being shattered. In going to the chief priests, he was trying to get what he could out of the situation. He wanted to be in good standing with the winning side and to get what he could.

> **"But it shall not be so among you: but whosoever will be great among you, let him be your minister; and whosoever will be chief among you, let him be your servant: even as the Son of man came not to be ministered unto, but to minister, and to give his life a ransom for many" (Mt.20:26-28).**

"And whosoever shall exalt himself shall be abased; and he that shall humble himself shall be exalted" (Mt.23:12).

"How can ye believe, which receive honour one of another, and seek not the honour that cometh from God only?" (Jn.5:44).

c. Greed. Judas was a thief, consumed with greed and the love of money. In fact, this is the sin of Judas that is stressed above all the others by Scripture. "What will ye give me, and I will deliver him unto you?" (Mt.26:15).

Thought 1. Note four significant facts about greed.

(1) Greed is a growing sin. It has to be fed to grow. We lust for more and more. Desiring is normal and natural. It is when we feed our desires that they become sin and grow and grow (see notes—Js.4:1-3; 4:2. These notes will stir additional thoughts for application in dealing with desires and lust.)

(2) Greed or covetousness, the desire for more and more, will eat at us just like a cancer. Judas had what he needed: food, clothing, and housing. He did not go without. What was he after? The sin of lusting for more and more ate away at him, causing him to put his hand into the till.

(3) Greed is sin. But note: it is not money that is sinful; it is the love of money (1 Ti.6:10). Money is a *thing*; it is *inanimate, lifeless*. It has no feelings, no desires, no will to act. Man is the culprit. Man is the one who lusts for more and more; therefore, man is the one who sins, not the piece of paper or metal.

(4) Greed is very, very dangerous. It is one of the most dangerous sins. (See *Ambition*, pt.2 above.)

"And he said unto them, Take heed, and beware of covetousness: for a man's life consisteth not in the abundance of the things which he possesseth" (Lu.12:15).

"For the love of money is the root of all evil: which while some coveted after, they have erred from the faith, and pierced themselves through with many sorrows" (1 Ti.6:10).

"Mortify therefore your members which are upon the earth; fornication, uncleanness, inordinate affection, evil concupiscence, and covetousness, which is idolatry" (Col.3:5).

"Your gold and silver is cankered; and the rust of them shall be a witness against you, and shall eat your flesh as it were fire. Ye have heaped treasure together for the last days" (Js.5:3).

"He that is greedy of gain troubleth his own house; but he that hateth gifts shall live" (Pr.15:27).

"He that loveth silver shall not be satisfied with silver; nor he that loveth abundance with increase: this is also vanity" (Ec.5:10).

"Yea, they are greedy dogs which can never have enough, and they are shepherds that cannot understand: they all look to their own way, every one for his gain, from his quarter. Come ye, say they, I will fetch wine, and we will fill ourselves with strong drink; and tomorrow shall be as this day and much more abundant" (Is.56:11-12).

Thought 2. Judas allowed his strength to become his weakness. This is often true with us.

⇒ Gifts of administration can lead to being overbearing.
⇒ Gifts of loveliness can lead to being sensual.
⇒ Gifts of humility can lead to no service.
⇒ Gifts of leadership can lead to being self-seeking.
⇒ Gifts of speaking can lead to being prideful or super-spiritual.

d. Devil-possessed. Judas actively denied Jesus and sought how to betray Him. Only a man possessed by the devil denies and betrays Jesus. The devil did enter into Judas (Jn.13:27). Apparently, Judas had filled his heart with the lust for more and more instead of filling it with Jesus. He went too long without repenting and letting Jesus into his life, and the devil was able to fill his being. The devil blinded and took control of his rationale. Hence, Judas was able to justify his betrayal in his own mind. He was, after all, helping the religious body and saving himself from being arrested as one of the followers of Jesus. Therefore, he betrayed Jesus of Nazareth, who apparently in Judas' mind was just another mistaken self-proclaimed messiah who was doomed to be arrested and condemned as an insurrectionist.

In looking at the bargain Judas agreed to in betraying Jesus, thirty pieces of silver seems a small price for betraying someone of the Lord's stature. It amounted to only about four or five months' wages. However, three things need to be kept in mind.

1. Judas probably expected to get much more, but he did not dictate the terms—the chief priests did. They were going to arrest Jesus in just a few days anyway, just as soon as the pilgrims left the city (Mt.26:5). All Judas did was move their schedule up a few days.

2. Judas felt that Jesus was doomed, without any hope of escape. He had become convinced that Jesus was not the true Messiah, but just another mistaken self-proclaimed messiah. There is a possibility that Judas betrayed Jesus because he was angry for having been deceived as well as for having been disillusioned. He was willing to get what he could, no matter how small the amount.

3. Once Judas had approached the leaders, he was forced to betray Jesus no matter how much or how little they were willing to pay him. If he attempted to back out of the deal, he felt they would arrest him right along with Jesus and His disciples.

2 (14:11) **Judas**: Judas forsook Christ: deceived and betrayed Him. Note the words, "He sought *how* he might conveniently [find a chance, an opportunity to] betray Him." The picture is that of being on the prowl, searching and seeking, looking here and there for the right moment. Judas' heart was set, full of intrigue, plotting evil and planning its strategy. He did *not* believe in Jesus, but even more, He *willed* to do evil against Jesus, to hurt Him, to destroy Him; and he sought opportunity to do so. Just how deceitful Judas was is clearly seen: immediately after bargaining with the authorities, he sat down to eat with Jesus. He sat at the very table where the Lord's Supper was being instituted.

Thought 1. Note that Judas not only rejected Jesus, but he also sought to destroy Him. Many reject Jesus, but they do not seek to harm and destroy Him.

⇒ Some curse Him, consciously or unconsciously dishonoring His name.
⇒ Some talk and teach against His divine nature, against the fact that He is the Son of God.
⇒ Some talk and teach against the written revelation of Himself and the truth, that is, the Word, the Holy Bible.
⇒ Some talk and teach against His active presence in the life of the genuine believer.

"Beware of false prophets, which come to you in sheep's clothing, but inwardly they are ravening wolves" (Mt.7:15).

"Now the Spirit speaketh expressly, that in the latter times some shall depart from the faith, giving heed to seducing spirits, and doctrines of devils; speaking lies in hypocrisy; having their conscience seared with a hot iron" (1 Ti.4:1-2).

"This know also, that in the last days perilous times shall come. For men shall be lovers of their own selves, covetous, boasters, proud, blasphemers, disobedient to parents, unthankful, unholy, without natural affection, trucebreakers, false accusers, incontinent, fierce, despisers of those that are good, traitors, heady, highminded, lovers of pleasures more than lovers of God; having a form of godliness, but denying the power thereof: from such turn away" (2 Ti.3:1-5).

D. Jesus' Last Chance to Sway Judas: The Appeal to a Sinner, 14:12-21
(Mt. 26:17-25; Lu. 22:21-23; Jn. 13:21-31)

1. The Passover was approaching
- a. The disciples asked where they were to observe the Passover
- b. It was Jesus' habit to worship

2. Jesus knew about Judas' denial & betrayal
- a. He kept His plans & movement secret
- b. He shared only with His trusted disciples
  - 1) He had preplanned the arrangements
  - 2) He sent trusted disciples to carry out the arrangements
- c. He kept His plans despite the betrayal

3. Jesus gave Judas every chance to repent
- a. The 1st chance: He tried to stir conviction
  - 1) Stirred sorrow in the faithful
  - 2) Stirred self-examination in the faithful
- b. The 2nd chance: Revealed monstrous deception

4. Jesus gave Judas a last warning

12 And the first day of unleavened bread, when they
killed the passover, his disciples said unto him, Where
wilt thou that we go and prepare that thou mayest eat the
passover?
13 And he sendeth forth
two of his disciples, and saith
unto them, Go ye into the
city, and there shall meet you
a man bearing a pitcher of
water: follow him.
14 And wheresoever he
shall go in, say ye to the
goodman of the house, The
Master saith, Where is the
guestchamber, where I shall
eat the passover with my disciples?
15 And he will show you a
large upper room furnished
and prepared: there make
ready for us.
16 And his disciples went
forth, and came into the city,
and found as he had said unto
them: and they made ready
the passover.
17 And in the evening he
cometh with the twelve.
18 And as they sat and did
eat, Jesus said, Verily I say
unto you, One of you which
eateth with me shall betray
me.
19 And they began to be
sorrowful, and to say unto
him one by one, Is it I? and
another said, Is it I?
20 And he answered and
said unto them, It is one of
the twelve, that dippeth with
me in the dish.
21 The Son of man indeed
goeth as it is written of him:
but woe to that man by whom
the Son of man is betrayed!
good were it for that man if
he had never been born.

DIVISION IX

THE SON OF GOD'S PASSION MINISTRY: JESUS' SUPREME SACRIFICE—REJECTED AND CRUCIFIED, 14:1-15:47

D. Jesus' Last Chance to Sway Judas: The Appeal to a Sinner, 14:12-21

(14:12-21) **Introduction**: Jesus was forced to make secret arrangements for keeping the Passover. This is clear from the present passage. Judas had just plotted with the authorities to betray Jesus (Mk.14:10-11). They wanted to arrest Him in a quiet spot where the people would not be present and rise to His defense. Judas was just waiting for the right place and time. The Upper Room would be an ideal place and time. Jesus knew this, so He made secret arrangements.

The point of the present passage is to show that Jesus knew about Judas' betrayal and to show how Jesus went about giving Judas a last chance to repent.

1. The Passover was approaching (v.12).
2. Jesus knew about Judas' denial and betrayal (vv.13-17).
3. Jesus gave Judas every chance to repent (vv.18-20).
4. Jesus gave Judas a last warning (v.21).

1 (14:12) **Passover**: the Passover was approaching. Jerusalem was astir with excitement. Josephus, the notable Jewish historian of that day, estimated that between two and three million people flooded into the city to observe the Passover. Pilgrims by the teeming thousands came from all over the world. The mass of people and the necessary housing, food, and commercial arrangements that had to be made—along with the commercial carnival atmosphere—can hardly be imagined.

Note that the disciples had to ask Jesus where they were to celebrate the Passover. He had not told them, not even given them a hint. The day of unleavened bread was at hand, and so far as they knew, no arrangement had been made to secure a place for them to observe the Passover. Considering the housing shortage with the mass of pilgrims, such apparent oversight was most unusual. The disciples must have wondered and questioned why He had not shared His plans earlier.

> **Thought 1.** Jesus worshipped and kept the feasts of the Jews. He did not neglect the assembling together with others. The disciples knew this.
>
> **"Not forsaking the assembling of ourselves together, as the manner of some is; but exhorting one another: and so much the more, as ye see the day approaching" (He.10:25).**

2 (14:13-17) **Judas—Denial—Betrayal**: Jesus knew about the denial and the betrayal of Judas. This seems to be the very point of what happened in these verses. Judas had just plotted with the chief priests against Jesus (Mk.14:10-11). Judas was denying and betraying Jesus. Jesus knew this, so He had to keep His plans and movements quiet and secret. He could not let Judas know, lest Judas lead the authorities to arrest Him in the Upper Room before He had completed His mission with the disciples. Note the point of the passage.

a. Jesus had kept His plans and movements secret. The disciples did not know where He wished to celebrate the Passover. He could not reveal the plans to a sinful, fallen disciple who was denying and betraying Him. That disciple (Judas) would only interrupt what Jesus was trying to do with the faithful disciples in the Upper Room. He would only create havoc, cause disturbance, hindering and hampering the work of Jesus.

b. Jesus could only share with His faithful and trusted disciples. Note that Jesus did have a plan, and He followed that plan even to the most minute detail. He had apparently pre-planned the arrangements. He sent two trusted disciples to carry out the arrangements. They followed His instructions exactly. But note how secretive the instructions were. Secret arrangements were necessary because Judas and the authorities were seeking to catch Jesus in a quiet place away from the people. The Upper Room would have been an ideal place to arrest Him.

1) There was a pre-planned sign: a man carrying a pitcher of water on his head. This was a most unusual sight. Women were usually the ones who carried pitchers on their heads. It was apparently a sign for the disciples to quietly follow.
2) Jesus did not name the homeowner or tell where the house was. He simply said to follow the man with the pitcher on his head and to tell the homeowner that "The Master" requests the room.

c. Jesus kept His plans despite the betrayer and those who would stop Him. Note the courage and power of Jesus to control the circumstances and events.

Thought 1. Note several striking and convicting points.

(1) Jesus knows about the denial and betrayal of any man, just as He knew about Judas.
(2) Jesus does not reveal His plans or movements to the man who is denying and betraying Him. The man who denies Jesus knows this. He has no sense, no consciousness, no awareness of Jesus' presence. The Lord's plans are not known to him and the movements of God's Spirit are not felt or experienced.
(3) Jesus shares His plans and movement only with faithful and trusted disciples.
(4) Jesus' plans are sure; they are fixed. Just as they could not be stopped by Judas, so they cannot be stopped now, no matter the denial and betrayal. Jesus keeps His plans, working out whatever is necessary to fulfill them.

"And we know that all things work together for good to them that love God, to them who are the called according to his purpose" (Ro.8:28).

"But the natural man receiveth not the things of the Spirit of God: for they are foolishness unto him: neither can he know them, because they are spiritually discerned" (1 Co.2:14).

"He that walketh in darkness knoweth not whither he goeth" (Jn.12:35).

3 (14:18-20) **Judas—Denial—Betrayal**: Jesus gave Judas every chance to repent.

a. The first chance was an attempt to stir conviction within Judas. Jesus said, "One of you which eateth with me shall betray me." Judas was seated there. He heard the words of Jesus. What were his thoughts? He had tried to hide his sin and he had done a good job. In his mind no one knew about his sin (plot), not even the disciples who were his closest associates. But he was wondering, "Does Jesus know; or is Jesus stabbing in the dark, guessing, suspicious, aware that something is brewing, but not quite sure what?" Scripture is silent about the betrayer's thoughts, but one thing is known: Judas was not convicted of his sin, not enough to repent. But note what happened to the faithful and trusted disciples.

1) They were stirred with deep sorrow (grieved) in their hearts. The word *sorrow* (lupeisthai) means to grieve, to sorrow with heaviness of heart. Their hearts were gripped with a real burden, a heavy weight of grieving.
2) They were stirred to examine their own hearts. They asked, "Is it I?" Note how they had matured. They knew the weakness of the flesh, that it could so easily fail. Each one feared lest a great fall lay ahead of them. Note also how they did not look for the fault or weakness in others, but they looked at themselves. What a lesson for us all!

Thought 1. The man who should have been...

- convicted, was not
- grieving, was not
- examining his own heart, was not
- sorrowing, was not
- repenting, was not

Thought 2. Two things are critical, even for the most faithful and trusted.

(1) To know the weakness of the human flesh, the great danger of falling.
(2) To always be examining oneself and not others.

b. The second chance given to Judas left him without excuse if he refused to heed it. Jesus revealed that He knew about the *monstrous deception* (v.20). "It is one of the twelve," one "that dippeth with me in the dish." What deception! The sinner sat with Jesus, partaking of His Last Supper and being guilty of the most terrible sin.

Note that Judas was told that his sin was known. Yet, even after he was told, he still felt he could get away with it. He refused to repent. He lived on in his deception, rejecting chance after chance.

"I tell you, Nay: but, except ye repent, ye shall all likewise perish" (Lu.13:3, 5).

"Repent ye therefore, and be converted, that your sins may be blotted out, when the times of refreshing shall come from the presence of the Lord" (Ac.3:19).

"Repent therefore of this thy wickedness, and pray God, if perhaps the thought of thine heart may be forgiven thee" (Ac.8:22).

4 (14:21) **Judas—Denial—Betrayal**: Jesus gave Judas a last warning. He warned Judas of the terrible judgment that was to come. Jesus knew the destiny of the sinner, the terrible fate that awaited him. It would be better never to have been born than to deny and betray Christ.

Thought 1. Note the grace of God in warning the sinner of judgment.

(1) The sinner is told in *advance*, before judgment ever comes or is ever pronounced. Judas was told. The sinner can still repent when he *first* hears about judgment. He can still be saved as long as he is living. It is God's grace that warns him of the consequences of his sin, of coming judgment.

(2) The sinner is never compelled to repent of his denial or betrayal of Christ. Judas was not forced to turn from his evil; neither is any other sinner. It is God's grace that respects our will and desires. God loves and cares, warns and speaks frankly, but He never forces obedience.

"Woe unto the world because of offences! for it must needs be that offences come; but woe to that man by whom the offence cometh! Wherefore if thy hand or thy foot offend thee, cut them off, and cast them from thee: it is better for thee to enter into life halt or maimed, rather than having two hands or two feet to be cast into everlasting fire. And if thine eye offend thee, pluck it out, and cast it from thee: it is better for thee to enter into life with one eye, rather than having two eyes to be cast into hell fire" (Mt.18:7-9).

"For the wages of sin is death; but the gift of God is eternal life through Jesus Christ our Lord" (Ro.6:23).

"How shall we escape, if we neglect so great salvation; which at the first began to be spoken by the Lord, and was confirmed unto us by them that heard him" (He.2:3).

"And as it is appointed unto men once to die, but after this the judgment" (He.9:27).

"The soul that sinneth, it shall die" (Eze.18:20).

Outline	Scripture	Scripture	Outline
	E. Jesus' Institution of the Lord's Supper, 14:22-26 *(Mt. 26:26-30; Lu. 22:7-20; Jn. 13:1-30)*	drank of it. 24 And he said unto them, This is my blood of the new testament, which is shed for many.	b. He gave it & they drank it c. He identified the cup as His blood which was to be poured out for many
1. The first act: Jesus took the bread a. He took & gave thanks b. He broke & gave it, identifying the bread as His body	22 And as they did eat, Jesus took bread, and blessed, and brake it, and gave to them, and said, Take, eat: this is my body.	25 Verily I say unto you, I will drink no more of the fruit of the vine, until that day that I drink it new in the kingdom of God.	**3. The third act: Jesus revealed the hope of a glorious kingdom, the Kingdom of God**
2. The second act: Jesus took the cup a. He took & gave thanks	23 And he took the cup, and when he had given thanks, he gave it to them: and they all	26 And when they had sung an hymn, they went out into the mount of Olives.	**4. The fourth act: Jesus & His disciples sang a hymn**

DIVISION IX

THE SON OF GOD'S PASSION MINISTRY: JESUS' SUPREME SACRIFICE—REJECTED AND CRUCIFIED, 14:1-15:47

E. Jesus' Institution of the Lord's Supper, 14:22-26

(14:22-26) **Introduction**: so much happened in the Upper Room. John is the only gospel writer to cover the Upper Room in great detail. He devotes five whole chapters to the event. In contrast, Mark covers only two events of the Upper Room, and both of these are given in only brief detail. Mark concentrates upon Judas' betrayal and the Lord's Supper. In five fully packed verses, he shares what Jesus did to institute the Lord's Supper.

1. The first act: Jesus took the bread (v.22).
2. The second act: Jesus took the cup (vv.23-24).
3. The third act: Jesus revealed the hope of a glorious kingdom, the Kingdom of God (v.25).
4. The fourth act: Jesus and His disciples sang a hymn (v.26).

1 (14:22) **Lord's Supper—Bread**: the first act of the Lord's Supper involves bread. Note that Jesus did four things with the bread.

a. Jesus took the bread into His hands. This symbolized that His death was a voluntary act. His destiny was in His hands. He did not have to die, but He willingly died.

> **"As the Father knoweth me, even so know I the Father: and I lay down my life for the sheep....Therefore doth my Father love me, because I lay down my life, that I might take it again. No man taketh it from me, but I lay it down of myself. I have power to lay it down, and I have power to take it again. This commandment have I received of my Father" (Jn.10:15, 17-18).**

b. Jesus gave thanks. He thanked God for *deliverance and the provision and assurance of life.*

c. Jesus broke the bread. This symbolized that His body was to be broken, that is, sacrificed as a victim for man's deliverance (Is.53:5). This act was so significant that the early church sometimes called the Lord's Supper simply *the breaking of bread* (Ac.2:42; 1 Co.10:16). Under the Old Testament the broken bread pictured the sufferings of the Israelites. Now, under the New Testament, the bread was to picture the broken body of Christ (1 Co.11:24).

> **"But he was wounded for our transgressions, he was bruised for our iniquities: the chastisement of our peace was upon him; and with his stripes we are healed" (Is.53:5).**

d. Jesus gave the bread to the disciples to eat. The words "Take, eat: this is my body," mean that a man is to take and receive Christ into his life. The moment a man takes and receives Christ is the moment of redemption. It is that moment of redemption that is to be remembered in this ordinance (see DEEPER STUDY # 2—Mt.26:26; note—Jn.6:52-58).

> **"This is the bread which cometh down from heaven, that a man may eat thereof, and not die. I am the living bread which came down from heaven: if any man eat of this bread, he shall live for ever: and the bread that I will give is my flesh, which I will give for the life of the world" (Jn.6:50-51).**

2 (14:23-24) **Lord's Supper—Cup, The**: the second act of the Lord's Supper involves the cup. Jesus did four things with the cup.

a. He took the cup into His hands. Again, Jesus was teaching that His death was voluntary. He held His own life in His hands. His life was not being taken from Him; He was laying it down (see Jn.10:11, 17-18).

b. He gave thanks. He thanked God for deliverance through sacrifice.

c. He gave the cup and they all drank of it. Jesus was again saying that He must become a part of man's very being if man wishes deliverance. Note the word *gave* (edoken) is in the Greek aorist tense. This means Christ gave the cup *once-for-all.* He died once and only once (Ro.6:10), and man partakes of His death once and only once (Ro.6:6).

> **"Knowing this, that our old man is crucified with him, that the body of sin might be destroyed, that henceforth we should not serve sin" (Ro.6:6).**
> **"For in that he died, he died unto sin once: but in that he liveth, he liveth unto God" (Ro.6:10).**

d. He identified the cup as His blood of the new testament. He simply meant that His blood established a new covenant with God. His blood allowed a new relationship between God and man. Note the Lord's exact words.

1) "This is my blood." His blood, which was shed from His body, was to become the sign, the symbol of the new covenant. His blood was to take the place of the sacrifice of animals.
2) "The new testament." His blood, the sacrifice of His life, established a new testament, a new covenant between God and man (see Heb.9:11-15). Faith in His blood, His sacrifice is the way man is now to approach God. Before, under the Old Testament, a man who wanted a right relationship with God approached God through the sacrifice of the animal's blood. The Old Testament believer believed that God accepted him because of the sacrifice of the animal. Now, under the New Testament, the believer believes that God accepts him because of the sacrifice of Christ. This is what Jesus said: "This is my blood of the new testament, which is shed for many" (Mk.14:24. See DEEPER STUDY # 4—Mt.26:28; note—Heb.9:18-22.) A man's sins are forgiven and he becomes acceptable to God by believing that Christ's blood was shed for him.

"In whom we have redemption through his blood, the forgiveness of sins, according to the riches of his grace" (Ep.1:7).

"But if we walk in the light, as he is in the light, we have fellowship one with another, and the blood of Jesus Christ his Son cleanseth us from all sin" (1 Jn.1:7).

"My little children, these things write I unto you, that ye sin not. And if any man sin, we have an advocate with the Father, Jesus Christ the righteous: and he is the propitiation for our sins: and not for ours only, but also for the sins of the whole world" (1 Jn.2:1-2).

The point is this: a man must receive what Christ has done for him. He must drink, partake, absorb, assimilate Christ's blood into his life. That is, a man must believe and trust the death of Christ to forgive his sins. He must allow Christ's death to become the very nourishment, the innermost part and energy, the very flow of his life (see DEEPER STUDY # 3—Mt.26:27-28).

"Whoso eateth my flesh, and drinketh my blood, hath eternal life; and I will raise him up at the last day. For my flesh is meat indeed, and my blood is drink indeed. He that eateth my flesh, and drinketh my blood, dwelleth in me, and I in him. As the living Father hath sent me, and I live by the Father: so he that eateth me, even he shall live by me. This is that bread which came down from heaven: not as your fathers did eat manna, and are dead: he that eateth of this bread shall live for ever" (Jn.6:54-58).

3 (14:25) **Promises—Great Marriage Feast of Christ**: the third act was the giving of two great promises.

⇒ There was the promise of a glorious kingdom (see DEEPER STUDY # 3—Mt.19:23-24).
⇒ There was the promise of a glorious celebration (see outline and notes—Mt.22:1-14 for discussion).

Both promises were due to the body and blood of Christ, and both promises were given to the person who partakes of the body and blood of Christ.

Jesus promised a day when all genuine believers would sit down with Him in the Kingdom of God. They would sit down at the great marriage feast of the Lamb. This is the promise of perfection, of living forever in the new heavens and earth, of sitting with Christ in the glorious Kingdom of God which is to be established in the future.

"The Spirit itself beareth witness with our spirit, that we are the children of God: and if children, then heirs; heirs of God, and joint-heirs with Christ; if so be that we suffer with him, that we may be also glorified together" (Ro.8:16-17).

"When Christ, who is our life, shall appear, then shall ye also appear with him in glory" (Col.3:4).

"For our light affliction, which is but for a moment, worketh for us a far more exceeding and eternal weight of glory" (2 Co.4:17).

"For so an entrance shall be ministered unto you abundantly into the everlasting kingdom of our Lord and Saviour Jesus Christ" (2 Pe.1:11).

4 (14:26) **Lord's Supper—Singing**: the fourth act of the Lord's Supper involved the singing of a hymn. Despite the sorrow, perplexity, and uncertainty of what lay ahead, they sang a hymn. They sang the hymn in celebration of the great *hope* which God gives of *deliverance and salvation.*

"These things have I spoken unto you, that my joy might remain in you, and that your joy might be full" (Jn.15:11).

"Rejoice in the Lord alway: and again I say, Rejoice" (Ph.4:4).

"As sorrowful, yet alway rejoicing; as poor, yet making many rich; as having nothing, and yet possessing all things" (2 Co.6:10).

	F. Jesus' Prediction of Peter's Denial: How Jesus Treats Failure, 14:27-31 *(Mt. 26:31-35; Lu. 22:31-34; Jn. 13:36-38)*	29 But Peter said unto him, Although all shall be offended, yet will not I.	**3. Jesus tried to get men to face their failures** a. Peter's verbal loyalty
		30 And Jesus saith unto him, Verily I say unto thee, That this day, even in this night, before the cock crow twice, thou shalt deny me thrice.	b. Jesus' appeal for conviction
1. Jesus showed tenderness in the face of weakness & failure*DS1*	27 And Jesus saith unto them, All ye shall be offended because of me this night: for it is written, I will smite the shepherd, and the sheep shall be scattered.	31 But he spake the more vehemently, If I should die with thee, I will not deny thee in any wise. Likewise also said they all.	**4. Jesus provoked men to exaggerate their failure: Peter's flaming self-confidence**
2. Jesus encouraged returning to Him after failure	28 But after that I am risen, I will go before you into Galilee.		

DIVISION IX

THE SON OF GOD'S PASSION MINISTRY: JESUS' SUPREME SACRIFICE—REJECTED AND CRUCIFIED, 14:1-15:47

F. Jesus' Prediction of Peter's Denial: How Jesus Treats Failure, 14:27-31

(14:27-31) **Introduction—Man, Weakness of—Flesh**: men are weak and they fail. There is one basic reason for failure conveyed by Scripture: men are not perfect. By nature, that is, by thought, act and being, men come short.

⇒ Their thoughts come short: their thoughts are imperfect, incomplete, never absolute nor all-embracing.
⇒ Their acts come short: their acts are imperfect, incomplete, never all that they can be, not in an absolute sense.
⇒ Their beings come short: their beings are imperfect, incomplete, corruptible and dying.

Men are weak; they do fail. They are short of perfection by nature. Scripture expresses the same thought another way. Men are flesh, beings with a nature that is basically driven by self-interest and raw urges. Men desire to please and pamper their flesh and will, body and mind. They seek to please and pamper...

- their flesh through comfort and ease, pleasure and excitement, stimulation and feelings, recognition and fame.
- their will through power and conquest, achievement and position, knowledge and development.

Note, it is not the urges and the goals that are wrong. It is man who is wrong. The urges within men are good and healthy when they are put in their proper place, that is, when they are used to the glory of God and for the benefit of man as Scripture dictates. When a man acts for the glory of God and the welfare of others, there is nothing wrong...

- with comfort and ease
- with pleasure and excitement
- with stimulation and feelings
- with recognition and fame

For example, God expects His people to possess power and to conquer (spiritually, mentally, and physically). He expects us to achieve and secure better positions, to gain more knowledge and more development, ever increasing and growing. The problem arises in that man is not able to control his flesh and will, body and mind. Too often he centers upon self, misusing and depriving other people to fulfill his own urges. His misusing and depriving other people can range all the way from minor deception to destroying life.

All this is what lies behind the present passage. Man has a weak and fallen nature that causes him to be imperfect and incomplete, corruptible and dying. Man's flesh is weak and failing; therefore, man must receive a new nature from God, a supernatural nature. He cannot trust in the arm of the flesh; he must trust in the arm of God. Man must receive a *God-given resurrected power* (nature) if he is to live a conquering and fulfilled life, a life that pleases God and makes him acceptable to God.

Peter and the disciples needed to learn this. They trusted their own flesh and their own strength. Therefore, they were destined to fail despite a determination that was as strong as it could be. Jesus needed to prepare them. They were to fail and fall away at His death because of the weakness of their flesh. But He was to arise. They would need to know they were not rejected because they had fallen away. And they would need to receive the power of the resurrection through the presence of the Holy Spirit so that they could conquer and not fail in the future.

1. Jesus showed tenderness in the face of weakness and failure (v.27).
2. Jesus encouraged returning to Him after failure (v.28).
3. Jesus tried to get men to face their failures (vv.29-30).
4. Jesus provoked men to exaggerate their failure: Peter's flaming self-confidence (v.31).

1 (14:27) **Failure—Jesus Christ, Care; Tenderness—Weakness**: Jesus showed tenderness in the face of weakness and failure. Jesus knew what was coming. "All ye shall be offended [stumble, fall] because of me this night." He was referring to His death. Note three things.

a. The word *offend* (skandalizo) means to stumble, to fall. Jesus saw their *scattering* as a sin, a stumbling, a falling away from Him.

b. Jesus clearly stated that God was behind His death. The Scripture says, "I [God] will smite the shepherd" (Zec.13:7). There was a Godly purpose for Jesus' dying, an eternal purpose.

"Him, being delivered by the determinate counsel and foreknowledge of God, ye have taken, and by wicked hands have crucified and slain: whom God hath raised up, having loosed the pains of death: because it was not possible that he should be holden of it" (Ac.2:23-24).

c. Jesus said that the disciples would tragically forsake Him. Not a single one would stand up for Him. The threat of the world and the weakness of their flesh would be too much to overcome. They would fail.

Note that Jesus *predicted* their failure. In so doing, He helped them in several ways.
⇒ He taught them the weakness and failure of human flesh.
⇒ He laid the groundwork of the resurrection, the basis for receiving the new power (nature) of God, the presence of the Holy Spirit.
⇒ Their remembering His words would stir them to remember His tenderness and care, and it would draw them back to Him more quickly and easily.
⇒ Their remembering His words would stir faith in Him as the Son of God who is omniscient, knowing all things.
⇒ Their faith would be strengthened by understanding how the Old Testament prophecy was fulfilled in Jesus and them: "I will smite the shepherd, and the sheep shall be scattered."

DEEPER STUDY # 1
(14:27) **Prophetic Reference**: see Zec.13:7.

2 (14:28) **Forgiveness—Repentance—Jesus Christ, Care**: Jesus encouraged returning to Him after failure. Jesus had been blunt: they would fall. But now He was just as clear. He would go before them into Galilee. Their failure, even in so crucial an hour, would not cause Him to reject them. Despite their failure, they could return to Him, and there would be a glorious reunion.

Note: Jesus again predicted His resurrection. It was His resurrection that made both *repentance* and the glorious *reunion* possible.

Thought 1. No matter how terrible the failure, we can repent and return to Christ and rest assured of being a part of the glorious reunion in the great day of His return.

"Repent therefore of this thy wickedness, and pray God, if perhaps the thought of thine heart may be forgiven thee" (Ac.8:22).

"If we confess our sins, he is faithful and just to forgive us our sins, and to cleanse us from all unrighteousness" (1 Jn.1:9).

"He that covereth his sins shall not prosper: but whoso confesseth and forsaketh them shall have mercy" (Pr.28:13).

3 (14:29-30) **Self-Confidence—Flesh, Weakness of**: Jesus tried to get men to face their weaknesses and failures. Only when man faces his weaknesses and failures will he work to correct them. This is the point of these two verses (and also the next three verses). Peter strongly declared his loyalty. So Jesus spelled out in detail that Peter would not only fall one time, but he would fall three times—and all three times would be in the same night. Note several points.

a. Peter was sincere and full of fervor for the Lord. He was thoroughly convinced he would not fall and fail his Lord.

b. Peter did not know the weakness of the flesh, not in great trial.

c. Peter looked at the weaknesses and failures of others, not at his own: "Although *all* shall be offended, yet will not I." He could see how others could perhaps fall, but not himself. He loved and cared for the Lord too much.

d. Peter boasted confidence in self, in his own natural strength. *As with all men*, his natural strength failed. The need for the Lord's strength, for the presence of the Holy Spirit, to conquer self was the great lesson Peter had to learn. Very simply, he and the others had to learn to trust the strength of Jesus and not their own flesh, not if they wished to please God and be acceptable to Him.

Thought 1. The cock's crowing was probably mentioned to trigger the warning about the weakness of the flesh in the mind of Peter and the others. For any who have the privilege of hearing the rooster crow, it is a good trigger to remind them of the weakness of their own flesh and the great need to walk with the Spirit of God.

"Wherefore let him that thinketh he standeth take heed lest he fall" (1 Co.10:12).

"He that trusteth in his own heart is a fool: but whoso walketh wisely, he shall be delivered" (Pr.28:26).

4 (14:31) **Self-Confidence—Flesh, Weakness of**: Jesus provoked men to exaggerate their failure. The message about the weakness of human flesh provoked Peter. Jesus had to get the point across, so He stressed the fact (v.30). But note Peter's refusal to accept the truth. In flaming self-confidence, he declared that he would not deny Jesus, even if he had to die for Him. Peter's over-confidence was caused by three things.

a. Peter's over-confidence was caused by being blind to the cross (Mt.26:34). Peter just did not see the cross. It was the image of Jesus' hanging upon the cross that was going to cause Peter to deny Him. Jesus had told Peter all about the cross, but he had refused to believe it (see notes—Mt.17:22; 18:1-2). The fact that human flesh was so sinful, so depraved that God would have to crucify the flesh was just too much to grasp (see outline, notes, and DEEPER STUDY # 1—Lu.9:23; notes—Ro.6:6-13; Gal.2:20; 5:24; 6:14. See Ro.6:2; Col.3:3.)

b. Peter's over-confidence was caused by not knowing himself, his own personal weaknesses, the weaknesses of his human flesh. Peter's self-image was strong. He saw himself above *serious* sin and failure. He asserted with all the confidence in the world that he would die for Jesus before denying Him.

Thought 1. Note several things.
(1) Peter was a strong believer, one of the strongest.
(2) Peter really failed to understand himself, his flesh. The one sin that a believer should not commit is to deny Jesus. To die for Jesus rather than to deny Him is the one thing a genuine believer would be expected to do.
(3) Peter believed strongly that he, his flesh, was above serious sin (see Ro.3:9f; 7:8, 14-18; Ga.5:19f).
(4) Peter failed not once, but three times, and all three times were in the same night with Christ right off to his side (Lu.22:61).

c. Peter's over-confidence was caused by contradicting Jesus instead of listening to Him—caused by not listening to the Word of Jesus, to what Jesus was saying. Jesus was warning the disciples about the deceitfulness and weakness of the human heart. Peter and the rest just refused to accept the fact. They denied personal weaknesses; they rejected the Word of Jesus.

Thought 1. Note that all the disciples declared their loyalty, boasting confidence in their flesh. Peter was only the spokesman for the group.

"Thus saith the LORD; Cursed be the man that trusteth in man, and maketh flesh his arm, and whose heart departeth from the LORD" (Je.17:5).

"Therefore by the deeds of the law there shall no flesh be justified in his sight: for by the law is the knowledge of sin" (Ro.3:20).

"In me [that is, in my flesh] dwelleth no good thing" (Ro.7:18).

"They that are in the flesh cannot please God" (Ro.8:8).

"It is the spirit that quickeneth; the flesh profiteth nothing" (Jn.6:63).

"Knowing that a man is not justified by the works of the law, but the faith of Jesus Christ, even we have believed in Jesus Christ, that we might be justified by the faith of Christ, and not by the works of the law: for by the works of the law shall no flesh be justified" (Ga.2:16).

Thought 2. We must listen and keep the Word of Jesus, do just what He said. It is when we fail to listen to the Words of Jesus, to the Holy Scriptures, that we fall.

⇒ Keeping the Words of Jesus assures eternal life.

"It is the spirit that quickeneth; the flesh profiteth nothing: the words that I speak unto you, they are spirit, and they are life" (Jn.6:63).

"Then Simon Peter answered him, Lord, to whom shall we go? thou hast the words of eternal life" (Jn.6:68).

"Verily, verily, I say unto you, If a man keep my saying, he shall never see death" (Jn.8:51).

⇒ Keeping the Words of Jesus assures the presence of the Holy Spirit.

"If ye love me, keep my commandments. And I will pray the Father, and he shall give you another Comforter, that he may abide with you for ever" (Jn.14:15-16).

⇒ Keeping the Words of Jesus assures fellowship with God and Christ.

"Jesus answered and said unto him, If a man love me, he will keep my words: and my Father will love him, and we will come unto him, and make our abode with him" (Jn.14:23).

⇒ Keeping the Words of Jesus assures our security, that we know Him.

"And hereby we do know that we know him, if we keep his commandments" (1 Jn.2:3).

⇒ Failing to keep the Words of Jesus dooms us to judgment.

"He that rejecteth me, and receiveth not my words, hath one that judgeth him: the word that I have spoken, the same shall judge him in the last day" (Jn.12:48).

	G. Jesus in the Garden of Gethsemane: Bearing the Weight of Great Trial, 14:32-42 *(Mt. 26:36-46; Lu. 22:39-46; Jn. 18:1; He. 5:7-8; 12:3-4)*	from me: nevertheless not what I will, but what thou wilt. 37 And he cometh, and findeth them sleeping, and saith unto Peter, Simon, sleepest thou? couldest not thou watch one hour?	**4. Picture 4: His disappointment in His friends**
1. Picture 1: His great need for prayer & for friends to be at His side[DS1]	32 And they came to a place which was named Gethsemane: and he saith to his disciples, Sit ye here, while I shall pray.	38 Watch ye and pray, lest ye enter into temptation. The spirit truly is ready, but the flesh is weak.	**5. Picture 5: His continuing ministry—even under trial**
2. Picture 2: His heavy agony & pressure	33 And he taketh with him Peter and James and John, and began to be sore amazed, and to be very heavy;	39 And again he went away, and prayed, and spake the same words. 40 And when he returned, he found them asleep again, (for their eyes were heavy,) neither wist they what to answer him.	**6. Picture 6: His perseverance in prayer—despite no answer from God** **7. Picture 7: His continued disappointment in friends**
3. Picture 3: His desperate search for relief	34 And saith unto them, My soul is exceeding sorrowful unto death: tarry ye here, and watch.		
a. He got all alone: Prostrated Himself b. He prayed for the cup of the hour, the cross, to pass from Him 1) For the cup to be taken away[DS2] 2) For God's will to be done	35 And he went forward a little, and fell on the ground, and prayed that, if it were possible, the hour might pass from him. 36 And he said, Abba, Father, all things are possible unto thee; take away this cup	41 And he cometh the third time, and saith unto them, Sleep on now, and take your rest: it is enough, the hour is come; behold, the Son of man is betrayed into the hands of sinners. 42 Rise up, let us go; lo, he that betrayeth me is at hand.	**8. Picture 8: His relief of soul & spiritual strength** **9. Picture 9: His acceptance of God's chosen path**

DIVISION IX

THE SON OF GOD'S PASSION MINISTRY: JESUS' SUPREME SACRIFICE—REJECTED AND CRUCIFIED, 14:1-15:47

G. Jesus in the Garden of Gethsemane: Bearing the Weight of Great Trial, 14:32-42

(14:32-42) **Introduction**: no man could ever understand the depth of sorrow and agony experienced by Jesus in the Garden of Gethsemane. His experience is the picture of a terrifying struggle—a struggle against sin and the awful judgment which is to fall upon sin. It is a picture which should cause every man to bow in humble adoration and worship of the Lord Jesus, for Jesus bore the sorrow and agony of sin for every man. He bore the punishment of sin for all.

1. Picture 1: His great need for prayer and for friends to be at His side (v.32).
2. Picture 2: His heavy agony and pressure (vv.33-34).
3. Picture 3: His desperate search for relief (vv.35-36).
4. Picture 4: His disappointment in His friends (v.37).
5. Picture 5: His continuing ministry—even under trial (v.38).
6. Picture 6: His perseverance in prayer—despite no answer from God (v.39).
7. Picture 7: His continued disappointment in friends (v.40).
8. Picture 8: His relief of soul and spiritual strength (v.41).
9. Picture 9: His acceptance of God's chosen path (v.42).

[1] (14:32) **Jesus Christ, Prayer Life—Prayer, Need for**: the first picture was the Lord's great need for prayer and for friends to be at His side. Gethsemane was apparently a beautiful garden just outside the city of Jerusalem. Gardens were not allowed behind the walls within the city because of the lack of space. Therefore, the wealthy secured beautiful spots right outside the walls and built their gardens. It was Jesus' habit to pray in Gethsemane. Judas knew exactly where to go (v.43). However, this time Jesus' need was much greater than before. He was facing the cross, unbelievable human suffering, and final separation from God (see notes—Mt.20:19). He needed not only prayer, He needed the very presence and strengthening of God, and He needed the presence and prayer of His closest companions. Note what He did.

a. He said to His disciples, "Sit ye here, while I shall pray." His words suggested that they too should begin to pray, for great trials were coming, and the billows of temptation would roll in upon them ever so heavily.

b. Taking Peter, James, and John, He walked farther into the garden to be more alone with these three. They were the closest to Him. And in His darkest hour, He especially needed their presence and prayer support. But note: His need was not to talk the problem over with them. He just needed their presence and prayer support *while* He talked and shared with God. He knew who had the true answer to His need. (See vv.34, 37-38, 40-41.)

Thought 1. Every believer should have his place for prayer, and it should be his habit to visit it, daily approaching the throne of God.

Thought 2. What a lesson! Too many talk their problems over with friends instead of with God. God is the One who holds the true answer to our problems. The proper order between friends and God is to seek God for the answer and friends for their prayer support.

> **"Seek the LORD and his strength, seek his face continually" (1 Chr.16:11).**
> **"Ask, and it shall be given you; seek, and ye shall find; knock, and it shall be opened unto you" (Mt.7:7).**
> **"And he spake a parable unto them to this end, that men ought always to pray, and not to faint" (Lu.18:1).**
> **"Is any among you afflicted? let him pray. Is any merry? let him sing psalms" (Js.5:13).**

DEEPER STUDY # 1
(14:32) **Gethsemane**: see DEEPER STUDY # 1—Mt.26:36.

2 (14:33-34) **Jesus Christ, Death—Gethsemane**: the second picture was the Lord's heavy agony and pressure. He "began" to experience extreme agony and pressure beyond imagination.

The words *sore amazed* (ekthambeisthai) are very strong words in the Greek. The words mean utter and extreme fright, horror, terror, bewilderment, amazement. Jesus was staggering under the "horror of great darkness," something like what fell upon Abraham, except Jesus' horror was much, much worse (Ge.15:12).

The words *very heavy* (ademonein) are expressive, perhaps as expressive as words can be. The words mean to be heavy, troubled, distressed—extremely so. However, when looking at the root of the word (ademos), it means much more. It means *being not at home*, *homeless*, *out of one's usual surroundings*. The meaning is probably twofold.

1. Jesus suffered beyond all imagination. Imagine this: whatever suffering and whatever pain were involved in the *Perfect and Ideal Man's* bearing all the sins of the world and the judgment for those sins—all of it fell upon Jesus. No one could bear any of the suffering with Jesus. He had to bear it all alone. Upon the cross He had to "*become* sin for us" (2 Co.5:21). In Gethsemane He was facing the loneliness of bearing all for us. He was alone, and He experienced all the terrible emotions and distress of the solitary, the lonely, the *homeless*.

2. Jesus had to be separated from God for the first time in His eternal existence. His *home*, His place, His very being was with God throughout all eternity. In Gethsemane Jesus was facing the separation from God which He was shortly to experience upon the cross. He was to be *cut off from God*, left all alone to bear the sins and judgment of men. He again felt the terrible emotions and distress of being left all alone, cut off from God, of being left *homeless*.

The terror (amazement) and heaviness were so painful they almost killed Him. And He shared this fact with the disciples: "My soul is exceeding sorrowful unto *death*." The sorrow and weight were life-threatening. The pressure was swelling up in Him to such a degree it was about to explode. He began to sweat great drops of blood (Lu.22:44). God had to send an angel to save His life and to strengthen Him. (See DEEPER STUDY # 2, *Jesus Christ, Suffering*—Mt.26:37-38.)

Note that Jesus told the three disciples to "watch," that is, to be praying. They knew a critical hour was at hand. They felt the pressure in the very atmosphere, and He had just shared His own great need. He needed and wanted their presence and prayer support.

> **"Reproach hath broken my heart; and I am full of heaviness: and I looked for some to take pity, but there was none; and for comforters, but I found none" (Ps.69:20).**
> **"And being in an agony he prayed more earnestly: and his sweat was as it were great drops of blood falling down to the ground" (Lu.22:44).**
> **"Greater love hath no man than this, that a man lay down his life for his friends" (Jn.15:13).**

3 (14:35-36) **Jesus Christ, Death**: the third picture was the Lord's desperate search for relief. In confronting the cross (death), Jesus did all He could: He turned to God. Five things are said in these two verses.

a. Jesus got all alone and prostrated Himself before God. Luke says He withdrew "about a stone's cast" from the three apostles. Two significant points. (1) He needed to be alone with God. He was desperate. (2) He fell on His face. The pressure and weight were unbearable.

b. Jesus prayed that the hour of the cross "might pass from Him." The term "the hour" or "My hour" is a constant symbol of His death (see note—Jn.12:23-24. See Mt.26:18, 45; Jn.7:6, 8, 30; 8:20; 12:27, 33; 13:1; 17:1.) He was definitely praying for God to choose another way to secure the redemption of the world.

c. Jesus prayed "Abba, Father." He addressed God as "Father." This was what a small child called his father from day to day. It was the address of a child's love and dependency. The child knew that His father would hear and turn to him when he called "Father." But note also the words, "*O my* Father." Jesus was broken, weighed down, fallen on His face, prostrated on the ground. In desperation He cried out "*O my* Father." Just like a child, He cried out to *His Father* in childlike brokenness and dependency, knowing that His Father would hear and turn to help Him.

d. Jesus said, "All things are possible unto thee [God]." Why then did God not choose another way? As simply stated as possible...

- God does only what He has willed to do; and He wills only what His love and righteousness tell Him to will. God's love and righteousness led Him to demonstrate His love and righteousness by giving His Son to die for the sins of men. The cross demonstrated in the very best way possible that "God so loved the world that He gave His only begotten Son" to bear the judgment of sin for every man. Therefore, God's will was subject to His love and righteousness.

In Gethsemane Jesus knew this, but He struggled in His flesh, in His humanity, for God to choose another way. The pressure of it all, of being cut off from His Father, was just too heavy. He cried out in desperation for God to deliver Him from the terrible load. He knew that God would not, yet He cried for God to do it; He cried *expressing* His great dependence and love for God. He loved His Father so much, He did not want to be separated from Him. He wanted His Father to know that, so He pleaded for deliverance by another way, *expressing* His love and dependence, knowing that God had determined the path of the cross. He was willing to bear it, to subject Himself to God's eternal will and love and righteousness.

e. Jesus asked God to remove the cup from Him. (See DEEPER STUDY # 4, Cup—Mt.26:39. Also see DEEPER STUDY #2—Mk 14:36; DEEPER STUDY # 1—Mt.27:26-44; see Mt.20:19.) The human nature and will of Jesus are clearly seen in this request. He was as much man as any man is. Therefore, He begged God to choose another way other than the cup if possible. The experience of being separated from God upon the cross was too much to bear.

f. The divine nature and will of Jesus are also clearly seen in this request. Note the Lord's words: "Let this cup pass from me: nevertheless...." The first act, the first impulse and struggle and movement of His will had come from His flesh: to escape the cup of separation from God. But immediately, the second act, the second impulse and struggle and movement of His will came from His divine nature: to do not as He willed, but as God willed.

Thought 1. Christ's surrender to do God's perfect will in the Garden of Gethsemane was critical.

⇒ It was through His surrender that He was made perfect and stood before God as the Ideal, Perfect Man.

⇒ It was through His surrender to be the Ideal, Perfect Man that His righteousness was able to stand for every man.

⇒ It was through His surrender to be the Ideal, Perfect Man that He was able to bear the cup of God's wrath against sin *for every man.*

⇒ It was through His surrender to be the Ideal, Perfect Man that His sacrifice and sufferings were able to stand for every man.

"But we see Jesus, who was made a little lower than the angels for the suffering of death, crowned with glory and honor; that he by the grace of God should taste death for every man. For it became him, for whom are all things, and by whom are all things, in bringing many sons unto glory, to make the captain of their salvation perfect through sufferings" (He.2:9-10).

"Though he were a Son, yet learned he obedience by the things which he suffered; and being made perfect, he became the author of eternal salvation unto all them that obey him" (He.5:8-9).

"For he hath made him to be sin for us, who knew no sin; that we might be made the righteousness of God in him" (2 Co.5:21).

DEEPER STUDY # 2

(14:36) **Cup**: Jesus Christ was not fearing nor shrinking from death itself. This is clearly seen in Jn.10:17-18. Death for a cause is not such a great price to pay. Many men have so died—fearlessly and willingly, some perhaps more cruelly than Jesus Himself. Shrinking from betrayal, beatings, humiliation, and death, increased by foreknowledge is not what was happening to Jesus. As stated, some men have faced horrible deaths courageously, even inviting martyrdom for a cause. The Lord knew He was to die from the very beginning, and He had been preparing His disciples for His death (see outlines and notes—Mk.8:31-33; 9:30-32; Mt.16:21-28; 17:22; 20:17-19). It was not just human and physical suffering from which Jesus was shrinking. Such an explanation is totally inadequate in explaining Gethsemane. The great cup or trial Jesus was facing was separation from God (see note, pt.1 and DEEPER STUDY # 2—Mt.26:37-38). He was to be the sacrificial Lamb of God who takes away the sins of the world (Jn.1:29). He was to bear the judgment of God for the sins of the world (see note—Mt.27:46-49; see Is.53:19). Jesus Himself had already spoken of the "cup" when referring to His sacrificial death (see DEEPER STUDY # 2—Mt.20:22-23; DEEPER STUDY # 2—Jn.18:11).

Scripture speaks of the cup in several ways.

1. The cup is called "the cup of the Lord's fury" (Is.51:17).
2. The cup is associated with suffering and God's wrath (see Ps.11:6; Is.51:17; Lu.22:42).
3. The cup is also associated with salvation. Because Jesus drank the cup of suffering and wrath for us, we can "take the cup of salvation and call upon the name of the Lord" (Ps.116:13).

4 (14:37) **Flesh, Weakness of—Dedication, Lack of—Prayer, Weakness in**: the fourth picture was the Lord's disappointment in His friends. The Lord returned to the three disciples and found them asleep.

a. Jesus spoke to all three, but He addressed Peter in particular. Peter was the one who had spoken up just an hour or two earlier declaring that he would stand with Jesus through anything. Yet he was unwilling to stand with Jesus in prayer. Jesus was speaking to Him very bluntly.

b. Jesus did not address Peter by his new name, Peter, but by his old name, Simon. The flesh had gotten the best of Peter, and Jesus was letting Peter know it.

c. Jesus had not asked Peter and the disciples to watch and pray all night. He had asked only for one hour of prayer. This is significant in seeing their failure and weakness.

"For I know that in me (that is, in my flesh,) dwelleth no good thing: for to will is present with me; but how to perform that which is good I find not" (Ro.7:18).

"So then they that are in the flesh cannot please God" (Ro.8:8).

"For the flesh lusteth against the Spirit, and the Spirit against the flesh: and these are contrary the one to the other: so that ye cannot do the things that ye would" (Ga.5:17).

5 (14:38) **Jesus Christ, Work—Ministry**: the fifth picture was the Lord's continuing ministry even under trial. He was pressured so heavily He was at the point of exploding. Yet He was concerned over the needs of the disciples. They were going to face great temptation, and He knew it. He wanted them to know it. They must watch and pray, be prepared. Despite His own need in this hour, He ministered all He could to them, helping them and trying to awaken them to watch and pray as never before.

Thought 1. The believer is to continue to minister even while He is in need or under fire. The believer's life is to be a life of ministry.

"Therefore watch, and remember, that by the space of three years I ceased not to warn every one night and day with tears" (Ac.20:31).

6 (14:39) **Prayer, Perseverance in**: the sixth picture was the Lord's perseverance in prayer, despite no answer from God. Note that Jesus had not yet found relief from God, yet He was not discouraged. He did not turn away from God; He went back, got alone, and sought God again. "And [He even] spoke the same words." He zeroed in on the same request: that the cup might pass from Him. He sought, wrestled, and agonized with God. He persevered, giving every indication that He was not going to quit praying until God heard and met His need.

"Ask, and it shall be given you; seek, and ye shall find; knock, and it shall be opened unto you" (Mt.7:7).

"Continue in prayer, and watch in the same with thanksgiving" (Col.4:2).

"Submit yourselves therefore to God. Resist the devil, and he will flee from you. Draw nigh to God, and he will draw nigh to you" (Js.4:7-8).

7 (14:40) **Flesh, Weakness of—Dedication, Lack of**: the seventh picture was the Lord's continued disappointment in His friends. Some commentators excuse the disciples, saying their bodies and eyes were so heavy with the pressure of the hour, they just could not stay awake. But their failure to watch and pray was just inexcusable and greatly disappointing to the Lord. Even after a rebuke (v.37), they would not struggle to stand with the Lord. They were guilty; they knew not "what to answer Him."

"Blessed are those servants, whom the lord when he cometh shall find watching: verily I say unto you, that he shall gird himself, and make them to sit down to meat, and will come forth and serve them" (Lu.12:37).

"Ye are all the children of light, and the children of the day: we are not of the night, nor of darkness. Therefore let us not sleep, as do others; but let us watch and be sober" (1 Th.5:5-6).

"Be sober, be vigilant; because your adversary the devil, as a roaring lion, walketh about, seeking whom he may devour" (1 Pe.5:8).

"O LORD, I know that the way of man is not in himself: it is not in man that walketh to direct his steps" (Je.10:23).

8 (14:41) **Jesus Christ, Submission**: the eighth picture was the Lord's relief of soul and spiritual strength. There were His words, the evidence of great release: "Sleep on now, and take your *rest*." Jesus' agony, His desperate need for friends to *watch* with Him, was now gone (vv.34, 38). God had given Him great relief of soul. The very tone of His words to His disciples revealed a calmness of spirit, a peace of mind, a relief of the physical and emotional strain that was about to kill Him. God had met His need in a most wonderful way.

"In the day when I cried thou answeredst me, and strengthenedst me with strength in my soul" (Ps.138:3).

"And there appeared an angel unto him from heaven, strengthening him" (Lu.22:43).

"Who in the days of his flesh, when he had offered up prayers and supplications with strong crying and tears unto him that was able to save him from death, and was heard in that he feared" (He.5:7; see He.5:7-9).

9 (14:42) **Jesus Christ, Submission**: the ninth picture was the Lord's acceptance of God's chosen path. His words were evidence of great courage: "It is enough, the hour is come; behold, the Son of man is betrayed into the hands of sinners." Note three things.

a. There was no shrinking now, no agony, no desperation. Jesus was relieved and strengthened, ready to face the sufferings necessary to secure the salvation of man.

b. Jesus said He was being "betrayed into the hands of sinners." All those taking part in His death were sinners. His death was the most heinous crime of history, for He, the Son of Man, the Ideal and Perfect Man, was killed by men. But there is more here: He died for the sins of the world. It was every man's sins that caused Him to be crucified. Every sin is an act of rebellion, of simply saying "No" to God (Ro.3:23). Therefore every man is guilty of putting Christ to death. There is a sense in which every sin, every act of rebellion crucifies "the Son of God afresh, and put[s] Him to an open shame" (He.6:6).

c. Jesus' relief of soul and infusion of strength did not come from resigning Himself to death. Rather, He relinquished His will in favor of the Father's will. He deliberately gave up His own will and actively pursued the Father's will. This was the victory He fought to gain in Gethsemane. It should also be said that His submission was voluntary—not forced. He had a choice even up until His death upon the cross. (See note—Mt.26:39.)

> **"I delight to do thy will, O my God: yea, thy law is within my heart" (Ps.40:8).**
>
> **"I can of mine own self do nothing: as I hear, I judge: and my judgment is just; because I seek not mine own will, but the will of the Father which hath sent me" (Jn.5:30).**
>
> **"Who gave himself for our sins, that he might deliver us from this present evil world, according to the will of God and our Father" (Ga.1:4).**
>
> **"And walk in love, as Christ also hath loved us, and hath given himself for us an offering and a sacrifice to God for a sweetsmelling savour" (Ep.5:2).**
>
> **"Then said, I, Lo, I come (in the volume of the book it is written of me,) to do thy will, O God. Above when he said, Sacrifice and offering and burnt offerings and offering for sin thou wouldest not, neither hadst pleasure therein; which are offered by the law; then said he, Lo, I come to do thy will, O God. He taketh away the first, that he may establish the second. By the which will we are sanctified through the offering of the body of Jesus Christ once for all....But this man, after he had offered one sacrifice for sins for ever, sat down on the right hand of God" (He.10:7-10, 12).**

Outline	Scripture	Scripture (cont.)	Outline
	H. Jesus' Arrest: A Study of Human Character, 14:43-52 *(Mt. 26:47-56; Lu. 22:47-53; Jn. 18:3-11)*	on him, and took him. 47 And one of them that stood by drew a sword, and smote a servant of the high priest, and cut off his ear.	**hands on Jesus: Arrested Him** **3. The disciple who was courageous, but mistaken**
1. The fallen disciple who was a traitor a. His tragedy 1) He was one of the disciples 2) He led a crowd against Jesus b. His prearranged sign	43 And immediately, while he yet spake, cometh Judas, one of the twelve, and with him a great multitude with swords and staves, from the chief priests and the scribes and the elders. 44 And he that betrayed him had given them a token, saying, Whomsoever I shall kiss, that same is he; take him, and lead him away safely.	48 And Jesus answered and said unto them, Are ye come out, as against a thief, with swords and with staves to take me? 49 I was daily with you in the temple teaching, and ye took me not: but the scriptures must be fulfilled. 50 And they all forsook him, and fled. 51 And there followed him a certain young man, having	**4. The Lord who showed a striking serenity in the midst of mass confusion** a. His piercing question b. His obedience to Scripture, to God's will **5. The disciples who allowed their faith to crack** **6. The young man who became terror-stricken when confronted**
c. His hypocritical deception **2. The men who misused their**	45 And as soon as he was come, he goeth straightway to him, and saith, Master, Master; and kissed him. 46 And they laid their hands	a linen cloth cast about his naked body; and the young men laid hold on him: 52 And he left the linen cloth, and fled from them naked.	

DIVISION IX

THE SON OF GOD'S PASSION MINISTRY: JESUS' SUPREME SACRIFICE—REJECTED AND CRUCIFIED, 14:1-15:47

H. Jesus' Arrest: A Study of Human Character, 14:43-52

(14:43-52) **Introduction**: Jesus was betrayed, arrested, and deserted within just a few minutes. The event is a dramatic study of human character.

1. The fallen disciple who was a traitor (vv.43-45).
2. The men who misused their hands on Jesus: arrested Him (v.46).
3. The disciple who was courageous, but mistaken (v.47).
4. The Lord who showed a striking serenity in the midst of mass confusion (vv.48-49).
5. The disciples who allowed their faith to crack (v.50).
6. The young man who became terror-stricken when confronted (vv.51-52).

1 (14:43-45) **Deception—Hypocrisy—Betrayal—Forsaking Christ**: the first study concerns the fallen disciple who was a traitor. Note the terrible tragedy. Judas was a professed follower of Jesus; he was actually a disciple, one of the twelve, yet he is seen taking the lead against Jesus. Remember, he had begun his downward fall by stealing just a little at a time; but as with all thieves, he became bolder and began to take more and more. Scripture calls him a thief and a robber (Jn.10:1). He fell so deeply that he was a betrayer, a leader against Jesus.

> **Thought 1.** How many disciples have forsaken Jesus? How many now stand against Him? How many began with *little sins* but are now involved in greater sins?

It was night and already dark, and some of the arresting party would not know Jesus, not well enough to arrest Him in the cover of darkness. So Judas arranged to identify Jesus with a kiss. It was the custom of the day for a disciple to greet his teacher with a slight kiss on the cheek. But note what Judas did: as he approached Jesus, he not only attempted to deceive Jesus, he poured it on. He said, "Master, Master," and kissed Him. The word kiss here is different from the word kiss in verse 44. In verse 44, the word is *philein* which is the respectful kiss of greeting. But in verse 45 when Judas kissed Jesus, the word is *kataphilein*, which is a kiss of intense feelings. Judas was not only portraying hypocritical deception, he was drenching Jesus with deception and soaking himself in hypocrisy. He was standing face to face with Jesus fervently declaring his discipleship, yet at that very moment, he was leading others in their sin against Jesus.

> **Thought 1.** How many approach Christ in church and pour it on? They profess discipleship, yet at the same time, they live in sin and shame. How many feel they are actually getting away with it, actually able to keep the truth from Christ? How foolishly we deceive ourselves and deceive others!

> **"Take heed, brethren, lest there be in any of you an evil heart of unbelief, in departing from the living God" (He.3:12).**
>
> **"[These] shall receive the reward of unrighteousness, as they that count it pleasure to riot [party] in the day time. Spots they are and blemishes, sporting themselves with their own deceivings while they feast with you [the church]; having eyes full of adultery, and that cannot cease**

from sin; beguiling unstable souls: an heart they have exercised with covetous practices; cursed children" (2 Pe.2:13-14).

"The heart is deceitful above all things, and desperately wicked: who can know it? I the LORD search the heart, I try the reins, even to give every man according to his ways, and according to the fruit of his doings. As the partridge sitteth on eggs, and hatcheth them not; so he that getteth riches, and not by right, shall leave them in the midst of his days, and at his end shall be a fool" (Je.17:9-11).

2 (14:46) **Jesus Christ, Response to—Man, Response to Christ**: the second study concerns the men who misused their hands on Jesus. This is a descriptive statement full of application. Note three simple things.

a. The hands laid upon Jesus were the hands of the rude, the abusive, the unconcerned, the neglectful, the violent. When they should have been concerned over Jesus and their own souls, they were rejecting and reacting against Him.

b. Jesus desired men to lay hold of Him in humility and belief, not in some sinful, negative reaction.

c. The hands of men can take hold of Jesus in reaction. They can arrest His messenger and message, and they can sense triumph, but only temporarily. God will always raise up His messengers to carry on the glorious news of salvation, even if the messengers have to be new ones. The triumph will always be the Lord's, and in that glorious day of redemption, He will triumph ultimately. It was this that Judas and his cohorts failed to grasp. It was their rejection of God's Son that led them to misuse their hands on Jesus.

"He was in the world, and the world was made by him, and the world knew him not. He came unto his own, and his own received him not" (Jn.1:10-11).

"For they that dwell at Jerusalem, and their rulers, because they knew him not, nor yet the voices of the prophets which are read every sabbath day, they have fulfilled them in condemning him" (Ac.13:27).

"Father, glorify thy name. Then came there a voice from heaven, saying, I have both glorified it, and will glorify it again" (Jn.12:28).

3 (14:47) **Jesus Christ, Submission—Witnessing—Courage**: the third study concerns the disciple who was courageous but mistaken. This disciple was a true disciple, a true follower of the Lord. As soon as Jesus was opposed, the disciple jumped to the Lord's defense. He was ready and prepared to stand with his Lord. But note: the way he went about defending Jesus was wrong. His courage was commendable, but his method was mistaken. He tried to attack and to defeat (kill) the enemy of Jesus with physical force. Physical force was not the way of Jesus. Jesus would have His attackers know His faith and trust, His gentleness and love, His submission and willingness to do the will of God. This is always the way into the presence of God.

Thought 1. Courage is needed—but spiritual courage, not physical courage. The believer must be courageous and zealous in his spirit, standing with Christ proclaiming the way of faith and trust, gentleness and love, submission and a willingness to do God's will.

"But sanctify the Lord God in your hearts: and be ready always to give an answer to every man that asketh you a reason of the hope that is in you with meekness and fear" (1 Pe.3:15).

"Not by might, nor by power, but by my spirit, saith the LORD of hosts" (Zec.4:6).

"As many as I love, I rebuke and chasten: be zealous therefore, and repent" (Re.3:19).

Thought 2. Many are too often involved in attacking instead of proclaiming. The opponents of Christ are often treated as though they are unreachable and untouchable by Christ. The wise disciple must treat everyone *in the truth*: the sinner must be loved and shown the way of Christ. His sin is to be despised, but not the sinner himself.

4 (14:48-49) **Love—Obedience—Indulgence—Truth**: study four concerns the Lord who showed a striking serenity in the midst of mass confusion. Jesus was serene through the whole affair. His serenity is a dynamic example as we face the trials of this life. He was able to be serene through it all because He lived moment by moment in obedience to the Scripture, that is, to the will of God. Note two things.

a. There was the piercing question of Jesus: "Are ye come out, as against a thief?" The world treated Him as a thief. They acted as though He had stolen from them, for He had not preached a message that allowed them to live as they wished. He had not praised them, nor boosted their egos; He had not honored their service and gifts. Rather, He had proclaimed that they were short of God's glory and were dying and doomed if they did not repent and begin to live as God commanded (see note—Mt.26:55-56).

Note a critical point too often overlooked: Jesus had to tell the truth in order for men to be saved. God is love, but His love is not the indulgence of the grandfather who accepts wrongdoing. His love is the ache and acceptance of a true father who receives a repentant and obedient son. *Only through repentance and obedience can a man ever know the love of God* (see Jn.14:21, 23-24; 15:10, 14). God does not accept a man who does wrong and lives unrighteously. Therefore, Jesus had to tell men the truth. He could not deceive men. If men wanted to be acceptable to God and live in His love, then they had to turn away from sin and come to God, believing that God exists and diligently seeking Him (He.11:6).

b. Jesus said the Scriptures, that is, God's will, must be fulfilled. Note two facts.

1) He had to die; Scripture said so. God's will was fixed and set in Scripture.
2) Jesus was dying willingly. He willingly laid down His life just as Scripture said.

"But he was wounded for our transgressions, he was bruised for our iniquities: the chastisement of our peace was upon him; and with his stripes we are healed. All we like sheep have gone astray; we have turned every one to his own way; and the LORD hath laid on him the iniquity of us all. He was opposed, and he was afflicted, yet he opened not his mouth: he is brought as a lamb to the slaughter, and as a sheep before her shearers is dumb, so he openeth not his mouth" (Is.53:5-7).

"Therefore doth my Father love me, because I lay down my life, that I might take it again. No man taketh it from me, but I lay it down of myself. I have power to lay it down, and I have power to take it again. This commandment have I received of my Father" (Jn.10:17-18).

"Him, being delivered by the determinate counsel and foreknowledge of God, ye have taken, and by wicked hands have crucified and slain" (Ac.2:23).

Again, it was Jesus' obedience to God's will that brought the serenity and peace to His heart in the midst of mass confusion.

Thought 1. We secure peace and serenity through living for God and obeying Him.

"If ye abide in me, and my words abide in you, ye shall ask what ye will, and it shall be done unto you" (Jn.15:7).

5 (14:50) **Faith**: the fifth study concerns the disciples who allowed their faith to crack. The disciples were not cowards (see v.47). Their problem was not lack of courage but weak faith and lack of spiritual understanding (carnality). When Jesus was arrested, their courage rose to the occasion. They were willing to stand up and fight although they were far outnumbered and had inferior weapons. What happened was this. When they saw Jesus' standing there not freeing Himself (Mt.26:52), they could not understand. They were disillusioned, wondering: "Why does Jesus not blast His enemies away? The Messiah could. He is supposed to have such power, and Jesus is the Messiah. Isn't He?" Their faith was bound to falter. Two things caused their weak faith.

First, they were close-minded. They had closed their minds to *part of the truth*, to His full mission and purpose. They had *refused* to accept His word about dying and rising again literally. They had failed to grasp the spiritual and eternal nature of His kingdom. They symbolized what He was saying. Now that it was happening, they were not prepared for it; their faith was too weak.

Second, they were worldly and materialistic minded. They had hung on to their earthly concept of the Messiah, that is, a Messiah who was coming to bring utopia to this material and physical world. They were, therefore, not prepared to deal with their earthly Messiah's being bound and taken prisoner by men of this earth. Their faith lacked the strength to bear such a trial.

"Ye therefore, beloved, seeing ye know these things before, beware lest ye also, being led away with the error of the wicked, fall from your own stedfastness. But grow in grace, and in the knowledge of our Lord and Saviour Jesus Christ. To him be glory both now and for ever" (2 Pe.3:17-18).

"And Jesus said unto him, No man, having put his hand to the plough, and looking back, is fit for the kingdom of God" (Lu.9:62).

"A double minded man is unstable in all his ways" (Js.1:8).

"Blessed is the man that endureth temptation: for when he is tried, he shall receive the crown of life, which the Lord hath promised to them that love him" (Js.1:12).

"Draw nigh to God, and he will draw nigh to you. Cleanse your hands, ye sinners; and purify your hearts, ye double minded" (Js.4:8).

6 (14:51-52) **Fear**: the sixth study concerns a young man who became terror stricken when confronted and attacked. Most commentators seem to think this young man was Mark, the author of this gospel. If so, he does not name himself out of modesty. Several facts lead to this conclusion.

a. Why is the event recorded if it were not Mark? There seems to be little, if any, point to the event's being mentioned if the young man were not Mark. Apparently Mark is saying, "I was there; I was an eyewitness to the happenings." (Not mentioning oneself by name is the practice of the Gospel writers. For example, John refers to many instances where he was an eyewitness, but he never gives his name.)

b. Mary, Mark's mother, lived in Jerusalem (Ac.12:12).

c. The detail of the account points to Mark's having been an eyewitness (see Judas' approach, "Master, Master," and the two different words for "kiss").

d. The trait of fleeing Jesus when the going got rough is the same picture of Mark in the book of *Acts* (Ac.13:13; 15:37-38).

Mark's mother, Mary, had a house large enough to hold a fairly large prayer meeting. Some commentators think the Upper Room was even in her home. If so, when Judas returned to the Upper Room with the arresting party, Mark was probably lying in his bed and heard the commotion. He quickly threw the sheet around him and struck out to warn Jesus. When Jesus was grabbed, one of the officers reached for the young man, but the young man was able to break loose and escape.

The point again is weak faith (if it were Mark) or lack of faith (if it were an unbelieving spectator). The young man failed to stand with Jesus. He had little if any faith in the Lord. His whole being surged with fear and terror. He sought to save himself at the expense of standing with the Messiah and witnessing for Him.

Thought 1. Many seek to escape embarrassment, ridicule, threats, and persecution instead of standing with Christ and being a testimony for Him. Why? Weak faith. Our faith is not strong enough to cast out fear.

> **"And he was sad at that saying, and went away grieved: for he had great possessions" (Mk.10:22).**
>
> **"Thou therefore, my son, be strong in the grace that is in Christ Jesus" (2 Ti.2:1).**
>
> **"Be not thou therefore ashamed of the testimony of our Lord, nor of me his prisoner: but be thou partaker of the afflictions of the gospel" (2 Ti.1:8).**
>
> **"Wherefore gird up the loins of your mind, be sober, and hope to the end for the grace that is to be brought unto you at the revelation of Jesus Christ" (1 Pe.1:13).**
>
> **"Behold, I come quickly; hold that fast which thou hast, that no man take thy crown" (Re.3:11).**

	I. Jesus' Trial Before the High Priest: A Look at Weak & Strong Characters, 14:53-65 *(Mt. 26:57-68; Lu. 22:54, 63-71; Jn. 18:12-14, 19-24)*		
1. The setting: Jesus was led before the High Priest & the Sanhedrin	53 And they led Jesus away to the high priest: and with him were assembled all the chief priests and the elders and the scribes.		
2. The confused, yet courageous Peter: He alone followed Jesus	54 And Peter followed him afar off, even into the palace of the high priest: and he sat with the servants, and warmed himself at the fire.		
3. The disturbed religionists: They sought testimony against Jesus	55 And the chief priests and all the council sought for witness against Jesus to put him to death; and found none		
a. The witnesses were false & did not agree	56 For many bare false witness against him, but their witness agreed not together.		
b. The final charge was formulated	57 And there arose certain, and bare false witness against him, saying, 58 We heard him say, I will destroy this temple that is made with hands, and within three days I will build another made without hands.		
		59 But neither so did their witnesses agree together.	c. The final witnesses did not even agree
		60 And the high priest stood up in the midst, and asked Jesus, saying, Answerest thou nothing? what is it which these witness against thee? 61 But he held his peace, and answered nothing. Again the high priest asked him, and said unto him, Art thou the Christ, the Son of the Blessed?	**4. The calm Lord: He stood silent before men, but assured before God**
		62 And Jesus said, I am: and ye shall see the Son of man sitting on the right hand of power, and coming in the clouds of heaven.	**5. The strong Lord: He claimed to be the Messiah, the Son of God**
		63 Then the high priest rent his clothes, and saith, What need we any further witnesses? 64 Ye have heard the blasphemy: what think ye? And they all condemned him to be guilty of death.	**6. The frenzied mob of religionists: They got their satisfaction—the death of their disturber** a. The true character of the High Priest
		65 And some began to spit on him, and to cover his face, and to buffet him, and to say unto him, Prophesy: and the servants did strike him with the palms of their hands.	b. The true character of men *DS1*

DIVISION IX

THE SON OF GOD'S PASSION MINISTRY: JESUS' SUPREME SACRIFICE—REJECTED AND CRUCIFIED, 14:1-15:47

I. Jesus' Trial Before the High Priest: A Look at Weak and Strong Characters, 14:53-65

(14:53-65) **Introduction**: there is a picture of both weak and strong character in this passage. The traits that one should avoid and follow are both seen.

1. The setting: Jesus was led before the High Priest and the Sanhedrin (v.53).
2. The confused, yet courageous Peter: he alone followed Jesus (v.54).
3. The disturbed religionists: they sought testimony against Jesus (vv.55-59).
4. The calm Lord: He stood silent before men, but assured before God (vv.60-61).
5. The strong Lord: He claimed to be the Messiah, the Son of God (v.62).
6. The frenzied mob of religionists: they got their satisfaction—the death of their disturber (v.63-65).

1 (14:53) **Jesus Christ, Trials—Sanhedrin**: Jesus was led before the High Priest and the Sanhedrin. He stood before them on trial for His life. The Sanhedrin was the official ruling body, the high court of the Jews. Note the word *assembled* (sunerchomai), which means to gather, to come together, to flock together, to resort. There is also the idea of accompanying in the word. The picture is that of the Jewish leaders' flocking or herding together around Jesus, of being called to accompany one another to their respective seats, ready to pounce on Jesus. There was no question about the evil of their hearts. They were ready to pounce on and eliminate Him. Several facts reveal the evil of their hearts.

⇒ They had hastily assembled the court *at night*, which was illegal. All criminals had to be tried in the day.
⇒ They were meeting in Caiaphas' palace (home), not in the official court. This, too, was illegal. All cases had to be tried in court.
⇒ Jesus was being tried during the Passover week, when no cases were to be tried.
⇒ They had not met to try Jesus but to secretly devise charges and to condemn Him to death.

Thought 1. Men *flock together* too often to do evil. Men also *flock together* to oppose Christ, even in the church. It is easier to do evil or to oppose Christ in a group than when alone.

"Wherefore come out from among them, and be ye separate, saith the Lord, and touch not the unclean thing; and I will receive you, and will be a Father unto you, and ye shall be my sons and daughters, saith the Lord Almighty" (2 Co.6:17-18).

Thought 2. A heart that wishes to do evil will twist the rules. If a man looks and lusts, he will usually figure out a way, rationalizing and justifying the matter in his mind.

> **"Beloved, follow not that which is evil, but that which is good. He that doeth good is of God: but he that doeth evil hath not seen God" (3 Jn.11).**
> **"Therefore to him that knoweth to do good, and doeth it not, to him it is sin" (Js.4:17).**

2 (14:54) **Jesus Christ, Love for**: there was the confused, yet courageous Peter. He had attempted to defend Jesus, but Jesus stopped him and even forbade him to come to His aid (Mk.14:47; Jn.18:10). In addition, Jesus was giving in to the injustices and indecencies of the mob instead of blasting them away and setting up His kingdom. Peter could not understand. In the Garden of Gethsemane, when Jesus stopped him from fighting the arresting party, Peter had to flee for his life. But Peter loved His Lord too much to flee too far away. His love for Jesus stopped him, turned him around, and led him back to Jesus. He followed the mob from a safe distance. The trail ended up in the courtyard of Caiaphas' palace. It took enormous courage for Peter to enter the courtyard, for Peter was risking his life by being there. But He had to see what happened to his Lord. He hoped against hope that Jesus was just waiting to act and take over. He had to see.

Thought 1. How much we need a deep love for Christ, a love so great that we would risk our lives to follow Him. Too often, our love is so weak we will not even risk ridicule or embarrassment to witness for Him, much less risk our lives.

> **"There is no fear in love; but perfect love casteth out fear: because fear hath torment. He that feareth is not made perfect in love" (1 Jn.4:18).**

Thought 2. Peter's love caused him to be courageous. Courage always needs to be rooted in love, and love must always rule over courage.

> **"Wherefore I put thee in remembrance that thou stir up the gift of God, which is in thee by the putting on of my hands. For God hath not given us the spirit of fear; but of power, and of love, and of a sound mind" (2 Ti.1:6-7).**

3 (14:55-59) **Jesus Christ, Trial**: there were the disturbed religionists—they sought testimony against Jesus. Imagine! It was the religionists who were actually seeking testimony against Jesus. They were so disturbed with Jesus, the kind of evidence they gathered was meaningless. Their minds were closed—they rejected Him and opposed Him. He was a threat to their way of life, their security and position, and their nation. Therefore, they were set on rejecting and opposing Him. The truth did not matter. He was to be denied and done away with. (See notes—Mt.12:1-8; note and DEEPER STUDY # 1—12:10; note—15:1-20; DEEPER STUDY # 2—15:6-9; DEEPER STUDY # 3—16:12 for a discussion of the reasons for their opposition.)

Note how far they went to formulate a charge against Jesus.

a. The witnesses were false witnesses (v.56). Many came charging Jesus, but they were all false and their testimonies would not stand up in court under the scrutiny of honest and objective minds. Therefore, the leaders faced a problem, for they had to formulate a charge that would convince Pilate and the Roman authorities that Jesus should die.

b. The witnesses could not agree. By law two witnesses had to agree for a formal charge to be made and a conviction secured. But note, two witnesses who agreed could not be found, despite "many" who came forward.

c. Finally, two witnesses did come forward with a charge that seemed to be strong enough to stand up and convince the Roman authorities. However, note three simple facts (see note—Mt.26:60-61 for detailed discussion).

1) The charge against Jesus was still said to be false. It came from "false witness against him."
2) The two witnesses distorted Jesus' words. Jesus had said, "Destroy *ye* this temple, and in three days I will raise it up" (Jn.2:19). Jesus had actually said the Jews were to be the destroyers; but the false witnesses said, "We heard him say, I will destroy this temple." They distorted His words, making Him the destroyer.
   The false witnesses also misunderstood Jesus' words. Jesus was referring to His body—to the temple of His body and to the resurrection of His body. The Jews apparently thought He meant He would destroy and rebuild the Jerusalem temple in three days. It was this charge—the charge of being a revolutionary—that the religionists believed they could use to convince the Romans to execute Jesus.
3) Mark reemphasizes that this charge was false.

Thought 1. Many today have closed minds; they reject Christ. Some even oppose Him and actively struggle to gather evidence against Him. Why? Primarily for the same reason the religionists of Christ's day rejected Him. They desire...

- to live as they wish.
- to build their image and live as they desire.
- to gain personal recognition, position, security, and wealth as they want.

> **"But his citizens hated him, and sent a message after him, saying, We will not have this man to reign over us" (Lu.19:14).**
> **"The world cannot hate you; but me it hateth, because I testify of it, that the works thereof are evil" (Jn.7:7).**
> **"If the world hate you, ye know that it hated me before it hated you....But this cometh to pass, that the word might be fulfilled that is written in their law, They hated me without a cause" (Jn.15:18, 25).**

Thought 2. The religionists did not understand, so they twisted and distorted the word of Christ. We abuse God's Word to our condemnation.

> **"And account that the longsuffering of our Lord is salvation; even as our beloved brother Paul also according to the wisdom given unto him hath written unto you; as also in all his epistles, speaking in them of these things; in which are some things hard to be understood, which they that are unlearned and unstable wrest, as they do also the other scriptures, unto their own destruction" (2 Pe.3:15-16).**

4 (14:60-61) **Jesus Christ, Trial**: there was the calm Lord who stood silent before men, but assured before God. Note three facts.

a. The two witnesses who charged Jesus with being a revolutionary could not agree (Mk.14:59).

b. Jesus "held His peace." He was silent; He said nothing in defending Himself against the false charges.

c. The High Priest and court became disturbed and perhaps confused by Jesus' silence. They needed Him to begin speaking, hoping He would add evidence to the charge and thereby incriminate Himself. The High Priest turned, brow-beating and attempting to pressure Jesus: "Answeredst nothing...?"

Thought 1. The example of Jesus under attack was forceful.
(1) There was the example of *patience*. He had to stand there patiently while *false* charge after *false* charge was leveled against Him.
(2) He had to *endure* it all.
(3) He had to *control* Himself, his emotions and tongue, and not retaliate.

Thought 2. How difficult it is to remain silent and to control the tongue! Especially when the accusations are false!

> **"For he that will love life, and see good days, let him refrain his tongue from evil, and his lips that they speak no guile" (1 Pe.3:10).**
>
> **"He that keepeth his mouth keepeth his life: but he that openeth wide his lips shall have destruction" (Pr.13:3).**
>
> **"Whoso keepeth his mouth and his tongue, keepeth his soul from troubles" (Pr.21:23).**

5 (14:62) **Jesus Christ, Claim—Trial**: there was the strong Lord—He claimed to be the Messiah, the actual Son of the Blessed (God). By *blessed* (eulogetos) is meant God. The Jews, when mentioning God's name, would usually say, "God, blessed for ever." The word *blessed* came to be a title for God. Note the strong assertion of Jesus' answer to the court.

a. Jesus' answer was a strong claim. He pulled no punches, left no room for doubt. He used the striking words of deity: *I am* (ego eimi). (See notes—Jn.6:20-21; DEEPER STUDY # 2—Mt.1:18 for discussion.)

b. He called Himself "the Son of Man" (see DEEPER STUDY # 3—Mt.8:20 for discussion).

c. He gave two proofs of His claim: His resurrection and exaltation and His second coming. Both would prove His person and authority. Note that the believer hopes in the resurrection and exaltation and in the second coming of Christ, but the emphasis of Jesus to these unbelievers was judgment.

⇒ His resurrection declared Him to be the Son of God with power.

> **"And declared to be the Son of God with power, according to the spirit of holiness, by the resurrection from the dead" (Ro.1:4).**

⇒ His exaltation declares His position and authority to rule and reign over all men (Ph.2:9-11).

> **"This Jesus hath God raised up, whereof we all are witnesses. Therefore being by the right hand of God exalted, and having received of the Father the promise of the Holy Ghost, he hath shed forth this, which ye now see and hear. For David is not ascended into the heavens: but he saith himself, The LORD said unto my Lord, Sit thou on my right hand, until I make thy foes thy footstool. Therefore let all the house of Israel know assuredly, that God hath made that same Jesus, whom ye have crucified, both Lord and Christ" (Ac.2:32-36).**
>
> **"Wherefore God also hath highly exalted him, and given him a name which is above every name: that at the name of Jesus every knee should bow, of things in heaven, and earth, and things under the earth; and that every tongue should confess that Jesus Christ is Lord, to the glory of God the Father" (Ph.2:9-11).**

⇒ His return will declare His execution of justice and judgment (Mt.24:30; Jn.5:28).

> **"And then shall appear the sign of the Son of man in heaven: and then shall all the tribes of the earth mourn, and they shall see the Son of man coming in the clouds of heaven with power and great glory" (Mt.24:30).**

"Marvel not at this: for the hour is coming, in the which all that are in the graves shall hear his voice, and shall come forth; they that have done good, unto the resurrection of life; and they that have done evil, unto the resurrection of damnation. I can of mine own self do nothing: as I hear, I judge: and my judgment is just; because I seek not mine own will, but the will of the Father which hath sent me" (Jn.5:28-30).

6 (14:63-65) **Man, Character of**: there was the frenzied mob of religionists—they got their satisfaction, the death of their disturber. Note two things.

a. The true character of the High Priest. The enmity and the bitter hatred of Caiaphas reached its peak when Jesus made the strong claim to be the Son of God. The High Priest ripped his clothes, which was a custom when God's name was disgraced (2 K.18:37; 19:1; see Is.36:22; 37:1; Ac.14:14), and he shouted out for the verdict. The whole scene was a travesty, a terrible abuse of justice. Caiaphas pictured for us the character of every man who chooses this world and its institutional religion over Jesus.

Thought 1. Two things got the best of Caiaphas:
⇒ He wished to have this world with its rewards of position and wealth, recognition and pleasure.
⇒ He wished to have a religion of self-image instead of God's image.

Too often, the same two things get the best of us.

b. The true character of men.
1) There was the ridicule of Jesus' claim and the heaping of sarcasm upon Him. This is seen in the religionists' shout to Him, "Prophesy," and in their calling Him "*thou* Christ" (Mt.26:68).
2) There was bitter behavior and hatred. Spitting in the face was a sign of monstrous disrespect. Beating with the fists and palms (the Greek says rods) was an outburst of the inner bitterness within the hearts of the religionists against Jesus.

"I gave my back to the smiters, and my cheeks to them that plucked off the hair: I hid not my face from shame and spitting" (Is.50:6; see Is.52:14).
"They shall smite the judge of Israel with a rod upon the cheek" (Mi.5:1).

DEEPER STUDY # 1
(14:65) **Jesus Christ—Spit Upon**: a sign of utter contempt (see Nu.12:14; De.25:9; Is.50:6).

	J. Peter's Denial: A Lesson in Failure, 14:66-72 *(Mt. 26:69-72; Lu. 22:54, 62; Jn. 18:15-18, 25-27)*	again, and began to say to them that stood by, This is one of them. 70 And he denied it again. And a little after, they that	**caused an emphatic denial** a. Charged before a crowd b. Gave an outright denial **4. Failure 3: Fearing a crowd—caused a cursing denial**
1. The cause of failure: Peter was below in the courtyard, among the worldly & unbelievers	66 And as Peter was beneath in the palace, there cometh one of the maids of the high priest:	stood by said again to Peter, Surely thou art one of them: for thou art a Galilaean, and thy speech agreeth thereto.	a. A crowd charged Peter
2. Failure 1: Fearing an individual—caused a denial & pretension a. A maid charged Peter with being a disciple	67 And when she saw Peter warming himself, she looked upon him, and said, And thou also wast with Jesus of Nazareth.	71 But he began to curse and to swear, saying, I know not this man of whom ye speak.	b. Gave a denial of cursing & swearing
b. Peter claimed ignorance & denied association with Christ: A denial of pretension c. The rooster crowed	68 But he denied, saying, I know not, neither understand I what thou sayest. And he went out into the porch; and the cock crew.	72 And the second time the cock crew. And Peter called to mind the word that Jesus said unto him, Before the cock crow twice, thou shalt deny me thrice. And when he	c. The rooster crowed a second time **5. The answer to failure: Repentance** a. Peter remembered b. Peter wept in repentance
3. Failure 2: Fearing a crowd—	69 And a maid saw him	thought thereon, he wept.	

DIVISION IX

THE SON OF GOD'S PASSION MINISTRY: JESUS' SUPREME SACRIFICE—REJECTED AND CRUCIFIED, 14:1-15:47

J. Peter's Denial: A Picture of Failure, 14:66-72

(14:66-72) **Introduction**: failing the Lord is very, very serious. Peter failed Jesus in several areas, and his failure reached its climax in an actual denial of the Lord. But he was forgiven, and there is forgiveness for any believer who fails.

1. The cause of failure: Peter was below in the courtyard, among the worldly and unbelievers (v.66).
2. Failure 1: fearing an individual—caused a denial and pretension (vv.67-68).
3. Failure 2: fearing a crowd—caused an emphatic denial (vv.69-70).
4. Failure 3: fearing a crowd—caused a cursing denial (vv.70-72).
5. The answer to failure: repentance (v.72).

1 (14:66) **Apostasy—Desertion—Sin, Cause**: the cause of failure is simply stated: "Peter was beneath in the palace." He was where he should not have been. He was with the crowd of rejecters, sitting with them and warming himself by their fire. As the case would be in any similar situation, the crowd was discussing the trial and mocking, joking, and cursing Jesus because of His claims. Peter should have been off alone or else with the other disciples in prayer, seeking an answer to their confusion.

Peter's failure seems to have been due to at least four things.

a. His misunderstanding of God's Word. In particular he misunderstood the teaching concerning the Kingdom of God. He thought of the Kingdom of God in physical and material terms only. He failed to see the spiritual Kingdom of God, that is...

- the death and resurrection of Christ.
- the Lord's indwelling power, His rule and reign within the human heart.
- the remaking of a new heavens and earth, which he was later to understand in the clearest of terms (2 Pe.3:10).

b. His confusion. Peter had drawn his sword and attacked. He had been ready to act in the flesh, to fight to establish the Lord's kingdom (Mk.14:47; Jn.18:10), but Jesus had rebuked him and stopped him. In addition, Jesus had not blasted His enemies nor made His move; but rather, He had allowed them to take Him, voluntarily surrendering to their abuse. Peter could not understand. He was confused. His mind was reeling and searching for answers.

c. His fear. Peter had created a bad situation for himself. He had attacked the arresting party (Mk.14:47; Jn.18:10). He had failed to wait upon the Lord's directive, acting in the arm of the flesh and doing what he thought best. Therefore, to some degree he was now a hunted man. In the scuffle, he had forsaken the Lord and fled for his life. But, as mentioned before, Peter's great love for Jesus and his great hope that Jesus might yet make His move had stopped Peter and turned him around. He followed Jesus, although from a safe distance (see note—Mk.14:54). Throughout the whole incident, his heart had probably been palpitating with fear—fear of being recognized, arrested, and killed.

d. His weak faith. Peter had failed to trust Jesus in the midst of confusing and threatening *circumstances*. Jesus was being tried and condemned to die before Peter's eyes, yet Jesus had said He would arise. Peter had chosen to interpret Jesus' words symbolically, probably thinking Jesus was referring to raising up the kingdom after a struggle with the Romans (symbolically viewed as death, the death of enemies or fallen governments). The point is, Peter never interpreted the Lord's words literally; therefore, his faith was based upon error. This led to weak faith and being unprepared for the events facing him.

Thought 1. One thing will always cause great temptation: being with a crowd of rejecters, associating with and moving among the worldly.

> **"Wherefore come out from among them, and be ye separate, saith the Lord, and touch not the unclean thing; and I will receive you, and will be a Father unto you, and ye shall be my sons and daughters, saith the Lord Almighty" (2 Co.6:17-18).**
>
> **"Now we command you, brethren, in the name of our Lord Jesus Christ, that ye withdraw yourselves from every brother that walketh disorderly, and not after the tradition which he received of us" (2 Th.3:6).**

Thought 2. Four things will cause failure:
⇒ misunderstanding God's Word
⇒ being confused
⇒ fear
⇒ weak faith (due to misinterpreting the Lord's words)

2 (14:67-68) **Apostasy—Denial—Fear—Pretension**: the first failure is that of fearing an individual, which caused pretension. Fearing an individual often makes a person pretend. Note what happened. A maid simply walked up to Peter and said that he had also been with Jesus of Nazareth. There seems to be no threat or danger in this statement to Peter. At worst, it seems that it would have led only to some bantering and ridicule. The rejecters standing around were naturally bantering back and forth about Jesus and His claims. In their minds and talk, He was but a fool. Peter had an opportunity, perhaps, to be a witness for Jesus, humbly sharing about the love and enormous care of Jesus for people. Perhaps he could have helped to turn some who were standing there to Jesus or at least stopped some of the mob from ridiculing. We must always remember that John was somewhere in the palace as well, and as far as we know, he was maintaining his composure and testimony for Jesus.

Peter cracked under his fear. He denied Jesus, pretending he knew nothing about Him nor had anything to do with Him. He just claimed ignorance of the whole matter.

Thought 1. The fear of ridicule and embarrassment often causes a person to deny Jesus. Sometimes the denial is...
- by voice
- by act (going along with the person or crowd)
- by silence

Thought 2. When out in the world, too many pretend not to know Jesus. They profess Jesus on Sundays and among believers yet never say a word about Him during the week. Or, they live no differently from the world. No one ever knows they are professing believers. Such pretension is denial.

> **"Whosoever therefore shall be ashamed of me and of my words in this adulterous and sinful generation; of him also shall the Son of man be ashamed, when he cometh in the glory of his Father with the holy angels" (Mk.8:38).**
>
> **"The fear of man bringeth a snare: but whoso putteth his trust in the LORD shall be safe" (Prov.29:25).**
>
> **"But sanctify the Lord God in your hearts: and be ready always to give an answer to every man that asketh you a reason of the hope that is in you with meekness and fear" (1 Pe.3:15).**

3 (14:69-70) **Apostasy—Denial—Fear**: the second failure is that of fearing a crowd. Fearing a crowd sometimes causes outright denial. It did with Peter. This time a maid recognized him and said to the crowd standing around, "This is one of them." The pressure upon Peter was stronger because a crowd was present. He denied it more emphatically this time. Matthew says "he denied with an oath" (Mt.26:72). Note four things.

a. Peter actually denied Jesus before men, and he denied Him using an oath. Instead of denying Jesus, he should have been upstairs in the courtroom standing by the Lord's side and testifying for Him.

b. Peter was falling (progressing) more and more into sin.
⇒ He was denying Jesus because he was not by His side; instead he was standing among the Lord's rejecters.
⇒ He was standing among the Lord's rejecters because he had fled the Lord.
⇒ He had fled the Lord because he had acted in the flesh.
⇒ He had acted in the flesh because he had not accepted the Lord's words. The Lord had told Peter and the others exactly what was to happen, yet Peter had refused to open his mind to the truth. Therefore, he was utterly confused and caught off guard.

c. Peter was fearing persecution. This was the first time he was standing face to face with life-threatening persecution. And he was failing to stand. He was failing despite the fact that Jesus had told him time and again that he must suffer for God.

d. Peter followed Jesus ever so readily when Jesus was popular and had a large following. But he could not stand the heat when Jesus was being opposed and rejected by most.

> **"But whosoever shall deny me before men, him will I also deny before my Father which is in heaven" (Mt.10:33).**

"Be not thou therefore ashamed of the testimony of our Lord, nor of me his prisoner: but be thou partaker of the afflictions of the gospel according to the power of God" (2 Ti.1:8).

"Be strong and of a good courage, fear not, nor be afraid of them: for the LORD thy God, he it is that doth go with thee; he will not fail thee, nor forsake thee" (De.31:6).

4 (14:70-72) **Fear—Denial**: the third failure is also that of fearing the crowd. Fearing a crowd will sometimes cause a cursing and swearing denial of Jesus. Note several things (see notes—Mt.26:73-74; 5:33-37).

a. It was the crowd that approached and confronted Peter this time. The pressure was much greater. It was his Galilaean speech that gave him away, and the crowd knew that Jesus and His disciples were from Galilee. Jesus had been arrested secretly, and few knew about it. They just figured no Galilaean would be out this time of night unless he was a follower of Jesus.

b. Peter's chest was bound to be pounding with emotion and fear. His thoughts were flying, trying to figure out how to escape. His emotions burst forth in a forceful cursing and swearing denial: "I know not this man." Note Peter called his Lord "this man," which was all He was to those standing around. (To all rejecters Jesus is no more than "this man.")

c. Immediately upon his denial the cock crew, and Peter heard it.

Thought 1. A worldly crowd can and will put undue pressure upon a believer. A believer does not belong in the midst of a worldly crowd, hanging around worldly places.

"And in nothing terrified by your adversaries: which is to them an evident token of perdition, but to you of salvation, and that of God" (Ph.1:28).

"And with many other words did he testify and exhort, saying, Save yourselves from this untoward generation" (Ac.2:40).

"And have no fellowship with the unfruitful works of darkness, but rather reprove them" (Ep.5:11).

5 (14:72) **Apostasy—Repentance**: the answer to failure is repentance. As soon as Peter heard the cock crow, he called to mind the words of the Lord; and "he thought thereon, [and] he wept." The word *thought* (epibalon) means to throw upon. Peter "threw his thought upon" what Jesus had said: that he, Peter, would deny Jesus three times. Peter's mind was fastened upon what Jesus had told him. His mind would not let Jesus' words go. Quickly, emotion and sorrow began to arise in his chest, and he felt the tears begin to come. He had failed his Lord and failed Him so miserably. Peter loved the Lord, and somehow he knew that he was not where he belonged. He might not understand what was happening to the Lord and the course the Lord had taken, but he should have been by His side all the time testifying for Him. As fast as he could, without attracting attention, he made his way out of the courtyard; and as soon as he reached the outside, he *burst into tears* (eklaie). The Greek is descriptive in illustrating Peter's repentance through godly sorrow and weeping. The idea is that Peter was utterly heartbroken and added weeping upon weeping. (See DEEPER STUDY # 1—2 Co.7:10; note and DEEPER STUDY # 1—Acts 17:29-30 for application.)

⇒ He wept, and the more he thought about the situation, the more he wept.
⇒ He fell to the ground and wept, being heartbroken.
⇒ He wept, being grieved with hurt and pain that was unbearable.
⇒ He wept and wept and continued to weep.

"If we confess our sins, he is faithful and just to forgive us our sins, and to cleanse us from all unrighteousness" (1 Jn.1:9).

"Repent therefore of this thy wickedness, and pray God, if perhaps the thought of thine heart may be forgiven thee" (Ac.8:22).

"Now therefore make confession unto the LORD God of your fathers, and do his pleasure: and separate yourselves from the people of the land" (Ezr. 10:11).

"He that covereth his sins shall not prosper: but whoso confesseth and forsaketh them shall have mercy" (Pr.28:13).

"Only acknowledge thine iniquity, that thou hast transgressed against the LORD thy God, and hast scattered thy ways to the strangers under every green tree, and ye have not obeyed my voice, saith the LORD" (Je.3:13).

1. **He was forced to make a decision concerning Jesus Christ**
   a. The religionists met to finalize their charge against Jesus
   b. They bound & took Jesus to Pilate
2. **He was indecisive & rejected strong evidence**
   a. Jesus' strong claim: He is King
   b. Jesus' strong control: Silence
   c. Jesus' strong, enduring purpose: Under repeated questioning
   d. Jesus' impact: Pilate marveled, but was still indecisive
3. **He attempted compromise**
   a. The custom of Rome to pacify the Jews
   b. The prisoner chosen: A murderer & an insurrectionist

CHAPTER 15

K. Jesus' Trial Before Pilate: The Picture of a Morally Weak Man,[DS1] **15:1-15**

(Mt. 27:1-2, 11-25; Lu. 23:1-25; Jn. 18:28-40)

And straightway in the
morning the chief priests held
a consultation with the elders
and scribes and the whole
council, and bound Jesus and
carried him away, and delivered him to Pilate.
2 And Pilate asked him, Art
thou the King of the Jews?
And he answering said unto
him, Thou sayest it.
3 And the chief priests
accused him of many things:
but he answered nothing.
4 And Pilate asked him again,
saying, Answerest thou nothing? behold how many things
they witness against thee.
5 But Jesus yet answered
nothing; so that Pilate marvelled.
6 Now at that feast he released unto them one prisoner, whomsoever they desired.
7 And there was one named
Barabbas, which lay bound
with them that had made insurrection with him, who had
committed murder in the insurrection.
8 And the multitude crying
aloud began to desire him to
do as he had ever done unto
them.
9 But Pilate answered them,
saying, Will ye that I release
unto you the King of the
Jews?
10 For he knew that the
chief priests had delivered
him for envy.
11 But the chief priests
moved the people, that he
should rather release Barabbas unto them.
12 And Pilate answered and
said again unto them, What
will ye then that I shall do
unto him whom ye call the
King of the Jews?
13 And they cried out again,
Crucify him.
14 Then Pilate said unto
them, Why, what evil hath he
done? And they cried out the
more exceedingly, Crucify him.
15 And so Pilate, willing to
content the people, released
Barabbas unto them, and delivered Jesus, when he had
scourged him, to be crucified.

   c. The frenzied mob
   d. The wish of Pilate: To release Jesus
   e. The reason: Pilate knew Jesus was innocent
4. **He ignored the influence of evil men upon people**
5. **He was too weak to act justly & responsibly**
   a. His first attempt at justice: Presented Jesus as king of the Jews
   b. His second attempt at justice: Declared Jesus to be innocent
6. **He gave in to worldly pressure**

DIVISION IX

THE SON OF GOD'S PASSION MINISTRY: JESUS' SUPREME SACRIFICE—REJECTED AND CRUCIFIED, 14:1-15:47

K. Jesus' Trial Before Pilate: The Picture of a Morally Weak Judge, 15:1-15

(15:1-15) **Introduction**: Pilate was morally weak both as a man and as a judge. His treatment of Jesus clearly demonstrated some of the shortcomings or failures of a morally weak person—failures that every man needs to reflect on.

1. He was forced to make a decision concerning Jesus Christ (v.1).
2. He was indecisive and rejected strong evidence (vv.2-5).
3. He attempted compromise (vv.6-10).
4. He ignored the influence of evil men upon people (v.11).
5. He was too weak to act justly and responsibly (vv.12-14).
6. He gave in to worldly pressure (v.15).

DEEPER STUDY # 1

(15:1-15) **Pilate**: Pilate was the procurator of Judea. He was directly responsible to the Roman Emperor for the administrative and financial management of the country. A man had to work himself up through the political and military ranks to become a procurator. Pilate was, therefore, an able man, experienced in the affairs of politics and government as well as the military. He held office for ten years, which shows that he was deeply trusted by the Roman government. However, the Jews despised Pilate; and Pilate despised the Jews, in particular their intense practice of religion. When Pilate became procurator of Judea, he did two things that aroused the people's bitter hatred against him forever. First, on his state visits to Jerusalem, he rode into the city with the Roman standard, an eagle sitting atop a pole. All previous governors had removed the standard because of the Jews' opposition to idols. Second, Pilate launched the construction of a new water supply for Jerusalem. To finance the project, he took the money out of the temple treasury. The Jews never forgot or forgave this act. They bitterly opposed Pilate all through his reign, and he treated them with equal contempt. On several occasions Jewish leaders threatened to exercise their right to report Pilate to the emperor. This disturbed Pilate tremendously, causing him to become even more bitter toward the Jews.

1 (15:1) **Jesus Christ, Trials—Religionists—Sanhedrin**: the ruling body of the Jews (the Sanhedrin) met to finalize its charges against Jesus. The charges had to be strong enough to convince the Romans. What happened was probably this. The false witnesses had been secured the evening before (see Mk.14:53-65). They had probably met until the wee hours of the morning and taken a break for a little rest and breakfast. They were now returning to formulate in writing the charges against Jesus. The charges had to be so strong that the Romans would be forced to condemn Him as a revolutionary. As soon as the charges were finalized, they bound Christ and led Him to Pilate.

Thought 1. Note the picture of sacrifice. In the Old Testament, sacrifices were to be bound with cords (Ps.118:27). Christ was "bound...and carried away; and delivered" as the great Sacrifice for us (He.10:5-14).

2 (15:2-5) **Indecisive**: the morally weak man was indecisive and rejected Jesus despite strong evidence.

a. The major charge and Jesus' critical answer. The major charge against Jesus was that He claimed to be the King of the Jews. Pilate asked Jesus about the charge. Note two things.

1) Jesus' meek and humble appearance. The Greek form of Pilate's question points to Jesus' meekness and humility. The question was emphatic: "Thou! Art thou the King of the Jews?"...the One who stands here...
   - with no revolutionary fire in your eyes or voice.
   - with such a humble and meek aire and look.
   - with no friends or followers supporting you.
   - with such poor clothing, the garb of a peasant.
   - How could *you* be a king?

2) Jesus' strong claim: *"Thou sayest it"* (su legeis). The meaning is "[unmistakably] what thou sayest is true." Jesus strongly claimed to be King. But it must always be noted: Jesus went on to explain that He was not a threat to Caesar nor to any other civil government. He was the King of man's spirit and of heaven, not of this earth (Jn.18:36-37). He wished to reign in men's hearts and lives, in the realm of the spiritual and eternal, not in the realm of the physical and temporal.

b. The barrage of charges and Jesus' enduring purpose. The leaders accused Him of many things, "but He answered nothing." He was stone silent before His accusers. Why would Jesus not defend Himself, not try to escape death? His purpose was to surrender to the *sinful behavior* of men. The *sinful behavior* to which He submitted was...
- the very depth of sin itself.
- the ultimate demonstration of sin.
- the greatest sin that could be committed.

The sin to which Jesus subjected Himself was the rejection and killing of the Son of God. Standing before His accusers, He said nothing, enduring their awful indignities. He endured because He was purposed to die for the sins of men.

Thought 1. Indecision is one of the gross mistakes of men, a mistake that dooms many. There is no excuse for indecision; the evidence that Jesus is the Savior of the world is clearly seen to an open and honest heart.

> **"No man can serve two masters: for either he will hate the one, and love the other; or else he will hold to the one, and despise the other. Ye cannot serve God and mammon" (Mt.6:24).**
> **"Ye cannot drink the cup of the Lord, and the cup of devils: ye cannot be partakers of the Lord's table, and of the table of devils" (1 Co.10:21).**
> **"A double minded man is unstable in all his ways" (Js.1:8).**
> **"How long halt ye between two opinions? if the LORD be God, follow him" (1 K.18:21).**

3 (15:6-10) **Compromise—Man, Morally Weak**: the morally weak man attempted compromise. The scene was set. Jesus had been accused and condemned to die by the Jewish court (Sanhedrin). He was delivered to the Gentile authority, Pilate, who had to pass the final sentence and actually carry out the execution. However, Pilate knew that Jesus was innocent and wished to release Him. But how? He must pacify and maintain fairly good relations with the Jewish authorities. It was the only way he could maintain peace and keep them from reporting him to Rome, threatening his own position (see DEEPER STUDY # 1, *Pilate*—Mk.15:1-15).

Pilate thought of a way to escape his predicament. It was his custom to release a prisoner, whomever the Jews wished, at every Passover. This was one way he used to gain good will with the Jews. He had a notorious criminal in prison at that very moment, Barabbas, who was a robber, an insurrectionist, and a murderer (Jn.18:40). Pilate felt sure that by pitting Barabbas against Jesus, the people would choose Jesus, the One who had ministered and helped so many of them. How wrong the man of compromise was. The world will always cry out against Jesus to get rid of Him.

Note the moral weakness of Pilate. He knew Jesus was innocent. He knew the Jews sought to kill Jesus because they envied Him. Jesus should have been released immediately, but Pilate attempted a compromise instead of standing up for the truth.

Thought 1. Note a crucial point: when the truth is known, it should be proclaimed and not compromised. Compromise results in three tragedies.
(1) Compromise weakens character and testimony.
(2) Compromise means that the truth is not being done or lived. A person is agreeing to do something less than what he should be doing.
(3) Compromise weakens principle, position, and life.

Thought 2. God accepts no compromise concerning His Son, Jesus Christ. A man either stands for Him or against Him. There is no neutral ground. Jesus is the innocent, sinless Son of God in whom all men are to place their trust and lives.

> **"He that is not with me is against me: and he that gathereth not with me scattereth" (Lu.11:23).**
>
> **"All men should honour the Son, even as they honour the Father. He that honoureth not the Son honoureth not the Father which hath sent him. Verily, verily, I say unto you, He that heareth my word, and believeth on him that sent me, hath everlasting life, and shall not come into condemnation; but is passed from death unto life" (Jn.5:23-24).**
>
> **"And this is the record, that God hath given to us eternal life, and this life is in his Son. He that hath the Son hath life; and he that hath not the Son of God hath not life" (1 Jn.5:11-12).**
>
> **"Submit yourselves therefore to God. Resist the devil, and he will flee from you. Draw nigh to God, and he will draw nigh to you. Cleanse your hands, ye sinners; and purify your hearts, ye double minded. Be afflicted, and mourn, and weep: let your laughter be turned to mourning, and your joy to heaviness. Humble yourselves in the sight of the Lord, and he shall lift you up" (Js.4:7-10).**

4 (15:11) **Evil, Ignoring**: the morally weak man ignored the influence of evil men. What happened now was tragic. The religionists moved out among the crowd, arousing and inflaming them to clamor for Barabbas' release. Note that Pilate did nothing. He just sat still and said nothing, ignoring the reality of evil influence.

Thought 1. Men who are set on evil will try to influence others in order to get their way.

Thought 2. The influence of wicked men upon other people cannot be ignored. Evil men do influence others. To ignore the fact is to allow the infiltration and growth of more and more evil.

> **"For the name of God is blasphemed among the Gentiles through you, as it is written" (Ro.2:24).**
>
> **"But evil men and seducers shall wax worse and worse, deceiving, and being deceived" (2 Ti.3:13).**
>
> **"Who is a liar but he that denieth that Jesus is the Christ? He is antichrist, that denieth the Father and the Son. Whosoever denieth the Son, the same hath not the Father....These things have I written unto you concerning them that seduce you" (1 Jn.2:22-23, 26).**

5 (15:12-14) **Man, Weakness of**: the morally weak man was too weak to act justly and responsibly. Pilate actually made two attempts to get Jesus released.

a. He presented Jesus to the people as their King, the One whom they call the King of the Jews. He was *appealing* to the hope they had for a deliverer. Many had, after all, called Jesus their King, the One for whom they had been looking. He had ministered to and cared for so many. He had declared His kingdom to be concerned only with the spiritual (Jn.18:36-37). He was no threat to Caesar. Why should the people condemn One who had shown so much care and interest in the needs of people? But the people cried out for Jesus' death. Pilate, surprised, made another attempt to free Jesus.

b. Pilate declared Jesus to be innocent. He had done no evil and Pilate knew it. He tried to persuade the crowd to think about the fact. He cried out loudly, "Why, what evil hath he done?" But it was all to no avail. They cried out, inflamed even more, "Crucify Him."

The point to note is the weakness of Pilate. He was a morally weak man.

⇒ He was not strong enough to do what he knew was right.
⇒ He lacked the moral strength to stand up for Christ.
⇒ He was too weak to declare the truth.

> **"I call heaven and earth to record this day against you, that I have set before you life and death, blessing and cursing: therefore choose life, that both thou and thy seed may live" (De.30:19).**
>
> **"And Elijah came unto all the people, and said, How long halt ye between two opinions? if the LORD be God follow him: but if Baal, then follow him. And the people answered him not a word" (1 K.18:21).**

6 (15:15) **Man, Weakness of—Worldliness**: the morally weak man gave in to worldly pressure.

a. Pilate was more willing to satisfy and please the people than to do what was right. Fear, of course, lay behind Pilate's action—the fear...

- of losing the people's favor.
- of causing problems for himself.
- of losing his position and security (see DEEPER STUDY # 1, *Pilate*—Mk.15:1-15).

b. He scourged Jesus (see note—Mt.27:26-38).

c. He released Barabbas and delivered Jesus to be crucified.

Note that Pilate had the authority and the duty to do what was right. But he failed. He was too weak...

- to stand for the truth.
- to declare the truth as the thing to do.
- to free himself from the evil influence of the world.

"Love not the world, neither the things that are in the world. If any man love the world, the love of the Father is not in him. For all that is in the world, the lust of the flesh, and the lust of the eyes, and the pride of life, is not of the Father, but is of the world" (1 Jn.2:15-16).

"And be not conformed to this world: but be ye transformed by the renewing of your mind, that ye may prove what is that good, and acceptable, and perfect, will of God" (Ro.12:2).

"By faith Moses, when he was come to years, refused to be called the son of Pharaoh's daughter; choosing rather to suffer affliction with the people of God, than to enjoy the pleasures of sin for a season" (He.11:24-25).

L. Jesus' Cross: An Outline of Its Mockery & Events, 15:16-41
(Mt. 27:26-56; Lu. 23:26-49; Jn. 19:16-37)

1. The abuse by Pilate's soldiers: A misunderstanding of Jesus' claim
  a. They called others to join in abusing Him
  b. They ridiculed & mocked Him
  c. They physically abused Him

2. The rechanging of Jesus' clothes: His life was valued less than royal clothing

3. The man who carried Jesus' cross: A picture of conversion by picking up the cross

4. The place of the crucifixion: A symbol of death—Jesus died just like all men

5. The refusal of drugs: A resolve to taste death at its bitterest

6. The gambling for Jesus' clothes: An indifferent & insensitive spirit

7. The crucifixion: The depth of sin & the summit of love

8. The inscription on the cross: A misunderstood charge

9. The two thieves crucified with Jesus: A picture of Jesus' life—to the end He was numbered with sinners, see Is. 53:12

10. The mocking of the people: A misunderstanding of His salvation
  a. The mockery by those passing by: Misunderstanding His resurrection
  b. The mockery by religionists: Misunderstanding God's Messiahship
  c. The mockery by two thieves: Misunderstanding His claim

11. The frightening darkness: A symbol of separation & loneliness

12. The terrible cry of separation: A horrifying judgment

13. The confused mob: A picture of the world's people
  a. A man of pity: Offered Jesus a narcotic drink
  b. A man of hardness: Ridiculed Jesus

14. The loud cry of death: A picture of glorious triumph

15. The torn veil of the temple: A symbol of open access into God's very presence

16. The centurion's confession: A picture of the great confession to be made by many

17. The women at the cross: A proof that Jesus lived & served well

16 And the soldiers led him
away into the hall, called
Praetorium; and they call together the whole band.
17 And they clothed him
with purple, and platted a
crown of thorns, and put it
about his head,
18 And began to salute him,
Hail, King of the Jews!
19 And they smote him on
the head with a reed, and
did spit upon him, and bowing their knees worshipped
him.
20 And when they had
mocked him, they took off
the purple from him, and
put his own clothes on him,
and led him out to crucify
him.
21 And they compel one
Simon a Cyrenian, who
passed by, coming out of the
country, the father of Alexander and Rufus, to bear his
cross.
22 And they bring him unto
the place Golgotha, which is,
being interpreted, The place
of a skull.
23 And they gave him to
drink wine mingled with
myrrh: but he received it
not.
24 And when they had crucified him, they parted his
garments, casting lots upon
them, what every man should
take.
25 And it was the third
hour, and they crucified him.
26 And the superscription
of his accusation was written
over, THE KING OF THE
JEWS.
27 And with him they crucify two thieves; the one on
his right hand, and the other
on his left.
28 And the scripture was
fulfilled, which saith, And he
was numbered with transgressors.
29 And they that passed by
railed on him, wagging their
heads, and saying, Ah, thou
that destroyest the temple,
and buildest it in three days,
30 Save thyself, and come
down from the cross.
31 Likewise also the chief
priests mocking said among
themselves with the scribes,
He saved others; himself he
cannot save.
32 Let Christ the King of
Israel descend now from the
cross, that we may see and
believe. And they that were
crucified with him reviled
him.
33 And when the sixth hour
was come, there was darkness over the whole land until the ninth hour.
34 And at the ninth hour
Jesus cried with a loud voice,
saying, Eloi, Eloi, lama
sabach thani? which is, being
interpreted, My God, my
God, why hast thou forsaken
me?
35 And some of them that
stood by, when they heard it,
said, Behold, he calleth Elias.
36 And one ran and filled a
spunge full of vinegar, and
put it on a reed, and gave
him to drink, saying, Let
alone; let us see whether Elias will come to take him
down.
37 And Jesus cried with a
loud voice, and gave up the
ghost.
38 And the veil of the temple was rent in twain from
the top to the bottom.
39 And when the centurion,
which stood over against
him, saw that he so cried out,
and gave up the ghost, he
said, Truly this man was the
Son of God.
40 There were also women
looking on afar off: among
whom was Mary Magdalene,
and Mary the mother of
James the less and of Joses,
and Salome;
41 (Who also, when he was
in Galilee, followed him, and
ministered unto him;) and
many other women which
came up with him unto Jerusalem.

DIVISION IX

THE SON OF GOD'S PASSION MINISTRY: JESUS' SUPREME SACRIFICE—REJECTED AND CRUCIFIED, 14:1-15:47

L. Jesus' Cross: An Outline of Its Mockery and Events, 15:16-41

(15:16-41) **Introduction**: the death of Jesus on the cross is the most phenomenal event in history; in fact, it is the most crucial focal point of history. Eternal salvation was secured for man in the death of Jesus upon the cross. Because Jesus died, man can live forever in a perfect state of being. Therefore, the events of the cross are all-important. They hold lesson after lesson for the man who seeks the truth of God's Son.

1. The abuse by Pilate's soldiers: a misunderstanding of Jesus' claim (vv.16-19).
2. The rechanging of Jesus' clothes: His life was valued less than royal clothing (v.20).
3. The man who carried Jesus' cross: a picture of conversion by picking up the cross (v.21).
4. The place of the crucifixion: a symbol of death—Jesus died just like all men (v.22).
5. The refusal of drugs: a resolve to taste death at its bitterest (v.23).
6. The gambling for Jesus' clothes: an indifferent and insensitive spirit (v.24).
7. The crucifixion: the depth of sin and the summit of love (v.25).
8. The inscription on the cross: a misunderstood charge (v.26).
9. The two thieves crucified with Jesus: a picture of Jesus' life—to the end He was numbered with sinners (vv.27-28).
10. The mocking of the people: a misunderstanding of His salvation (vv.29-32).
11. The frightening darkness: a symbol of separation and loneliness (v.33).
12. The terrible cry of separation: a horrifying judgment (v.34).
13. The confused mob: a picture of the world's people (vv.35-36).
14. The loud cry of death: a picture of glorious triumph (v.37).
15. The torn veil of the temple: a symbol of open access into God's very presence (v.38).
16. The centurion's confession: a picture of the great confession to be made by many (v.39).
17. The women at the cross: a proof that Jesus lived and served well (vv.40-41).

1 (15:16-19) **Jesus Christ, Death—Tortured**: the first event was the abuse by Pilate's soldiers—they misunderstood the claim of Jesus. Jesus had explained to Pilate that His kingdom was a spiritual kingdom, but Pilate had not understood what He meant (Jn.18:36-37). The soldiers, of course, knew little if anything about the conversation between Jesus and Pilate. But they had heard about the man Jesus, a carpenter from Nazareth who claimed to be the Messiah, the Son of God. Now Jesus of Nazareth stood before them, guilty of insurrection and of claiming to be the King of the Jews. This, of course, was a threat to their own rule and power. In their eyes, seeing Jesus standing there as a captive, beaten and bloody, He was anything but a King. He was a man condemned as a threat to their power as soldiers and to their government which they had sworn to uphold. To them, He was worthy of death. Two things caused the soldiers to torture Jesus so severely...

- His claim to be the Messiah and the Son of God
- His being condemned as an insurrectionist

Note what the soldiers did.

a. They called all the other soldiers to join in on the "fun" (torture). They were in the Praetorium, which was the main quarters of the soldiers. It was a large court within the palace itself. There were between two and six hundred soldiers taunting and torturing Jesus (see note, pt.2—Mt.27:26-38).

b. They ridiculed and mocked His claim. They stripped Him and took an old, faded, worn-out soldier's cloak, purple in color, and threw it upon His bleeding body. The cloak was a mocking symbol of the royal cloak worn by kings. Then, several soldiers went outside and wove a crown from a thorn bush. Returning, they thrust the crown of thorns upon His head and brow. And they mocked His claim to be the King of the Jews.

c. They abused Him physically. They took the reed, which they had given to Him as a sceptre (Mt.27:29), and beat the crown of thorns down upon His head. They also spat upon Him and continued their ridicule.

> **Thought 1**. What the soldiers did in mocking Jesus demonstrates perfectly the *nature* of the Lord's Kingship. Earthly royalty is symbolized by a royal robe, gold crown, sceptre, and bowing of the knee—all standing for the pomp and power of earthly royalty. Christ could not accept such, not at His first coming.
>
> The worn, faded robe, the crown of thorns, the reed sceptre, the mocking—all show that the nature of Christ's Kingship is love, *sacrificial love.*
>
> > **"[Christ] being in the form of God, thought it not robbery to be equal with God: but made himself of no reputation, and took upon him the form of a servant, and was made in the likeness of men: and being found in fashion as a man, he humbled himself, and became obedient unto death, even the death of the cross" (Ph.2:6-8).**

2 (15:20) **Jesus Christ, Death—Clothes**: the second event was the rechanging of Jesus' clothes—His life was valued less than royal clothing. This verse is both interesting and revealing. It shows the depth of human depravity. The soldiers would save a worn-out, faded robe, yet the life of an innocent person (even more, the very Son of God) would be destroyed. The cloak was no good; it was a throw-away. They never would have put a *good* cloak upon such a beaten, bloody mass of flesh. The blood and the continued torture would have ruined a good cloak.

The soldiers, of course, did not want a criminal's wearing a soldier's cloak through the streets, even if it were a throw-away. So they stripped the cloak from Him. The dried blood had naturally caused the robe to stick to the Lord's back; therefore, the wounds were reopened and bled again.

The point is twofold.

First, the cloak and what it stood for were valued and honored more than the life of Jesus, more than the very One who had come to reveal God's love and salvation to man. What men need is not to value things more highly than Jesus but to value Jesus more highly than all else combined.

"I counsel thee to buy of me...white raiment, that thou mayest be clothed, and that the shame of thy nakedness do not appear; and anoint thine eyes with eyesalve, that thou mayest see" (Re.3:18; see Ep.4:23-24).

"These are they which...have washed their robes, and made them white in the blood of the Lamb" (Re.7:14).

"Love not the world, neither the things that are in the world. If any man love the world, the love of the Father is not in him. For all that is in the world, the lust of the flesh, and the lust of the eyes, and the pride of life, is not of the Father, but is of the world" (1 Jn.2:15-16).

Second, the soldier's robe had been only a mockery of kingly authority, but it symbolized the world's attitude toward giving homage to God's Son. No man determines the authority of God's Son. He possesses authority because He is God's Son, not because man gives Him authority. God has given Him all authority and rule because He bore the sufferings and death of the cross for man.

"And Jesus came and spake unto them, saying, All power is given unto me in heaven and in earth" (Mt.28:18).

"For the Father judgeth no man, but hath committed all judgment unto the Son: that all men should honor the Son, even as they honor the Father. He that honoreth not the Son honoreth not the Father which hath sent him" (Jn.5:22-23).

3 (15:21) **Jesus Christ, Death—Simon of Cyrene**: the third event was the man who carried Jesus' cross—a picture of conversion by picking up Jesus' cross. Note several things.

a. There is God's plan or providence. Nothing happens by chance, not to the Christian believer. God oversees the life of His people. Thus, Simon's being pressed into carrying the cross for Jesus was in the plan of God.

b. Simon was standing along the roadway watching the armed procession make its way through the streets. Apparently, there was some expression of concern and sympathy for Jesus, something within his heart that was touched and reached out to Jesus. God knew this, and directed the soldiers to enlist his help in carrying the Lord's cross.

c. Simon was "the father of Alexander and Rufus." The comment by Mark is interesting. Evidently they were known believers at the time of Mark's writing (see Acts 13:1; Ro.16:13). The indication is that Simon, or at least his two sons, were eventually converted.

Thought 1. The symbol and application are clear. The man who takes up the cross and dies to self will be converted and become a true follower of Christ.

"And he said to them all, If any man will come after me, let him deny himself, and take up his cross daily, and follow me" (Lu.9:23).

4 (15:22) **Jesus Christ, Death—Golgotha**: the fourth event was the place of death—a symbol of death. Jesus died just like all other men. Golgotha was a hill outside Jerusalem. It was known as a place of death, a place where executions took place. The very word "Golgotha" means the place of a skull. It stirred the thoughts of death and corruption. The very place where Jesus was crucified symbolized death itself. Every act seemed to point to His dying for the deliverance of man. Here upon Golgotha was the picture and thought of death. And here upon Golgotha, He was to die to deliver all men from the bondage of death.

"Forasmuch then as the children are partakers of flesh and blood, he also himself likewise took part of the same; that through death he might destroy him that had the power of death, that is, the devil; and deliver them who through fear of death were all their lifetime subject to bondage" (He.2:14-15).

5 (15:23) **Jesus Christ, Death—Offered Drugs**: the fifth event was the refusal of drugs—a resolve to taste death at its bitterest. The drink was strong and intoxicating, deadening the senses to some degree. It was given to crucifixion victims as a narcotic to somewhat ease the pain.

Jesus was to die for man. God's will was not to be done in a drunken stupor, in a drugged, insensitive, and unthoughtful state. He was to taste death for man, being fully conscious of doing God's will, being as mentally alert as possible.

"But we see Jesus, who was made a little lower than the angels for the suffering of death, crowned with glory and honour; that he by the grace of God should taste death for every man" (He.2:9).

"In burnt offerings and sacrifices for sin thou hast had no pleasure. Then said I, Lo, I come (in the volume of the book it is written of me,) to do thy will, O God....by the which will we are sanctified through the offering of the body of Jesus Christ once for all" (He.10:6-7, 10).

6 (15:24) **Jesus Christ, Death—Clothes, Gambled for**: the sixth event was the gambling for Jesus' clothes—an indifferent and insensitive spirit. Note two facts.

a. Mary, Jesus' mother, was standing by the cross; yet the soldiers showed no compassion whatsoever in sharing His belongings with her. (See Ps.22:18.)

"For what shall it profit a man, if he shall gain the whole world, and lose his own soul?" (Mk.8:36).

b. Jesus was stripped by the soldiers, stripped of His mortal clothes. He allowed all His mortality to be stripped so that He might abolish death and bring life and immortality to light.

"But is now made manifest by the appearing of our Savior Jesus Christ, who hath abolished death, and hath brought life and immortality to light through the gospel" (2 Ti.1:10).

7 (15:25) **Jesus Christ, Death—Crucifixion**: the seventh event was the crucifixion—the summit of sin and love. Note two things.

a. Jesus was crucified at 9 a.m. (the third hour), and darkness swept the land from 12 noon until 3 p.m. (the sixth to the ninth hour, vv.33-34) (see DEEPER STUDY # 1—Mk.6:48; see Mt.27:45-46; Mk.15:33-34; Lu.23:44).

b. Man demonstrated the height of depravity by rejecting and putting God's Son to death. God demonstrated the height of love by not sparing His Son, but by allowing Him to die for man's sins.

"But God commendeth his love toward us, in that, while we were yet sinners, Christ died for us" (Ro.5:8).

"For God so loved the world, that he gave his only begotten Son, that whosoever believeth in him should not perish, but have everlasting life" (Jn.3:16).

8 (15:26) **Jesus Christ, Death—Inscription**: the eighth event was the inscription on the cross—a misunderstood charge. The sign placed above His head, "The King of the Jews," was placed there by Pilate. Pilate intended to mock the Jewish authorities and to reproach Jesus' claim. However, God overruled and used the title to proclaim the truth of Jesus' Lordship to the whole world (Lu.23:38). The very charges against Jesus proclaimed His deity and honor.

"He humbled himself, and became obedient unto death, even the death of the cross. Wherefore God also hath highly exalted him, and given him a name which is above every name: that at the name of Jesus every knee should bow, of things in heaven, and things in earth, and things under the earth; And that every tongue should confess that Jesus Christ is Lord, to the glory of God the Father" (Ph.2:8-11).

"Our Lord Jesus Christ: which in his times he shall shew, who is the blessed and only Potentate, the King of kings, and Lord of lords; who only hath immortality, dwelling in the light which no man can approach unto; whom no man hath seen, nor can see: to whom be honour and power everlasting. Amen" (1 Ti.6:14-16).

9 (15:27-28) **Jesus Christ, Death—Two Thieves**: the ninth event was that of the two thieves' being crucified with Jesus—a picture of His life; to the end He was numbered with sinners.

"Therefore will I divide him a portion with the great, and he shall divide the spoil with the strong; because he hath poured out his soul unto death: and he was numbered with the transgressors; and he bare the sins of many, and made intercession for the transgressors" (Is.53:12).

"This is a faithful saying, and worthy of all acceptation, that Christ Jesus came into the world to save sinners" (1 Ti.1:15).

"For Christ also hath once suffered for sins, the just for the unjust, that he might bring us to God, being put to death in the flesh, but quickened by the Spirit" (1 Pe.3:18).

10 (15:29-32) **Jesus Christ, Death—Mockery**: the tenth event was the mocking of the people—a misunderstanding of Jesus' salvation.

a. There was the mockery of the mob. They misunderstood His resurrection. As people travelled in and out of the city, they slowed down, and some stopped to see what was going on. When they stopped, they saw the charge above the cross that Jesus claimed to be "The King of the Jews." They were told about His claim of enormous power—power to destroy and rebuild the temple in three days. Such was ridiculous in their minds. Therefore, they joined in the mocking and verbal abuse.

"He was oppressed, and he was afflicted, yet he opened not his mouth: he is brought as a lamb to the slaughter, and as a sheep before her shearers is dumb, so he openeth not his mouth" (Is.53:7).

b. There was the mockery of the religionists. They misunderstood God's Messiahship.

"...Christ [Messiah] Jesus who gave himself a ransom for all, to be testified in due time" (1 Ti.2:5-6).
"Christ [Messiah] Jesus came into the world to save sinners" (1 Ti.1:15).

c. There was the mockery of the two thieves. They misunderstood His claim. The thieves heard the mob's mockery about Jesus' claiming to be the Messiah. A man's making such a claim while dying seemed to be insane and to merit abuse. Thus, they joined the mockers.

"Who, when he was reviled, reviled not again; when he suffered, he threatened not....Who his own self bare our sins in his own body on the tree, that we, being dead to sins, should live unto righteousness: by whose stripes ye were healed" (1 Pe.2:23-24).

11 (15:33) **Jesus Christ, Death—Darkness**: the eleventh event was the frightening darkness—a symbol of separation and loneliness. The darkness told man something (see note—Mt.27:45 for detailed discussion).

a. Man was separated from the light.

"And this is the condemnation, that light is come into the world, and men loved darkness rather than light, because their deeds were evil. For every one that doeth evil hateth the light, neither cometh to the light, lest his deeds should be reproved" (Jn.3:19-20).

b. Man stood all alone. He could not see in the dark, not well. He was, so to speak, standing in the world all alone, responsible for his own behavior. And because of what he has done, man must face God someday all alone to give an account for his behavior.

"And it is appointed unto men once to die, but after this the judgment" (He.9:27).

12 (15:34) **Jesus Christ, Death—Separation from God**: the twelveth event was the terrible cry of separation—a horrifying judgment. What did Jesus mean when He cried out that God had forsaken Him?

a. Jesus did not mean the suffering and ill treatment of the cross, the suffering at the hands of men which He was going through. All through His ministry He knew suffering and foretold of suffering for His followers, even martyrdom.

b. Scripture tells us what Jesus meant (see note—Mt.27:46-49 for detailed discussion).

1) He was being made sin for us.

"For he hath made him to be sin for us, who knew no sin; that we might be made the righteousness of God in him" (2 Co.5:21).

2) He was bearing our sins as the sacrificial Lamb of God.

"For if the blood of bulls and of goats, and the ashes of an heifer sprinkling the unclean, sanctifieth to the purifying of the flesh: how much more shall the blood of Christ, who through the eternal Spirit offered himself without spot to God, purge your conscience from dead works to serve the living God....So Christ was once offered to bear the sins of many; and unto them that look for him shall he appear the second time without sin unto salvation" (He.9:13-14, 28).

3) He was suffering for sins, the just for the unjust.

"For Christ also hath once suffered for sins, the just for the unjust, that he might bring us to God, being put to death in the flesh, but quickened by the Spirit" (1 Pe.3:18).

4) He was bearing the curse of the law.

"Christ hath redeemed us from the curse of the law, being made a curse for us" (Ga.3:13).

Note a critical point: the only thing that could have caused God to separate Himself from Christ was sin (Is.59:2; Ro.5:12. See DEEPER STUDY # 1—Heb.9:27.) Sin is the only thing that causes God to withdraw from anyone. Since Christ was perfect and sinless, it was not His own sin that caused God to forsake Him—it was our sin (2 Co.5:21; Heb.4:15; 7:26; 1 Pe.1:10; 2:22).

13 (15:35-36) **Jesus Christ, Death—World, Confused**: the thirteenth event was the confused mob—a picture of the world's people.

a. There was the picture of hardness. When Jesus called out to God, some thought He was calling out to Elijah. They mockingly wanted to see what would happen, ridiculing the fact that Jesus would call upon a prophet of old to save Him.

b. There was the picture of pity. Jesus had said, "I thirst" (Jn.19:28-29). One man sensed compassion for the Lord and offered to wet His lips. But the other men standing around—those with hard hearts—stopped Him.

Jesus was seen hanging and suffering on the cross, expressing the utmost pity for man. Yet, when one man tried to show compassion for Christ, the man was stopped.

"But God commendeth his love toward us, in that, while we were yet sinners, Christ died for us" (Ro.5:8).

"And this is his commandment, That we should believe on the name of his Son Jesus Christ, and love one another, as he gave us commandment" (1 Jn.3:23).

14 (15:37) **Jesus Christ, Death—Finished**: the fourteenth event was the loud cry of death—a picture of glorious triumph. What Jesus cried out was one word in the Greek, *Tetelestai*, "It is finished" (Jn.19:30). It is a cry of purpose, a shout of triumph. He was dying for a specific purpose and that purpose was now fulfilled (see note—Mt.27:50 for detailed discussion).

> **"I am the door: by me if any man enter in, he shall be saved, and shall go in and out, and find pasture....I am the good shepherd: the good shepherd giveth his life for the sheep....As the Father knoweth me, even so know I the Father: and I lay down my life for the sheep....Therefore doth my Father love me, because I lay down my life, that I might take it again. No man taketh it from me, but I lay it down of myself. I have power to lay it down, and I have power to take it again. This commandment have I received of my Father" (Jn.10:9, 11, 15, 17-18).**

15 (15:38) **Jesus Christ, Death—Temple, Veil Torn**: the fifteenth event was the torn veil of the temple—a symbol of open access into God's very presence. Note four facts.

a. The veil (curtain) that was torn was the *inner veil* (katapetasma), the curtain which separated the Holy of Holies from the Holy Place. There was another veil, an *outer curtain* (kalumma), which separated the Holy Place from the outer court of the temple.

The Holy of Holies was the most sacred part of the temple, the place where the very presence of God was symbolized as dwelling in a very special way. It was closed *forever* to everyone except the High Priest. But even he could enter the Holy of Holies only once a year, on the Day of Atonement (Ex.26:33).

b. At the very hour that Jesus died, the High Priest was rolling back the outer curtain in order to expose the Holy Place to the people, to those who had gathered to worship in the surrounding court. As he rolled back the outer curtain, exposing the Holy Place for worship, both he and the worshippers stood in amazement. They saw the inner veil rent from the top to the bottom. There they stood, seeing and experiencing for the very first time the Holy of Holies, the very special presence of God Himself.

c. The veil was torn from top to bottom. This symbolizes that it was torn by an act of God Himself. It symbolized God's giving direct access into His presence (He.6:19; 9:3-12, 24; 10:19-23). Now through the body of Christ, any man can enter the presence of God anytime, anyplace.

> **"By the which will we are sanctified through the offering of the body of Jesus Christ once for all" (He.10:10).**

d. The torn veil symbolized that all men could now draw near God by the blood of Christ.

> **"But now in Christ Jesus ye who sometimes were far off are made nigh by the blood of Christ. For he is our peace, who hath made both one, and hath broken down the middle wall of partition between us" (Ep.2:13-14).**

16 (15:39) **Jesus Christ, Death—Centurion, Confession of**: the sixteenth event was the centurion's confession—a picture of the great confession to be made by many.

a. The centurion was bound to be a thoughtful and honest man. He was in charge of the crucifixion. He was responsible for overseeing all that took place. As the events unfolded upon the cross, he was striken more and more with the claim of Jesus and the way in which the events were happening. When Jesus shouted out that His purpose was finished, that His death was the climax of His purpose upon earth, the centurion was convinced. The very fact that Jesus' death was purposeful sealed his conviction. God quickened the soldier's heart to the glorious truth: "Truly this man was the Son of God."

b. The centurion was a Gentile. He symbolized all who were to confess Jesus in coming generations.

> **"That if thou shalt confess with thy mouth the Lord Jesus, and shalt believe in thine heart that God hath raised him from the dead, thou shalt be saved. For with the heart man believeth unto righteousness; and with the mouth confession is made unto salvation" (Ro.10:9-10).**

17 (15:40-41) **Jesus Christ, Death—Women at Cross**: the seventeenth event is the women at the cross—a proof that Jesus lived and served well. Note that the women were at the cross despite the danger. They stood off some distance away, but they were there nonetheless. They still loved and cared, no matter what. They symbolized that Christ's life was not in vain.

> **"For whosoever will save his life shall lose it; but whosoever shall lose his life for my sake and the gospel's, the same shall save it" (Mk.8:35).**

	M. Jesus' Burial: A Discussion of Courage, 15:42-47 *(Mt. 27:57-66; Lu. 23: 50-56; Jn. 19:38-42)*	calling unto him the centurion, he asked him whether he had been any while dead.	**God's cause: Seen in Christ's early death**
		45 And when he knew it of the centurion, he gave the body to Joseph.	
1. The need for haste because the Sabbath was approaching	42 And now when the even was come, because it was the preparation, that is, the day before the sabbath,	46 And he bought fine linen, and took him down, and wrapped him in the linen, and laid him in a sepulchre which was hewn out of a rock, and rolled a stone unto the door of the sepulchre.	**4. The courage to make an unashamed commitment to Jesus** a. Took Jesus down from the cross b. Cared for and buried the body of Jesus
2. The courage to request & to look after the body of Jesus	43 Joseph of Arimathaea, an honourable counsellor, which also waited for the kingdom of God, came, and went in boldly unto Pilate, and craved the body of Jesus.		
3. The courage to experience a broken heart & to die for	44 And Pilate marvelled if he were already dead: and	47 And Mary Magdalene and Mary the mother of Joses beheld where he was laid.	**5. The courage to take a public stand by the cross**

DIVISION IX

THE SON OF GOD'S PASSION MINISTRY:JESUS' SUPREME SACRIFICE—REJECTED AND CRUCIFIED, 14:1-15:47

M. Jesus' Burial: A Discussion of Courage, 15:42-47

(15:42-47) **Introduction**: the burial of Jesus presents a strong picture of courage, the kind of courage that sets a dynamic example for all to follow.

1. The need for haste because the Sabbath was approaching (v.42).
2. The courage to request and to look after the body of Jesus (v.43).
3. The courage to experience a broken heart and to die for God's cause: seen in Christ's early death (vv.44-45).
4. The courage to make an unashamed commitment to Jesus (v.46).
5. The courage to take a public stand by the cross (v.47).

1 (15:42) **Sabbath—Jesus Christ, Burial**: the need for the haste was threefold.

a. The Sabbath was the day of worship for Jews. The day began at 6 p.m. (Jewish days began at 6 p.m. and ran until 6 p.m. the next night, that is from sundown to sundown.) Strict Jewish law said that once the Sabbath began, no work could be done including the burial of the dead.

b. Jesus died at 3 p.m. (see Mk.15:33-34, 37). He died on Friday, the day of preparation for the Sabbath. If anything was to be done with Jesus' body, it had to be done immediately and quickly. Only three hours remained for work.

c. The Romans either dumped the bodies of crucified criminals in the trash heaps or left the bodies hanging upon the cross for the vultures and animals to consume. The latter served as an example of criminal punishment to the public. If Jesus' body was not removed quickly within these three hours, the fate of His body was set. The Romans would not care what happened to Him, and no Jew could remove Him until the Sabbath was over.

2 (15:43) **Courage—Boldness—Discipleship, Secret**: courage boldly requested to look after the body of Jesus. This was a striking picture. A man, Joseph of Arimathaea, was stirred to step forth for Jesus. Several important facts are given by the gospel writers about him.

⇒ He was from Arimathaea.
⇒ He was now a permanent citizen of Jerusalem. He had bought a tomb in Jerusalem for his burial.
⇒ He was an honorable counsellor, that is, a member of the Sanhedrin (Mk.15:43).
⇒ He was a good and just man (Lu.23:50).
⇒ He waited for the Kingdom of God (Mk.15:43).
⇒ He was rich (Mt.27:57).
⇒ He did not vote for Jesus' death in the Sanhedrin (Lu.23:51).
⇒ He was a disciple, but a secret one, fearing his fellow Jews (Jn.19:38).

It was this last fact that revealed a marked change in Joseph. Up until the death of Jesus, he had been a secret disciple. He had probably had several meetings with Jesus when the Lord had visited Jerusalem; but now, after the Lord's death, he was no longer a secret disciple. He became bold in standing forth for Jesus.

Joseph actually marched in "boldly to Pilate" and requested permission to look after the body of Jesus. This was a tremendous act of courage, for Pilate was extremely upset and wearied with the whole situation. He had been forced to give in to the Jewish authorities who were always causing problems for him. He just despised them. He could react severely and cause some serious problems for Joseph, especially since Joseph was one of the leaders of the nation.

The thing that turned Joseph from being a secret disciple to a bold disciple seems to be the phenomenal events surrounding the cross (for example, the behavior and words of Jesus, the darkness, the earthquake, and the torn veil). When Joseph witnessed all this, his mind connected the claims of Jesus with the Old Testament prophecies of the Messiah, and Joseph saw the prophecies fulfilled in Jesus. He stepped forward, braved all risks, and took his stand for Jesus. A remarkable courage! A courage stirred by the death of Jesus.

Thought 1. The primary thing that stirs courage in the believer is the cross. Seeing the cross and what the cross really means will stir a secret disciple to courageously step forward for Christ.

Thought 2. Joseph courageously asked to take care of the body of Jesus. Today the body of Jesus is the church (Ep.1:22). We are to boldly step forward and take care of the church, in particular when there are special times of need. But note: special courage is often needed to step forward and show care. In those times a fresh look at the cross will be helpful. God can use the cross to stir us.

"For I determined not to know any thing among you, save Jesus Christ, and him crucified" (2 Co.2:2).

"Knowing that he which raised up the Lord Jesus shall raise up us also by Jesus, and shall present us with you. For all things are for your sakes, that the abundant grace might through the thanksgiving of many rebound to the glory of God" (2 Co.4:14-15).

"And that he died for all, that they which live should not henceforth live unto themselves, but unto him which died for them, and rose again" (2 Co.5:15).

3 (15:44-45) **Courage—Boldness**: courage was willing to experience a broken heart and to die for God's cause. Note: Pilate marvelled that Jesus was already dead. Victims usually lingered for days before dying from exposure to the sun and from thirst and loss of blood due to the scourging and nail wounds. In fact, the victims' legs were often broken to hasten death (Jn.19:31).

All indications point to Jesus' dying from a broken heart. The weight of sin and its inevitable separation and judgment from God were just too much to bear (see notes—Mk.15:34; Mt.27:46-49). The weight began in the Garden of Gethsemane and continued up to the point of His death upon the cross. (See note—Mk.14:33-34. See notes and DEEPER STUDY # 2—Mt.26:37-38 for detailed discussion.)

The point is the courage of Jesus. He was willing to bear terrible sorrow and pain, so much suffering that it would actually burst His heart and bring death (see note, pt.2—Jn.19:31-37). Just imagine! He did it for us.

"Who his own self bare our sins in his own body on the tree, that we, being dead to sins, should live unto righteousness: by whose stripes ye were healed" (1 Pe.2:24).

"For Christ also hath once suffered for sins, the just for the unjust, that he might bring us to God, being put to death in the flesh, but quickened by the Spirit" (1 Pe.3:18).

Thought 1. The heart of Jesus was broken over sin and the sinner. He loved the sinner (all of us). He was always seeking for, praying for, and weeping over the sinner. He ached so much for the sinner to personally know God, *ached* so much that He never knew what it was to be free from *suffering in heart* for the sinner. His hurt was so deep for the sinner that eventually it was the pain of sin and the sinner that crushed His heart.

Note the great lesson. It took enormous, unswerving courage to bear a broken heart for the sinner. What a lesson for us in courage—the courage to experience brokenness for the sinner, brokenness in prayer, weeping and seeking.

4 (15:46) **Courage—Boldness**: courage made an unashamed commitment to Jesus. Four acts show that Joseph made a courageous commitment to Jesus.

a. Joseph personally took Jesus down from the cross, wrapped the linen cloth around Him, and laid Jesus in his own sepulchre. Joseph personally took care of Jesus. Remember the disciples had fled and forsaken Jesus. But Joseph, witnessing the events of the cross, became thoroughly convinced of Jesus' Messiahship and made a firm commitment to Him. It was doubtful that Joseph understood all that was surrounding the cross and all that was about to take place in the resurrection. No one did. But he apparently believed and courageously acted on that belief.

b. Joseph risked the disfavor and discipline of the Sanhedrin. They were the ruling body who had instigated and condemned Jesus, and Joseph was a member of the council. There was no question that he would face some harsh reaction from some of his fellow Sanhedrin members and from some of his closest friends.

c. Joseph demonstrated a care, even an affection, for Jesus. He gave by giving his own tomb for the burial of Jesus. This act alone would leave no question about his stand for Jesus.

d. Joseph also eliminated himself from taking part in the great Passover Feast—and this was never done, even for the most serious reasons. Joseph, by handling Jesus' body, was considered defiled for seven days for having come in contact with a corpse. Once defiled, Jewish law forbade a person from taking part in Jewish ceremonies.

Simply stated, Joseph, who had been a secret disciple, now stepped forward making an unashamed commitment to Jesus. Everyone would know that he stepped forward to take care of Jesus' body. They would know that he had even given his own tomb for Jesus' burial. Joseph was risking his position, esteem, wealth, and even his life by making such a pronounced commitment to the affairs of Jesus.

Thought 1. The courage demonstrated by Joseph is desperately needed by all.
(1) The courage to make an unashamed commitment to Christ.
(2) The courage to risk all for Christ, even if it does cost our position, esteem, wealth, and life.
(3) The courage to unashamedly care for the body of Christ, His church and its affairs.
(4) The courage to be an unashamed witness for Christ, no matter the cost.

> **"Be strong and of a good courage, fear not, nor be afraid of them: for the LORD thy God, he it is that doth go with thee; he will not fail thee, nor forsake thee" (De.31:6).**
> **"Be ye therefore very courageous to keep and to do all that is written in the book of the law of Moses, that ye turn not aside therefrom to the right hand or to the left" (Jos.23:6).**
> **"The LORD is on my side; I will not fear: what can man do unto me?" (Ps.118:6).**
> **"Behold, God is my salvation; I will trust, and not be afraid: for the Lord JEHOVAH is my strength and my song; he also is become my salvation" (Is.12:2).**

5 (15:47) **Courage—Boldness**: courage took a public stand by the cross. The women stood by the cross (Mk.15:40-41, 47). They loved Jesus and felt deep affection and loyalty for Him. They did not understand, but they did *love and believe*. The men may forsake Jesus, but not them. They stood by the cross from beginning to end despite the danger and possible threat of being arrested as a follower of Jesus. Apparently, they loved and believed so strongly that nothing could have driven them away.

What happened seems to be this. Many women followers were present at the cross (v.41). After Jesus died, all but two women either returned to their own home or else escorted Mary, the mother of Jesus, to her residence. The two women who remained behind saw Joseph come to bury Jesus. They watched, probably even accompanied him, so they would know where their Lord was buried.

The women had courage, the kind of courage that takes a stand by the cross. The women...
- were not ashamed to stand by the cross.
- did not allow the fear of men to run them away from the cross.
- did not allow discouragement to defeat them despite not understanding what was going on.

> **"Be not thou therefore ashamed of the testimony of our Lord" (2 Ti.1:8).**
> **"For I am not ashamed of the gospel of Christ: for it is the power of God unto salvation to every one that believeth; to the Jew first, and also to the Greek" (Ro.1:16).**

CHAPTER 16

X. THE SON OF GOD'S SUPREME MINISTRY: JESUS' VICTORY OVER DEATH & HIS GREAT COMMISSION, 16:1-20

A. The Proofs of the Resurrection,[DS1] **16:1-13**
(Mt. 28:1-15; Lu. 24:1-49; Jn. 20:1-23)

1. The sad & despairing women
- a. They witnessed His death & burial
- b. They bought spices to anoint His body
- c. They were strict religionists who obeyed the law
- d. They were practical, sensible, thinking women—not hysterical, deceived women

2. The rolled away stone

3. The young man dressed in a white robe
- a. He sat on the right side
- b. He made a frightening appearance

And when the sabbath was
past, Mary Magdalene, and
Mary the mother of James,
and Salome, had bought
sweet spices, that they might
come and anoint him.
2 And very early in the
morning the first day of the
week, they came unto the
sepulchre at the rising of the
sun.
3 And they said among
themselves, Who shall roll us
away the stone from the door
of the sepulchre?
4 And when they looked,
they saw that the stone was
rolled away: for it was very
great.
5 And entering into the
sepulchre, they saw a young
man sitting on the right side,
clothed in a long white garment;
and they were affrighted.
6 And he saith unto them,
Be not affrighted: Ye seek
Jesus of Nazareth, which was
crucified: he is risen; he is
not here: behold the place
where they laid him.
7 But go your way, tell his
disciples and Peter that he
goeth before you into Galilee:
there shall ye see him, as
he said unto you.
8 And they went out quickly,
and fled from the sepulchre;
for they trembled and
were amazed: neither said
they any thing to any man;
for they were afraid.
9 Now when Jesus was risen
early the first day of the week,
he appeared first to Mary
Magdalene, out of whom he
had cast seven devils.
10 And she went and told
them that had been with him,
as they mourned and wept.
11 And they, when they had
heard that he was alive, and
had been seen of her, believed not.
12 After that he appeared
in another form unto two of
them, as they walked, and
went into the country.
13 And they went and told
it unto the residue: neither
believed they them.

- c. He commanded authority

4. The missing body of Jesus

5. The compassionate, encouraging word to Peter

6. The fulfillment of the Lord's promise

7. The fright & silence of the women

8. The appearance to Mary Magdalene[DS2]

9. The immediate unbelief of the disciples

10. The appearance to two disciples

11. The continued unbelief of other disciples

DIVISION X

THE SON OF GOD'S SUPREME MINISTRY: JESUS' VICTORY OVER DEATH AND HIS GREAT COMMISSION, 16:1-20

A. The Proofs of the Resurrection, 16:1-13

(16:1-13) **Introduction**: there are eleven proofs (events) of the resurrection in these verses—proofs that should stir faith in the Lord Jesus Christ.

1. The sad and despairing women (vv.1-3).
2. The rolled away stone (v.4).
3. The young man clothed in a white robe (vv.5-6).
4. The missing body of Jesus (v.6).
5. The compassionate, encouraging word to Peter (v.7).
6. The fulfillment of the Lord's promise (v.7).
7. The fright and silence of the women (v.8).
8. The appearance to Mary Magdalene (vv.9-10).
9. The immediate unbelief of the disciples (v.11).
10. The appearance to two disciples (v.12).
11. The continued unbelief of other disciples (v.13).

DEEPER STUDY # 1

(16:1-13) **Jesus Christ—Resurrection**: the order of the resurrection events seems to be as follows: (1) Mary discovers the empty tomb (Jn.20:1-2), and (2) runs to inform Peter and John; (3) they in turn run to see and verify for themselves (Jn.20:3-10).

Then some of the resurrection appearances begin. It should be noted that just how long Jesus stayed with the apostles when He visited them is not given. Some of the visits may have been for days upon days. In fact, He may have even appeared to some of whom we have no record. The exact order of the appearances mentioned by Scripture is hazy, but some order is possible (see 1 Co.15:5-11): (1) to Mary Magdalene (Mk.16:9-11; Jn.20:11-18); (2) to the women running to tell the disciples about the empty tomb (Mt.28:8-10); (3) then apparently to Peter, probably to assure him of restoration (Lu.24:34; 1 Co.15:5); (4) to the two Emmaus disciples sometime in the early evening (Mk.16:12; Lu.24:13-42); (5) to the disciples, with Thomas absent (Mk.16:14; Lu.24:36-43; Jn.20:19-25). (6) The next recorded appearance seems to be one week later, on Sunday evening, when Jesus appears to the disciples who had gone fishing (Jn.21:1-25). There were also other appearances although the order is unknown: (7) to 500 believers (1 Co.15:6); (8) to the apostles (Mt.28:16-20; Mk.16:15-18); (9) to James, the Lord's half-brother (1 Co.15:7); (10) then there was the appearance to the believers at His ascension (Mk.16:19-20; Lu.24:44-53; Acts 1:3-12).

1 (16:1-3) **Resurrection—Women, At Cross & Resurrection**: the first proof of the resurrection was the sad and despairing women. Several facts point to the women as proofs of the resurrection.

a. They were actual witnesses of His death and burial. They knew He was dead, and they knew where He had been laid. They had followed along behind the procession to the tomb (Mk.15:40-41, 47; see Mt.27:55-56, 61; Lu.23:55-56). There was no question in their minds whatsoever about His being dead and buried.

b. They bought spices and came to anoint His body. Apparently, they had bought the spices Saturday evening after 6 p.m. when the Sabbath ended. Note they arose "very early in the morning, the first day of the week [Sunday]" to go and embalm Him. Again, they knew He was dead; but they cared, so they wanted to take care of His body just as loved ones would do.

c. They were religionists who strictly obeyed the law. They were strict in the observance of the Sabbath. Imagine, their loved One was dead, yet they would not break the Sabbath law even to take care of Him (see Lu.23:56). The women were obedient to the commandments of God. They were moral, truthful women who would never think about or even consider lying about the death and resurrection of Jesus.

d. They were practical, sensible, thinking women, not hysterical or deceived. Note what was on their minds: how they were going to remove the stone from the entrance of the tomb. Their senses were present; they were thinking about solving the practical problems facing them. Note also that they had stayed right with Joseph of Arimathaea until he had closed the tomb. They knew that a large stone had sealed the entrance. Luke even says they "beheld the sepulchre, and how the body was laid" (Lu.23:55). Apparently they went in, looked over the sepulchre, and perhaps helped Joseph and Nicodemus (and probably their servants) all they could. They probably stayed with them until the *great* stone was rolled into the entrance.

The point is this: the women, despite their sadness and bereavement, were sensible. They knew Jesus was dead. They were not mistaken or deceived. Every step they took was evidence that what they experienced was true: Jesus did arise from the dead.

2 (16:4) **Stone**: the second proof of the resurrection was the rolled-away stone (see DEEPER STUDY # 1—Mt.27:65-66 for a detailed description of the stone). The stone was not rolled back for the benefit of Jesus but for the witnesses to the resurrection. When Jesus arose, He was in His resurrection body, the body of the spiritual dimension of being which has no physical bounds. However, the witnesses needed to enter the tomb to see the truth. The tomb was rolled back for their benefit (see outline and notes—Jn.20:1-10).

Note also that soldiers were guarding the tomb (Mt.27:65-66. See 27:62-66; 28:2-4, 11-15.) The fact that the stone was rolled back is a proof of the resurrection.

3 (16:5-6) **Angel**: the third proof of the resurrection was the young man clothed in a long white robe. He was an angel sent by God as proof of the resurrection. God sent him for four reasons.

a. To roll the stone back for the witnesses (Mt.28:2).

b. To take care of the soldiers guarding the tomb (Mt.28:4).

c. To reassure the women (Mk.16:5-6). They were already grieving over Jesus' death. If they found the tomb empty without any explanation, they would have been devastated even more. The angel was a ministering spirit of God, one who ministered by reassuring God's people (see DEEPER STUDY # 1,2—Heb.1:4-14).

d. To validate and proclaim the resurrection and to give directions (Mk.16:6-7).

4 (16:6) **Jesus Christ, Resurrection**: the fourth proof of the resurrection was the missing body of Jesus. Note several facts, all giving evidence of the resurrection.

a. The women entered the tomb (v.5).

b. The angel verified that Jesus "was crucified" (dead).

c. The angel proclaimed, "He is risen; He is not here: behold [look, contemplate] the place where they laid Him." And the women did.

d. The women "beheld" (saw, contemplated) that Jesus was not there. They saw the place where He had been laid, and the body was missing.

5 (16:7) **Peter—Jesus Christ, Resurrection**: the fifth proof of the resurrection was the compassionate and wise word to Peter. The compassion and wisdom of God are clearly seen in this personal word sent to Peter. God knew that Peter was crushed, despite his repentance, and that it would be extremely difficult for him to face the other disciples. He had proclaimed his loyalty too loudly and failed too greatly, even to the point of denying his Lord (see Mk.14:26-31, 66-72). Peter was devastated, more than most believers could ever imagine. This is evident from the fact that he needed both this personal word of encouragement from an angel and a personal visit from the resurrected Lord. Apparently, the Lord had to visit him first, all alone, before He appeared to the rest of the disciples (Lu.24:34; 1 Co.15:5).

This personal word to Peter points to God's being behind the whole event. It demonstrates God's compassion and perfect wisdom. It is evidence of the resurrection.

> **"And when I saw him, I fell at his feet as dead. And he laid his right hand upon me, saying unto me, Fear not; I am the first and the last: I am he that liveth, and was dead; and, behold, I am alive for evermore, Amen; and have the keys of hell and of death" (Re.1:17-18).**
> **"Fear thou not; For I am with thee: be not dismayed; for I am thy God: I will strengthen thee; yea, I will help thee; yea, I will uphold thee with the right hand of my righteousness" (Is.41:10).**
> **"But now thus saith the LORD that created thee, O Jacob, and he that formed thee, O Israel, Fear not: for I have redeemed thee, I have called thee by thy name; thou art mine. When thou passest through the waters, I will be with thee; and through the rivers, they shall not overflow thee: when thou walkest through the fire, thou shalt not be burned; neither shall the flame kindle upon thee" (Is.43:1-2).**

6 (16:7) **Jesus Christ, Resurrection—Promises, Fulfilled**: the sixth proof of the resurrection was the fulfillment of the Lord's promise. Jesus had told the disciples that He would go into Galilee after He had arisen (Mk.14:28). Fulfilling His promise was proof that Jesus had arisen. Being told to meet Him in Galilee would do two things.

a. It would stir their hearts with some degree of wonder and hope. It would give them hope that their relationship with the Lord could be restored. They would know that everything could be explained to them in Galilee.

b. It would stir them to remember His promise and give evidence that Jesus had actually arisen from the dead. The very fact that He met them in Galilee, fulfilling His promise, is evidence of His resurrection. The promise could not be fulfilled if He had not risen, and since He arose, the promise was to be fulfilled.

> **"And being fully persuaded that, what he had promised, he was able also to perform" (Ro.4:21).**
> **"For all the promises of God in him are yea, and in him Amen, unto the glory of God by us" (2 Co.1:20).**
> **"If we believe not, yet he abideth faithful: he cannot deny himself" (2 Ti.2:13).**
> **"Whereby are given unto us exceeding great and precious promises: that by these ye might be partakers of the divine nature, having escaped the corruption that is in the world through lust" (2 Pe.1:4).**

7 (16:8) **Jesus Christ, Resurrection—Fear**: the seventh proof of the resurrection was the fright and silence of the women. Note the women were as anyone would be: trembling, amazed, silent, and afraid. As they ran to tell Peter and the disciples, why were they silent and afraid, saying nothing to anyone?

a. The angel had told them to tell only "His disciples and Peter." They were to tell no one else.
b. They feared others might think them *crazy*, so grieved that they were imagining things.
c. They feared the Jewish and Roman authorities, that they might be accused of stealing the body.

Every emotion of the women and their very reaction (trembling, being amazed and afraid) are proof of the resurrection. They reacted in a normal way, just as any group would react, and their normal reaction is evidence of the resurrection. (Note: despite the effect upon their emotions, their thought processes were still very active. They did exactly as the angel instructed. They reasoned and knew to keep silent and quiet about the matter.)

8 (16:9-10) **Mary Magdalene—Devotion**: the eighth proof of the resurrection was the appearance of Jesus to Mary Magdalene (see outline and notes—Jn.20:11-18). The very fact that Jesus visited Mary first, before He visited anyone else, is evidence of the resurrection. It is just like Jesus. He *responds* to love and deep devotion. And Mary, above all others, seems to have loved Jesus more and held Him closer to her heart with more devotion than anyone else. Her need for Him seems to have been greater and felt more than anyone else's.

- ⇒ She had been forgiven and healed from so much. (Note that even in this reference to her, mention is made that Jesus cast seven devils out of her.)
- ⇒ She was at the cross through the whole ordeal and her name is one of the names always given, even above Jesus' own mother, Mary (Mk.15:40-41).
- ⇒ She was present when Jesus was taken down from the cross and until the very last moment at His burial (Mk.15:47; Lu.23:55).
- ⇒ She was foremost in making preparations for embalming the body over the weekend (Mk.15:56).
- ⇒ She visited the tomb after the Sabbath at the earliest possible moment, arising very early in the morning when it was still dark (Mk.16:1-2; Jn.20:1).
- ⇒ She refused to leave the tomb after Peter and John verified that the body was missing (Jn.20:11f).

Mary was a most unusual follower of the Lord, a woman of deep devotion and love, humility and grace; a precious saint who felt the loss of her Lord perhaps more deeply than anyone else. Therefore, Jesus responded to her, meeting her need first of all. This definitely lends proof to the fact that the Lord was risen. (Every genuine believer can attest to the same glorious truth that Mary's experience proclaims: Jesus is risen, for He is ever present with us, responding to our love and devotion and meeting our every need. How precious and strong the presence of our wonderful Lord!)

> **"Greater love hath no man than this, that a man lay down his life for his friends" (Jn.15:13).**

"If ye love me, keep my commandments. And I will pray the Father, and he shall give you another Comforter, that he may abide with you for ever" (Jn.14:15-16).

"For the Father himself loveth you, because ye have loved me, and have believed that I came out from God" (Jn.16:27).

"Who shall separate us from the love of Christ? shall tribulation, or distress, or persecution, or famine, or nakedness, or peril, or sword?" (Ro.8:35).

DEEPER STUDY # 2
(16:9-10) **Scripture**: these verses are not in the two oldest manuscripts, the Sinaiticus and Vaticanus. Only portions are found in other manuscripts and then in various forms. However, they are found in the Vulgate and Syriac Versions.

9 (16:11) **Disciples, Weak Faith**: the ninth proof of the resurrection was the immediate unbelief of the disciples. Again, the disciples are painted in a bad light, a picture that most likely would not be shown if the resurrection had not really happened. The disciples would be seen as stalwarts of great belief and heroic examples if the resurrection were being fabricated. The very fact that they are seen failing again and again and that they are actually the ones to fail the most tragically and are to be blamed the most, is clear evidence of the resurrection.

"Afterward he appeared unto the eleven as they sat at meat, and upbraided them with their unbelief and hardness of heart, because they believed not them which had seen him after he was risen" (Mk.16:14).

"He that believeth on him is not condemned: but he that believeth not is condemned already, because he hath not believed in the name of the only begotten Son of God" (Jn.3:18).

"Take heed, brethren, lest there be in any of you an evil heart of unbelief, in departing from the living God" (He.3:12).

"Let us labour therefore to enter into that rest, lest any man fall after the same example of unbelief" (He.4:11).

10 (16:12) **Jesus Christ, Resurrection—Appearance**: the tenth proof of the resurrection was the appearance of Jesus to two disciples. This probably refers to the appearance to the two on the road to Emmaus (Lu.24:13-35). Just who they were is not known. They were simply two disciples of the Lord who were to go to the apostles and prepare them even more for the Lord's appearances to them. Again, the very way in which the Lord appeared and went about preparing His disciples for confrontation with Him is evidence of His having truly risen. His perfect wisdom, tenderness, and care—which is so evident in the way everything is handled—are clear evidence.

11 (16:13) **Jesus Christ, Resurrection—Disciples, Unbelief**: the eleventh proof of the resurrection was the continued unbelief of the disciples. Again, no fabricated story would paint its main characters in such a bad light, not time after time. In fact, the disciples were not heroes but tragic failures throughout the whole gospel story. This is seldom remembered and mentioned by preachers and teachers, yet they are seen as tragic failures, unbelievably weak time and again. They were a far cry from the type of men we would want as heroes. Why does Scripture paint them in such a bad light? Because what they said *did* happen. It is the truth. Jesus arose and appeared to Mary and the two disciples, and when they shared their experiences with the apostles, the apostles refused to believe. (They were without excuse. For many months Jesus had drilled the fact of His death and resurrection into them. See notes—Mt.16:21-28; 17:1-13; 17:22; 17:24-27.) The weakness of the disciples and their continued unbelief are evidence that what happened was true. It is proof of the resurrection. The truth—exactly what happened—is being told simply and clearly by honest and moral eyewitnesses.

"Then he said unto them, O fools, and slow of heart to believe all that the prophets have spoken" (Lu.24:25).

"And he said unto them, Why are ye so fearful? how is it that ye have no faith?" (Mk.4:40).

"He that believeth on the Son hath everlasting life: and he that believeth not the Son shall not see life; but the wrath of God abideth on him" (Jn.3:36).

"I said therefore unto you, that ye shall die in your sins: for if ye believe not that I am he, ye shall die in your sins" (Jn.8:24).

Outline	Scripture	Scripture	Outline
	B. The Lord's Great Commission, 16:14-20 *(Mt. 28:16-20; Lu. 24:46-49; Jn. 20:21. See Jn. 17:18; Ac. 1:8)*	17 And these signs shall follow them that believe; In my name shall they cast out devils; they shall speak with new tongues;	**4. The promise to the believer as he carries out the Great Commission: Power**
1. The two hindrances to the Great Commission a. Unbelief b. A stubborn refusal to believe, go forth, & bear witness	14 Afterward he appeared unto the eleven as they sat at meat, and upbraided them with their unbelief and hardness of heart, because they believed not them which had seen him after he was risen.	18 They shall take up serpents; and if they drink any deadly thing, it shall not hurt them; they shall lay hands on the sick, and they shall recover.	
2. The Great Commission: Go—preach a. What: The gospel b. Where: All the world	15 And he said unto them, Go ye into all the world, and preach the gospel to every creature.	19 So then after the Lord had spoken unto them, he was received up into heaven, and sat on the right hand of God.	**5. The confirmation of the Great Commission** a. The Lord's ascension to the position of power
3. The reason for the Great Commission a. If believe: Saved[DS1] b. If disbelieve: Condemned	16 He that believeth and is baptized shall be saved; but he that believeth not shall be damned.	20 And they went forth, and preached every where, the Lord working with them, and confirming the word with signs following. Amen.	b. The Lord's working through the disciples' ministry

DIVISION X

THE SON OF GOD'S SUPREME MINISTRY: JESUS' VICTORY OVER DEATH AND HIS GREAT COMMISSION, 16:1-20

B. The Lord's Great Commission, 16:14-20

(16:14-20) **Introduction—Jesus Christ, Resurrection**: this was the first appearance of Jesus to all the disciples. It is important to keep in mind that it was Sunday evening, the same day that Jesus had arisen from the dead. He had undergone an extremely busy day, encouraging those who had needed special attention and sending word of His resurrection to the disciples. They were hovered behind closed doors in fear of the Jews. Jesus needed to send word of His resurrection to them bit by bit so they would be prepared to see Him risen and in His resurrected body. The day included the following appearances.

⇒ The appearance to Mary Magdalene (Mk.16:9-11).
⇒ The appearance to the women as they were going to tell the disciples (Mt.28:9).
⇒ The appearance to Peter, which probably was a long conference lasting for hours (Lu.24:34).
⇒ The appearance to two disciples on the road to Emmaus (Mk.16:12-13).
⇒ The appearance to the disciples mentioned in this passage (Mk.16:14. This appearance is discussed more fully in Lu.24:36f; Jn.20:19f.)

Note what Mark stresses in this passage (this is the close of His gospel): he stresses the Great Commission. The Great Commission is the whole focus of his attention.

1. The two hindrances to the Great Commission (v.14).
2. The Great Commission: go—preach (v.15).
3. The reason for the Great Commission (v.16).
4. The promise to the believer as he carries out the Great Commission: power (vv.17-18).
5. The confirmation of the Great Commission (vv.19-20).

1 (16:14) **Unbelief—Heart, Hardness of**: there are two major hindrances to the Great Commission—unbelief and hardness of heart. Standing before the apostles, Jesus upbraided them for their unbelief and hardness of heart. The word *upbraid* (onedise) means to rebuke, reproach, reprove, scold. Note three things.

a. They deserved the rebuking and scolding. Their unbelief and hardness were inexcusable.
   1) They had witnessed Jesus' power, that is, God's power, throughout His ministry. They had seen His power over both nature and disease, and they had even witnessed His power over death when He raised up Jairus' daughter and a young man and Lazarus, and perhaps others of which there is no record.
   2) They had witnessed His life, His purity and holiness and sinlessness. And they had been taught that sin caused death, that is, that a man dies because of sin (Jn.3:19; see 3:16-21; 5:24-29; 8:34-35. See Ro.5:12; 6:23.) Jesus was without sin; therefore, death could never hold Him and enforce its power over Him. They should have been able to reason and see this glorious fact, especially in light of the Scriptures.

> **"Neither wilt thou suffer thine Holy One to see corruption" (Ps.16:10; Ac.2:27; 13:35).**
> **"Jesus Christ our Lord....declared to be the Son of God with power, according to the spirit of holiness, by the resurrection from the dead" (Ro.1:3-4).**

   3) They had been taught month after month that He was to die and be raised again.
   4) They had rejected the testimony of His resurrection. He had sent them word by Mary Magdalene and the other two disciples (Mk.15:9-11, 12-13).

b. The disciples' unbelief and hardness of heart was very, very serious. Jesus' rebuke (and Mark's stress) of their unbelief and hardness show this (Mk.15:11, 13, 14). It had to be dealt with if the Great Commission were to be carried out.

Thought 1. Jesus dealt with the matter of unbelief and hardness of heart. How much more should we! When we begin to believe that souls are lost and doomed unless they hear and receive Jesus, then we will take the Great Commission seriously and preach the gospel to the whole world. It has now been two thousand years, and a place as small as our world has not even been reached. Unimaginable, when we have had the means of transportation and communication as well as the resources at our disposal to do the job.

c. The *root cause* of unbelief and hardness of heart was very simply the misinterpretation of Scripture and of Jesus' words. The disciples had been told that Jesus was to die and arise from the dead. Jesus had told them time and time again. But the disciples refused to believe the word of Christ; they...

- refused to see the Messiah as a suffering Savior, choosing instead to think in terms of a conquering King (Lu.24:44-45. See notes—Lu.3:24-31; 7:21-23.)
- refused to see the Kingdom of God as a spiritual kingdom, choosing instead to think in terms of a physical kingdom, a kingdom on earth.
- refused to see the death and resurrection of Jesus as a literal fact, choosing instead to think of it in symbolic terms (see note, pt.5—Mt.20:20-21).

Thought 1. Unbelief and hardness of heart are inexcusable within a believer.

"Then he said unto them, O fools, and slow of heart to believe all that the prophets have spoken" (Lu.24:25).

"Then saith he to Thomas, Reach hither thy finger, and behold my hands; and reach hither thy hand, and thrust it into my side: and be not faithless, but believing" (Jn.20:27).

"But exhort one another daily, while it is called To day; lest any of you be hardened through the deceitfulness of sin" (He.3:13).

"Let us labour therefore to enter into that rest, lest any man fall after the same example of unbelief" (He.4:11).

"As many as I love, I rebuke and chasten: be zealous therefore, and repent" (Re.3:19).

"Happy is the man that feareth always: but he that hardeneth his heart shall fall into mischief" (Pr.28:14).

"He, that being often reproved hardeneth his neck, shall suddenly be destroyed, and that without remedy" (Pr.29:1).

"He that believeth on him is not condemned: but he that believeth not is condemned already, because he hath not believed in the name of the only begotten Son of God" (Jn.3:18).

"He that believeth on the Son hath everlasting life: and he that believeth not the Son shall not see life; but the wrath of God abideth on him" (Jn.3:36).

"I said therefore unto you, that ye shall die in your sins: for if ye believe not that I am he, ye shall die in your sins" (Jn.8:24).

2 (16:15) **Commission, Great—Ministry**: the Great Commission is a straightforward command. It is brief, yet forceful and uncompromising: *go—preach.* Jesus made two critical points.

a. It is the gospel that is to be preached. We are not to preach our own thoughts and ideas, humanistic and man-centered beliefs, world religions and philosophies. We are to preach the gospel. The gospel of Jesus Christ is the news which the world desperately needs to hear.

"Moreover, brethren, I declare unto you the gospel which I preached unto you, which also ye have received, and wherein ye stand; by which also ye are saved, if ye keep in memory what I preached unto you, unless ye have believed in vain. For I delivered unto you first of all that which I also received, how that Christ died for our sins according to the scriptures; and that he was buried, and that he rose again the third day according to the scriptures" (1 Co.15:1-4).

"The gospel of God (which he had promised afore by his prophets in the holy scriptures,) concerning his Son Jesus Christ our Lord, which was made of the seed of David according to the flesh; and declared to be the Son of God with power, according to the spirit of holiness, by the resurrection from the dead" (Ro.1:1-4).

b. The gospel is to be carried "into all the world" and preached "to every creature." The gospel is the news which everyone needs to hear. Note two simple facts.

1) The Great Commission was given to the whole church, to every believer. It is a permanent commission given to the church of every generation, not only to the first disciples. Note the words, "He that believeth" (v.16) and "them that believe" (v.17). After a person believes and is baptized, Jesus says the person goes forth with power and signs while he preaches the gospel (vv.16-17). Every believer who is genuinely saved is to preach the gospel (v.16; see Mt.28:19-20; Jn.20:21; Ac.1:8; 2 Ti.2:2; 1 Pe.3:15).
2) The Great Commission does not consider difficulties, dangers, or barriers to be reasons for not going. Jesus did not discuss excuses for not sharing the gospel. His command was an *uncompromising demand.* The issue of eternal life vs. eternal damnation is too critical an issue to allow anything to stop the gospel from going forth. The gospel has to be carried forth. No land is to be neglected, no people are to be

ignored. The believer is to be undaunted and unswerved from the Great Commission. The believer is commanded: "Go ye into all the world" (v.15).

3 (16:16) **Salvation—Belief**: the reason for the Great Commission is twofold. Men are either saved or condemned. If the gospel is shared with them and they believe and are baptized, they shall be saved; but if they disbelieve, they shall be condemned. (See DEEPER STUDY # 1, *Baptism*—Mk.16:16 for additional discussion.)

a. A man can now be saved. He no longer needs to walk about, wandering throughout life seeking and searching for fulfillment and completeness, questioning if there is really any purpose to life. Man can be saved and live eternally. He can be delivered...

- from sin and its power (Ro.6:6-7).
- from death and its fear and corruption (Jn.5:24; He.2:14-15).
- from hell and its torture and separation from God (see DEEPER STUDY # 2—Mt.5:22; DEEPER STUDY # 1—He.9:27).

The message that life is now available must be carried to the whole world.

b. A man is lost and condemned if he disbelieves the gospel. The words *believeth not* (apistesas) mean to disbelieve. And the word *damned* (katakrithesetai) means to be condemned. The man who rejects Jesus Christ, who refuses to believe and follow Him, shall be condemned. Condemned to what?

⇒ To the power and enslavement of sin (Jn.3:19; Ro.3:12, 23).
⇒ To the fear and corruption of death (Ro.5:12; 6:23).
⇒ To the torture and separation of hell (see DEEPER STUDY # 2—Mt.5:22; DEEPER STUDY # 1—He.9:27).

Therefore, the great motive for reaching the world is the desperate need of man to be saved: saved from sin, death, and hell—saved to the uttermost—saved to live forever in the presence of God Himself (Jn.3:16; 5:24-29).

DEEPER STUDY # 1

(16:16) **Baptism—Belief—Salvation—Obedience**: two things are said to be essential for salvation—belief and baptism. There are two basic positions on baptism: first, one must be baptized to be saved, and, second, baptism is a symbol or sign that one believes and has been saved. Note four things.

1. Perhaps what is often overlooked by both positions is this: *belief* is an *act of obedience* to God's demand if a person wishes to be saved, and *baptism* is an *act of obedience* to God's demand if a person believes.

Baptism is an act of obedience to God's demand just as belief is an act of obedience to God's demand. Very simply, if a man wishes to be saved, God says (demands that he) *believe*; and if a man believes, God says (demands that he) *be baptized.*

A legitimate and straightforward question needs to be asked: "How can a person honestly be saved if he immediately rebels against being baptized? How can a person really believe, be genuine in his confession, if he rebels at obeying His Lord about baptism?"

Facing the reality of the situation, Scripture is strong: a person who truly believes in the Lord will not refuse to follow His Lord *in baptism* or in anything else (Lu.9:23). To believe and to obey are the same thing. The two, belief and obedience, are one and the same.

> **"He became the author of eternal salvation unto all them that *obey him*" (He.5:9. See DEEPER STUDY # 1—He.5:9 as well.)**

Another way to say the same thing is this. There is no such thing as faith alone, not without works or fruit. Faith without obedience is not what the Scripture means by faith. In the Scripture, faith is the movement of the heart which embraces the Lord, the Lord who is the fulfillment of the law (Mt.5:17-18. See note—Mt.5:17-18 as well.) Faith is that which "cometh to God believing that He is, and...*diligently seeking* Him" (He.11:6). Faith, Biblical faith, diligently seeks to obey the Lord. Therefore, the man who truly believes will follow the Lord in baptism and in everything else.

This does not mean the person will be perfect and never fail. Far from it. He will fail, but he will *not continue in sin.* He will get up out of his sin, ask God to forgive him, and begin to follow the Lord even more diligently. His faith works and bears fruit, for He knows that God exists and that He is a rewarder of them that diligently seek Him.

> **"What doth it profit, my brethren, though a man say he hath faith, and have not works? can faith save him?" (Js.2:14).**
>
> **"Faith, if it hath not works, is dead, being alone. Yea, a man may say, Thou hast faith, and I have works: show me thy faith without thy works, and I will show thee my faith by my works" (Js.2:17-18).**
>
> **"But wilt thou know, O vain man, that faith without works is dead? Was not Abraham our father justified by works, when he had offered Isaac his son upon the altar? Seest thou how faith wrought with his works, and by works was faith made perfect? And the scripture was fulfilled which saith, Abraham believed God, and it was imputed unto him for righteousness: and he was called the Friend of God. Ye see then how that by works a man is justified, and not by faith only" (Js.2:20-24).**

Thought 1. There is no such thing as cheap salvation, not the kind that is too often preached and stressed. Following Jesus or being saved costs. It costs all that a person *is and has*. A man is not saved without following Jesus (Lu.9:23), and following Jesus means being baptized and diligently seeking Him (living righteously).

2. The person who is condemned is said to be the person who disbelieves, not the person who is not baptized. This is a matter for close attention. The word "baptized" is omitted from *disbelieveth*. Not being baptized is not mentioned as a reason for being condemned. This does point toward *disbelief's* being the reason for condemnation, and conversely, toward belief's being the reason for salvation. However, as discussed above, it is very difficult to explain how a person can be genuinely saved and not be baptized if he is physically able to be baptized. Believing is commitment, doing what God says, and commitment is believing (see DEEPER STUDY # 1—Jn.2:24). Therefore, a man is saved by doing what God says: believing, being baptized, living righteously. A man is not saved if he does not believe, that is, refuses to do what God says. To truly be saved, a person must be committed to Jesus Christ, committed to being baptized and to living righteously.

3. Something that should be looked at is the nature of belief and baptism. Belief and baptism are two different substances, of two different natures, of two different dimensions. In dealing with belief, the same things can be said about belief that is said about salvation. Both are of the spirit, not of the body nor of the physical world of man. Belief is a spiritual thing or substance. Its nature is spiritual; it is of the spiritual dimension of being; it is an act of the spirit of man.

However, baptism is of a different nature. It is man's physical body being placed into water (a material thing or substance). Baptism is of the physical or material dimension of being; it is an act of the body of man.

4. Very practically, in a world of billions of people, some are born mentally alert and responsible; yet they are tragically deformed, or injured, or diseased. Some are so deformed and physically affected they could never be immersed in the waters of baptism. Some of these do come to believe in Christ and do live righteously, obeying God in so far as their heart and body allows them.

In conclusion, the thrust of Scripture seems to be that a person who genuinely believes *is* baptized and will not fail to be baptized unless it is physically impossible, nor will he fail to live righteously. Yet the moment of salvation is not at baptism nor at any other act or work of doing righteousness. It is at the moment of believing in the Lord Jesus Christ. When a man really believes and really *entrusts* his life into the hands of Christ, *God knows that moment*, the very second of trust. Therefore, at that very moment God quickens his spirit, causing him to be *born again*, and making him alive spiritually (not physically. It is not a physical thing or substance.) Then the man arises from confession on his knees, is baptized, and begins to follow the Lord in righteousness.

4 (16:17-18) **Power**: the promise to the believer as he carries out the Great Commission is critical. The believer must have *supernatural power* as he goes forth throughout the world. The world is a dangerous place. The believer will sometimes be called upon to face treacherous land, violent storms within nature, savage and poisonous animals, unbelieving and hostile men, spiritual evil of unbelievable force. The evil of men, of nature, and of spirits can be so threatening to the believer that the believer's witness would be stopped if God did not provide His strength and power. This is the point of this passage. God does give power to the believer—all the power necessary to carry the gospel "into all the world" and "to every creature."

This, of course, does not mean that every believer will be delivered from every threat and from ever being martyred. Some believers are persecuted and some even martyred. As God wills, He teaches and touches lives and moves history and society itself through the persecution and martyrdom of believers. Things do not always run smoothly for believers. But God does give power to believers—the power to walk through the difficulties in His confidence and peace, even through the fire of martyrdom if faced. It is often the witness of the God-given power, confidence, and peace that reaches others for Christ and that causes an enormous movement toward God.

To repeat, this is the point of these two verses. As the believer carries out the Great Commission, God promises power, the power needed to get the task done. Note the power or signs mentioned by Mark. Such power will be present in the life of the believer (when needed) as he proclaims the gospel around the world.

⇒ Casting out devils (see Ac.16:18).
⇒ Speaking with new tongues (see DEEPER STUDY # 4—Ac.2:4).
⇒ Taking up serpents (Ac.28:5).
⇒ Drinking any deadly thing (Mk.16:18).
⇒ Laying hands on the sick and healing them (Ac.28:7-8).

"But ye shall receive power, after that the Holy Ghost is come upon you: and ye shall be witnesses unto me both in Jerusalem, and in all Judaea, and in Samaria, and unto the uttermost part of the earth" (Ac.1:8).

"And my speech and my preaching was not with enticing words of man's wisdom, but in demonstration of the Spirit and of power" (1 Co.2:4).

"That he would grant you, according to the riches of his glory, to be strengthened with might by his Spirit in the inner man" (Ep.3:16).

"For our gospel came not unto you in word only, but also in power, and in the Holy Ghost, and in much assurance" (1 Th.1:5).

"For God hath not given us the spirit of fear; but of power, and of love, and of a sound mind. Be not thou therefore ashamed of the testimony of our Lord, nor of me his prisoner: but be thou partaker of the afflictions of the gospel according to the power of God" (2 Ti.1:7-8).

"But truly I am full of power by the spirit of the LORD, and of judgment, and of might, to declare unto Jacob his transgression, and to Israel his sin" (Mi.3:8).

"Not by might, nor by power, but by my spirit, saith the LORD of hosts" (Zec.4:6).

5 (16:19-20) **Commission, Great**: the confirmation of the Great Commission is seen in two acts.

a. There is the Lord's ascension to the right hand of God, that is, the position of power (see Lu.24:50-51; Acts 1:9-11). The ascension assures (proves, confirms) that seven things are absolutely certain. (See note, *Ascension*—Jn.6:62 for more discussion.)

1) The ascension assures us that God is and that He is alive. Christ could be raised from the dead and received up into heaven *only* by the power of God. The fact that Christ was raised up from the dead and "carried up into heaven" (Lu.24:51) proves that God exists. Only God could do such a thing. (1 Co.6:14; 2 Co.4:14; see Jn.3:16. See Ac.2:24, 32; 3:15, 26; 4:14; 5:30; 10:40; 13:30, 33-34; 17:31.)
2) The ascension assures us that Christ is God's Son. The very fact that God raised up Christ and "received [Him] up into heaven" proves that Christ is God's Son (Ro.1:3-4; Ph.2:5-11).
3) The ascension assures us that heaven is real (Ph.3:20-21).
4) The ascension assures us that the gospel is true. When God raised up Christ and received Him into heaven, God showed that the message of Christ is true. What Christ proclaimed and revealed is true. The problem with man is sin and death, a future of condemnation and separation from God. But man can be saved, saved by the cross of Christ (Mk.16:16; 1 Pe.2:24).
5) The ascension assures us that the Great Commission is the call and mission of believers. Two things show this.
   - ⇒ First, Christ has ascended into heaven. He is gone, no longer on earth. If the gospel is to be carried to the ends of the earth, believers have to do it. They are the ones left on earth to do it.
   - ⇒ Second, it is the risen and ascended Lord who gave the Great Commission. As the ascended Lord, He demands that His commission be fulfilled (Mk.16:15; see Mt.28:19-20).
6) The ascension assures us that power is available to carry out the Great Commission (Mt.28:18; see Mk.16:20).
7) The ascension assures us that we have a very special Helper in heaven, One who really loves and cares for us. He is One who is "touched with the feelings of our infirmities, One who was in all points tempted like we are, yet without sin" (He.4:15). Therefore, He is ever ready to forgive us and to look after us and to carry us through all of life.

b. The Great Commission is confirmed by the Lord's working through the disciples' ministry. The Great Commission is to be carried out. The early disciples "went forth" immediately and "preached everywhere." The believers of every generation are to go forth immediately and preach the gospel everywhere.

Note two simple facts.
1. "The Lord worked" with them.
2. "The Lord...confirmed the Word [of God] with signs."

> **"And with great power gave the apostles witness of the resurrection of the Lord Jesus: and great grace was upon them all" (Ac.4:33).**

THE
OUTLINE & SUBJECT INDEX

REMEMBER: When you look up a subject and turn to the Scripture reference, you have not just the Scripture but also an outline and a discussion (commentary) of the Scripture and subject.

This is one of the GREAT FEATURES of *The Preacher's Outline & Sermon Bible®*. Once you have all the volumes, you will have not only what all other Bible indexes give you, that is, a list of all the subjects and their Scripture references, but in addition you will have...

- an outline of every Scripture and subject in the Bible
- a discussion (commentary) on every Scripture and subject
- every subject supported by other Scripture, already written out or cross referenced

DISCOVER THE UNIQUE VALUE for yourself. Quickly glance below to the first subject of the Index:

ABOMINATION OF DESOLATION (See **ANTICHRIST**)
Discussed. Mk.13:14-23

Turn to the first reference. Glance at the Scripture and the outline, then read the commentary. You will immediately see the TREMENDOUS BENEFIT of the INDEX of *The Preacher's Outline & Sermon Bible®*.

OUTLINE AND SUBJECT INDEX

OUTLINE BIBLE RESOURCES

This material, like similar works, has come from imperfect man and is thus susceptible to human error. We are nevertheless grateful to God for both calling us and empowering us through His Holy Spirit to undertake this task. Because of His goodness and grace, ***The Preacher's Outline & Sermon Bible***® New Testament is complete and the Old Testament volumes are releasing periodically.

The Minister's Personal Handbook and other helpful **Outline Bible Resources** are available in printed form as well as releasing electronically on WORDsearch software.

God has given the strength and stamina to bring us this far. Our confidence is that as we keep our eyes on Him and grounded in the undeniable truths of the Word, we will continue working through the Old Testament volumes. The future includes other helpful Outline Bible Resources for God's dear servants to use in their Bible Study and discipleship.

We offer this material first to Him in whose Name we labor and serve and for whose glory it has been produced and, second, to everyone everywhere who preaches and teaches the Word.

Our daily prayer is that each volume will lead thousands, millions, yes even billions, into a better understanding of the Holy Scriptures and a fuller knowledge of Jesus Christ the Incarnate Word, of whom the Scriptures so faithfully testify.

You will be pleased to know that Leadership Ministries Worldwide partners with Christian organizations, printers, and mission groups around the world to make Outline Bible Resources available and affordable in many countries and foreign languages. It is our goal that *every* leader around the world, both clergy and lay, will be able to understand God's Holy Word and present God's message with more clarity, authority, and understanding—all beyond his or her own power.

LEADERSHIP MINISTRIES WORLDWIDE
PO Box 21310 • Chattanooga, TN 37424-0310
(423) 855-2181 • FAX (423) 855-8616
info@outlinebible.org
www.outlinebible.org - FREE Download materials

2/11

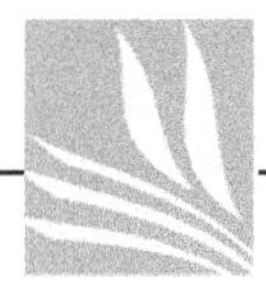

PURPOSE STATEMENT

LEADERSHIP MINISTRIES WORLDWIDE

exists to equip ministers, teachers, and laymen in their understanding, preaching, and teaching of God's Word by publishing and distributing worldwide *The Preacher's Outline & Sermon Bible®* and related **Outline Bible Resources**; to reach & disciple men, women, boys and girls for Jesus Christ.

MISSION STATEMENT

1. To make the Bible so understandable – its truth so clear and plain – that men and women everywhere, whether teacher or student, preacher or hearer, can grasp its message and receive Jesus Christ as Savior, and...

2. To place the Bible in the hands of all who will preach and teach God's Holy Word, verse by verse, precept by precept, regardless of the individual's ability to purchase it.

The **Outline Bible Resources** have been given to LMW for printing and especially distribution worldwide at/below cost, by those who remain anonymous. One fact, however, is as true today as it was in the time of Christ:

THE GOSPEL IS FREE, BUT THE COST OF TAKING IT IS NOT

LMW depends on the generous gifts of believers with a heart for Him and a love for the lost. They help pay for the printing, translating, and distributing of **Outline Bible Resources** into the hands of God's servants worldwide, who will present the Gospel message with clarity, authority, and understanding beyond their own.

LMW was incorporated in the state of Tennessee in July 1992 and received IRS 501 (c)(3) nonprofit status in March 1994. LMW is an international, nondenominational mission organization. All proceeds from USA sales, along with donations from donor partners, go directly to underwrite our translation and distribution projects of **Outline Bible Resources** to preachers, church and lay leaders, and Bible students around the world.

5/10

www.ingramcontent.com/pod-product-compliance
Lightning Source LLC
LaVergne TN
LVHW081250100826
845148LV00009B/1181

* 9 7 8 1 5 7 4 0 7 0 0 3 3 *